Lecture Notes in Computer Science 6985

Commenced Publication in 1973
Founding and Former Series Editors:
Gerhard Goos, Juris Hartmanis, and Jan van Leeuwen

Erik Altman   Weisong Shi (Eds.)

Network and Parallel Computing

8th IFIP International Conference, NPC 2011
Changsha, China, October 21-23, 2011
Proceedings

 Springer

Volume Editors

Erik Altman
IBM T.J. Watson Research Center
19 Skyline Drive, Hawthorne, NY 10532, USA
E-mail: ealtman@us.ibm.com

Weisong Shi
Wayne State University
Department of Computer Science
5057 Woodward Avenue, Detroit, MI 48202, USA
E-mail: weisong@wayne.edu

ISSN 0302-9743   e-ISSN 1611-3349
ISBN 978-3-642-24402-5   ISBN 978-3-642-24403-2 (eBook)
DOI 10.1007/978-3-642-24403-2
Springer Heidelberg Dordrecht London New York

Library of Congress Control Number: 2011936739

CR Subject Classification (1998): D.1, C.2.4, D.2, F.2, D.4, H.3

LNCS Sublibrary: SL 1 – Theoretical Computer Science and General Issues

Typesetting: Camera-ready by author, data conversion by Scientific Publishing Services, Chennai, India

Printed on acid-free paper

Springer is part of Springer Science+Business Media (www.springer.com)

Program Chairs' Welcome

Welcome to the proceedings of NPC 2011 which was held in Changsha. We had a strong and diverse Program Committee (PC), who selected 27 papers for presentation. Of the 67 committee members, 23 were from Asia, 8 from Europe, and 36 North America. In addition 46 were from academia, 17 from industry, and 4 from government.

77% of the submitting authors, were from China, 11% from the USA, 6% from the Republic of Korea, with the remaining authors from Algeria, Canada, Egypt, France, and Italy.

The committee reviewed the 54 submissions over a 6-week period from mid-April to the end of May, with an average of 3.7 reviews per paper. The committee then conducted a virtual and electronic PC meeting over the first 2 weeks of June to discuss papers and make selections for the conference. The EasyChair reviewing system used for the conference facilitated this virtual meeting and discussion. Comments made by any PC member on the EasyChair site were emailed to all other PC members assigned that paper, to the two of us as PC Chairs, and to any other PC members interested in that paper. In addition, we tried to seed discussions especially around controversial papers by commenting on the key points of reviews and highlighting differences of opinion. To avoid any hint of bias in selecting papers, discussion was double-blind throughout. There was clear consensus on almost all papers, and we had discussions and majority rule of PC members who reviewed a paper in the small set of cases where there was continuing disagreement.

Based on these discussions, we selected 17 papers as our top "select" papers (a 31% rate), and another 11 papers as regular papers. In addition, the six strongest papers from the PC were put in two special sessions, from which NPC 2011 attendees could select the best overall paper.

Two papers required shepherding, and we thank Xipeng Shen and Peter Sweeney for their extra efforts in working with the authors to ensure that the needed improvements were made.

Pulling together this program of course required lots of help beyond the committee and the 13 external reviews the committee employed. We thank the General Chairs, Jack Dongarra and Nong Xiao, for all of their advice and help. We also thank the NPC 2011 Publicity Chairs, Wenbin Jiang and Xiaoming Li, for their strong efforts to publicize the Call for Papers. Mingche Lai was also very organized in getting the NPC 2011 registration set up many months before the conference. Finally, Kemal Ebcioglu as Chair of the Steering Committee provided us with lots of background on previous conferences and other advice. Last year's Program Chairs, Chen Ding and Zhiyuan Shao, were also very helpful and forthcoming with advice.

We hope that you find the proceedings of NPC 2011 interesting.

Erik Altman
Weisong Shi

Organization

General Co-chairs

Jack Dongarra   University of Tennessee, USA
Nong Xiao   NUDT, Changsha, China

Program Co-chairs

Erik Altman   IBM Research, USA
Weisong Shi   Wayne State University, USA

Workshop Chair

Li Shen   NUDT, China

Registration Chair

Mingche Lai   NUDT, Changsha, China

Local Arrangements Chairs

Fang Liu   NUDT, Changsha, China
Mingche Lai   NUDT, Changsha, China
Libo Huang   NUDT, Changsha, China

Publicity Chairs

Wenbin Jiang   HUST, Wuhan, China
Xiaoming Li   University of Delaware, USA

Finance Chair

Fang Liu   NUDT, Changsha, China

Steering Committee

Chair: Kemal Ebcioglu	Global Supercomputing, USA, Turkey
Chen Ding	University of Rochester, USA
Jack Dongarra	University of Tennessee, USA
Guangrong Gao	University of Delaware, USA
Jean-Luc Gaudiot	University of California-Irvine, USA
Hai Jin Huazhong	University, China
Guojie Li	Institute of Computing Tech, China
Yoichi Muraoka	Waseda University, Japan
Daniel Reed	University of North Carolina, USA
Yang Xiang	Central Queensland University, Australia
Zhiwei Xu	Institute of Computing Tech, China

Program Committee

Tor Aamodt	U-British Columbia, Canada
Ajith Abraham	Machine Intelligence Research Labs
Ishfaq Ahmad	University of Texas at Arlington, USA
Vasanth Bala	IBM
Rajesh Bordawekar	IBM
Luc Bouge	IRISA/ENS Cachan Brittany, France
Arun Chauhan	Indiana University, USA
Wenguang Chen	Tsinghua University, China
Randy Chow	University of Florida, USA
Yeh-Ching Chung	National Tsing Hua University, China
Lieven Eckhout	Ghent University, Belgium
Yaoqing Gao	IBM Toronto, Canada
Christian Grothoff	University of Munich, Germany
Ajay Gulati	VMWare
Hwansoo Han	Sungkyunkwan University, Korea
JianJun Han	Huazhong University of Science and Technology, China
Wei-Chung Hsu	National Chiao Tung University, Taiwan
Weijia Jia	City University of Hong Kong
Song Jiang	Wayne State University, USA
Lizy John	UT-Austin, USA
David Kaeli	Northeastern
Kuan-Ching Li	Providence University, Taiwan
Ruidong Li	NICT
Xiao-Feng Li	Intel
Zhiyuan Li	Purdue University, USA
Guiquan Liu	University of Science and Technology of China
Shaoshan Liu	Microsoft
Paul Lu	University of Alberta, Canada

External Reviewers

Jed Kao-Tung Chang
Justin Gottschlich
Zhimin Gu
Ganghee Jang
Yunlian Jiang
Johnny Kuan
Yiming Ma
Karim Seada
Kai Tian
Bo Wu
Changjiu Xian
Hongtao Yu
Zhijia Zhao

Table of Contents

_____

[*] Papers are "Select Papers" as chosen by the Program Committee.

Session 4: Trust and Authentication

Session 5: Monitor, Diagnose, and Then Optimize

Session 6: Best Paper – 1

(*) Papers are "Select Papers" as chosen by the Program Committee.

Session 7: Best Paper – 2

Session 8: Microarchitecture

Session 9: Network and Mobile Computing

(*) Papers are "Select Papers" as chosen by the Program Committee.

Elastic Phoenix: Malleable MapReduce for Shared-Memory Systems

Adam Wolfe Gordon and Paul Lu

Department of Computing Science, University of Alberta,
Edmonton, Alberta, T6G 2E8, Canada
{awolfe,paullu}@cs.ualberta.ca

Abstract. We present the design, implementation, and an evaluation of Elastic Phoenix. Based on the original Phoenix from Stanford, Elastic Phoenix is also a MapReduce implementation for shared-memory systems. The key new feature of Elastic Phoenix is that it supports *malleable jobs*: the ability add *and* remove worker processes during the execution of a job. With the original Phoenix, the number of processors to be used is fixed at start-up time. With Elastic Phoenix, if more resources become available (as they might on an elastic cloud computing system), they can be dynamically added to an existing job. If resources are reclaimed, they can also be removed from an existing job. The concept of malleable jobs is well known in job scheduling research, but an implementation of a malleable programming system like Elastic Phoenix is less common.

We show how dynamically increasing the resources available to an Elastic Phoenix workload as it runs can reduce response time by 29% compared to a statically resourced workload. We detail the changes to the Phoenix application programming interface (API) made to support the new capability, and discuss the implementation changes to the Phoenix code base. We show that any additional run-time overheads introduced by Elastic Phoenix can be offset by the benefits of dynamically adding processor resources.

Keywords: MapReduce, parallel programming, malleable, shared-memory systems.

1 Introduction

In many programming systems, the number of processes, threads, or workers is fixed at start-up time. After all, creating and initializing per-thread data structures is most easily handled at the beginning of the job. Furthermore, the classic batch schedulers (e.g., Load Sharing Facility (LSF), Portable Batch System (PBS), Sun Grid Engine (SGE), LoadLeveler) either do not support a dynamically changing allocation of processors in the middle of running a job, or support it awkwardly. However, with the emergence of elastic cloud computing systems (e.g., Amazon EC2 [1], Eucalyptus [11]) comes a new resource provisioning model where it is feasible to allocate more processors on demand. With additional processors, a MapReduce job might finish with a lower response time. But, what programming model or system can support *malleable jobs* [8] that have the ability to add (and remove) processor resources during job execution?

E. Altman and W. Shi (Eds.): NPC 2011, LNCS 6985, pp. 1–16, 2011.

Custom applications can, of course, create and destroy threads on demand. But, one of the most appealing aspects of the MapReduce programming model [6] is the separation of the application code from the management of processes and data, for a large class of data-parallel problems. Extending a MapReduce system to support malleable execution seems like a natural thing to do, with minimal additional complexity for the application developer. And, although the benefits of running malleable jobs on elastic cloud systems depends greatly on the specific application, the option of dynamically adding processors to a job is desirable, as long as the overheads are reasonable and the benefits are significant.

We present the design, implementation, and an evaluation of Elastic Phoenix, a MapReduce implementation for shared-memory multiprocessors. With a few minor changes to the original Phoenix [14] application programming interface (API) (Table 1) and some changes to MapReduce applications (Table 2), Elastic Phoenix maintains the original data-parallel programming model and has reasonable overheads. In our empirical evaluation, we show the overheads to be small (6% to 8%) for many applications (Figure 2). And, in a synthetic workload experiment (Figure 4), we show that Elastic Phoenix can improve the response time of the workload by up to 29%, over an equivalent workload where processor allocations can change only at job start-up time.

Phoenix [14] is a MapReduce framework written in C for shared-memory computers. Unlike other MapReduce frameworks, such as Google's MapReduce [6] and Hadoop [2], Phoenix is not distributed: a Phoenix application runs entirely in one address space on a single host, using only the local filesystem and memory. But, we argue that as the core count of individual servers increases over time, and if they have sufficient I/O capacity, the desire to run a MapReduce application on a single, shared-memory server will also grow.

One limitation of the original Phoenix system is that, because all worker threads run in the same process, an application cannot take advantage of additional resources that become available after a job is started. That is, if a Phoenix application is started with four threads, and four more processors become idle while the application runs, there is no way to use these additional processors to accelerate the Phoenix application. In this way, we say that Phoenix is not malleable, or in the terminology of cloud computing, Phoenix is not *elastic*.

Elastic Phoenix is a modification to the original Phoenix framework that allows worker threads to be added or removed while a job is running, which makes our new system elastic and malleable.[1]

2   Background

Phoenix [14] is a MapReduce framework designed for shared-memory systems. A Phoenix application is written in C and linked with the Phoenix library into a single executable. A Phoenix job runs in a single process, within which there are multiple worker threads and a single master thread. As in other MapReduce frameworks, execution proceeds in four stages: split, map, reduce, and merge. Input data is usually stored

---

[1] Elastic Phoenix is an open-source project and can be obtained from
https://github.com/adamwg/elastic-phoenix

in a file on the local filesystem. The split stage is performed by the master thread, generating map tasks. The map tasks are executed by the worker threads, generating intermediate key-value pairs in memory. This intermediate data is consumed by the reduce tasks, which are also executed by the worker threads. The final data emitted by the reduce tasks is merged in multiple rounds by the worker threads. The merged data can be written to a file or processed further by the master thread.

The main function of a Phoenix application is provided by the application, not by the framework. The application configures a MapReduce job by filling in a data structure which is passed to the framework. The application must provide a map function. Most applications provide a reduce function, although an identity reduce function is provided by the framework. The application can optionally provide a splitter function for dividing input data (the default splitter treats the input data as an uninterpreted byte array and splits it into even parts); a combiner that merges intermediate values emitted by a map thread; a partitioner that divides the intermediate data among reduce tasks; and a locator function that helps the framework assign each input split to an appropriate map thread based on the location of the data. The application must also provide a comparator for the application-defined intermediate data keys.

Phoenix creates a worker thread pool, which is used for map, reduce, and merge tasks during execution of a job. Tasks are placed in a set of queues, one for each worker thread, by the master thread. The worker threads in the pool get work by pulling tasks from their queues. If a worker's queue runs out of tasks, it will steal work from other threads to avoid sitting idle.

Map tasks emit intermediate key-value pairs into a set of arrays. Each map thread has an output array for each reduce task (the number of reduce tasks is defined by the application). A reduce task processes the data produced for it by each map thread, emitting final data into another array of key-value pairs. These final data arrays are merged pairwise until a single, sorted output array is produced.

To avoid confusion, we will henceforth refer to Phoenix as "original Phoenix," in contrast to our Elastic Phoenix framework. We use the name Phoenix on its own only for discussion applicable to both frameworks.

3   Related Work

Malleable Programming Environments. Malleable applications are supported by the Message Passing Interface (MPI) through its dynamic process management capability [9]. However, this technique is only applicable to applications developed directly on top of MPI, which offers a low level of abstraction.

At a higher level, support for malleability has been implemented in the Process Checkpointing and Migration (PCM) library, which is built using MPI [7]. PCM is similar to Elastic Phoenix in that it adds malleability to an existing API. However, unlike Elastic Phoenix, the PCM implementation uses explicit splitting and merging of MPI processes; that is, the application developer is required to reason about malleability in order to support it.

An unrelated project, also called Phoenix [12], provides a non-MPI-based message-passing API that supports malleability by allowing nodes in a cluster to join and leave a computation while it runs. Unlike Elastic Phoenix, it is not intended for shared-memory systems.

MapReduce Improvements. Other research groups have also tried to reduce the response time of MapReduce jobs by modifying the framework or semantics of the programming model. The Hadoop Online Prototype (HOP) [5] improves response time of jobs in the Hadoop framework by modifying the flow of data during execution. In HOP, intermediate key-value pairs are sent directly from map workers to reduce workers, before a map task is completed. The framework can also produce partial results by running the reducer on partial map output, though the reducer must be executed over all the map output to produce a final result. By better pipelining and overlapping the work between the map and reduce stages, response time can be improved.

Verma *et al.* [13] present a Hadoop-based MapReduce framework in which reduce tasks not only receive but consume map output as it is produced, eliminating the effective barrier between the map and reduce stages. This technique changes the semantics of the MapReduce model, since the reducer no longer has guarantees about the ordering of its input data. Application developers are thus required to store and sort the data if necessary. Evaluation shows that if careful and efficient techniques are used to handle intermediate data, this modification to MapReduce can improve response time for certain classes of problems.

Chohan *et al.* [4] explore the advantages of using Amazon EC2 Spot Instances (SI), inexpensive but potentially transient virtual machines, to accelerate Hadoop jobs. This is similar to our work in that it provides a type of malleability to a MapReduce framework: a job can be accelerated by adding worker nodes in SIs. However, because of the nature of Hadoop, termination of a spot instance is expensive, since completed work often needs to be re-executed. Elastic Phoenix does not encounter this expense in reducing the number of workers, since the data produced by all completed tasks is in shared memory and will not be lost. We note, though, that our current implementation is not suitable for the semantics of SIs, in which the worker node is terminated without warning, since an Elastic Phoenix worker requires a signal and a little bit of extra time to clean up when it is removed.

The Intermediate Storage System (ISS) [10] for Hadoop improves the response time of MapReduce jobs when faults occur. Hadoop normally stores map output data on local disk until it is required by a reduce worker, requiring the map task that produced the data to be re-executed if a fault occurs on the worker node. The ISS asynchronously replicates the intermediate data, saving the re-execution time if only one replica incurs a fault. However, this technique induces overhead in the absence of faults.

4   Design Goals

Our design goals for Elastic Phoenix were:

- **Elasticity.** The user should be able to add (or remove) worker threads to a running MapReduce job in order to accelerate it. The framework should not make assumptions about the stage of computation during which workers will be added.

- **Design Flexibility.** The implementation described in this paper uses the POSIX shared-memory mechanism, but our design assumes as little as possible about the mechanism being employed, such that it can be ported to other data-sharing mechanisms in the future.
- **API compatibility.** It should take minimal effort to make an original Phoenix application work with Elastic Phoenix.

These design goals are sometimes conflicting. In particular, maintaining the API of the original Phoenix framework, which was not designed for elasticity, made it more difficult to achieve the other goals.

5   Implementation

The basic design change that enables Elastic Phoenix is separation of the master thread and worker threads into different processes, as illustrated in Figure 1. This presents a number of challenges, since original Phoenix was designed with a shared address space in mind. In addition, our implementation does not assume that all worker processes share a kernel or filesystem, allowing future versions to support distributed operation using another distributed data-sharing mechanism such as distributed shared memory or message passing.

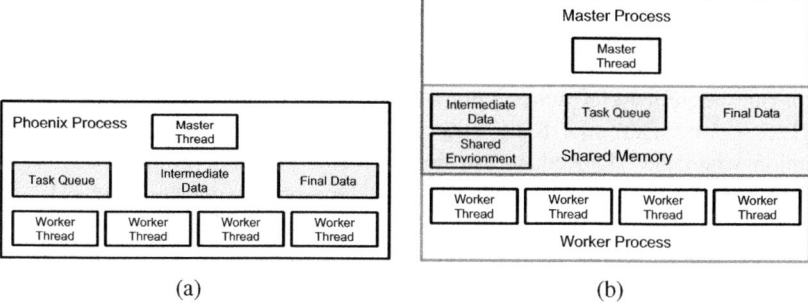

(a)   (b)

Fig. 1. High-level architecture of (a) original Phoenix and (b) Elastic Phoenix

5.1   Sharing Data

One challenge in designing Elastic Phoenix was how to get input data to the worker threads. The master thread splits the input data, but the worker threads then need to access this data for the map phase. A common idiom in original Phoenix applications is to mmap an input file, then have the splitter calculate offsets into the mapped file. Since Elastic Phoenix threads do not share an address space, this clearly will not work. In the interest of flexibility, we also assume that the worker processes cannot access the input file.

Our initial design, which made no changes to the original Phoenix API, required splitter functions to return pointers to the actual input data. The framework then copied this data into shared memory. This was a simple requirement, but one that did not exist in original Phoenix. As a result, some original applications returned pointers to structures that describe the input data, rather than pointers to the actual data itself. This design allows applications to continue using the mmap method described above, with most applications requiring no changes to the splitter code.

However, copying the input data into shared memory after it has been split is a performance bottleneck. Most application-provided splitters must examine at least some portion of the data in order to generate sane splits. Therefore, the copying strategy ends up reading in the data from disk during the split, then copying the data into the shared-memory region, and possibly reading the data off disk again if the buffer cache has been recycled.

Our final design changes the API for splitter functions by adding an argument: a structure containing pointers to memory-allocation functions, which we require the splitter use to allocate space for the input data. The functions we pass to the splitter are custom memory-allocation functions that allocate space in the shared-memory region, keeping all allocation metadata in the region itself. The common design for splitters using this API is to allocate memory for a split, read data directly into this memory, then reduce the size of the split as necessary to reflect application-specific restrictions on the split data.

In addition to the input data, the master and the workers must share the intermediate and final data arrays. The intermediate data is straightforward to move into the shared-memory region, using the previously mentioned memory allocators to dynamically allocate the arrays. The only complication is that there is a set of intermediate data arrays for each worker thread, and in Elastic Phoenix the total number of worker threads is not known at initialization time. We deal with this by setting an upper bound on the number of map threads and pre-allocating space for the necessary pointers.

There is one additional issue with the final data array: it is returned to the application when the MapReduce job finishes. This causes a problem because many applications free this array when they are done processing the results it contains. This works in original Phoenix because the framework allocates the final data array with malloc. In Elastic Phoenix this array resides in the shared-memory region and is allocated with our custom allocator. We deal with this by adding a function to the API: map_reduce_cleanup. The cleanup function mirrors the framework's map_reduce_ init function, and is called by the application when it is finished with the results of the MapReduce job.

5.2 Assigning Tasks

In original Phoenix, there is one task queue for each worker thread. The framework does allow threads to steal work from other queues when their own queue runs out, so pre-allocating a task queue for each of the maximum number of worker threads is one potential solution. However, given that Elastic Phoenix will rarely have the maximum number of worker threads, this would lead to the threads exhausting their own queues, then all sharing the other queues until they are exhausted. Given this, we opted for a simpler design with a single task queue. The task queue is pre-allocated in shared memory with a maximum number of tasks, and all worker threads take work from the queue. Since the task queue in original Phoenix was already thread-safe for dequeue operations, we re-used nearly all of its code.

The pre-allocation design causes an issue for the splitter: there is a maximum number of map tasks, so the splitter can only create so many splits. Elastic Phoenix uses the application-provided unit size estimate to request an appropriate number of data units for each split such that the task queue is filled but not exceeded. However, an application's estimated unit size will, in some cases, be inaccurate because the data is not uniform and not known beforehand. In this case, the framework may run out of space for map tasks before all the data has been split. We deal with this situation by requiring that splitters be "resettable". When the splitter is passed a special argument, it should thereafter operate as if it has not yet been called. When we run out of space for map tasks, we reset the splitter and re-split the data, requesting more units for each task. This is a rare case, as many applications provide good unit size estimates. We have observed that when re-splitting is required it often takes only one try, which tends to be fast due to filesystem caching.

5.3 Coordinating Workers

An Elastic Phoenix job is started by first running the master process, then running one or more worker processes. Coordinating the worker threads is somewhat different from original Phoenix, since the master does not create the worker threads.

We use two basic mechanisms for coordination in Elastic Phoenix: a worker counter and a barrier, both stored in shared memory. When the master starts, it executes the split phase, then waits for workers to join the computation. The first thing a worker process does when it starts is acquire a worker ID using the counter in shared memory. This is done using atomic operations to avoid the need for a lock.

Because we do not assume that all workers run under the same kernel, we cannot use a blocking barrier for synchronization between computation phases. Instead, we have implemented a barrier using spinlocks and polling. The barrier is used after each stage to synchronize the master and worker threads. The master thread reaches the barrier first, since it does no work in the map, reduce, and merge phases. To make the barrier code simpler, we give each worker process a constant number of threads; in our current implementation the default is four. In addition, we use a shared spinlock to prevent new workers from joining the computation at inconvenient times, such as after the first worker thread reaches the barrier (since this would change the number of threads expected, complicating the barrier code) or before the master has finished setting up the necessary shared environment.

Elastic Phoenix keeps track of the current phase of execution using a flag in shared memory. This allows workers to join during any stage of execution: split, map, reduce, or merge. A worker that joins during a later phase skips the previous phases entirely.

An additional coordination problem in Elastic Phoenix is that because we have attempted to preserve the original Phoenix API as much as possible, the application code is not intended to be executed in multiple processes. Many original Phoenix applications contain code that should be executed only once as part of initialization or cleanup. We add two optional application-provided functions to the API to deal with this: `prep` and `cleanup`. If an application may provides these functions, Elastic Phoenix guarantees that they will be executed only in the master process. The `prep` function is called before any other work is done, and can be used to, for example, open the input file and set up data for the splitter. The `cleanup` function is called by the `map_reduce_cleanup` function described earlier. These functions reduce the need for applications to explicitly manage concurrency, and allow our implementation to handle initialization and cleanup differently in future versions.

6   Porting Phoenix Applications

One of our design goals, as described in Section 4, was to allow original Phoenix applications to be easily ported to Elastic Phoenix. In this section, we describe our experiences porting applications, and try to quantify the amount of change required. Table 1 lists the complete set of API changes.

The biggest change that is required in every application is to the splitter function. Since Elastic Phoenix requires that the splitter use a framework-provided memory allocator for allocating input splits, it has an additional argument. In some splitters, this is simply a matter of replacing calls to `malloc` with calls to the provided allocator, but most need to be restructured to read in a file incrementally instead of using `mmap`, as described in Section 5.1.

Table 1. API changes from original Phoenix to Elastic Phoenix

Description	Original Phoenix	Elastic Phoenix
Splitter function signature	`int splitter(void *, int, map_args_t *)`	`int splitter(void *, int, map_args_t *, splitter_mem_ops_t *)`
Splitter uses provided allocator	`free(out->data); out->data = malloc(out->length);`	`mem->free(out->data); out->data = mem->alloc(out->length);`
Splitter can be reset	N/A	`if(req_units < 0) { lseek(data->fd, 0, SEEK_SET); data->fpos = 0; }`
New cleanup API function	`printf("Num. values: %d\n", mr_args.result->length); return(0);`	`printf("Number of values: %d\n", mr_args.result->length); map_reduce_cleanup(&mr_args); return(0);`
New application prep function	`int main(int argc, char **argv) { ... struct stat s; stat("in", &s); data.fd = open("in"); mr_args.data_size = s.st_size; ...`	`int prep(void *data, map_reduce_args_t *args) { struct stat s; stat("in", &s); ((app_data_t*)data)->fd = open("in"); args->data_size = s.st_size; }`
New application cleanup function	`int main(int argc, char **argv) { ... close(data.fd); ...`	`int cleanup(void *data) { app_data_t *ad = (app_data_t *)data; close(ad->fd); }`
API init modifies argc and argv	`int nargs = argc; char *fname = argv[1]; map_reduce_init();`	`map_reduce_init(&argc, &argv); int nargs = argc; char *fname = argv[1];`

In Phoenix applications, most of the code in `main` serves one of four purposes: setting up the splitter; setting up the MapReduce job; processing the results; and cleaning up. The first can usually be moved verbatim into the `prep` function. The second is usually idempotent, operating only on local data structures, and can remain intact without harm. The third and fourth can usually be moved to the `cleanup` function to ensure they execute only in the master process.

Table 2. Porting MapReduce applications: original to Elastic Phoenix (lines of code)

Application	Original	Elastic	Lines altered
Histogram	245	285	110
Word Count	234	202	114
Linear Regression	230	243	97
Matrix Multiply	168	185	48

The original Phoenix framework includes seven sample applications: histogram, k-means, linear regression, matrix multiply, PCA, string match, and word count. Of these, we have ported histogram, word count, and linear regression. PCA and k-means require multiple MapReduce jobs, a feature not currently supported in Elastic Phoenix (we discuss this limitation in Section 8). The matrix multiply included in original Phoenix is not written in the MapReduce style: the map tasks calculate the resultant matrix directly into a known output location, rather than emitting the calculated values as intermediate data. We wrote a new matrix multiply for original Phoenix that uses the MapReduce style, emitting a key-value pair for each entry in the resultant matrix, then ported it to Elastic Phoenix. String match also does not emit any intermediate or final data; in fact, it produces no results at all.

To quantify the amount of work required to convert an application to Elastic Phoenix, we analyzed the applications we converted. First, we calculated the lines of code for each application before and after conversion using SLOCCount [3]. Second, we estimated how many lines were altered by taking a `diff` of the two source files and counting the number of altered lines in the Elastic Phoenix version. This does not entirely account for the fact that many of the changes simply involved moving code from one function to another. The results of this analysis are displayed in Table 2. Of course, lines of code are an incomplete and controversial metric for programming effort, but we include it as a data point for consideration.

Word count was the first sample application we ported, and we modified it incrementally during the development of Elastic Phoenix. Therefore, it underwent more change than would an application being ported directly to the final version of Elastic Phoenix. We ported histogram and linear regression to one intermediate version of Elastic Phoenix, then to the final version, so they display less change than word count. We developed our new version of matrix multiply for original Phoenix first, then we ported it directly to the final version of Elastic Phoenix. Therefore, matrix multiply provides the best indication of the effort needed to directly port an application. Anecdotally, a single developer wrote the new matrix multiply application for original Phoenix in several hours, and took only a few minutes to port it to Elastic Phoenix.

7   Evaluation

We evaluated Elastic Phoenix in two ways. First, we evaluated the overhead of using Elastic Phoenix by running our ported applications with both frameworks. Then, we explored the advantages of Elastic Phoenix by developing a workload of repeated MapReduce jobs on a system where the availability of processors varies over time. All experiments were performed on an Intel Xeon X5550 (2.67 GHz) server with two sockets, eight cores, 16 hyperthreads, and 48 GB of RAM. We compiled original Phoenix with its default tuning parameters, and used the default four worker threads per process for Elastic Phoenix.

Table 3. Applications and inputs for evaluation

Application	Description	Input Size
Histogram	Counts the frequency of each color value over pixels in a bitmap image	1.4 GB
Word Count	Counts the frequency of each word in a text file	10 MB
Linear Regression	Generates a linear approximation of a set of points	500 MB
Matrix Multiply	Parallel matrix multiplication using row and column blocks	1000x1000

7.1   Overhead

The performance advantage of malleability is that MapReduce jobs can be accelerated as they run by adding threads to the computation. If the overhead of Elastic Phoenix is so large that, for example, using four threads in original Phoenix is faster than using eight threads in Elastic Phoenix, then this advantage disappears. In this section we evaluate the overhead of using Elastic Phoenix, showing that for some applications it is possible to increase performance by adding threads.

To evaluate the overhead of our design, we ran four applications under both original and Elastic Phoenix. For each application, we used the largest input data we could given 4 GB of shared memory (we discuss these limits in Section 8). The applications we used and their input sizes are shown in Table 3. All times are averages over five runs, with cold filesystem caches.

We divide these applications into two classes, which we will discuss separately: I/O-bound and CPU-bound. Histogram, word count, and linear regression are I/O-bound. This is due to the fact that the computation performed in the map and reduce stages is quite trivial, even with large input. The bottleneck, therefore, is reading and splitting the input data, which must be done serially in both original and Elastic Phoenix. Our matrix multiply application is CPU-bound because its input is generated in the splitter function, avoiding any file I/O.

Benchmark results for the I/O-bound applications are presented in Figure 2. Being I/O-bound, we do not expect any speedup as we add threads. We observe that Elastic Phoenix has little overhead compared to original Phoenix for the histogram and linear regression applications (8% and 6%, respectively, on average), showing some slowdown as we add more threads due to the additional coordination overhead. These applications have large input data, and generate intermediate data with a fixed number of keys.

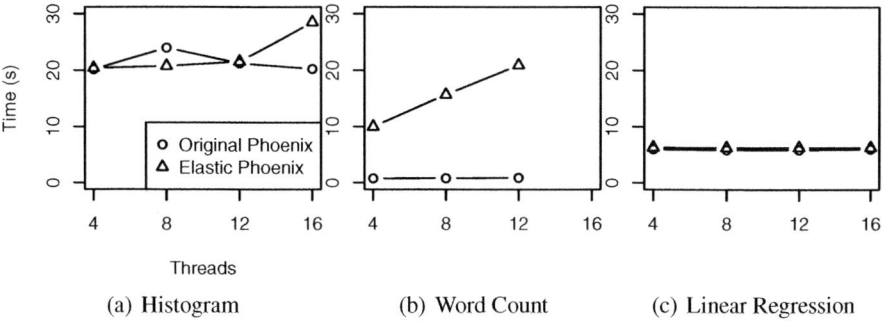

Fig. 2. Overhead experiment results for I/O-bound applications

In contrast, we observe significant overhead (1792% average) in the word count application. This overhead likely stems from the fact that the input size is small, and that the application produces a large amount of intermediate data with diverse keys, since many more words appear infrequently in the input than appear frequently. This causes a large amount of extra shared memory to be allocated but never used, as the framework allocates space for multiple values (10, by default) with the same key when the first value for a given key is emitted. In fact, word count, with only 10 MB of input data, can be run with at most 12 worker threads in Elastic Phoenix; with more threads, the small amount of additional per-thread allocation in shared memory causes it to exceed the 4 GB limit. Our shared-memory allocator is simple, and does not match the efficiency of the system's `malloc`, which is used in original Phoenix.

Benchmark results for our single CPU-bound application (i.e., matrix multiply) are shown in Figure 3. Here we observe significant speedup from four to eight threads, then moderate speedup as we increase to 12 and 16 threads. We theorize that the extreme speedup from four to eight threads is caused by the fact that our CPUs are quad-core, and with eight threads Phoenix uses both sockets. Original Phoenix pins threads to cores, spreading work out as much as possible, but we have configured it to use the same number of processors as threads, so the four threads are pinned onto one CPU. Using both sockets doubles the total usable cache size and the total memory bandwidth available. The decline in speedup beyond eight threads is likely due to the fact that we have only eight real CPU cores, and the hyperthreaded cores offer little advantage in an application such as matrix multiply with regular memory access patterns, few branches, and no disk I/O.

With four threads (i.e., a single worker process), Elastic Phoenix adds no overhead compared to original Phoenix. Elastic Phoenix adds a moderate amount of overhead when more than one process is used, due to the added overhead of coordinating threads in multiple processes, such as increased contention on spinlocks. Overall, the overhead averages 38%. Nonetheless, Elastic Phoenix with eight threads is significantly faster than original Phoenix with four threads, suggesting that the ability to add additional workers as a job runs can improve performance in some cases.

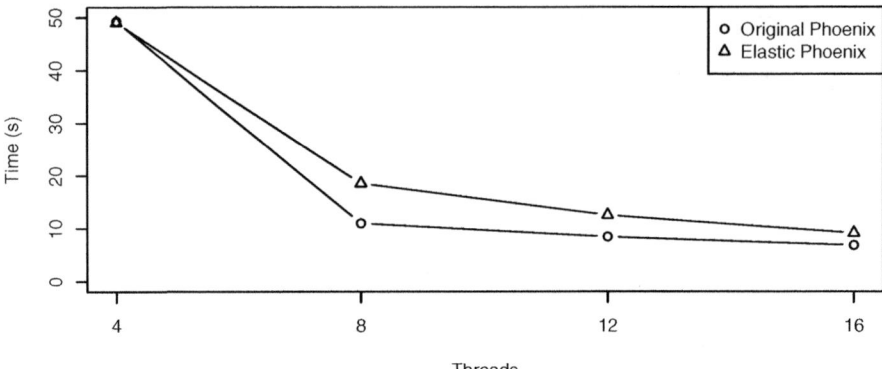

Fig. 3. Overhead experiment results for the CPU-bound matrix multiply application

7.2 Elasticity Advantages

Elastic Phoenix can improve throughput and job latency by allowing idle processors to be used immediately by a running MapReduce job. A performance improvement is possible when the overhead of using Elastic Phoenix does not exceed the speedup provided by the additional threads. As we showed earlier, this is the case for some applications. In this section, we evaluate how much performance can be gained in such a situation. For this benchmark, job latency can be reduced by 29% by adding threads as processors become available.

Consider a scenario in which a sequence of MapReduce jobs is run repeatedly, starting again each time it finishes. For example, the sequence may consist of a job that creates a link graph from a set of hypertext pages, then a job that computes the most popular page. Assume the jobs run on a system where CPU resources become available unpredictably, as is typical in a multi-user, batch-scheduled environment. Original Phoenix always uses the number of CPUs that are available when it starts, while in Elastic Phoenix CPUs are added to the computation as they become available.

Our benchmark uses alternating linear regression and matrix multiply jobs with random-sized inputs of 250 MB to 500 MB for linear regression and 500 x 500 to 1000 x 1000 for matrix multiply. This sequence represents a typical workload of an I/O-bound job that generates input for a compute-bound job, although we do not actually use the linear regression output as input for the matrix multiply. With one worker thread, the jobs take between 1 second and 5 minutes each. For this experiment, we compiled Elastic Phoenix with one thread per worker process, so that it can take advantage of a single processor becoming available.

We generated a set of random CPU availability changes, where every 5 seconds the number of CPUs available can change, with at least 2 and at most 8 CPUs always being available, since our host has 8 CPU cores (we do not employ the 8 hyperthreaded cores). The workload we generated contains 500 jobs in total: 250 linear regression jobs interleaved with 250 matrix multiply jobs.

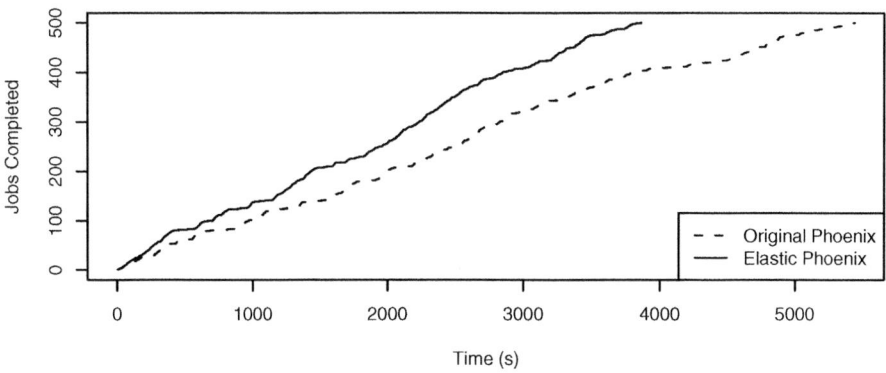

Fig. 4. Job completion over time in the elasticity benchmark

The results of the experiment are displayed in Figure 4. Original Phoenix completed the jobs in 5,451 seconds and Elastic Phoenix completed the jobs in 3,866 seconds, a 29% improvement. We see from these results that adding processors as they become available can drastically speed up a workload of this type.

Note that we have successfully tested the ability to dynamically remove workers from a running Elastic Phoenix job, for proper malleability, but we do not present a performance evaluation in this paper.

8   Limitations and Future Work

The design of Elastic Phoenix introduces a number of limitations not present in original Phoenix. Some of these are inherent to the design we have chosen; others are due to our current implementation and could be eliminated in the future without a significant design change. There are also some ways in which Elastic Phoenix could be improved, orthogonal to these limitations.

Job Size. Currently, the size of the shared-memory region used with Elastic Phoenix limits the amount of input data that can be used. This is because the input data must all fit in shared memory, and will share the space with some of the intermediate data (input data is freed immediately after being used by a map task, but intermediate values are stored to shared memory as they are produced). Similarly, the intermediate data must share the space with some final data, so this data is also limited in size. The input size limit is not the same for all applications and cannot be calculated in advance. As mentioned in Section 7.1, the number of intermediate key-value pairs, as well as the diversity of the keys, affects the maximum input size.

Combiners. The original Phoenix framework allows applications to provide a combiner function, which performs a partial reduce on the map output of a single worker thread. This can speed up the reduce stage, and reduce the amount of space used for intermediate data. In particular, it helps applications that have a large number of repeated intermediate keys.

Elastic Phoenix currently does not support combiners. The application may specify a combiner, to keep the API consistent with original Phoenix, but it will not be used by the framework. This is a limitation of the current implementation and could be changed in the future. It is possible that this modification would help with the job size limitation by compacting intermediate data.

Multiple MapReduce Jobs. A common idiom in MapReduce applications, including Phoenix applications, is to run multiple MapReduce jobs in sequence. For example, one might run a job to do a large computation, then another job to sort the results by value. In original Phoenix, multiple jobs can be performed without writing data to disk: the output data from one job becomes the input data to another job. That is, multiple calls are made to the Phoenix MapReduce scheduler within a single executable application.

The current Elastic Phoenix implementation does not support running multiple MapReduce jobs in one execution, due to the way in which Elastic Phoenix initializes data that will be shared among the master and worker processes. This limitation could be eliminated through some further design.

Number of Workers. Elastic Phoenix pre-allocates a number of data structures that in original Phoenix are allocated based on the number of threads being used. In particular, there is one set of intermediate data queues and one final data queue for each worker thread, and the pointers for these are pre-allocated. They could be allocated dynamically as workers join the computation, but this would require using a linked list or similar structure, making lookups slower when inserting data.

In order to pre-allocate this data, we set a fixed limit on the number of worker tasks that can join a MapReduce job. The default limit in our current implementation is 32 threads, which allows for eight worker processes with four threads each. On any given system, the number of worker threads is naturally limited by the number of processors, so this is a minor limitation.

Other Future Work. Elastic Phoenix makes extensive use of spinlocks instead of blocking locks. This is because we designed Elastic Phoenix with flexibility in mind, and for a potential hybrid shared-memory and distributed-memory version of Elastic Phoenix where the worker processes may not share a kernel, making the use of standard blocking locks, such as pthreads mutexes and semaphores, impossible. One potential performance improvement would be to use blocking locks when they are available, or to exploit optimistic concurrency by making more extensive use of atomic operations. This would likely involve abstracting locking and atomic operations so that they could be implemented in an appropriate way for any given data sharing system.

The original Phoenix software implemented many optimizations to improve cache usage and memory locality for worker threads. In the process of building Elastic Phoenix, we have eschewed many of these optimizations, either because they do not apply in the case where worker threads are in different processes or because getting the initial version of Elastic Phoenix was easier without them. In the future, we may re-introduce some of these optimizations.

9   Concluding Remarks

We have presented the design, implementation, and an evaluation of Elastic Phoenix, a MapReduce implementation for shared-memory multiprocessors. Based on the Stanford Phoenix system, Elastic Phoenix adds the ability to support malleable jobs that can dynamically add processors to the computation, with the goal of reducing the turnaround time of the job or workload.

Using a synthetic workload (Figure 4), we have shown that Elastic Phoenix can improve the response time of the workload by up to 29%, over an equivalent workload where processor allocations can only change at job start-up time. Although the benefits of malleability or an elastic programming system will vary from application to application, Elastic Phoenix provides those benefits while maintaining the MapReduce programming model and much of the Phoenix API.

Acknowledgements. This research was supported by a grant from the Natural Sciences and Engineering Research Council of Canada (NSERC).

References

1. Amazon Elastic Compute Cloud (Amazon EC2),
   `http://aws.amazon.com/ec2`
2. Apache Hadoop,
   `http://hadoop.apache.org/`
3. SLOCCount,
   `http://sourceforge.net/projects/sloccount/`
4. Chohan, N., Castillo, C., Spreitzer, M., Steinder, M., Tantawi, A., Krintz, C.: See spot run: using spot instances for mapreduce workflows. In: 2nd USENIX Conference on Hot Topics in Cloud Computing, HotCloud 2010 (June 2010)
5. Condie, T., Conway, N., Alvaro, P., Hellerstein, J.M., Elmeleegy, K., Sears, R.: MapReduce online. In: 7th USENIX Symposium on Networked Systems Design and Implementation (NSDI 2010), USENIX Association (2010)
6. Dean, J., Ghemawat, S.: MapReduce: Simplified data processing on large clusters. In: 6th Symposium on Operating Systems Design and Implementation (OSDI 2004), USENIX Association (2004)
7. El Maghraoui, K., Desell, T.J., Szymanski, B.K., Varela, C.A.: Dynamic Malleability in Iterative MPI Applications. In: IEEE International Symposium on Cluster Computing and the Grid (CCGrid 2007), pp. 591–598. IEEE, Los Alamitos (2007)
8. Feitelson, D., Rudolph, L., Schwiegelshohn, U., Sevcik, K., Wong, P.: Theory and practice in parallel job scheduling. In: Feitelson, D.G., Rudolph, L. (eds.) IPPS-WS 1997 and JSSPP 1997. LNCS, vol. 1291, pp. 1–34. Springer, Heidelberg (1997)
9. Gropp, W., Lusk, E.: Dynamic process management in an MPI setting. In: 7th IEEE Symposium on Parallel and Distributed Processing. IEEE Computer Society, Los Alamitos (1995)
10. Ko, S.Y., Hoque, I., Cho, B., Gupta, I.: Making cloud intermediate data fault-tolerant. In: Proceedings of the 1st ACM Symposium on Cloud Computing, SoCC 2010, pp. 181–192. ACM, New York (2010)
11. Nurmi, D., Wolski, R., Grzegorczyk, C., Obertelli, G., Soman, S., Youseff, L., Zagorodnov, D.: The Eucalyptus Open-Source Cloud-Computing System. In: 2009 9th IEEE/ACM International Symposium on Cluster Computing and the Grid, pp. 124–131. IEEE, Los Alamitos (2009)

12. Taura, K., Kaneda, K., Endo, T., Yonezawa, A.: Phoenix: a parallel programming model for accommodating dynamically joining/leaving resources. ACM SIGPLAN Notices 38(10) (October 2003)
13. Verma, A., Zea, N., Cho, B., Gupta, I., Campbell, R.: Breaking the MapReduce Stage Barrier. In: IEEE International Conference on Cluster Computing, Heraklion, Greece, pp. 235–244 (2010)
14. Yoo, R.M., Romano, A., Kozyrakis, C.: Phoenix rebirth: Scalable MapReduce on a large-scale shared-memory system. In: 2009 IEEE International Symposium on Workload Characterization (IISWC), pp. 198–207. IEEE, Los Alamitos (2009)

A Load-Aware Data Placement Policy on Cluster File System

Yu Wang[1,2], Jing Xing[1], Jin Xiong[1], and Dan Meng[1]

[1] National Research Center for Intelligent Computing Systems,
Institute of Computing Technology, Chinese Academy of Sciences
[2] Graduate University of Chinese Academy of Sciences
{wangyu,xingjing,xj,md}@ncic.ac.cn

Abstract. In a large-scale cluster system with many applications running on it, cluster-wide I/O access workload disparity and disk saturation on only some storage servers have been the severe performance bottleneck that deteriorates the system I/O performance. As a result, the system response time will increase and the throughput of the system will decrease drastically. In this paper, we present a load-aware data placement policy that will distribute data across the storage servers based on the load of each server and automatically migrate data from heavily-loaded servers to lightly-loaded servers. This policy is adaptive and self-managing. It operates without any prior knowledge of application access workload characteristics or the capabilities of storage servers. It can make full use of the aggregate disk bandwidth of all storage servers efficiently. Performance evaluation shows that our policy will improve the aggregate I/O bandwidth by 10%-20% compared with random data placement policy especially under mixed workloads.

Keywords: Cluster File System, Data Placement.

1 Introduction

Cluster computing has been widely used in many fields such as weather research, geophysics, finance, information service and so on [1]. These applications not only need high-performance computing ability, but also generate large amount of data, hence I/O performance has a significant influence on the execution time of the applications. Moreover, the data set size of many applications can be petabyte and is increasing gradually now and in the future [2, 3, 4].

In almost all of the environments, the file size distribution is approximately lognormal or a mixture of lognormal [5, 6, 7]. The file size among files differs so great that it will arise some problems if files are not placed properly. If large files from applications are all stored on the same servers, the disk space of these servers will be exhausted while that of others will be under-used. However, if the server's disk is over-utilized, its I/O performance will degrade acutely [8] and even worse, the write operation may fail if there is no space left in the disk for the newly created files. It will be the bottleneck and failure point of the whole system despite the average disk usage of the system is so low that it has much large space left really. Additionally, in

E. Altman and W. Shi (Eds.): NPC 2011, LNCS 6985, pp. 17–31, 2011.

some environments, the read/write requests are distributed uniformly among storage servers [9], while in others, the distribution is so uneven [6] that the data access workloads are very different among storage servers. The I/O performance of those I/O-overloaded servers will decline because there are many read/write requests waiting for disk I/O. Hence, those servers will be the performance bottleneck of the whole system and the response time will increase drastically. With the rapidly growing I/O demand of data-intensive or I/o-intensive applications [10], the impact of disk I/O on overall system performance is becoming more and more important.

In general, I/O load imbalance and disk space saturation will engender the system bottleneck, decrease the read/write performance and increase system response time. It is a vital issue to avoid such situations as possible .An efficient data placement policy is potentially one of the best ways to relieve or eliminate these problems by distributing and arranging the application's data among the storage servers intelligently and efficiently.

In this paper, we propose a load-aware data placement policy to adaptive distribute data among storage servers. It defines method to evaluation the load of storage system, which will consider both workload and disk utilization. Based on the evaluation result, it chooses the location of a new created file. Multiple locations will be chosen if the file keeps multiple replicas. When load imbalance or disk saturation occurs, the evaluation method can also guide data migration process to achieve system balance. The evaluation shows that our data placement policy can diminish the situation of disk saturation. By adjusting data distribution through evaluating system load, higher I/O throughput can be achieved as we can maintain workload balance in most of the time.

The rest of this paper is organized as follows. In section 2 that follows, related work in the literature is briefly reviewed. In section 3, we describe the prototype file system DCFS3. Section 4 describes the load-aware data placement policy for cluster file system. Evaluation is given in section 5. Finally we will conclude this paper in section 6.

2   Related Work

Pseudo-random hash method has been widely used in file systems and storage systems to distribute files among storage servers. All of the hash related works do not consider the I/O access difference of storage servers. However, some of them have taken the heterogeneity of disks into account. Chord [12] adapts consistent hashing[11] to select the data storage location. However, it does not take the difference of I/O workload and storage usage among servers into account. Choy [13] has proposed extendible hashing for perfect distribution of data to disks. But it does not support necessary features such as weighting of storage servers and data replication. Honicky[14] presents the RUSH algorithms for balanced distribution of data to disks, which support weighting of disks and data replication. However, these algorithms rely on iteration for producing the same sequence of numbers regardless of the number actually required, and the large-scale iterations increase the allocation time. CRUSH[15] most closely resembles the RUSH family of algorithms upon which it is based. It fully generalizes the useful elements of $RUSH_P$ and $RUSH_T$ which resolving previous issues. But it also does not consider I/O load balance of servers. Brinkmann[16] proposes an efficient, distributed data placement policy of pseudo-random distribution data to multiple disks using partitioning of the unit ranges for SAN. Wu and Burns [17] build on this work to provide a storage system which can balance metadata workload by moving file sets among storage servers. These methods can relocate data sets to rebalance the load. However, they all do not support the placement of replicas.

A large body of work can be found in the literature that addresses the issue of balancing the load of disk I/O. Many dynamic load management techniques for parallel systems are designed for homogeneous clusters. Workload is transferred from heavily loaded servers to lightly loaded ones. Another series of techniques allow for server heterogeneity but requires all servers to periodically broadcast I/O load and available storage space. Utopia [18] uses prior knowledge of non-uniform server capabilities and makes load adjustment decisions based on the available CPU utilization, free memory size and disk bandwidth updates for each server. Zhu et al [19] use knowledge of server storage capacity and employ a metric that combines available CPU cycles and storage capacity of each server to select a server to process the incoming requests. Lee et al. [20] propose two file assignment algorithms that balance the load across all disks. The I/O load balancing policies in these studies have been shown to be effective in improving overall system performance by fully utilizing the available hard drives. Xiao Qin et al. [21] develop two effective I/O-aware load balancing schemes, which make it possible to balance I/O load by assigning I/O-intensive sequential and parallel jobs to the node with light I/O load. However, the above techniques are insufficient for automatic computing platforms due to the lack of adaptability. Dynamo [22] is a distributed replicated storage system used in Amazon. It maps the virtual node which is I/O-intensive to the server node which can provide higher I/O bandwidth to achieve the I/O load balance. It also distributes all virtual storage nodes to the hash ring uniformly to achieve the balance of storage utilization. It is only suitable when the request size is similar. In the system Sorrento, Tang et al [24] weight two factors of storage utilization and I/O workload of the providers to get an integral load factor, which will be used to choose the segment's storage location. The system dynamically adjusts the segments' location to balance I/O load and storage usage among the providers. But it relies on the prior-knowledge of the applications to determine how to combine these two factors together efficiently and its I/O workload factor can only reflect the disk I/O status of one special moment. BASIL[28] achieves load balancing by modeling of workloads and devices, however, it only solve balance problem with focus on I/O workload and not space utilization.

Existing data placement methods considers either disk usage or I/O load. And some of them requires almost equal request size, or rely on prior knowledge of workload characteristics. We propose an adaptive and self-managing data placement method that takes both disk storage and I/O load into account. Our method is designed for common environments with very diverse I/O requests. And it operates without any prior knowledge of workload characteristics or the capabilities of storage servers.

3   Background

In this section, we will give a brief overview of the basic architectural features of DCFS3 which is the fundamental system for this work. DCFS3 is a high performance cluster file system designed for supercomputers. It consists of Metadata Server (MDS), Object-based Storage Device (OSD) and Client, which are connected by AMP (Asynchronous Message Passing). The architecture of DCFS3 is shown in Figure 1.

Fig. 1. DCFS3 architecture

The primary goals of this architecture are scalability, performance and reliability. DCFS3 maximizes the separation of file system metadata management from the storage of file data. Metadata information and operations are collectively managed by MDS. In DCFS3, MDS doesn't only maintain namespace metadata, but also maintain data location. To provide high performance management, MDS holds all the metadata in memory [27]. Clients interact directly with OSDs to perform file I/O operations. All OSDs are divided into multiple OSD groups, and OSDs within the same group have the same hardware configurations. When creating a new file, MDS will choose an OSD group and stripe the new file across all the OSD within the same group. To support high availability, replica technology is implemented in data storage. If a file will be maintained with 3 replicas, MDS will choose 3 OSD groups to place its 3 replicas when creating this file.

4   Load-Aware Data Placement and Load Balance Mechanism

In this section, we first describe how to measure the storage server's load and how to choose file's storage location based on the load. Then we will discuses load balance mechanism.

4.1   Storage Server Load

Due to unexpected data access workload and big difference of file size and file life time, the following two conditions are unavoidable. One is that some storage servers are saturated while others are relatively vacant. The other is that some servers' disk I/O is heavy while others' is light. In these two conditions, those overloaded servers will be the bottleneck of the whole system. As a result the throughput will decrease and the response time will increase. Therefore, we should combine the server's I/O workload and its disk storage utilization efficiently when measuring its load.

We use an ordered pair to define the load f, $f = (f_l, f_s)$ where f_l is I/O workload of the server and f_s is disk storage utilization. In our data placement policy and load balance mechanism, we will first consider its I/O workload f_l, then its disk utilization f_s. In the following sections, we will treat these two factors separately and orderly.

For the server's I/O workload, we measure it by the average bandwidth utilization ratio of the disk during the two contiguous load collections. By extending the method of Linux command *iostat* when computing the disk bandwidth utilization ratio of a special hard disk during a small time interval, we can get the average disk bandwidth utilization ratio $f_l \in [0,1]$ during the load collection time interval. For the server's storage utilization, we measure it by disk space usage of the disk, which can be computed from the fields by calling *vfs_statfs*. We use it as the storage utilization factor $f_s \in [0,1]$.

An efficient data placement policy should consider the disparity of I/O workload among storage servers when arranging the data locations. To fully utilize all storage server's disk bandwidth, the I/O workload should be averaged among all storage servers. Meanwhile, storage utilization must also be taken into account to avoid disk saturation, which is also the cause of performance bottleneck.

4.2 Loads-Aware Data Placement

When creating a new file, the Client will send a message to MDS which will determine the OSD location for this new file and MDS must avoid the previously mentioned bottleneck problems. Due to this, we propose a location selection method based on the probability distribution of the loads on all OSDs. Each OSD group has a load factor *f* which we discussed before. The selection probability of one OSD group is determined by its load proportion of all OSD groups load. The larger the percentage, the smaller probability it will be selected. The proportion is negatively correlated to the selection probability. During the load collection interval, all the newly created files will be distributed among all the OSD groups statistically.

Let's take an example to explain how this method works. We assume that there are 3 OSD groups and every OSD group has a load 0.2, 0.8, 0.4. The load can be either *fl* or *fs*. The selection probability of each OSD group is like the following:

$$p_1 = \frac{1/0.2}{1/0.2 + 1/0.8 + 1/0.4} = \frac{4}{7}, p_2 = \frac{1/0.8}{1/0.2 + 1/0.8 + 1/0.4} = \frac{1}{7} \quad p_3 = \frac{1/0.4}{1/0.2 + 1/0.8 + 1/0.4} = \frac{2}{7}.$$

Then [0, 1) can be divided into 3 sub-ranges, [0, 4/7) is assigned to OSD group 1, [4/7, 5/7) is assigned to OSD group 2, [5/7, 1) is assigned to OSD group 3. When creating a new file, a random real number $\varepsilon \in [0,1)$ will be generated and the OSD group whose range contains ε will be selected. With this method, the newly created files will be distributed among all OSD groups statistically according to their load.

To maximize the system performance by fully utilizing the aggregate disk bandwidth, when evaluating the load of storage system, we firstly considered the workload and then the disk utilization. After an OSD group is chosen in Formula-1, its dist utilization must be checked to skip disk saturation. If any OSD in the group exceeds 95%, it will be discarded and the selection procedure will repeat. The pseudo-code is shown in Figure 2.

```
1: Algorithm: File Storage Based on Load (FSBL)
2: find_flag = 0;
3: unavail_osd_group = Φ ;
4: cur_group_ok = 1;
5: if  fl_i∈[μ(f_l)−3×σ(f_l),μ(f_l)+3×σ(f_l)],∀i=1,2,···,group_num  then
6:        calculate p_i with Formula- 2 for each group i;
7: else
8:        calculate p_i with Formula -1 for each group i;
9: endif
10: while find_flag == 0 do
11:      generate a real random number E in [0, 1);
12:      for each group i in the system do
                         i
13:                if E < Σ p_j   then
                        j=0
14:                          cur_group_id  =  i ;
15:                          break;
16:                endif
17:      endfor
18:      for each osd in osd_group[cur_group_id] osd_ i do
19:                if osd_i.disk_usage >= SATURATION_FLAG then
20:                          cur_group_ok = 0;
21:                          break;
22:                endif
23:      endfor
24:      if cur_group_ok == 1 then
25:                find_flag = 1;
26:                return cur_group_id;
27:      else
28:                if unavail_osd_group == all_osd_group then
29:                          retrun -1;    // file allocation failed.
30:                else
31:                          add cur_group_id to unavail_osd_group;
32:                          continue;
33:                endif
34:      endif
35: endwhile
```

Fig. 2. Pseudo-code of load-aware data placement

1) Check if I/O workload of OSD groups in the system is balanced.
2) If not, use the I/O workload as the load factor to choose the file storage location. By applying the above method, the probability of selecting OSD group i is as follows, N is the number of OSD groups.

$$p_i = \frac{1/f_{li}}{\sum_{j=1}^{N} 1/f_{li}}, i = 1,2,\cdots,N \qquad (Formula-1)$$

3) If yes, use the storage utilization as the load factor to choose the file storage location. By applying the above method, the probability of selecting OSD group i is

$$p_i = \frac{1/f_{si}}{\sum\limits_{j=1}^{N} 1/f_{si}}, i = 1,2,\cdots,N \qquad (Formula-2)$$

4)   When we get an OSD group based on the p_i and the Random value $\varepsilon \in [0,1)$ (Algorithm FSBL line 10-17), we need to check the disk usage of all OSDs in this group (Algorithm FSBL line 18-23). If there is someone whose disk usage exceeds 95%, then go back to step 1) to choose another OSD group (Algorithm FSBL line 24-26). If all the selections fail, it returns error as it indicates that the average disk usage of the system has exceeded 95% (Algorithm FSBL line 28-29). The system need to be expanded by mean of adding new storage servers.

4.3   Load Balance Mechanism

After files are stored based on storage server's load, disparity of I/O workload and disk saturation may also take place as the application workload is keep changing and unpredictable. We first identify these two conditions and then take actions as data migration to eliminate them.

4.3.1   Load Balance Measurement

The above two circumstances should be differentiated separately in that they are two different aspects that influence the system performance. For I/O workload imbalance, we identify it by using the general method that combines mean deviation and standard deviation, that is $\mu(f) \pm C \times \sigma(f)$. The constant C can be adjusted. Through evaluation in section 5.1 we set it to 3 to achieve the best balance between performance and efficiency. Then we can get the confidential interval $[\mu(f_l) - 3 \times \sigma(f_l), \mu(f_l) + 3 \times \sigma(f_l)]$. When I/O workload of all storage servers is within the range, it means that I/O workload of the whole system is balanced. If there is one server whose I/O workload goes beyond the upper bound, it indicates that this server's I/O workload is so heavy that I/O workload of the whole system is imbalance. In this situation, data migration must be triggered to rebalance the load. In our system, we will use OSD group as unit to determine its I/O workload balance. Because the data of a file is striped across an OSD group and the variance of file access frequency results in I/O workload difference among OSD groups. And I/O workload of OSDs within the same OSD group is almost balanced. Hence, load balance of all OSD groups is equivalent to system-wide load balance.

For the server disk space saturation, we identify it by determining whether the disk usage is more than or equal to a SATURATION_FLAG, which we set it as 95% to achieve balance between disk utilization and disk availability. In a cluster system which runs with many applications, there will be numerous fragments in the disk. When the disk usage ratio exceeds 95%, not only the write performance will decrease rapidly, but also the server is in danger of running out of disk. This server will be the access bottleneck or the write failure point. Herein, some data from the saturated disk should migrate to other disks as soon as possible.

MDS collects the two load information periodically, and determines whether the load is balance. If not, the data migration will happen.

4.4   Data Migration

Each object file has a dynamic access frequency, which will change over time. A hot object file is the one that is being actively accessed recently, while a cold object file is the one that has not been accessed for quite a while. Usually, the hot ones are more likely to be accessed in the near future than the cold ones. The last access time (LAT) will be used to measure the temperature of the object file, that is, a more recent LAT stands for a higher temperature while an ever long LAT represents a lower temperature. And the distribution of object files in relation to temperature is typically bimodal. Almost all of the object files are either hot or cold, with few lukewarm ones between them.

We should adopt different data migration strategies for access overload and disk saturation respectively. However, they are all including the following four key aspects. The pseudo-code is shown in Figure 3 and it includes two sub-algorithms DMDS and DMII.

1)   Data Migration Occasion. We will trigger the data migration operation under two situations. When MDS has got the system's load information, it first   check whether there is a server whose disk usage ratio has achieved or exceeded 95% (Algorithm DMDS line 2-7). If there is, it should check if there exists some server whose disk usage is smaller than 95%. If it exists, the data migration will happen, otherwise, it indicates that the disk usage of all the servers is greater than 95%. At this situation, new storage devices need to be added to the cluster file system to provide continuous high performance disk I/O. Second, if the workload of a OSD group beyond the confidential interval as in Algorithm DMII line 2-3, data migration must be triggered to cool the hot OSD group.

2)   Data Migration Source and Destination. That means data will be moved from which OSD and to which OSD. For I/O workload imbalance, data will be moved out from OSD group with the highest I/O workload and to one OSD group with the lowest I/O workload (Algorithm DMII line 4). Each OSD within the source OSD group and the destination OSD group will be one-to-one corresponded as the source and destination. For server disk saturation, its data will be moved to one or several OSDs whose disk usage is low (Algorithm DMDS line 8-23). The reason that we choose several destinations is to avoid the destination to be the bottleneck after data migration.

3)   Data Migration Object. That means what data and how much should be migrated. For I/O workload imbalance, hot data will be migrated preferably. The proportion of data migrated can be adjusted according to the data scale of applications (Algorithm DMII line 5-11). For server disk saturation, cold data will be migrated preferably so that the impact to the normal file access will be minimized. We can compute the optimal quantity of migrated data with reference to the OSD's current disk usage, the average disk usage of the whole system and the destination OSD's disk usage ratio (Algorithm DMDS line 24-31).

4)   Data Migration Manner. That is how the data will be migrated. For I/O workload imbalance, we have determined the one-to-one relationship of the source OSD and the destination OSD. Data migration will take place among every pair of these OSDs in parallel. And within every OSD, multi-thread will be used to move object files. For server disk saturation, the source OSD will use multi-thread to migrate some object files from itself to other OSDs.

```
1: Algorithm: data migration
2: collect_osd_load(osd_disk_usage[], osd_ioload[]); //osd_disk_usage[] is ascendant
3: call Algorithm DMDS    // to handle the situation of disk saturation
4: call Algorithm DMII     // to handle the situation of I/O workload imbalance


1: Algorithm: Data Migration of Disk Saturation (DMDS)
2: osd_disk_saturation[] = Φ ;
3: for each osd osd_i in system do
4:       if osd_i.disk_usage >= SATURATION_FLAG then
5:             add osd_i to osd_disk_saturation;
6:       endif
7: endfor
8: for each osd osd_i in osd_disk_saturation do
9:       data_migration_quantity=
10:             osd_i. disk_capacity*(osd_i.disk_usage–system_average_disk_usage);
11:      index = temp = 0;
12:      initilize dest_osd_data[];
13:      for each osd osd_iter in osd_disk_usage[] do
14:             avail_space=
15:             osd_iter.disk_capacity*(system_average_disk_usage-osd_iter.disk_usage);
16:             temp += avail_space;
17:             if temp <= data_migration_quantity then
18:                    dest_osd_data[index ++] = avail_space;
19:             else
20:                    dest_osd_data[index ++] = temp - data_migration_quantity;
21:                    break;
22:             endif
23:      endfor
24:      total_migration_size = 0;
25:      for osd_iter = 0 to index do
26:             migrate cold object files preferably to the osd_iter;
27:             update total_migration_size;
28:             if total_migration_size >= dest_osd_data[osd_iter] then
29:                    break;
30:             endif
31:      endfor
32: endfor


1: Algorithm: Data Migration of Ioload Imbalance (DMII)
2: for each group osd_group_i in system do
3:    if   fl_i ∈ [μ(f_l)−3×σ(f_l),μ(f_l)+3×σ(f_l)],∀i=1,2,···,group_num   then
4:    find the osd group with the lowest ioload: dest_osd_group ;
5:    for osd_index=0 to nr_osd_in_group in osd_group_i do
6:       total_migration_size = 0;
7:       migrate hot files from osd_group_i[osd_index] to dest_osd_group[osd_index];
8:       update total_migration_size;
9:       if total_migration_size >= osd_group_i[osd_index].total_size*5% then
10:          break;
11:       endif
12:    endfor
13:    endif
14: endfor
```

Fig. 3. Pseudo-code of data migration

5   Performance Evaluation

This section evaluates the performance of our load-aware data placement policy. The system configuration of DCFS3 consists of one MDS, 3 OSD groups with 2 OSDs in each group and six Clients. MDS is configured with two AMD Opteron 2.2 GHz processors and 2GB RAM. All OSDs and Clients are configured of virtual servers created by VMware which include one Intel Xeon Processor (2.0GHz) and 1 GB RAM. All of the servers have one 146GB, 10k rpm Seagate SCSI disk and are connected by Gigabit Ethernet.

5.1   Load Balance Interval Constant

We have shown that constant C of the confidential interval is set to 3 when determining the I/O load balance. We will compare different constant set (C=1, 2, 3, 4) from running time, data migration frequency and data migration quantity. We simulate the burst I/O requests in some occasion of scientific computing applications [9] to evaluate the impact of constant C. File number that will be created is 500. The file size distribution is suitable for the lognormal distribution [9]. The total size of each Client is about 22GB. Table 1 shows the test results. The interval range of constant 4 is so broad that almost all servers I/O workload belong to the interval even if the I/O workload disparity is extremely large and running time increases by 6%. The running time of constant 1 and 2 increases by 8% and 5% because there are so many data migration operations and a large amount of data has been migrated. And there are some data thrashing that consumes the system disk bandwidth. Therefore, 3 is the optimal value of constant C.

Table 1. Test results of constant C

C	Running time	Migration frequency	Migration quantity
1	+8%	8/10	4.8GB
2	+5%	5/10	2.9GB
3	0	1/10	402MB
4	+6%	0/10	0

5.2   Throughput

We simulate three scenarios of system I/O workload balance, imbalance [9] and no I/O workload to compare the system throughput between random data placement (RDP) and load-aware data placement policy with (LADP-with migration) or without data migration (LADP-without migration). For load imbalance, we make the following scene: the average disk bandwidth utilization of the first two OSDs is 100%, the middle two OSDs is 50%, and the last two OSDs has no I/O workload. For load balance, we make the following scene: the average disk bandwidth utilization of all OSDs is 40-50%. The test will be taken under 1, 2, 4, 6 client configurations and all clients execute the test example as in section 5.1 concurrently.

Figure 4 shows throughput under circumstance of no I/O workload. We can see from the figure that throughput of LADP-without migration improves by 3.3%, 5.02%, 5.12% and 5.4% compared with RDP. Figure 5 shows throughput under circumstances of balanced load. We can see from the figure that throughput of LADP-without migration improves by 2.5%, 3.0%, 3.7% and 5.6% compared with

RDP. Figure 6 shows throughput under of load imbalance. We can see from the figure that throughput of LADP-with migration improves by 2.3%, 17.5%, 18.1% and 21.2% compared with RDP and throughput of LADP-without migration improves by 1.9%, 9.1%, 10.3% and 11.2% compared with RDP.

In the circumstance of no load and load balance, the system will undertake some I/O burden because several clients are writing files concurrently. LADP-without migration can consider the real-time load distribution of the system and choose the suitable servers to store the newly created files. Hence, its throughput will be improved for uniformly utilizing the system aggregate disk bandwidth. In circumstance of load imbalance, the system will undertake mixed I/O burden, not only because several clients are writing files concurrently but also other applications have brought out the current load imbalance. LADP-without migration can consider the current load distribution of the system and choose the suitable file storage servers. In addition to this, LADP-with migration can fully utilize the system aggregate disk bandwidth and improve throughput by data migration.

Therefore, the system resource contention on data servers can significantly degrade the overall I/O performance, and skipping hot-spots can substantially improve the I/O performance when load on storage servers is highly imbalanced.

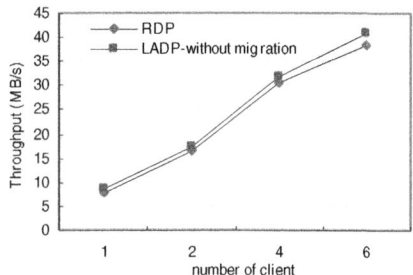

Fig. 4. Throughput when the current system has no workload

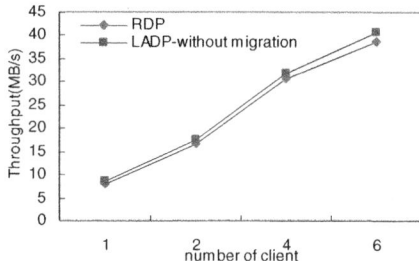

Fig. 5. Throughput when the current system has some workload and the load is balance

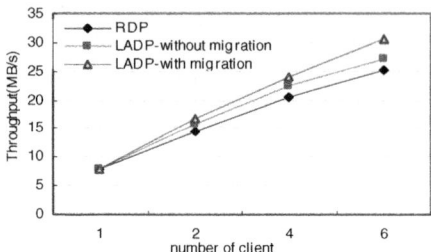

Fig. 6. Throughput when the current system has some workload but the load is not balance

5.3   mpiBLAST Application

The mpiBLAST [25] is the parallel implementation of the biological sequence search tool BLAST. By utilizing distributed computational resources through database fragmentation, query fragmentation and parallel I/O, mpiBLAST improves performance of BLAST by several orders of magnitudes. Since DCFS3 provides cluster-wide shared name space and mpiBLAST runs directly on them through parallel I/O interfaces, the worker does not need the copying procedure in the parallel I/O implementations. It is separated into two steps. The first one is to divide the whole database into multiple segments, that is *mpiformatdb*. The second one is *mpiexec*, which is each worker searches one database fragment using the entire query. Previous research has shown that the length of 90% of the query sequences used by biologists is within the range of 300-600 characters [26] and the second step usually takes a few minutes. But the first step will take dozens of minutes. Therefore, our focus is to decrease the run time of the first step *mpiformatdb*.

We use the sequence database month.est_others and est_mouse, which are the nucleotide sequence databases in non-redundant form, freely available from download at NCBI web site. We compare the running time between RDP and LADP-with migration. The fragmentation number is 25, 50 and 100, and Figure 7 and 8 show the experiment results. In these three fragmentation number, the fragmentation time decreases by 10.2%, 13.9%, and 17.1% for month.est_others and the fragmentation time decreases by 7.5%, 9.1%, and 9.2%s for est_mouse. Our experiments show that with the load-aware data placement, mpiBLAST greatly outperforms random data placement.

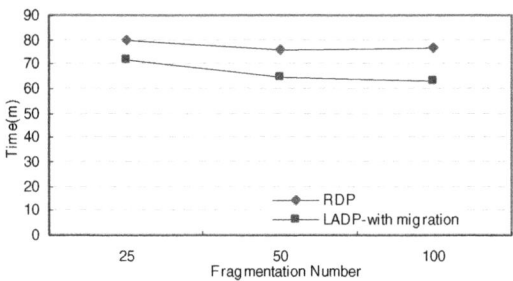

Fig. 7. mpiBLAST fragmentation time of month.est_others

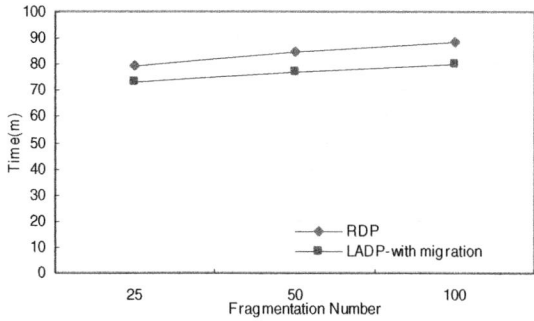

Fig. 8. mpiBLAST fragmentation time of est_mouse

6   Conclusion

In this paper, we present a load-aware data placement policy which is implemented on a large-scale cluster file system DCFS3. In order to avoid performance bottleneck, both I/O workload and storage utilization should be considered when measuring the load of storage system. Data migration is triggered to balance the system-wide load when it is imbalanced. We distinguish two different scenes of load imbalance and take different actions. We propose a probability-based load-aware data placement method. When creating a new file, its location is chosen based on I/O workload first, then the storage utilization. Our experiments show that by considering these two load factors and data migration, disk bandwidth of all servers can be fully utilized and the throughput increases obviously.

In this work, we only evaluate the influence of disk resource contention. Clearly, the load conditions of CPU, memory and network can also influence the throughput and response time. We will study the impact of contention of these resources in the future work.

Acknowledgments. This work is supported by the National High-Tech Research and Development Program of China under grant no. 2006AA01A102 and grant no. 2009AA01Z139.

References

1. http://www.top500.org/
2. DOE National Nuclear Security Administration and the DOE National Security Agency. SGS file system (April 2001)
3. Kramer, W.T.C., Shoshani, A., Agarwal, D.A., Draney, B.R., Jin, G., Butler, G.F., Hules, J.A.: Deep scientific computing requires deep data. IBM J. Res. Dev. 48(2), 209–232 (2004)
4. http://public.web.cern.ch/public/
5. Wang, F., Xin, Q., Hong, B., Brandt, S.A., Miller, E.L., Long, D.D.E., McLarty, T.T.: File system workload analysis for large scale scientific computing applications. In:

Proceedings of the 21st IEEE / 12th NASA Goddard Conference on Mass Storage Systems and Technologies, College Park, MD (April 2004)

6. Leung, A.W., Pasupathy, S., Goodson, G., Miller, E.L.: Measurement and analysis of large scale network file system workloads. In: Proceedings of the 2008 USENIX Annual Technical Conference (June 2008)

7. Evans, K.M., Kuenning, G.H.: Irregularities in file-size distributions. In: Proceedings of the 2nd International Symposisum on Performance Evaluation of Computer and Telecommunication Systems, SPECTS (July 2002)

8. McKusick, M., Joy, W., Leffler, S., Fabry, R.: A Fast File System for UNIX. ACM Trans. on Computer Systems 2(3), 181–197 (1984)

9. Lawrence Livermore National Laboratory. IOR software,
   http://www.llnl.gov/icc/lc/siop/downloads/download.html

10. Zhu, Y., Jiang, H., Qin, X., Swanson, D.: A Case Study of Parallel I/O for Biological Sequence Analysis on Linux Clusters. In: Proceedings of Cluster 2003, Hong Kong, December 1-4 (2003)

11. Karger, D., Lehman, E., Leighton, T., Levine, M., Levin, D., Panigraphy, R.: Consistent hashing and random trees: Distributed caching protocols for relieving hot spots on the World Wide Web. In: Proceedings of ACM Symposium on Theory of Computing (STOC 1997), pp. 654–663 (1997)

12. Stoica, I., Morris, R., Karger, D., Kaashoek, F., Balakrishnan, H.: Chord: A scalable peer-to-peer lookup service for internet applications. In: Proc. of the 2001 Conference on Applications, Technologies, Architectures, and Protocols for Computer Communications (SIGCOMM 2001), San Diego, CA (August 2001)

13. Choy, D.M., Fagin, R., Stockmeyer, L.: Efficiently extendible mappings for balanced data distribution. Algorithmica 16, 215–232 (1996)

14. Honicky, R.J., Miller, E.L.: Replication under scalable hashing: A family of algorithms for scalable decentralized data distribution. In: Proceedings of the 18th International Parallel & Distributed Processing Symposium (IPDPS 2004), Santa Fe, NM (April 2004)

15. Weil, S.A., Brandt, S.A., Miller, E.L., Maltzahn, C.: CRUSH: Controlled, scalable, decentralized placement of replicated data. In: Proc. of the 2006 ACM/IEEE Conference on Supercomputing, Tampa, FL (November 2006)

16. Brinkmann, A., Salzwedel, K., Scheideler, C.: Efficient, distributed data placement strategies for storage area networks. In: In Proceedings of the 12th ACM Symposium on Parallel Algorithms and Architectures SPAA (2000)

17. Wu, C., Lau, F.: Load Balancing in Parallel Computers: Theory and Practice. Kluwer Academic Publishers, Boston (1997)

18. Zhou, S., Wang, J., Zheng, X., Delisle, P.: Utopia: A load-sharing facility for large heterogeneous distributed computing systems. Software Practice and Experience 23(12) (1993)

19. Zhu, H., Yang, T., Zheng, Q., Watson, D., Ibarra, O.H.: Adaptive load sharing for clustered digital library servers. International Journal on Digital Libraries 2(4) (2000)

20. Lee, L., Scheauermann, P., Vingralek, R.: File Assignment in Parallel I/O Systems with Minimal Variance of Service time. IEEE Trans. on Computers 49

21. Xiao, Q., Jiang, H., Zhu, Y., Swanson, D.: Toward load balancing support for I/O intensive parallel jobs in a cluster of workstation. In: Proc. of the 5th IEEE International Conference Cluster Computing, Hong Kong (December 14, 2003)

22. DeCandia, G., Hastorun, D., Jampani, M., Kakulapati, G., Lakshman, A., Pilchin, A., Sivasubramanian, S., Vosshall, P., Vogels, W.: "Dynamo: Amazon's Highly Available Key-Value Store". In: ACM SOSP (2007)

23. Chang, F., Dean, J., Ghemawat, S., Hsieh, W., Wallach, D., Burrows, M., Chandra, T.: Bigtable: A Distributed Storage System for Structured Data. In: Proc. of OSDI 2006 (2006)
24. Tang, H., Gulbeden, A., Chu, L.: A Self-Organizing Storage Cluster for Parallel Data-Intensive Applications. In: Proc. of SC 2004, PA (November 2004)
25. http://www.mpiblast.org/
26. Pedretti, K.T., Casavant, T.L., Roberts, C.A.: Three complementary approaches to parallelization of local BLAST service on workstation clusters. In: Malyshkin, V.E. (ed.) PaCT 1999. LNCS, vol. 1662, Springer, Heidelberg (1999)
27. Xing, J., Xiong, J., Ma, J., Sun, N.: Main Memory Metadata Server for Large Distributed File Systems. In: GCC 2008 (October 2008)
28. Gulati, A., Kumar, C., Ahmad, I., Kumar, K.: BASIL: automated IO load balancing across storage devices. In: Proceedings of the 8th USENIX Conference on File and Storage Technologies (FAST 2010), pp. 13–13. USENIX Association, Berkeley, CA, USA (2010)

H-Fuzzing: A New Heuristic Method for Fuzzing Data Generation

Jinjing Zhao[1,2], Yan Wen[1,2], and Gang Zhao[1,2]

[1] Beijing Institute of System Engineerring, Beijing, China
[2] National Key Laboratory of Science and Technology on Information System Security,
Beijing, China
misszhaojinjing@sina.com.cn, celestialwy@gmail.com,
zg@public.bise.ac.cn

Abstract. How to efficiently reduce the fuzzing data scale while assuring high fuzzing veracity and vulnerability coverage is a pivotal issue in program fuzz test. This paper proposes a new heuristic method for fuzzing data generation named with H-Fuzzing. H-Fuzzing achieves a high program execution path coverage by retrieving the static information and dynamic property from the program. Our experiments evaluate H-Fuzzing, Java Path Finder (JPF) and random fuzzing method. The evaluation results demonstrate that H-Fuzzing can use fewer iterations and testing time to reach more test path coverage compared with the other two methods.

Keywords: Fuzzing test, static analysis, dynamic analysis, program slicing, control flow graph, program security testing.

1 Introduction

Fuzzing, according to its basic definition, might be characterized as a blind fishing expedition that aims at uncovering completely unsuspected problems in the software. If the program contains a code slice that may lead to exceptions, crash or errors, it can be determined that a vulnerability has been discovered. Generally, fuzzers are good at finding buffer overflow, DoS, SQL Injection, XSS, and Format String bugs, but always suffer the difficulty of finding vulnerabilities that does not cause program to crash, such as information disclosure, encryption flaws and so on.

Because of its random nature, the fuzzing data space must be huge enough to achieve high veracity and vulnerability coverage. For many applications, injecting random bits is almost infeasible. Consequently, completely random fuzzing is a comparatively ineffective way to uncover problems in an application.

To address this limitation, this paper presents a new heuristic fuzzing data generation method, namely H-Fuzzing. H-Fuzzing collects the information of key branch predictions and builds its relations with the program input variables. Besides, H-Fuzzing supervises how the fuzzing data space shrinks with the branch predictions and input variables. By abstracting these static information and dynamic property from the analyzed program, it accomplishes high program execution path coverage.

E. Altman and W. Shi (Eds.): NPC 2011, LNCS 6985, pp. 32–43, 2011.

The remainder of this paper is organized as follows. Section 2 is a brief introduction of the related work. Before the description of our method, the program model is built in section 3. The details of H-Fuzzing is described in section 4 and an experimental evaluation is presented in section 5. Finally, we conclude our work with a brief summary and discussion of open problems in section 6.

2   Related Work

The term fuzzing is derived from the fuzz utility [1], which is a random character generator for testing applications by injecting random data at their interfaces [2]. In this narrow sense, fuzzing just means injecting noise at program interfaces. For example, one might intercept system calls made by the application while reading a file and make it appear as though the file containing random bytes. The idea is to look for interesting program behavior that results from noise injection. Such behavior may indicate the presence of vulnerability or other software fault.

A simple technique for automated test generations is random testing [3-8].In random testing, the tested program is simply executed with randomly-generated inputs. A key advantage of random testing is that it scales well in the sense that generating random test input takes negligible time. However, random testing is extremely unlikely to expose all possible behaviors of a program. For instance, the "then" branch of the conditional statement "if (x= =10) then" has only one in 2^{32} chances of being executed if x is a randomly chosen 32-bit input variable. This intuitively explains why random testing usually provides low code coverage.

Several symbolic techniques for automated test generation [9-13] have been proposed to ameliorate the limitations of manual and random testing. Grammar-based techniques [14, 15] have recently been presented to generate complex inputs for software systems. However, these techniques require a grammar to be given for generating the tested program's input, which may not always be feasible.

There are several other works including some more intelligent techniques. For example, fuzzing tools are aware of commonly used Internet protocols, so that testers can selectively choose which parts of the data will be fuzzed. These tools also generally let testers specify the format of test data. This is very useful for applications that do not use the standard protocols. These features overcome the limitations discussed in the previous paragraph. In addition, fuzzing tools often let the tester systematically explore the input space. Such tester might be able to specify a range of input variables instead of having to rely on randomly generated inputs.

To sum up, existing traditional fuzzing ways suffer the following deficiencies:

1) They lack general fuzzers because they have to put focus on special objects to reduce the complexity and scale of fuzzing data generation.
2) The random methods suffer poor test efficiency.
3) They only have a low execution path coverage rate, which denotes the execution path number divided by the total number of branches in the program.

3 Program Model

A program P in a simple imperative programming language consists of a set of functions $F = \{f_1, f_2, ..., f_n\}$, one of which is distinguished as *main*, i.e., the program execution entry function. Each function f_i is denoted as $\{$ *Entry$_i$, Input$_i$, Exit$_i$* $\}$, wherein *Entry$_i$* is the function executing entrance, $Input_i = \{I_{i1}, I_{i2}, ..., I_{im}\}$ is the function input set, and $Exit_i = \{E_{i1}, E_{i2}, ..., E_{it}\}$ is the set of function return points. The function f_i is executed as a call, namely $call(f_i)$. In its body, $m := e$ means assigning the value e to the memory location m, an expression free of side effects and a conditional *if p then goto l*, wherein l is the label of another statement in the same function and p is a predicate free of side effects.

The execution of program P with inputs $Input_P$ which the customers give proceeds through a sequence of labeled program statements $p_0; ...; p_k$, with $p_0 = l_{main;0}$: $Entry_{main}$, the first statement of the main function.

The program P consisting of functions $f_1, ..., $ and f_n. Its combined control flow and static call graph CFCG$_P$ is a directed graph whose vertices are the statements of P. The edges of CFCG$_P$ begin from each statement $l_{i;j} : s_{i;j}$ and end at its immediate successors.

$$
\begin{cases}
none & if \ s_{i,j} = Exit_{f_i} \\
l' \ and \ l_{i,j+1} & if \ s_{i,j} = if \ p \ goto \ l' \\
Entry_{f_i} \ and \ l_{i,j+1} & if \ s_{i,j} = call(f_i) \\
l_{i,j+1} & otherwise
\end{cases}
\tag{1}
$$

To describe the rest of this paper more clearly, the following definitions are proposed.

Definition 1 (Control Flow Graph, CFG). The control flow graph G denotes a directed graph. Each of its nodes is a basic module with only one entry and exit, symbolized with *Entry* and *Exit* correspondingly. If the control flow can reach the basic module B from the basic module A directly, there is a directed edge from node A to node B. Formally, the control flow graph of program P can be represented with a quadruple G $(IV, E, Entry, Exit)$. IV is the node set which symbolizes the basic modules. E denotes the edge set. Each edge is symbolized by an ordered couple $<n_i, n_j>$ which represents a possible control transition from n_i to n_j (n_j may be executed just after n_i has been executed).

Definition 2 (Branch Path Tree, BPT). The branch path tree of program P, namely T_f, is the set of all the possible execution paths of P. Each node T_f is the set of a branch node along with all the non-branch nodes between this branch node and previous branch node, or the *Exit* of P. The root of T_f denotes the initial state of P.

Definition 3. With the denotation that l represents any node of a control flow graph *CFG*, we can reach the following definitions.

a)   ***The Definitions Set***, $Def(l) = \{$ $x|x$ is a variable changed in the sentence l $\}$.
b)   ***The References Set***, $Ref(l) = \{$ $x|x$ is a variable referred in the sentence l $\}$.

Definition* 4 *(Data Dependence). If node *n* and *m* satisfy the following two conditions, *n* is data-dependent on *m*.
   a)   There is a variable *v*, and *v* belongs to *Def (m)* ∩ *Ref (n)*.
   b)   There is a path *p* in *G* from *m* to *n*, and for any node *m'*∈*p - { m , n }* , *v* ∣ *def(m')*.

Definition* 5 *(Control Dependence). If node *n* and *m* meet the following two conditions, *n* is control-dependent on *m*.
   a)   There is a path *p* in *G* from *m* to *n*, and for any node *m'*□*p - { m , n}*, n is the successive dominator of *m'*.
   b)   *n* is not the successive dominator of *m*.

Definition* 6 *(Program Slicing). A slice *S* of a program is an executable sub-program. For a variable *v* located in some interest point *l* (*l* and *v* is termed as the Slicing Rules), *S* is composed of all the sentences which may influence *v* in *l*. In the functionality point of view, the slice *S* is equivalent with *P*. The so-called influencing *v* refers to having data-dependence or control-dependence on *v*.

   Slicing a program is supposed to follow some slicing rules. While slicing the same program, the slices worked out will differ with the selected slicing rules. A dynamic slicing rule is represented with an ordered triple $<Input_p, S_k, v>$, wherein $Input_p$ denotes the input set of a program. *S* is a sentence of the program, and then S_k indicates that the sentence *S* is executed at step *k*. It can also be symbolized with *S:lk*. *v* denotes a variable. It can represent a single variable or a subset of the program's variable set.

4   Heuristic Program Fuzzing Data Generation Method

H-Fuzzing is composed of two processes: static analysis process and fuzzing process. Fig. 1 illustrates the working flow of H-Fuzzing. Firstly, the information of all branch predictions and possible execution paths is collected, especially their relations with the input variables. Secondly, an initial input is generated, and then a new path will be chosen to be analyzed next time according to the execution path selecting rules. With the information supervised in the static analysis process, a new input variable set will be generated to run the program continually. If it works, the fuzzing process will get the next path until all the paths in the program are covered. Otherwise, the process will iterate the input variable again.

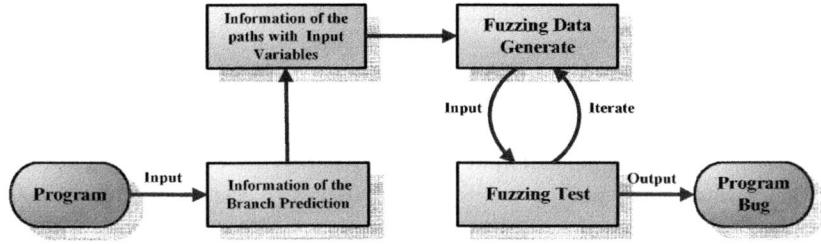

Fig. 1. The Work Flow Chart in H-Fuzzing Method

4.1 The Program Static Analysis Procedure

The static analysis is responsible for analyzing the relations between the possible execution paths and the input variables. The program tested here can be source code, inter-procedure language or even Java byte code. The working steps of the static analysis are listed as follows, as shown in Fig.2.

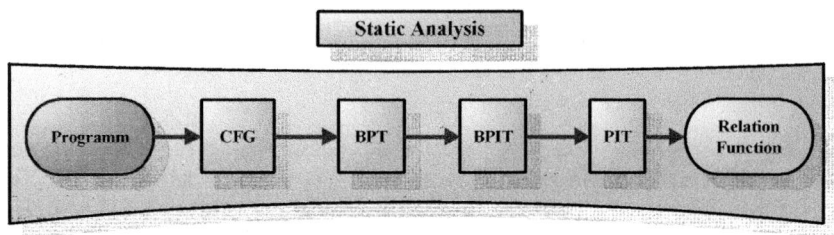

Fig. 2. The Output Information of The Static Analysis

1) Construct the CFG of the fuzzed program;
2) Build the branch path tree (BPT) of the program with the CFG information;
3) Slice the program with every branch prediction variable in branch lines, and record its data & control dependence information, especially with the input variables.
4) Deduce the relation functions between execution paths and input variables. All such information is organized with a table, called Branch Prediction Information Table (BPIT).
5) According to the BPT and BPIT, deduce the information of every possible path in the fuzzed program, and work out a Path Information Table (PIT) which records the relations between execution paths and input variables.

One entry in BPIT includes four elements: { *Line Number, Branch Predication, Corresponding Input, Relation Function*}. *Line Number* is line no. of the branch sentence. *Branch Predication* is the variables which make the branch be executed. *Corresponding Input* is the input variable set which has effect on the branch prediction. *Relation Function* defines the relation function between the branch prediction and the input variable set.

One entry in PIT is composed of five elements: *{ID, Path, Branch Point, Corresponding Input, Relation Function}*. *ID* is the exclusive number of path. *Path* is the set of line numbers of the path. *Branch Point* contains all the line numbers of branch sentences. *Corresponding Input* is the input variable set which has effect on this path. *Relation Function* defines the relation function between the path branches and the input variable set.

Because the generation algorithms of the program CFG and the BPT have been fully studied and lots of related tools are available, they would not be discussed here.

The process of calculating the prediction slicing is listed as follows: Firstly, H-Fuzzing finds all the nodes which the prediction variable v in the branch sentence S has data or control dependence on directly. Secondly, it keeps finding the nodes which new nodes have data or control dependence on directly, until no new nodes is added. Finally, it parallels these nodes according to the sequence in the program sentences. Then, the slice of the variable v in the branch sentence S is generated.

```
Algorithm "H-Fuzzing Static Analysis Procedure"
Input: P
Output: PIT
Begin
        Begin at the Entrymain in P, add every object to Object[] in P

        While Object[] ≠ φ {

                For oᵢ ∈ Object[]{
10:                 add every function to Functionᵢ [] in oᵢ;

                    While Functionᵢ [] ≠ φ {

20:                         For fⱼ ∈ Functionᵢ []{
                                Build CFG_fⱼ;
                                Build BPT_fⱼ;
                                For each branch node Bnᵢ ∈ BPT_fⱼ          {
        Get the information of its { Line Number, Branch Predication, Corresponding Input, Relation
        Function};          }
                                Build BPIT_fⱼ;
                                For each path Ptₗ ∈ BPT_fⱼ {
        Get the information of its { ID, Path, Branch Point, Corresponding Input, Relation Function }; }
                                Build PIT_fⱼ;   }
                                Find the related function fₘ   to fⱼ;
                                Get their exchanged information;
                                fⱼ = fₘ ;
                            Delete fₘ from  Functionᵢ [];
                            Goto 20;
                            }
                    Find the related object oₙ to oᵢ;
                    Get their exchanged information;
                    oᵢ =oₙ ;
                    Delete oₙ from  Object[];
                    Goto 10;
                    }
                }
End
```

Fig. 3. H-Fuzzing Static Analysis Procedure

In the concrete analyzing process, H-Fuzzing introduces the hierarchical decomposing method. H-Fuzzing need to separate the program into data layer, function layer, object layer and class layer, abstract the hierarchical slicing models, and figure out all kinds of dependence relations between them. Following that, H-Fuzzing builds the CFGs and BPTs in different layers, and then utilize the prediction slicing algorithm to calculate different granularity slices in every layer from the top level to the bottom. When the slicing process is working among layers, the escalating algorithm is adopted. This concrete static analysis algorithm is described in Fig. 3.

4.2   The Fuzzing Data Generation Algorithm

The fuzzing data generation process of H-Fuzzing is listed as follows. H-Fuzzing firstly constructs an initial input in a random or manual way. Then, it records the execution pathes and adjusts one or more input variables following the relation functions. In this way, a new input will be generated and make the tested function execute the specified path iteratively. H-Fuzzing will repeat the above process until the whole paths have been executed.

The branch prediction includes the following symbols.

Relation symbols: ">", "<", "==", ">=", "<=", "$\neq$".

Operator symbols: "+", "—", " *", " $/$".

Conjoint symbols: "&", "‖".

The branch predictions can be categorized into several types, such as atom predictions, twice-dimension predictions, triple-dimension predictions, and so on.

The input variable generation algorithm of the atom predictions is listed as follows.

(1) If "nl+n2+···+ni>m" , then nl =N, n2=N+1, ...,ni =N+i-1, m=-1+i(2N+i-1)/2.

(2) If "nl+n2+···+ni <m", then nl =N, n2=N+1, ...,ni =N+i-1, m=1+i(2N+i-1)/2.

(3) If "nl+n2+···+ni =m", then nl =N, n2=N+1, ...,ni =N+i-1, m= i(2N+i-1)/2.

(4) If "nl+n2+···+ni$\neq$m", then nl =N, n2=N+1, ...,ni =N+i-1, m $\neq$ i(2N+i-1)/2.

The input variable generation algorithm of twice-dimension predictions is illustarted as follows.

(1) "&" conjunction

① If "a>(<, =, >=, <=)N1 & b>(<, =, >=, <=)N2 & a+(-, *,/)b>(<, =, >=, <=)N3", then H-Fuzzing takes a, b for the axis and choose the points surrounded by three lines to establish dimensional rectangular coordinate system.

② If "a$\neq$ N & b$\neq$ M", then H-Fuzzing takes a, b for the axis and choose the points outside the two lines to establish dimensional rectangular coordinate system.

(2) "‖" conjunction

① If "a>(<, =、 >=、 <=)b ‖ c>(<、 =、 >=、 <=)d", then generate three set values, i.e., (a=N+l, b=N, c=M, d=M+l), (a=N, b=N+1, c=M+1, d=M), and (a=N+1, b=N, c=M+1, d=M).

② If "a$\neq$b ‖ c$\neq$ d", then generate three set values, i.e., (a$\neq$N, b=N, c=M, d=M), (a=N, b=N, c$\neq$M, d=M), and (a$\neq$N, b=N, c$\neq$M, d=M).

The search method for more complex three-dimensional predicated coverage test is shown as follows.

(1) "&" conjunction ("$\neq$"conjunction is not considered).

① Reduce inequalities to linearly independent inequalities.

② Figure out the critical values for the one-dimensional expression variables, in accordance with the direction of the critical value inequality +1 or -1 (eg, "a> N" will take "a = N + 1").

③ Adjust another variable conditioning variables included in the two-dimensional variables inequalities, which have been identified, to satisfy the two-dimensional variable inequality.

④ Adjust the value of third variable to meet the three-dimensional variable inequality, regulate the value of the fourth variable to meet the four-dimensional variable inequality ..., and finally adjust the value of i-variables to satisfy the N-dimensional variable inequality.

(2) "‖" conjunction ("≠"conjunction is not considered).

The values are that satisfying the i-th expression accordance with the "‖" conjunction input variable generation method of the two-dimensional complex predicate coverage

(3) Conjunctions contain the relation symbol "≠"

Following the above two-step search algorithm, H-Fuzzing can puzzle out any value, which satisfies the expression, and the other variable values.

In order to improve the efficiency of fuzzing data generation algorithm, H-Fuzzing defines the following rules.

Rule 1. Maximum Iteration Times Rule: The search will terminate into failure if it runs out of branches to select, exhausts its budget of test iterations, or uncovers no new branches after some set number of iterations.

Rule 2. The Minimum Variable Changing Rule: If one branch prediction is influenced by several input variables, H-Fuzzing will change the numbers of inputs as least as possible during the fuzzing data reducing process.

Rule 3. DFS and Nearest Rule: While choosing the next execution path, H-Fuzzing will follow the depth first order and the path nearest to the current execution path because they have the most same code.

```
Algorithm "H-Fuzzing Fuzzing Procedure"
Input: P,{x_init,y_init},PIT,Al_max
Output: Bug
Begin
        Execute the program P with input {x_init,y_init};
        According to the Rule 3, find the next path_i in PIT;
10:    for (j= Al_max;0;j--) {
                    Find the Branch Point set BP_i[] in path_i;
                    Find Corresponding Input fset In_i[] in path_i;
                    Generate {x_j,y_j} according to the Relation Function Rf() in path_i;
                        Execute the program P with input {x_i,y_i};
                    if (the path follows path_i){
                            if   ((Bug found) or (path_i= φ ))   return (Bug) ; else Break; }   }
            Printf("Could find the inputs to execute s%", path_i.path);
            find the next path_i in PIT;
        if   ((path_i= φ ))    return (0)         ;
        else{             path_i= path_i;  goto 10; }
End
```

Fig. 4. H-Fuzzing Fuzzing Procedure

5   Experimental Evaluation

Table 1. The Key Attributes of The Tested Programs

	Jar File Size	Code Line	Class Count	Function Count
JLex	50	7874	21	146
SAT4J	428	19641	120	1056
JCL2	56984	3586	35	179
JLine	91183	5636	36	324
checkstyle	627333	49029	328	1982

We have implemented H-Fuzzing based on the official Java platform, viz., OpenJDK. In this section, we will evaluate H-Fuzzing and compare it with JPF and random fuzzing method to demonstrate its effectiveness. The testbed is equipped with an Intel i7 920 processor, 4G RAM, Windows XP SP3 operating system, and OpenJDK (version b71). We test five open source Java projects, exploring JLex, SAT4J, Java Class Loader 2 (JCL2), JLine and checkstyle. Table 1 lists the key attributes of their source code.

In our experiment, the time for each test is limited within one hour. The evaluation makes statistic on the input file numbers and the paths covered by H-Fuzzing, JPF and random fuzzing method. The evaluation results demonstrate that H-Fuzzing can use fewer fuzzing iterations and testing time to reach higher test path coverage than the other two methods.

Due to the page limitation, the static analysis results are only presented for JLex. For the other programs, just the evaluation results (the path coverage comparisons) are illustrated.

```
public class JLex.Main extends java.lang.Object
{
    ......
    public static void main(java.lang.String[]) throws java.io.IOException
    {
        java.lang.String[] r0;          JLex.CLexGen r1, $r4;
        java.lang.Error r2, $r6;        int $i0;
        java.io.PrintStream $r3, $r7; java.lang.String $r5, $r8;
        [1] r0 := @parameter0;
        [2] $i0 = lengthof r0;
        [3] if $i0 >= 1 goto label0;
        [4] $r3 = java.lang.System.out;
        [5] $r3.println("Usage: JLex.Main <filename>");
        [6] return;
        [7]      label0:          $r4 = new JLex.CLexGen;
        [8] $r5 = r0[0];
        [9] specialinvoke $r4.<init>($r5);
        [10] r1 = $r4;
        [11] r1.generate();
        [12]     label1:          goto label3;
        [13]     label2:          $r6 := @caughtexception;
        [14] r2 = $r6;
        [15] $r7 = java.lang.System.out;
        [16] $r8 = r2.getMessage();
        [17] $r7.println($r8);
        [18]     label3:          return;
        [19] catch java.lang.Error from label0 to label1 with label2;
    }
}
```

Fig. 5. Static Decompiled Results of The Main Function of JLex

● **JLex**

JLex is a Lex file parser generator. Its input is just the path of a Lex file. The static analysis process of H-Fuzzing analyzes 162 functions of JLex, however there are only 146 methods in its source code. This is because that some functions will be added by the Java compiler during the compiling procedure, such as class's default constructor, destructor and so on. The static analysis process also generates the control flow graph and pollution spreading graph, which contains the Java intermediate language expressions of the branch nodes dependent on the input variables. Fig. 5 is the static decompiled results of the main function of JLex. As shown in this figure, the statement, tagged with [3], is the branch statement dependent on the input variables.

H-Fuzzing constructs the heuristic fuzz data referring to both the control flow graph and the static decompiled results. The static analysis shows there are 775 branch statements in its source code. Fig. 6 (a) is the evaluation results of H-Fuzzing, JPF and random fuzzing method. The horizontal axis is the number of fuzzing iterations. The vertical axis is the number of covered branches. When the iteration number is over 2,100 times, the number of covered branches almost does not change.

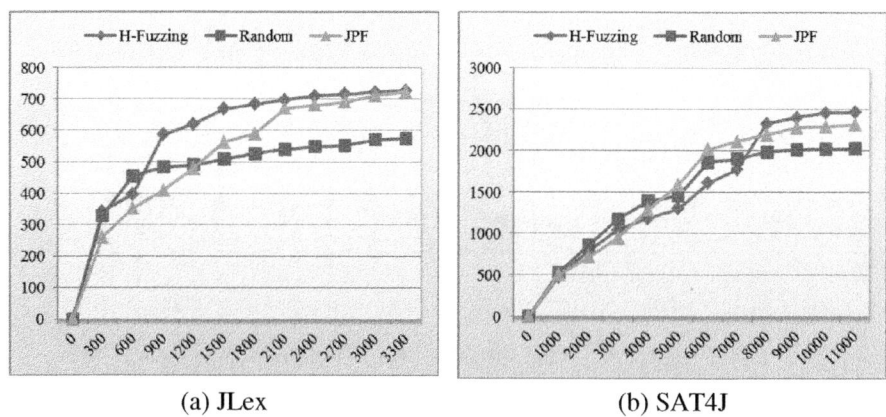

(a) JLex   (b) SAT4J

Fig. 6. Trend Graph of JLex & SAT4J Branch Coverage

● **SAT4J**

SAT4J is a Java language Boolean SAT tool. Its input parameters is a set of real numbers. 2610 functions of SAT4J are analyzed during the static analysis process. There are 3074 branch statements in its source code. Fig. 6 (b) shows the comparison results of H-Fuzzing, JPF and random fuzzing method. As shown in this figure, when the iteration number exceeds 8,000 times, the number of covered branches almost does not increase.

● **JCL2**

JCL2 is a configurable, dynamic and extensible custom class loader that loads java classes directly from Jar files and other sources. There are 1356 branch statements in JCL2 program. The comparison results are shown in Fig. 7 (a). As illustrated in this figure, when the iteration number is more than 4,100 times, the number of covered branches reaches a relatively stable state.

● **JLine**

JLine is a Java library for handling console input. It is similar in functionality to BSD editline and GNU readline. There are 1987 branch statements in JLine program. As shown in Fig. 7 (b), after the iteration number run overs 5,900 times, the number of covered branches begins to keep about 1800.

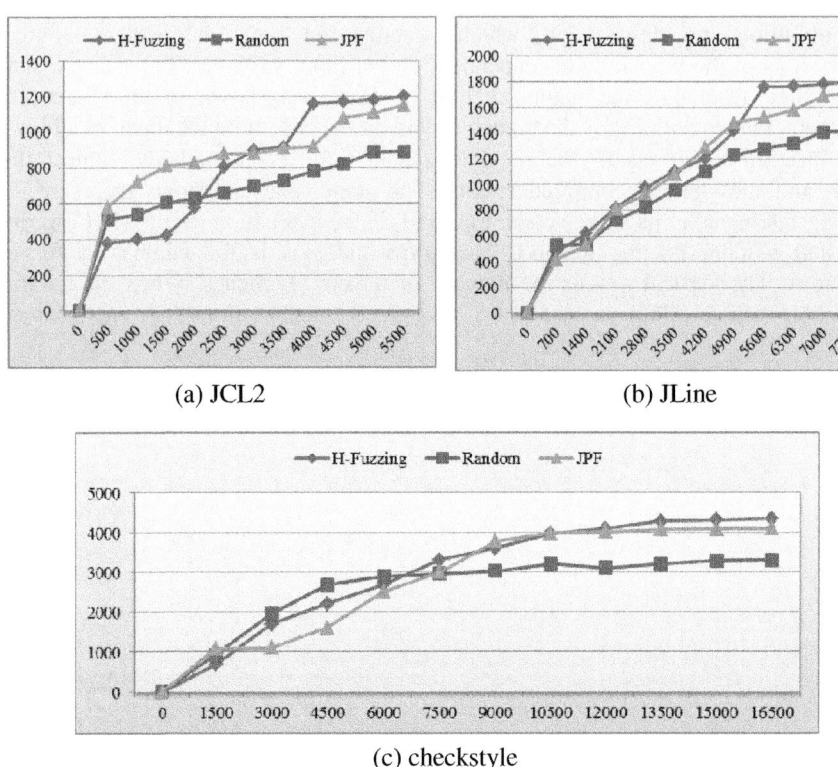

(a) JCL2   (b) JLine

(c) checkstyle

Fig. 7. Trend Graph of JCL2, JLine & checkstyle Branch Coverage

- **checkstyle**

Checkstyle is a development tool to help programmers write Java code that adheres to a coding standard. It automates the process of checking Java code to spare humans of this boring task. There are 4729 branch statements in checkstyle program. Fig. 7 (c) illustrates the comparison results of H-Fuzzing, JPF and random fuzzing method. As demonstrated in Fig. 7 (c), after the iteration number is over 141,000 times, the number of covered branches begins to keep about 4300.

5   Conclusion and Discussion

In this paper, we present a new method named H-Fuzzing for program fuzzing data generation. H-Fuzzing achieves high program execution path coverage by virtue of the the static analysis information and the program dynamic property.

In order to effectively reduce the fuzzing data set, H-Fuzzing figures out the key branch predictions information and builds its relations with the program input variables.

During the iterative input variable generating procedure, H-Fuzzing abstracts the dynamic property from the tested program. Besides, H-Fuzzing introduces a series of fuzzing data reduction rules to improve the efficiency of the fuzzing data generation algorithm and reach a high execution path coverage rate.

H-Fuzzing has high practical value for the program security testing. In the future study, more efforts will be involved to perfect our fuzzing method, for example, recording and recovering the variable information if the next chosen path has the same execution part with the previous one. In addition, we will further improve its performance to apply it in large-scale program security testing.

References

1. Fuzz utility, `ftp://grilled.cs.wisc.edu/fuzz`
2. Miller, B.P., Fredriksen, L., So, B.: An empirical study of the reliability of UNIX utilities. Communications of the ACM 33(12), 32–44 (1990)
3. Bird, D., Munoz, C.: Automatic Generation of Random Self-Checking Test Cases. IBM Systems Journal 22(3), 229–245 (1983)
4. Offut, J., Hayes, J.: A Semantic Model of Program Faults. In: Proceedings of International Symposium on Software Testing and Analysis (ISSTA 1996), pp. 195–200 (1996)
5. Forrester, J.E., Miller, B.P.: An Empirical Study of the Robustness of Windows NT Applications Using Random Testing. In: Proceedings of the 4th USENIX Windows System Symposium (2000)
6. Csallner, C., Smaragdakis, Y.: JCrasher: An Automatic Robustness Tester for Java. Software: Practice and Experience 34, 1025–1050 (2004)
7. Pacheco, C., Ernst, M.D.: Eclat: Automatic Generation and Classification of Test Inputs. In: Proceedings of 19th European Conference Object-Oriented Programing (2005)
8. King, J.C.: Symbolic Execution and Program Testing. Communications of the ACM 19(7), 385–394 (1976)
9. Clarke, L.: A System to Generate Test Data and Symbolically Execute Programs. IEEE Transaction on Software Engineering 2, 215–222 (1976)
10. Visvanathan, S., Gupta, N.: Generating Test Data for Functions with Pointer Inputs. In: Proceedings of 17th IEEE International Conference on Automated Software Engineering, ICASE 2002 (2002)
11. Visser, W., Pasareanu, C.S., Khurshid, S.: Test Input Generation with Java PathFinder. In: Proceedings of 2004 ACM SIGSOFT International Symposium on Software Testing and Analysis (ISSTA 2004), pp. 97–107 (2004)
12. Beyer, D., Chlipala, A.J., Henzinger, T.A., Jhala, R., Majumdar, R.: Generating Test from Counterexamples. In: Proceedings of the 26th International Conference on Software Engineering (ICSE 2004), pp. 326–335 (2004)
13. Xie, T., Marinov, D., Schulte, W., Notkin, D.: Symstra: A Framework for Generating Object-Oriented Unit Tests Using Symbolic Execution. In: Halbwachs, N., Zuck, L.D. (eds.) TACAS 2005. LNCS, vol. 3440, pp. 365–381. Springer, Heidelberg (2005)
14. Majumdar, R., Xu, R.: Directed test generation using symbolic grammars. In: Foundations of Software Engineering, pp. 553–556 (2007)
15. Godefroid, P., Kiezun, A., Levin, M.: Grammar-based Whitebox Fuzzing. In: Proceedings of the ACM SIGPLAN 2002 Conference on Programming Language Design and Implementation, PLDI 2008 (2008)
16. Majumdar, R., Sen, K.: Hybrid concolic testing. In: Proceedings of 29th International Conference on Software Engineering (ICSE 2007), pp. 416–426. IEEE, Los Alamitos (2007)

Improved Compact Routing Schemes
for Power-Law Networks

Mingdong Tang[1,2], Jianxun Liu[1], and Guoqing Zhang[2]

[1] Key Laboratory of Knowledge Processing and Networked Manufacturing,
Hunan University of Science and Technology, Xiangtan 411201, China
[2] Institute of Computing Technology, Chinese Academy of Sciences, Beijing 100093, China
{tangmingdong,gqzhang}@ict.ac.cn

Abstract. Compact routing intends to achieve good tradeoff between the routing path length and the memory overhead, and is recently considered as a main alternative to overcome the fundamental scaling problems of the Internet routing system. Plenty of studies have been conducted on compact routing, and quite a few universal compact routing schemes have been designed for arbitrary network topologies. However, it is generally believed that specialized compact routing schemes for peculiar network topologies can have better performance than universal ones. Complex network research has uncovered that most real-world networks have degree distributions exhibiting power law tails, i.e., a few nodes have very high degrees while many other nodes have low degrees. High-degree nodes play a crucial role of hubs in communication and networking. Based on this fact, we put forward two highest-degree landmark based compact routing schemes, namely HDLR and HDLR$^+$. Theoretical analysis on random power law graphs shows our schemes can achieve a better space-stretch tradeoff than prior compact routing schemes. Simulations conducted on random power law graphs and real-world AS-level Internet graph validate the effectivity of our schemes.

Keywords: compact routing, power law, stretch, routing table size, algorithm.

1 Introduction

Routing is a basic function of a network on which many upper-layer applications rely. For the efficient use of network resources (link capacities, etc.) it is desirable to design schemes which route along paths as short as possible. This is measured by the metric called stretch, which can be represented by (α, β), meaning the path between any two nodes u, v is no longer than $\alpha d(u,v) + \beta$, where $d(u,v)$ is the length of the shortest path between u and v. A scheme with stretch $(\alpha, 0)$ is said to have multiplicative stretch, whereas one with stretch $(1, \beta)$ is said to have additive stretch β. In addition to stretch, with the exponential growth of network size, the routing table size also grows rapidly and becomes a bottleneck of the network, so, it becomes equally important to reduce the routing table size.

E. Altman and W. Shi (Eds.): NPC 2011, LNCS 6985, pp. 44–58, 2011.

However, these two objectives are contradictive in that optimizing one will typically deteriorate the other. At one extreme, the shortest path routing ensures the minimum stretch (i.e. with a multiplicative stretch of 1) but requires a $O(n \log n)$ table size at each node (one entry for every node in the network). At the other extreme, the flooding scheme does not need to maintain any state information at each node, but has a worst-case multiplicative stretch $O(n)$ for general graphs. Both of these two solutions do not scale well. It is evident that there is a tradeoff between the space requirement and the stretch. It is desirable, therefore, to develop schemes with good tradeoff between them. Such schemes typically have the property of near-optimal stretch but with substantially smaller routing tables.

The routing schemes that balance between routing table size and stretch are usually called compact routing schemes. Compact routing schemes on arbitrary network topologies (also termed as universal schemes) [1-3] and specific networks such as trees [4-5], planar graphs[6], growth bounded graphs [7] and graphs with low doubling dimension [8-9] have attracted wide research attentions. Presently, the most optimized universal compact routing scheme could restrict the routing table size on each node to $\tilde{O}(n^{1/2})$ [1]bits, and meanwhile, achieve a multiplicative stretch of 3, i.e., the length of the path between any node pair taken by the routing is no more than 3 times the length of the shortest path between the node pair. Although it has been proved that no routing scheme can achieve multiplicative stretch less than 3 with sub-linear space for generic networks [3], it is generally believed that routing schemes specialized for peculiar network topologies can achieve better performance than universal ones. This is because, unlike the TZ scheme, specialized routing schemes can exploit the topological properties of special networks.

Recent researches on complex networks have uncovered that many real-world networks, such as the Internet [10], P2P [11], WWW [12], have scale-free topologies, i.e., the degree distribution follows a power law. Compact routing on power law networks has attracted increasingly more attention [13-17]. Many researchers even consider compact routing as a promising alternative to overcome the scaling limitations of the Internet routing system [18-20]. Although previous work has experimentally showed that specialized routing schemes can outperform the optimal universal routing scheme on power law networks, they seldom give theoretical analysis and guaranteed performance on stretch and routing table size.

In this paper, we focus on compact routing in power law graphs, and present two high-degree landmark based routing schemes, namely HDLR and HDLR$^+$. Based on the RPLG (Random Power Law Graph) model [21-22], theoretical analysis shows: 1) HDLR can achieve a multiplicative stretch of 3 and average routing table size of $\tilde{O}(n^{1/3})$ with high probability.2) HDLR$^+$ can achieve a stretch of $\min\{(3,0),(2,D_A)\}$ and average routing table size of $\tilde{O}(n^{1/3})$ with high probability, where n is the number of nodes in the graph, and D_A is the diameter of the subgraph induced by the landmark set, bounded by some constant with high probability. Simulations conducted on both random power law graphs and real-world AS graph validate our theoretical results.

---

[1] $\tilde{O}()$ notation indicates complexity similar to $O()$ notation up to poly-logarithmic factors.

2   Related Work

Since 1990s, several excellent compact routing schemes are proposed for generic networks [1-3][23], among which the Cowen scheme [2] and the TZ scheme [1] are two prominently referenced ones. Cowen scheme is the first universal compact routing scheme that reduces the stretch to (3,0), and produces sublinear routing table size whose upper bound is $\tilde{O}(n^{2/3})$. TZ scheme improves the Cowen scheme's routing table size upper bound to $\tilde{O}(n^{1/2})$. Both these two schemes are landmark-based and differ only in how landmarks are selected. Cowen scheme adopts a greedy algorithm to find the dominating set of the graph, and obtains the landmark set based on this dominating set, whereas the TZ scheme relies on random techniques for landmark selection. Since Gavoille and Gengler [3] showed that no universal routing scheme with a multiplicative stretch < 3 can produce $o(n)$ routing table size, and Thorup and Zwick [24] proved that any routing scheme with multiplicative stretch strictly below 5 cannot guarantee space smaller than $\tilde{O}(n^{1/2})$, it thus follows that the TZ scheme is nearly optimal as far as the stretch and routing table size are concerned.

All the above schemes are designed for generic networks. However, recent studies revealed that most real networks, for example, the Internet, WWW and unstructured P2P networks, can all be categorized as power-law networks [25-28], i.e., the degree distribution $p(k)$ satisfies $p(k) \sim k^{-\gamma}$, where γ is called the power-law exponent, typically between 2 and 3. It has been shown that on power-law networks, high degree nodes play the hub role for network connectivity and routing [16][21], most nodes are directly connected to these nodes or separated by only a few hops, and the path between these high degree nodes are typically very small[29]. So recently, compact routing schemes on power-law networks have attracted much attention. Krioukov [13] first evaluated the performance of the TZ scheme on Internet-like power-law graphs, and found that the performance is far better than the worst case theoretic results, e.g., the average multiplicative stretch is only 1.1. Brady and Cowen [14] introduced the concept of additive stretch, and proposed a compact routing scheme with additive stretch $(1,d)$ and logarithmic routing table scaling, i.e. $O(e\log^2 n)$. Simulations showed that d and e can both take small values on power-law networks, and the average stretch is lower than the TZ scheme. Other specialized compact routing schemes on power-law networks can be found in recent works [15-17].

Although the aforementioned work is effective, none of them gave theoretical bounds on stretch and routing table size. Most recently, Chen et al. [28] proposes a compact routing scheme, which is the first routing scheme guarantees a better space-stretch tradeoff on power law graphs than universal ones. The theoretical analysis is based on the RPLG (Random Power Law Graph) model [21-22], and shows the routing table size can be reduced to $\tilde{O}(n^{1/3})$ or less using address length of $O(\log n \log \log n)$ bits and stretch of (3,0). However, Ref. [28] makes no progress in the worst-case stretch compared to the universal optimal scheme. Our proposed scheme HDLR$^+$ is the first compact routing scheme that achieves a better stretch than (3,0) on power law networks. Furthermore, HDLR and HDLR$^+$ are superior to the scheme by Ref. [28] by using addresses and packet headers both with $O(\log n)$ bits.

3   Definitions and Notations

We model a communication network as an undirected, unweighted graph $G=(V,E)$, with vertices representing routers and edges representing communication links. For convenience, we use the terms vertex and node, edge and link interchangeably throughout this paper. The distance between any two nodes $u,v \in V$, is defined as the number of edges on the shortest path between them, denoted by $d(u,v)$.

A routing scheme R is a distributed algorithm for packet delivery between any two nodes in the network. R can only be called compact if it has routing tables with sizes sublinear in n and message header sizes polylogarithmic in n. There are two classes of compact routing schemes: Name-dependent schemes are allowed to add labels to node addresses to encode useful information for routing purposes, where each label has length at most polylogarithmic in n. Name-independent schemes do not allow renaming of node addresses, instead they must function with all possible addresses. We consider name dependent routing in this paper. Denote the length of the path traversed by a packet from u to v according to a routing scheme R by $d_R(u,v)$.

The quality of a routing scheme is primarily measured by two metrics: the storage space of the distributed data structures established by the preprocessing procedure, typically referring to the size of routing table; and the routing efficiency, measured by the stretch. Other metrics include packet header length, routing table convergence time and communication cost. In this paper, we only consider routing on static topologies, hence the convergence time and communication cost are out of our consideration.

4   Our Routing Schemes

This section introduces the design of our routing schemes—HDLR and HDLR$^+$, which are both landmark-based schemes. The basic idea of landmark based routing is to select a small proportion of nodes from the network as landmarks. The routing table of each node only stores routing entries for the landmarks and its vicinity. As a result, suppose a node is sending a packet to some destination, if the destination node could be found in the source node's routing entries, then the packet can be delivered along the shortest path; otherwise, the packet is first sent towards the nearest landmark of the destination, and then will be delivered to the target by the landmark.

HDLR is adapted from the TZ scheme by using a highest degree landmark selection method instead of a random one, and HDLR$^+$ extends HDLR by optimizing its stretch.

4.1   HDLR

Let $A \subseteq V$ represent the landmark set. For any $u \in V$, define u's ball $B(u)$ to be $B(u) = \{v \in V | d(u, v) < d(u, A)\}$, where $d(u, A)$ is the minimum shortest path length among all the shortest paths from u to all the landmarks in A, and define u's cluster $C(u)$ to be $C(u) = \{v \in V | u \in B(v)\}$. Take the graph in Fig.1 as an example, Table 1 illustrates these definitions.

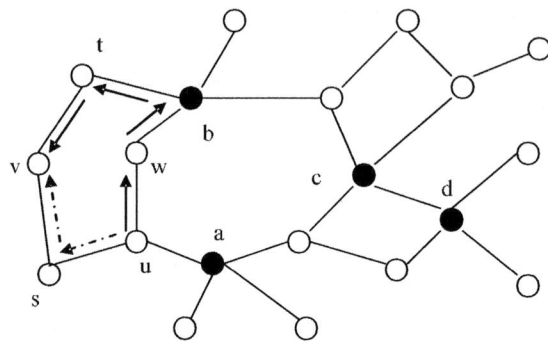

Fig. 1. An example of the HDLR scheme. Filled nodes are landmarks. It illustrates the forwarding path form *u* to *v* taken by the HDLR scheme. Solid lines are the actual path used by HDLR scheme, and the dashed lines compose the shortest path.

Tabel 1. Balls and clusters of the nodes in Fig.1

	s	*t*	*u*	*v*	*w*
$B()$	$\{u,v\}$	ϕ	ϕ	$\{s,t\}$	ϕ
$C()$	$\{v\}$	$\{v\}$	$\{s\}$	$\{s\}$	ϕ

In HDLR, The preprocessing procedure consists of the following steps:

1) Landmark selection: sort the nodes in decreasing order of their degrees, and choose the first n^x nodes as the landmarks, where $0 < x < 1$ is a tunable parameter;

2) Address assignment: for each non landmark $u \in V-A$, assign $(u, A(u), e_{A(u)}(u))$ as its address, denoted as *Address(u)*, where $A(u)$ is the name of the nearest landmark to *u*, and $e_{A(u)}(u)$ is the identifier of the port at $A(u)$ that lies on the shortest path from $A(u)$ to *u*; for each landmark, its address is identical to its name.

3) Routing table setup: for each non landmark $u \in V-A$, its routing table is *Table (u)* $= \{(v, e_u(v)) | v \in A \cup C(u)\}$. In other words, *u* stores the routing entries to nodes in A and $C(u)$, where $e_u(v)$ is the identifier of the port at *u* that lies on the shortest path from *u* to *v*; for each landmark $l \in A$, its routing table only contains the routing information to other landmarks, i.e., $Table(l) = \{(v, e_l(v)) | v \in A-\{l\}\}$.

We can see the routing table at each node is much smaller than generic shortest path routing schemes. For example, in Fig. 1, the routing tables of *u* contain only 5 routing entries for $\{a, b, c, d, s\}$, as a contrast to 19 entries for all other nodes if a shortest path routing scheme is adopted.

The packet forwarding procedure of HDLR is very similar to the TZ scheme. Assuming a packet with a destination address $(v, A(v), e_{A(v)}(v))$ arrives at node u, u makes the following decision:

1) If $u = v$, then the packet reaches its destination;
2) otherwise, if $u = A(v)$, then forward the packet using the port $e_{A(v)}(v)$ that found in the packet header;
3) otherwise, if $Table(u)$ contains the routing entry for v, forward the packet using the port $e_u(v)$;
4) otherwise, forward the packet to $A(v)$ using the port $e_u(A(v))$ found in $Table(u)$.

The above forwarding algorithm is likely to use non-shortest paths, with a worst-case stretch of $(3,0)$, as will been proved in Section 5. For example, in Fig. 1, when sending a packet from u to v, the actual forwarding path would be $u–w–b–t–v$, but the shortest path between u and v is $u–s–v$.

4.2 HDLR$^+$

The HDLR$^+$ scheme is an extension of HDLR, with the purpose to optimize the worst-case stretch for compact routing in power law graphs. Based on HDLR, we store limited more information at each node u, by adding entries for nodes in $B(u)$ to $Table(u)$. Therefore, for any non-landmark node u, $Table\ (u) = \{(v, e_u(v))|$ $v \in A \cup B(u) \cup C(u)\}$. While for each landmark l, its routing table is still only composed by entries for nodes in A, as both $B(l)$ and $C(l)$ are empty. By this means, as we will show through analysis in Section 5, the worst-case stretch of HDLR$^+$ is superior to HDLR.

Except the routing table setting, the other aspects of HDLR$^+$ such as the landmark selection and address assignment scheme, and the forwarding algorithm are identical to HDLR. Therefore, we omit unnecessary details of HDLR$^+$.

5   Analytical Performance Analysis

In this section, we use the random power law graph theory [21-22] to analyze the space-stretch tradeoff of the proposed two schemes, and present the bounds for address length, stretch and routing table size.

5.1   Theory of Random Power-Law Graphs

The random power-law graph model extends the generic random graph theory for power-law networks.

Definition 1(Random Power Law Graph [21,22]). Let $G(\mathbf{k})$ represent the ensemble of all random graphs satisfying the expected degree sequence $\mathbf{k} = (k_1, k_2, ..., k_n)$, where k_i is the expected degree of node v_i. The probability that there is an edge connecting two nodes v_i and v_j is given by $k_i k_j / \sum_{z=1}^{n} k_z$. If $\mathbf{k} = (k_1, k_2, ..., k_n)$ follows power-law distribution, then $G \in G(\mathbf{k})$ is called a random power-law graph.

An important reason to work with this random graph model is that the edges are independent. This independence makes several graph properties easier to analyze. Actually, there are already many analytical results for the topological properties of random power-law graphs, in the following we introduce some useful ones, which offer basic proofs for the analysis in this section.

Let $S_{G(\mathbf{k})}^k$ denote the set of nodes in $G(\mathbf{k})$ whose expected degrees are no less than k, then the following property holds for the subgraph induced by $S_{G(\mathbf{k})}^k$.

Lemma 1. Suppose $G \in G(\mathbf{k})$ is a power-law graph instance with the power-law exponent satisfying $2 < \gamma < 3$. Given $t \geq n^\delta$ ($0 < \delta < \frac{3-\gamma}{\gamma-2}$), then the diameter of the subgraph induced by $S_{G(\mathbf{k})}^t$ has probability $1 - n^{-2}$ not exceeding $(1 + o(1)) \frac{\log n}{(3-\gamma)\log t}$.

Proof. Readers can refer to Ref. [21], page 62, Lemma 12, for the proof of this Lemma.   □

From Lemma 1, we can see that the subgraphs induced by high-degree vertices of power law graphs usually have very small diameters, approaching some constant when the graph size increases.

Lemma 2. Let $\beta = \frac{\gamma-2}{2\gamma-3} + \varepsilon$, $\beta' = \frac{1-\beta}{\gamma-1}$, and $\alpha = \beta'(\gamma-2) + \frac{(2\gamma-3)\varepsilon}{\gamma-1}$, where ε is any positive real number that satisfies $n^{\frac{(2\gamma-3)\varepsilon}{\gamma-1}} \geq \frac{2(\gamma-1)}{\gamma-2} \ln n$ (apparently, when n is sufficiently large, ε could be very small). Let G is an instance of $G(\mathbf{k})$, then for all $u \in V(G)$, the following property holds with probability at least $1 - 3n^{-2}$: $|B(u)| = |\{u \in V(G): d(u, v) < d(u, S_{G(\mathbf{k})}^\tau)\}| = O(n^\alpha)$, where $\tau = n^{\beta'}$.

Proof. Please refer to Ref. [28], Lemma 7, for the proof of this Lemma.   □

Lemma 2 indicates that for power law graphs, if high-degree nodes are selected as landmarks, the ball size of any node u is high likely to has an upper bound much smaller than the size of the graph. This might be partly caused by the reason that ordinary nodes in power law graphs usually have very small hop distances to high-degree nodes, which limits the range of neighborhood expansions and thus ball sizes.

5.2 Analysis

In the following, we analyse the routing performance of HDLR and HDLR$^+$ on random power law graphs, using the metrics such as address length, stretch and routing table size.

The address length of HDLR or HDLR$^+$ is $O(\log n)$ bits, which arises from the following observations. For any node v, its address is $(v, L(v), e_{A(v)}(v))$. Since the node name and interface identifier can both be represented using $O(\log n)$ bits, so the address length is $O(\log n)$. Because each packet of HDLR or HDLR$^+$ only includes the destination address, the packet header length of HDLR or HDLR$^+$ is also in $O(\log n)$ bits. For the stretch of HDLR or HDLR$^+$, we have the following analytical results.

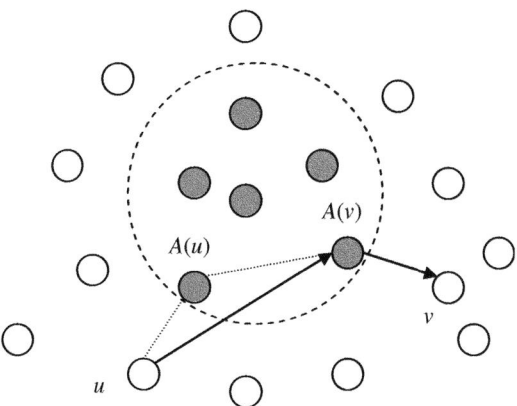

Fig. 2. Proving the stretch of HDLR and HDLR$^+$. Filled nodes denote the landmark set. Assuming node u is to send a packet to node v, which is not stored in *Tabel(u)*.

Theorem 1. The worst-case stretch of HDLR and HDLR$^+$ are (3, 0) and $\min\{(3,0),(2,DA)\}$ respectively, where $D_A = \max_{u,v \in A} d(u,v)$ is the maximum distance between any two landmarks.

Proof. Let's first consider the HDLR scheme. Suppose a node u is to send a packet to node v. Let $d_R(u,v)$ denote the length of the route taken by HDLR between u and v. If v is stored in u's routing table, u can route along the shortest path to v, in this case the stretch is (1,0). Otherwise, u will forward the packet to $A(v)$, as is shown in Fig. 2. When the packet reaches $A(v)$, $A(v)$ will forward the packet along the shortest path to v. Therefore we have

$$d_R(u,v) \le d(u, A(v)) + d(A(v), v) \tag{1}$$

According to the triangle inequality, we know

$$d(u, A(v)) \le d(u,v) + d(A(v), v)) \tag{2}$$

Combine Equation (1) and (2), we can get

$$d_R(u,v) \le d(u,v) + 2d(A(v), v) \tag{3}$$

Since v is not contained in u's routing table, i.e. $v \notin A \cup C(u)$, we certainly have $d(u,v) \ge d(A(v),v)$. Thus we get

$$d_R(u,v) \le 3d(u,v) \tag{4}$$

This produces a stretch (3,0) for HDLR.

For the HDLR$^+$ scheme, It's not difficult to see, Equation (1), (2), (3) and (4) also hold according to its forwarding algorithm and routing table setting. This means the

HDLR$^+$ scheme also has a worst-case stretch (3,0). Besides, we'll prove HDLR$^+$ can achieve another stretch (2,D_A).

As the dash lines in Fig.2 show, according to the triangle inequality, we have

$$d(u, A(v)) \leq d(u, A(u)) + d(A(u), A(v))$$ (5)

Combine Equation (1) and Equation (5), we get

$$d_R(u,v) \leq d(u, A(u)) + d(A(u), A(v)) + d(A(v), v)$$ (6)

Since v is not contained in u's routing table, i.e. $v \notin A \cup B(u) \cup C(u)$, thus both $d(u,v) \geq d(u, A(u))$ and $d(u,v) \geq d(A(v), v)$ hold. Therefore

$$d_R(u,v) \leq 2d(u,v) + d(A(u), A(v)) \leq 2d(u,v) + D_A$$ (7)

This produces a stretch (2, D_A). Combining Equation (4) and Equation (7), we can see HDLR$^+$ can achieve the stretch $\min\{(3,0), (2, D_A)\}$.   □

In Theorem 1, one critical problem is what the D_A will be on a typical power-law network. In the following, we show that with high probability D_A is bounded by a constant in random power-law graphs.

Corollary 1. Let G to be an instance of $G(k)$, and the landmark set A to be composed of the $n^x(0 < x < 1)$ nodes with the highest expected degrees, then D_A has probability 1 − n^{-2} to be bounded by a constant.

Proof. Assuming the degree distribution of $G(\mathbf{k})$ follows $P(k) \propto k^{-r}$, then the cumulative degree distribution can be represented by $P(z \geq k) = ck^{1-r}$, where c is a constant. Denote the smallest expected node degree in A as τ . According to the cumulative degree distribution, we have $c\tau^{1-r} \approx n^x / n$, so

$$c\tau^{1-\gamma} \approx n^x / n$$
$$\Rightarrow \log c - (\gamma-1)\log \tau \approx (x-1)\log n$$
$$\Rightarrow \log \tau \approx (1-x)\log n /(\gamma-1) + \log c /(\gamma-1)$$
$$\Rightarrow \tau \approx c_1 n^{(1-x)/(\gamma-1)}$$

where c_1 is a constant depending on γ and c.

A can be treated as $S^t_{G(\mathbf{k})}$ of $G(\mathbf{k})$. According to Lemma 1, the diameter of the subgraph induced by A has probability $1 - n^{-2}$ not exceeding $(1 + o(1)) \frac{\log n}{(3-\gamma)\log \tau} = (1 + o(1)) \frac{(\gamma-1)\log n}{(3-\gamma)((1-x)\log n + \log c)}$. Since γ, c and x can all take constant values, this expression will be bounded by a constant as $n \to \infty$. According to the definition of D_A, D_A is no greater than the diameter of the subgraph induced by A, hence D_A is bounded by a constant with probability $1 - n^{-2}$.   □

The routing table size of HDLR and HDLR$^+$ can be analyzed separately for landmarks and non landmarks. For each landmark l, HDLR and HDLR$^+$ have the same routing table setting, i.e., $Table_{HDLR}(l) = Table_{HDLR^+}(l) = \{(v,\ e_l(v))|v \in A - \{l\}\}$. Since the landmark set A has a size of $n^x (0 < x < 1)$, the routing table size of each landmark   must be bounded by $O(n^x)$. In the following, we analyze the routing table size of non-landmark nodes for HDLR and HDLR$^+$.

We denote the routing table of node u as $Table_{HDLR}(u)$ according to HDLR and $Table_{HDLR^+}(u)$ according to HDLR$^+$, respectively. As defined earlier, for each non landmark node u, $Table_{HDLR}(u) = \{(v,\ e_u(v))|v \in A \cup C(u)\ \}$, and $Table_{HDLR^+}(u) = \{(v,\ e_u(v))|v \in A \cup C(u) \cup B(u)\}$. Apparently, since the size of the landmark set A is given, the routing table sizes critically depend on the size of $B(u)$ and $C(u)$. Again, we analyze the size of $B(u)$ and $C(u)$ by means of the power-law random graph theory.

Corollary 2. Let G be an instance of $G(k)$, A be the landmark set consisting of the n^x nodes with the highest expected degrees, then for any $u \in V(G)$, the probability that $|B(u)| = O(n^\alpha)$ is at least $1 - 3n^{-2}$, where $\alpha = \frac{(1-x)(\gamma-2)}{\gamma-1} + \xi$, ξ is sufficiently small.

Proof. According to Corollary 1, the least expected degree $\tau = c_1 n^{(1-x)/(\gamma-1)}$, which can be rewritten as $\tau = c_1 n^{\frac{1-x}{\gamma-1}+\varepsilon'}$, where $\varepsilon' = o(1)$ being sufficiently small. According to Lemma 2, we know that $\alpha = (\frac{1-x}{\gamma-1}+\varepsilon')(\gamma-2)+\frac{(2\gamma-3)\varepsilon}{\gamma-1}$, i.e., $\alpha = \frac{(1-x)(\gamma-2)}{\gamma-1}+\xi$, where $\xi = (\gamma-2)\varepsilon'+\frac{(2\gamma-3)\varepsilon}{\gamma-1}$, Since ε and ε' can both take sufficiently small values, so can ξ.   □

For all $u \in V(G)$, Corollary. 2 gives the upper bound of $|B(u)|$. However, it is impossible to analyze the bound of $|C(u)|$ for each u in this way. We however, could provide the upper bound of the average size of $C(u)$.

Lemma 3. For any arbitrary graph G, $\sum_{u \in V(G)}|B(u)| = \sum_{u \in V(G)}|C(u)|$, i.e., $|C(u)|$ and $|B(u)|$ have the same average size.

Proof. According to the definitions of $C(u)$ and $B(u)$, it follows that for any $v \in B(u)$, we have $u \in C(v)$, and vice versa. Since these u, v occur pairwise, so Lemma 3 holds.   □

Based on the above analysis, we have the following Theorem.

Theorem 2. Let G be an instance of $G(k)$, and let A be the landmark set containing the n^x nodes with the highest expected degrees, then for any non landmark node $u \in V(G)$, with probability at least $1 - 3n^{-2}$, the average routing table sizes of $Table_{HDLR}(u)$ and $Table_{HDLR^+}(u)$ are both in $O(n^x + n^\alpha)$, where $\alpha = \frac{(1-x)(\gamma-2)}{\gamma-1} + \xi$ and ξ is sufficiently small.

Proof. Since $|A| = O(n^x)$, $|B(u)| = O(n^\alpha)$, thus both $|C(u)|$ and $|B(u)|$ have an average size $O(n^\alpha)$, so it is easy to see that $Table_{HDLR}(u)$ and $Table_{HDLR^+}(u)$ have an average size of $O(n^x + n^\alpha)$. □

Corollary 3. In HDLR and HDLR$^+$, For any γ satisfying $2 < \gamma < 3$, the average routing table size of non landmark nodes can be bounded by $O(n^{\frac{1}{3}+\xi})$ with high probability .

Proof. Since $2 < \gamma < 3$, $\alpha = \frac{(1-x)(\gamma-2)}{\gamma-1} + \xi \le \frac{(1-x)}{2} + \xi$, so $Table_{HDLR}(u)$ and $Table_{HDLR^+}(u)$ have average sizes of $O(n^x + n^{\frac{1-x}{2}+\xi})$ with high probability, which results in $O(n^{\frac{1}{3}+\xi})$ by setting $x = 1/3$. □

So far, we have completed the analytical performance analysis for HDLR and HDLR$^+$. The results show HDLR and HDLR$^+$ can achieve excellent bounds for address length, packet header size, stretch and routing table size.

6   Simulations

In order to provide an insight into the real performance of our proposed scheme on power-law networks, we perform simulations on both the synthesized graphs generated by the random power-law graph (RPLG) model and the real AS-level Internet topology. The AS graph is acquired from CAIDA [29], having a total of 9204 nodes, 28959 edges, and a power law component about 2.1. The random power law graphs are generated with different size and different power law component (e.g., $\gamma = 2.1, 2.3, 2.5$, and $n = 1000, 2000, ..., 10000$).

6.1   Diameter of the Subgraph Induced by Landmarks

Fig.3 reports D_A, the diameter of the subgraph induced by the landmark set A, for random power law graphs with different network size and different power law exponents. We can see that D_A remains relatively stable as the network expands. Also, we observe that when γ increases, D_A increases accordingly. This is because when γ increases, the degrees of landmarks in A will decrease, making the edges connecting landmarks more sparse, thus D_A increases. It is worth noting, for

AS graph, D_A is only 2, much smaller than those in the corresponding random power law graphs. This is due to the rich-club structure in AS graph, i.e., high degree nodes are prone to connect with each other directly, which does not happen in random power law graphs.

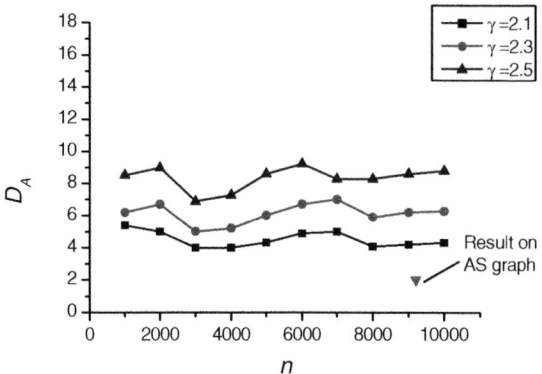

Fig. 3. Diameter of landmarks on random power law graphs and AS graph

6.2 Average Routing Table Size

Fig.4 shows the average routing table size obtained by our schemes and the TZ scheme on random power law graphs with $\gamma = 2.1$ and AS graph. For each random power law graph, the number of landmarks is set to be $|A| = n^{1/2}$, where n denotes the graph size. For AS graph with 9204 nodes, we set $|A| = n^{1/3} = 21$.

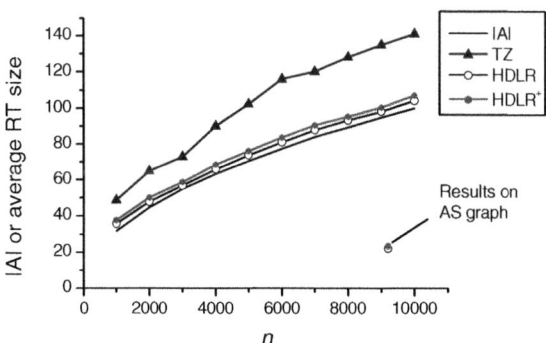

Fig. 4. Average routing table size on random power law graphs and AS graph: comparison of our routing schemes and the TZ scheme

It is evident that with our schemes, the routing table size can be significantly reduced compared to the TZ scheme. With our schemes, the average routing table size is very close to |A|, implying the size of the local cluster and the ball of a node are usually very small. For AS graph, the average routing table size achieved by HDLR or HDLR$^+$ is about 22 or 23. It is not surprising that the routing table size produced on AS graph is remarkably smaller than those on random power law graphs. The reason may be that in AS graph, the highest degree nodes have much higher degrees than those in a random power law graph with comparable size. For example, the highest degree of AS graph with 9204 nodes is 2070, while the highest degree of a random power law graph with similar size is only about 60. This implies that in AS graph a majority of nodes are directly connected with a very small set of highest degree landmarks, thus markedly decreasing the size of the routing table.

6.3   Average Stretch

Fig.5 shows the average multiplicative stretch achieved by our schemes and the TZ scheme on AS graph and random power law graphs with different exponents. Again, for random power law graphs we set $|A| = n^{1/2}$, and for AS graph we set $|A| = n^{1/3} = 21$. It is observed that our schemes outperform the TZ scheme with non marginal improvement For random power law graphs, HLDR or HDLR$^+$ achieves a 1.06~1.09 average stretch, whereas the TZ scheme can only achieve a much higher average stretch in the range of 1.14~1.20. For AS graph, our schemes have an average multiplicative stretch about 1.09 while the TZ scheme with an average multiplicative stretch about 1.17. The average stretch of HDLR$^+$ is very close to that of HDLR, with only negligible improvement. This is due to the fact that the routing table size of HDLR$^+$ is only slightly larger than HDLR. We also notice that, when γ increases, the average stretch of all routing schemes are decreasing. The reason may be, when γ increases, the average routing table size increases, thus a node knows more routing information, resulting more shortened stretched paths.

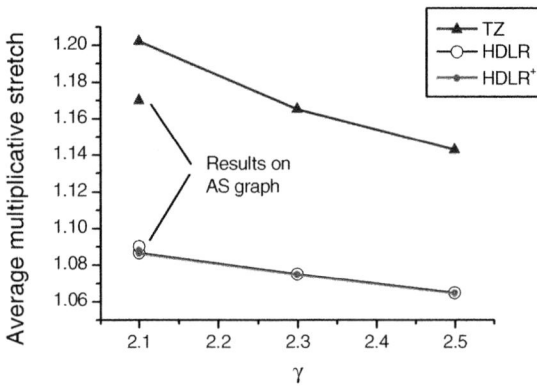

Fig. 5. Average stretch on random power law graphs and AS graph: comparison of our routing schemes and the TZ scheme

7 Conclusions

In this paper we present two compact routing schemes, HDLR and HDLR$^+$, aiming to improve the space-stretch tradeoff for routing in power law graphs. Based on the fact that in a power law network graph a few nodes usually have very high degrees, and play the important role of hub in communication and networking, we select high-degree nodes as landmarks.

Analytic study on random power law graphs shows: 1) HDLR can achieve a multiplicative stretch of 3 and an average routing table size of $\tilde{O}(n^{1/3})$ with high probability. 2) HDLR$^+$ can achieve a stretch of $\min\{(3,0),(2,D_A)\}$ and an average routing table size of $\tilde{O}(n^{1/3})$ with high probability, where D_A is the diameter of the sub-graph induced by the landmark set and is almost surely bounded by some constant. Both HDLR and HDLR$^+$ improve the space-stretch tradeoff obtained by the TZ scheme, whose bounds for stretch and routing table size are $(3,0)$ and $\tilde{O}(n^{1/2})$. Simulations conducted on networks generated by synthetic random power law graph model with different parameter settings and real-world AS graph validate our results.

Acknowledgments. The authors are supported by the National Natural Science Foundation of China under Grant No. 90818004 and 60973129.

References

[1] Thorup, M., Zwick, U.: Compact routing schemes. In: 13th ACM Symposium on Parallel Algorithms and Architecture, pp. 1–10. ACM Press, New York (2001)

[2] Cowen, L.: Compact routing with minimum stretch. Journal of Algorithms 38(1), 170–183 (2001)

[3] Gavoille, C., Gengler, M.: Space-Efficiency for routing schemes of stretch factor three. Journal of Parallel and Distributed Computing 61(5), 679–687 (2001)

[4] Fraigniaud, P., Gavoille, C.: Routing in trees. In: Yu, Y., Spirakis, P.G., van Leeuwen, J. (eds.) ICALP 2001. LNCS, vol. 2076, pp. 757–772. Springer, Heidelberg (2001)

[5] Laing, K.A.: Name-independent compact routing in trees. Information Processing Letters 103(2), 57–60 (2007)

[6] Lu, H.: Improved compact routing tables for planar networks via orderly spanning trees. In: 8th International Computing and Combinatorics Conference, pp. 57–66. Springer, Heidelberg (2002)

[7] Abraham, I., Malkhi, D.: Name independent routing for growth bounded networks. In: 17th Annual ACM Symposium on Parallel Algorithms and Architectures (SPAA 2005), pp. 49–55. ACM Press, New York (2005)

[8] Konjevod, G., Richa, A., Xia, D.: Optimal scale-free compact routing schemes in networks of low doubling dimension. In: 18th ACM-SIAM Symposium on Discrete Algorithms, pp. 939–948. ACM Press, New York (2007)

[9] Abraham, I., Gavoille, C., Goldberg, A.V., Malkhi, D.: Routing in networks with low doubling dimension. In: 26th International Conference on Distributed Computing Systems. IEEE Computer Society, Washington, DC (2006)

[10] Faloutsos, M., Faloutsos, P., Faloutsos, C.: On power-law relationships of the Internet topology. Computer Communications Review 29, 251–262 (1999)
[11] Ripeanu, M., Iarmnitchi, A., Foster, I.: Mapping the Gnutella network. IEEE Internet Computing, 50–57 (2002)
[12] Albert, R., Jeong, H., Barabasi, A.L.: Dimeter of the world wide web. Nature 401, 130–131 (1999)
[13] Krioukov, D., Fall, K., Yang, X.: Compact routing on Internet-like graphs. In: IEEE INFOCOM 2004, IEEE Computer Society, Washington, DC (2004)
[14] Brady, A., Cowen, L.: Compact routing on power law graphs with additive stretch. In: 8th Workshop on Algorithm Engineering and Experiments, pp. 119–128. SIAM, Philadelphia (2006)
[15] Carmi, S., Cohen, R., Dolev, D.: Searching complex networks efficiently with minimal information. Europhysics Letters 74, 1102–1108 (2006)
[16] Enachescu, M., Wang, M., Goel, A.: Reducing maximum stretch in compact routing. In: IEEE INFOCOM 2008, pp. 977–985. IEEE Computer Society, Washington, DC (2008)
[17] Norros, I.: Powernet: compact routing on Internet-like random networks. In: 5th Euro-NGI Conference on Next Generation Internet Networks. IEEE Press, New York (2009)
[18] Meyer, D., Zhang, L., Fall, K.: Report from the IAB workshop on routing and addressing. RFC4984 (2007)
[19] Huston, G.: Analyzing the Internet's BGP routing table. The Internet Protocol Journal 4(1) (2001)
[20] Krioukov, D., Claffy, K.: On compact routing for the Internet. ACM SIGCOMM Computer Communication Review 37(3), 43–52 (2007)
[21] Chung, F., Lu, L.: The average distances in random graphs with given expected degrees. Internet Mathematics 1, 15879–15882 (2002)
[22] Lu, L.: Probabilistic methods in massive graphs and Internet computing. Ph D thesis, University of California San Diego (2002)
[23] Eilam, T., Gavoille, C., Peleg, D.: Compact routing schemes with low stretch factor. In: 17th Annual ACM Symposium on Principles of Distributed Computing, pp. 11–20. ACM Press, New York (1998)
[24] Thorup, M., Zwick, U.: Approximate distance oracles. In: ACM Symposium on Theory of Computing, pp. 183–192. ACM Press, New York (2001)
[25] Barabasi, A., Albert, R.: Emergence of scaling in random network. Science 286, 509 (1999)
[26] Zhang, G.Q., Zhang, G.Q., Yang, Q.F., Cheng, S.Q., Zhou, T.: Evolution of the Internet and its cores. New Journal of Physics 10, 123027 (2008)
[27] Zhou, S., Mondragon, R.J.: The rich-club phenomenon in the Internet topology. IEEE Communications Letters 3, 180–182 (2004)
[28] Chen, W., Sommer, C., Teng, S.-H., Wang, Y.: Compacting routing in power-law graphs. In: Keidar, I. (ed.) DISC 2009. LNCS, vol. 5805, pp. 379–391. Springer, Heidelberg (2009)
[29] CAIDA, http://www.caida.org

Accelerating the Requirement Space Exploration through Coarse-Grained Parallel Execution

Zhongwei Lin and Yiping Yao

School of Computer, National University of Defense Tecnology
{zwlin,ypyao}@nudt.edu.cn

Abstract. The design and analysis of complex systems need to determine suitable configurations for meeting requirement constraints. The Monotonic Indices Space (MIS) method is a useful approach for monotonic requirement space exploration. However, the method is highly time and memory-Consuming. Aiming to the problem of low efficiency of sequential MIS method, this paper introduces a coarse-grained parallel execution mechanism to the MIS method for accelerating the process of requirement space exploration. The task pool model is used to receive and deploy hyperboxes for work balancing. To validate our approach, the speedup is estimated by a mathematical analysis and then an experiment is conducted in a PC cluster environment. The results show that high speedup and efficiency is achieved through our approach.

Keywords: requirement space exploration, coarse-Grained parallel execution, task pool model.

1 Introduction

A lot of practical problems, such as getting the system capability requirement indices [1, 2, 3, and 4], getting the effective light intensity space [5], and getting the effective radar coverage [5], can be transformed into the problem of requirement space exploration. These problems have a common feature: the requirement measure of these systems is related with several factors (indices), and their combination forms a huge parameter space in which we should explore to make the measurement satisfying requirement constraints. For example, the response time (requirement measure) of a web server is affected by several factors, including the CPU's frequency, memory, network, operating system, and current load, so we are anxious about what configurations of these factors which can satisfy the demand on the response time.

The problem of requirement space exploration can be defined formally as follows.

Definition 1. *Requirement space: suppose R^n is n-Dimensional Euclidean space, P is non-Empty subset of R^n, then $P \subset R^n$ and $P \neq \emptyset$, there exists a function f defined in P, $f : P \to R$, the requirement space S satisfies: $S \subset P$ and $\forall p \in S, f(p) \geq \alpha$, where α is the threshold.*

E. Altman and W. Shi (Eds.): NPC 2011, LNCS 6985, pp. 59–70, 2011.

Due to the complexity and uncertainty of some practical problems, it is very difficult or even impossible to get the analytic form of the function f, thus we need to determine the require space in other ways, rather than analytic way.

A few classic methods have been used to solve the requirement space determining problem. The system effectiveness analysis method [1] compares the system capabilities and the mission requirements in a common attribute space, while attaining the system mission requirements locus is difficult. ADC model [6] is a very strict mathematical method, but the calculation will increase exponentially with the increase of system state dimensions. In multi-Attribute analysis method [7], the design of the weights of each attribute should be very skillful, but very difficult. The Monotonic Indices Space (MIS) method [4] introduced by Hu Jianwen takes the typical complex system characteristics into account, and turns out an efficacious way.

Coarse-Grained Multicomputer (CGM) model is a well-known parallel method for multi-Replication simulations. Frank Dehne presented the method [8], described and proofed the time cost of the method, and employed it to solve Hausdorff Voronoi Diagrams problem [9]. CGM has been widely used, and turned out effective. Thierry Garcia and David Sem' employed CGM to solve the Longest Repeated Suffix Ending problem [10], Albert Chan introduced CGM to the next element search problem [11]. According to their results, CGM is highly effective.

The paper is organized as follows. In section 2, we introduce the MIS method in detail. The coarse-Grained approach is described in section 3. We analyze the speedup of our approach formally, and then present some experimental results in section 4 and 5. Future work is arranged in section 6.

2   Monotonic Indices Space (MIS) Method

The main idea of the MIS method is divide-and-conquer strategy: the whole parameter space is partitioned into a lot of hierarchical sub-spaces which are isomorphic with their parental space. Any sub-space is called a hyperbox which is an important concept of MIS. A hyperbox can be imaged as a hypercube, and it is a description of parameter space.

2.1   MIS Method

The MIS method is mainly applied in monotonic vector space. In monotonic vector space P, f should be n-Dimensional monotonic function, that means $\forall p(x_1, x_2, \cdots, u, \cdots, x_n), q(x_1, x_2, \cdots, v, \cdots, x_n) \in P$, if $u \geq v$, then $f(p) \geq f(q)$ or $f(p) \leq f(q)$. For example: $P = [0, 2] \times [0, 2] \subset R^2$, $f(x, y) = x^2 + y^2$, the requirement space $S = \{p : p \in P, f(p) \leq 4\}$. In this case, the initial hyperbox is P, and the partition point is $p^*(\sqrt{2}, \sqrt{2})$ which is on the diagonal of the current hyperbox, and then it produces 4 sub-hyperboxes, as illustrated by Fig. 1.

The main operation of the MIS method is resolving hyperbox, and the resolving includes two procedures: search and partition:

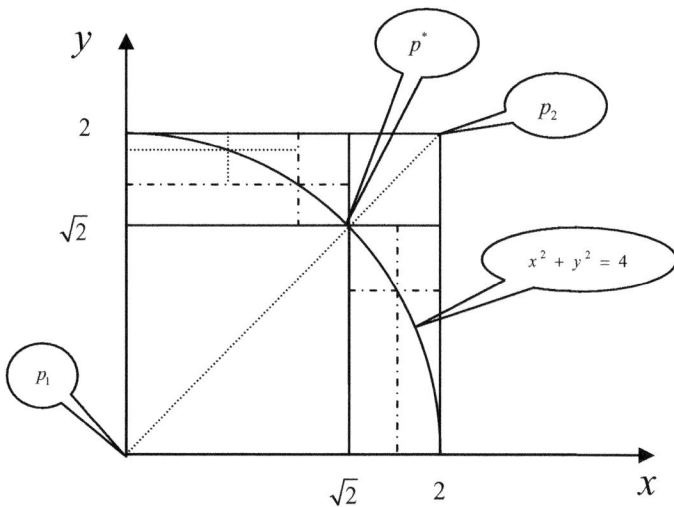

Fig. 1. An example of the MIS method. The root hyperbox is determined by point p_1 and p_2, and the partition point p^* ($f(p^*) = \alpha$) is on the diagonal. The partition point cuts the current hyperbox into 4 sub-hyperboxes, one of them (determined by p_1 and p^*) belongs to requirement space, one (determined by p^* and p_2) of them doesn't, and the other two should be inspected again.

1. Search: search the partition point along the diagonal of the hyperbox. As shown in Fig. 1, the current hyperbox is determined by point p_1 and p_2, let $a_0 = p_1$, $b_0 = p_2$, $c_0 = (p_1 + p_2)/2$, if $f(c_i) \leq \alpha$, then $a_{i+1} = c_i, b_{i+1} = b_i, c_{i+1} = (a_{i+1} + b_{i+1})/2$, if $f(c_i \geq \alpha)$, then $a_{i+1} = a_i, b_{i+1} = c_i, c_{i+1} = (a_{i+1} + b_{i+1})/2$, repeat this operation. Since there must be at least one partition point on the diagonal[4], thus the point c_i can be considered as the partition point when $\|a_i - b_i\| \leq \theta l_0$, where θ is a parameter called cut rate, and l_0 stands for the length of the diagonal of the root hyperbox.
2. Partition: each component of the partition point will divide the same dimension of the current hyperbox into two segments, and the combination of all the segments will produce 2^n sub-hyperboxes, see Fig. 1, and the undetermined $2^n - 2$ sub-hyperboxes should be inspected again. In the partition procedure, sub-hyperboxes that are too little to affect the requirement space (or affect a little bit) will be abandoned directly. Suppose V is the volume of some sub-hyperbox, we can abandon this subhyperbox when $V \leq \gamma V_0$, where γ is a parameter called stop rate, and V_0 stands for the volume of the root hyperbox.

During the above two procedures, we can get a hyperbox tree, see Fig. 2:

After the above two procedures, we can get a requirement-Satisfied hyperbox s_i (i stands for the identifier of the hyperbox on the hyperbox tree) determined by p_1 and p^*, see Fig. 1, obviously $s_i \subset S$, then the requirement space can be determined as follows:

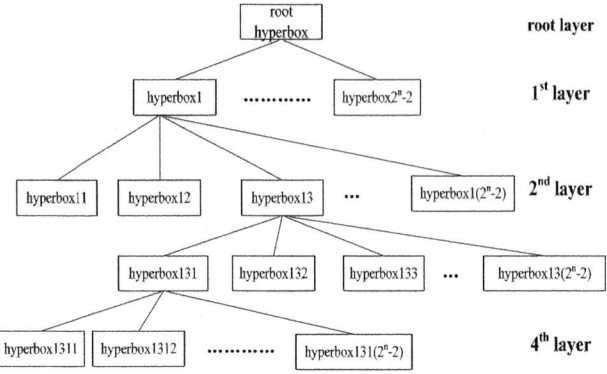

Fig. 2. Hyperbox tree. Resolving the current hyperbox will produce $2^n - 2$ undetermined sub-hyperboxes, and the current hyperbox is the parent of these sub-hyperboxes, then all the hyperboxes form a tree structure.

$$S = \bigcup_{i=0}^{\infty} s_i \tag{1}$$

2.2 Time and Memory Costs of the MIS Method

The MIS method is highly recursive, thus it is very suitable to implement it by recursive program. However the depth of the recursion is the key for precision. We can't get the precise requirement space with low depth. While deep depth will bring in a very large amount of calculation and memory need (as shown in Fig. 2, the hyperbox scale is $O\left((2^n - 2)^k\right)$, and the memory need is $O\left(n(2^n - 2)^k\right)$, where n is the dimension of the requirement space, and k stands for the maximal depth of recursion.) which exceed a single computer's capability in a certain period of time. Additionally, extra cost brought by recursion to operating system makes the execution ineffective.

Most practical problems are related with high-Dimensional model, they need much more calculation and memory, compared to low-Dimensional model. In some cases, the calculation and memory need are so large that it makes a single computer exhausted or even halted. Thus we come to the edge that we must process the calculation and satisfy the memory need in other way.

Above all, our task becomes accelerating the execution of the MIS method, promising a certain depth of recursion.

3   Coarse-Grained Approach

Reviewing the MIS method, we can find that the algorithm has immanent parallelism: the resolving of hyperboxes is all independent. Any hyperbox determined by the initial parameters can be resolved without communicating with other hyperboxes, thus the hyperboxes can be resolved concurrently.

A Coarse-Grained Multicomputer model: p processors solving a problem on n data items, each processor has $O(n/p) \gg O(1)$ local memory, and all the processors are connected via some arbitrary interconnection network [8], can be represented as $CGM(n, p)$. In the MIS method, each hyperbox is one data item, thus the key is to assign the hyperboxes to the processors, and keep load-Balanced for each processor.

In most cases, the requirement space is not evenly distributed in the parameter space, thus it is not suitable to partition the items (hyperboxes) according to their location in the parameter space. While it is very hard or impossible to predict the requirement space, thus we almost can't partition the items and assign them to the processors before the execution, and we have to do this work during resolving dynamically. New hyperboxes will come out during resolving their paternal hyperbox, and the hyperboxes can be stored into a container (usually called pool), and then a hyperbox will be taken out and assigned to each idle processer if there exists idle processers.

3.1   Parallelized Resolving in C/S Mode

There are two core operation of the MIS method: resolving hyperbox and maintaining the hyperbox tree. Generally speaking, resolving hyperbox is a kind of compute-intensive procedure which needs a large amount of calculation, while maintaining the hyperbox tree is a kind of communicate-intensive procedure which needs to communicate with others frequently. Therefore, the two operation should be implemented separately and execute on separate computers.

Basing on the analysis before, the computer which executes resolving hyperbox is called calculative node, and it is in charge of resolving hyperbox. The computer which executes maintaining hyperbox tree is called control node, and it is in charge of receiving and deploying hyperbox. Therefore the calculative nodes and the control node form a client-Server structure.

Resolving Hyperbox on Client. The MIS method will generate a lot of hyperboxes, and the faster the generated hyperboxes resolved the faster the experiment completes, thus we always assign a few calculative nodes in the system. A procedure called clientProcedure is running on each calculative node, and it will process the fundamental tasks of calculative node: resolving the hyperbox and interacting with the control node. The action of calculative node is driven by the commands from the control node, and the command can be packed into a message, such as a socket message, thus the messages can be classified and identified according to the command type. The main body of clientProcedure is to operate according to the message received from the control node.

```
clientProcedure :
    Initialize ;
    Connect  to  the  Server ;
    Listen  message  from  Server ;
    switch ( message )
```

```
        case information of experiment:
            save the imformation;
        case hyperBox:
            call resolveProcedure;
        case collectResults:
            collect the local results and send them to
                server;
```

A procedure called resolveProcedure is in charge of searching the partition point and generating sub-hyperboxes and it will be called after the calculative node receiving a message telling a hyperbox from the control node. Two n-Dimensional points can determine a hyperbox uniquely, see Fig. 1, and they also determine the diagonal on which the partition point locates. Thus we can search the partition point along the diagonal of the hyperbox. The model is used to calculate the requirement measure, and it is always implemented as a program whose input is a single point. So the search can be divided into two iterative sub-courses: calculating the input point, and calling the model program. Once the partition point has been determined, $2^n - 2$ sub-hyperboxes will be produced and filtered. Any hyperbox can be determined by two n-Dimensional points, and the two points can be packed into a message, and then the message will be sent to the control node, telling a hyperbox. Sub-hyperbox is filtered according to its volume, and the one that is too little to affect the requirement space will be abandon directly. After the resolving completed, a message will be sent to the control node to tell that this calculative node has become idle.

Maintain the Hyperbox Tree on Server. Maintaining the hyperbox tree is the main task of the control node, and it includes two fundamental operations: receiving the subhyperboxes generated by the calculative nodes and deploying hyperbox to them. A procedure called serverProcedure is running on the control node, and it will process the above two operations.

```
serverProcedure:
    Initialize;
    the user choose an experiment configuration file;
    deploy the necessary files to the connected clients;
    start the experiment;
    Listen message from the connected clients;
    switch(message)
        case finish://means client completes resolving
            put the client from which the message came
                into idle clients queue;
            if(the hyperbox queue is empty && all the
                clients are idle)
                call resultProcessProcedure;
            else
                call deployProcedure;
        case hyperBox:
```

```
            receive the hyperbox and put it into the
                hyperbox queue
        case resultFile:
            receive the result file
```

3.2   Task Pool Work Balancing

Task pool is one of implementations of work stealing [12], and it can be used for load balancing. In this paper, the hyperboxes generated by the calculative nodes will be put into a hyperbox queue which is assigned on the control node and plays the task pool. Once a message telling a hyperbox has been received by the control node, the serverProcedure will unpack the message to get the two n-Dimensional points, and then construct a hyperbox according to the two points. The constructed hyperbox will be put into the hyperbox queue.

The control node maintains a list to record the information of the calculative nodes. In the beginning, the whole parameter space will be constructed as the first hyperbox, and then the hyperbox will be put into the hyperbox queue. After starting the execution , the front hyperbox of the hyperbox queue will be taken out and assigned to the front idle calculative node of the calculative nodes list. To use the calculative nodes fully, we hope that the nodes are keeping resolving hyperboxes if there are unresolved hyperboxes in the hyperbox queue. Once the control node finds an idle calculative node, a hyperbox will be taken out and assigned to the idle node. To decrease the overhead of preparing the message of assigning a task to the idle calculative node, the server always gets the front hyperbox of the hyperbox queue out(time consuming $O(1)$), and then packs it into the assigning message. Therefore, the calculative nodes are keeping resolving hyperbox controlled by the calculative node. The terminal condition of the whole execution is that the hyperbox queue on the control node is empty and all the calculative nodes are idle.

4   Speedup Analysis

For the sequential MIS method, the total execution time is the summary of the time of resolving each sub-hyperbox, and suppose T_s is the period of time which the sequential MIS method costs, then

$$T_s = \sum_{i=1}^{N} t_i \geq \sum_{i=1}^{N} t_{min} \tag{2}$$

where N is the total number of hyperboxes in the experiment, t_i is the period of time which resolving ith hyperbox costs, and $t_{min} = \min\{t_i\}$. T_p is the period of time which the parallel algorithm costs, then

$$T_p = \sum_{j=1}^{\lceil N/m \rceil} t_j \leq \sum_{j=1}^{\lceil N/m \rceil} t_{max} \tag{3}$$

where m is the number of calculative nodes, and $t_{max} = \max\{t_j\}$, then the speedup is the ratio

$$speedup = \frac{T_s}{T_p} \geq \frac{t_{min}}{t_{max}} \cdot \frac{N}{\lceil N/m \rceil} \approx \frac{t_{min}}{t_{max}} \cdot m \qquad (N \gg m) \tag{4}$$

In the sequential MIS method, the period of resolving a hyperbox is mainly composed of two parts: time of model calls and the extra cost of the system (including the OS and the program itself). While in the parallel algorithm, the period is mainly composed of five parts: overhead of the server preparing message, the delay of transferring message from the server to the clients (determined by the bandwidth of the network), overhead of the client receiving message, the overhead of the client preparing message (above four are the communication cost), and time of model calls. The communication cost can be represented as following

$$t_{com} = o_s + L + o_c + (2^n - 2)o_c \tag{5}$$

then the period can be represented as

$$t_j = t_{com} + t_{call} \tag{6}$$

Suppose the period of single execution of the model f is const T, then the period of model calls t_{call} is proportional to the number of times of the model calls. Reviewing the search procedure of the MIS method, the repeat will have the length of the distance between a_i and b_i to halve again and again, then the terminal condition of binary search can be described as following

$$\frac{l_k/2^r}{l_0} = \theta \tag{7}$$

where k is the depth of the current hyperbox on the hyperbox tree, l_k is the length of the diagonal of the current hyperbox, r is the number of times of the model calls, l_0 is the length of the diagonal of the root hyperbox, and θ is the cut rate. Statistically, $l_k = 2^{-k}l_0$ is correct, then

$$r = -\log_2 \theta - k \tag{8}$$

In the partition procedure, a sub-hyperbox will be abandoned directly, if its volume is too little to affect the requirement space of the problem. Statistically, $V_k = 2^{-nk}V_0$ (n is the dimension of the parameter space) is correct, then

$$\frac{2^{-nk}V_0}{V_0} = \gamma \tag{9}$$

$$k = \frac{\log_2 \gamma}{n} \tag{10}$$

formula (10) is also the maximal depth of recursion. Let

$$h_1(\theta, \gamma, n) = \frac{t_{min}}{t_{max}} = \frac{(-\log_2 \theta - k_0)T}{(-\log_2 \theta - k_{max})T + \max\{t_{com}\}}$$
$$\underset{k_0=0}{\equiv} \frac{T \log_2 \theta}{(\log_2 \theta + \frac{\log_2 \gamma}{n})T - \max\{t_{com}\}} \quad (11)$$

For a certain experiment, the dimension of the requirement space is station-ary, thus the variable n in formula (11) can be considered as const, and then $h_1(\theta, \gamma, n)$ becomes

$$h_2(\theta, \gamma) = \frac{\log_2 \theta}{(\log_2 \theta + \frac{\log_2 \gamma}{n}) - \frac{\max\{t_{com}\}}{T}} \quad (12)$$

$$speedup \geq h_2(\theta, \gamma) \cdot m \quad (13)$$

5   Experimental Results

To test our approach, we take the system mentioned by Hu Jianwen in [4] as an example. It is an air defense information system consisting of three entities: long-Distance warning radar, command and control center, and enemy's aircraft. The scenario is following: one of enemy's aircraft is flying direct to target T which is protected by us, and once the long-Distance warning system discovers the air-craft, it sends the information of the aircraft to the command and control center, and then the center sends firing order to the air defense missiles after processing the information. In this case, the requirement measure is destroying the enemy's aircraft more than 0.7 success probability, and the indices are abstracted into long-Distance warning radar detecting index, system processing delay index, and tracking index of the tracking radar.

The model f is implemented by a program, and the sequential algorithm is implemented as a recursive program. The parallel algorithm is implemented and running in a group of PCs (PC of same type) connected by 100M Ethernet with each other. In the group, one PC is assigned as control node to execute the serverProcedure, and several other PCs are assigned as calculative node to execute the clientProcedure. Test the sequential algorithm and the parallel al-gorithm separately, and then add up the period of their execution. We played two schemes: increase calculative nodes, keeping the parameters (θ and γ) un-changed, and change one of the parameters, keeping the other parameter and calculative nodes unchanged, the results are shown in Table 1.

In this case, the period of single execution of the model call is tens of seconds. For the PCs are connected by 100M Ethernet, then the latency of transferring message is very tiny, and the overhead of the server preparing message is also very tiny because of the dequeue operation. Compared to t_{call}, t_{com} is too tiny to affect $h_2(\theta, \gamma)$ much, then we can ignore it to estimate the speedup.

We can attain pretty speedup through our parallel algorithm, and the speedup increases almost linearly with the number of calculative node, see Fig. 3. But

Table 1. results table. T_s: time of sequential MIS, T_p: time of parallel execution, m: number of calculative nodes, θ: cut rate, γ: stop rate, *speedup*: T_s/T_p, PE: Practical Efficiency (*speedup/m*), TE: Theoretical Efficiency (formula (12)).

$T_s(s)$	$T_p(s)$	m	θ	γ	*speedup*	PE	TE
5888	3552	2	0.05	0.05	1.658	0.829	0.750
5888	2518	3	0.05	0.05	2.338	0.779	0.750
5888	1913	4	0.05	0.05	3.078	0.769	0.750
5888	1546	5	0.05	0.05	3.809	0.762	0.750
5888	1456	6	0.05	0.05	4.044	0.674	0.750
5888	1258	7	0.05	0.05	4.680	0.669	0.750
5888	1133	8	0.05	0.05	5.197	0.650	0.750
1789	1121	2	0.05	0.10	1.600	0.798	0.796
1789	601	4	0.05	0.10	2.977	0.744	0.796
7158	4567	2	0.0375	0.05	1.567	0.784	0.767
7158	2375	4	0.0375	0.05	3.014	0.753	0.767

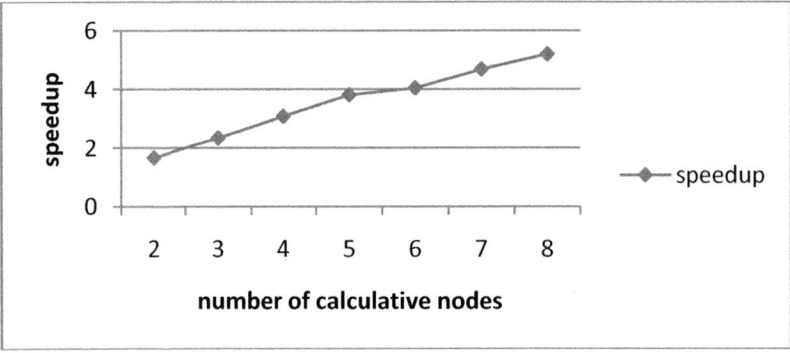

Fig. 3. Speedup. Keep the parameters(θ and γ) unchanged, and increase calculative node step by step, add up the period of sequential execution and the period of parallel execution, and then calculate speedup.

there is a trend that the speedup with more nodes (6, 7, 8 nodes) increases more slowly than that with fewer nodes (2, 3, 4, 5 nodes). The main reason for this trend: during the execution, we found that the calculative nodes were not well-Balanced, in spite of using task pool model. We found that: at some time, several nodes are busy, while the others are idle (the hyperbox queue is empty at that time), but after the busy nodes completing resolving, they will make the idle nodes busy (because the resolving will produce sub-hyperboxes, and the hyperbox queue will not still empty after resolving completed), that means some calculative node were wasted. Therefore, the more calculative nodes we have the more nodes will be idle, and the more speedup will decrease. The cause of the waste is that the deploying of hyperboxes is blindly, thus the realistic work of the calculative nodes are not exactly symmetrical, and the faster ones have to wait for the slower ones.

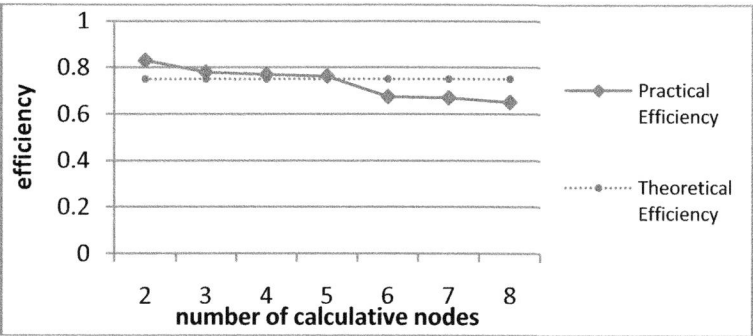

Fig. 4. efficiencies. Keep the parameters(θ and γ) unchanged, and increase calculative nodes step by step, add up the period of sequential execution and the period of parallel execution, and then calculate parallel efficiency.

In our test, the practical efficiency is very close to the theoretical efficiency which is determined by formula (12), and it indicates that formula (12) is useful to estimate the parallel efficiency in this algorithm, see Fig. 4. As same as the speedup, the practical efficiency will decrease with the increasing of number of calculative node. The main reason for the decrease includes two points: 1) the calculative nodes are not well-balanced; 2) extra work which is brought in by parallelization goes up when the number of calculative node goes up.

6   Conclusions and Future Work

Basing on the analysis of the MIS method, this paper digs the immanent parallelism of the algorithm, and then introduces a coarse-grained parallel execution mechanism to the MIS method for accelerating the process of requirement space exploration. We implement the algorithm and then test it on PC clusters. The results indicate that the parallel algorithm is much more effective than the sequential algorithm.

In spite of the high parallel effectiveness of our parallel algorithm, we find the communication delay can decrease more, and the memory pressure for the control node can decrease more. In our parallel algorithm, the hyperboxes generated by the calculative nodes should be sent to the control node, and then sent to some calculative node back. In this course, one hyperbox is double-sent, and the delay between the time of generating and resolving will increase logically. In fact, the source and destination of hyperboxes are both calculative nodes, thus a hyperbox can be sent from one calculative node to some other calculative nodes directly or stay on itself controlled by the control node.

In our test, we find that the calculative nodes are not well load-Balanced. In fact, some feature (such as volume, bound, and so on) of hyperbox can be used to estimate the calculation which resolving the hyperbox needs, and the estimated information can be used to improve the deploy policy to adjust the load of each calculative node for load balancing.

References

1. Bouthonnier, V., Levis, A.H.: System Effectiveness Analysis of C3 Systems. IEEE Trans On Systems, Man, and Cybernetics 14(1), 48–54 (1984)
2. Levis, A.H., et al.: Effectiveness Analysis of Automotive System. Decision Syst., MIT, Cambridge (1984); LIDS-P-1383
3. Christine, B.M.: Computer Graphics for System Effectiveness Analysis.M.S.thesis, Dept.Elect.Eng.Comput.Sci, MIT, Cambridge, MA (1986)
4. Hu, J., Hu, X., Zhang, W., et al.: Monotonic Indices Space Method and Its Application in the Capability Indices effectiveness analysis of a Notional Anti-Stealth Information System. IEEE Transaction on System, Man, Cybernetics Part A 39(2), 404–413 (2009)
5. Hu, J.: Analysis and design of search for weapon system indices. National Defense Industry Press, Beijing (2009) (胡剑文: 武器装备体系能力指标的探索性分析与设计.国防工业出版社,北京(2009))
6. Prediction Measurement. New York: WSEIAC, Final Report of Task Group 2, 1,2,3 (January 1965)
7. Hwang, C.L., et al.: Multiple Attribute Decision Making. Springer, Berlin (1981)
8. Dehne, F., Fabri, A., Rau-Chaplin, A.: Scalable Parallel Computational Geometry For Coarse Grained Multicomputers. International Journal of Computational Geometry & Applications 6(3), 379–400 (1996)
9. Dehne, F., Maheshwari, A., Taylor, R.: A Coarse Grained Parallel Algorithm for Hausdorff Voronoi Diagrams. In: Proceedings of the 2006 International Conference on Parallel Processing, ICPP 2006 (2006)
10. Garcia, T., Sem', D.: A Coarse-Grained Multicomputer algorithm for the Longest Repeated Suffix Ending at Each Point in a Word. In: 11-th Euromicro Conference on Parallel Distributed and Network Based Processing (PDP 2003),
11. Chan, A., Dehne, F., Rau-Chaplin, A.: Coarse Grained Parallel Geometric Search. Journal of Parallel and Distributed Computing 57, 224–235 (1999)
12. Dinan, J., Larkins, D.B., Krishnamoorthy, S., Nieplocha, J.: Scalable Work Stealing. In: Proceeding SC 2009 Proceedings of the Conference on High Performance Computing Networking, Storage and Analysis. ACM, New York (2009)

A Global Benefit Maximization Task-Bundle Allocation

Meiguang Zheng[1], Zhigang Hu[1], Peng Xiao[1], Meixia Zheng[2], and Kai Zhang[3]

[1] School of Information Science and Engineering, Central South University,
Changsha, China
[2] School of Foreign Language, Xinyu College, Xinyu, China
[3] Central Research and Design Institute, ZTE Nanjing, Nanjing, China
zhengJo@gmail.com,
zghu@csu.edu.cn

Abstract. Obtaining maximal benefit is usually the most important goal pursued by Grid resource/service provider. As providers and users being non-cooperative inherently, it is a fundamental challenge to design a resource allocation strategy which seems to be fair. In order to adapt to large-scale Grid environment, we adopted a hierarchical grid structure with bundle tasks to describe the Grid system. A model called Intra-Site Cooperative-game of Task-bundle (ISCT) was proposed, in which all subordinate resources participated in making profits. We calculated task market price based on the theoretical proof that the system would gain maximal global benefit if and only if it was in a balanced state. Then we determined the task allocation solution with solving the task assignment amount vector. An Intra-Site Global Benefit Maximization Allocation for Task-bundle (ISGBMAT) was presented, which converted the Grid task-bundle allocation problem into an iteration process involving retail price, market price and assignment amount of tasks. Extensive simulation experiments with real workload traces were conducted to verify our algorithm. The experimental results indicated that ISGBMAT could provide an effective solution with global benefit and completion time optimization and also adapt to dynamic Grid market.

Keywords: cooperative game, pricing, global benefit maximization, intra-site allocation, grid computing.

1 Introduction

As one of the fundamental challenges in enabling computational grid [1] systems, task scheduling has been widely studied in the last decade. Large-scale scientific or engineering applications are usually mapped onto multiple distributed resources, so how to provide an efficient strategy without complicated coordination is a hard problem. Considering grid resource owners being similar to rational market participants, economic model becomes a topic of great interest in grid task scheduling strategies which are designed similarly to market supply-demand mechanisms[2][3]. Although the grid resource provider, also being the scheduling decision maker, usually attempts to obtain maximum commercial profits, it has to design a seemingly fair allocation strategy since an obvious unreasonable allocation will arouse users'

E. Altman and W. Shi (Eds.): NPC 2011, LNCS 6985, pp. 71–85, 2011.

dissatisfaction. Current market-oriented paradigms have two following limitations: (1) most models have a selecting tendency in the bargain process. For example, commodity market model is biased towards grid user while auction mechanism favors resource owner; (2) the difficulty of resource pricing obscures evaluating allocation performance.

For above two reasons, a hierarchical grid structure with bundles of individual tasks in a Bags-of-Tasks (BoT) fashion [4] is used in this paper to characterize the grid system of large-scale environment. We propose a novel model called Intra-Site Cooperative-game of Task-bundle (ISCT), in which each subordinate resource participates in making profits. We provide a pricing scheme including market price and retail price of tasks, based on the theoretical proof that the system will obtain maximal global benefit if and only if it is in a balanced state. We determine the task allocation via solving the task assignment amount vector. Then the resource allocation problem is converted into an iterative computing process involving retail price, market price and assignment amount of tasks. Thus an Intra-Site Global Benefit Maximization Allocation for Task-bundle (ISGBMAT) is presented. Our contributions are theoretical and experimental: (1) We propose a task scheduling mechanism ISGBMAT which realizes global benefit maximization of the system; (2) We analytically and experimentally demonstrate important features of ISGBMAT, including efficient outcome with performance optimization and adaptive property of market self-selection.

The remainder of this paper is organized as follows. Section 2 reviews related work and compares them with the work proposed in this paper. Section 3 presents the grid system model, formulates specific problem and proposes our pricing scheme. Section 4 derives the ISGBMAT algorithm and analyzes its key properties. Section 5 presents experimental details and simulation results. The final Section 6 concludes the paper and highlights future directions.

2   Related Work

The work in this paper will focus on task scheduling algorithm. The problem of resource allocation and grid scheduling has been extensively investigated. Up to now, scheduling of tasks on the grid remains to be a complex optimization problem in which different objectives of grid system and users are need to be considered.

Kim [5] conducted a survey to provide detailed comparisons among lots of traditional resource allocation algorithms, which argued that policy performance is much affected by different user QoS demand. To this end, with the progressing of grid technologies towards a service-oriented paradigm and the developing of users' more sophisticated requirements, researchers have provided many economy-based approaches for more efficient management of grid resources.

Buyya [6] proposed a famous distributed computational economy-based framework called the Grid Architecture for Computational Economy (GRACE) [7], and developed a grid resource broker called Nimrod-G [8] to support economic scheduling algorithms for scheduling parameter sweep applications on the grid. Later, according to different metrics of either system or users in specified application scenarios, researchers have designed the improved commodity-market-based algorithms. Current market-oriented researches mainly fall into auction-based mechanism [9-13] and game-based mechanism [14-16][19][20] two categories.

Popcorn [11] is a Web-based computing system for parallel application scheduling, in which jobs are auctioned in different mechanisms including Vickrey and first-price and k-price double auction. Garg [12] designed a meta-scheduler which used Continuous Double Auction (CDA) to map user applications onto resources. Within this CDA-based scheduler, job valuation was considered as a bid while resource valuation was considered as an ask. Zhao [13] proposed the BarSAA (barging based self-adaptive auction) grid task-bundle allocation algorithm. Our work has some similarities with BarSAA in the sense that we both handle allocation of bundle tasks, and view task as a commodity sold in the commercial market. However, BarSAA fixed market clearing price via searching tentative price vector, which could not always guarantee algorithm convergence.

In grid computing, game theory is extremely helpful in modeling behaviors of benefit-driven agents. The typical approaches define the objective utility functions and converge at the system equilibrium state on the basis of benefit maximization. Li [14] proposed a resource allocation strategy which used sequential game method to predict resource load for time optimization. Kwok [15] investigated the impact of selfish behaviors of individual machine by taking account of non-cooperativeness of machines. Considering that the gird scheduler has full control of processor's schedules, Rzadca [16] tried to produce solutions which are fair to all the participants by modeling scheduling as an extension of the well-known Prisoner's Dilemma (PD) game. However, due to the extreme complexity of the game process, the time complexity of his algorithm is usually very high. Even if there are only two organizations, the number of Pareto-optimal grid schedules is still very large.

Khan [17] classified game-based co-allocation models into three types: cooperative, semi-cooperative and non-cooperative. By extensive simulations, they concluded that the cooperative method leads to better task rejection, utilization and turnaround time as well as comparable load fairness and makespan. Inspired by this, we use cooperative game to model resource behaviors. With reference to the above mentioned related work, our models and formulations are novel in that we consider the cooperativeness of subordinate resources and the inherent non-cooperativeness between providers and users. Our work is also the first of its kind in providing a proven global benefit maximization allocation.

3   Problem Formulation

3.1   System Model

Kwok argued that a hierarchical structure is more feasible for the large-scale open grid computing system [15]. We follow the approach and our two-tier system model is shown in Fig. 1.

The up-tier consists of grid users, grid sites and a global scheduler. The global scheduler is responsible for handling users' applications submitted to the grid. Applications are inserted into a global FIFS (first in first service) queue. Global scheduler could use our former inter-site gaming strategy [20] to dispatch applications onto grid sites.

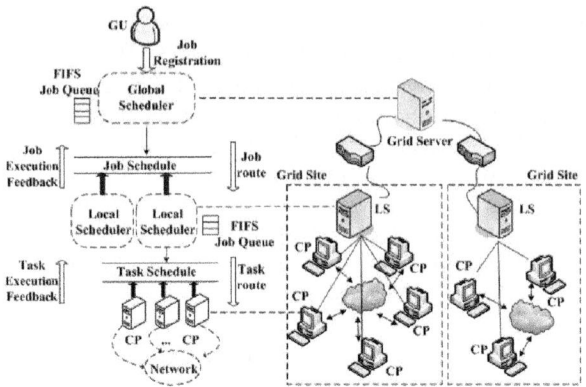

Fig. 1. Structure of hierarchical grid system

The down-tier contains computing peers (CPs) participating in making up of grid site and a local scheduler (LS). In each grid site there is a LS to allocate local resources, such as Portable Batch Scheduler (PBS) and Load Sharing Facility (LSF) used in GRAM. LS is critical in our model which behaves in dual mode. As a site agent, LS contends for its own site profits. As a local resource manager, LS breaks applications into tasks and generates the current available list of computing peers, further specifies the intra-site mapping rule. CPs contend tasks for their own utility.

In this paper we focus on the down-tier in which core problem is intra-site scheduling. Our grid system is limited in a single site domain.

Based on our former inter-site scheduling strategies [18-20], within a site we assume that tasks are colleted in mode of task-bundle [13], denoting a large set of identical independent tasks with no communications involved. The BoT size is much larger than Medium class [4] such as of size 1000 and over. We assume that after some time there are m tasks arrived. These tasks have identical attributes including computational size (S_{cp}) and communication size (S_{cm}). Current available CP list contains n computing peers. Since our system model is built upon a virtual grid market, the following definitions are critical and will be throughout this paper.

Definition 1. Task Retail Price.
Let $v_i (i = 1, 2, ..., n)$ denote the monetary value of one task setup by every CP. Every task should pay v_i for successful execution on CP_i.

Definition 2. Task Market Price.
Let p* denote the monetary value of one task setup by LS. Every CP should pay LS p* for getting a task.

Definition 3. Task assignment amount vector $A = (A_1, ..., A_i, ..., A_n)$.
Let $A_i (i = 1, 2, ..., n)$ denote the task assignment amount which will maximize CP_i's utility at current task market price. Obviously, A_i satisfies $\forall i, A_i \in N$ and $A_i \leq m$.

Grid system performs as follow: LS sells tasks to available CPs at a uniform price called task market price. Every task will pay CP's retail price for the successful execution. Different CP will demand its own task retail price according to its resource performance. All CPs' profits constitute grid system's benefit and CPs cooperate with LS aiming at maximizing global resource benefit. Based on this critical property, we name our model Intra-Site Cooperative-game of Task-bundle (ISCT) in the following text. Note that tasks and CPs are inherently non-cooperative. Tasks hope to minimize their cost, which would inevitably lower down the profits of CPs.

The utility function of LS is defined as

$$U^L = p * \cdot \sum_{i=1}^n A_i, \quad \sum_{i=1}^n A_i = m \tag{1}$$

The utility function of CP_i is defined as

$$U_i^C = A_i \cdot v_i - A_i \cdot p * \tag{2}$$

The global benefit is the sum of all the CPs' profits and the LS's revenue, which equals to the sum cost of n tasks:

$$U^G = U^L + \sum_{i=1}^n U_i^C = \sum_{i=1}^n (A_i \cdot v_i) \tag{3}$$

As the task provider, LS should determine reasonable $p*$ and A. The solution of cooperative model can be viewed as a distribution of benefit and will be characterized by the 2-tuple $< p*, A >$. Indeed, solution space of A is the set of scheduling schemes.

3.2   Pricing

We use t_i to represent estimated completion time (ECT) of CP_i finishing one task. Let Cm_i denote CP_i's communication capacity and Cp_i denote CP_i's computation capacity. ECT contains setup time t^{setup}, transmission time t^{trans} and execution time t^{exec} three parts in which t^{setup} is fixed. t_i is calculated as follow:

$$t_i = t^{setup} + t^{trans} + t^{exec} = t^{setup} + \frac{S_{cm}}{Cm_i} + \frac{S_{cp}}{Cp_i} \tag{4}$$

Generally users would like pay more money for faster service. Here we map the ECT to task retail price by $v_i = 1/t_i$. We use a discount rate considering different deal price at different quantities. Let $k(k \in N, k \le m)$ represent different quantities of tasks and $v_i(k)$ represent mean deal price for k tasks on CP_i, then $v_i(k)$ satisfies

$$v(0) = 0, \quad \forall i, k_1 < k_2 \Rightarrow v_i(k_1) > v_i(k_2) \tag{5}$$

Let V_i^k be the sum deal price for k tasks on CP_i, $\alpha(0 < \alpha < 1)$ be the discount rate and $q = 1 - \alpha \ (0 < q < 1)$, we can get

$$V_i^1 = v_i(1) = v_i = \frac{1}{t_i}, \quad V_i^k = \frac{1}{t_i} \cdot \sum_{j=1}^{k}(1-\alpha)^{j-1} = \frac{1}{t_i} \cdot \frac{1-q^k}{\alpha} \tag{6}$$

We assume that different CPs have the identical discount rate. v_i can be regarded as the base price from which we can evaluate performance of CP_i. As V_i^1 has the same value with v_i, V_i^1 is denoted as V_i^b. We can get

$$V_i^k = V_i^b \cdot \frac{(1-q^k)}{\alpha}, \quad v_i(k) = \frac{V_i^b}{k} \cdot \frac{(1-q^k)}{\alpha} \tag{7}$$

4   Design and Analysis of ISGBMAT Algorithm

For the convenience of representation, some definitions are given as follows.

Definition 4. $CPs^+(p^*)$, $CPs^-(p^*)$ and $CPs^0(p^*)$.

At p^*, $CPs^+(p^*) = \{CP_i \mid U_i^C > 0, i \in [1,...,n]\}$ is the set of CPs with positive profits; $CPs^-(p^*) = \{CP_i \mid U_i^C < 0, i \in [1,...,n]\}$ and $CPs^0(p^*) = \{CP_i \mid U_i^C = 0, i \in [1,...,n]\}$ respectively are the set of CPs with negative and zero profits.

Definition 5. Balanced State.
At $< p^*, A_i >$, CP_i will be in a balanced state if $CP_i \in CPs^0(p^*)$; at $< p^*, A >$, the ISCT system will be in a balanced state if $\forall CP_i$ satisfies $CP_i \in CPs^0(p^*)$.

4.1   Calculation Method for ISCT

For each CP_i in the available CP list, we assume A_i is positive. So $\forall i$, $1 \leq i \leq n$ satisfies $A_i \in N^+$.

Theorem 1. If ISCT system is in a balanced state at $< p^*, (A_1,...,A_n) >$, adjusting $< p^*, (A_1,...,A_n) >$ will not affect the global benefit U^G.
Proof Let $(U_1^C, U_2^C,..., U_n^C)$ represent the profits of CPs at $< p^*, (A_1,...,A_n) >$ and $(U_1^C, U_2^C,..., U_n^C)$ represent   the   profits   of   CPs   at $< p^*+\Delta p^*, (A_1+\Delta A_1,...,A_n+\Delta A_n) >$.

   At $< p^*, (A_1,...,A_n) >$, according to definition 4 and definition 5, it can be known that $\forall CP_i$ satisfies $U_i^C = A_i \cdot (v_i - p^*) = 0$, then

$$U^G = U^L + \sum_{i=1}^{n} U_i^C = U^L + \sum_{i=1}^{n} 0 = U^L.$$

Assumed   after   adjusting,   ISCT   system   is   being   at $<p*+\Delta p*, (A_1+\Delta A_1,..., A_n+\Delta A_n)>$. According to Formula (2), we can get

$$U_i^C = A_i \cdot (v_i - p*) - \Delta p* \cdot (A_i + \Delta A_i) + \Delta A_i \cdot (v_i - p*) = -\Delta p* \cdot (A_i + \Delta A_i)$$

Provided that the total task amount m is fixed, then $\sum_{i=1}^{n}(A_i + \Delta A_i) = \sum_{i=1}^{n} A_i$. It can

be known that at $<p*+\Delta p*, (A_1+\Delta A_1,..., A_n+\Delta A_n)>$, the global benefit $U^{G'}$ is

$$U^{G'} = U^L + \sum_{i=1}^{n} U_i^C = (p*+\Delta p*) \cdot (\sum_{i=1}^{n}(A_i + \Delta A_i)) - \Delta p* \cdot \sum_{i=1}^{n}(A_i + \Delta A_i)$$

$$= p* \cdot \sum_{i=1}^{n}(A_i + \Delta A_i) = p* \cdot \sum_{i=1}^{n} A_i = U^L = U^G$$

Theorem 2. If ISCT system is in an unbalanced state at $<p*, (A_1,..., A_n)>$, the global

benefit U^G can always be increased by adjusting $<p*, (A_1,..., A_n)>$.

Proof: At $<p*, (A_1,..., A_n)>$, if system is in an unbalanced state, according to

Formula (3) we can get $U^G = \sum_{i=1}^{n}(A_i \cdot v_i)$ and U^G is independent of $p*$. If $p*$ is

adjusted to p_0^* and $p_0^* = v_k, 1 \le k \le n$, the system will satisfy the following

conclusions at $<p_0^*, (A_1,..., A_n)>$.

(a)The system is still in unbalanced state or else it will contradict with the precondition of the theorem.

(b) According to formula (3), the global benefit remains the same.

(c) Provided $p_0^* = v_k$, the CP_k is in a balance state, that is $CP_k \in CPs^0(p_0^*)$.

According to (a), it can be known that $\exists CP_i$ satisfies $CP_i \in CPs^+(p_0^*)$ or

$CP_i \in CPs^-(p_0^*)$, where $i \ne k$.

If $CP_i \in CPs^+(p_0^*)$, task assignment amount of CP_k and CP_i can be adjusted to

$A_k' = A_k - \Delta \delta$ and $A_i' = A_i + \Delta \delta$ respectively, where $\Delta \delta > 0$.

For $CP_k \in CPs^0(p_0^*)$, adjustment of CP_k will not affect the global benefit. For

$CP_i \in CPs^+(p_i^*)$, increasing CP_i's task assignment amount will increase the global

benefit. Thus the global benefit at $<p_0^*, (A_1,...A_k',...A_i',..., A_n)>$ could be larger than

that at $<p*, (A_1,..., A_n)>$.

If $CP_i \in CPs^-(p_0^*)$, the analysis and conclusion are similar to the above, and the

only difference is $\Delta \delta < 0$.

Theorem 3. ISCT system will obtain maximal global benefit if and only if it is in a balanced state.

Combining Theorem 1 and Theorem 2, it is easy to get Theorem 3. So, the system can improve its global benefit by repeatedly adjusting $<p*, (A_1,..., A_n)>$ to make the system in or near to a balanced state.

Given the system is in an unbalanced state at $<p^*,(A_1,...A_n)>$ and would be adjusted to $<p_0^*,(A_1',...,A_n')>$. If p_0^* satisfies $\min\sum_{i=1}^n(v_i-p_0^*)^2$, system is the nearest to a balanced state. It is clear that the solution is

$$p_0^* = \frac{1}{n}\cdot\sum_{i=1}^n v_i \tag{8}$$

4.2   Solution of Task Assignment Amount Vector

LS will assign tasks to the CPs according to their task retail price v_i. Generally, tasks tend to be executed on the CP with faster resource for better time metric or with lower retail price to meet cost metric. This may arise two extremities: the most expensive or the cheapest CP will occupy too much tasks. As mentioned in section III our pricing scheme use discount, and mean deal price $v_i(k)$ is a decreasing function of task quantity k. Similar with the case in a commodity market, a CP can get more tasks assigned by lowering its mean deal price. However, the mean deal price can not be too low or CP will benefit zero or negative considering that CP still should pay LS p^*. This constraint avoids aforementioned extremities. According to Formula (7), as mean deal price of CP_i being a function of its task assignment amount A_i, utility function defined in Formula (2) can be rewritten as $U_i^C = A_i \cdot v_i(A_i) - p^*\cdot A_i$. Since $v_i(A_i) = \frac{V_i^b}{A_i}\cdot\frac{(1-q^{A_i})}{\alpha}$, we have $U_i^C = V_i^b\cdot\frac{(1-q^{A_i})}{\alpha} - p^*\cdot A_i$. To solve $\frac{d(U_i^C)}{d(A_i)}=0$ we can get the equation $\frac{V_i^b}{\alpha}\cdot q^{A_i}\cdot\ln q + p^* = 0$, so the solution of A_i is

$$A_i = \log_q(\frac{-\alpha\cdot p^*}{\ln q\cdot V_i^b}) \tag{9}$$

In Formula (9) A_i may be negative, which means it lose money in business for CP_i to execute tasks. According to our pricing scheme, utility of CP_i executing kth task can be defined as

$$U_i^C(k) = V_i^b\cdot q^{k-1} - p^*, \quad 0<q<1. \tag{10}$$

Provided $U_i^C(k)$ is a decreasing function of k, it is easy to know that CP_i's utility U_i^C is maximal as long as the lowest utility for single task $U_i^C(k)$ is not negative, which is represented as follow:

$$V_i^b\cdot q^{A_i-1} - p^* \geq 0, \quad 0<q<1 \tag{11}$$

So we can get $A_i \leq 1+\log_q(p^*/V_i^b)$ and task assignment amount can be modified as

$$A_i = \left\lfloor 1 + \log_q (p^* / V_i^b) \right\rfloor \tag{12-1}$$

In some extreme cases, some CPs with super capability may get most of tasks. In order to alleviate this monopoly phenomenon, here we introduce N_{max} to limit the maximum quantity of tasks that a CP of super capability can get. Hence Formula (12-1) can be modified as follow:

$$A_i = \begin{cases} A_i, & \text{if } A_i < N_{max} \\ N_{max}, & \text{if } A_i \geq N_{max} \end{cases} \tag{12-2}$$

```
INPUT:  m, n, S_cp, S_cm, α, N_max .
OUTPUT: p*, A .
1.   Begin
2.      Initialization flagCon=1, A = LF = F = 0 , UB = N_max ;
3.      for i=1 to n do
4.            calculate V_i^b ;  v_i = newV_i^b = V_i^b ;
5.      end for
6.      calculate p*;
7.      while Σ_{i=1}^{n} A_i + Σ_{i=1}^{n} F_i ≠ m  do
8.            for i=1 to n do
9.                LF_i = F_i ;  calculate F_i ;
10.           end for
11.           flagCon=any(LF~=F);
12.           if ~flagCon
13.              for i=1 to n do
14.                   A_i = A_i + F_i ; newV_i^b = V_i^b · q^{A_i} ;
15.                   UB_i = UB_i − F_i ; F_i = LF_i = 0 ;
16.              end for
17.           end if
18.           for i=1 to n do
19.                v_i = newV_i^b * (1 − q^{F_i}) / α / F_i ;
20.           end for
21.           update p*;
22.      end while
23.      for i=1 to n do
24.         Calculate CP_i's income from tasks, the payment
25.         from CP_i's to LS and CP_i's profits
26.      end for
27.   output p*, A
28.end.
```

Fig. 2. Intra-Site Global Benefit Maximization Allocation for Task-bundle (ISGBMAT)

4.3   ISGBMAT Algorithm

The ISGBMAT algorithm is described in Fig.2.

Based on our previous analysis result, ISGBMAT uses an iteration adjustment in the sequence of retail price, market price and assignment amount of tasks. We save the latest task assignment amount in F_i and the task assignment amount of last round in LF_i. In step4, for each CP_i, V_i^b is initialized according to Formula (6). In step 6, p* is calculated with Formula (8).

A flag 'flagCon' is used to partition the iteration into inner and outer. The transition of flagCon from 1 to 0 represents that a round assignment is over. In a round, task assignment amount of each CP adjusts according to Formula (12) and F_i should satisfy $0 \le LF_i \le F_i \le UB_i$ (Step 9). Accordingly, the mean retail price of CP changes by Formula (7) (Step 19) and the latest p* is calculated with Formula (8) (Step 21). After getting the result of F_i, it need compare F_i with LF_i to update flagCon (Step 11). The equality denotes that the amount can not be updated anymore and the inner iteration ends. Then it should set flagCon zero and update retail price of CPs (Step 14). Here $newV_i^b$ is used to memorize V_i^b of every round.

Here UB is used to save the realtime remaining maximum assignment amount, which is uniformly initialized with N_{max} (Step 2) and will be updated according to the latest assignment mount (Step 15). Set task assignment amount to be UB if it figures larger than UB (Step 9).

The time complexity of the algorithm is $O(n \cdot S)$ where n is the number of computing peers and S is the iteration times of the outside loop (Step7-Step22). It is easy to know that the maximum value of S is equal to m. So the complexity of ISGBMAT is lower than $O(n \cdot m)$.

5   Performance Evaluation

5.1   Experimental Setup

The performance of ISGBMAT proposed in this paper is evaluated based on a prevalent grid simulator GridSim 5.0 [21]. A multi cluster computational grid model is constructed, consisting of 12 clusters which referenced to the related data in the American large-scale grid application TeraGrid [22]. Fig. 3 illustrates system snapshots of available computing and network resources that each CP is willing to contribute. The computing speed is represented in MIPS and network bandwidth is represented in bps. In Fig. 3, system's $H_D = 11.0468$ (see Definition 6).

Our experiment uses real workload traces gathered from existing supercomputers and collected in the Parallel Workload Archive [23]. The basic workload consists of 1000 tasks. Based on Formula (4), we classify tasks to three categories according to compute communication ratio, which are (1) computation-intensive: $S_{cp}/S_{cm} = 1000:1$; (2) neutrality (Cp size and Cm size are equal): $S_{cp}/S_{cm} = 500:500$; (3) communication-intensive: $S_{cp}/S_{cm} = 1:1000$. Setup time t^{setup} is fixed to 5ms. The following two metrics are important in our experiment.

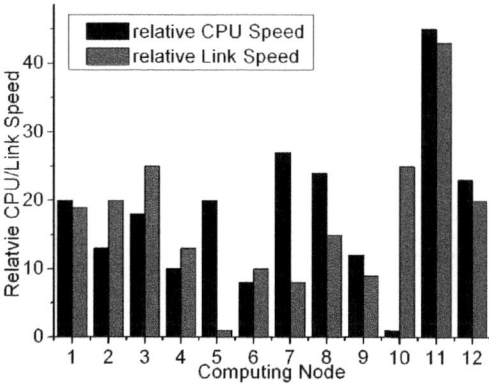

Fig. 3. System snapshot of CPU/Link

Definition 6. Heterogeneous degree H_D.

$H_D \geq 0$, which indicates the resource performance difference between CPs, is defined as:

$$H_D = \frac{1}{2} \cdot \left(\sqrt{\frac{1}{n} \cdot \sum_{i=1}^{n} (Cp_i - \overline{Cp})^2} + \sqrt{\frac{1}{n} \cdot \sum_{i=1}^{n} (Cm_i - \overline{Cm})^2} \right) \qquad (13)$$

Where $\overline{Cp}$ and $\overline{Cm}$ represent the mean computing and network ability respectively.

Definition 7. Workload Fairness FI.

$FI \in (0,1]$ indicates workload balance situation concerning ECT in every CP. We quantity the workload fairness by using the Jain's fairness index [24]:

$$FI = \frac{(\sum_{i=1}^{n} T_i)^2}{n \cdot \sum_{i=1}^{n} T_i^2} \qquad (14)$$

T_i is the ECT for CP_i to finish all the assigned tasks. The strategy is perfectly fair if the value of FI is 1.

In the simulation experiments, ISGBMAT is compared with three other economy models: Commodity Market (CM) Model (Flat) [6], Proportional Share [6] and Double Auction [12], in terms of global benefit, completion time and total time. Completion time is the longest completion time on single CP while total time is the sum of completion time on all CPs. The benefit and payments in ISGBMAT are expressed with virtual grid dollars (G$). For each scenario, we did the experiments 50 times independently and took the average value for different metrics.

5.2   Experimental Results and Analysis

1) Performance comparison

As shown in Table 1, we observe that our algorithm outperforms others in terms of global benefit and can obtain fairly good time metrics. CM(flat) has performed the

Table 1. Scheduling Result Comparison with three other algorithms

Algorithm	Performance metrics		
	Global benefit *(G$)*	*Completion time* *(h:m:s)*	*Total time* *(h:m:s)*
CM(flat)	60424	2:00:37	18:21:03
Double Auction	61976	1:49:51	17:43:27
Proportional Share	60790	1:23:46	16:56:31
ISGBMAT	62765	1:37:50	16:48:25

worst in every case. The reason for this behavior is that CM(flat) with static price could not adapt to dynamic market. Proportional Share fairly allocates tasks among various CPs on the basis of CP prices, which leads to good time metric but poor global benefit. In Double Auction, it is prone to allocate tasks to expensive (high performance) CPs which results in high global benefit at the expenses of time. In ISGBMAT, task market price adjusts iteratively until the equilibrium is reached. The Global benefit is increased by adjusting task assignment amount of CPs and retail price of CP is updated accordingly. We have proved global benefit maximization property of ISCT. Contrasting with conventional economy model in commodity market, we introduce dynamic task market price as leverage to the proposed ISGBMAT, which leads to workload balance and reduction of the completion time.

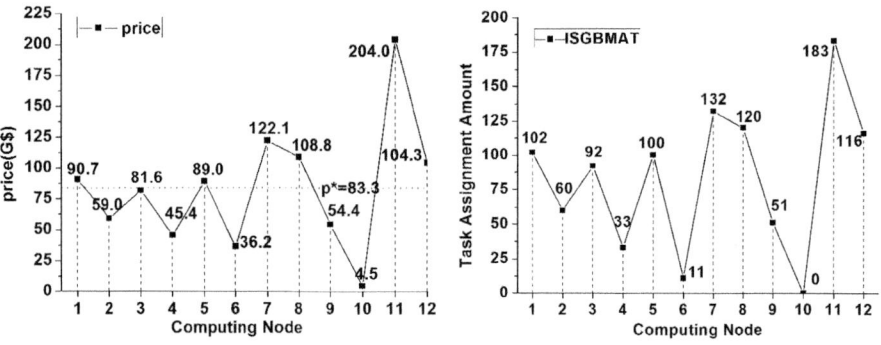

Fig. 4. (a)Retail price of CPs   (b) Allocation result of ISGBMAT

2) Self-selection property of ISGBMAT
ISGBMAT preserves self-selection property which is inherited from market model. For more deep explanation, details of each CP's retail price and allocation result are shown in Fig.4(a) and Fig.4(b) respectively. In this set of experiments, CPs are configured just as they are in Fig.3 and tasks attribute is set to be computation-intensive. As shown in Fig.4(b), there is no task assigned to CP10 which means CP10 has been knocked out. We observe that CP10's relative CPU Speed is so low (Fig.3) that it will be priced (in Fig.4(a), PriceCP10=4.5) far behind market price ($p^*=83.3$) when executing computation-intensive tasks.

3) Interplay of N_{max}, FI *and* H_D

In the last set of experiments we demonstrate how N_{max}, FI and H_D interplay. In Fig. 5, for simplicity, we define mean assignment amount $A_{mean} = \lfloor m/n \rfloor$. Here N_{max} will set to be λ times of A_{mean}. There are three curves which represent different groups of CPs with resource capability, referencing to different H_D. Results show that higher degree of heterogeneity will decrease FI of allocation, which is coincident with our common cognition that 'diversity calls forth unfairness'.

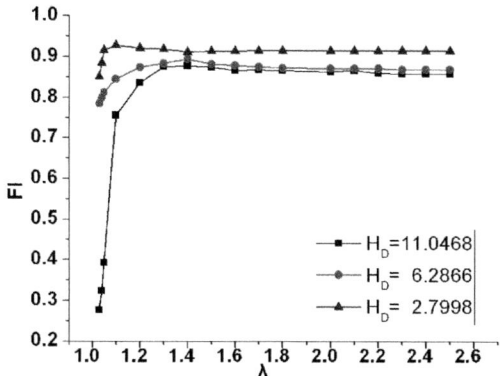

Fig. 5. Interplay of N_{max}, FI and H_{Degree}

We observe that these three curves have similar sketch. In the condition $\lambda = 1$, workload is enforced to be distributed balancedly, which will lead to poor FI. As λ going up, N_{max} becomes bigger and bigger, and the system will have better FI accordingly. FI will converge with λ getting to a certain maximum constraint. Then task assignment amount has no limit so that N_{max} is useless. This analysis result gives advice for more effective solution with a feasible N_{max}.

6   Conclusion

In this paper we propose an efficient Intra-Site Global Benefit Maximization Allocation for Task-bundle (ISGBMAT) based on our model called Intra-Site Cooperative-game of Task-bundle (ISCT) in hierarchical computational grids. There are two major contributions of our design. First of all, our solution of ISCT will realize maximal global benefit of system which has been validated by mathematical analysis. In addition, based on ISCT, ISGBMAT is designed by formulating resource allocation as an iteration process involving retail price, market price and allocation amount of tasks. It provides a novel economy-based scheme for resource allocation. Extensive simulations verify the efficiency of ISGBMAT. In our ongoing work, we will explore different discount rate α setting to different CPs for more balanced workload and further adapt our strategy to other workload mode and pricing schemes.

Acknowledgements. This paper is supported by the NSFC project (Grant No. 60970038).

References

1. Foster, I., Kesselman, C.: The Grid: Blueprint for a New Computing Infrastructure. Morgan Kauffman, San Francisco (2004)
2. Chun, B.N., Culler, D.E.: User-centric Performance Analysis of Market-based Cluster Batch Schedulers. In: 2nd IEEE/ACM International Symposium on Cluster Computing and the Grid, pp. 30–38. IEEE Computer Society, Berlin (2002)
3. Yeo, C.S., Buyya, R.: Service Level Agreement based Allocation of Cluster Resources: Handling Penalty to Enhance Utility. In: 7th IEEE International Conference on Cluster Computing, pp. 1–10. IEEE Press, Boston (2005)
4. Losup, A., Sonmez, O., Anoep, S., Epema, D.: The Performance of Bags-of-tasks in Large-scale Distributed Systems. In: 17th International Symposium on High Performance Distributed Computing, pp. 97–108. ACM, Boston (2008)
5. Kim, J.K., Shivle, S., Siegel, H.J., Maciejewski, A.A., Braun, T.D., Schneider, M., et al.: Dynamic Mapping in a Heterogeneous Environment with Tasks Having Priorities and Multiple Deadlines. In: 17th International Symposium on Parallel and Distributed Processing, pp. 98–112. IEEE Computer Society, Nice (2003)
6. Buyya, R.: Economic-based Distributed Resource Management and Scheduling for Grid Computing. Monash University, Australia (2002)
7. GRACCE: Grid Application Coordination, Collaboration and Execution, http://www.cs.uh.edu/~gracce
8. Buyya, R., Abramson, D., Giddy, J.: Nimrod/G: An Architecture for a Resource Management and Scheduling System in a Global Computational Grid. In: Proceedings of International Conference/Exhibition on High Performance Computing in Asia-Pacific Region, Beijing, pp. 283–289 (2000)
9. Lai, K., Rasmusson, L., Adar, E., Zhang, L., Huberman, A.: Tycoon: An Implementation of a Distributed, Market-based Resource Allocation System. Multiagent and Grid System 1(3), 169–182 (2005)
10. AuYoung, A., Chun, B., Snoeren, A., Vahdat, A.: Resource Allocation in Federated Distributed Computing Infrastructures. In: 1st Workshop on Operating System and Architectural Support for the On-Demand IT Infrastructure (2004)
11. Regev, O., Nisan, N.: The POPCORN Market Online Markets for Computational Resources. Decision Support System 28(1-2), 177–189 (2000)
12. Garg, S.K., Venugopal, S., Buyya, R.: A Meta-scheduler with Auction based Resource Allocation for Global Grids. In: 14th IEEE International Conference on Parallel and Distributed Systems, pp. 187–194. IEEE, Melbourne (2008)
13. Zhao, H., Li, X.L.: Efficient Grid Task-Bundle Allocation using Bargaining Based Self-adaptive Auction. In: 9th IEEE/ACM International Symposium on Cluster Computing and the Grid, pp. 4–11. IEEE Computer Society, Shanghai (2009)
14. Li, Z.J., Cheng, C.T., Huang, F.X., Li, X.: A Sequential Game-based Resource Allocation Strategy in Grid Environment. Journal of Software 17(11), 2373–2383 (2000)
15. Kwok, Y.K., Song, S., Hwang, K.: Selfish Grid Computing: Game Theoretic Modeling and NAS Performance Results. In: 5th IEEE/ACM International Symposium on Cluster Computing and the Grid, vol. 2, pp. 1143–1150. IEEE Computer Society, Cardiff (2005)

16. Rzadca, K., Trystram, D., Wierzbicki, A.: Fair Game-theoretic Resource Management in Dedicated Grids. In: 7th IEEE/ACM International Symposium on Cluster Computing and the Grid, pp. 343–350. IEEE Computer Society, Rio de Janeiro (2007)

17. Khan, S.U., Ahmad, I.: Non-cooperative, Semi-cooperative, and Cooperative Games-based Grid Resource Allocation. In: 20th IEEE International Symposium on Parallel and Distributed Processing, p. 10. IEEE Press, Rhodes Island (2006)

18. Xiao, P., Hu, Z.G.: A novel QoS-based Co-allocation Model in Computational Grid. In: IEEE Global Communications Conference 2008, pp. 1562–1566. IEEE Press, New Orleans (2008)

19. Hu, Z.J., Hu, Z.G., Ding, C.S.: Game-theory-based Robust-enhanced Model for Resource Allocation in Computational Grids. Systems Engineering-Theory&Practice 29(8), 102–110 (2009)

20. Zheng, M.G., Hu, Z.G., Zhang, K.: Performance-efficiency Balanced Optimization based on Sequential Game in Grid Environments. Journal of South China University of Technology 38(1), 92-96+107 (2010)

21. GridSim, http://www.cloudbus.org/gridsim

22. TeraGrid, http://www.teragrid.org

23. Parallel Workloads Archive,
    http://www.cs.huji.ac.il/labs/parallel/workload

24. Jain, R., Chiu, D., Hawe, W.: A quantitative measure of fairness and discrimination for resource allocation in shared computer systems. In: CoRR (1998)

Service Quality Assurance Mechanisms for P2P SIP VoIP

Xiaofei Liao, Fengjiang Guo, and Hai Jin

Services Computing Technology and System Lab
Cluster and Grid Computing Lab
School of Computer Science and Technology
Huazhong University of Science and Technology, Wuhan, 430074, China
hjin@hust.edu.cn

Abstract. Recently P2P (Peer-to-Peer) has been proposed to improve the scalability of the traditional VoIP (voice over IP) systems. However, P2P makes VoIP service unreliable because P2P networks probably scale up and the service nodes are very likely to fail or leave the P2P networks when VoIP service is offering. To deal with this issue, we propose a service quality assurance mechanism. The whole proposition includes a relay overlay algorithm and a dynamic relay algorithm. In the scheme, VoIP system can select the successor of the failed relay nodes without adding extra backup nodes. The simulation results demonstrate that our algorithms maintain 70% voice dialogs correctly in the presence of relay nodes failure with the delay remaining below 150ms. The results also show that the system architecture is feasible and scalable.

Keywords: Voice over IP, Service quality, Backup links, Dynamic switching.

1   Introduction

Voice over IP (VoIP) system is gradually replaying traditional PSTN (Public Switched Telephone Network) telephone and becoming the key pattern of voice transportation in NGN (Next Generation Network) due to its low cost, high flexibility and ability of integrating multimedia information.

The P2P technology enhances VoIP system performance, but also brings some problems. P2P overlay network is open and extensible, but also has great differences and dynamics. The characteristic makes P2P networks unable to meet the requirements of VoIP system which is a kind of real-time application. When two VoIP nodes communicate in this network, the system often has quality of service problems.

The unreliability of service is a common issue in traditional VoIP systems, and it is mainly due to the breakdown or departure of the service node. Traditional service quality improvement mechanisms use RSVP (Resource Reservation Protocol) in application-layer, and MPLS (Multi-protocol Label Switching) in physical layer for improving service quality. The main disadvantages of those solutions are as follows:

- High costs: the cost of hardware and maintenance is increased, because it is based on the redundant mechanisms.
- Poor scalability: the scalability of the system is subject to the constraints of the server capacity, and the increasing number of the user means that the service of the system is needed to be upgraded constantly.

E. Altman and W. Shi (Eds.): NPC 2011, LNCS 6985, pp. 86–98, 2011.

- Performance bottleneck: those solutions do not take the property of P2P network into account. The delay of restoration does not meet the requirement of real-time systems.

On the other hand, in currently VoIP system, the more popular solution for traversing the firewall is to add a relay node between the users. However, due to property of the relay node, the system often has quality of service problems because the service node may leave the relay overlay. In that case the VoIP call is likely to fail.

The relay overlay consists of relay nodes and relay servers. The relay node is selected by relay server in VoIP system. In our VoIP system, the user applies to relay server for appropriate node before initiating a call. The unreliability of this relay service has extreme impact on the call process, because the call will be forced to be suspended once the failure or departure of caller's relay node.

As mentioned above, how to design an affective mechanism to find a successor of the failed relay node is still a problem. We propose a solution of a dynamic relay algorithm based on ICE (Interactive Connectivity Establishment) protocol. The main idea is that a lightweight redundant mechanism for relay server is adopted. If two users need to relay when communicating, one can use the relay server find the appropriate node to relay. We will explain the relay-node finding mechanism between two relay servers in the paper in detail. Before the call is initialized, the callee does not hold the information of the caller. It will select the relay node for accomplishing ICE process. At the same time, when the VoIP system makes the call with that relay node, it can dynamically switch the relay node which can provide better service. The callee automatically detects the voice quality and sends RE-INVITE (a command in SIP protocol) request. Then the callee is staying on the phone with the caller in the case of poor voice quality. In this case, the callee who holds the caller's information such as the position of its relay server could use a better relay node detecting algorithms.

In this paper we study the framework of P2P-SIP system and relay detecting algorithms. The problem proposed is how to design service quality assurance mechanism for P2P-SIP VoIP system to take full advantage of the properties of relay overlay to achieve high reliability and low investment VoIP system.

The rest of this paper is organized as follows. Section 2 discusses the related work. The detail system architecture is described in section 3. Section 4 describes our simulation and presents the performance evaluation. We conclude this work in section 5.

2   Related Work

In this section, we give a brief overview of Skype, a real VoIP system, and related technologies including an application-layer relay algorithm.

2.1 Skype Relay Calls

Skype is the most popular P2P-based commercial VoIP system, which works around NAT (Network Address Translation) and firewall issues by routing calls through the machine of another Skype user with unrestricted connectivity to the Internet.

Skype client (SC) maintains a list of other Skype peers called a host cache (HC) [4]. Other Skype peers list is empty when a SC is running for the first time, and is built during the lifetime of a Skype client. Then, a SC can contact nodes in the host cache

(HC). Additionally, a SC has a built-in list of about seven default Skype nodes, which are called bootstrap nodes and are used to help peers join the Skype overlay for the first time after installation.

After joining successfully, a Skype client establishes a TCP connection with another Skype user or a super node (SN). There are two types of nodes in the Skype overlay: super node (SN) and ordinary node. Both SN and ordinary node run the same Skype software. SNs are responsible for detecting online SCs, and transmitting signaling messages between SCs [3]. To establish a call, a SC searches for the callee machine. If they successfully contact with each other, they can directly exchange media data with the callee machines. We can select a node as a relay node (RN) and the call can be routed. A RN is a SN, which has sufficient bandwidth to relay a voice or a video call.

A key aspect of Skype's robust connectivity is its ability to traverse NAT and firewalls by routing a video or voice call through one or more Skype relays. The network conditions between the caller and callee machines are configured so that they are forced to use a RN.

The success rate of relay calls depends on the network conditions, the presence of a host cache, and caching of the callee's reachable address. From our experiments, we have found that Skype relay mechanism can be further improved. Because the Skype uses private protocol and the most important problem is how to guarantee the relay node steady and dependable.

2.2   Application-Layer Relay Algorithm

The application-layer relay algorithm is a one-hop relay algorithm. It sets an overall server in relay overlay. This server is called relay server and manages other peers. The peers in the overlay keep the information of other nodes in the network and divide them into some parts. This information of other nodes will be stored in a ring-structure called Meridian [1]. It sets the radius of every ring according to the delay. The peers ping each other and get the delay among them, and put the other nodes in its rings. These nodes are used when the system needs a relay call.

While one peer wants to join the network, it will ask the relay server for some node lists according to its network environment. After detecting the peers in these lists, the new node can initialize its own rings. It will update their delay information by using timer. The nodes send update packets to some of the peers in their rings. According to the approach, the node can update the peers in their rings.

When users need a relay call, it sends the search packet including the information of another user. The search algorithm will send the result back to the user who requests the relay call. The process is as follows. First, the source peer sends the search packets to some of its neighbors in its inner ring. The packets include IP address of the destination node. The nodes who receive the search packets continue to transfer the packet to the node in its own neighbors until it finds the destination node. By defining survival time of these search packets, it can reach some nodes so that there will be more opportunity to find the relay.

The application-layer relay algorithm is used in our early system which is called as Cutephone. But the relay node plays important role, and its network condition is crucially important for the call completion and service quality. Unfortunately, the relay call is used to solve the problem when users are behind NAT and firewall. The callee does not know the caller's information before initializing a call in most call cases. The relay path it selects may not be the best option.

3   Design and Architecture

There are two levels in our VoIP system architecture, the signal overlay and the media relay overlay, as shown in Figure 1. The upper level is signal overlay, which consists of super node client (SN-C). The SN-C is responsible for signal transferring. The lower level is media relay overlay, and it consists of relay servers and relay nodes. Their respective functions are described in the following sections. A UE (the VoIP client) could be standard traditional SIP clients or our own P2P-SIP client called Cutephone. Cutephone is more flexible than tradition SIP clients by adding some functions to support ICE (Interactive Connectivity Establishment).

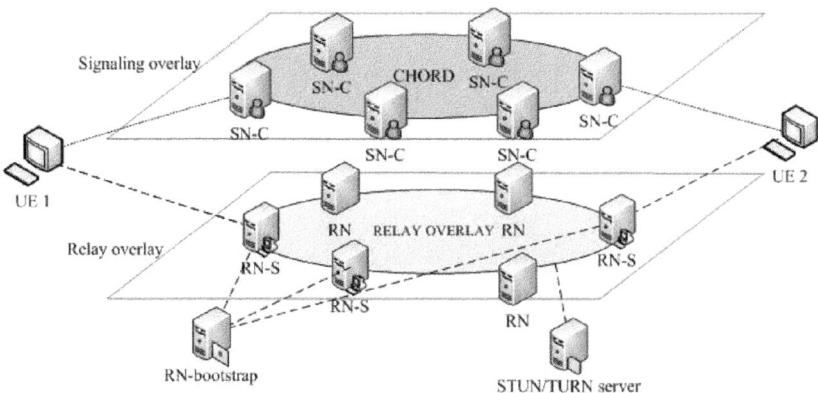

Fig. 1. P2P VoIP system structure

3.1   Design Principle

The system consists of Super Node Client (SN-C), Relay Node Server (RN-S), and Relay Node (RN). They play different roles in the VoIP system.

SN-C combines the functions of SIP register server, SIP redirect server, and SIP agent server. Actually SN-C has two layers. One is the tradition SIP layer, called SIP server, and the other is the P2P overlay layer. P2P overlay is maintained by the SN-C mainly for user orientation and user information publishing, the specific algorithm of P2P overlay is Chord protocol.

RN-S manages the peers in relay overlay. It keeps the information of other nodes in the network and divides them into some parts according to the delay among them. This information of other nodes will be kept in a Meridian rings.

RN transfers RTP (Real-time Transport Protocol) packets between UEs if necessary. Besides, RN helps UEs which involves NAT traversal problem. The UEs use ICE to traverse NAT and firewall. The relay node's address is one of the candidate addresses in ICE process. ICE details will be described below.

The service quality assurance mechanisms should meet the following principles:

- The system should backup the relay call link before the call initializing. Otherwise the delay of the whole relay node switching cannot be ignored.

- The relay detecting algorithm should be divided into two different parts. As mentioned above, the relay node which is selected before may not be the best option. So the relay detecting algorithm must be distinguished before and after first relay call.
- The RN-S plays an important role in relay call. Its stability will have influence on the ICE and the relay call procedures. So we should consider the RN-S reliability.

3.2 System Architecture Overview

According to the above principle, we adopt redundant communication mechanisms in RN-S management of UEs. The whole architecture of relay overlay is shown in Figure 2.

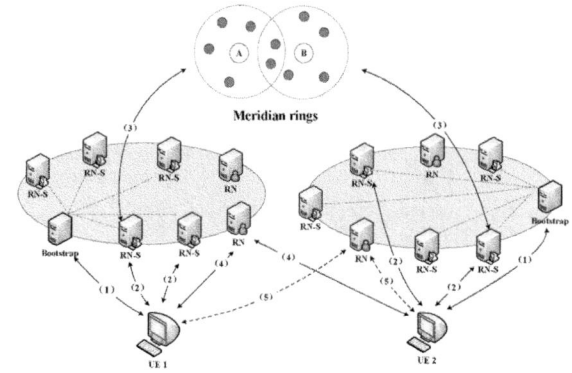

Fig. 2. Relay call procedure

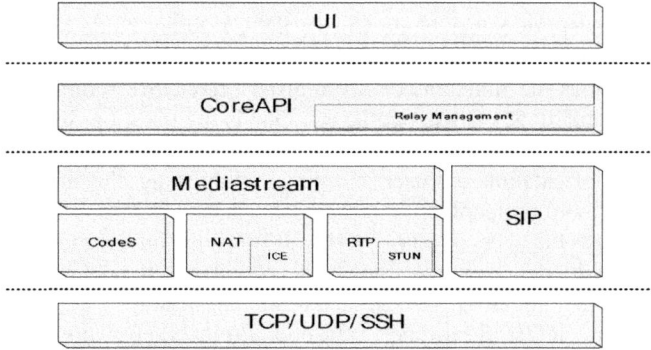

Fig. 3. Cutephone application modules

In Cutephone, the above relay call process and service quality assurance mechanism are replaced by relay overlay structure. The software is four-layer structure, as shown in Figure 3. The top layer is UI (User Interface) module, which analyzes UE's operation command and calls the functions provided by lower layer.

The Core API module provides the relay management function which can decide the call modes. There are two kinds of call modes, direct and relay call, respectively. The Media stream module uses codes module to encode and decode the audio/video data. The NAT module uses ICE to traverse NAT and firewall. The RTP and STUN module defines a standardized packet format for delivering audio and video over IP networks and traverse them. The SIP module handles SIP request and response.

3.3 RN-S Register

As shown in Figure 4, the process that UEs register in the relay overlay network is the same as that UEs register in the P2P network according to a bootstrap node.

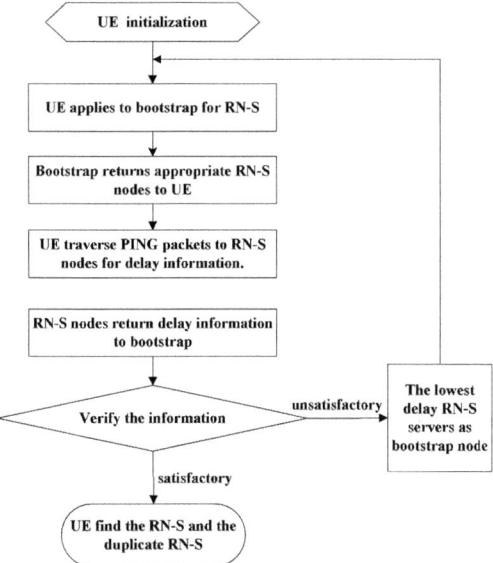

Fig. 4. RN-S registration

Specific registration process is as follows:

1) When a UE starts up, it will register in relay overlay with the bootstrap node in the list of bootstrap it maintains.
2) UE sends requests to bootstrap node for its RN-S nodes. Then the bootstrap node returns appropriate RN-S nodes according to UE's geographic information.
3) UE tests the delay between itself and the RN-S nodes returned by bootstrap node. Then it will check if the delay values can meet its requirements.
4) If satisfied, the registration is finished and the lowest delay nodes will be UE's RN-S node. Otherwise, it will serve as bootstrap node and take step 1.

The actual UE registration in relay overlay involves more than one bootstrap node. The multi-bootstrap nodes will ensure UE's registration in the relay overlay successfully.

3.4   Redundancy Detecting

The process that UEs request its RN-S nodes through relay overlay network is not different from ordinary detecting algorithm if the RN-S response acknowledgement message is available. However, it may be failed because of the unreliable characteristic of the overlay network. In these cases, UE will send request to its duplicate RN-S, and then wait for the returned relay node, as shown in Figure 5. The timer in our mechanism asks the UEs to see if the relay node server is failed or departed.

After sending request message to the RN-S and waiting for the response, the UEs must finish the process of relay detecting. If the UEs work behind the symmetric NAT, the relay call mode is necessary. Moreover, the relay node is important for candidate address collection and connectivity checks in ICE technology.

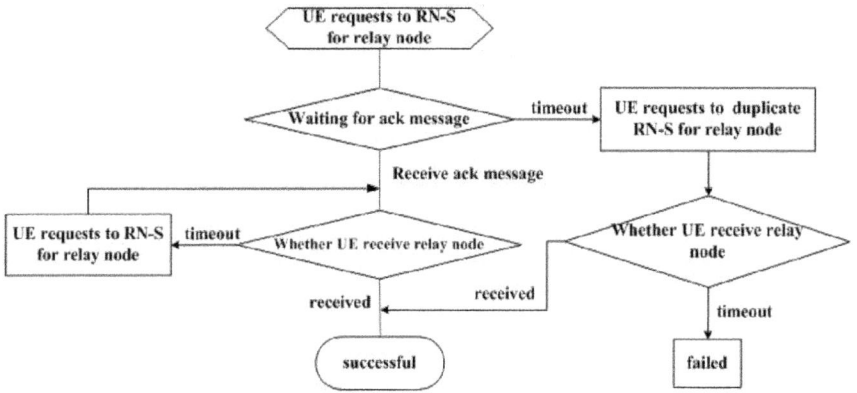

Fig. 5. Redundancy detecting

3.5   NAT Traversal

The problem of NAT traversal can be resolved by ICE technology. The IETF (Internet Engineering Task Force) has devised a suite of protocols, namely STUN (Session Traversal Using NAT) [9], TURN (Traversal Using Relay NAT) [10], and ICE [11], to address the limitations of the currently available NAT traversal solutions. Making a call starts by sending a SIP INVITE message with an SDP describing on which IP address and port the application can receive audio and/or video packets. These addresses and ports are known as candidates. Candidates are obtained from any firewall engine and are inserted into the SDP of a SIP INVITE message, which is sent to the callee.

There are 3 types of candidates: local candidate, a local IP address of the client; reflexive or STUN candidates, an IP address of the client's NAT (assuming they are only behind a single NAT); and relay candidate, an address on a relay node that has been allocated by the client.

After gathering the candidates, the caller encodes them in the SIP INVITE message, and sends the message to the callee according to signaling overlay. In response to the SIP INVITE, the callee sends its ICE candidates within the SDP of a SIP provisional response, such as a SIP 183 (Session Progress), to the caller. Once the callee has sent its ICE candidates and the caller receives them, they will start performing ICE connectivity checks. At this time, both parties know about their peer's potential transport candidates. Each possible pair of local and remote candidates is formed. A connectivity check is done by sending STUN messages from the local candidate to the remote candidate for each pair, starting with the highest priority candidate pair first. Both parties exchange STUN messages in this way to determine the best possible candidate pair based on that they can communicate. Once a successful message has been sent both ways on a single candidate pair, the connectivity check may stop and media can be sent/received using that candidate pair.

3.6 Dynamic Relay Algorithm

The dynamic relay algorithm is based on the ICE protocol (draft-ietf-mmusic-ice-19) and the relay detecting algorithm. It provides a self-testing and failure restoration mechanism. Due to the breakdown or departure of relay node, the relay call service is unreliable. For that reason, the UEs must dynamically switch relay links. In SIP messages, the re-INVITE can modify the dialog and the parameters of the sessions at the same time. Consequently, we use the re-INVITE message and send it to the callee for new relay link establishment.

The other important procedure is the inquiry for a relay node. As we have said, the relay detecting algorithm can be divided into two parts. Before the call is initialized, we use ICE technology to determine the call link. When UEs are likely to switch the relay links, the process of choosing relay nodes is as follows:

Step 1. UE A requests the relay node corresponding to RN-S A and RN-S B;
Step 2. for each relay Ai **in** Meridian rings of RN-S A;
       For each relay Bi **in** Meridian rings of RN-S A;
         if ($Ai == Bi$) **do** return relay Ai;
         Else do Bi+1;
       Endif;
       Ai+1;
Step 3. RN-S A returns the relay node Ai to UE A, UE A makes it as relay node. Then UE A makes a call start by sending a SIP re-INVITE message with a SDP describing on relay node's IP address and port the application can receive audio and/or video packets.

Algorithm 1.   Relay node detecting algorithm before switching

---

The specific process of dynamic relay algorithm is shown in Figure 6 and the detailed message flow is as follows:

1) SIP-client-A (UE 1) finds the poor quality of audio or video service, according to the parameter such as packet loss ratio and delay.
2) UE 1 requests a new relay node to its relay server (RN-S 1) with the information of UE 2's relay server RN-S 2. According algorithm 1, the RN-S 1 and RN-S 2 work together and return the appropriate new relay node to UE 1.
3) UE 1 makes a new call by sending re-INVITE message with a SDP message on new relay node's address and port the application can receive audio and/or video packets.
4) UE 1 transmits STUN packets to new relay node's address and port. On the other hand, UE 2 transmits the RTP packets to the address.

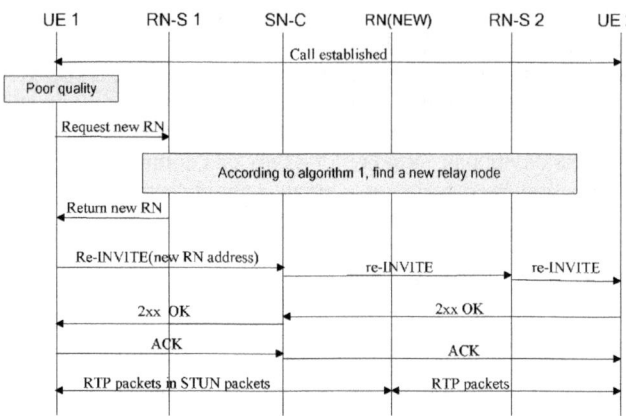

Fig. 6. AAA structure of P2PSIP

Considering the condition that all of the SIP clients are our applications, there may be a problem if they send the re-INVITE message at the same time. UEs must return a 491 error message for the re-INVITE message. The clients who receive a 491 error message will check if it is a caller. Then the caller startup a timer at the average from 2.1 to 4 second, and the callee's timer is from 0 to 2 second.

4   Performance Evaluations

4.1   Evaluation Environment

We test our service quality assurance mechanism in the NS-2 (Network Simulation Version 2), which is running on a node of the high performance computing cluster in our lab. The node has two dual-processor Intel Xeon CPU and 8GB memory. We adopt the network model of random connecting of Transit AS with Stub AS, which is similar to the real network. With different sets of delay between, we run the system in different network scales to evaluate the performance.

By checking the results of the simulation, we will estimate the re-hit ratio of the relay nodes, the dialog completion ratio, and the latency in our system, which is to test the stability of the relay mechanism.

4.2   Re-Hit Ratio

The re-hit ratio is an important indicator of efficiency in our algorithm. The re-hit ratio indicates the probability that system switches relay nodes dynamically. According the algorithm described in section 3, the relay node is crucial to service quality assurance mechanism. Higher re-hit ratio brings better reliability of relay sub-system.

From section 3, we can see that a higher percentage of RNs in our relay overlay does not imply that more relay calls are requested. We set the number of RN from 400-2400.The results of re-hit ratio equals to the successful switching relay link ratio are shown in Figure 7.

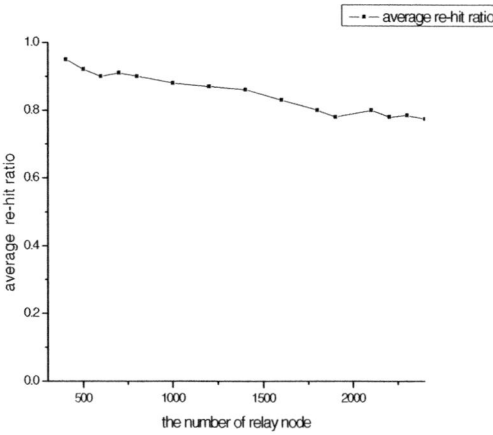

Fig. 7. Re-hit Ratio

As shown in Figure 7, the average re-hit ratio of the system decreases along with the number of RN. The average re-hit ratio refers to the finding rate of fresh relay nodes when UEs switch the relay links under a certain node scale. The algorithm ensures a high re-hit rate in the low node scale. The average re-hit rate is about 90%. But with the expansion of the RN nodes, the re-hit ratio of the algorithm also decreases, because with the increasing of RN nodes number, the coverage TTL of searching packets will be reduced. But exceeding a certain number of the RN nodes, the hit rate stabilizes at a certain range, which is more than 75%, and proves the stability of the dynamic search algorithm.

4.3 Dialog Completion Ratio

The dialog completion ratio is another important indicator of efficiency in system. Dialog completion ratio is defined as the number of successfully completed dialogs in a certain period of time to total dialogs. This value can be used to indicate the quality of VoIP service.

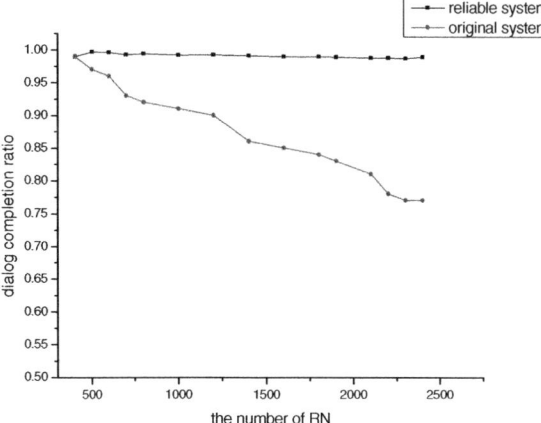

Fig. 8. Dialog completion ratio

In order to illustrate the unreliability of original VoIP system and the effectiveness of our algorithm, we run simulations for both the original VoIP system and our reliable system, which contains the ICE user software. In our simulation, we uniformly set the disabled nodes among the network and the node disabling time according to the overall simulation time, and we run the overall 1000 sessions with relay call. The results are shown in Figure 8.

The average re-hit ratio of the system decreases with the increasing of the number RN. In spite of the relay node could fail in our system, the algorithm maintains around 98% dialogs correctly to provide the reliable SIP service. On the other hand, the dialog completion ratio in the original VoIP system decreases along with the number of RN. The main reason of the low ratio may be the performance of the relay detecting algorithm, which also degrades along with the RN node scale. In our system, if the first relay node fails, the UEs will dynamically switch another relay node.

Figure 9 shows the dialog completion ratio changing with the node failure ratio. In the simulation we change the node failure ratio and keep the number of relay nodes about 500. Then we can find the difference between our system and original VoIP system. As shown in Figure 9, the dialog completion ratio decreases with the growth of the relay node failure ratio. The original VoIP system fails even faster, under 30% when the failure ratio is 50%, while our system is 70% at the same condition.

4.4   Latency of Switching Relay Nodes

The latency of switching relay nodes refers to the average delay of changing a relay node between two UEs under certain situation. We will test the latency from the time when the UE detects the poor quality to the time when one relay node has been decided. The feasibility of the strategy also should be still useful with the expansion of the nodes scale. If the delay value is too big or only be limited within a small node scale, this system can not be used. In our simulation, as the shown in Figure 10, when the system switches relay node, the latency remains about 250ms. The delay is not satisfied, and the user can feel conversation interrupts, which comes mainly from the delay of ICE process and relay detecting.

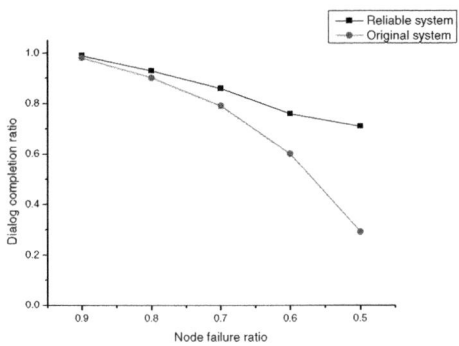

Fig. 9. Dialog completion ratio with node failure ratio

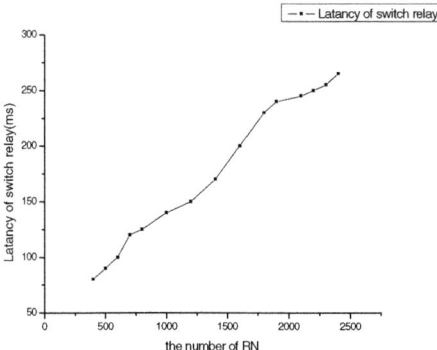

Fig. 10. Latency of switch relay

5 Conclusions

In this paper, we propose a service quality assurance mechanism, which maintains the VoIP servers quality in a relay overlay effectively. Simulation results indicate that the system architecture is feasible and scalable.

The whole design includes relay detecting algorithm and dynamic relay algorithm. When the VoIP system builds a call with a relay node, it can dynamically switch the relay node with another one which can provide better service. The callee automatically detects the voice quality and sends re-INVITE request for poor voice quality. Our work provides an initial study on the reliable structure of P2P-SIP VoIP system.

Acknowledgments. This work is supported by Program for New Century Excellent Talents in University under grant NCET-08-0218, China National Natural Science Foundation (NSFC) under grant 60973133, FOK YING TUNG Education Foundation under grant No.122007, the National Science and Technology Major Project of the Ministry of Science and Technology of China under grant No.2010ZX-03004-001-03 and the Fundamental Research Funds for the Central Universities under grant No.No.2010QN013.

References

1. Wong, B., Slivkins, A., Sirer, E.G.: Meridian: A Lightweight Framework for Network Positioning without Virtual Coordinates. In: The Annual ACM Conference of the Special Interest Group on Data Communication (SIGCOMM 2005), Philadelphia, PA (2005)
2. Singh, K., Schulzrinne, H.: Peer-to-Peer Internet telephony using SIP. In: the 15th International Workshop on Network and Operating Systems Support for Digital Audio and Video (NOSSDAV 2005), pp. 63–68 (2005)
3. Baset, S.A.: An Analysis of the Skype Peer-to-Peer Internet Telephony Protocol. In: INFOCOM 2006, Barcelona, Spain (2006)
4. Jennings, C., Lowekamp, B., Rescorla, E., Baset, S., Schulzrinne, H.: REsource LOcation And Discovery (RELOAD). IETF draft draft-ietf-p2psip-reload-04 (2008)

5. Baset, S., Gupta, G., Schulzrinne, H.: OpenVoIP: An Open Peer-to-Peer VoIP and IM System. In: ACM SIGCOMM 2008 (demo), pp. 517–517 (2008)
6. Hardie, T.: Pointers for Peer-to-Peer overlay networks, nodes, or resources. IETF Draft draft-hardie-p2psip-p2p-pointers-00 (2008)
7. Jiang, X.F., Zheng, H.W.: Service extensible P2P protocol. IEFT Draft draft-jiang-p2psip-sep-01 (2008)
8. Song, H., Zheng, H., Jiang, X.: Diagnose P2PSIP overlay network failures. IETF Draft draft-zheng-p2psip-diagnose-02 (2008)
9. Rosenberg, J., Mahy, R.: Session Traversal Utilities for NAT. IETF STUN draft behave-rfc3489bis-10 (2008)
10. Behave, W.G., Rosenberg, J.: Obtaining Relay Addresses from Simple Traversal Underneath NAT. IETF TURN draft behave-turn-04 (2008)
11. Rosenberg, J.: Interactive Connectivity Establishment (ICE): A Protocol for Network. IETF ICE draft mmusic-ice-18 (2007)
12. Address Translator (NAT) Traversal for Offer/Answer Protocols
13. Guha, S., Daswani, N.: An Experimental Study of the Skype Peer-to-Peer VoIP System. In: IPTPS 2006 (2006)
14. Xie, H., Reng, Y.: A Measurement based Study of the Skype Peer to Peer VoIP Performance. In: IPTPS 2007, Bellevue, WA (2007)
15. Fei, T., Tao, S., Guerin, R.: How to select a good alternate path in large peer-to-peer system. In: IEEE INFOCOM 2006 (2006)
16. Shansi, R., Lei, G., Zhang, X.: ASAP: an AS-Aware Peer-Relay Protocol for High Quality VoIP. In: The 26th IEEE International Conference On Distributed Computing System (2006)
17. Shu, T., Kuai, X., Antonio, E.: Improving VoIP quality through path switching. In: IEEE INFOCOM 2005 (2005)

VSCM: A Virtual Server Consolidation Manager for Cluster

Yang Liu, Yunchu Liu, and Hanli Bai

Computational Aerodynamics Institute
China Aerodynamics Research & Development Center,
621000 Mianyang, China
cai@cardc.cn

Abstract. Virtual server consolidation is to use virtual machines to encapsulate applications which are running on multiple physical servers in the cluster and then integrate them into a small number of servers. Nowadays, with the expanding of enterprise-class data centers, virtual server consolidation can reduce large number of servers to help the enterprises reduce hardware and operating costs significantly and improve server utilization greatly. In this paper, we propose the VSCM manager for virtual cluster, which solves the problems in the consolidation from a globally optimal view and also takes migration overhead into account. Experiment results in virtual cluster demonstrate that, VSCM can greatly reduce the number of servers and the migration overhead.

Keywords: Virtual Server Consolidation, Virtual Cluster, Virtual Machine Bin Packing, Virtual Machine Migration.

1   Introduction

With the development of information technology, to meet the growing business, many companies start to build their own data centers. In the twenty-first century, enterprise-class data centers have been expanding, in which the growth rate of the number of servers is very impressive. However, the high costs of hardware and operation and the low utilization of these servers become very important problems. Virtual Server Consolidation (VSC), which can greatly reduce the number of servers, becomes a widespread-used technology for enterprise-class data centers to reduce hardware and operating costs and improve the server utilization. To use virtual machines (VM) to encapsulate applications which are running on multiple physical servers (PS) in the cluster and then integrate them into a small number of servers, VSC can reduce the number of servers greatly and improve their utilization significantly.

Several approaches [1-2] to VSC have been proposed. However, these approaches use heuristics from a locally optimal perspective according to some strategies, in which resource demands of VMs and resource residuals of PSs could not be considered from a globally optimal perspective. As a result, missing many chances to reduce the number of servers, these approaches could hardly achieve the minimum number of servers. Furthermore, they focus on how to make a new placement in

E. Altman and W. Shi (Eds.): NPC 2011, LNCS 6985, pp. 99–110, 2011.

which a VM is able to migrate to another PS, ignoring the migration overhead. Making use of constraint programming (CP) [3], Hermenier et al. [4] have solved above problems. But, they make this accomplishment in a homogeneous cluster environment, and one PS is allowed to run only one VM at a time which is much different from the real cluster of data center. In the real environment, using CP will produce significant time overhead that data center can not afford.

In this paper, we propose a new approach to VSC in virtual cluster that consider both the problem of allocating the VMs to available PSs and the problem of how to migrate the VMs to these servers. Our consolidation manager Virtual Server Consolidation Manager (VSCM) works in two phases. In the first phase, according to the measurements of CPU and memory usages of VMs and servers, VSCM uses Globally Optimal Virtual Machine Bin Packing (GOVMBP) algorithm to calculate a VM placement from the point of globally optimal view, with the objective of reducing the number of servers as much as possible. And in the second phase, based on the feedback mechanism, VSCM uses Feedback based Virtual Machine Migration (FVMM) algorithm to improve the placement and remove the constraints on migration. In our experiment, we simulate such a cluster environment in which there are 64 PSs and 100 VMs that are randomly generated. Compared to consolidation based on previously-used First Fit Decreasing (FFD), GOVMBP saves 10.22% of PSs in average. And FVMM gains a saving of 67.6% of migration step and 34.7% of migration overhead. Promising experiment results show that VSCM not only greatly reduces the number of servers but also significantly reduces the migration overhead.

The rest of the paper is organized as follows. We state the problems in the two phases of VSCM in Section 2. In Section 3, we describe our Virtual Server Consolidation Manager in details. Results from our experimental evaluation are reported in Section 4. We compare our work with related research efforts in Section 5 and conclude in Section 6.

2   Problem Statements

As mentioned above, VSCM works in two phases. The first phase calculates the minimum number n of servers that are necessary to hold all the VMs. We refer to this problem as the Virtual Machine Bin Packing Problem (VMBPP). The second phase reduces the migration overhead as much as possible, giving the number n. We refer to this problem as the Virtual Machine Migration Problem (VMMP).

2.1   The Virtual Machine Bin Packing Problem

The goal of the VMBPP is to calculate the minimum number n of servers that are necessary to hold all the VMs, according to the measurements of CPU and memory usages of VMs and servers. Consider the servers as bins, their resource capacity as bins' volume, VMs as items, and VMs' resource demands as items' volume, this problem can be expressed as Bin Packing problem [5], a classic NP-hard problem.

A VM cannot be allocated to a PS until the server has enough resource, for example, CPU, memory and etc. Taking into account that we do not study the quantity of VM allocated to one CPU core, for simple, we prescribe that one Virtual CPU (VCPU) of VM occupy one CPU core. Considering these two factors, CPU and memory, VMBPP can be reduced to 2-D Bin Packing problem [6].

Used by previous approaches [1, 7-8] as the solution to VMBPP, FFD works as follows: firstly, based on latest resource measurements of VMs and PSs, ranks the VMs in the decreasing order of resource demands; then, for each VM, if the residual resource of PS is enough for the VM, the VM will stay, if not, migrate this VM to the first PS which can hold it; if there's no active PS that can be migrated to, activate a new PS to hold the VM. The description of FFD discloses a strict restriction: VM can not migrate to a PS that has not enough residual resource. Although ensuring the feasibility of the VM migration, this restriction makes FFD a locally optimal solution which misses many opportunities to reduce the number n.

Therefore, FFD can not be competent for VMBPP, and only a solution standing from a globally optimal view is able to dig out the relationship between the demands of VMs and residuals of PSs, to make a plan that needs less number of servers.

2.2   The Virtual Machine Migration Problem

Given the minimum number n, the objective of VMMP is to make a placement to reduce the migration overhead as much as possible, and guarantee the feasibility of VM migration at the same time. Therefore, this problem is divided into two parts.

Which PS a single VM should migrate to is the first part of VMMP. Previous approaches [1-2] pay too much attention to whether a VM could migrate to some PS or not, ignoring the overhead that the migration itself brings. It may not be possible to migrate a VM to the destination PS immediately in the real environment, so the migration overhead plays an important role in the process of migration.

In the second part, migration constraints are taken into account. Hermenier [4] points out that the placement made by the preceding part may force a VM to migrate to some unqualified PS. In fact, the PS has the capacity to hold that VM at the end, but it may have not enough resources in the middle of the placement. There are two types of constraints on migration: sequential constraint and cyclic constraint.

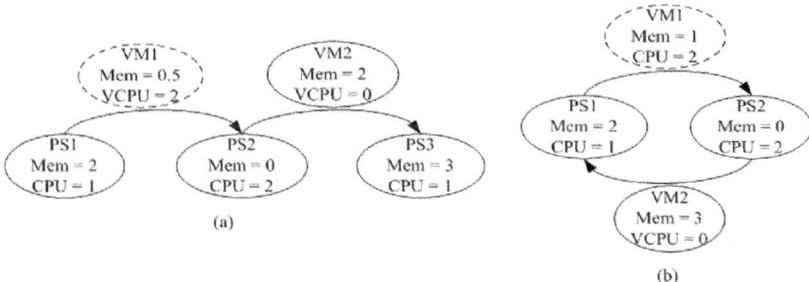

Fig. 1. Examples of migration constraints. The *Mem* and *CPU* in *PS* represent the residual resource capacity of the PS, and the *Mem* and *VCPU* in *VM* represent the resource demands of the VM. The dashed circle denotes that *VM1* is going to be activated. The *0* of *VCPU* denotes *VM2* is not active.

A sequential constraint takes place when one migration can not start until another migration has finished. Fig. 1(a) shows an example. Once VM1 is activated, it finds deficiency in CPU residual in PS1, so it has to migrate to PS2. However, the residual memory in PS2 can not meet the need of VM1, so a migration of VM2 from PS2 to PS3 should be executed at first. These two migrations can not occur in parallel, that is, the migration of VM1 has to wait till VM2's has completed.

A cyclic constraint occurs when multiple migrations form a cycle. Fig. 1(b) shows an example. Once VM1 is activated, it finds deficiency in CPU residual in PS1, so it has to migrate to PS2. However, the residual memory in PS2 can not meet the need of VM1, so a migration of VM2 from PS2 to PS1 is needed at first. Unfortunately, PS1 has not enough memory for VM2, which requires that the migration of VM1 should be done in the first place. These two migrations can not happen because the two VMs both lock the resources that the other need.

These two types of constraints have severe influence in the establishment of the placement. The migration can not be executed unless these constraints are removed, and the feasibility of migration is greatly threatened. Most of previous approaches [1-2, 7] may not encounter the migration constraints, because they guarantee the feasibility in each step of migration. However, as mentioned above, the locally optimal solution they adopt can not achieve a global optimization. When a migration is not feasible, Wood07 [8] identifies a set of VMs to swap to free resources on the destination server. However, this method temporarily needs some space for hosting VMs and the placement issue it is able to solve can not be complex. Girt [9] take an offline strategy in which they suspend the VMs that need migrate till the destination PS is qualified. Yet, this does not work for live migration.

3   Design and Implementation of VSCM

A typical virtual cluster consists of one management server without virtual environment and multiple computing servers (PSs as mentioned above) with Xen [10] virtual environment in which the VMs are placed. System architecture of VSCM is showed in Fig. 2. VSCM is made up of one *Control Center* in the *Management Server*

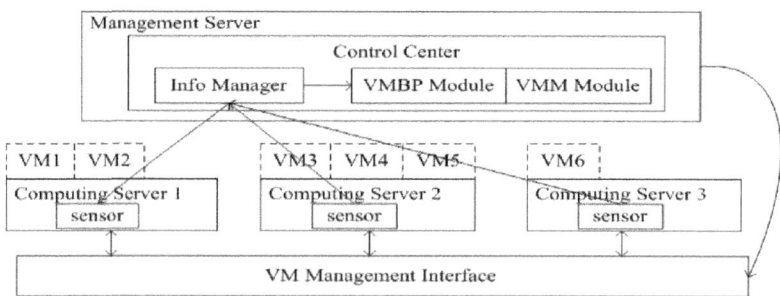

Fig. 2. VSCM system architecture. Modules of *VMBP* and *VMM* constitute the core of VSCM and the *sensor* and *Info Manager* are used to collect and arrange the info from VMs and PSs.

and one *sensor* in each *Computing Server*. These sensors and the *Info Manager* in the *Control Center* are components of Prospector [11], a Xen virtual cluster monitor, which is used to iteratively collect the measurements of resources in PSs and VMs and detect the change of their state. After arranged by *Info Manager*, the information that is collected by sensors is sent to the core of VSCM, *VMBP* and *VMM*, two modules in the *Control Center*. *VMBP Module* uses GOVMBP algorithm to solve VMBPP and then *VMM Module* uses FVMM algorithm to solve VMMP. Once the core finds the current placement not viable, or new placement needs fewer servers, VSCM will call the *VM Management Interface* to execute the consolidation corresponding to the new plan.

3.1 The Globally Optimal Virtual Machine Bin Packing Algorithm

To dig out the possible opportunities to reduce the minimum number n, VMBP module uses a globally optimal algorithm, the GOVMBP, to solve the VMBPP. Making a new placement according to the current one is the limitation of FFD, so the essence of GOVMBP is to initialize the placement no matter what the current one is. That is, at the beginning of determining the placement, GOVMBP ignores the current placement, and hypothesizes that each PS is in its initial state, without any VM. Therefore, when considering the placement, GOVMBP faces a brand new cluster instead of complicated placement, which helps to completely take demands of all VMs and residuals of all PSs into account from a globally optimal view before making the decision.

GOVMBP firstly takes current placement and measurements of VMs and PSs as input, and save the current placement as *begin_cluster*. The next step, the kernel of this algorithm, is to initialize the placement to the situation in which there are no VMs on any PS. The following part is based on FFD. Firstly, on the basis of latest resource measurements of VMs and PSs, ranks the VMs in the decreasing order of resource demand; then, for each VM, if the residual of PS is enough for the VM, the VM will stay, if not, migrate this VM to the first PS which can hold it; if there's no active PS that can be migrated to, activate a new PS to hold the VM. Finally, we get the new placement *mid_cluster* as the output.

As initializing the placement, GOVMBP is no longer limited to the current placement, and finds more possibilities to reduce the number n, the number of active servers in new placement. However, this algorithm introduces migration constraints that are mentioned in Section 2.2 and we are going to solve them in Section 3.2.2.

There's another point to emphasize that, *mid_cluster* is just a plan which is not executed immediately, and the real placement in the cluster does not change.

3.2 Feedback Based Virtual Machine Migration Algorithm

Given the minimum number n, VMM module adopts FVMM algorithm to solve the VMMP. Taking current placement as feedback, FVMM improves the new placement made by GOVMBP to reduce the migration overhead, and then removes the migration constraints introduced by GOVMBP to guarantee the feasibility of the migration.

The Feedback Mechanism. Previous approaches [1-2, 7] focus on the right PS that the VM should be moved to, ignoring the migration overhead. Therefore, to reduce the migration overhead as much as possible, the feedback mechanism (FM) tries its best to avoid the migration. So, the essence of this mechanism is that, if a migration is avoidable, avoid it. After comparing the new placement with the current one, FM tries to restore the placement. That is, for each migration in the new placement, if canceling this move still guarantees that the PS has the capacity to hold the VMs and the number n is not increased, this migration will be dropped. The final objective of FM is to make every VM stay on the PS where it is placed now.

The FM works as follows. A VM that needs to move (MVM) is the one whose host server in the new placement *new_host* is not the same one in the current placement *old_host*. For each MVM v, the FM will make a judgment whether v could stay on the *old_host* or not by the analysis of the resource measurements of all the VMs and PSs in the new placement. If the following situations happen, v is allowed to stay, and the migration for v in the new placement is cancelled.

(1) The *old_host* has enough resource residual to hold v

(2) The *old_host* could move some MVMs that are hosted on it to other PSs to free the resources to hold v.

(3) Some MVM that are hosted on *old_host* could exchange the position with v, without exceeding the resources limits on both servers.

If, unfortunately, above situations do not happen, v has to move from *old_host* to *new_host*. The FM will produce a new placement *end_cluster* in which more VMs are hosted on its *old_host* than *mid_cluster*. This leads to fewer migrations and the overhead will be reduced greatly.

The *end_cluster* is the final placement which will be the real placement after this process of consolidation is done. The migrations in *end_cluster* can not be avoided and they are put on a list *move_list*. Like *mid_cluster*, *end_cluster* is not executed immediately and the real placement at this moment in the cluster does not change.

Methods to Remove Migration Constraints. As GOVMBP introduces migration constraints and the FM aggravates this situation, the feasibility of migration in the latest placement can not be guaranteed. As mentioned above in Section 2.2, there are two types of constraints on migration.

For sequential constraints, the solution lies in the description of this problem. One move M_1 can not be executed until another one M_2 has finished. As a result, finishing M_2 and M_1 in order will remove this constraint. So, for all migrations in *move_list*, search the feasible ones and remove them from the list. These migrations are executed earlier and free the resources for the ones still on the list. Repeat this process till there are no feasible migrations, and those left on the list are limited by cyclic constraints. The feasible migrations found in the same iteration can be done in parallel because there are no longer constraints between them.

For cyclic constraints, we give the following definition.

A VM vm_i needs to move from server s_i to server s_j while another VM vm_j needs to move from s_j to s_i. If the resource limits both moves, we define this situation as a (s_i, s_j, s_i) cycle. By extension, if vm_j needs to move from s_j to s_k while VM vm_k needs to move from s_k to s_i, this forms a (s_i, s_j, s_k, s_i) cycle.

According to above definition, a cyclic constraint is hard to find, and we need find a way to recognize the cycle by using Graph Theory. Given k PSs, we construct a digraph $G = (V, E)$. Vertex v_i denotes server s_i, and vertex set $V = (v_0, v_1, ..., v_{k-1})$ is the set of all vertexes. A directed edge $e_{i,j} = <v_i, v_j>$ from v_i to v_j denotes that there is a

VM that needs to move from v_i to v_j and edge set $E = (e_{0,1}, e_{1,2}, ..., e_{k-1,k-2})$ is the set of all directed edges. If there is directed edge $e_{i,j} = <v_i, v_j>$, we define v_j as the neighbour of v_i. We also call $v_i e_{i,i+1} v_{i+1} e_{i+1,i+2} v_{i+2}...e_{k-1,k} v_k$ a directed path that connect v_i to v_k. If there is a directed path $v_i e_{i,i+1} v_{i+1} e_{i+1,i+2} v_{i+2}...e_{k-1,k} v_k$ from v_i to v_k, we say v_k is accessible from v_i. So, the cycle (s_i, s_j, s_i) denotes the directed path that goes from v_i to v_j by the directed edge $e_{i,j}$ and then back to v_i by $e_{j,i}$, that is, v_i is accessible from v_i itself. We define this path from v_i back to v_i as a directed cycle (DC) $v_i e_{i,j} v_j e_{j,i} v_i$. Therefore, to recognize a cycle is to recognize the corresponding DC in the graph G. For example, there are two DCs in Fig. 3 which are $v_1 e_{1,2} v_2 e_{2,5} v_5 e_{5,6} v_6 e_{6,1} v_1$ and $v_3 e_{3,4} v_4 e_{4,3} v_3$ respectively.

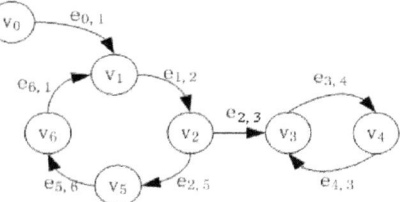

Fig. 3. An example of directed graph G in which there are two DCs, $v_1 e_{1,2} v_2 e_{2,5} v_5 e_{5,6} v_6 e_{6,1} v_1$ and $v_3 e_{3,4} v_4 e_{4,3} v_3$

This paper introduces a method to recognize the DC in graph G on the basis of Depth First Search (DFS) algorithm. The essence of this method is that if v_i is in a DC $v_i e_{i,j} v_j e_{j,k} v_k...e_{m,i} v_i$, v_i is accessible from v_i itself. So, in the graph G' which is built by cutting the edge $e_{i,j}$, there is certainly a path from v_j to v_i, that is, v_i is accessible from v_j. Furthermore, in the graph G'' built from G' by cutting the edge $e_{j,k}$, v_i is accessible from v_k. Taking advantage of DFS, we can test a vertex v whether it is accessible from itself. If accessible, v is in a DC that includes v.

Pseudo-code of the method to test whether vertex *end* is accessible from vertex *begin* on the basis of DFS.

```
1   def test_access(begin, end):
2     for v in begin.neighbours:
3       if v.des == end:
4         add begin into cycle
5         return True
6       if v.des not visited:
7         test_access(v.des, end)
```

The above pseudo-code tests whether vertex *end* is accessible from vertex *begin* on the basis of DFS. For each vertex v in the neighbors of *begin*, if its destination node *v.des* happens to be *end*, *end* is accessible from *begin*. If not, test whether *end* is accessible from *v.des* on the premise that *v.des* has not been visited before.

Take Fig. 3 as an example. Starting with v_0, the search sequence is $v_0 -> v_1 -> v_2 -> v_3 -> v_4$, and then we find a unique path from v_4 to v_3, so we step back to v_2. However, we will soon find that, after $v_2 -> v_5 -> v_6$, v_6 can only reach v_1. That is, v_0 is not accessible from itself. If we start with v_1, we will recognize a DC

$v_1e_{1,2}v_2e_{2,5}v_5e_{5,6}v_6e_{6,1}v_1$. Similarly, another DC $v_3e_{3,4}v_4e_{4,3}v_3$ is found if we take v_3 as the beginning vertex.

The next step is to untie this cycle, that is, to remove this cyclic restraint. Comparing with the method to recognize the cycle, the one to untie it is much simpler. Search all servers and find one to be a springboard. That is, for each MVM vm in this cycle, if some server s can be found enough resource residual to hold vm, we firstly move vm to s and then move it from s to its original destination. This server s is used as a springboard to hold vm temporarily.

During the process to remove the migration constraints, VSCM generates feasible migration commands for consolidation and calls the VM management interface to execute them. After the consolidation is done, the real placement in the cluster is finally changed to *end_cluster*.

4   Evaluation

This section presents results from a number of experiments we conducted to evaluate our algorithms.

4.1   Design of Migration Overhead

As one of the simplest overhead, migration step is the number of the migrations that the consolidation needs to change the current placement to the new one, directly evaluating various migration algorithms. However, resource usages on servers play a great role in moving one VM from source server to destination server. The higher the CPU or memory usage is, the longer the process of migration takes, for example. And the most important factor is the memory requirement of VM which determine the time of the process.

Therefore, we design the migration overhead as follows.

The total overhead of placement $O(p)$ is the sum of each migration overhead $O(v)$ made by VM v moving from source server s_{src} to destination server s_{des} in this migration. (Equation 1)

$$O(p) = \sum_{v \in p} O(v) \; \cdot \tag{1}$$

As involving the source server and destination server, $O(v)$ is made up of the overhead to source $f(s_{src}, v)$ and the overhead to destination $f(s_{des}, v)$. (Equation 2)

$$O(v) = f(s_{src}, v) + f(s_{des}, v) \; . \tag{2}$$

In consideration of the only focus on CPU and memory in Section 2.1, the overhead $f(s, v)$ made by VM v to server s is determined by following factors: CPU usage of the server $s.cpu\_util$, memory usage of the server $s.mem\_util$ and the memory requirement of the VM $v.mem$. Since $v.mem$ dominates the time of migration process, we construct Equation 3 as follows.

$$f(s, v) = (s.cpu\_util + s.mem\_util) * v.mem \; . \tag{3}$$

4.2 Experimental Setup

Limited by real environment, we have to evaluate our algorithms on simulation data, to illustrate the range of benefit that VSCM can provide. The virtual cluster we simulate consists of 64 PSs and 100 VMs that are generated randomly. Each PS has 4 CPU cores and 4 GB of memory. For each VM, we generate the VCPU demand randomly in the range of [0, 4] and the memory demand in the range of (0.0, 2.0] GB. For simple, the memory is going to be 0.5 or 1.0 or 1.5 or 2.0GB.

The computer configuration for this simulation is shown as follows: Intel(R) Core(TM)2 Duo CPU P8400@2.26GHz, 2x1G DDR3 memory and the operating system is CentOS 5.3. VSCM is implemented in this OS by Python 2.4.3.

4.3 Results and Analysis

GOVMBP vs FFD. To test whether GOVMBP uses fewer PSs, we compare it with FFD which is used by most of the previous approaches. The initial cluster is made up of 64 PSs without any VM and then we randomly generate 100 VMs. For the initial placement, both the algorithms adopt the same policies to allocate these VMs to the PSs, and the number of PSs in use is the same. Then we change the configuration of the 100 VMs to simulate the various situations in the real environment. Facing to the new placements in which there are already 100 VMs hosted on the PSs, GOVMBP and FFD will take different policies. As a result, the number of PSs used may not be the same, and neither do the new placements the algorithms produce.

Fig. 4 shows the comparison between GOVMBP and FFD in 20 experiments. The numbers on the right denotes the numbers of servers that GOVMBP saves. We divide them into four classes and find that, in most cases (45%), GOVMBP uses 6-10 fewer servers than FFD. Furthermore, in the vast majority of cases (95%), GOVMBP uses fewer servers than FFD. On the basis of statistics, we find that GOVMBP uses 5.9 fewer servers than FFD and saves 10.22% of servers in average, verifying the superiority of this globally optimal solution.

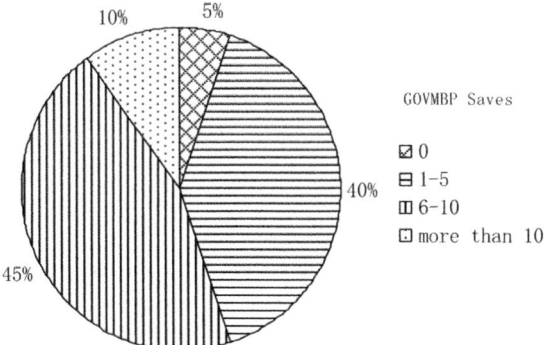

Fig. 4. Comparison between GOVMBP and FFD. The numbers on the right represents the numbers of servers that GOVMBP saves.

Effect of the Feedback Mechanism. The FM is the kernel of FVMM, so we conduct this experiment to evaluate the effect of the FM on the consolidation. In this comparison, one is the VSCM with FM and the other one is without FM. For the initial cluster where there are 64 PSs without any VM, we randomly generate 100 VMs. Without preceding placement to feed back, VSCM with FM adopt the same policy to allocate VMs to PSs as the one without FM does. Then we change the configuration of the 100 VMs to simulate the various situations in the real environment. With current placement as the feedback, the one with FM and the other one without FM will take different policies. As a result, the overhead which is produced by all the migrations will be different.

Fig. 5 shows the comparison migration overhead between VSCM with FM and the one without FM in 20 experiments. The left part compares migration step. In average, the one with FM needs 34.25 steps to finish the placement while the one without FM needs 106.25 steps which is 3.1 times the former. The right part compares the migration overhead designed by Section 4.1. The result also verifies the benefit of the FM that, the overhead produced by the one without FM is 1.5 times that produced by the one with FM. According to the statistics, the FM is able to save 67.6% of migration step and 34.7% of migration overhead designed by Section 4.1.

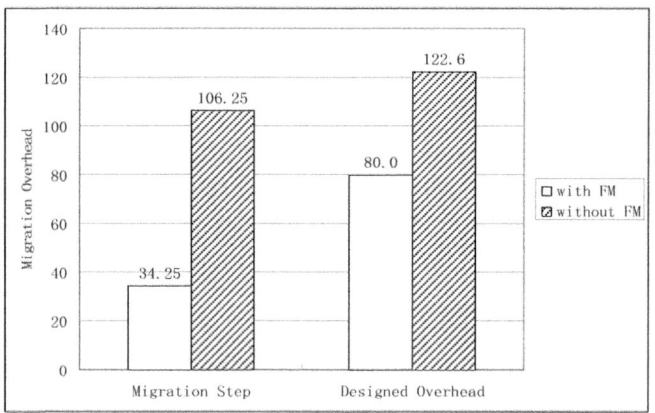

Fig. 5. Migration overhead comparison between VSCM with FM and the one without FM. The left part compares the average migration step and the right part compares the average migration overhead designed by Section 4.1.

5   Related Work

Most of previous approaches use heuristics from a locally optimal perspective to solve VMBPP, so they lose many opportunities to reduce the number of servers, and they often ignore the migration overhead which is very important for the real cluster.

Bobroff et al. [1] establishes the virtual server consolidation on a forecast mechanism. They predict the resource demands of VMs on the basis of history, rank the VMs in the decreasing order of the demands, and then use FFD to allocate VMs to PSs in arranged order. For each server, they take the sum of all the VMs' resource demands as the predicted resource overload. If this overload does not exceed the threshold of the server and the resource capacity is enough to handle the resource demand, they allocate the VM to the most suitable server. Strictly speaking, the placement algorithm they use is based on BFD.

Though Khanna et al. [12] use heuristics to solve VMBPP, it is gratifying that they pay more attention to the migration overhead while determining the placement. They rank VMs in non-decreasing order of the resource usages of VMs from which migration overhead is calculated. In other words, they rank the VMs in the order of the overhead. They choose the VM whose usage is the lowest on the unqualified PS, and move it to the qualified PS which has the least resource residuals. Wood07 et al. [8] also use a greedy algorithm to determine a sequence of moves to migrate overloaded VMs to underloaded servers, in which the migration overhead is considered in the form of defined volume. However, these approaches still base their placement algorithm on the locally optimal solution.

Some approaches mention the migration constraints in their work. Girt et al. [9] try to solve the VMMP with the help of Shirako [13], a system for on-demand leasing of shared networked resources in federated clusters. When a migration can not proceed because of the migration constraint, the VM will be suspended till the destination server is available. This simple method is not qualified in the real-time environment where needs live migration. Wood07 et al. [8] identify a set of VMs to swap to free resources on the destination server. This approach is only able to solve simple placement issue and needs some space for hosting VMs temporarily.

Unlike the above approaches, Hermenier et al. [4] develop the Entropy by Choco [14] to perform consolidation based on constraint programming. From the globally optimal point of view, Entropy solves VMBPP and VMMP pretty well. Comparing to FFD, Entropy greatly reduces the number of servers and the migration overhead. However, Entropy aims at homogenous cluster and one PS is allowed to run only one VM at a time. This is much different from the real cluster of data center where there are usually many VMs placed on one PS. As a result, using CP in a real cluster environment will produce significant time overhead that data center can not afford.

6   Conclusions

Virtual server consolidation which can reduce large number of servers helps the enterprises reduce hardware and operating costs significantly and improve server utilization greatly in the enterprise-class data center.

In this paper, we propose a new approach to virtual server consolidation that considers both the problem of allocating the VMs to available PSs and the problem of how to migrate the VMs to these servers. Experiment results demonstrate that, our consolidation manager VSCM can indeed reduce the number of servers greatly, as compared to previously used FFD. While reducing the migration overhead significantly, VSCM also guarantees the feasibility of each migration operation.

In future work, we plan to improve the Globally Optimal Virtual Migration Bin Packing algorithm on the basis of more complicated bin-packing algorithm. We also expect to apply VSCM to the real cluster to get convincing experiment results.

References

1. Bobroff, N., Kochut, A., Beaty, K.: Dynamic Placement of Virtual Machines for Managing SLA Violations. In: IEEE Conf. Integrated Network Management, pp. 119–128 (2007)
2. Hyser, C., Mckee, B., Gardner, R., Watson, B.J.: Autonomic Virtual Machine Placement in the Data Center. Technical Report HPL-2007-189, HP Labs (2007)
3. Benhamou, F., Jussien, N., O'Sullivan, B.: Trends in Constraint Programming. ISTE, London (2007)
4. Hermenier, F., Lorca, X., Menaud, J.M., Muller, G., Lawall, J.: Entropy: a Consolidation Manager for Clusters. In: Proceedings of the ACM/Usenix International Conference On Virtual Execution Environments (VEE 2009), pp. 41–50 (2009)
5. Coffman Jr., E.G., Garey, M.R., Johnson, D.S.: Approximation algorithms for bin-packing - An updated survey. Approximation Algorithms for Computer System Design, pp. 49-106 (1984)
6. Lodi, A., Martello, S., Vigo, D.: Recent advances on two-dimensional bin packing problems. Discrete Appl. Math. 123(1-3), 379–396 (2002)
7. Verma, A., Ahuja, P., Neogi, A.: Power-aware dynamic placement of HPC applications. In: Proceedings of the 22nd Annual International Conference on Supercomputing (ICS 2008), pp. 175–184 (2008)
8. Wood, T., Prashant, S., Arun, V., Yousif, M.: Black-box and Gray-box Strategies for Virtual Machine Migration. In: Proceedings of the Fourth Symposium on Networked Systems Design and Implementation (NSDI), pp. 229–242 (2007)
9. Grit, L., Irwin, D., Yumerefendi, A., Chase, J.: Virtual Machine Hosting for Networked Clusters: Building the Foundations for Autonomic Orchestration. In: Proc. VTDC 2006, pp. 1–8 (2006)
10. Barham, P., Dragovic, B., Fraser, K., Hand, S., Harris, T., Ho, A., Neugebauery, R., Pratt, I., Warfield, A.: Xen and the Art of Virtualization. In: Proc. of ACM SOSP, vol. 37(5), pp. 164–177 (2003)
11. Liu, Y., Xiao, N., Shen, L.: Design and Implementation of Xen Virtual Cluster Monitor. Jounal of Wuhan University of Technology 32(20), 184–188 (2010)
12. Khanna, G., Beaty, K., Kar, G., Kochut, A.: Application Performance Management in Virtualized Server Environments. In: Network Operations and Management Symposium, pp. 373–381 (2006)
13. Irwin, D., Chase, J., Grit, L., Yumerefendi, A., Becker, D.: Sharing networked resources with brokered leases. In: ATEC 2006: Proceedings of the Annual Conference on USENIX 2006 Annual Technical Conference, pp. 18–18. USENIX Association (2006)
14. Jussien, N., Rochart, G., Lorca, X.: The CHOCO constraint programming solver. In: CPAIOR 2008 Workshop on Open-Source Software for Integer and Constraint Programming (OSSICP), Paris (2008)

Informed Live Migration Strategies of Virtual Machines for Cluster Load Balancing*

Xing Li, Qinming He, Jianhai Chen, Kejiang Ye, and Ting Yin

College of Computer Science, Zhejiang University,
Zheda Rd. 38, Hangzhou 310027, China
{lix,hqm,chenjh919,yekejiang,yintingeye}@zju.edu.cn

Abstract. Virtualization technology brings great conveniences to cluster and data center management. By using this technique, we can reconstruct a new computing environment quickly and easily. Compared to the traditional cluster environment, load balancing in a virtualized environment needs to address several new problems. This paper focuses on live migration strategies for load balancing in the virtualized cluster. We first divide the whole balancing process into three sub-problems, namely, the selection of the VM being migrated to, the choice of destination host and the determination of the migration execution sequence. Then we perform a series of experiments to investigate the particular features of the live migration of virtual machines in the balancing scenario. Based on our experiment results, we propose an informed live migration strategy which includes affinity-aware decision making and workload-aware migration to improve the efficiency of configuration of the virtualized cluster.

Keywords: Virtualization, Live Migration, Workload Aware.

1   Introduction

Virtualization has recently emerged as an essential technology to the modern computing cluster and data center mainly due to its capabilities of virtual machine isolation, consolidation and migration [1]. The enabled hardware independence and rapid deployment using QCOW technology [2], permit one to construct a computing cluster within minutes.

Live migration is an extremely powerful tool for cluster management. It facilitates typical functions such as: load balancing, online maintenance, power saving, and high availability. For example, if a physical machine needs to be removed from a cluster for maintenance, we can simply migrate the virtual machine (VM) from the original host to another available host. Similarly, VMs can be reallocated across the physical servers in the cluster to relieve the workload

---

* This work is funded by the National 973 Basic Research Program of China under grant NO.2007CB310900 and National Natural Science Foundation of China under grant NO. 60970125.

E. Altman and W. Shi (Eds.): NPC 2011, LNCS 6985, pp. 111–122, 2011.

on congested servers. In these situations the combination of virtualization and migration significantly improves the manageability of clusters.

At present, most of the virtualization platforms use memory Pre-Copy[3] as the default algorithm to implement live migration due its ability to decrease the VM downtime to the order of milliseconds which is imperceptible to users. However, the Pre-Copy algorithm will cause workload performance degradation during live migration. It will also produce an inevitable overhead.

In fact, not only the memory transferring mechanism affects the cost of live migration, the choice of the actual migration strategy also impacts greatly on the performance of a migrating VM. Especially, in the scenario of performing load balancing for virtualized cluster, there are often multiple VMs that must be migrated to multiple destination hosts . In such case, the migration strategy of these multiple VMs will be even more important.

In this paper, we study the behaviors of various live migration strategies. We found that some particular features will impact the performance of load balancing. These features include the affinity relationship between migrating VMs and the actual sequence of migration. We then propose an informed live migration strategy that incorporates affinity-aware decision and workload-aware migration. The strategy makes migration decisions according to the VMs' characteristics and the migration sequence. It will improve the reconstruction efficiency of virtualized cluster.

The rest of this paper is organized as follows. Section 2 introduces the background of load balancing in the virtualized cluster and the motivation to study the effective balancing approach. In Section 3, we present our experiments and results, followed by the proposed strategies. Section 4 describes related work and Section 5 presents our conclusions and future work.

2   Background and Motivation

In this section, we briefly introduce the virtual machine technology and the motivation to investigate the live migration strategies.

Live-migration technology. At present, many commercial corporations have their own live migration technology available within their software products. For example, Microsoft has Hyper-V [4] live migration, Cirtix integrates XenMotion [6] with their xenserver, and VMware uses VMotion [5]. Among a number of live migration algorithms, Memory Pre-Copy is the most prevailing one. The main advantage of the Pre-Copy algorithm is that it produces the minimum downtime. The actual time taken could be as low as 60ms[3], so users will not detect the event that the services have been interrupted and the virtual machine is migrating from one host to another. This algorithm copies and sends memory pages from the current host to the destination host iteratively, while ensures that services on the migrating VM are still available. Until the writable working set becomes small enough, will the virtual machine monitor (VMM) suspend the VM and then send the last remaining dirty pages and the CPU state. The network bandwidth being occupied may affect other VMs when network connection is involved in migration.

The performance metrics of live migration. To measure the performance and efficiency of live migration, four typical metrics are used: migration time, downtime, data transferred and workload performance degradation [7]. The migration time measures the time elapsed from the start of a migration process to the end of it. The downtime measures the time period when the migrating VM is stopped to transfer the remaining data. The VM is not responsible during the downtime . The data transferred reflects the total size of virtual machine memory data that has been sent during the migration. The workload performance degradation reflects the performance lose caused by live migration compared to the no-migration case.

Three problems of reconstructing the virtualized cluster. In order to balance the load of a virtualized cluster, three important problems must be addressed in making a wise choice on a good live migration strategy. Firstly, how to select the candidate virtual machine from the overloaded host to migrate out? The different VM selections will result in different outcomes. Criterions of minimum migration costs and earliest completion of reallocation procedure are both very necessary. Secondly, how to choose the destination host for each candidate migrating virtual machines? In other words, how to find the mapping relationship between migrating VMs and those idle hosts. Lastly, if there are many VMs to be migrated at one time, what would be the migration execution sequence of these candidate VMs, that will produce less marginal impact the other VMs. It can be expected that the migration sequence plays a significant role in the overall performance.

3   Experimental Evaluation and Analysis

In this section, we describe our detailed migration experiments for different scenarios, and then analyze the measurement results. These results will reveal key characteristics of many migration algorithms when used for load balancing purpose.

3.1   The Migrating VMs Selection Problem

In order to release the overloaded host fast, we need to choose the correct candidate VMs for migration to assure the minimum migration costs and make the reallocation procedure finished as quickly as possible. Table 1 displays the migration time, down time and overheads of selected typical workloads.

As we can see, the migration of different workloads will use different lengths of time and cause different overhead. Workloads such as OLTP and SPEC-jbb, which have many memory accesses, need long periods of time to migrate and generate more overhead. The network-intensive workload like webbench will prolong the migration procedure, and cause extra overheads. The pure CPU-intensive workload like SPEC-CPU will have the least impact in all three metrics.

Table 1. The typical workload behavior in migration

workloads	Migration-time(s)	Downtime(ms)	Overhead( )
IOZONE	214.51	1028	7.93
WEBBENCH	47.67	113	29.03
OLTP	69.32	998	33.26
SPEC-CPU	26.69	88	3.31
SPEC-jbb	31.25	232	8.29

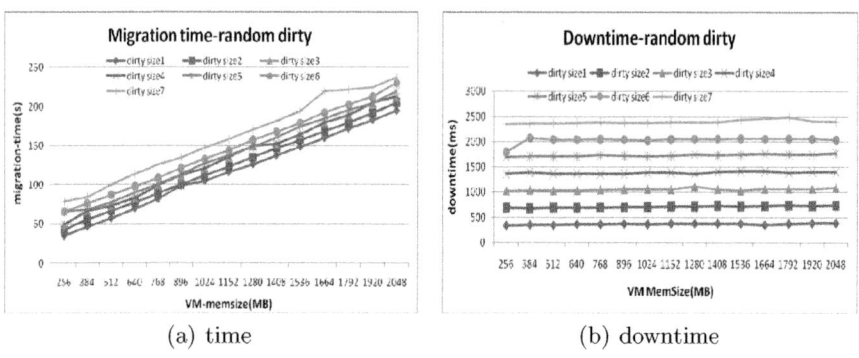

(a) time   (b) downtime

Fig. 1. Factors of Migration time&downtime

In the next experiment, we run a scalable memory dirty workload in the testing VM. We change the VM memory size during the process. The dirty workload was implemented by updating an array continuously and randomly. This was written using the C programming language so that the memory would have a consistently high dirtying rate and would be hard to migrate.

The Figure 3 shows that the migration time of a virtual machine is influenced by both the memory size and the memory dirty size. This is because that Xen uses a pre-copy algorithm to transfer the memory data to the destination host iteratively in its live migration implementation.

Figure 4 illustrates that the migration downtime is proportional to the memory dirty size and is unrelated to the memory size. When Xen detects that some parts of the memory are getting dirty frequently, it considers it not worthy to send it repeatedly. In this case, Xen will stop this virtual machine and turn to the Stop-and-Copy phase. Xen then transfers the remainder of the dirty data during the Stop-and-Copy phase. However, this approach leads to the case that the downtime is proportional to size of the dirty memory of the migrating VM.

When there is a need to select several virtual machines to migrate out, both the procedure completion time and migration overhead have to be taken into account. As the above experiments illustrated, we can choose some virtual machines which are running CPU workloads to migrate, and consider additionally criteria such as the small memory size and small dirty size. The dirty logging switch tool we have mentioned in previous section are especially useful in monitoring the dirty rate and dirty size in each domains to support the migration strategies.

3.2   The Destination Host Choose Problem

Deciding which host be the suitable destination will greatly impact the migration perfformance. We have designed a group of experiments, the first one runs the SPEC-CPU workload in two virtual machines which are placed on different physical hosts. Then one of the virtual machines will be migrated from its original host to the other, making the two virtual machines running together. To get clear experiment results, one additional condition imposed was that the two virtual machines are pined to a single physical CPU, and share the same L2 cache.

Table 3 shows that, there are visible affinity relationship between some workloads. Theworkload pairs like libquantum and gamess can work well together, but not the other workload pairs like two bwaves not. This is because that the latter two workload would mutual restrain each other and need very long time to complete.

Table 2. SPEC-CPU workload affinity, the values in the table display the running time of each workloads

Destination	Workloads be migrating				
	milc	bwaves	bzip2	libquantum	Games
mig-to-milc	1100	1280	824	1530	1270
mig-to-bwaves	961	1500	633	1470	1270
mig-to-bzip2	824	1160	628	1190	1240
mig-to-libquantum	1070	1340	886	1760	1290
mig-to-gamess	843	1180	588	1100	1240
max-difference	25.1	22.7	33.6	37.5	3.9

Table 3 and Figure 2(a) show that choosing different migration destination hosts will dramatically impact the virtual machine performance. The difference may even reach 37.5% in some cases. The reasons for these differences are that these CPU-bounded workload have different cache accessing types: some workloads like bwaves and libquantum will pollute cache block, while some other workloads like bzip2 and gmaess will not.

Figure 2(b) shows that when placing the two virtual machines, which have a large number of communications, together on the same host, they will get better performance.

We also designed experiments to deploy a virtual cluster of e 16 virtual machines in different number of physical hosts, from one physical host, to 2 hosts each has 8 VMs, and to 4 hosts each has 4 VMs. The comparisons of the three cases are shown in Figure 2(c). In general, the three configurations show similar

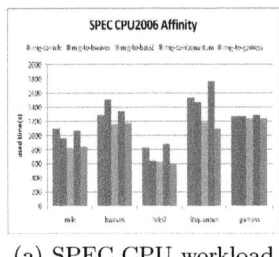 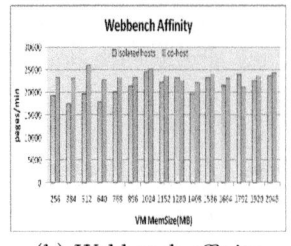 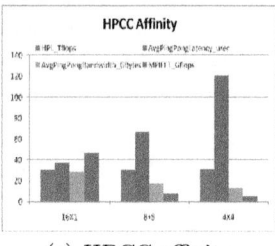

(a) SPEC CPU workload   (b) Webbench affinity   (c) HPCC affinity

Fig. 2. (a)The affinity of SPEC CPU workload.(b)Comparison of webbench on 2 isolated-hosts VMs with co-host.(c)Comparison of HPCC VMs isolated and co-host.

HPL performance. But the communication performance decreases a lot when deploying these virtual machines to more different hosts. When there are 4 physical hosts, the MPIFFT shows the worst performance. It means that the communication performance of virtual machines is more effective when deployed on the same physical host.

On the other hand, the Xen memory sharing mechanism and grant table could be used to communicate between domains. By using this mechanism, the domain could lease one of its memory block to another domain temporarily. This method will be more effective than communication through a physical network. However theis memory sharing mechanism is only implemented in the virtual machine monitor Xen.

Figure 3 illustrates that, when two disk-I/O-bounded virtual machines working together, there will be a significant degradation in performance. In contact, a disk-I/O-bounded virtual machine and a CPU-intensive one could work well together. It is easy to see that consolidating multiple disk-I/O-bounded workloads has to consider the nonsharable usage of the physical disk I/O operations which restricted the capacity. In summary, we have the following observations when

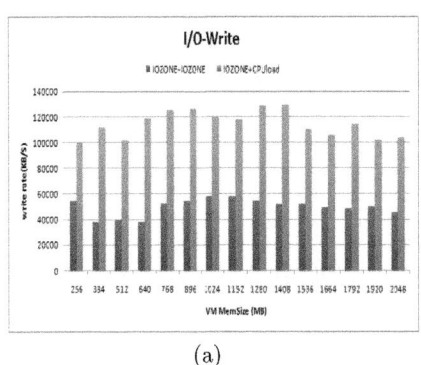 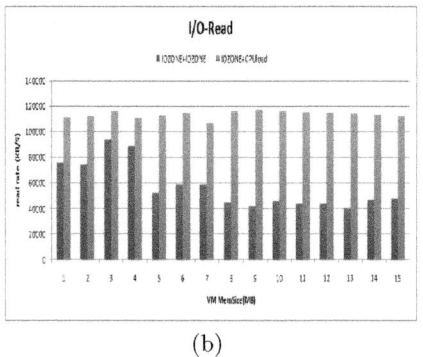

(a)   (b)

Fig. 3. Two I/O type VMs working together

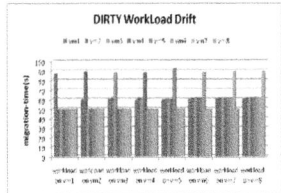
(a) The impact of memory dirty workload

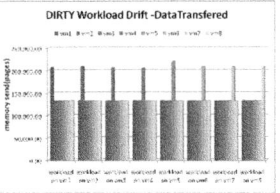
(b) Data transfer

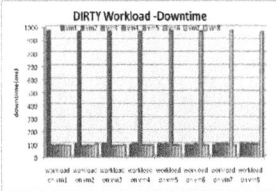
(c) migration downtime

Fig. 4. (a)Memory dirty workload VMs will affect these VMs migrated before it.(b)Data transferred of each migrated VMs.(c)Downtime of each migrated VMs

determining a suitable server to host a migrating VM: (1) it would be better to choose the kinds of virtual machines as neighbors, the kinds that have well affinity with the migrating one; (2) it would be better to make the virtual machines that communicate with each other to work on the same host; (3) it would be better to avoid migrating two workloads that have the same nonsharable type of resources together.

3.3   The Migration Sequence

When migration involves multiple VMs, the migration sequence becomes a critical issue because it will dramatically affect the whole reconfiguration procedure of the cluster. Our next experiments will show the influence. In this set of experiments, we migrate 8 virtual machines one after the other. One of the 8 virtual machines has a workload running on it, others are idle. By altering the location of the workload VM in the migration sequence, we can observe clearly that the different migration order of the workload virtual machine will affect the other virtual machine that are co-hosted with it. Firstly, we place a memory-dirty workload on the first virtual machine, named VM1, in the migration sequence, and migrate these 8 virtual machines one by one from VM1 to VM8. Then, we place the dirty workload on the second virtual machine VM2 and migrate all the virtual machines in succession. Repeatedly, we place the memory-dirty workload on the VM3, VM4 until VM8.

Figure 4(a) illustrates memory dirty workload virtual machine will significantly affect the migration time of these co-hosting virtual machines migrate before it, and these virtual machines which migrate behind the dirty workload VM don't suffer impact. As Figure 4(b)(c) show, the memory dirty workload will not affect the performance of the migration downtime and migration data transferred of the other VMs. It is clear that the memory dirty workload causes large page fault and slows down the other virtual machines' memory copy procedure. The conclusion is simple, We must ensure that the memory dirty workload always have the higest priority to migrate. However, not all the cases own this phenomenon as we can see a complete different situation in the next experiment.

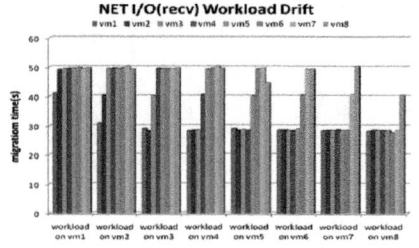
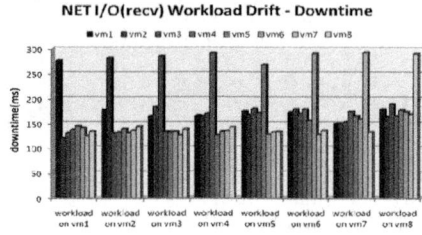

(a) The impact of migration time   (b) The impact of migration downtime

Fig. 5. The impact of NET I/O(receive) VMs on (a)migration time or (b)migration downtime of the other VMs migrated before

This time we changed the memory dirty program into a NET I/O workload.Thus the workload virtual machine continuously receives the data sent from remote server. In the remainder, we just repeat the process as described in previous experiment.

Figure 5(a) shows NET I/O(receive) virtual machine will greatly impact the migration time of the other virtual machines migrated after it, this is because when the net I/O receiver workload migrates to the destination host, it reduces the destination host's ability to receive the memory data being transferred, and also slows down the migration time of other followed virtual machines. However, this is not the same as previous case. It seems that we need to migrate these virtual machine with NET I/O(receive) workload as late as possible. Figure 5(b) shows that NET I/O will prolong the migration downtime, because when it comes to stop-copy step, it will take a longer time to send the remaining memory data.

In this case, we need a compromise approach to balance the migration time and downtime. For these virtual machines tend to have short migration time. We choose to migrate it before the NET I/O (recv) workload virtual machine. On the other hand, for these virtual machine tend to have short downtime, we choose to migrate it after the workload virtual machine migration.

Then, we change the workload into web server application and repeat the experiment.

As Figure 6 shows, the web server workload VM will dramatically impact both of the migration time and migration downtime of its co-hosting virtual machines. Obviously, toese virtual machines migrated before the workload VM will have a long migration time and downtime. This is because the web server load sends data through the network continuous,which occupies large bandwidth, and will slow down both the migration time and downtime. It is easy to reach the conclusion: for these web server workloads, we need to migrate them out as soon as possible.

Our experiments also show that the disk I/O load and CPU workload will not affect the neighboring virtual machine migration performance.

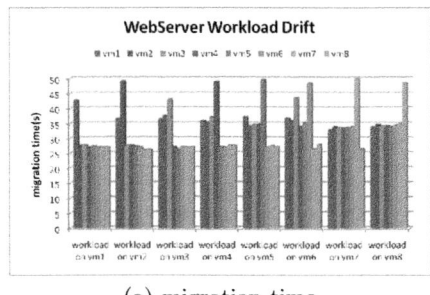

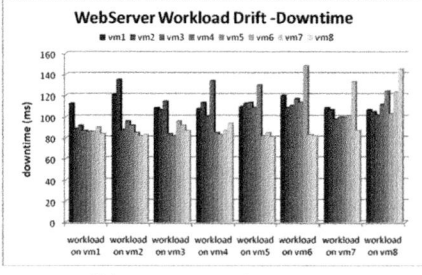

(a) migration time   (b) migration downtime

Fig. 6. WebServer VMs will impact the migration (a)time,(b)downtime of some other VMs migrated before it

At last, we can assemble these experiments described above together and take an overview. With the workload virtual machine migrating backwards in the migration order, the average migration time of whole migrating VMs sequence will have different features. For the sequence having memory dirty workload, the workload virtual machine gets migrated later the average migration time gets larger?" For the sequence which having NET I/O (recieve) workload virtual machine, the average migration time will be smaller but will have a longer average downtime; For these sequence having web server workload, the later migration will cause both larger migration time and down time. For these having disk I/O or CPU workload sequences, the migration order causes no effect.

3.4   Informed Live Migration Strategies

By analyzing the above experimental results, we have found interesting features of the live migration in the scene of virtual cluster load balancing: (1) Different kinds of workloads result in a diversity in the migration time and different performance overheads; (2) Besides the total memory size, the memory dirty rate and dirty area size will also affect the migration time and downtime; (3) There are certain affinity relationship between some workloads, e.g., some kinds of workload consolidation will cause large performance degradation, while others will not; (4) Migrating two virtual machines which communicate through network on the same physical host will obtain performance improvement; (5) The migration sequence of a group of VMs with different kinds of workloads will greatly affect the whole reconfiguration efficiency.

Based on these specific features, we propose affinity-aware decision making and workload-aware migration to improve the efficiency of live migration.

The strategy contains a set of rules: (1) choosing proper virtual machines to achieve shorter migration procedure time and less migration overheads; (2) taking the virtual machine affinity into consideration to decide suitable destination host; (3) Understanding the virtual machine workload features and determining an optimal migration sequence. In our implementation of the strategy, we tend to choose the VMs that have less total memory and smaller memory dirty size as candidate migrating VMs./ The types of the workloads are also considered (see Table 3.2), the CPU workload and Disk I/O are currently preferred in our testing. When choosing the migration destination host, it's important to avoid consolidating the same type of virtual machine with nonsharable ; but the VMs having network communications should be set to work together. When determining the migration sequence of a group of VMs, the VMs which have dirty memory or web server workload should be considered first. For the VM which have Network I/Os (receiving) and web application running on it, for example, online video, webgame, etc, we need to migrate it at the end of the migration process. This is because it will impact the destination server's bandwidth, slow down the pre-copy operation and increase the downtime of the subsequent migration. So, the VMs which have NET I/O(receive) workload need to be migrated at last. For the VMs which have CPU or disk I/O workload, we just need to ensure that the smaller VM is migrated early using the principle of SJF (Shortest Job First). This will lead to the least average completion time of each migrating VM.

Based on the aforementioned discoveries and mechanisms, we are in a position to implement the features of affinity-aware decision making and workload-aware migration into the balancing system, which establishes our informed live migration strategies for live migration.

4   Related Work

Many efforts have been made to improve the efficiency of live migration. Some research has been done into improving the efficiency of the live migration mechanism. H.Jin et al. [14] presents an implementation of a novel memory-compression based VM migration approach to improve the migration efficiency ; Liu et al.[16] described a design and implementation of a novel approach that Adopts checkpointing-recovery and trace-replay technology to Provide fast, transparent VM migration. Luo et al. [11] describe a whole-system live migration scheme, which transfers the whole system run-time state, including CPU state, memory data, and local disk storage, of the virtual machine (VM). There are also many efforts have been made to the dynamic placing and consolidation of the virtualized resources. Hermenier et al. [15] provide substantial improvement over static server consolidation in reducing the amount of required capacity and the rate of service level agreement violations. Choi et al. [13] describe a learning framework that autonomously finds and adjusts thresholds at runtime. Verma et al. [8] presented the pMapper architecture and placement algorithms to minimize the power used to a fixed performance requirement. Hermenier et al. [15] propose the Entropy resource manager for homogeneous clusters, which performs dynamic consolidation and takes migration overhead into account. Differing from the above work, This paper studied the live migration strategies in the scenario of load balancing in a virtualized cluster.

5 Conclusions and Future Work

In this paper, we study the live migration features in the load balancing scenario of a virtualized cluster, our experiments showed several interesting observations that help to establish rules for live migration to achieve the goal of load balancing. Our proposed informed live migration strategy includes affinity-aware decision making and workload-aware migration. It improves the efficiency of reconfiguration a virtualized cluster.

Our future work will include more comprehensive performance metrics and use workload automatic monitoring to support the informed live migration strategy. Additionally, we will use mathematical modeling methods to evaluate and integrate the multiplicity of factors that influence live migration.

References

1. Barham, P., Dragovic, B., Fraser, K., Hand, S., Harris, T., Ho, A., Neugebauer, R., Pratt, I., War eld, A.: Xen and the art of virtualization. In: Proceedings of the 19th ACM Symposium on Operating Systems Principles, pp. 164–177 (2003)
2. COW, http://en.wikipedia.org/wiki/Qcow
3. Clark, C., Fraser, K., Hand, S., Hansen, J.G., Jul, E., Limpach, C., Pratt, I., Wareld, A.: Live migration of virtual machines. In: Proceedings of the 2nd Conference on Symposium on Networked Systems Design & Implementation, pp. 273–286 (2005)
4. Hyper-V, http://www.microsoft.com/hyper-v-server/en/us/default.aspx
5. VMware VMotion, http://www.vmware.com/products/vmotion/overview.html
6. XenServer XenMotion, http://www.citrix.com
7. Huang, D., Ye, D., He, ., Chen, J., Ye, K.: Virt-LM: A Benchmark for Live Migration of Virtual Machine. In: Proceeding of the Second Joint WOSP/SIPEW International Conference on Performance Engineering, pp. 307–316 (2011)
8. Verma, A., Ahuja, P., Neogi, A.: pMapper: Power and Migration Cost Aware Application Placement in Virtualized Systems In: IFIP International Federation For Information Processing, pp. 243–264 (2008)
9. Ye, K., Jiang, X., He, ., Li, X.: Evaluate the performance and scalability of image deployment in virtual data center. In: Network and Parallel Computing, pp. 390–401 (2010)
10. Voorsluys, W., Broberg, J., Venugopal, S.: Cost of virtual machine live migration in clouds: A performance evaluation. In: IEEE International Conference of Cloud Computing, pp. 254–265 (2009)
11. Luo, Y., Zhang, B., Wang, X., Wang, Z., Sun, Y., Chen, H.: Live and incremental whole-system migration of virtual machines using block-bitmap. In: 2008 IEEE International Conference on Cluster Computing, pp. 99–106 (2008)
12. Bobroff, N., Kochut, A., Beaty, K.: Dynamic placement of virtual machines for managing sla violations. In: 10th IFIP/IEEE International Symposium on Integrated Network Management, IM 2007, pp. 119–128 (2007)
13. Choi, H., Kwak, H., Sohn, A., Chung, K.: Autonomous learning for efficient resource utilization of dynamic VM migration. In: Proceedings of the 22nd Annual International Conference on Supercomputing, pp. 185–194 (2008)

14. Jin, H., Deng, L., Wu, S., Shi, X., Pan, X.: Live virtual machine migration with adaptive, memory compression. In: IEEE International Conference on Cluster Computing and Workshops, CLUSTER 2009, pp. 1–10 (2009)
15. Hermenier, F., Lorca, X., Menaud, J., Muller, G., Lawall, J.: Entropy: a consolidation manager for clusters. In: Proceedings of the 2009 ACM SIGPLAN/SIGOPS International Conference on Virtual Execution Environments, pp. 41–50 (2009)
16. Liu, H., Jin, H., Liao, X., Hu, L., Yu, C.: Live migration of virtual machine based on full system trace and replay. In: Proceedings of the 18th ACM International Symposium on High Performance Distributed Computing, pp. 101–110 (2009)
17. Jin, X., Chen, H., Wang, X., Wang, Z., Wen, X., Luo, Y., Li, X.: A Simple Cache Partitioning Approach in a Virtualized Environment. In: Proceedings of IEEE International Symposium on Parallel and Distributed Processing with Applications, pp. 519–524 (2009)

Dynamic Advance Reservation for Grid System Using Resource Pools

Zhiang Wu, Jie Cao, and Youquan Wang

Jiangsu Provincial Key Laboratory of E-Business, Nanjing University of Finance
and Economics, Nanjing, P.R. China
{zawuster,youq.wang}@gmail.com, caojie690929@163.com

Abstract. Dynamic behavior of resources is a non-negligible feature in
grid system, and most research efforts on advance reservation cannot effectively deal with the negative effect resulted from the dynamic feature.
In this paper, a new grid system architecture using resource pool is proposed firstly. Theoretical analysis demonstrates that resource pool can
well adapt to dynamic behavior of resources. Secondly, uality of Service (oS) distance computation method for hybrid variable types is presented. Then, k-set Availability Prediction Admission Control (kAPAC)
algorithm is described in detail. Experimental results show that kAPAC
can significantly increase success ratio of reservation, resource utilization
and stability of grid system.

Keywords: grid computing, advance reservation, resource pool, oS.

1   Introduction

The last decade has witnessed tremendous progress of various distributed computing infrastructures aiming to support Internet-wide resources collaboration
and sharing. Grid technology flourished worldwide in the early 2000's, and grid
community requires participants to exhibit some degree of trust, accountability,
and opportunities for sanctions in response to inappropriate behavior. This relative close community facilitates Quality of Service (QoS) guarantee mechanism.

Virtualization, a software-based technology for building shared hardware infrastructures in Grid computing, helps to achieve greater system utilization while
lowering total cost of ownership and responding more effectively to changing
business conditions [1]. Cloud computing also employs virtualization technology to provide dynamic resource pool. Therefore, virtualization will be a widely
used technology for next generation computing platforms. Various resources are
virtualized as a resource pool, and are managed as a whole.

In the meanwhile, with the advent of Web services, Internet computing (i.e.
grid, cloud) has become a use case for Web Services. World is modeled as a
collection of services: computational resources, storage resources, networks, programs, databases, and the like are all represented as services [2]. Seamless QoS
(Quality of Service) is required to be delivered by this convergence between the
architecture of grid system and service-oriented architecture. Google and IBM

E. Altman and W. Shi (Eds.): NPC 2011, LNCS 6985, pp. 123–134, 2011.

have proposed WS-resource framework (WSRF) to support stateful web services widely applied in Internet computing [3].

Advance reservation is a well-known and effective mechanism to guarantee QoS. Grid Resource Agreement and Allocation Protocol (GRAAP) work group of Global Grid Forum(GGF) has defined advance reservation [4]: an advance reservation is a possibly limited or restricted delegation of a particular resource capability over a defined time interval, obtained by the requester from the resource owner through a negotiation process. Advance reservation in grid environment is a complex issue due to the following reasons: (i) Since availability and performance of resources both exhibit dynamic variability, it is difficult to guarantee availability of resources at reserved time in the future. (ii) To satisfy users' requirements strictly often leads to an increase of miss-reject ratio, because some secondary requirements determine whether this reservation request will be admitted or not.

This paper focuses on dynamic advance reservation for the grid system utilizing resource pools. Firstly, three kinds of Service Level Agreements (SLAs) are introduced for QoS negotiation. Secondly, enabling system architecture employing resource pools to alleviate negative influence of grid dynamic behaviors is presented. Then, a new admission control approach, called k-Set Availability Prediction Admission Control (kAPAC), is proposed. At last, we demonstrate the effectiveness and efficiency of our kAPAC algorithm in experiments.

2   Related Work

Foster et al. propose general-purpose architecture for reservation and allocation (GARA) in early stage [5]. GARA supports reservation and adaptation, which simplifies the development of end-to-end QoS management strategies in service-oriented grid environment. This is the initial work on grid architecture to support QoS. Li et al. propose layered QoS scheduling aiming to maximize global user satisfaction degree at application layer [6]. Siddiqui et al. introduce 3-layered negotiation protocol for the advance reservation also aiming to achieve global optimization of application utility [7]. Service Negotiation and Acquisition Protocol (SNAP) is proposed in [8], which provides lifetime management and an at-most-once creation semantics for remote SLAs (Service Level Agreements). Three different types of SLAs are included in SNAP. They are task service level agreements (TSLAs), resource service level agreements (RSLAs) and binding service level agreements (BSLAs). We define a new SLA and extend states transition among SLAs in this paper.

Grid resources exhibit dynamic availability due to the unexpected failure, or due to dynamic joining and leaving and also exhibit dynamically varying performance due to the varying local load and unpredictable latency of today's Internet [9]. Our work takes this feature into consideration and utilizes resource pool to alleviate the negative influence of dynamic behavior. Resource pool is proposed in [10] and its performance is analyzed using queuing theory. This performance analysis method is expanded in this paper.

3   SLAs for QoS Negotiation

In our architecture proposed in Section 4, reservation requests are not bound with resources directly, but with resource pool. Three SLAs defined by SNAP cannot meet this requirement. We should define new SLA to support the dynamic binding between reservation request and resource pool.

A new SLA called Virtual Binding Service Level Agreement (VBSLA) is introduced, and states transition among SLAs is extended as shown in Fig. 1. Three kinds of SLAs defined by SNAP are still used in this paper. TSLA is used to negotiate for the performance of a task, which is characterized in terms of its service steps and QoS requirements. RSLA is used to negotiate for the right to consume a resource and each resource is characterized in terms of its service capabilities. BSLA associates a TSLA with the RSLA and the resource service capabilities should satisfy the task's requirements. In Fig. 1, S0, S1, S3 and S4 are original states in SNAP, and S2 is extended state for VBSLA. User submits reservation request at S1, and establishes VBSLA with resource pool at S2. When the start time of advance reservation request reaches, BSLA is established with certain resource at S3, and SLA state migrates to run-state S4.

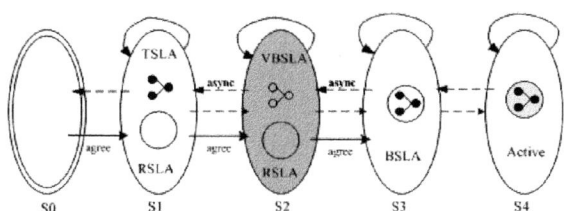

Fig. 1. Extended SLA States Transition

4   Grid Architecture Using Resource Pool for Advance Reservation

In this section, we first present a grid system architecture using resource pool. Then, we conduct theoretical analysis for resource pool.

4.1   Grid System Architecture

Resource pool aggregates resources provided by multiple physical sites. Physical sites control the amount of resources contributed to resources pool. The architecture of a resource pool supporting advance reservation is illustrated in Fig. 2. Admission control manager makes decisions about whether to accept a reservation request based on kAPAC algorithm which will be discussed in Section 5. Central pool sensor negotiates with local resource managers (LRM) of sites to determine the kind and ratio of resources contributed to the resource pool. Central pool actuator monitors the status of resource pool and gathers data for grid information center.

When reservation request is directly bound with specific resource, the reject rate of reservation requests will increase in a great extent, because the availability and performance of this bound resource cannot be guaranteed at runtime. Now, reservation request is firstly bound with resource pool at its arrival time, and this request will be bound with resource at its runtime according to the latest resource information. This dynamic binding method will alleviate negative influence of grid resources' dynamic behavior.

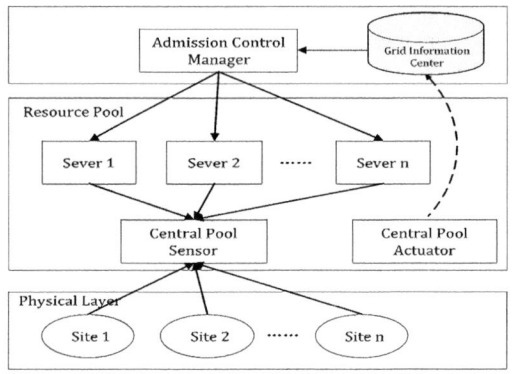

Fig. 2. Advance Reservation Architecture of a Resource Pool

4.2   Theoretical Analysis

It is obvious that little resources in resource pool cannot effectively guarantee QoS, but a large number of resources in resource pool may lead to resource profligacy. Let the arrival process of reservation requests be a *Poisson process* with an arrival rate λ. Assume service time conforms any probability distribution, which is the general form. Then, a resource pool aggregating c resources is modeled as $M/G/c$ queuing system. The average waiting time of $M/G/c$ is given by Eq.(1).

$$W_c = \frac{\overline{h^2}}{2\overline{h}(c - \lambda\overline{h})}[1 + \sum_{n=0}^{c-1} \frac{(\lambda\overline{h})^n}{n!} \frac{(c-1)!(c - \lambda\overline{h})}{(\lambda\overline{h})^c}]^{-1} \qquad (1)$$

In Eq.(1) $\overline{h}$ is the first moment of service time and $\overline{h}^2$ is the second moment of service time. Since file length in Web server and response time of websites are deemed to conform a heavy-tailed distribution [11], we assume that service time conforms *Bounded Pareto* (BP) distribution which is a typical heavy-tailed distribution. The probability density function of BP distribution is shown in Eq.(2).

$$f(x) = \frac{\alpha k^\alpha}{1 - (k/p)^\alpha} x^{-\alpha-1} \qquad k \leqslant x \leqslant p \qquad (2)$$

The first moment and second moment of BP distribution can be computed by Eqs. (3) and (4).

$$\overline{h} = \frac{\alpha}{\alpha - 1} \frac{k^{\alpha}}{1 - (k/p)^{\alpha}} \left(\frac{1}{k^{\alpha - 1}} - \frac{1}{p^{\alpha - 1}} \right) \tag{3}$$

$$\overline{h}^{2} = \frac{\alpha}{\alpha - 2} \frac{k^{\alpha}}{1 - (k/p)^{\alpha}} \left(\frac{1}{k^{\alpha - 2}} - \frac{1}{p^{\alpha - 2}} \right) \tag{4}$$

Table 1 lists five cases with different k and p values. We set α to 1.1 and $p = 10000 * k$. We reveal the relation between the average waiting time and the number of resources in five cases as shown in Fig. 3.

Table 1. Experiment Parameters (k,p) and The Mean and Variance of BP Distribution

	Case 1	Case 2	Case 3	Case 4	Case 5
k	0.1	1	10	30	50
p	1000	10000	100000	300000	500000
Mean	0.66211	6.6211	66.211	198.63	331.05
Variance	48.209	4820.9	20900000	388000000	520000000

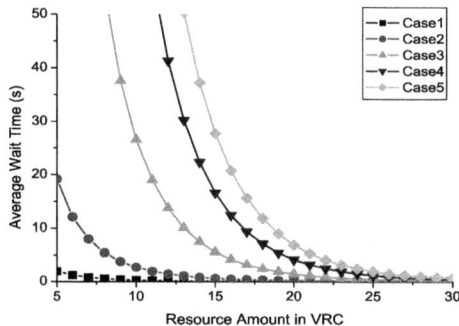

Fig. 3. Resource Amount in VRC vs. Average Wait Time

Fig.3 shows that the average waiting time decreases dramatically at the beginning, but once resource amount reaches threshold, average waiting time decreasing rate reduces in evidence. This threshold is inflection point of this group of curves, and from theoretical view, it is optimal resource amount provisioned in resource pool. Since Eq. (1) is non-continuous, we can not obtain precise X-coordinate of its inflection point. We just design an algorithm to find approximate optimal amount of resources. Approximate optimal amount is the first point that decreasing extent between two neighbor points reaches threshold. This threshold is set as average wait time that most users can endure. We observe kept W_c unchanged (means non-degraded QoS level), the permitted workload ratio (means service ability) will be increased with the increase of amount of resources integrated by resource pool. Therefore, the resource pool can avoid negative influence of grid resource dynamic fluctuation effectively, but without degrading the performance of advance reservation.

5   *k*APAC Algorithm

Admission control manager aims to determine whether grid resource pool accepts reservation requests. Most systems compare RSLA with TSLA, and only when all QoS requirements specified in TSLA are satisfied by RSLA, request can be accepted by system. The accepted requests are bound with fixed resources. There are two significant limitations in this method. First, some secondary QoS attributes determine requests whether to be accepted or not. The success rate of reservation requests decreases in extreme extent. Second, *availability* of resources are not considered. In fact, resources will be utilized by reservation requests in future time. Therefore, resources with low availability leads to the failure of the bound requests in a high probability.

This section presents a new admission control algorithm named *k*APAC. QoS distance computation method is presented firstly. Then, the procedure of *k*APAC is proposed.

5.1   QoS Distance Computation

Variable types of QoS attributes are widely different. For example, response time, bandwidth and delay are interval-scale variables; the level of security is discrete ordinal variable enumerating *low, middle, high* in-order. QoS distance computation method proposed in this paper deals with these hybrid variable types in a uniform framework. Let Q_i and Q_j denote two QoS vectors, and $d(Q_i, Q_j)$ is given by Eq. (5).

$$d(Q_i, Q_j) = \frac{\sum_{f=1}^{p} \delta_{ij}^f d_{ij}^f}{\sum_{f=1}^{p} \delta_{ij}^f} \tag{5}$$

In Eq.(5), if Q_i or Q_j do not assign a value to the f-th variable (x_{if} or x_{jf} are missing), $\delta_{ij}^f=0$; otherwise $\delta_{ij}^f=1$. The distance of the f-th variable between Q_i and Q_j is written d_{ij}^f which relies on the variable type. We consider binary variable, categorical variable, interval-scale variable and discrete ordinal variable respectively.

- the f-th variable is binary variable or categorical variable: if $x_{if} = x_{jf}$, d_{ij}^f =0; otherwise d_{ij}^f =1.
- the f-th variable is interval-scale variable: can be computed by Eq. (6).

$$d_{ij}^f = \frac{|x_{if} - x_{jf}|}{max_h x_{hf} - min_h x_{hf}} \tag{6}$$

- the f-th variable is discrete ordinal variable: assume the f-th variable has M_f states. We define ranking 1,2,$\cdots$,M_f for these M_f states, and the ranking corresponding to x_{if} is written r_{if}. Then, we convert r_{if} to interval-scale variable which is written z_{if}. z_{if} is given by Eq.(7), and Eq.(6) can be utilized to compute d_{ij}^f.

$$z_{if} = \frac{r_{if} - 1}{M_f - 1} \tag{7}$$

Moreover, we suppose there exists m service QoS parameters and namely p-m provisional QoS parameters. Let h_i denote whether all service QoS parameters of task request are satisfied perfectly. Adjusted distance between Q_i and Q_j is written $d'(Q_i, Q_j)$. If h_i =0, this reservation request cannot be satisfied and $d'(Q_i, Q_j)$ is infinite. $d'(Q_i, Q_j)$ is computed by Eq. (8).

$$d'(Q_i, Q_j) = \begin{cases} +\infty, h_i = 0 \\ d(Q_i, Q_j), h_i = 1 \end{cases} \tag{8}$$

With Eqs. (5) to (8), we can compute distance between reservation request and resource and distance between two requests.

5.2   Algorithm Design

kAPAC algorithm aims to accept reservation requests which will be executed in the future in a high probability. The data structure $RAQueue$ holds the requests that have been accepted but do not be executed. The pseudo-code of kAPAC algorithm is presented in Table 2.

Table 2. Pseudo-code Describing the kAPAC algorithm

kAPAC is deployed to Admission Control Manager, and is used to determine whether to accept a reservation request or not
1: **while** (*TRUE*) **do**
2: wait_request(q)   //reservation request q arrives
3: compute the number of similar requests with q in $RAQueue$, which is written $Index_{rej}$
4: **if** ($Index_{rej}$ >= k) **then** //the similar requests are enough to reject q
5:     reject_request(q)
6: **else**
7:     select k nearest neighbors (kNN) of q in resource set
8:     compute the availability of q's kNN, which is written $availability\_k\_set(q)$
9:     **if** ($availability\_k\_set(q) > threshold_{acp}$) **then**
10:       accept_request(q) and $RAQueue$.enqueue(q)
11: **end of while**

The process of kAPAC is that: when a reservation request arrives, it first selects top-k resources with small distance as much as possible to form k-set; then it judges whether availability of k-set resources is bigger than accept threshold; if it is, system accepts this task. But when lots of similar task requests arrive, selected k-set will also be similar. If availability of this k-set is bigger than accept threshold, these similar task requests are all accepted. Since these accepted tasks will occupy lots of similar resources in future and last for an interval, when similar task requests increase much more than k, these k resources will be busy in future in great probability and surplus requests will be aborted at runtime.

To avoid this case, kAPAC firstly judges whether the number of similar requests in $RAQueue$ is bigger than k. If it is, system aborts this reservation request.

To facilitate our study, we utilize a simplified model to predict resource availability. This model conforms to two observations: (i) Availability of recent used resource will be much higher in the future, and thus future availability is estimated by both historical and recent information. (ii) Historical availability decreases with the increase of idle time. We use recent availability A_{recent} to represent recent information and use $A_{cur} * g(t)$ to represent historical information. $g(t)$ is a non-incremental function here and t is the interval from last used time. Recent availability and current availability are calculated by Eqs. (9) and (10) respectively.

$$A_{recent} = \frac{T_{active}}{T_{total}} = \frac{T_{active}}{T_{active} + T_{down}} \qquad (9)$$

$$A_{cur} = \omega \cdot A_{cur} \cdot g(t) + (1 - \omega) * A_{recent} \quad 0 < g(t) < 1 \qquad (10)$$

Every time when resource is used, Eq. (9) is used to measure most recent availability, in which T_{active} is total time when this resource is active (not down) and of course T_{total} equals sum of T_{active} and T_{down}. Eq. (10) is used to estimate current availability. Current availability is weighted sum of historical availability and recent availability, the right A_{cur} in Eq. (10) is the old current availability that is calculated last used time. Current availability decreases with the increase of t.

6   Experimental Results

Our experiment is conducted in Southeast University Grid (SEUGrid) developed based on Globus Toolkit [12]. SEUGrid is designed for Alpha Magnetic Spectrometer (AMS-02) experiment. The Monte Carlo (MC) production, an important jobs in AMS experiment, is a kind of typical parameter sweep application. There are also no inter-task communication or data dependencies in MC production. We utilize part of computational resources in SEUGrid to conduct our experiments, containing two clusters each with 32 blade servers and one PowerLeader server. The total number of CPU reaches 140.

To simulate the dynamic performance fluctuation, all grid nodes produce local *High Performance Linpack* (HPL) test jobs randomly to form local workload. Thus, system workload ratio can be easily estimated according to size of HPL jobs. Another type of job, MC production jobs including various QoS constraints, submits advance reservation request to Admission Control Manager. All reservation requests mentioned below refer to MC production jobs. We firstly define some evaluation metrics that will be used in our experiments.

1. W_r **(Workload Ratio):** This metric is used to measure workload of overall system in a given time interval. It is determined by mount and size of HPL jobs within an interval, and can be calculated by Eq. (11).

$$W_r = \frac{\sum_{i=1}^{m}\left(\frac{2}{3} \cdot N_i^3 - 2 \cdot N_i^2\right)}{t \cdot \sum_{i=1}^{n} Rpeak_i} \tag{11}$$

Where N_i is the size of one HPL job, and $2/3 * N_i^3 - 2 * N_i^2$ is its actual calculation flops, which is defined in HPL specification. $Rpeak_i$ is theoretical peak of one CPU, and the denominator is total peak of system during a time interval.

2. R_s (**Success Ratio**): This metric is the percentage ratio of reservation requests that are successfully completed.
3. R_a (**Accept Ratio**): This metric is the percentage ratio of reservation requests that are accepted by admission control manager.
4. E_r (**Effectiveness Ratio**): This metric is the average percentage ratio of successfully completed requests in total accepted requests. R_s is always smaller than R_a since part of accepted requests may be aborted at their start time due to sudden unavailability of estimated available resources, or due to resource contention. E_r reflects how many accepted requests are aborted at start time. The less accepted requests are aborted, the higher E_r is. High E_r shows that this system performs good effectiveness and brings good trust to users. In contrast, bad system effectiveness may lost their users.
5. U_r (**Utilization Ratio**): This metric is the average percentage ratio of total resources that used by tasks, and can be calculated by Eq. (12).

$$U_r = \frac{\sum_{i=1}^{m} Request(i)}{(1 - W_r) \cdot t \cdot \sum_{i=1}^{n} Rpeak_i} \tag{12}$$

Where $Request(i)$ is the computation amount of a MC production job. W_r is the workload ratio of overall system in a time interval, and so the denominator is actual computation amount provided by system during this time interval.

6.1 Impact of k-set Length and Recent Queue Length

In kAPAC, recent queue length L is set as a times of k-set length k. That is $L = a * k$. In this experiment, we investigate how a and k affect on U_r and E_r. We range k from 1 to 10 and set a to 3, 2, and 1.5 respectively. We also set average request inter-arrival time to 80s. Fig. 4 and Fig. 5 show U_r and E_r obtained by increase of k from 1 to 10 with different a, in which each plots is measured in 30 minutes.

Comparing the plots both in Fig. 4 and Fig. 5 indicates that with the increase of k, U_r increases but E_r decreases. It also indicates that the increase of a brings the same results as the increase of k. Since with the increase of k, grid system becomes more open and more requests can be admitted, causing that resources become more busier and resource contention often happens. Thus, U_r will increase. But the opening characteristic also results that more admitted requests will be aborted at their start time due to resource contention, and then system effectiveness ratio E_r will reduce. Therefore, we conclude that open

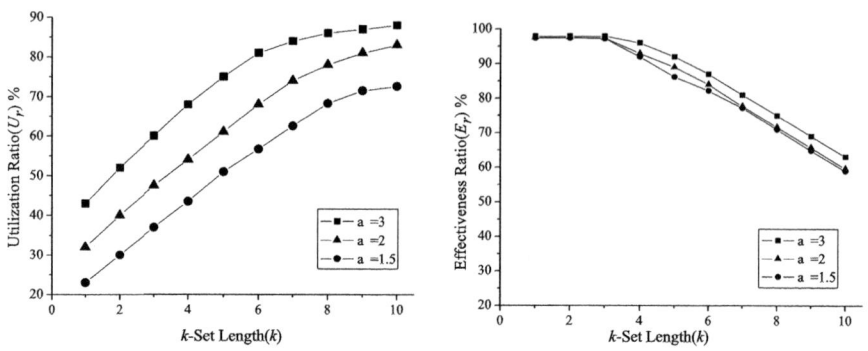

Fig. 4. k-set length (k) vs. U_r **Fig. 5.** k-set length (k) vs. E_r

system has high accept ratio and high resource utilization, but has low system effectiveness ratio. Conversely, conservative system which sets k and a to small values has high system effectiveness ratio, but low accept ratio and low resource utilization. Thus, k and a have to be carefully chosen to achieve good tradeoff between U_r and E_r.

6.2 kAPAC vs. SNAP Strict Negotiation

Most advance reservation architectures compare TLSA with RSLA strictly, called SNAP strict negotiation in this paper. If QoS requirements of a request specified in TSLA can be satisfied by one resource, this request can be admitted. The difference with kAPAC is that this method only considers one resource to satisfy reservation request and compares QoS requirements strictly but not based on QoS Euclidian distance. We assume reservation request arrival process of MC production is a Poisson process, and vary average request inter-arrival time from 500 to 20s. And we set k to 5 and a to 2. Fig. 6 and Fig. 7 compare success ratio S_r and utilization ratio U_r between kAPAC and strict negotiation respectively, whose plots are also measured in 30 minutes. When request arrival rate becomes high, Fig. 6 shows that although S_r reduces in both two cases, kAPAC has higher S_r than strict negotiation all the time and also reduces less slowly. Since when resource contention becomes not negligible, kAPAC can choose resources in great range for it takes QoS Euclidian distance as metric, which satisfies service QoS parameters strictly and bears degradation of provisional QoS parameters. Fig. 7 indicates that kAPAC also leads higher U_r than strict negotiation and brows up quickly when request arrival rate increases. In strict negotiation once one resource can satisfy reservation request this request is admitted, but lack of consideration on availability of this resource. Thus, more requests will be aborted after they are admitted, which results the decrease of U_r.

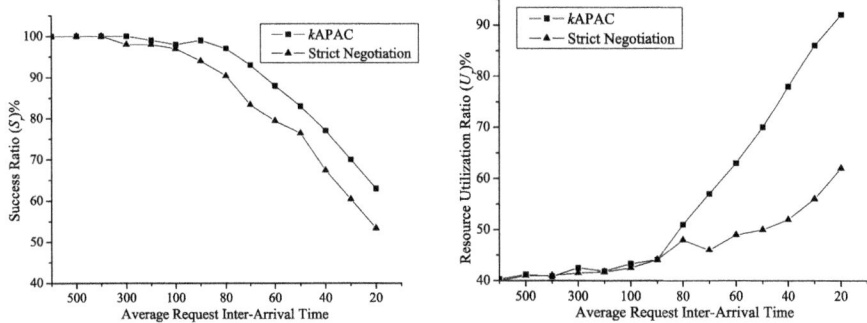

Fig. 6. Comparison between k-APACA and Strict Negotiation on S_r

Fig. 7. Comparison between k-APACA and Strict Negotiation on Resource U_r

7   Conclusion

In this paper, grid system architecture using resource pool is proposed and theoretical analysis for resource pool is conducted. Theoretical analysis demonstrates that the number of resources in pool should be moderate and an algorithm determining approximate optimal resource amount is proposed. Since variable types of QoS attributes are widely different, a uniform framework for computing QoS distance is presented. QoS distance can be utilized to compare the similarity of two requests or between request and resource. kAPAC algorithm proposed in this paper proceeds based on QoS distance comparison. Experiments are conducted in SEUGrid designed for AMS-02 experiment. Comparison between kAPAC and SNAP strict negotiation shows that kAPAC can increase success ratio of reservation, resource utilization and stability of grid system remarkably.

Acknowledgments. This research is supported by National Natural Science Foundation of China under Grants No.71072172, National Soft Science Foundation of China under Grants No. 2010GXS5D208, Jiangsu Provincial Key Laboratory of Network and Information Security (Southeast University) under Grants No.BM2003201, Transformation Fund for Agricultural Science and Technology Achievements under Grants No. 2011GB2C100024 and Innovation Fund for Agricultural Science and Technology in Jiangsu under Grants No. CX(11)3039.

References

1. Gmach, D., Rolia, J., Cherkasova, L., Kemper, A.: Resource Pool Management: Reactive Versus Proactive or Let's be Friends. Computer Networks 53, 2905–2922 (2009)
2. Malik, Z., Rater, B.A.: Credibility Assessment in Web Services Interactions. World Wide Web: Internet and Web Information Systems 12(1), 3–25 (2009)

3. Czajkowski, K., Ferguson, D.F., Foster, I., et al.: The WS-resource Framework, Version 1.0 (2004),
   http://www-106.ibm.com/developerworks/library/ws-resource/ws-wsrf.pdf
4. MacLaren, J.: Advance Reservations: State of the Art, GGF GRAAP-WG (2003),
   http://www.fz-juelich.de/zam/RD/coop/ggf/graap/graap-wg.html
5. Foster, I., Roy, A., Sander, V.: A uality of Service Architecture That Combines Resource Reservation and Application Adaptation. In: International Workshop on uality of Service, pp. 181–188 (2000)
6. Li, C., Li, L.: Utility -based Scheduling for Grid Computing under Constraints of Energy Budget and Deadline. Computer Standards & Interfaces 31(6), 1131–1142 (2009)
7. Siddiqui, M., Villazon, A., Fahringer, T.: Grid Capacity Planning with Negotiation-based Advance Reservation for Optimized   oS. In: Proceedings of the ACM/IEEE Supercomputing Conference, Tampa, Florida, USA, pp. 21–36 (2006)
8. Czajkowski, K., Foster, I., Kesselman, C., Sander, V., Tuecke, S.: SNAP: A Protocol for Negotiating Service Level Agreements and Coordinating Resource Management in Distributed Systems. In: Feitelson, D.G., Rudolph, L., Schwiegelshohn, U. (eds.) JSSPP 2002. LNCS, vol. 2537, pp. 153–183. Springer, Heidelberg (2002)
9. Liu, Y.H., Liu, X.M., Ni, L.M., Zhang, X.D.: Location-Aware Topology Matching in P2P Systems. In: Proceedings of IEEE INFOCOM 2004, pp. 2220–2230 (2004)
10. Wu, Y., Yang, G., Mao, J., Shi, S., Zheng, W.: Grid Computing Pool and Its Framework. In: International Conference on Parallel Processing Workshops (2003)
11. Subrata, R., Zomaya, A.Y., Landfeldt, B.: Game-Theoretic Approach for Load Balancing in Computational Grids. IEEE Trans. on Parallel and Distributed Systems 19(1), 66–76 (2008)
12. Luo, J., Song, A.-B., Zhu, Y., Wang, X., Ma, T., Wu, Z.-A., Xu, Y., Ge, L.: Grid Supporting Platform for AMS Data Processing. In: Chen, G., Pan, Y., Guo, M., Lu, J. (eds.) ISPA-WS 2005. LNCS, vol. 3759, pp. 276–285. Springer, Heidelberg (2005)

A Way of Key Management in Cloud Storage Based on Trusted Computing

Xin Yang[1,2,3], Qingni Shen[1,2,3,*], Yahui Yang[1], and Sihan Qing[1,4]

[1] School of Software and Microelectronics,
Peking University, Beijing, China
[2] MoE Key Lab of Network and Software Assurance,
Peking University, Beijing, China
[3] Network & Information Security Lab., Institute of Software,
Peking University, Beijing, China
[4] Institute of Software, Chinese Academy of Sciences, Beijing 100086, China
yangxin@pku.edu.cn, {qingnishen,yhyang,qsihan}@ss.pku.edu.cn

Abstract. Cloud security has gained increasingly emphasis in the research community, with much focus primary concentrated on how to secure the operation system and virtual machine on which cloud system runs on. We take an alternative perspective to consider the problem of building a secure cloud storage service on top of a public cloud infrastructure where the service provider is not completely trusted by the customer. So, it is necessary to put cipher text into the public cloud. We describe an architecture based on Trusted Platform Module and the client of cloud storage system to help manage the symmetric keys used for encrypting data in the public cloud and the asymmetric keys used for encrypting symmetric keys. The key management mechanism includes how to store keys, how to backup keys, and how to share keys. Based on the HDFS (Hadoop Distributed File System), we put a way of key management into practice, and survey the benefits that such an infrastructure will provide to cloud users and providers, and we also survey the time cost it will bring to us.

Keywords: cipher text, key management, symmetric keys, asymmetric keys, backup, public cloud.

1 Introduction

With the development in networking technology and the increasing need for computing resources, many companies have been prompted to outsource their storage and computing needs. This new economic computing model is commonly regarded as cloud computing and includes various types of services[1] such as: infrastructure as a service (IaaS), where a customer makes use of a service provider's computing, storage or networking infrastructure; platform as a service (PaaS), where a customer leverages the provider's resources to run custom applications; and finally software as a service (SaaS), where customers use software that is run on the providers infrastructure.

---

* Corresponding author.

E. Altman and W. Shi (Eds.): NPC 2011, LNCS 6985, pp. 135–145, 2011.

Cloud can be commonly classified as either private or public. In a private cloud, the infrastructure is managed and owned by the company or individual which means accessing to data is under its control and is only granted to parties they trusts. However, in a public cloud the infrastructure is owned and managed by a cloud service provider, which means that customer's data is beyond of its control and therefore could be acquired by illegal parties [7, 10].

Storage services based on public clouds such as Microsoft's Azure storage service and Amazon's S3 provide customers with scalable and dynamic storage. By moving their data to the cloud customers can avoid the costs of building and maintaining a private storage infrastructure, opting instead to pay a service provider as a function of its needs. For most customers, this provides several benefits including availability (i.e. we cannot access data from anywhere) and reliability (i.e. we do not have to worry about backups) at a relatively low cost.

Although the benefits of using a public cloud infrastructure are apparent, it introduces significant security and privacy risks. In fact, it seems that the biggest difficulty is how to guarantee the confidentiality and the integrity of data [4, 10]. While, so far, consumers have been willing to trade privacy for the convenience of software services (e.g., for web-based email etc), this is not the case for enterprises and governments, and especially for military departments. Any customers do not want to store mission-critical data or private data like personally identifiable information, or medical and financial records [7, 8, 9]. So, unless the problem of confidentiality and integrity are addressed properly, many potential customers are reluctant to use the public cloud instead of the traditional computing facility.

As a customer, there are many reasons to consider that the public cloud is unsafe [8]. Importing our data into public cloud enables us to face at least the following threats.

First, as a result of the limit of our law and technology, while we can trust the cloud providers, they cannot guarantee if one of the operators of the cloud will steal our data directly, because they can have the capacity and the authority to get data easily.

Second, the traditional network attack. When we upload data into public cloud, it is totally possible that attackers can intercept or destroy our data.

Third, unlike data stored in our personal computer, the data stored in the cloud is not isolated from other people's data. As a result, the risk of being attacked of our data in the cloud is increasing.

Last but not least, the same to the traditional storage system, the public cloud is also faced the threat of attacker from all over the world.

To address the concerns stated above and increase the usage of cloud storage. We are suggesting designing *Private Data Protecting Service (PDPS)* based on the architecture of Trusted Computing and the client of public cloud. Such a service should aim to encrypt the data that will be uploaded into cloud and protect the keys used for encryption. More precisely, such a service should provide:

- Confidentiality: the encryption before data is uploaded to the public cloud and decryption service after data is downloaded from the cloud.
- Key management: be responsible for the protection the keys from various kinds of attack, at the same time, the relationship between data and keys will also be maintained in this part.

- Data sharing: customers can share data by ways sharing their keys safely which are related to the data.
- Key backup: it is possible that our client which stores keys will collapse suddenly. So there must be a mechanism for key backup, and more importantly the backup must not be used by illegal customer.

PDPS is built based on the client of public cloud, the coupling factor between the public cloud and *PDPS* is nearly zero, so we can retain the main benefits of a public cloud:

- Availability: customer's data is accessible from any machine with a TPM and at all times.
- Reliability: customer data is reliably backed up by backing up the keys.
- Data sharing: customers can share their data with trusted parties by sharing keys.

2   Background and Motivation

With the development of Trusted Computing Organization, TPM 1.2 they produced (Trusted Platform Module) serves a very important part to key storage, data signing, IMA and remote attestation.

2.1   Key Management and Cloud

As shown in [5], there are tremendously large amount of files in the cloud, if we encrypt them one by one, there must be the same amount of keys we should manage safely. If we encrypt thousands of files by the same key, it is very easy for attackers to get the key by analysis of the encrypted text [6]. One of techniques that TPM use for storing data and keys in a secure fashion is to use encryption to store data, and to use encryption and decryption to control access to that data. Although a TPM is somewhat similar to a smart card chip, one difference is that it is attached (through the PC) to a large amount of persistent storage. One of the design goals for secure storage is to take advantage of the persistent storage to store a large amount of private keys and symmetric keys [2]. As a result, we can store a large amount of encrypted data that is associated with the TPM. However, TPM does not help us to manage the map between the Keys and the data. So we should add the mapping service into the private data protecting service.

2.2   RNG

As stated in [2], in order to generate keys internally, it is necessary for the TPM to have an internal random number generator (RNG). Typically, instead of having a true random number generator (it is difficult to do), many TPMs have pseudo random number generators (PRNGs) that are periodically fed with entropy from timing measurements or other sources of entropy within the TPM itself. This entropy is then distilled into the current seed, so entropy is always increasing. The output of the PRNG or RNG is used to generate keys, nonce, and seeds in the PKCS#1 V2.0 blob creation. Hence, in the solution, the keys are provided by the TPM instead of customs. At the same time TPM provide a series of interfaces for legal customs to manage the keys in a simple way.

2.3   Key Structure

Figure 1 shows the basic setup of keys inside a TPM. In the figure, if Key 2 is directly below Key 1, then Key 2 is encrypted (Asymmetric Encryption) with the public key corresponding to Key 1. Thus, we see that User 1 migratable storage is wrapped with the platform migratable key, which is in turn wrapped with the SRK. User 1's non-migratable storage key is also wrapped with the SRK. Hence, the architecture of keys is a tree structure.

```
┌──────────────────────────────────────────────────────┐
│                          TPM                          │
│                                                        │
│  Base Key(non-migratable):SRK    Key4:User 1 Non-mig Storage Key │
│                                                        │
│  Key1:Platform Mig Storage Key   Key5:                 │
│                                                        │
│  Key2:User 1 Mig Storage Key     Key6:                 │
│                                                        │
│  Key3:                           Key7:                 │
└──────────────────────────────────────────────────────┘
```

Fig. 1. Basic key structure of TPM

2.4   Migratable Keys versus Non-migratable Keys

Migratable keys are meant for two purposes. As shown in [3], the first is to provide a quick way to transfer keys from one platform to another in the event that a user wants to change his or her facilities, either because of upgrading or other reasons. The second is to provide the capability for more than one system to use a key. Keys can be valuable if they have associated certificates, or store a lot of data. For example, if a key is used for signing e-mail, a person might want to use it at home and at work or on multiple systems. A key that is used to store symmetric keys might be shared among a group, so only members of that group have access to the keys necessary to decrypt a shared file.

2.5   Motivation

First, using persistent storage appears to have a major problem. It is possible that the computer that stores key collapses or some other disasters happen, our solution needs to take into account disaster recovery. So we add *Backup Service* into the architecture. Second, as a customer in the cloud, it is totally possible that customers need to share data with some other ones safely. In other words, he should send related keys to others. In our solution, we provide *Key Sharing Service* to help customers to share their keys safely by constructing a backup structure, and the whole process for sharing keys and backing up keys is maintained by the structure. Third, as to data that has high confidentiality, customers do not wanted them to be shared, so in this solution, we provide a interface to enable customer to decide the confidential level of their data neatly.

3   Architecture of a Private Data Protecting Service

We now describe a possible architecture for PDPS, as shown in Figure 2, the architecture includes four sub services (also called functional modules): *data encryption service*, which processes data before it is sent to the cloud; *data decryption service*: which processes data after it is received from the cloud; *backup service*, which backs up keys in a safe way; *data sharing service*, which enables customers to share data among trusted parties. In the figure, the right side shows four basic modules, among these modules RNG (random number generator), the structure of key tree, and the operation of migration are maintained by the function of TPM. The structure of *key data mapping* is implemented outside TPM. As shown in Figure 2, the thick lines represent the key flow between modules, while the thin ones indicate the call of function between functional modules.

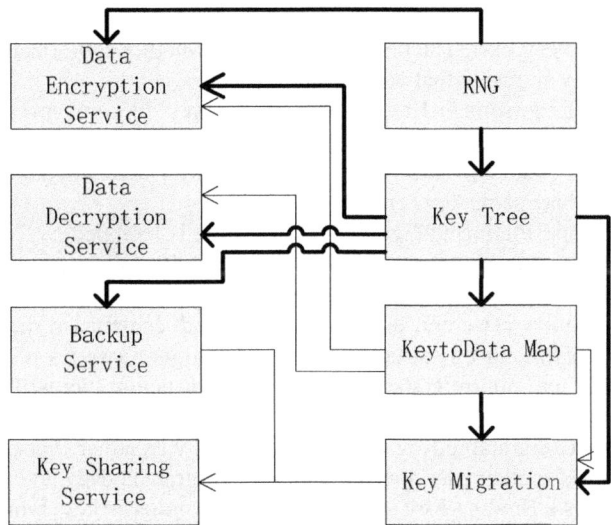

Fig. 2. Architecture of PDPS

3.1   Create Key Structure of Cloud

As show in Figure 3, we design a logical structure of keys we will use in the client end of cloud storage system. The characters shown in every square represents in which step the key will be generated. Every square in Figure 3 represents a key. The process of creating such a structure includes (the creation process is based on the assumption that the TPM in the cloud client have not been used, it is just a new TPM):

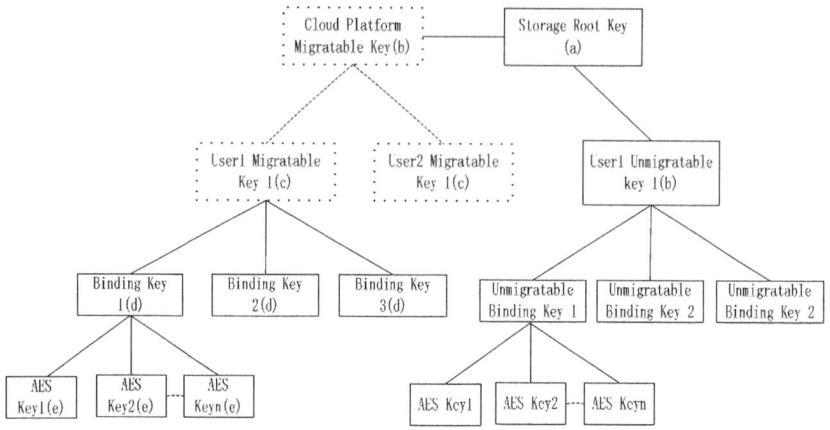

Fig. 3. Key Structure of Cloud

- Upon activating the TPM (or upon reset), the TPM will use its random number generator to create a new base 2048-bit SRK key. The SRK is required to be non-migratable and to be a 2048 (or greater) storage key, but other parameters are left to the end user. The parameters include whether authorization is required to use the key and what that authorization is.
- Create EK (Endorsement Key), especially this key does not involve in the Key Tree, When a TPM comes to a new user, it typically does not include anything other than an endorsement key (EK), EK is used for authentication when the user needs to share some keys or use others' keys.
- Create a Cloud Platform Migratable Key which is wrapped by its father key—SRK, the construction of a RSA Key contains the following steps: first, call RNG method to generate a 1024 bits or 2048 bits pair that includes public key and a private key p(we choose 1024 bits); second, construct a structure that can be used by TPM, in this structure, we can configure a series of attributes like "migratable" or "non-migratable", after the construction, we will move the key from the inner of the TPM to persistent storage.
- Create User1 Migratable Key which is wrapped by its father Platform Key. If the client end has another user, then create User2 Migratable Key.
- User1 creates a Binding Key (used for encrypt symmetric key) which is wrapped by User1 Migratable Key.
- If user1 want to encrypt a file, he will create a AES Key(a leaf in the key structure) and wrap the key by one of his binding key.
- If user1 have some classified data and he is sure that he does not need to share it with some other ones. hence, he can create a User1 Non-migratable Key, the rest steps are same to a Use1 Migratable Key.

3.2   Data Processing Service

Data Processing Service contains Data Encryption Service and Data Decryption Service.

A user Alice stores her data in the cloud. Before it is sent to the cloud, the data encryption service will call the function of RNG to generate a symmetric key (we adopt a 256 bits AES key), then the service uses the symmetric key to encrypt the upload filter of the data. After the encryption, the service encrypt the symmetric key by one of the user's binding key, then input the relation between the symmetric key and the binding key and the relation between the encrypted file and binding key into a map.

When Alice gets a file from the cloud, after the authentication of TPM, the client will open a download filter. The Data Decryption Service will get the key related to the file according to the map stated in the 3.2, then use the Key to decrypt the download filter, then Alice get the plaintext.

3.3   The Backup Service

As stated in Specification of Trusted Computing, the non-migratable key cannot be migrated out from the TPM. So, in this section, we talk about the backup of migratable keys. In addition, as all we know, public key in the migratable key is not sensitive. The goal we will achieve is to ensure the private key must not be got by illegal parties when we move this private part of key out of TPM.

1.   We design a structure to describe the migration authentication. In Figure 4, TPM owner authorize three kind of authority to the migratable key. The first is use authority that means the key can be used by legal customers. The second is migration authority that means the key can be migrated by the owner of the key. The third is encryption authority that means the key can be encrypted by trusted third parties (generally, trusted third party indicates the customer whom you want to share your key with). Combine the three authorization we get a migration authentication structure:

```
Struct TPM_MIGRATIONKEYAUTH{
        TPM_PUBKEY migrationKey;
        TPM_MIGRATE_SCHEME migrationScheme;
        TPM_DIGEST digest;} TPM_MIGRATIONKEYAUTH;

Digest= SHA-1(migrationKey || migrationScheme
                ||TPM_PERMANENT_DATA -> tpmProof)
```

Fig. 4. Migration Authentication Structure

Migrationkey represents the public key provided by the trusted party. Migration Scheme represents the scheme in which key will be migrated. When TPM owner change, the TPM Proof changes too, hence the digest, at this case, the MIGRATIONKEYAUTH will be invalid.

2.   Check the migration authentication structure to see if the key is migratable and if the wrapping key has the authority to wrap the migratable key. If both checks are passed, we can get the migratable key from key structure stated in Chapter 3.1.

3.   Construct the backup structure, as shown in Figure 5, the construction contains three steps:

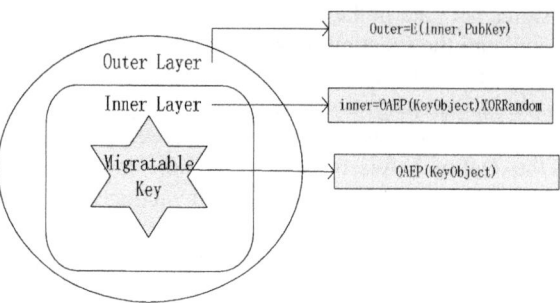

Fig. 5. Backup structure

- Use OAEP (defined in RSA PKCS1 V2.1) to codify the key object that is attained in the step 2. The process protects the key from being tampered by vicious cloud storage manager.
- Call the RNG method to generate a random, and XOR it with OAEP(Key Object), then we get the inner layer.
- Use the authorized public key to encrypt the inner layer, then we get the outer layer

4. The backup object can be stored in many ways. When we need to inject the backup object, the process contains 4 steps.
    - Customer input password get the authority to communicate with TPM in the target platform.
    - The target platform receives the backup object, and then, the TPM gets the private key from the key structure.
    - Decrypt the backup object with the private key, then we get the inner layer
    - After the Key owner provides the random which is used in the backup construction process, we can use the random to XOR the inner layer to get the key object.

3.4   The Key Sharing Service

The key sharing service will use the backup structure stated in Chapter 3.3. The sharing process concludes:

- When customer Alice needs to share a file with Bob, first, Bob will send a public key (the corresponding private key has existed in the key tree in Bob's TPM) to Alice.
- Alice use the public key to create a backup object by the process stated in Chapter 3.3, after the process, Alice sends the backup object to Bob.
- After Bob receives the backup object, he will use the process stated in the chapter 3.3 to inject the key object into Bob's TPM. After the injection, Bob can use the key freely.

4　Constructing the Prototype and the Performance Evaluation

We implement PDPS in HDFS (Hadoop Distributed File System). Our experiment is constructed using four computers with an Intel Core 2 processor running at 1.86 GHz, 2048 MB of RAM, and a 7200 RPM Western Digital 250 GB Serial ATA drive with an 8 MB buffer – one namenode, two datanodes, and one client. As shown in Figure 6, they are all in the same Ethernet.

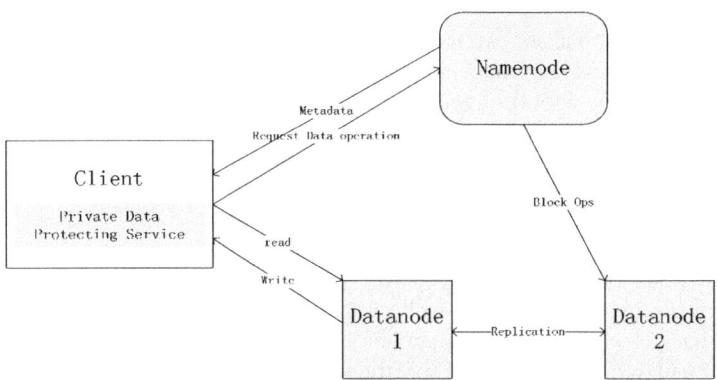

Fig. 6. Architecture of HDFS with PDPS

Compared to HDFS without a PDSP, the time we will used for PDPS (when uploading a file) includes the time it costs to generate a symmetric key, the time it costs for encryption of the file upload filter, and the time it costs for encryption of the symmetric key and persistence of the symmetric key. Especially, the time cost for encrypting the file upload filter is offset by the time cost for uploading the file. Table1 shows the time we cost when we upload various kinds of data with the PDSP comparing the uploading without a PDSP.Table2 shows the time we cost when we download files of various amounts.

Table 1. Time consumption of uploading a file

File size	1K	1M	32M	128M	1G
with PDSP (ms)	635	1322	3133	12227	93744
without PDSP (ms)	523	1088	2746	11601	92532
Cost percentage	21.4	21.1	14.1	4.54	1.21

Table 2. Time consumption of downloading a file

File size	1K	1M	32M	128M	1G
with PDSP (ms)	1456	3056	10056	35452	3065256
without PDSP (ms)	1178	2532	8999	32669	2955235
Cost percentage	23.6	20.7	11.7	8.5	3.7

From Table1 and Table2, we can see the cost percentage decreases when the file size is growing. So we can make a conclusion that the PDSP suits for the cloud storage system that cope with files with large size like HDFS.

5   Conclusions and Future Work

In this paper, we have presented the architecture of private protecting service to keep the data in cloud safe. In the service, we explored a new fashion of data backup in a more flexible way. If user1 want to backup all his keys, he just needs to construct only one backup object—user1 migratable key. If the cloud system platform needs backup all its keys, it just needs to construct only one backup object—cloud platform migratable key. So, the same cost to the key sharing service. In the further study, we will implement the smaller unit of data process like Chunk in GFS, or block in HDFS and propose detailed designs for the authentication framework that will be used in key sharing service based on signature, remote attestation. The private data protecting service can be adopted by almost all of the cloud storage system, because it is based on the client end and have no interaction with the server or cloud provider.

Acknowledgement. This work is supported by National Natural Science Foundation of China under Grant No. 60873238, 61073156, 61070237, 60970135, and our IBM SUR 2009 Project.

References

1. Kmara, S., Lauter, K.: Cryptographic Cloud Storage. In: Proceedings of Financial Cryptography: Workshop on Real-Life Cryptographic Protocols and Standardization 2010, pp. 111–116 (January 2010)
2. Challener, D., Yoder, K.: A Practical Guide To Trusted Computing, pp. 17–18. IBM Press (2009)
3. Balacheff, B., Chen, L.: Trusted Computing Platforms, pp. 166–167. Prentice Hall PTR, Englewood Cliffs (2009)
4. Wang, C., Wang, Q., Ren, K., Lou, W.: Ensuring data storage security in cloud computing. In: Proc. of IWQoS 2009, Charleston, South Carolina, USA (2009)
5. Ateniese, G., Di Pietro, R., Mancini, L.V., Tsudik, G.: Scalable and efficient provable data possession. In: Proc. of SecureComm. (2008)

6. Stallings, W.: Cyptography and Network Security Principles and Practices, 4th edn., pp. 59–60 (2006)
7. Christodorescu, M., Sailer, R., Schales, D.L., Sgandurra, D., Zamboni, D.: Cloud Security is not (just) Virtualization Security. In: Proc. CCSW (2009)
8. Dean, J., Ghemawat, S.: Mapreduce: Simplied data processing on large clusters. In: Proc. OSDI (2004)
9. Haeberlen, A., Kuznetsov, P., Druschel, P.: PeerReview:Practical Accountability for Distributed Systems. In: Proc. SOSP (2007)
10. Jensen, M., Schwenk, J., Gruschka, N., Iacono, L.L.: On Technical Security Issues in Cloud Computing. In: Proc. CLOUD (2009)

A Trust-Based Defensive System Model for Cloud Computing

Qian Zhou[1], Jiong Yu[1], and Feiran Yu[2]

[1] College of Information Science and Engineering, Xin jiang University,
Urumqi, Xin jiang, China
{zhouqian,yujiong}@xju.edu.cn
[2] Control & Computer Technology School, North China Electric Power University,
Beijing, China
yufeiran@yahoo.com.cn

Abstract. Because of the dynamic and open characteristics of the cloud computing, continuing malicious attacks happen frequently. Combining the idea of trusted cloud, a trust-based defensive system model for cloud computing has been constructed to guarantee the cloud security. Through real-timely monitoring, users' behavior evidences have been obtained and standardized; a new method for users' trust evaluation based on fuzzy AHP (Analytic Hierarchy Process, AHP) has been presented, it gradually determines the weights of behavior evidences, achieves quantitative assessment of behavioral trust; to provide great security defense for users, multiple detection engines have been used to conduct a comprehensive inspection of suspicious files and integrated decisions have been made. Experimental results show the system model can effectively eliminate the malicious behaviors from undesirable users, reduce users' damages caused by virus and achieve a two-way defense for both cloud and client.

Keywords: cloud security, trusted cloud, trust, behavioral evidence, fuzzy AHP, multiple detection engines.

1   Introduction

In the face of continuing malicious attacks, the simple methods of intrusion detection, virus detection and secure login protocol have been unable to cope with a variety of network attacks and damages, therefore cloud security and trusted cloud [1] came into being. Cloud security is intended to eliminate existing viruses, trojans and malicious files in the network. Trusted cloud is guaranteed safe from the user terminals; combining the idea of trusted network [2], it evaluates, forecasts, monitors and manages user behaviors to eliminate malicious attacks to data center from undesirable users and hackers in the cloud to enhance the security of the cloud environment.

In recent years, many scholars began the research of the trust mechanism to make up the defect of traditional security mechanisms that the trust of user behaviors was not considered. Song et al.[3] propose a dynamic trust model based on fuzzy logic under

E. Altman and W. Shi (Eds.): NPC 2011, LNCS 6985, pp. 146–159, 2011.
© IFIP International Federation for Information Processing 2011

grid environment, this model has better capacities of detecting and defending malicious entities, while the downside is that the convergence of computing and system scalability are poor, it does not consider the calculation of the indirect trust and the trust can not reflect the overall credibility. Power-Trust[4] is a P2P reputation system based on the power law distribution, the system uses power law to collect feedback from local nodes, and gets global reputation through the super-nodes generated from queuing mechanism, significantly improves the accuracy of global reputation and accelerates the rate of polymerization. Jameel introduces vector operation mechanism to establish the trust model [5], its most notable feature is the introduction of the trust factor, historical factors and the time factor to reflect dynamic trust relationship, but it can not solve the cheating behaviors when recommending and has no risk analysis. A new trust quantitative model based on multi-dimensional decision-making properties is proposed in paper [6]; it introduces direct trust, risk function, feedback trust, activation function and physical activity level and other decision-making attributes to assess the complexity and uncertainty of trust relationship from various angles.

Through analyzing and comparing the existing trust models, studying the trusted cloud and reputation technology of the client cloud [7], in this paper we change traditional ideas of network defense which are for their own business and propose a trust-based defensive system model in the cloud environment. This model has integrated trust and risk evaluation mechanisms and provides maximum security defense to customers in the cloud and the network security and defense functions are provided as services to end customers.

2   Architecture of Defensive Model

Cooperation between network services, resources, applications provided by cloud computing and customers depends on the trust relationship between them. In this paper, the system model is built by borrowing the idea of trusted network, therefore the network entities' behavioral states can be monitored, behavioral outcomes can be assessed and abnormal behaviors can be controlled [8].

2.1   Physical Structure

The system consists of Cloud Client (CC), File Monitoring and Analyzing center (FMA), Behavior Monitoring center (BM) and Trust Management center (TM) in which CC is a lightweight terminal located in the client and the rest are high-performance large-scale servers in the cloud. Figure 1 shows model's physical structure.

CC is responsible for submitting samples of suspicious files and executes the final decision.

FMA is composed of file detecting engines and file behavior analyzing engine. Using virtualization technology and multi-engine detection mechanism, FMA takes a full inspection to the uploaded suspicious files and returns the test results to the customer.

BM is consisted of a behavioral evidence obtaining module and a standardizing module. It monitors customers' behaviors continuously, obtains and standardizes users' behavioral evidences.

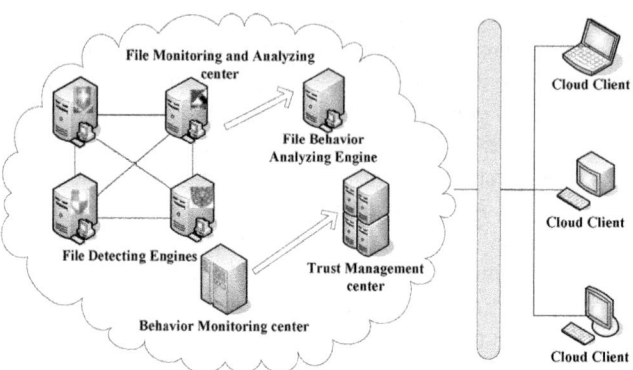

Fig. 1. Physical structure of the defensive system

TM is consisted of a behavior database, a behavioral trust evaluating module and a trust database. It stores users' behavioral evidences, evaluates users' trust degree and saves users' overall trust degree.

2.2   Logical Structure

To provide security and defensive services for the massive clients, this model is designed to take full advantages of the high computing power and storage power of the cloud computing. At the same time, the system monitors and assesses users' behaviors to eliminate malicious attacks from undesirable users which are in interaction in the cloud to achieve a two-way defensive purpose. Figure 2 shows the flow chart of the model.

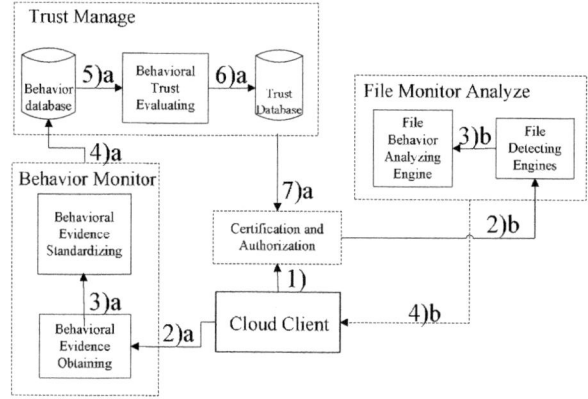

Fig. 2. Flowchart of the defensive system

The system flow can be divided into the following steps: 1) When a user login to the cloud, the cloud's certification and authorization module queries Trust Management center to give the user a trust level and the corresponding operating authorities; 2)a The user is monitored by Behavior Monitoring center continuously and behavioral evidence obtaining module gets the user's behavioral evidences; 3)a Evidences obtained from the user will be standardized by Behavioral standardizing module; 4)a Behavior Monitoring center dumps standardized behavioral evidences to the behavior trust database in Trust Management center; 5)a Trust evaluation module uses the data in the behavior database to evaluate the user's trust value; 6)a Trust evaluation module sends the user's trust value to the trust database; 7)a In the basis of the user's trust value, the certification and authorization module authorizes real-time permission to the user; 2)b Suspicious file samples are submitted to File Monitoring and Analyzing center through Cloud Client by the client; 3)b Suspicious files that are unable to be determined by file detecting engines are submitted to file analyzing engine for real-timely dynamic behavioral analysis; 4)b The final decisive results of the suspicious files are returned to the client by Files Monitoring and Analysis center and the final decision is taken by the user.

The system's processing flow is composed by two extensions: 'a' process provides defense for the cloud through evaluating the user's behavior trust and giving the appropriate operating authorities to the user; 'b' process contains detecting and analyzing malicious files uploaded by the end user, establishing the latest and most complete trusted/malicious file database to provide maximum defense for users in the cloud.

2.3   Relevant Description

Definition 1. Suppose there are m measure items for measuring users trust degree, let $E=\{E_1, E_2, ..., E_m\}$ denote m kinds of behavioral evidence and the measured values are expressed as $I=\{I_1, I_2, ..., I_m\}$. Let w_i ($1\leq i\leq m$) represents the importance of the ith piece of evidence relative to the other evidences, and meet

$$0 \leq w_i \leq 1, \quad \sum_{i=1}^{m} w_i = 1$$

Definition 2. Let Tr denote the overall trust degree of the user evaluated by the cloud, denoted as Overall Trust Degree (OTD) and OTD is the basis for the user to get authorities during the interaction with the cloud.

Definition 3. Suppose set C is the behavior trust classification space, denoted as $C=\{C_1, C_2,...,C_p\}$, respectively represents $p+1$ trust levels for Tr, where $0<C_p<1$ and $1\leq p\leq m$. C has following properties: $C_i\cap C_j=\Phi(i\neq j)$, $C_1<C_2<...<C$, and C_{k+1} is stronger than C_k, then we say C is an ordered partition class.

Definition 4. Suppose the cloud provides k levels of services denoted $Se=\{Se_1, Se_2,..., Se_k\}$, Se is an ordered partition class, and the mapping function between Se and Tr is

$$fs(Tr) = \begin{cases} Se_k, & C_{k-1} < Tr \le 1 \\ \cdots \\ Se_2, & C_1 < Tr \le C_2 \\ Se_1, & 0 < Tr \le C_1 \end{cases} \tag{1}$$

Where C_k etc. are defined by definition 3. When a user requests to the cloud for services, the user will be decided his service level based on his trust level to reduce existing potential risk of the user.

For example, some cloud operator provides 3 levels of services, then Se={Se_1, Se2, Se3}. Which, Se_1 denote services are denied, Se_2 denote files are read only, Se_3 denote files can be edited. Trust level space is set to C={C_1, $C2$}={0.3, 0.6}, the decision-making function for services is

$$fs(Tr) = \begin{cases} Se_3, & 0.6 < Tr \le 1 \\ Se_2, & 0.3 < Tr \le 0.6 \\ Se_1, & 0 < Tr \le 0.3 \end{cases}$$

If Tr = 0.7, then the decision-making process is $fs(Tr) = f(0.7) = Se_3$= file can be edited.

Definition 5. Let $Trp(0 \le Trp \le 1)$ denote the trust properties of the suspicious files after being detected by the cloud; suspicious files trust level space is denoted by V={V_1, V_2}, and $V_1 < V_2 \in (0, 1)$. So, the decision-making function for suspicious files trust levels is

$$fp(Trp) = \begin{cases} Trusted, & V_2 \le Trp < 1 \\ Unknown, & V_1 \le Trp < V_2 \\ Malicious, & 0 \le Trp < V_1 \end{cases} \tag{2}$$

3   Behavioral Evidences

3.1   Obtaining Evidences

User's behavioral evidences (evidences for short) can be obtained directly from the detection of system software and hardware, which are the base values for quantitatively assessing user's overall behaviors [9]. Current methods for obtaining evidences are: intrusion detection systems, such as Snort, which can detect worms, vulnerabilities, port scanning and a variety of suspicious behaviors; network traffic detection and analysis tools, such as Bandwidthd, you can view highly detailed IP traffic and network status; professional network data collection tools, such as Flunk's NetFlow Tracker, which can get real-time network bandwidth utilization and bandwidth usage of different users and so on.

3.2   Standardizing Evidences

Evidences have many forms: specific values, such as the number of scanning an important port; percentage, such as CPU utilization; binary, such as data integrity (1 if data is complete, 0 if data is incomplete). In order to facilitate numerical calculation and assessment to user behavior, evidences need to be standardized as positive increasing dimensionless values in the interval [0, 1].

Let $A = (a_{ij})_{m \times n}$ denote initial evidences matrix and we normalize A to evidences matrix $E = (e_{ij})_{m \times n}$, the rules are:

① Evidences of percentage and binary forms are already in [0,1] and they are translated into positive increasing values using equation (3)

$$e_{ij} = \begin{cases} a_{ij} & , when \ a_{ij} \ is \ positive \ increasin g \\ 1 - a_{ij} & , when \ a_{ij} \ is \ positive \ decreasin g \end{cases} \tag{3}$$

② Evidences of specific values are normalized into positive increasing values in [0,1] using equation (4)

$$e_{ij} = \begin{cases} \dfrac{a_{ij} - \left(a_{ij}\right)_{min}}{\left(a_{ij}\right)_{max} - \left(a_{ij}\right)_{min}} & , when \ a_{ij} \ is \ positive \ increa \sin g \\ \dfrac{\left(a_{ij}\right)_{max} - a_{ij}}{\left(a_{ij}\right)_{max} - \left(a_{ij}\right)_{min}} & , when \ a_{ij} \ is \ positive \ decrea \sin g \end{cases} \tag{4}$$

Where, $(a_{ij})_{min}$ and $(a_{ij})_{max}$ respectively express the minimum and maximum evidence.

4   Evaluation Model Based on FAHP

AHP (Analytic Hierarchy Process) is a system analysis method combining qualitative and quantitative analysis [10]. The traditional AHP has following shortcomings [11]: it uses nine scales to construct judgment matrix and this is too complex in practice; it needs to judge and build matrix continuously until the matrix meets consistency verification with large calculation and low precision.

In order to overcome the problems in AHP, this paper uses fuzzy analytic hierarchy process (Fuzzy AHP). FAHP uses three scales to construct a judgment matrix to facilitate decision-makers easily decide in two factors which is relatively important; and the initial judgment matrix is transformed into the fuzzy consistent matrix that satisfies the consistency condition without consistency test.

4.1   A Hierarchical Structure of Evidences

Evidences are divided into several trust properties gradually by layer, and then broken down into specific evidences' types, which can effectively resolve the general and uncertain problems of user's behavioral trust under cloud computing. A hierarchical structure of evidences is shown in Figure 3.

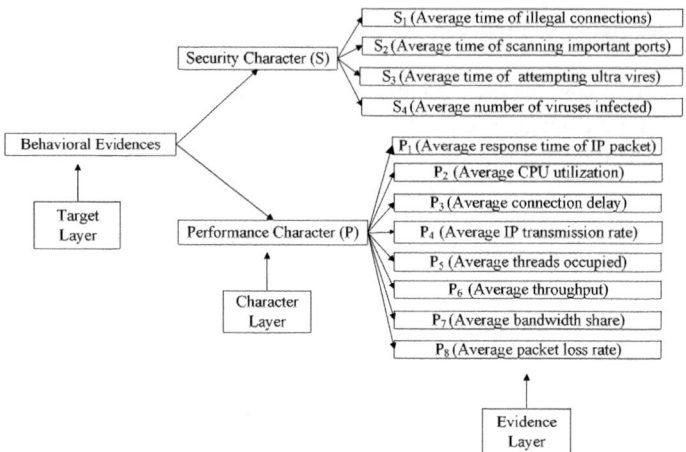

Fig. 3. Hierarchical structure of user's behavioral evidences

4.2   The Weight Determined by FAHP

(1) Establish an initial judgement matrix

In Figure 3, suppose there are m evidences related to the performance character, respectively denoted as $\{ep_1, ep_2, ..., ep_m\}$. For the m evidences, according to their importance relevant to the performance character, through pairwise comparison we get an m-order initial judgment matrix $EP = (ep_{ij})_{m \times m}$

$$ep_{ij} = \begin{cases} 0.5 & , c(i) = c(j) \\ 1 & , c(i) > c(j) \\ 0 & , c(i) < c(j) \end{cases} \tag{5}$$

Where, $c(i)=c(j))$ express evidence ep_i is equally important as ep_j; $c(i)>c(j)$ express evidence ep_i is important than ep_j; $c(i)<c(j)$ express evidence ep_i is less important than ep_j.

(2) Steps of sum and transformation of line are used to convert the initial judgment matrix $EP=(ep_{ij})_{m \times m}$ to the fuzzy consistent matrix $Q=(q_{ij})_{m \times m}$ without consistency verification.

$$q_{ij} = \frac{q_i - q_j}{a} + 0.5 \tag{6}$$

$$\left(q_i = \sum_{k=1}^{m} ep_{ik}, i = 1, 2, ..., m; a = 2m \right)$$

(3) When conducting sum of line for the fuzzy consistent matrix Q, self-comparison (i.e., diagonal element) is not contained. The weight vector $W= (w_1, w_2...w_m)^T$ is Calculated using equation (7)

$$w_i = l_i \bigg/ \sum_i l_i \tag{7}$$

Where, l_i denote evidence p_i's importance relative to the upper performance character

$$l_i = \sum_{k=1}^{m} q_{ik} - 0.5, \quad i = 1,2,\ldots m \tag{8}$$

$$\sum_i l_i = m(m-1)\big/2 \tag{9}$$

4.3   The Assessment of User Behavior Character

Suppose user behavior contains n items of features, and k denote the largest item value of the feature (if the item number does not reach k, the corresponding elements are 0); we use Section 3.2 to get standardized evidence matrix $E=(e_{ij})_{m \times n}$, $e_{ij} \in [0,1]$ represents the j th evidence of the i th character and its weight is $w_{ij} \in [0,1]$. Matrix diagonal values calculated by equation (10) are the assessment values of user character.

$$E \times W^T = \begin{pmatrix} e_{11} & e_{12} & \cdots & e_{1k} \\ e_{21} & e_{22} & \cdots & e_{2k} \\ \vdots & \vdots & \ddots & \vdots \\ e_{n1} & e_{n2} & \cdots & e_{nk} \end{pmatrix} \begin{pmatrix} w_{11} & w_{12} & \cdots & w_{1k} \\ w_{21} & w_{22} & \cdots & w_{2k} \\ \vdots & \vdots & \ddots & \vdots \\ w_{n1} & w_{n2} & \cdots & w_{nk} \end{pmatrix}^T \tag{10}$$

4.4   The Overall Trust Evaluation of User Behavior

Set the user feature vector is $F=(f_1,f_2,\ldots,f_n)^T$, the weight vector of the features is $W_f^T=(w_1,w_2,\ldots,w_n)^T$, user's overall trust degree Tr is calculated using equation (11)

$$Tr = 1 - F \times W_f^T = 1 - \sum_{i=1}^{n} f_i w_i \tag{11}$$

5   Evaluation Model for Suspicious Files

Suspicious files may be user's normal files, original virus files, files infected by virus, files corrupted by virus, malicious software and so on. In order to reduce the losses caused by viruses and malicious software, we use multi -engine detection mechanism and dynamic behavior analysis to test comprehensively the suspicious files uploaded by the user.

5.1   Multi-engine Detection Mechanism

As a single engine can not conduct a comprehensive inspection to suspicious files, file detection engine in File Monitoring and Analysis center (FMA) then uses multi-engine detection mechanism.

(1) Suppose we use n kinds of detection engines denoted as $Eg=\{Eg_1,Eg_2,...,Eg_n\}$ and the accuracy of the engines is $Per=\{Per_1,Per_2,...,Per_n\}$.

(2) Using n kinds engines to test a single suspicious file, we can get n kinds detection results $R=\{R_1, R_2, ...R_n\}$ ($R_i \in \{0,1\}$, 0 indicates that no virus is found, 1 indicates virus is found). Integrated trust property value Trp of the suspicious file is calculated using equation (12)

$$Trp = 1 - \left. \sum_{i=1}^{n} Per_i \times R_i \middle/ n \right.$$

(12)

(3) According to equation (2), the file's trust level can be determined. When the file is *Trusted* or *Malicious*, FMA will directly return the results to the user for the final decision.

5.2   Dynamic Behavior Analysis of Suspicious Files

When the file's trust level is *Unknown*, FMA will hand the file to the file behavior analyzing engine, which is consisted of feature database of malicious files and the virtual machine. The *Unknown* file will be run in the virtual machine for real-timely dynamic analysis of behaviors.

6   Simulation and Analysis

6.1   Experimental Simulation and Description

Experimental environment consists of 3 servers, 1 router and 6 clients. We use C#.Net to realize the certification and authorization module, the behavioral evidence standardizing module, the file detection engines and the behavioral trust evaluating module; suspicious files are run in VMware workstation and analyzed dynamically; kinds of services under the experimental environment are monitored continuously by NetFlow Tracker and the test scenario is a small cloud storage system.

(1) According to Section 2.3 Definition. 3, the user trust level is set C={0.3, 0.6}; user is authorized according to Definition. 4, this small cloud storage system provides three levels of service Se={Se_1,Se_2,Se_3} (Se_1 denote services are denied, Se_2 denote files are read only, Se_3 denote files can be edited and download); according to Definition. 5, suspicious files trust level is set V={0.4, 0.5}. Parameter settings are shown in Table 1.

Table 1. Parameter Settings

	OTD: *Tr*	[0,0.3)	[0.3,0.6)	[0.6,1)
User	Trust level	Low	Normal	High
	Service level	S_1	S_2	S_3
Malicious	*Trp*	[0,0.4)	[0.4,0.5)	[0.5,1)
Files	Trust level	*Malicious*	*Unknown*	*Trusted*

(2) When a user is in the process of interaction with the cloud, BM continuously monitors the user and puts his behavioral evidences into the behavior database, the trust evaluating module assesses the trust degree of the user to identify and predict the possible unforeseen circumstances and real-timely informs the certification and authorization module to revise to the service level of the user.

(3) This system uses multiple detection engines and their accuracy *Per* are shown in the following [12]: GData(*Per*=99.9%)、AntiVir(*Per*=99.8 %)、AVAST (*Per*=99.3%)、Norman(*Per*=96.6%)、Trend Micro(*Per*=90.3%), Kingsoft(*Per*=80.1%).

6.2   Example of Trust Evaluation

12 kinds of evidences (see evidence level in Figure 3) in a half-hour from a client are obtained by Behavior Monitoring center. Through Section 3.2, evidences are normalized and convert to average evidence values that are shown in Table 2.

Table 2. The average evidence values in a half-hour of a client

Performance Character (P)							
P	P	P	P	P	P	P	P
1	2	3	4	5	6	7	8
0	0	0	0	0	0	0	0
.62	.51	.88	.83	.74	.67	.73	.54

Security Character (S)			
S	S	S	S
1	2	3	4
0	0	0	0
.33	.28	.15	.08

We use Section 3.2 to determine the weight of performance and security characters respectively and take per- formance character for instance: Experience has shown that response time of IP packet, IP transmission rate, throughput and bandwidth share are the best reflection to user's performance character and they are of equal importance, therefore $[c(P_1)=c(P_4)=c(P_6)=c(P_7)]>[c(P_2)=c(P_8)]> [c(P_3)=c(P_5)]$. Construction of the Initial judgment matrix is constructed by equation (5)

$$EP = \begin{pmatrix} 0.5 & 1 & 1 & 0.5 & 1 & 0.5 & 0.5 & 1 \\ 0 & 0.5 & 1 & 0 & 1 & 0 & 0 & 0.5 \\ 0 & 0 & 0.5 & 0 & 0.5 & 0 & 0 & 0 \\ 0.5 & 1 & 1 & 0.5 & 1 & 0.5 & 0.5 & 1 \\ 0 & 0 & 0.5 & 0 & 0.5 & 0 & 0 & 0 \\ 0.5 & 1 & 1 & 0.5 & 1 & 0.5 & 0.5 & 1 \\ 0.5 & 1 & 1 & 0.5 & 1 & 0.5 & 0.5 & 1 \\ 0 & 0.5 & 1 & 0 & 1 & 0 & 0 & 0.5 \end{pmatrix}$$

The fuzzy consistent matrix is converted from EP by equation (6):

$$Q = \begin{pmatrix} 0.5 & 0.6875 & 0.8125 & 0.5 & 0.8125 & 0.5 & 0.5 & 0.6875 \\ 0.3125 & 0.5 & 0.625 & 0.3125 & 0.625 & 0.3125 & 0.3125 & 0.5 \\ 0.1875 & 0.375 & 0.5 & 0.1875 & 0.5 & 0.1875 & 0.1875 & 0.375 \\ 0.5 & 0.6875 & 0.8125 & 0.5 & 0.8125 & 0.5 & 0.5 & 0.6875 \\ 0.1875 & 0.375 & 0.5 & 0.1875 & 0.5 & 0.1875 & 0.1875 & 0.375 \\ 0.5 & 0.6875 & 0.8125 & 0.5 & 0.8125 & 0.5 & 0.5 & 0.6875 \\ 0.5 & 0.6875 & 0.8125 & 0.5 & 0.8125 & 0.5 & 0.5 & 0.6875 \\ 0.3125 & 0.5 & 0.625 & 0.3125 & 0.625 & 0.3125 & 0.3125 & 0.5 \end{pmatrix}$$

The weight vector of evidences relevant to the performance character can be calculated by equation (7)~(9): $W_P^T=\{0.161,0.107,0.071,0.161,0.071,0.161,0.161,0.107\}^T$. Through pairwise comparison, the importance of evidences relevant to security character is $[c(S_3)=c(S_2)]>c(S_1)>c(S_4)$, similarly, the results of their weight vector is: $W_S^T= \{0.208, 0.333, 0.333, 0.125\}^T$. The importance of user behavior character is $c(P)<c(S)$, then the weight vector of the characters is $W_f^T=\{0.25, 0.75\}^T$. According to equation (10), the assessed values of user behavioral characters are $F=E \times W^T=(0.656,0.222)^T$, then the evaluated value of user behaviors is calculated by equation (11): $Tr=0.67$. According to Section 6.1 we can see, this user has high credibility level that can edit and download files in the small cloud storage system.

6.3   Experimental Comparison

Experiment 1: The experimental comparison result of two different trust evaluation mechanisms respectively based on FAHP and AHP.

Figure 4 shows the following circumstance: In the interaction between the client and the cloud, when we gradually increase the proportion of malicious acts such as illegal connections and scanning important port, the changes of the overall trust degree. With increase in the proportion of malicious behaviors, trust value calculated by mechanism based on FAHP has a large decline compared to that of AHP and is more compatible with human reasoning. Combined with the settings in Section 6.1, we find that user with low credibility can be monitored out by FAHP earlier and faster than AHP, which is conducive for certification and authorization module to update the client's service level and reduce the risk of the cloud.

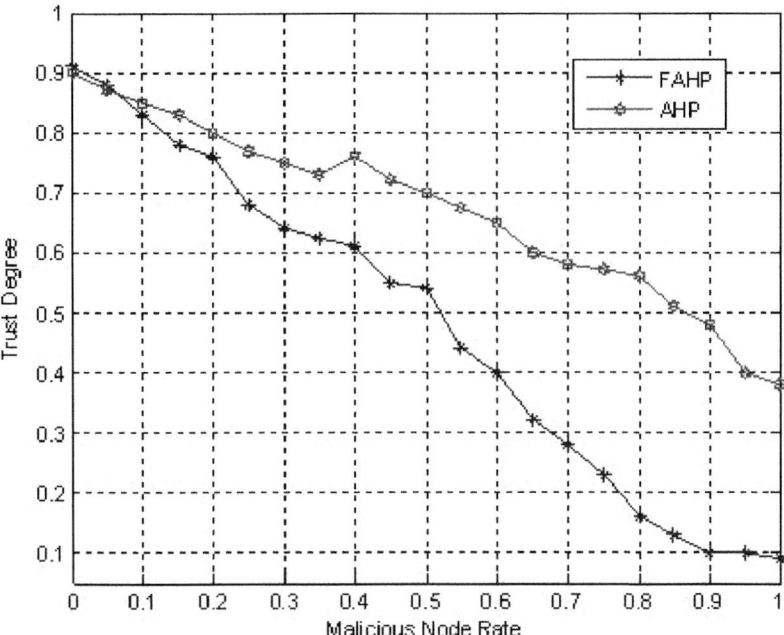

Fig. 4. Changes of a client's trust value

When using FAHP to construct the initial judgment matrix, because of the subjectivity of decision makers, determination of each element should be comprehensively evaluated by a number of experts. Also, the environment of the client should be considered when constructing a judgment matrix, if the client is in an unsafe environment (such as Internet cafes), the security character is important than performance character. Thus for the same client, even if evidences obtained are the same, the judgment matrix would be different under different environment, so do the assessed values of their behaviors.

Experiment 2: The comparison result of suspicious files detection based on multi-engines and single engine.

100 suspicious files are uploaded to the cloud and comprehensively detected by FMA. Experiments were carried out for the following three cases: 1) case is using multi-engines detection mechanism proposed in this paper to conduct a comprehensive inspection to suspicious files and determine their trust level; 2), 3) are using different single-engine to test, as a reference for the first case. Test results of suspicious files are shown in Table 3.

Table 3. Test results of suspicious files

	Trusted	Unknown	Malicious
Multi-engines	70.8%	4.2%	25%
Single-engine (AntiVir)	16.7%	0	83.3%
Single-engine (AVAST)	76%	0	24%

From Table 3, we can see that even for the same suspicious files, test results show great difference because of different detection engine (AntiVir and AVAST), so *Trusted* file could be mistaken for the *Malicious* one, thereby the client may be affected to make final decisions to suspicious files. Our system is based on multi-engines detection mechanism and conducts the integrated decision-making to test results, which can effectively avoid the above situations.

6.4   Performance Comparison

Using AHP to determine the weight of evidence, consistency test is needed. Because AHP uses nine scales to conduct the judgment matrix, excessive subjective judgments can easily bring deviation so that the matrix does not meet the consistency condition. At this point, the matrix need to be adjusted by number of experts' re-determine and a series of iterative computing, as the evidence layer is larger and the order of judgment matrix is higher, which means a large computing and communication overhead. In this paper, the experiment found that the average adjusted time is 3 when conducting the judgment matrix that meet the consistency condition using AHP method.

Without iterative calculation, FAHP method used in this paper can construct the fuzzy consistent matrix that meets the consistency condition just one-off. Therefore, under the same computation and communication, the computing time of our model can be shortened 1/3, so user's trust level and authorities can be judged faster. Therefore, the complex and time cost is greatly reduced.

7   Conclusion

Due to the severe security problems that cloud computing faces, combining the idea of trusted cloud, this paper presents a defensive system model based on trust. Taking the diversity of users' behavioral evidences into account, in order to conduct a more scientific and accurate trust evaluation, our system introduces FAHP to achieve the quantitative assessment of behavioral trust; considering the huge losses caused by viruses to the user, this system model uses multiple detection engines to conduct a comprehensive inspection of suspicious files. Experiments show that our model can not only effectively monitor and assess users' behaviors, but also provide users with security and protection services to achieve a two-way defense.

References

1. Li, H., Li, H.: The key technology and realization of trusted cloud security. Posts & Telecom press, Beijing (2010)
2. Lin, C., Peng, X.-h.: Research on trustworthy networks. Chinese Journal of Computer 28(5), 751–758 (2005)
3. Song, S.S., Hwang, K., Macwan, M.: Fuzzy trust integration for security enforcement in grid computing. In: Jin, H., Gao, G.R., Xu, Z., Chen, H. (eds.) NPC 2004. LNCS, vol. 3222, pp. 9–21. Springer, Heidelberg (2004)
4. Zhou, R.-F., Hwang, K.: Power-Trust: A robust and scalable reputation system for trusted Peer-to-Peer computing. IEEE Transactions on Parallel and Distributed Systems 18(4), 460–473 (2007)
5. Jameel, H.: A trust model for ubiquitous systems based on vectors of trust values. In: The 7th IEEE Int'l Symp. on Multimedia, pp. 674–679. IEEE Computer Society Press, Washington (2005)
6. Li, X.-y., Gui, X.-l.: Trust quantitative model with multiple decision factors in trusted network. Chinese Journal of Computer 32(3), 405–415 (2009)
7. A white paper of the network defense solutions of Secure Cloud from Trend Micro, http://www.chinacloud.cn/show.aspx?id=339&cid=29
8. Lin, C., Tian, L.-q., Wang, Y.-z.: Research on user behavior trust in trustworthy network. Journal of Computer Research and Development 45(12), 2033–2043 (2008)
9. Ji, T.-g., Tian, L.-q., Hu, Z.-x.: AHP-based user behavior evaluation method in trustworthy network. Computer Engineering and Applications 43(19), 123–126 (2007)
10. Wang, L.-f., Xu, S.-b.: The introduction of AHP. China Renmin University press, Beijing (1990)
11. Liu, L., Wang, H.-q., Liang, Y.: Evaluation method of service-level network security situation based on fuzzy analytic hierarchy process. Journal of Computer Applications 29(9), 2327–2331 (2009)
12. A test report of anti-virus softwares, http://www.av-comparatives.org/images/stories/test/ondret/av c_od_aug2010cns.pdf

A New Method for Authentication Based on Covert Channel

Yanan Sun, Xiaohong Guan, and Ting Liu

Ministry of Education Key Lab for Intelligent Networks and Network Security,
School of Electric and Information Engineering, Xian Jiaotong Uinversity

Abstract. Authentication is of great importance in information security. Traditional method only focus on encryption of the content itself, which is the same with the later proposed methods named information hiding and digital watermark. Since data transmission is in the open network, it can easily be detected and intercepted by the malicious party. In this paper, we put forward a new method which utilize the communication channel, not the content, as the data carrier, and guarantee the validation of the user's identity during the common data transmission. Specifically, by manipulating the inter-packet delays, we implement a prototype system for authentication and embed the authentication tag within the packet intervals based on network covert channel. By conducting a series of experiments, we prove that our method performs well in LAN and Campus Network.

Keywords: Network security, network covert channel, authentication, time intervals.

1   Introduction

With the development of modern technology, Internet is deeply involved with our daily life, the flaws and attacks within the network will lead to potential huge loss. As a result, information security is of great importance in order to maintain the security of the whole network, in which authentication plays an important part.

Authentication is critical for network security. Traditional authentication method is based on modern cryptography, which lay great emphasis on the study of the complexity of algorithm. It can be divided into symmetric and asymmetric key cryptography. Symmetric key cryptography is easy for encryption, but is not secure in key distribution; Asymmetric key cryptography introduce the new concept for PKI, which provide a new field and technical support for information security, but has a high requirement for system overhead. Relied on asymmetric key cryptography, digital signature is brought out as a new way to validate user's identity. Later, with the development of digital media, information hiding and digital watermark is proposed as a new thread to protect the copyright of digital media and also the validity and integrity of its content.

Traditional methods and the later proposed information hiding and digital watermark both make use of the content transmitted to do encryption and authentication. They are restricted in the information transmitted and appear to be vulnerable. Since

E. Altman and W. Shi (Eds.): NPC 2011, LNCS 6985, pp. 160–165, 2011.

the communication is in the open network, the transmitting data is easy to be intercepted by malicious middleman or third party, and if there is enough information, he can modify and fake the data, which emerge as a huge threat to information security. Thus, we propose a new scheme to do authentication from the respective of the communication channel, namely covert channel, which utilize the packet stream to indicate the cipher text. In this way, even though the malicious middleman intercept the packets for data transmission, he cannot determine if there is cipher text only from the overt communication, therefore covert channel can be a much more stealthy and secure way for authentication, which can be a supplement for the traditional methods.

2   Theory

2.1   Covert Channel

Covert channel is a communication channel that violates a security policy by using shared resources in ways for which they were not initially designed[2], which makes use of sharing resources to bypass the security policy to establish malicious communication for sensitive information leakage. Fig 1 shows the simple structure of covert channel.

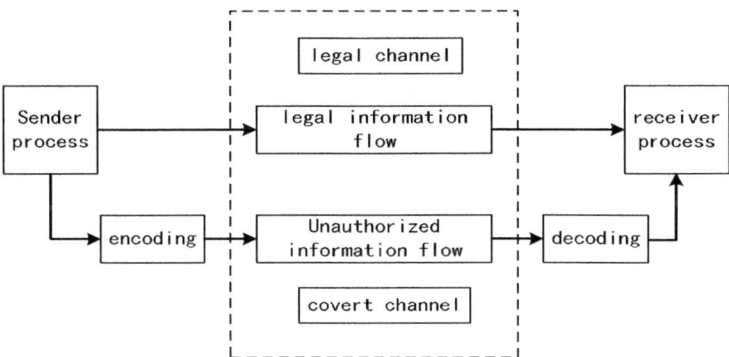

Fig. 1. Simple structure of Covert Channel

2.2   Categories of Covert Channel

Basically covert channels can be classified into two categories according to the type of the shared resources, namely storage covert channel and timing covert channel.
Storage covert channel means "the indirect or direct writing of a storage location by one process and the indirect or direct reading of the storage process by another process" [1].
    Timing covert channel means "a sender process which signals information to another by modulating its own use of system resources in such a way that the response time observed by the second process is changed" [1].

2.3   Comparison between Storage and Timing Covert Channel

In the real network environment, timing covert channel is much more difficult to be detected compared with the storage one [3]. The reason for which is that sometimes the modification of TCP / IP header is illegal and quite obvious, but for the timing covert channel, it can hardly be recognized unless analyzing the characteristics of traffic stream during the whole communication process. However, on the other hand, the synchronization of the clock and the sequence of the packet order have a significant influence on the accuracy of decryption. So considering this, storage covert channel can be much more accurate. What's more, storage covert channel is more effective than the timing one due to the packet delay.

3   Methodology

Taking stealth, effectiveness and accuracy into consideration, we decide to utilize timing covert channel [4] [5] [6] which embeds the authentication tag within the packet intervals.

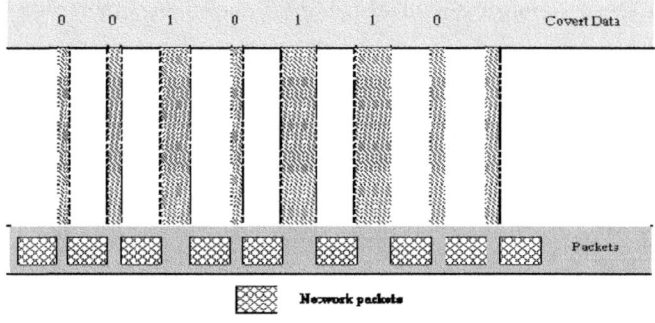

Fig. 2. A diagram to illustrate timing covert channel by manipulating the packet interval

In our design, the sender manipulate the interval between the two packets which is sent during the overt communication ,then use a certain kind of algorithm to encode these interval to represent certain information. And after these packets are received, the receiver decodes and obtains the information according to the "Key" which has been predetermined before. As Fig 2 illustrates, the sender process manipulates the inter-packet delays, and use the long intervals to indicate "1", the short intervals to indicate"0". And after the receiver process receives these packets, it records their arrival time and calculates the packet intervals, then decode and obtain the covert information the sender process transmit.

By using Winsock2 SPI and Winpcap interface, we implement a prototype system to do authentication as Fig 3 illustrates. In our proposed system, we exploit a module for FTP client to monitor the network traffic packets and embed the authentication tag within the packet intervals through encoding, and also a module for FTP server to decode the covert information and validate the client's identity, which is the authentication process.

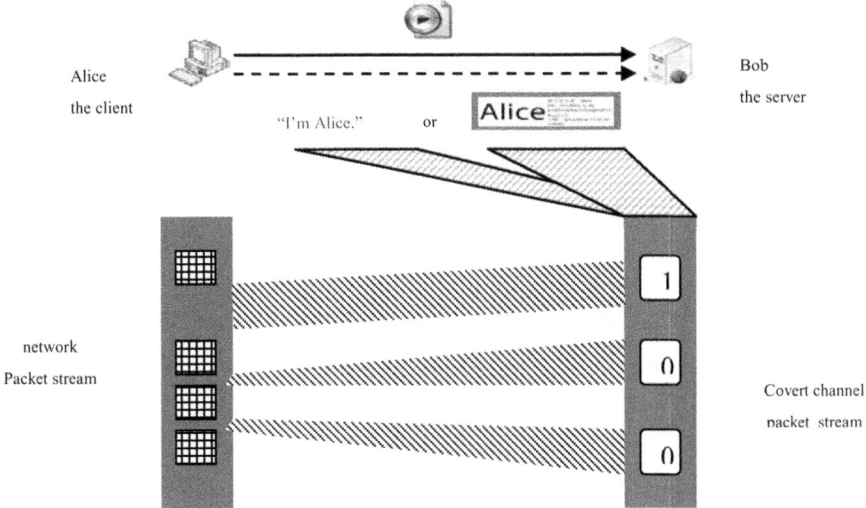

Fig. 3. The infrastructure of the model for authentication using timing covert channel

4 Result

From Fig 4, we can find that traffic stream distribution of covert channel is quite different from the legal one, no matter in LAN or Campus Network, the covert traffic stream shows an alternating long and short packet intervals, especially at the beginning of the communication process, the reason for which is that the sender process manipulate the inter-packet delays in order to transmit the authentication information. While the statistical charts are similar with each other, and this is because the packets used to transmit authentication tag is only a small portion of the total packets for the whole communication process, and most of the packets still belong to the overt channel.

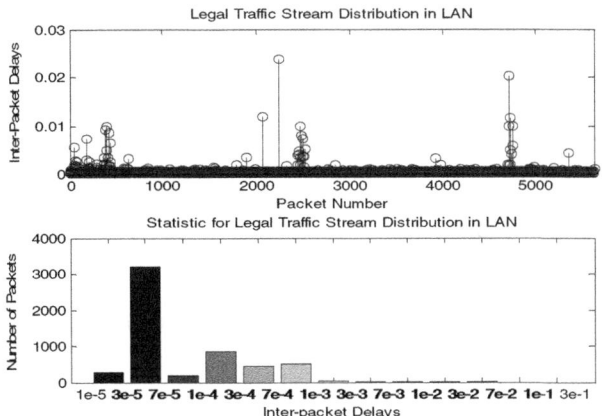

Fig. 4. Traffic Stream for legal and Covert Communication

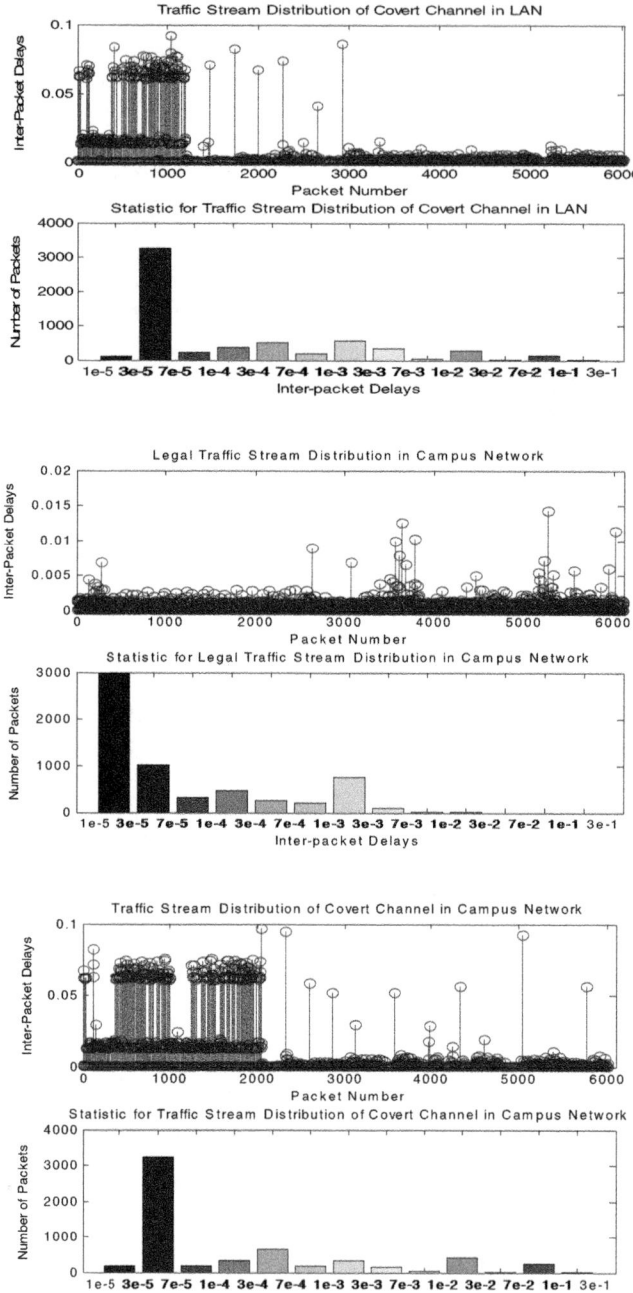

Fig. 4. (*continued*)

5   Conclusion and Future Work

In this paper, a new method for authentication by using communication channel—timing covert channel is proposed, and by conducting a series of experiments in LAN and Campus Network, we find timing covert channel may lead to certain delays and the packet stream is not similar to the regular ones, but it still proves to be a much more secure and stealthy way for authentication. Our future work is focus on evaluating the performance of the proposed system and further analyzing the difference of the traffic stream between legal and covert communication.

References

[1] Cabuk, S.: Network Covert Channels: Design, Analysis, Detection, and Elimination, Ph.D. thesis (2006)
[2] Lampson, B.W.: A Note on the Confinement Problem. Communications of the ACM 16(10), 613–615 (1973)
[3] Ahsan, K., Kundur, D.: Practical Date Hiding in TCP/IP, MMSec. (2002)
[4] Cabuk, S., et al.: IP Covert Timing Channels: An Initial Exploration. In: CCS 2004, Washington, DC, USA, October 25-29 (2004)
[5] Cabuk, S., Brodley, C.E., Shields, C.: IP Covert Timing Channels: Design and Detection. In: Proceedings of the 11th ACM Conference on Computer and Communications Security, CCS 2004 (2004)
[6] Sellke, S.H., Wang, C.-C., Bagchi, S.: TCP/IP Timing Channels: Theory to Implementation. In: Proceedings of the 28th, Conference on Computer Communications, INFOCOM (April 2009)

A Layered Detection Method for Malware Identification

Ting Liu, Xiaohong Guan, Yu Qu, and Yanan Sun

SKLMS Lab and MOE KLNNIS Lab, Xi'an Jiaotong University, P.R. China
{tingliu,xhguan}@mail.xjtu.edu.cn,
{yqu,ynsun}@sei.xjtu.edu.cn

Abstract. In recent years, millions of new malicious programs are produced by Pa mature industry of malware production. These programs have tremendous challenges on the signature-based anti-virus products and pose great threats on network and information security. Machine learning techniques are applicable for detecting unknown malicious programs without knowing their signatures. In this paper, a *Layered Detection (LD)* method is developed to detect malwares with a two-layer framework. The *Low-Level-Classifiers (LLC)* are employed to identify whether the programs perform any malicious functions according to the API-calls of the programs. The *Up-level-Classifier (ULC)* is applied to detect malwares according to the low level function identification. The *LD* method is compared with many classical classification algorithms with comprehensive test datasets containing 16135 malwares and 1800 benign programs. The experiments demonstrate that the *LD* method outperforms other algorithms in terms of detection accuracy.

Keywords: Machine learning, Network security, Malware detection, Malicious function identification.

1   Introduction

Exponential growth and development of Internet has created unprecedented opportunities to access and share information. Millions of online users and ubiquitous Internet accesses have cultivated not only a great number of convenient services and fast-developing companies, but also innumerable malicious programs and a huge underground economy. Malicious tools enable attackers to gain access to a variety of valuable resources such as identities, credentials, hacked hosts, and other information and services. The attackers sell the information and services on the underground market, and then reinvest the profits into the development of new malicious tools and services. This profitable cycle leads to a dramatic increase in the significant proliferation of malicious codes. In 2008, Symantec detected 1,656,227 new malicious programs which took up over 60% of the approximately 2.6 million malicious programs that Symantec has detected in total over time[1].

Malware is defined as a program that performs a malicious function, such as compromising a system's security, damaging a system or obtaining sensitive information without the user's permission. The malwares can be generally divided into the

E. Altman and W. Shi (Eds.): NPC 2011, LNCS 6985, pp. 166–175, 2011.

following categories: viruses, worms, Trojans and others. In recent years, Trojans and worms have been ranked as the top security threats, which occupied 68% and 29% of all new malwares and took over all top 10 malware families in 2008[1]. This paper concentrates on the Trojan and worm classification.

Due to inestimable damages caused by malicious programs, malware detection has become one of the primal research interests in the field of network and information security. Over the past decade, the signature-based detection, employed by most commercial antivirus products, such as Kaspersky Anti-Virus (KAV) and Symantec Norton AntiVirus, is the most widely used for detecting malware. In 2007, Kaspersky added 250,000 new signatures into their antivirus databases and released more than 10,000 database updates [2]. The rapidly-growing signature database would cause significant increase of computational cost to check all the signatures, and missing frequent updates would cause security loop holes.

Dynamic analysis is considered as an effective approach to detect unknown malwares. In 1991, researchers managed to determine what the programs attempt to do by observing and analyzing their actions at run-time in a controlled environment [3]. The major drawback of this technique is that the detection can only be done after at least a part of the malicious code is executed and has generated suspicious behaviors in the system. Therefore, many researchers have proposed that the suspected programs could be run and analyzed on the virtual machine (VM) before proceeding on an actual system [4, 5]. Since more and more malwares do not carry out malicious activities directly but only "activated" by a particular instruction, this method may not be effective in "normal" operation.

Applying machine learning in network security is regarded as one of the alternative effective solutions with integrated consideration of security and privacy with massive and ubiquitous information. The ability of machine learning to detect unknown attacks is demonstrated in the context of intrusion detection systems[6-8]. In recent years, many machine learning techniques have been applied to detect unknown malwares. Machine learning approach is based on the assumption that malwares have certain characteristics not presented in benign programs. The supervised classifier is trained to distinguish malicious codes based on the known instances of malicious and benign programs [9]. Thereby, the performance of this method critically depends on the me-thods of feature extraction, feature selection and classification. Another issue is that few of machine learning based approach could identify the malware's functions which are useful for selecting defense strategy.

In this paper, a *Layered Detection (LD)* method is developed to detect malwares with a two-layer framework. The *Low-Level-Classifiers (LLC)* are employed to identify whether the programs perform any malicious functions according to the API-calls of the programs. The *Up-level-Classifier (ULC)* is applied to detect malwares according to the low level function identification. A hybrid structure (Type-function), constituting of the classification results of *LLC* and *ULC*, is proposed to describe the malware.   The *LD* method is compared with many classical classification algorithms with compre-hensive test datasets containing 16135 malwares and 1800 benign programs. The experiments demonstrate that the *LD* method outperforms other algorithms in terms of detection accuracy. Moreover, the Type-function is proved as an unprejudiced and effective method for describing malware functions. In fact, the *LD* method can accurately identify 98% of all malwares' functions, much higher than the other methods do. Furthermore, we also apply our method to distinguish malicious and benign programs. The experimental results demonstrated that the *LD* method integrated with *J48 Tree* outperformed others classifiers including *Boosting-J48*.

The rest of this paper is organized as follows. Section 2 presents the methods of feature extraction, feature selection, classification and measurement which will be used in this paper. The framework of the *LD* method is introduced in the Section 3. The experimental results are discussed in Section 4, which show the *LD* method outperforms other methods. Section 5 is the conclusions of this paper.

2   Machine Learning Based Approach

The primary goal of this study is to explore the performance of various machine learning techniques in detecting known and unknown malwares based on the API calls. A large number of programs, including the benign and the malicious, have been collected to train and evaluate the classifiers. The methods of feature extraction and definition are firstly presented in this section. And then, the feature selection methods, classification algorithms and performance measurements are briefly described.

2.1   Feature Extraction and Definition

17935 Windows PE programs have been gathered, consisting of 16135 malicious and 1800 benign executables. The malicious executables are collected from malwares database of Kaspersky Corporation and Honey-Net in our lab, including 6377 Downloader Trojans, 4795 Spy Trojans, 2214 PSW Trojans, 1458 Email Worms, 532 P2P Worms and 759 Net Worms (which are expressed as M_1 to M_6 respectively). The benign programs are collected from a freshly installed Windows XP SP2 system, including DLL and EXE files. 2710 standard Windows API calls [10] are selected as the attributes of the program in this paper. By searching the Import Address Table of the programs, the Windows API calls of the programs are extracted and recorded in original dataset. The attribute is defined as $\{A_1, A_2, ...A_i, ..., A_{2710}, R\}$, where A_i identifies the *ith* API call (absence is 0 and presence is 1) and R represents the program category (benign is 0 and malicious is 1).

To facilitate the presentation, the notations are defined as follow:

R is the type of the sample. R_B, R_M and R_{Mi} means the sample is a benign, malicious and *i*th malware type program.

A_i is the *i*th API, A_{i1} means that the *ith* API is called; and A_{i0} means not.

S is the set of samples and defined as $\{A_1, A_2, ...A_m, R\}$.

2.2   Performance Measures

To measure the performance of previous feature selection and classification algorithms, several performance measures are selected in this work to represent and compare the results.

Confusion Matrix constitutes of the statistics of actual and predicted values. True Positive (*TP*) and True Negative (*TN*) are the number of correctly classified malicious and benign programs. False positive (*FP*) and False negative (*FN*) are the number of falsely classified benign and malicious programs. $N(R_M)$ and $N(R_B)$ are the number of the actual malicious and benign programs. $N(R_{PM})$ and $N(R_{PB})$ are the number of the predicted malicious and benign programs. N is the number of all samples.

True Positive Rate (TPR) is the rate of correctly classified malwares, which presents the detection rate.

$$TPR = TP/(TP+FN) = TP/N(R_M)$$

False Positive Rate (FPR) is the rate of misclassified benign programs in benign class.

$$FPR = FP/(TN+FP) = FP/N(R_B)$$

Accuracy is the rate of the entire correctly classified instances in whole set.

$$Accuracy = (TP+TN)/N$$

Kappa is used to measure the agreement between predicted and observed categorizations of a dataset, while correcting for agreement that occurs by chance.

$$Kappa = (Accuracy - Pe)/(1 - Pe)$$

where *Pe* is the hypothetical probability of chance agreement, using the observed data to calculate the probabilities of each observer randomly selecting category[11].

2.3 Feature Selection

A large number of features in many domains result in a huge challenges on the efficiency and accuracy of the classification. Typically, some of the features do not contribute to the accuracy of the classification task and may even hamper it. Therefore, identifying the most representative features is significant in minimizing the classification error and the resource consumption. In present research, three measurements: *Information Gain, One-Rule* [12] and *Chi-Square* [13] are employed to evaluate the contribution of each API in malware classification. The top ranked features are selected.

2.4 Classification Algorithm

Naive Bayes is one of the most successful learning algorithms for text categorization. It is based on the Bayes rule assuming conditional independence between classes. In this study, Naive Bayes algorithm is implemented by *WEKA NaiveBayes(NB) classifier* [14].

Decision Tree is a decision support tool that uses a tree-like graph or model of decisions and their possible consequences, including chance event outcomes, resource costs, and utility. In decision tree classifiers, the internal nodes are tests on individual features, and leaves are classification decisions. Typically, a greedy top-down search method is used to find a small decision tree that correctly classifies the training data [13]. *C*4.5, a classical algorithm for generating a decision tree and an extension of *ID3* algorithm, is performed by *WEKA **J48** classifier* in this study.

Boosting refers to a general and provably effective method of producing a very accurate prediction rule by combining rough and moderately inaccurate rules of thumb. This technique trains successive component classifiers with a subset of the training data that is "most informative" given the current set of component classifiers. Classification of a test point is based on the outputs of the component classifiers. Boosting can achieve a very low training error, even a vanishing training error if the problem is separable [15]. *Adaptive Boosting (AdaBoost)* is one of the most popular boosting algorithms, formulated by Yoav Freund and Robert Schapire. In this work, it is used in conjunction with NB and J48 to improve their performance, which is executed by WEKA **AdaBoost** classifier [14].

3   Layered Framework and Method for Detecting Malwares

Many machine learning techniques have been applied to detect unknown malwares. In our study, it is demonstrated that the common classification algorithms are significantly affected by: 1) the imbalanced numbers of benign and malicious programs; 2) the known differences among various malwares; 3) the multiple correlated functions of malwares.

For most classification algorithms, the imbalanced numbers of different classes results in un-uniform classification criteria of different classes. In fact, most users only use a number of required software products, but are threatened by thousands of malwares. In this paper, 16135 malwares and 1800 Windows XP SP2 initial executables are collected as the training and testing dataset. When the *NB* and *J48* classifiers are applied to categorize all these programs with 10-fold cross-validation, the *FPR* of them are as high as 32% and 18%.

Table 1. The probability of API to be called by various of programs

API	Probability to be called						
	Benign	DLoader	PSW	SPY	Email	P2P	Net
DisableThreadLibraryCalls	39.5%	2.6%	0.3%	1.9%	0.0%	0.0%	0.5%
InterlockedIncrement	53.8%	7.4%	3.4%	13.5%	7.4%	11.5%	15.0%
InterlockedDecrement	53.2%	9.0%	3.3%	13.4%	7.8%	11.1%	14.0%
GetLastError	77.2%	26.7%	18.4%	26.8%	22.2%	29.9%	30.3%
SetLastError	45.2%	6.1%	5.2%	6.0%	3.4%	2.6%	6.1%
ExitProcess	17.6%	62.5%	64.7%	63.8%	75.0%	79.3%	68.4%
HeapFree	40.1%	12.3%	4.7%	10.3%	11.1%	9.2%	14.9%
GetProcAddress	59.3%	78.6%	92.4%	88.6%	90.2%	89.8%	93.3%
ReadProcessMemory	*0.9%*	*1.5%*	*15.1%*	*4.2%*	*1.0%*	*0.8%*	*1.8%*
HeapAlloc	40.4%	15.0%	5.7%	10.4%	11.2%	9.2%	14.9%

Furthermore, the differences among various malwares also cause many difficulties for malware detection. Table 1 displays the probabilities of 10 APIs to be called by various programs, which represents the highest *Information Gain* in all APIs. It is noticed that *ReadProcessMemory* is scarcely called by the benign programs, Downloader Trojan, Email Worm and P2P Worm, but called by 15.1% of PSW Trojans. Obviously, the calling of *ReadProcessMemory* is a positive evidence to identify a program as the *PSW Trojan*. However, it is a dilemmatic evidence for the classifiers to identify whether that program is malicious when all malwares are set in one class.

The malware's type is useful and important for selecting defense strategy. However, it is extremely difficult to identify the type, since the most malwares perform multiple correlated functions. Even the security experts and companies define the malwares depending on their subjective judgments. For example, the *Rustock* is employed to create one of today's most extensive zombie networks for sending spam, exploiting the *Rootkit* techniques [16]. It is defined as *Backdoor* by Symantec, and as *Rootkit* by Kaspersky and MCafee.

To address the above issues, a new method - *Layered Detection (LD)* is proposed for malware detection. It applies a two-layer framework to identify the malware's function and detect the malware, and uses a Type-function structure to express the malware classification result. The *LD* method will be introduced from two phases: training and testing.

As illustrated in Fig.1.a, the training phase of *LD* classifier is constituted of two steps.   In the first step, all malwares are divided into several sub-datasets according to their type. These sub-datasets are applied to train the *Low-Level-Classifiers (LLC)* for identifying whether the programs perform the various malicious functions. Since these sub-datasets present better balance between the benign and malicious programs and retain the characteristics of various malware types, the *LLC* can identify the program's malicious functions with low *FPR* and high *Accuracy*. In the second step, the training programs are evaluated by all *LLCs* in parallel. The identification results are used to train the *Up-level-Classifier (ULC)* for detecting malwares. If a *LD* classifier employs *NB* and *J48* to train the *LLCs* and *ULC*, it is named as *LD-NB-J48*.

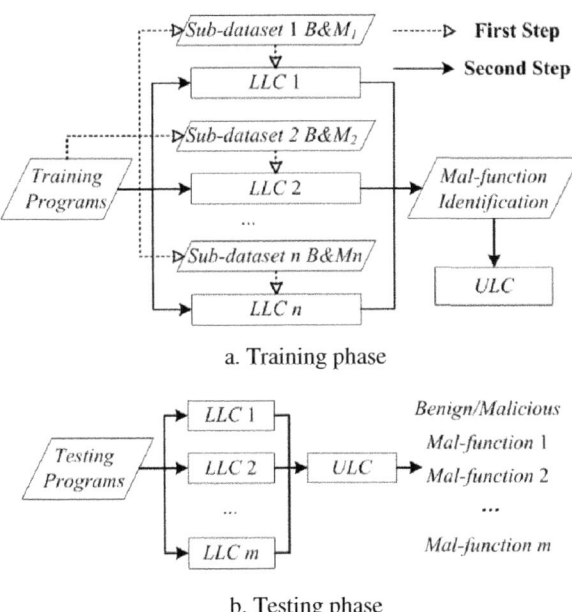

a. Training phase

b. Testing phase

Fig. 1. The model of Layered Detection Classifier

In the testing phase, all programs are first evaluated by the *LLCs* to identify whether they perform malicious functions, and are then estimated by the *ULC* to determine whether they are malwares, as shown in Fig.1.b. Both classifications of LLCs and ULC are output as Type-function structure for providing unprejudiced and comprehensive information to users.

4   Experiment and Discussion

4.1   Feature Selection

In all 2710 Windows standard APIs, there are 1559 APIs that are never called by any program. These APIs seldom contribute to the malware classification, but reduce the accuracy and exponentially increased the computation consumption. By filtering these useless APIs, a new subset was generated, consisting of the rest 1151 APIs (called as S_{1151}), to replace the original dataset in the following part. Then, three supervised feature selection methods: *IG, One-Rule* and *Chi-Square* are employed to evaluate and rank the value of all APIs on classification. For each selection method, the top 25, 50, 75, 100, 150, 200, 250, 300, 400, 600, 800 and 1000 valuable attributes are selected as new sets. (These sets were marked as $S_{Method\ Num}$, for example S_{IG100} expresses 100 APIs are selected with *IG* measure.) The *NB* and *J48* classifiers are applied to categorize all subsets using 10-fold cross-validation. For reliable results, every classifier is repeated 10 times on each set. The average *Kappa* is calculated to evaluate various feature selection methods, feature sizes, and classification algorithms.

Kappa describes the agreement between predicted and actual value by deducting the random success from the classifier's success. Hence, it is employed to evaluate the methods of feature selection and classification which showed oppositely on accuracy and *FPR* in this study.

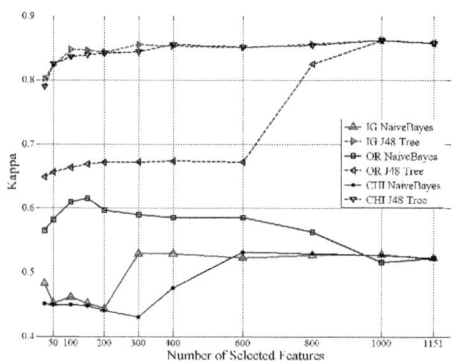

Fig. 2. Kappa of 3 feature selection methods

As illustrated in Fig 2, the *Kappa* of *NB* classifier is 0.522 on the S_{1151}. On the *OR* sets, it increases slowly but surely when more and more features are removed and exceeds 0.6 when the feature size is 100 and 150. On the *IG* and *CHI* sets, it quickly reduces about 20% when the feature size decreases from 600 to 200. That proves the *OR* method selects more effective and reliable features for the *NB* classifier than the *IG* and *CHI*. Considering the computational costs of classification, the feature size is expected to be as small as possible. As demonstrated in Fig.2, *J48* classifier presents integrated performance on the S_{IG100}. The *Kappa* is more than 0.6 only on the S_{OR100} and S_{OR150} (the *Kappa* of a substantial classifier should be more than 0.6 [11]). Therefore, the IG and OR are chosen for the *J48* and *NB* classifier, and the feature size is 100.

4.2   Malware Classification

In this subsection, we employ many classification algorithms to detect malwares, and compare their performance using different measurements. Besides *J48* and *NB*, the *LD* method employs *Multilayer Perceptron* (*MP*) and *IBk* as its *ULC* algorithm. *MP* is a back propagation neural network classifier, and *IBk* is a k-nearest-neighbor classifier that uses the Euclidean distance metric [14, 15]. (*k* is set as 6 in this paper.) Moreover, the *AdaBoost*, collaborating with *J48* and *NB* algorithms, is employed to compare with the *LD* method.

Table 2. Malware detection collaborating with *LD-J48* on S_{IG100}

Method	TP	TN	FP	FN	FPR	Accuracy	Kappa
J48	15986	1484	316	149	17.56%	97.41%	0.8503
Multi-J48	15935	1523	277	200	15.39%	97.34%	0.8499
AdaBoost-J48	16016	1590	210	119	11.67%	98.17%	0.8961
LD-J48-J48	16036	1639	161	99	8.94%	98.55%	0.9185
LD-J48-NB	15369	1734	66	766	3.67%	95.36%	0.7809
LD-J48-MP	16040	1640	160	95	8.89%	98.58%	0.9200
LD-J48-IBk	16035	1636	164	100	9.11%	98.53%	0.9172

Table 3. Malware detection collaborating with *LD-NB* on S_{OR100}

Method	TP	TN	FP	FN	FPR	Accuracy	Kappa
NB	15860	982	818	275	45.44%	93.91%	0.6103
Multi-NB	15101	1247	553	1034	30.72%	91.15%	0.5620
AdaBoost-NB	15872	976	824	263	45.78%	93.94%	0.6104
LD-NB-NB	15277	1313	487	858	27.06%	92.50%	0.6195
LD-NB-J48	15674	1218	582	461	32.33%	94.18%	0.6680
LD-NB-MP	15731	1147	653	404	36.28%	94.11%	0.6523
LD-NB-IBk	15667	1220	580	468	32.22%	94.16%	0.6672

Various classification algorithms are applied to detect malwares according to the program's function which are identified by the *LD-J48*. As reported in Table 3, *LD-J48*, *LD-J48-MP* and *LD-J48-IBk* misclassify no more than 100 malwares; and their *Accuracy* and *Kappa* are as high as 98.5% and 0.92. Although the *LD-J48-NB* shows the worst *Accuracy*, it falsely classifies only 95 benign programs (the *FRP* is as low as 3.67%). The *AdaBoost* method obviously improves the ability to identify malwares of *J48*: the *FP* and *FN* reduce 33.5% and 20.1%, and the *Kappa* increases from 0.8503 to 0.8961. The *Multi-J48* falsely classifies fewer benign programs, but misclassifies more malwares than the *J48*.

Table 4 shows the malware detection results when various methods are collaborated with *LD-NB*. Generally speaking, the performances of *LD-NB* on dataset S_{OR100} are not as good as that of *LD-J48* on S_{IG100}, and the performances of various methods collaborating with *LD-NB* are similarly to the *LD-J48*.

The experimental results demonstrate that the *LD* method significantly improves the detection accuracy of many classifiers. In more specific terms, *LD-J48-MP* is recommended to pursue high *Accuracy* and *Kappa*, and *LD-J48-NB* is suggested to chase low *FPR*.

5   Conclusions

In paper we demonstrate that the accuracy of malware detection is significantly affected by: 1) the imbalanced numbers of benign and malicious programs; 2) the known differences among various malwares; 3) the multiple correlated functions of malwares. A new method based on machine learning is developed for malware detection. To address the above issues, a layered detection framework is established and the malwares are divided into several *sub-datasets* to train the *low-level-classifiers* for identifying malicious functions and are detected based on the identified functions by the up-level-classifier. Since the malwares can be well categorized in the framework, it is helpful for selecting defense strategy.

The experiments with 17935 collected programs show that the new method can correctly identify the functions of 98.5% malwares and detect 98.6% of all malwares. Moreover, many feature selection methods and classification algorithms are also investigated. It is demonstrated that the *IG* and *OR* feature selection methods are amenable for *J48* and *NB* classifiers respectively and the best feature size is 100. The new method demonstrates more than 95% accuracy, about twice as high as *Multi-J48* and *Multi-NB*, for malicious function identification, and outperforms other classification algorithms including *Boosting* for malware detection.

References

[1] Gostev, A.: Kaspersky Security Bulletin. In: Statistics 2008 (2009)
[2] Lo, R., Kerchen, P., Crawford, R., Ho, W., Crossley, J., Fink, G., Levitt, K., Olsson, R., Archer, M.: Towards a testbed for malicious code detection. In: Compcon Spring 1991, Digest of Papers, pp. 160–166 (1991)
[3] Wang, X., Yu, W., Champion, A., Fu, X., Xuan, D.: Detecting worms via mining dynamic program execution. In: Third International Conference on Security and Privacy in Communications Networks and the Workshops, SecureComm (2007)

[4] Jiang, X., Wang, X., Xu, D.: Stealthy malware detection and monitoring through VMM-based "out-of-the-box" semantic view reconstruction. ACM Transactions on Information and System Security 13 (2010)

[5] Wenke, L., Stolfo, S.J., Mok, K.W.: A data mining framework for building intrusion detection models.: Security and Privacy. In: Proceedings of the 1999 IEEE Symposium on Security and Privacy, pp. 120–132 (1999)

[6] Berral, J.L., Poggi, N., Alonso, J., Gavald, R., Torres, J., Parashar, M.: Adaptive distributed mechanism against flooding network attacks based on machine learning. In: Proceedings of the 1st ACM Workshop on AISec, pp. 43–50. ACM, Alexandria (2008)

[7] Kloft, M., Brefeld, U., Pessel, D., Gehl, C., Laskov, P.: Automatic feature selection for anomaly detection. In: Proceedings of the 1st ACM Workshop on AISec, pp. 71–76. ACM, Alexandria (2008)

[8] Renchao, Q., Tao, L., Yu, Z.: An immune inspired model for obfuscated virus detection. In: 2009 International Conference on Industrial Mechatronics and Automation, ICIMA 2009, Chengdu, China, pp. 228–231 (2009)

[9] Windows: Windows API Reference: http://msdn.microsoft.com/en-us/library/aa383749(VS.85).aspx

[10] Landis, J.R., Koch, G.G.: The measurement of observer agreement for categorical data. Biometrics 33 (1977)

[11] Holte, R.C.: Very simple classification rules perform well on most commonly used data-sets. Mach. Learn. 11, 63-91 (1993)

[12] Moskovitch, R., Elovici, Y., Rokach, L.: Detection of unknown computer worms based on behavioral classification of the host. Computational Statistics and Data Analysis 52, 4544–4566 (2008)

[13] Witten, I.H., Frank, E.: Data Mining: Practical Machine Learning Tools and Techniques, 2nd edn. Morgan Kaufmann, San Francisco (2005)

[14] Duda, R.O., Hart, P.E., Stork, D.G.: Pattern Classification, 2nd edn. Wiley-Interscience, Hoboken (2000)

[15] Gostev, A.: Rustock and All That (2008)

Pedestrian Detection and Tracking Using HOG and Oriented-LBP Features

Yingdong Ma, Xiankai Chen, and George Chen

Center for Digital Media Computing,
Shenzhen Institutes of Advanced Technology, Shenzhen, China

Abstract. During the last decade, various successful human detection methods have been developed. However, most of these methods focus on finding powerful features or classifiers to obtain high detection rate. In this work we introduce a pedestrian detection and tracking system to extract and track human objectives using an on board monocular camera. The system is composed of three stages. A pedestrian detector, which is based on the non-overlap HOG feature and an Oriented LBP feature, is applied to find possible locations of humans. Then an object validation step verifies detection results and rejects false positives by using a temporal coherence condition. Finally, Kalman filtering is used to track detected pedestrians. For a 320×240 image, the implementation of the proposed system runs at about 14 frames/second, while maintaining an human detection rate similar to existing methods.

Keywords: Pedestrian detection, support vector machine, Oriented Local Binary Pattern, Histograms of Oriented Gradient.

1 Introduction

Pedestrian detection has attracted considerable attention from the computer vision community over the past few years. One of the important reasons is its wide variety of applications, such as video surveillance, robotics, and intelligent transportation systems. However, detecting humans in video streams is a difficult task because of the various appearances caused by different clothing, pose and illumination. Moving cameras and cluttered background make the problem even harder.

Many human detection methods have been developed but most of these methods are focus on finding powerful features or classifiers to obtain high detection rate. For applications such as on-line human detection for robotics and automotive safety, both efficiency and accuracy are important issues that should be considered carefully. In this work, we study the issue of finding a feature set for human detection from onboard video streams. In particular it combines the non-overlap histograms of oriented gradient (HOG) appearance descriptor [1] and an oriented Local Binary Patterns (LBP) feature. Temporal coherence condition is employed to reject false positives from detection results and Kalman filtering is used to track detected pedestrians. The aim of the proposed system is to achieve accurate human detection, while maintains efficient for applications that require fast human detection and tracking.

E. Altman and W. Shi (Eds.): NPC 2011, LNCS 6985, pp. 176–184, 2011.
© IFIP International Federation for Information Processing 2011

The paper is structured as follows. Section 2 briefly reviews some recent works in human detection in static and moving images. Section 3 describes the proposed features and Section 4 provides a description of the object validation and object tracking system. The implementation and comparative results are presented in Section 5. Finally, Section 6 summarizes the results.

2   Previous Work

Within the last decade a number of pedestrian detection systems have been presented to tackle the problem of finding humans from a moving platform. In this section we briefly review some more recent works on pedestrian detection. Systematic overviews of related work in this area can be found in [2] and [3].

While some pedestrian detection approaches are based on key-point detectors [4] or use a parts-based approach [5, 6], most up-to-date human detection approaches make use of the sliding-window analysis scheme. The performance of a sliding-window based method can be influenced by choosing various features and classifiers. Some widely used features extracted from the raw image data include Haar wavelet [7], HOG [1], edge orientation histogram (EOH) [8], edgelet [9], shapelet [10], region covariance [11], and LBP [12]. The most common classifiers, those employ statistical learning techniques to map from features to the likelihood of a pedestrian being present, usually either some variant of boosting algorithms [13, 14] or some types of support vector machines [15]. Researchers also explore different ways to combine various features to improve detection accuracy, such as the combination of gradient feature, edgelet, and Haar wavelets in [16] and the combined feature pool (Haar wavelets, EOH, edge density) in [13].

As an important visual feature, motion descriptors are widely used in video-based person detectors. Viola et al. [17] build a detector for static camera video surveillance by applying extended Haar wavelets over two consecutive frames of a video sequence to obtain motion and appearance information. In order to use motion for human detection from moving cameras, motion features derived from optic flow such as histograms of flow (HOF) are proposed by Dalal et al. [18]. These motion features are widely used in recent pedestrian detection systems [19, 20].

3   Feature Pool and Classifier

The proposed system aims to extract and track human objectives from onboard video streams. Efficiency and accuracy are two important issues of the system performance. In the following we describe the employed features including our proposed oriented Local Binary Patterns (Oriented LBP) feature and the HOG feature. This section also describes the classifier which we deployed in the sliding-window based system.

3.1   Feature Pool

Feature extraction is the first step in most object detection and tracking applications. The performance of these applications often relies on the extracted features. As mentioned above, a wide range of features have been proposed for pedestrian detection. We tried different successful features and their combination to choose suitable features for our moving camera pedestrian detection system. In particular we evaluate HOG, HOF, region covariance, LBP, and the color co-occurrence histograms [19]. The HOG and a new LBP features are chose because of the following reasons.

Firstly, the motion information is not included in the proposed system because the global motion caused by moving camera cannot be eliminated efficiently. The changing background also generates a large optical flow variance. Secondly, calculation of the region covariance feature and the color co-occurrence histograms (CH) is a time consuming task. For example, CH tracks the number of pairs of certain color pixels that occur at a specific distance. For a fixed distance interval and a quantized n_c representative colors, there are $n_c(n_c + 1)/2$ possible unique, non-ordered color pairs with corresponding bins in the CH. That is, in the case of $n_c = 128$, CH has 8128 dimensions [19].

HOG. Histograms of oriented gradients, proposed by Dalal and Triggs [1], are one of the most successful features in pedestrian detection applications. HOG features encode high frequency gradient information. Each 64×128 detection window is divided into 8×8 pixel cells and each group of 2×2 cells constitute a block with a stride step of 8 pixels in both horizontal and vertical directions. Each cell consists of a 9-bin histogram of oriented gradients, whereas each block contains a 36-D concatenated vector of all its cells and normalized to an L^2 unit length. A detection window is represented by 7×15 blocks, giving a total of 3780-D feature vector per detection window.

Although dense HOG features achieve good results in pedestrian detection, processing a 320×240 scale-space image still requires about 140ms on a personal computer with 3.0GHz CPU and 2GB memory. Hence, in our experiments we compute histograms with 9 bins on cells of 8×8 pixels. Block size is 2×2 cells with non-overlap (stride step 16 pixels). Each 64×128 detection window is represented by 4×8 blocks, yielding a total of 1152-D feature vector per detection window. According to [1], large stride step might decrease system performance. However, in our experiments, combining with other complementary features can significantly improve the system performance (see Fig. 2).

Oriented LBP. As a discriminative local descriptor, LBP is originally introduced in [22] and shows great success in human detection applications [12]. LBP feature has several advantages such as it can filter out noisy background using the concept of uniform pattern [12] and it is computational efficiency. To calculate the LBP feature, the detection window is divided into blocks and computes a histogram over each block according to the intensity difference between a center pixel and its neighbors. The histograms of the LBP patterns from all blocks are then concatenated to describe the texture of the detection window. For a 64×128 detection window with 32 non-overlap 16×16 blocks, its LBP feature has a 1888-D feature vector.

The HOG feature can be seen as an oriented gradient based human shape descriptor, while LBP feature serves as a local texture descriptor. Recent researches have shown that combination of these two features can achieve very good results in pedestrian detection [21]. However, extraction of the HOG-LBP feature is computational expensive. Each 64×128 detection window has a 5668-D (3780+1888) feature vector .

In this work we introduce a lower-dimensional variant of LBP, namely the oriented LBP. We define the arch of a pixel as all continuous "1" bits of its neighbors. The orientation $\theta(x,y)$ and magnitude $m(x,y)$ of a pixel is defined as its arch principle direction and the number of "1" bits in its arch, respectively (see Fig.1). The pixel orientation is evenly divided into k bins over $0°$ to $360°$. Then, the orientation histograms $F_{i,k}$ in each orientation bin k of cell C_i are obtained by summing all the pixel magnitudes whose orientations belong to bin k in C_i

$$F_{i,k} = \sum_{\substack{(x,y)\in C_i \\ \theta(x,y)\in bin_k}} m(x,y) \tag{1}$$

In our implementation, k is 8 for $LBP_{8,1}$, C_i has the size of 8×8 pixels. In this way, a 64×128 detection window with 32 non-overlap 16×16 blocks has a 1024-D ($4\times 8 \times 32$) oriented LBP feature vector. Finally, we have a 2176-D (1152+1024) HOG-Oriented LBP feature vector for each detection window. Fig. 1 illustrates the computation of Oriented LBP feature.

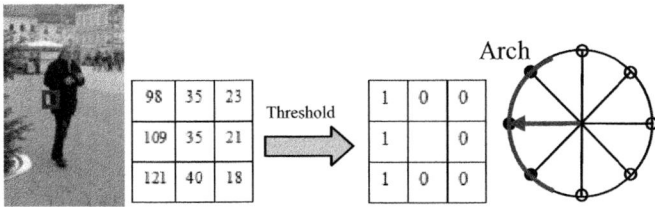

Fig. 1. Computing pixel orientation and magnitude of Oriented LBP feature. In this example we use a threshold of 20.

3.2   Classifier

Most pedestrian detection systems choose either SVMs or Adaboost as classifiers. We evaluate these classifiers using various common features and find the linear SVMs has better detection rate than that of boosting algorithms (see Fig.2 (b)). Moreover, with the lower-dimensional feature vector of the HOG-Oriented LBP feature, the processing speed of the same video frame using linear SVMs is similar to Adaboost. Therefore, we choose linear SVMs as classifier in the proposed pedestrian detection system.

4   Pedestrian Tracking

The output of the pedestrian detection step is a set of independent bounding boxes show possible locations of human objectives. Due to the cluttered background and limited number of positive/negative samples, the detection might have some false alarms. In order to recover from these problems, we employ a detection validation step before pedestrian tracking.

4.1   Detection Validation

Small objects with their height less than 40 pixels are discarded. After that, we compute a confidence measurement for each detected object based on its distance to the hyperplane of the SVM classifier. The distance between an example and the hyperplane can be calculated as follow:

$$d(x_i) = \frac{sgn(\omega x + b)}{|\omega|} = sgn(\sum_{j=1}^{i} y_j \alpha_j K(x_j, x_i + b)/|\omega| \tag{2}$$

where $K(x_j, x_i)$ is the kernel function.

The confidence measure of a pedestrian detection is in direct proportion to its distance to the hyperplane. Therefore, the confidence measure of an example is computed as:

$$conf(x_i) = \rho exp\left(-1/|d(x_i)|\right) \tag{3}$$

where ρ is a normalizing factor. Objects with their confidence measure less than τ are discarded as false positives. In practice, we found that setting the threshold as $\tau \in [0.65, 0.75]$ can provide good results.

In the next step, bounding boxes that do not satisfy the temporal coherence condition are removed. We define this condition as follow. When the first object is detected, a Kalman filter is initialized to start pretracking. The Kalman filter predicts its location in the next frame. A new detection in a consequent frame is assigned to this track if it coherently overlaps with the tracker prediction. In practice we set the overlap rate as 0.7. Only candidates meeting this condition in three consecutive frames are considered as a stable pedestrian objective and are labeled as positive.

4.2   Pedestrian Tracking

Once a candidate is validated as a pedestrian, pretracking stops and pedestrian tracking starts. In the object tracking step, each newly detected pedestrian with a positive mark is tracked by an individual Kalman filter. The detection validation and pedestrian tracking steps efficiently remove false positives from detection results.

5   Experimental Results

The proposed system is implemented on a personal computer with 3.0GHz CPU and 2GB memory running the Windows XP operating system and OpenCV libraries. For 320×240 pixel images, the implementation of the proposed system runs at about 13 to 15 frames/second, depending on the number of pedestrians being tracked.

We created several training and test video sequences containing thousands of positive (pedestrians) and negative (non-pedestrians) samples in different situations. The well-known INRIA person dataset is employed to evaluate the performance of the HOG-Oriented LBP feature. We also compare the detection results between the proposed system and several common pedestrian detection methods on both the INRIA dataset and the created video streams.

5.1   Performance of Different Features with SVM Classifier

First we implement the Dalal and Triggs algorithm using the same dataset and the same parameters suggested in their paper [1]. We compare its performance with other features, including non-overlap HOG, LBP, and HOG-LBP, using a linear SVMs classifier. As shown in Fig.2 (a), the HOG-LBP outperforms other features. However, the best performance of HOG-LBP is obtained by using a more complicated feature. As a result, the processing time of a 320×240 pixel video stream is about 7.7 frames per second (fps) using the HOG-LBP feature, whereas the cell-structured LBP feature has the fastest processing speed. The processing speed of various features on the same video stream using a linear SVMs classifier is shown in Table 1.

In our experiment, the HOG feature has block spacing stride of 8 pixels and the value of non-overlap HOG feature is 16 pixels. As Fig.2 (a) shows, overlapping blocks introduce redundant in the final descriptor vector but increase the performance. The miss rate decreases by 3% at 10^{-3}FPPW when we change from HOG feature to non-overlap HOG feature. The advantage of non-overlap HOG is its high processing speed, about 40% faster than that of HOG feature.

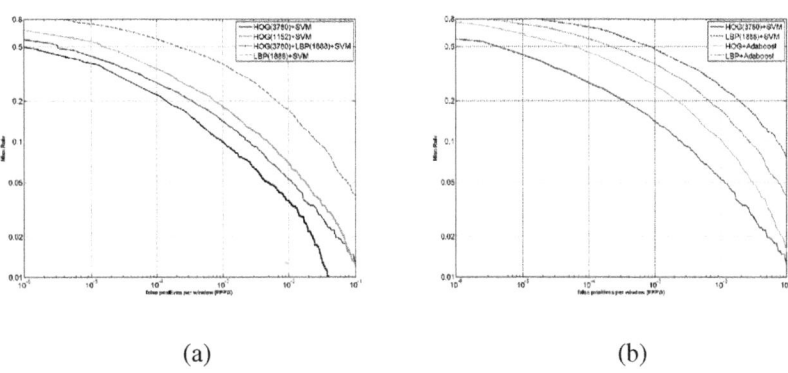

(a)   (b)

Fig. 2. Performance comparison of different features (a) and different classifiers (b)

Table 1. Precessing speed of different features

Features	HOG	Non-overlap HOG	LBP	HOG-LBP	Non-overlap HOG-Oriented LBP
Precessing time (fps)	11.8	16.0	17.4	7.7	14.1

5.2   Comparison of SVM and Adaboost Classifier

SVM and Adaboost are the two most popular classifiers and are widely used in various pedestrian detection systems. We evaluate the performance of these classifiers using Haar wavelet, HOG, and LBP features on the INRIA dataset.

As shown in Fig.2 (b), using HOG and LBP features with SVM classifier outperforms Adaboost classifier on the INRIA dataset. We observe that the performance of Haar wavelet feature is worse than HOG and LBP features, which reflects the fact that the intensity pattern of human face is simple than that of human body. Hence, Haar wavelet feature is more suitable for human face detection applications.

By treating each bin of HOG feature as an individual feature, we implement HOG-Adaboost pedestrian detection on the INRIA dataset in order to comparing its performance to HOG-SVM detector. The block size changes from 12×12 to 64×128. We observe performance decrease by about 9% at 10^{-3}FPPW when we change from SVM detector to Adaboost detector. Moreover, processing time of the two classifiers is similar when using the HOG feature. This is caused by the reason that computing histograms of oriented gradient for a sub-window spends much more time than computing intensity difference, even with the help of cascade structure and the integral images.

5.3   Detection Results with HOG-Oriented LBP Feature

As our main contribution is integrating the non-overlap HOG feature with the Oriented LBP feature to achieve efficient and accurate human detection, we compare the performance of our non-overlap HOG-Oriented LBP feature with the HOG-LBP feature on the INRIA dataset. As we can see from Fig.3, the HOG-LBP feature achieves detection rate about 91% at 10^{-3}FPPW, better than the proposed non-overlap HOG-Oriented LBP feature by about 3%. However, the processing speed of our proposed feature is about 2 times faster than the HOG-LBP feature.

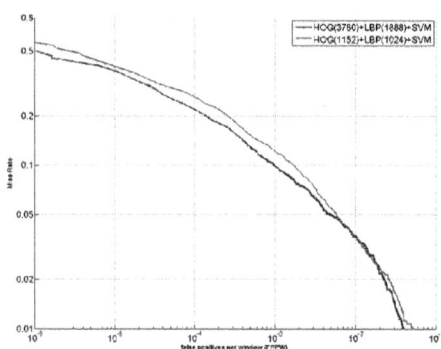

Fig. 3. Performance comparison between HOG-LBP and the proposed feature

Fig.4 shows some pedestrian detection results of the augmented system on the INRIA dataset and our video sequences. Some examples with false positives are shown in the bottom row. As mentioned in section 4, using the detection validation method can efficiently remove most of these false alarms.

Fig. 4. Pedestrian detection examples using the proposed system; Top row: examples from INRIA dataset; Middle row: examples of video streams; Bottom row: examples with false alarms

6 Conclusions

We introduce a new pedestrian detection system in this work, which aims at extracting and tracking human objectives from video streams with high efficiency and accuracy. We demonstrate the proposed human detection algorithm that has similar detection rate of up-to-date methods with an up to 2 times speedup. This is achieved by integrating the non-overlap HOG feature with an Oriented LBP feature. In this way, a lower dimensional and high discriminative feature vector is obtained for each detection window. Detection validation based on temporal coherence condition is employed to reject possible false alarms.

Acknowledgments. This work was supported in part by the NSFC research project (Grant No. 61003297).

References

1. Dalal, N., Triggs, B.: Histograms of Oriented Gradients for Human Detection. In: IEEE Computer Society Conference on Computer Vision and Pattern Recognition, CVPR, vol. 1, pp. 886–893 (2005)
2. Geronimo, D., Lopez, A.M., Sappa, A.D., Graf, T.: Survey of Pedestrian Detection for Advanced Driver Assistance Systems. IEEE Transactions on Pattern Analysis and Machine Intelligence 32(7), 1239–1258 (2010)

3. Enzweiler, M., Gavrila, D.M.: Monocular Pedestrian Detection: Survey and Experiments. IEEE Transactions on Pattern Analysis and Machine Intelligence 31(12), 2179–2195 (2009)
4. Seemann, E., Fritz, M., Schiele, B.: Towards robust pedestrian detection in crowded image sequences. In: IEEE Computer Society Conference on Computer Vision and Pattern Recognition, CVPR, pp. 1–8 (2007)
5. Alonso, I.P., Llorca, D.F., Sotelo, M.A., Bergasa, L.M., Toro, P.R., Ocana, M., Garrido, M.A.G.: Combination of Feature Extraction Methods for SVM Pedestrian Detection. IEEE Transactions on Intelligent Transportation Systems 8(2), 292–307 (2007)
6. Wu, B., Vevatia, R.: Detection of Multiple, Partially Occluded Humans in a Single Image by Bayesian Combination of Edgelet Part Detectors. In: IEEE International Conference on Computer Vision (ICCV), vol. 1, pp. 90–97 (2005)
7. Papageorgiou, C., Poggio, T.: A trainable system for object detection. International Journal of Computer Vision 38(1), 15–33 (2000)
8. Levi, K., Weiss, Y.: Learning Object Detection from a Small Number of Examples: the Importance of Good Features. In: IEEE Computer Society Conference on Computer Vision and Pattern Recognition, CVPR, pp. 53–60 (2004)
9. Wu, B., Nevatia, R.: Detection and Segmentation of Multiple, Partially Occluded Objects by Grouping, Merging, Assigning Part Detection Responses. International Journal of Compute Vision 82, 185–204 (2009)
10. Sabzmeydani, P., Mori, G.: Detecting Pedestrians by Learning Shapelet Features. In: IEEE Conference on Computer Vision and Pattern Recognition, CVPR, pp. 1–8 (2007)
11. Paisitkriangkrai, S., Shen, C., Zhang, J.: Fast Pedestrian Detection Using a Cascade of Boosted Covariance Features. IEEE Transactions on Circuits and Systems for Video Technology 18(8), 1140–1151 (2008)
12. Mu, Y., Yan, S., Liu, Y., Huang, T., Zhou, B.: Discriminative Local Binary Patterns for Human Detection in Personal Album. In: IEEE Computer Society Conference on Computer Vision and Pattern Recognition, CVPR, pp. 1–8 (2008)
13. Chen, Y., Chen, C.: Fast Human Detection Using a Novel Boosted Cascading Structure With Meta Stages. IEEE Transactions on Image Processing 17(8), 1452–1464 (2008)
14. Kim, T., Cipolla, R.: MCBoost: Multiple Classifier Boosting for Perceptual Co-clustering of Images and Visual Features. In: Neural Information Processing Systems Foundation, NIPS (2008)
15. Lin, Z., Davis, L.S.: A pose-invariant descriptor for human detection and segmentation. In: Forsyth, D., Torr, P., Zisserman, A. (eds.) ECCV 2008, Part IV. LNCS, vol. 5305, pp. 423–436. Springer, Heidelberg (2008)
16. Hu, B., Wang, S., Ding, X.: Multi Features Combination for Pedestrian Detection. Journal of Multimedia 5(1), 79–84 (2010)
17. Viola, P., Jones, M.J., Snow, D.: Detecting Pedestrians Using Patterns of Motion and Appearance. In: IEEE International Conference on Computer Vision, ICCV (2003)
18. Dalal, N., Triggs, B., Schmid, C.: Human Detection Using Oriented Histograms of Flow and Appearance. In: Leonardis, A., Bischof, H., Pinz, A. (eds.) ECCV 2006 Part II. LNCS, vol. 3952, pp. 428–441. Springer, Heidelberg (2006)
19. Walk, S., Majer, N., Schindler, K., Schiele, B.: New Features and Insights for Pedestrian Detection. In: IEEE Conference on Computer Vision and Pattern Recognition, CVPR, pp. 1030–1037 (2010)
20. Wojek, C., Walk, S., Schiele, B.: Multi-Cue Onboard Pedestrian Detection. In: IEEE Computer Society Conference on Computer Vision and Pattern Recognition, CVPR, pp. 794–801 (2009)
21. Wang, X., Han, T.X., Yan, S.: A HOG-LBP Human Detector with Partial Occlusion Handling. In: IEEE International Conference on Computer Vision, ICCV (2009)
22. Ojala, T., Pietikäinen, M., Harwood, D.: A comparative study of texture measures with classification based on featured distributions. Pattern Recognition 29(1), 51–59 (1996)

An Efficient Checkpointing Scheme Using Price History of Spot Instances in Cloud Computing Environment

Daeyong Jung[1], SungHo Chin[1], KwangSik Chung[2], HeonChang Yu[1],
and JoonMin Gil[3,*]

[1] Dept. of Computer Science and Education, Korea University, Seoul, Korea
[2] Dept. of Computer Science, Korea National Open University, Seoul, Korea
[3] School of Computer & Information Communications Engineering,
Catholic University of Daegu, Daegu, Korea
{karat,wingtop,yuhc}@korea.ac.kr,
kchung0825@knou.ac.kr,jmgil@cu.ac.kr

Abstract. The cloud computing is a computing paradigm that users can rent computing resources from service providers as much as they require. A spot instance in cloud computing helps a user to utilize resources with less expensive cost, even if it is unreliable. When a user performs tasks with unreliable spot instances, failures inevitably lead to the delay of task completion time and cause a seriously deterioration in the QoS of users. Therefore, we propose a price history based checkpointing scheme to avoid the delay of task completion time. The proposed checkpointing scheme reduces the number of checkpoint trials and improves the performance of task execution. The simulation results show that our scheme outperforms the existing checkpointing schemes in terms of the reduction of both the number of checkpoint trials and total costs per spot instance for user's bid.

Keywords: Cloud computing, Checkpointing, Spot instances, Price history.

1 Introduction

Cloud computing is a type of parallel and distributed system consisting of a collection of interconnected and virtualized computers that are dynamically provisioned and presented as one or more unified computing resources based on service-level agreements established through negotiation between the service provider and consumers [1]. Typically, cloud computing services provide high level of scalability of IT resources with combined Internet technology to multiple customers [2].

Many definitions of cloud computing have been suggested [3, 4, 5]. Recently, several commercial cloud systems have been developed, such as Amazon EC2 [6], GoGrid [7], and FlexiScale [8]. Open-source cloud computing middlewares such as Eucalyptus [9], OpenNebula [10], and Nimbus [11] have been also provided in this literature. In the most of these clouds, the concept of an instance unit is used to provide users with resources in a cost-efficient way. An instance means the VM (Virtual

---

* Corresponding author.

E. Altman and W. Shi (Eds.): NPC 2011, LNCS 6985, pp. 185–200, 2011.
© IFIP International Federation for Information Processing 2011

Machine) which is suitable for users' requirements. Generally, instances are classified into two types: on-demand instances and spot instances. The on-demand instances have a task execution for compute capacity by the hour with no long-term commitments. This frees users from the costs and complexities of planning, purchasing, and maintaining hardware and transforms what are commonly large fixed costs into much smaller variable costs [6]. While, the spot instances allow users to bid on unused cloud computing capacity and run those instances for as long as their bid exceeds the current spot price. The spot price changes periodically based on supply and demand, and users whose bids meet or exceed it gain access to the available spot instances. If users have flexibility in when applications can run, spot instances can significantly lower users' costs [6]. For task completion, therefore, spot instances have lower costs than on-demand instances. However, there is a problem that task failures can be incurred by the use of spot instances with higher cost than user suggested bid.

In this paper, we attempt to find a solution for an efficient checkpointing scheme in unreliable cloud computing environments and propose a price history based checkpointing scheme, by which users can pay the optimal cost based on SLA (Service Level Agreement). In the scheme, SLA management is done by the coordinator. The coordinator supports and manages SLA between users and instances. The failure of instances results in the delay of task completion time, so we design the cost-efficient checkpointing algorithm to solve the failure problem. In our proposed scheme, the checkpoints are taken on two points. One is the checkpoint taken on the rising edge in an execution bid when spot prices are more than a given threshold. The other is the checkpoint taken on the point when failure occurrence time is predicted by average execution time and failure possibility in an execution bid. Moreover, we carry out simulations to demonstrate the effectiveness of our scheme. Simulation results show that our scheme outperforms the existing schemes, such as hour-boundary checkpointing [17] and rising edge-driven checkpointing [14], in term of the reduction of both the number of checkpoint trials and total costs per spot instance for user' bid.

The rest of this paper is organized as follows: Section 2 briefly describes related work on checkpoint and SLA in cloud computing. Section 3 presents our system architecture and its components. Section 4 presents our SLA and checkpoint algorithms based on the price history of spot instances. Section 5 presents performance evaluations with simulations. Lastly, Section 6 concludes the paper.

2   Related Work

The unreliable cloud computing environment (spot instances) is less cost than reliable cloud computing environment (on-demand instances) in task processing environment. However, in unreliable cloud computing, it is difficult to estimate the total execution time of tasks and the total cost to be paid by users. Moreover, since task failures frequently occur according to the supply of instances and the demand of users on instances in unreliable cloud computing, many systems have used the checkpoint mechanisms to minimize task loss and reduce the rollback time of tasks.

In [12], authors proposed spot instance scheme that users can decide a minimum cost according to an SLA agreement between users and instances in Amazon's EC2. The scheme is based on a probabilistic model for the optimization of cost, performance and reliability and improved the reliability of services by changing dynamical-ly conditions to satisfy user requirements. To improve the reliability of services, this paper focuses on user costs rather than the point to be taken a checkpoint.

Due to the dynamic nature of the cloud computing, continuous monitoring on Quality of Service (QoS) attributes is necessary to enforce SLAs. In [13], authors proposed a mechanism for managing SLAs in cloud computing environment using the Web Service Level Agreement (WSLA) framework developed for SLA monitoring and SLA enforcement in a Service Oriented Architecture (SOA).

In [2], cloud platforms host several independent applications on a shared resource pool with the ability to allocate computing power to applications on per-demand ba-sis. This paper proposed an autonomic resource manager to control the virtualized environment which decouples the provisioning of resources from the dynamic place-ment of virtual machines. This manager aims to optimize a global utility function which integrates both the degree of SLA fulfillment and computational costs.

In [13] and [2], authors focuses on cloud resource management in the reliable cloud computing environment, but this paper focuses on the unreliable cloud compu-ting environment for the resource management applied to the SLA.

[14] introduced the spot instances of the Amazon Elastic Compute Cloud (EC2) to offer less resource costs in exchange for reduced reliability. Based on the actual price history of EC2 spot instances, authors compared several adaptive checkpointing schemes in terms of monetary costs and the improvement of job completion time.

In this paper, we propose checkpoint scheme based on SLA to satisfy user require-ments. Moreover, we compare our proposed checkpointing scheme with the existing checkpointing schemes (hour boundary checkpointing [17] and rising edge check-pointing [14]).

3   System Architecture

Fig. 1 shows the cloud computing environment assumed in this paper. This cloud computing environment basically consists of four entities: a cloud server, a storage server, cluster servers, and cloud users. The cloud server is connected to cluster

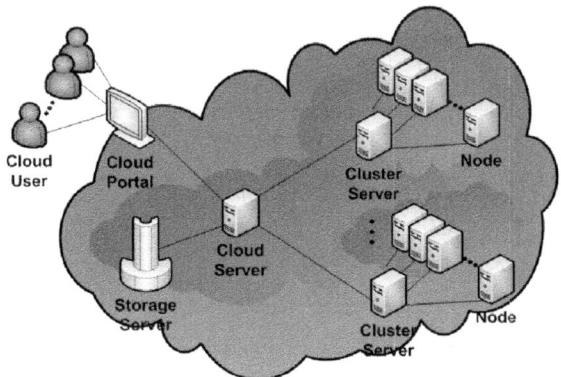

Fig. 1. Cloud computing environment

servers and storage servers. The cluster server is composed of a lot of nodes. The cloud users can access the cloud server via the cloud portal to utilize the nodes in the cluster servers as resources. Therefore, the cloud server takes the responsibility of finding virtual resources to satisfy the user's requirements, such as SLA requirements and QoS requirements. The coordinator in the cloud server manages tasks and is responsible for the SLA management. We focus on the coordinator and the VM, which play an important role in our checkpointing scheme.

3.1   Layer Structure

Fig. 2 shows the structure of coordinator in the cloud server that is composed of scheduler, VM Information Manager, History Manager, SLA Manager, QoS Manager and VM Information Collector. In the coordinator, the four managers are responsible for generating and maintaining a list of available VMs, based on the information collected from VM Information Collector. The VM Information Collector collects VM information and provides it for VM information Manager. The VM Information Manager generates a list of CPU utilization, available memory and storage space, network bandwidth, and so on. The History Manager manages the history data, in which the past bid and execution time of spot instances are accumulated. SLA Manager and QoS Manager manage the SLA requirements and the QoS requirements, respectively. When a cloud user requests job execution, the Scheduler allocates the requested job to the selected VM.

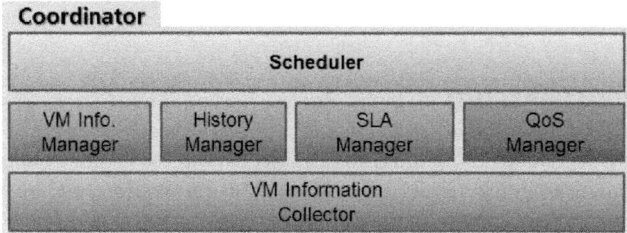

Fig. 2. The structure of Coordinator

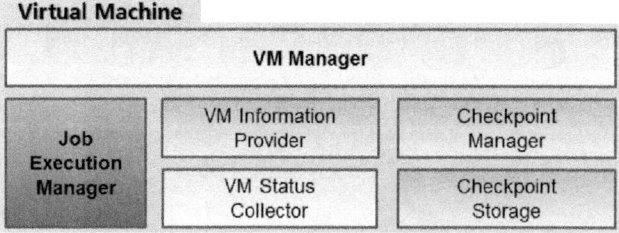

Fig. 3. The structure of Virtual Machine

Fig. 3 shows the structure of the VM. In this figure, VM Status Collector collects the status information of the VM, such as CPU utilization and memory space. VM Information Provider extracts resource information needed for job execution using the VM status Collector and delivers the resource information to VM Manager. Job execution Manager executes a requested job from the coordinator and returns a job result to VM Manager, and then VM Manager delivers the result to the coordinator. Checkpoint Manager manages checkpointing status and the data checkpointed by the Checkpoint Manager is stored to Checkpoint Storage.

3.2   Instances Types

An instance means the VM that a cloud user uses. The instances are classified into two types: on-demand instances and spot instances. In on-demand instances, users can use VM resources after paying a fixed cost to lend instances per hour. On the other hand, using the spot instances, users can use VM resources only when the price of instances is smaller than other users' bid. The difference between the two instance types is as follows: in on-demand instances, a failure does not occur during task execution, but the cost is comparatively high. On the contrary, the cost of spot instances for task completion is lower than that of on-demand instances. However, task failures are inevitably encountered when there exist the instances with higher price than a user's bid.

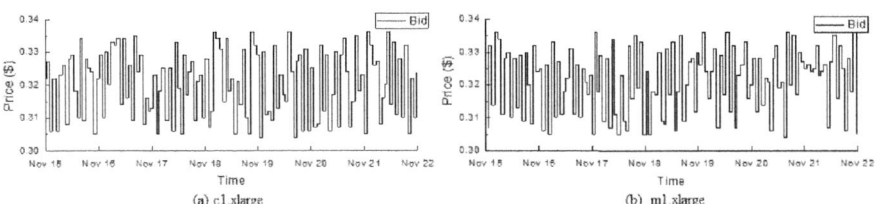

Fig. 4. Price history of EC2's spot instances

Amazon allows users to bid on unused EC2 capacity provided as 42 types of spot instances [15]. Their prices that are called *spot prices* are changed dynamically based on supply and demand. Fig. 4 shows examples of fluctuations of spot price for c1-xlarge (Standard Spot Instances - Extra Large) and m1-xlarge (High-Memory Spot Instances - Extra Large) during 7 days on November 2010 [16]. Our proposed system model is based on the characteristics of Amazon EC2's spot instances.

- The system provides a spot instance when user's bid is greater than the current price.
- The system stops immediately without any notice when user's bid is less than or equal to the current price. We call this an out-if-bid event or a failure.
- The system does not charge the latest partial hour when the system stops an instance.

- The system charges the latest partial hour when the user terminates an instance.
- The system provides the history of spot price.

4   The SLA Based Checkpointing Scheme

In this section, we propose the SLA (Service Level Agreement) based checkpointing scheme in the spot instances.

4.1   SLA Based on Price History Using Spot Instances

Fig. 5 shows the process of SLA between a user and an instance. A user determines an instance type and the user's bid to begin tasks in the instance. The coordinator calculates a task execution time based on user configurations, such as the user's bid and the instance type. Then, the coordinator sends a request message to the selected instance to investigate the performance of the instance and calculates the expected execution time, the expected failure time and the expected cost. In addition, the coordinator sends a user the expected execution time and cost. When a task is completed in the selected instance, the coordinator receives task results from the instance and sends them to the user. In Fig. 5, the prediction function plays an important role in our SLA processing because it performs the estimation process of the expected failure time, the expected execution time, and the expected cost using price history. The following shows a detailed description for the prediction function.

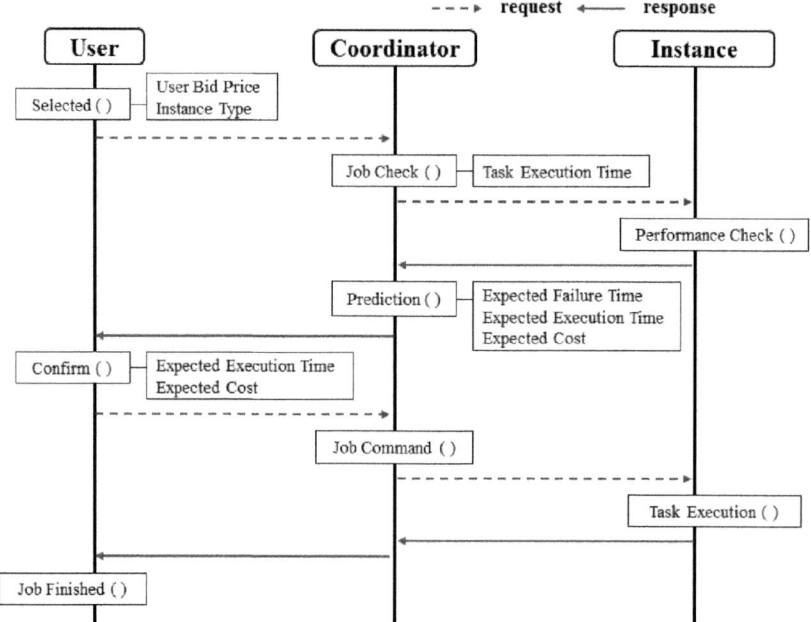

Fig. 5. SLA processing

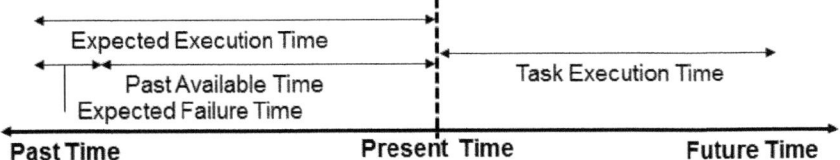

Fig. 6. Extraction of expected execution time from price history

Fig. 6 shows an illustrative example for task execution time, past available time, expected execution time, and expected failure time. The detailed definition for them is as follows:

- Task execution time: the total time needed to execute a task in the selected instance without failures.
- Past available time: the average execution time performed on the selected instance in the past time, excluding failure time. It is extracted from price history.
- Expected failure time: the time period when the spot price extracted from the price history exceeds a user's bid; *i.e.*, a total sum of failure time in the past time.
- Expected execution time: the sum of the past available time and the expected failure time.
- Total expected cost: the sum of costs that is charged for task execution.

4.2   Fault Tolerance Mechanisms Using Checkpoints

In the spot instance environment, a task fails when the cost exceeds the user's bid. Typically, this problem has been solved by using the checkpointing scheme, one of fault tolerance mechanisms [14]. In this section, we explain the existing checkpointing schemes and our proposed checkpointing scheme.

4.2.1   Hour-Boundary Checkpointing Scheme

Fig. 7 illustrates the hour-boundary checkpointing scheme. This scheme takes a checkpoint in time boundaries, and a user pays the cost per hour without the user's bid. If the failure of a task is occurs, the running task is stopped. The task is restarted at the position of the last checkpoint.

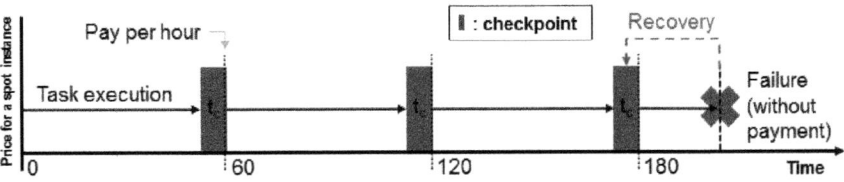

Fig. 7. Hour-boundary checkpointing

4.2.2   Rising Edge-Driven Checkpointing Scheme

Fig. 8 shows the rising edge-driven checkpointing scheme. This scheme takes a checkpoint when the cost is less than user's bid and the cost of spot instances is raised. It will increase the number of checkpoints significantly when cost is frequently fluctuated. The critical problem associated with this scheme is that the rollback time becomes long in case that the rising edge is not appeared in spot price for a long period after a checkpoint is taken. This leads to longer task completion time.

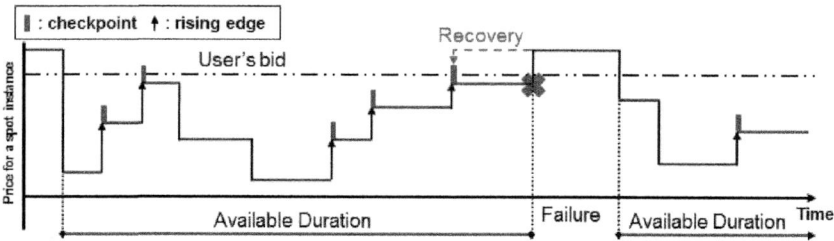

Fig. 8. Rising edge-driven checkpointing

4.2.3   Our Proposed Checkpointing Scheme

Fig. 9 illustrates our proposed checkpointing scheme. This scheme basically performs checkpointing operation using two kinds of thresholds, price threshold and time threshold, based on the expected execution time of the price history. Now, let t_a and t_b denote, respectively, a start point and an end point in the expected execution time. Based on t_a and t_b, we obtain the price threshold ($PriceTh$) and the time threshold ($TimeTh_{p_i}$), which are used as thresholds in our proposed checkpoint scheme.

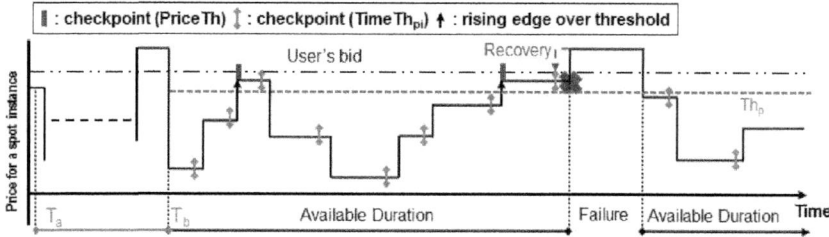

Fig. 9. Our proposed checkpointing scheme

The price threshold, $PriceTh$, can be calculated by

$$PriceTh = \frac{P_{min} + User_{bid}}{2}$$

where $User_{bid}$ represents the bid suggested by the user. P_{min} represents an available minimum price in a period between t_a and t_b as follows:

$$P_{min} = PriceMin(t_a, t_b)$$

The time threshold of price P_i, $TimeTh_{p_i}$, can be calculated by

$$TimeTh_{p_i} = AvgTime_{P_i}(t_a, t_b) \times (1 - F_{p_i})$$

where F_{p_i} is the failure probability of price P_i and $AvgTime_{P_i}(t_a, t_b)$ represents the average execution time of P_i in a period between t_a and t_b.

```
1:   Boolean flag = false              // a flag representing occurrence of a task failure
2:   while (!task execution finishes) do
3:       if (spot prices < User's bid ) then
4:           if (flag) then
5:               Recovery ( );
6:               flag = false;
7:           end if
8:           if (!flag) then
9:               if (rising edge && Price Threshold ≤ spot prices) then
10:                  Checkpoint ( );
11:              end if
12:              if (Time Threshold < execution time in current price) then
13:                  Checkpoint ( );
14:              end if
15:          end if
16:      end if
17:      if (failure is occurred) then
18:          flag = true;
19:      end if
20:  end while
21:  Function Checkpoint ( )
22:      take a checkpoint on the spot instance;
23:      send the checkpoint to the storage;
24:  end Function
25:  Function Recovery ( )
26:      rollback the checkpoint to the storage;
27:      restart the job execution;
28:  end Function
```

Fig. 10. Checkpointing and recovery algorithms

Using these two thresholds, our proposed checkpointing scheme performs checkpoint operations according to two cases: first case is that a checkpoint is performed when there is a rising edge between the user's bid and the price threshold. Second case is based on the failure probability and average execution time of each price. A checkpoint is performed when the time threshold exceeds the execution time of current price.

Fig. 10 shows the checkpointing and recovery algorithms used in our proposed scheme. In the algorithms, the flag representing the occurrence of a task failure is initially set to false. The checkpointing process repeats until all tasks are completed. When task execution is normal (i.e., the flag is false), the scheduler performs check-point process to provide against job failure (lines 2-20). Recovery process is per-formed when the flag is true (lines 4-7). Two cases of checkpoints are performed (lines 8-15). If the rising spot price is between user's bid and price threshold, the scheduler performs checkpointing operation (lines 9-11). If the execution time is greater than the time threshold, the scheduler also performs checkpointing operation (lines 12-14). When task failure event occurs, the flag is set to true to invoke the re-covery function (lines 17-19). Lines 21-24 and 25-28 show a detail process of the checkpointing and recovery, respectively.

Our proposed scheme can reduce checkpointing overhead because the number of checkpoints is less than that of the existing checkpointing schemes (hour-boundary checkpointing and rising edge-driven checkpointing). In our proposed scheme, the two thresholds and expected failure time are calculated based on price history. The thresholds are dynamically changed according to the price behavior of instances in the price history.

5   Performance Evaluation

In this section, we evaluate the performance of our checkpointing scheme using simu-lations and compare it with that of the other checkpointing schemes.

5.1   Simulation Environments

Our simulations are conducted using the history data obtained from the Amazon EC2's spot instances [16], which is accumulated during a period from 11-15-2010 to 11-22-2010 as shown in Fig. 4. The history data before 11-18-2010 are used to extract the expected execution time and failure occurrence probability for our checkpointing scheme. The applicability of our checkpointing scheme is tested using the history data after 11-18-2010, which are also used for hour-boundary checkpointing and rising edge-driven checkpointing schemes.

In the simulations, two types of spot instances are applied to show the effect of two different resource types on the performance of three checkpointing schemes; one resource type is a computing-type instance and another type is a memory-type in-stance. Table 1 shows the resource types used in our simulation. In this table, c1.xlarge offers more compute units than other resources and can be used for com-pute-intensive applications. On the other hand, m1.xlarge offers much memory capac-ity than other resources and can be used for high-throughput applications, including database and memory caching applications. Under the simulation environments, we compare the performance of our checkpointing scheme with that of the two check-pointing schemes in terms of the task execution time, the failure time, the number of failures, and the number of checkpoints.

Table 1. Resource types

Instance type name	Compute unit	Virtual cores	Memory	Storage	Platform
c1.xlarge (computing Instance)	8 EC2	4core (2 EC2)	15GB	1690GB	64-bit
m1.xlarge (high-memory Instance)	6.5 EC2	2core (3.25 EC2)	17.1GB	420GB	64-bit

5.2 The Analysis of Computing-Type Instances

Before analyzing the performance of our checkpointing scheme, we firstly extract parameter values from the spot history presented in Fig. 4(a). Table 2 shows the simulation parameters and values used for the analysis of computing-type instances.

Table 2. Simulation parameters and values for c1.xlarge instance

Simulation parameter	Task time	Max Bid	Average bid	Min bid	Checkpoint time	Recovery time
Value	259200(s)	0.336($)	0.319($)	0.304($)	300(s)	300(s)

We also extract the failure occurrence probability for each price from the spot history (11-15-2010 ~ 11-18-2010) presented in Fig. 4(a). The extracted failure occurrence probability is used to determine the time threshold in our checkpointing scheme. Fig. 11 shows the failure occurrence probability for c1.xlarge instance. In this figure, X and Y-axis mean spot price and failure occurrence probability per spot price for a given user's bid, respectively.

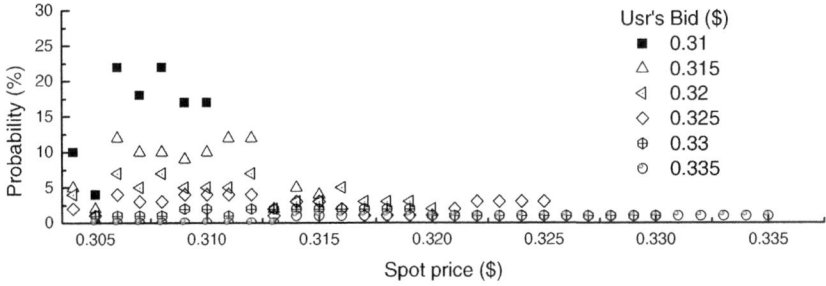

Fig. 11. Failure occurrence probability for c1.xlarge instance

Fig. 12 shows the performance comparison of our checkpointing scheme with hour-boundary checkpointing and rising edge-driven checkpointing schemes when tasks in c1.xlarge instance are used. Fig. 12(a) shows the effect of total task execution time and total failure time on the performance of three checkpointing schemes. Fig. 12(b) shows the effect of the number of failures and checkpoints in each user's bid on the performance of three checkpointing schemes.

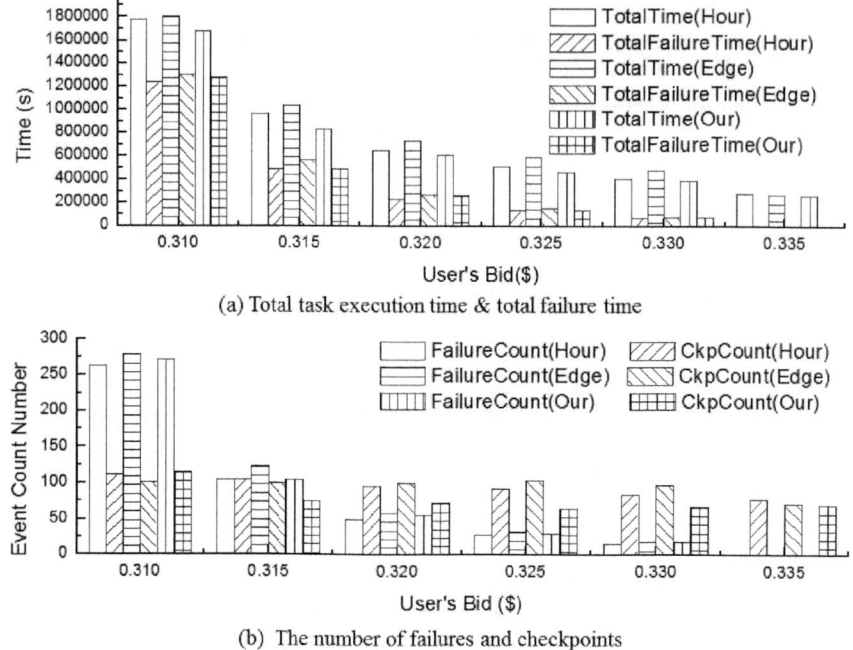

(a) Total task execution time & total failure time

(b) The number of failures and checkpoints

Fig. 12. Performance comparison of checkpointing schemes in c1.xlarge

From this figure, we can find that our checkpointing scheme achieves performance improvements in an average task execution time of 7.9% over the hour-boundary checkpointing scheme and in an average task execution time of 14.3% over the rising edge-driven checkpointing scheme. We can also find that our scheme reduces the number of checkpoints by average of 17 times over the hour-boundary checkpointing scheme and by average of 18 times over the rising edge-driven checkpointing scheme.

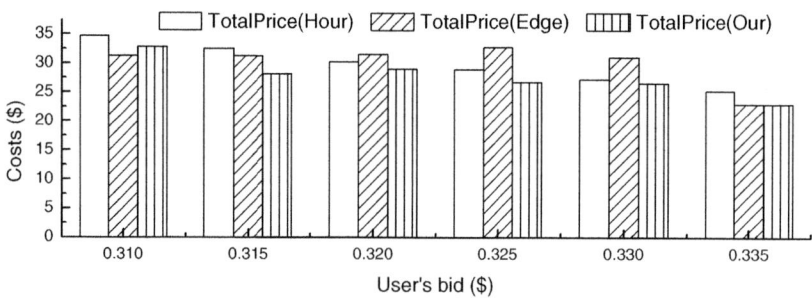

Fig. 13. Comparison of total costs in c1.xlarge

Fig. 13 shows the total costs in each user's bid. From this figure, we can see that our checkpointing scheme reduces the costs by average of $2.08 over the hour-boundary checkpointing scheme and by average of $2.42 over the rising edge-driven checkpointing scheme.

5.3 The Analysis of Memory-Type Instances

Now, we present the performance evaluation of our checkpointing scheme when memory-type instances are used. As the analysis presented in previous subsection, we firstly extract parameter values from the spot history presented in Fig. 4(b). Table 3 shows the simulation parameters and values used for the analysis of memory-type instances.

Table 3. Simulation value of m1.xlarge instance

Simulation parameter	Task time	Max bid	Average bid	Min bid	Checkpoint time	Recovery time
Value	259200(s)	0.76($)	0.32($)	0.304($)	300(s)	300(s)

We also extract the failure occurrence probability for each price from the spot history (11-15-2010 ~ 11-18-2010) in Fig. 4(b). Fig. 14 shows the failure occurrence probability for m1.xlarge instance. In this figure, X and Y-axis mean spot price and failure occurrence probability per spot price for a given user's bid, respectively.

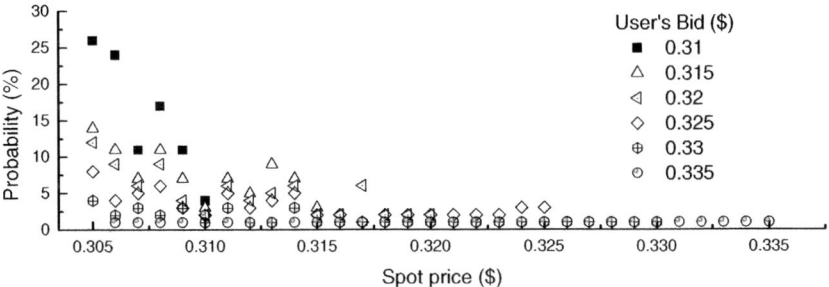

Fig. 14. Comparison of fault occurrence probability in m1.xlarge

Fig. 15 shows the performance comparison of our checkpointing scheme with hour-boundary checkpointing and rising edge-driven checkpointing schemes when tasks in the m1.xlarge instance are used. Fig. 15(a) shows the effect of total task execution time and total failure time on the performance of three checkpointing schemes. Fig. 15(b) shows the effect of the number of failures and checkpoints in each user's bid on the performance of three checkpointing schemes.

From this figure, we can find that our checkpointing scheme achieves performance improvements in an average task execution time of 14.35% over the hour-boundary checkpointing scheme and in an average task execution time of 23.83% over the rising edge-driven checkpointing scheme. We can also find that our scheme reduces the number of checkpoints by average of 28 times over the hour-boundary checkpointing scheme and by average of 31 times over the rising edge-driven checkpointing scheme.

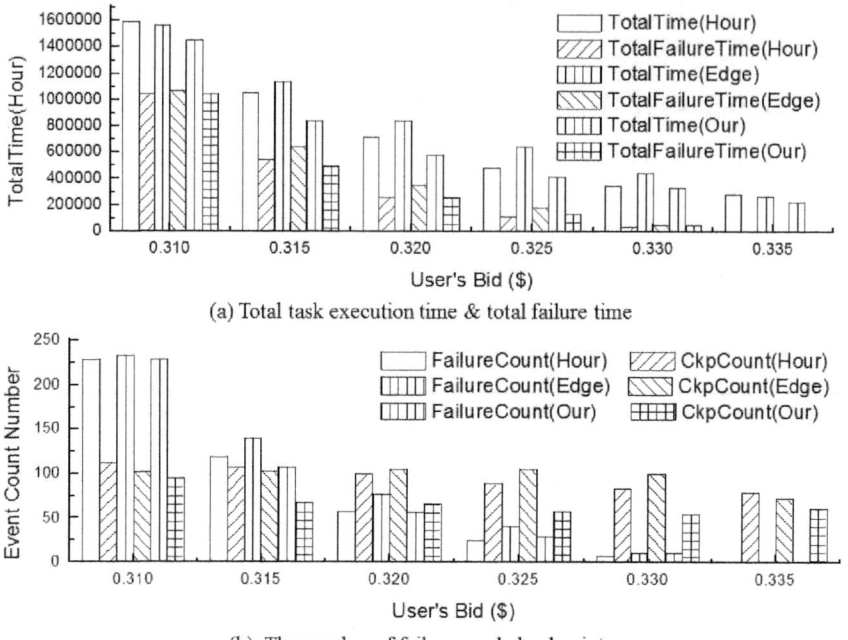

(a) Total task execution time & total failure time

(b) The number of failures and checkpoints

Fig. 15. Performance comparison of checkpointing schemes in m1.xlarge

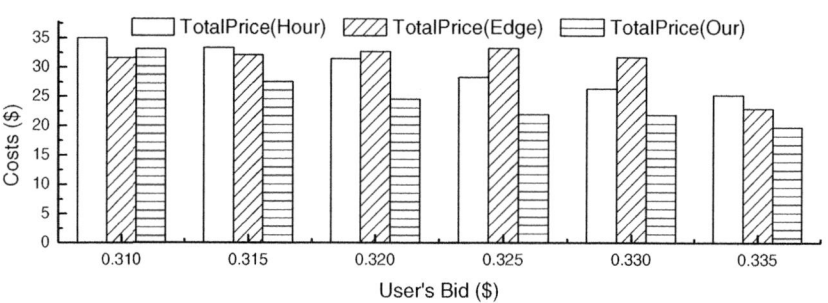

Fig. 16. Comparison of total costs in m1.xlarge

Fig. 16 shows the total costs in each user's bid. From this figure, we can see that our checkpointing scheme reduces the costs by average of $5.15 over the hour-boundary checkpointing scheme, and by average of $5.93 over the rising edge-driven checkpointing scheme.

6   Conclusion

In this paper, we proposed an efficient checkpointing scheme using the price history of spot instances to improve the stability of task processing in unreliable cloud computing environment. Our proposed scheme basically performs checkpointing operation based on two kinds of thresholds, price threshold and time threshold. These two thresholds were extracted from the price history of spot instances and used to determine checkpointing position in cost-efficient way in the presence of the failures of spot instances arisen from price fluctuation. As a result, our scheme can significantly reduce the number of checkpoint trials compared to the existing checkpointing schemes. Furthermore, the rollback time of our scheme can be much lesser than that of the existing checkpointing schemes because our scheme can adaptively perform checkpointing operation according to the time and price of spot instances. Simulation results showed that our scheme can achieve cost efficiency by reducing rollback time per instance for a given user's bid regardless of the resource types of spot instances. In the future, we have a plan to expand our environment into a combination of spot instances and on-demand instances for various cloud computing services.

Acknowledgments. This research was supported by Basic Science Research Program through the National Research Foundation of Korea (NRF) funded by the Ministry of Education, Science and Technology (No. 2010-0015637).

References

[1] Buyya, R., Chee Shin, Y., Venugopal, S.: Market-Oriented Cloud Computing: Vision, Hype, and Reality for Delivering IT Services as Computing Utilities. In: Proceeding of the 10th IEEE International Conference on High Performance Computing and Communications, pp. 5–13 (2008)

[2] Van, H.N., Tran, F.D., Menaud, J.-M.: SLA-Aware Virtual Resource Management for Cloud Infrastructures. In: Proceedings of the 2009 Ninth IEEE International Conference on Computer and Information Technology, vol. 2, pp. 357–362. IEEE Computer Society, Los Alamitos (2009)

[3] Armbrust, M., Fox, A., Griffith, R., Joseph, A.D., Katz, R.H., Konwinski, A., Lee, G., Patterson, D.A., Rabkin, A., Stoica, I., Zaharia, M.: Above the Clouds: A Berkeley View of Cloud Computing. EECS Department, University of Californi, Berkeley (2009)

[4] Youseff, L., Butrico, M., Da Silva, D.: Toward a Unified Ontology of Cloud Computing. In: Grid Computing Environments Workshop, GCE 2008, pp. 1–10 (2008)

[5] Foster, I., Yong, Z., Raicu, I., Lu, S.: Cloud Computing and Grid Computing 360-Degree Compared. In: Grid Computing Environments Workshop, GCE 2008, pp. 1–10 (2008)

[6] Elastic Compute Cloud, EC2 (2011), http://aws.amazon.com/ec2

[7] GoGrid (2011), http://www.gogrid.com

[8] FlexiScale (2011), http://www.flexiscale.com

[9] Nurmi, D., Wolski, R., Grzegorczyk, C., Obertelli, G., Soman, S., Youseff, L., Zagorodnov, D.: The Eucalyptus Open-Source Cloud-Computing System. In: Proceedings of the 2009 9th IEEE/ACM International Symposium on Cluster Computing and the Grid, pp. 124–131. IEEE Computer Society, Los Alamitos (2009)

[10] OpenNebula (2011), http://www.opennebula.org

[11] Nimbus (2011), http://workspace.globus.org

[12] Andrzejak, A., Kondo, D., Yi, S.: Decision Model for Cloud Computing under SLA Constraints. In: Proceedings of the 2010 IEEE International Symposium on Modeling, Analysis and Simulation of Computer and Telecommunication Systems, pp. 257–266. IEEE Computer Society, Los Alamitos (2010)

[13] Patel, P., Ranabahu, A., Sheth, A.: Service Level Agreement in Cloud Computing. In: Proceedings of Conference on Object Oriented Programming Systems Languages and Applications, pp. 212–217 (2009)

[14] Yi, S., Kondo, D., Andrzejak, A.: Reducing Costs of Spot Instances via Checkpointing in the Amazon Elastic Compute Cloud. In: Proceedings of the 2010 IEEE 3rd International Conference on Cloud Computing, pp. 236–243. IEEE Computer Society, Los Alamitos (2010)

[15] Amazon EC2 spot Instances (2010), http://aws.amazon.com/ec2/spot-instances/

[16] Cloud exchange (2011), http://cloudexchange.org

[17] Yi, S., Heo, J., Cho, Y., Hong, J.: Taking point decision mechanism for page-level incremental checkpointing based on cost analysis of process execution time. Journal of Information Science and Engineering 23(5), 1325–1337 (2007)

Towards a Universal Sketch for
Origin-Destination Network Measurements

Haiquan (Chuck) Zhao[1], Nan Hua[1], Ashwin Lall[2],
Ping Li[3], Jia Wang[4], and Jun (Jim) Xu[1]

[1] Georgia Tech
{chz,nanhua,jx}@cc.gatech.edu
[2] Denison University
lalla@denison.edu
[3] Cornell University
pingli@cornell.edu
[4] AT&T Research
jiawang@research.att.com

Abstract. Despite its importance in today's Internet, network measurement was not an integral part of the original Internet architecture, i.e., there was (and still is) little native support for many essential measurement tasks. Targeting the inadequacy of counting/accounting capabilities of existing routers, many data streaming and sketching techniques have been proposed to estimate the important statistics of traffic going through a network link. Most of these techniques are, however, developed to track one specific statistic and/or answer a specific type of query. Since there are a large number of such statistics and queries of interest, it is very difficult, if not impossible, for network vendors and operators to implement and deploy data streaming/sketching solutions for all of them, due to router resource (memory, CPU, bus bandwidth, etc.) constraints.

In this paper, we propose a general-purpose solution that can not only answer a wide range of queries, but also be able to answer types of queries that were not known *a priori*. In particular, we introduce the use of the Conditional Random Sampling (CRS) sketch data structure for succinctly capturing network traffic data between a set of nodes in the network. This sketch is the first step towards a "universal" sketch data structure in the sense that it is not tied to measurement of a single quantity. We show that the CRS sketch can compute unbiased estimates for any linear summary statistic in the intersection of a pair of traffic streams, e.g., traffic and flow matrix information, flow counts, and entropy. We present detailed experiments, using data collected at a tier-1 ISP, that show that our sketch is capable of estimating this wide range of statistics with fairly high accuracy.

1   Introduction

As the Internet continues to grow and evolve, network traffic measurement is essential to Internet service providers (ISPs) and application service providers (e.g., Google, Yahoo, Akamai) for a variety of network operation tasks and business decision-making. Despite its importance in today's Internet, network measurement was not an integral part of the original Internet architecture, i.e., there was (and still is) little native support for many

E. Altman and W. Shi (Eds.): NPC 2011, LNCS 6985, pp. 201–213, 2011.

essential measurement tasks. Besides some basic SNMP counters (e.g., total packet and byte counts across a link) and simple flow collection facilities (e.g., Cisco Netflow), today's routers still lack sophisticated measurement functionality. Such limitations have constrained many network management tasks, and forced significant research and engineering efforts to be expended on finding creative solutions. In particular, targeting the aforementioned inadequacy of counting/accounting capabilities of existing routers, many data streaming and sketching techniques (e.g., [14, 15, 33]) have been proposed to estimate the important statistics of, and to approximately answer various queries concerning, traffic going through a network link.

Most existing data streaming and sketching techniques are developed to track one specific statistic (e.g., second moment [1]) and/or answer a specific type of query (e.g., existence and identities of elephants [9, 16]). Since there are a large number of such statistics and queries of interest, it is very difficult, if not impossible, for network vendors and operators to implement and deploy data streaming/sketching solutions for all of them, due to router resource (memory, CPU, bus bandwidth, etc.) constraints. We believe this partly explains the lack of commercial success of these solutions. An emerging solution to this problem is so-called universal data sketches, each of which is a single versatile data structure that can track several different types of statistics and/or answer a wide range of queries, including those that were not known *a priori*, simultaneously. Overall a universal sketch consumes much less resources than individual sketches for tracking/answering all these statistics/queries combined. A conceivable tradeoff here is that a universal sketch might not provide as accurate answers to a type of query as data sketches designed specifically for it, given the same resource consumption.

In this paper we introduce the Conditional Random Sampling (CRS) sketch [19–21], a universal sketch for succinctly summarizing network traffic data. The CRS sketch, if deployed across multiple routers, can perform a type of "coordinated" sampling wherein the flows sampled at different locations can be highly correlated. This permits the accurate computation of statistics of the *intersection* of the data at both locations (i.e., origin-destination measurements) using the sketches at each. Moreover, CRS is not tied to measurement of a single quantity. We show that it is capable of computing any linear summary statistic of the intersection of streams. Examples of these statistics include (but are not limited to) computation of the traffic matrix, counting numbers of distinct flows, entropy estimation, and computation of higher moments for detection of large changes in the traffic distribution. A key contribution of this paper is to show that the estimator for the sketch is unbiased, settling an open problem raised implicitly in [21].

We perform a thorough analysis of CRS on packet trace data collected from a tier-1 ISP at the core of the Internet. Whereas CRS has been studied before [19, 21] for natural language applications, we had to tune parameters and make non-trivial adaptations to make it work on networking data. We were able to show that for most applications, such as traffic matrix, entropy estimation, etc., the sketch performed remarkably well while using very little memory. For most of the common measurement statistics that we estimated, it gave low measurement error while using memory comparable with a specialized algorithm for any single statistic.

The rest of this paper is organized as follows. Section 2 defines the problem that we solve in this paper. Section 3 presents the CRS sketch and how we apply it on network traffic measurement. We evaluate the CRS sketch using data collected from a tier-1 ISP in Section 4. Finally, we discuss related work in Section 5 before concluding in Section 6.

2   Problem Statement

Throughout this paper, we assume that there are ℓ spatially-separated nodes (say, ingress and egress nodes in a network). Each node encounters a stream of tuples of the form $\langle i, c \rangle$, where i is an element from a universe of size n (e.g., in the case of IP flows, $n = 2^{96}$, where $96 = 32 + 32 + 16 + 16$ is the length of the flow label consisting of source and destination IP addresses and port numbers) and c is the increment to the count for this element (e.g., the packet size in bytes). The classic streaming problem is to compute functions of the frequency distribution of the streams at individual nodes. In this paper, we expand this definition to answering queries for arbitrary *pairs* of nodes based on the sketches at the ℓ nodes. Note that this is a much harder problem since we must be able to answer $\binom{\ell}{2} = \Theta(\ell^2)$ queries from just ℓ sketches.

While previous work in data streaming has focused on sketches for a specific query/statistic, our goal is to have a single sketch that can be used to compute unbiased approximations for multiple types of queries performed on the intersection of traffic seen at any pair of nodes. In particular, we aim to compute any linear summary statistic, i.e., any function of the form $\sum_x g(x)$ where the sum is over the flow sizes in the OD-flows between pairs of streams. Examples of the types of queries that we expect to answer include:

1. The F_1 count between pairs of distributed streams, or simply put, the amount of traffic between two nodes in the network. Using the sketch proposed in this paper, we can estimate the traffic between all pairs of nodes and hence construct the traffic matrix [12].
2. The F_0 count is simply the number of distinct flows that are in the intersection of the two streams. This quantity is useful for network provisioners to determine the *number* of flows between a source-destination pair, rather than the aggregate traffic.
3. Prior work [33] has looked at the computation of the entropy norm of traffic between origin-destination pairs. This is defined as $\sum x \ln x$, where the sum is over the all the flows in OD-flow between a given pair of nodes. It is also often useful to compute the entropy, which is defined to be $\log L - (1/L) \sum x \ln x$, where L is the F_1 count of the OD-flow.
4. The higher-order moments $F_2, F_3, \ldots$ (where F_p is defined as $\sum_x x^p$) are also useful for detecting skewness and major shifts in the traffic distribution.

3   Conditional Random Sampling

We propose the use of Conditional Random Sampling [19–21] to sketch network data at ingress and egress nodes in the network. The CRS sketch has been shown to be capable of computing arbitrary linear summary statistics of the intersection of pairs of streams, and we evaluate its performance on networking data. Additionally, we show in Section 3.3 that it is possible to extract an *unbiased* estimate of any linear statistic of the intersection, a fact that was unknown to the authors of [21].

Algorithm 1. CRS Sketch

1: initialize shared permutation function π
2: initialize max-heap *heap*
3: **for** each packet p in the stream **do**
4:    let $flow := \pi(flow\_id(p))$
5:    **if** $flow \leq heap.maxElement$ **then**
6:        **if** $flow$ is in *heap* **then**
7:            update the record of $flow$ in *heap*
8:        **else**
9:            **if** $size(heap) \geq k$ **then**
10:               evict the max element
11:           **end if**
12:           insert $flow$ into the heap
13:       **end if**
14:    **end if**
15: **end for**

3.1 The CRS Algorithm

The CRS algorithm is executed independently at any set of ingress and egress points in the network (more generally at any router or interface of interest), and produces a sketch of the local stream. There is no requirement of universal deployment (e.g., allowing it to be run on only a subset of routers) and is capable of answering queries for any pair of participating routers.

At the heart of CRS lies a random permutation of the flow records in the streams. By ensuring that all the measurement interfaces all use the same permutation, we are able to perform "coordinated" sampling to accurately estimate statistics of the intersection of multiple streams. More precisely, each copy of the CRS sketch is maintained by retaining the k flows with smallest permuted flow IDs in a balanced max-heap data structure that is pruned to have at most k items in it at any time.[1] Here, k is the maximum number of flow records that can be retained in the sketch. Flows in the sketch are updated, and whenever a new flow enters the sketch (by replacing a flow with a larger permitted flow ID) a new record is created for it. See Algorithm 1 for details. By the monotonicity of the *min* operation, we are guaranteed to have complete counts for all the records in the sketch at the termination of the stream.

The CRS sketch strictly controls its memory consumption by guaranteeing that it never maintains more than k records. In contrast, most other sampling mechanisms such as uniform sampling, flow sampling [7, 8], sample-and-hold [9], etc., can only provide probabilistic guarantees on how much space they will consume.

After the sketches are computed, they can be shipped (due to their small size) to a central location for storage. To compute any linear summary statistic of an arbitrary pair of sketches, we compute the sum of the statistic over the set of flows that are in the intersection of the two sketches, excluding the max element of the two sketches. This sum is a sample of the desired statistic, and we can compute an estimate by reverting by

---
[1] Each sketch can use a different k.

Algorithm 2.. CRS Intersection

1: **INPUT:** A pair of CRS sketches c_1 and c_2, function g
2: $Z_1 :=$ largest ID in c_1
3: $Z_2 :=$ largest ID in c_2
4: $Z := \min(Z_1, Z_2)$
5: $n :=$ total number of possible flows
6: $sum := 0$
7: **for** each record f in both c_1 and c_2, and $f.ID < Z$ **do**
8:     $sum := sum + g(f.size)$
9: **end for**
10: **OUTPUT** $sum \times n/(Z-1)$

---

factor $n/(Z-1)$, where n is the cardinality of the space of flow IDs and Z is the minimum of the largest permuted ID of the two sketches. This is illustrated is Algorithm 2. In Section 3.3 we show that this factor is precisely the one needed to get an unbiased estimate for any linear summary statistic. We next discuss some implementation issues for the CRS sketch.

3.2 Implementation Details

Since a random permutation is expensive to implement, in an actual implementation we would use a hash function with a large range and maintain the k flows with the smallest hash signature. Such approximation has also been used in [2]. The range can be smaller than the domain of flow IDs but should be much larger than F_0^2 so that the probability of hash collisions is negligible. In Algorithm 2 we replace n with the size of the range.

Since this sketch has to work on streaming packet data, it is critical that the update time per packet should be extremely fast: inter-packet arrival times may be as small as 10–20 nanoseconds. The CRS sketch is extremely well-suited for updating at high speeds. For almost all the packets in the stream, the only processing necessary is the computation of two hashes: one to compute the hash of the flow ID, and another to perform a hash table lookup of the flow in the table (in a real implementation, the heap will contain pointers to the flows in the hash table). Since the hashes do not need to be of cryptographic strength, low-complexity hash functions such as Carter-Wegman's H_3 hashes [3] can be used. Alternatively, hardware support for hash functions are also available [26]. For a very small subset of updates, specifically when the first k distinct flows are seen in the stream and when a flow is replaced in the heap (lines 9-12 in Algorithm 1), we have to perform heap operations that cost $O(\log k)$ operations for a balanced heap (e.g., Red-Black tree). The former case happens precisely k times in the stream and the latter can be shown experimentally to be infrequent, and hence these slower operations do not significantly affect the run-time performance of CRS.

3.3 Unbiasedness of CRS

The CRS algorithm described in [21] can handle multiple streams and any linear summary statistic over all the streams. The flow size distribution of each stream is viewed as a vector over the space of all flow IDs. Consider a matrix of m row vectors of length n, denoted $\{x_{ij}\}$. If we construct a CRS sketch for each row, then we can get an estimate for any linear statistic of the form $\sum_{j=1}^{n} g(x_{1,j}, \cdots, x_{m,j})$. The CRS algorithm we described in Section 3.1 is simply a special case, with $m = 2$, $g(0,*) = 0, g(*,0) = 0$, and the assumption that $x_{1,j} = x_{2,j}$ whenever $x_{1,j} \neq 0, x_{2,j} \neq 0$.

While [21] only claimed CRS to be unbiased for F_0 estimation for one stream, we discovered that CRS is strictly unbiased in the general case. This follows as a corollary of the following theorem.

Theorem 1. *Consider m rows of n balls each. The balls are either red or white, and we denote this as an $m \times n$ $\{0,1\}$-valued matrix $\{a_{i,j}\}$ where 1 stands for red. Let $k_i \geq 2, \forall 1 \leq i \leq m$ be integer constants.*

Let $\pi : [n] \to [n]$ be a random permutation that is applied to the column indices. We will collect the columns from the left until for at least one row i we have collected k_i red balls. Let Z_i be the index of the k_i^{th} red ball in the ith row of the permuted matrix, i.e., $a_{i,\pi^{-1}(Z_i)} = 1$ and $\sum_{j=1}^{Z_i} a_{i,\pi^{-1}(j)} = k_i$. If there are less than k_i red balls in the ith row, let $Z_i = n + 1$. Let $Z = \min_i Z_i$. Then the first $Z - 1$ columns are an unbiased sample of all the columns, i.e.,

$$\mathrm{E}_{\pi}\left[\frac{1_{\{1 \leq \pi(j_0) \leq Z-1\}}}{Z-1}\right] = \frac{1}{n}, \forall 1 \leq j_0 \leq n.$$

Remark: $\mathrm{E}_{\pi}\left[1_{\{1 \leq \pi(j_1) \leq Z-1\}}\right] = \mathrm{E}_{\pi}\left[1_{\{1 \leq \pi(j_2) \leq Z-1\}}\right]$ is not true in general.

Proof. Let $h(m,n,a,k,j_0) \equiv \mathrm{E}_{\pi}\left[\frac{1_{\{1 \leq \pi(j_0) \leq Z-1\}}}{Z-1}\right]$. We want to prove by induction on n that $h(m,n,a,k,j_0) = \frac{1}{n}$ for any m,a,k,j_0.

When $n = 1$, since we require $k_i \geq 2$, we have $Z_i = 2, \forall i$, so $Z = 2$, and the statement is true.

Now assume it is true for $n - 1$, and we prove it for n.

We observe that if k_i is larger than the number of red balls on the ith row, i.e., $k_i > \sum_{j=1}^{n} a_{i,j}$, then $Z_i = n + 1$ always, and Z_i has no effect on Z, so we can remove the ith row from a. If there is only one row left, and $k_1 > \sum_j a_{1,j}$, then $Z = Z_1 = n + 1$, and the equation holds true. So we only need to prove for the cases where $k_i \leq \sum_{j=1}^{n} a_{i,j}, \forall i$.

We write the expectation conditioned on which column is mapped to n:

$$h(m,n,a,k,j_0) = \mathrm{E}\left[\mathrm{E}\left[\frac{1_{\{1 \leq \pi(j_0) \leq Z-1\}}}{Z-1} \middle| \pi^{-1}(n)\right]\right]$$

$$= \sum_{j'=1}^{n} \mathrm{E}\left[\frac{1_{\{1 \leq \pi(j_0) \leq Z-1\}}}{Z-1} \middle| \pi^{-1}(n) = j'\right] \Pr[\pi^{-1}(n) = j'].$$

For $j' = j_0$, i.e., $\pi(j_0) = n$, we get a zero term. This is because we assumed $k_i \leq \sum_{j=1}^{n} a_{i,j}$, so $Z_i \leq n$, therefore $Z - 1 \leq n - 1$, so $1_{\{1 \leq \pi(j_0) \leq Z-1\}} = 0$.

For $j' \neq j_0$, i.e., $\pi(j_0) \neq n$: Let us consider the same algorithm with the last column removed, i.e., with parameter m, n', a', k, j'_0 where $n' = n - 1$, a' is matrix a with the j'^{th} column removed, and j'_0 is the position of j_0 among $\{1, ..., j' - 1, j' + 1, ..., n - 1\}$. Each permutation π with $\pi(j') = n$ has a one-to-one correspondence with a permutation π'. We will argue that $Z_i = Z'_i$, given our assumption that $k_i \leq \sum_{j=1}^{n} a_{i,j}$.

- If $a_{i,j'} = 0$, i.e., it's a white ball; Or if $a_{i,j'} = 1$ and $k_i < \sum_{j=1}^{n} a_{i,j}$, i.e., it's a red ball but there are at least k_i red balls left in the ith row of a', then the position of the k_i^{th} red ball is the same with or without the last ball, so $Z_i = Z_i'$.
- If $a_{i,j'} = 1$, and $k_i = \sum_{j=1}^{n} a_{i,j}$, then $Z_i = n$. There are less than k_i red balls left in the ith row of a', so $Z_i' = (n-1) + 1 = n$.

Therefore $Z = Z'$, so $E\left[\frac{1_{\{1 \leq \pi(j_0) \leq Z-1\}}}{Z-1} \middle| \pi^{-1}(n) = j'\right] = h(m, n-1, a', k, j_0') = \frac{1}{n-1}$ by induction assumption. So

$$h(m,n,a,k,j_0) = \sum_{\substack{1 \leq j' \leq n \\ j' \neq j_0}} \frac{1}{n-1}\frac{1}{n} + 0\frac{1}{n} = \frac{1}{n-1}\frac{n-1}{n} + 0\frac{1}{n} = \frac{1}{n}.$$

Corollary 1. *Let ball (i,j) be assigned value $x_{i,j}$. Let $g : \mathbb{R}^m \to \mathbb{R}$ be any function. We have*

$$E_\pi\left[\frac{1}{Z-1}\sum_{j=1}^{Z-1} g(x_{1,\pi^{-1}(j)}, \ldots, x_{m,\pi^{-1}(j)})\right] = \frac{1}{n}\sum_{j=1}^{n} g(x_{1,j}, \ldots, x_{m,j}).$$

Proof.

$$E_\pi\left[\frac{1}{Z-1}\sum_{j=1}^{Z-1} g(x_{1,\pi^{-1}(j)}, \ldots, x_{m,\pi^{-1}(j)})\right]$$

$$= E_\pi\left[\frac{1}{Z-1}\sum_{j=1}^{n} 1_{\{1 \leq \pi(j) \leq Z-1\}} g(x_{1,j}, \ldots, x_{m,j})\right]$$

$$= \sum_{j=1}^{n} g(x_{1,j}, \ldots, x_{m,j}) E_\pi\left[\frac{1_{\{1 \leq \pi(j) \leq Z-1\}}}{Z-1}\right]$$

$$= \frac{1}{n}\sum_{j=1}^{n} g(x_{1,j}, \ldots, x_{m,j}).$$

Thus we see that the CRS algorithm is unbiased for multiple streams for any linear summary statistic.

4   Experiments

In this section we evaluate the performance of our algorithm using real Internet traffic traces obtained from a tier-1 ISP. We will investigate the impact of different sketch sizes on the estimation of the F_0, F_1, F_2, entropy and entropy norm and also investigate the distribution of relative error of the estimations. The results are compared with the entropy norm estimated by [33] and the F_2 estimated by stable random projection (SRP) [13]. We would also investigate the impact of the number of flows on the estimation error.

The traffic traces in use were collected from an ingress router of the tier-1 ISP. We also obtained the routing table at the ingress router to determine the egress router for

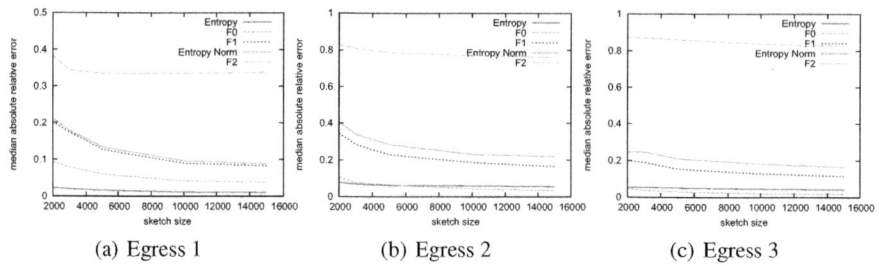

(a) Egress 1   (b) Egress 2   (c) Egress 3

Fig. 1. Median Absolute Relative Error with Varying Sketch Sizes. Summary statistics are listed in decreasing order of MARE.

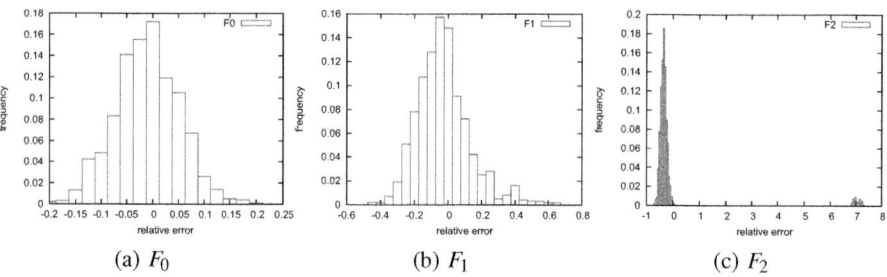

(a) F_0 (b) F_1 (c) F_2

Fig. 2. Distribution of relative error of F_0, F_1, F_2 of the intersection, with sketch size fixed at 10,000

each packet, thus determining the OD flows to each possible egress router. Because we do not have traffic traces collected at egress routers, we generate synthetic traffic traces at egress routers in addition to the OD flows observed at the ingress router. The synthetic traffic is generated with an identical distribution to that of the ingress. For the following experiments we pick a five-minute trace which contains 227,722 flows, and we pick three different egress router whose OD traffic contains 5,442 flows (Egress 1), 5,362 flows (Egress 2), and 25,276 flows (Egress 3).

We use H_3 hash function [3] in the simulations, since we notice that hash functions based on Linear Feedback Shift Register (LFSR) do not work well for our application. This is because some flows differ from each other by only a few bits in the flow label. For example, different HTTP sessions from the same client to the same web server only differ in the source port number field. An LFSR-based hash function often does not distribute the hash values uniformly in such cases while H_3 does. To compute an H_3 hash function, the input bit vector is multiplied by a fixed (randomly-chosen) $\{0,1\}$-valued matrix modulo 2 to get the hashed bit vector. This hash function has been also shown to be very amenable for hardware implementation [26] since it involves only simple logic such as bitwise XOR and parity computation. Therefore, we recommend that H_3 functions be used in implementing CRS on future Internet routers.

We run the experiments 1000 times for each configuration of varying sketch sizes. Figure 1 depicts the median absolute relative error (MARE) for different statistics using different sketch sizes on all three egresses. The results for the three egresses are similar. We observe that for F_0, F_1, and entropy norm, the relative error decreases as sketch size increases, just as expected. For entropy, the error is very small even at small sketch sizes. On the other hand, the relative error of F_2 remains large even at large sketch sizes. The F_0 errors of Egress 1 and Egress 2 are similar, however the F_1 error of Egress 2 is worse than Egress 1 and 3 since the traffic to Egress 2 is actually more heavy-tailed than the other two. The errors of Egress 3 are smaller than Egress 2 due to the larger number of flows to Egress 3.

The entropy estimation error is much smaller than the error for F_1 and entropy norm, the two components for estimating entropy. This is because the CRS sketch will either overestimate both F_1 and entropy norm, or underestimate both, so the errors end up largely canceling each other out. Compared with the method in [33], our method achieves MARE of around 10% with a sketch of 10,000 entries for entropy norm, which is comparable with [33] using 200,000 entries. (The size of each entry in our sketch , however, is a little over twice that of [33].) Our explanations for this is as follows: The estimation of entropy norm in [33] is based on the estimation of $F_{1-\alpha}$. The formulae (3) and (4) in [33] show that any error for estimating $F_{1-\alpha}$ will go opposite ways for F_1 and entropy norm, thus causing larger errors for the estimation of entropy.

We now fix the sketch size to 10000 entries and investigate the distribution of the relative error. Figure 2 shows the distribution of relative errors of F_0, F_1, and F_2 estimates of traffic from the ingress to Egress 1. The distributions for Egress 2 and 3 are similar and hence omitted. We see that for F_0 and F_1, the distribution function are both roughly bell curves centered slightly off 0. However, there are two modes of the distribution of F_2 error, one centered around -0.3 and the other around 7. This means that F_2 estimation most likely underestimates by 30%, and occasionally overestimates by 700%. This is caused by the presence of a large elephant in the OD flow.

An alternative algorithm for estimating F_2 is to use random stable projections (RSP) [13]. In Figure 3 we compare the theoretical standard deviation (SD) of the CRS sketch and the random stable projection sketch for this dataset. We see that the stable projection sketch would perform better, due to the heavy tailed nature of this OD flow. However we need to emphasize that a single CRS sketch can be used to measure many quantities, while a stable sketch for F_2 can only be used for F_2 measurement alone.

We also plotted the sample SD of the CRS sketch from 1000 runs in Figure 3. We could see the sample SD is very close to the theoretical SD for large sketch sizes, which validates our experiments. However the variance of the SD is so high that for small sketch sizes the sample SD cannot accurately capture the true SD with 1000 runs, which explains that deviations for sketch sizes below 6000.

Finally, we change the number of flows for Egress 1 while maintaining the same set of OD flows. We plot the errors in Figure 4. We can see that the left side of the error curves are flat when the number of egress flows is no more than the number of ingress flows, but the right side goes up. This demonstrates that the performance of CRS sketch depends on the max of the number of flows of ingress and egress. In other words, the greater the traffic at either node relative to the OD traffic, the less accuracy we expect from the CRS sketch.

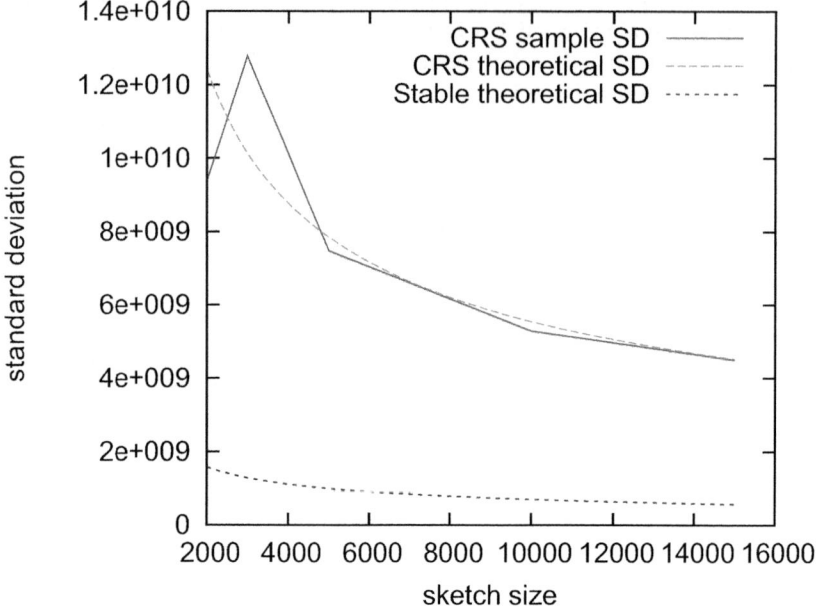

Fig. 3. Comparison with stable distribution sketch for F_2 estimation (varying sketch size)

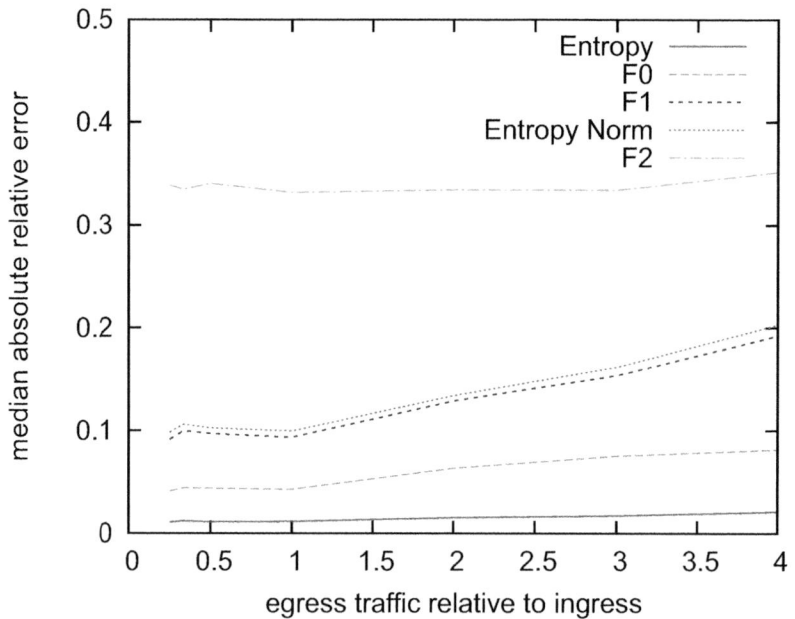

Fig. 4. Varying Egress Flows (Egress 1)

5   Related Work

This work is most similar to, and in fact was inspired by, the Conditional Random Sampling sketch [21]. The CRS sketch was initially proposed for sparse language data, and we show in this paper how it can be adapted to the networking context. Since the target goals and data characteristics are extremely different in these two domains, the issues in adapting this sketch were far from trivial. In addition, we present a novel proof in this paper that the CRS sketch can give *unbiased* estimates of arbitrary functions of the intersection of a pair of streams.

The key idea of bottom-k sketch [4, 5] is close to that of the CRS sketch. The bottom-k sketch also maintains the k items with the lowest-k hashed values, and its hashing can be also coordinated hence supporting queries on intersections. However, although the bottom-k sketch can be applied to streaming applications, it is only for the situations in which the weight of each item is known and fixed. The estimators derived are for the aggregate of functions of these weights. In comparison, the CRS sketch performs coordinated sampling of a subset and then estimates any function of the whole set based on the sampled set.

The idea of coordinated sampling can be traced back to Trajectory sampling [6]. Trajectory sampling samples and stores the flows with hashed flow IDs in the same range. Compared with our method, the size of sketch sampled by Trajectory sampling on each router would be in proportion to the amount of traffic passing through it. Hence it lacks flexibility with regard to traffic fluctuations and traffic imbalance among routers. A recent work c-Samp [27] also leverages coordinated flow sampling. However, its design goal is to assign different sampling ranges for different routers in order to achieve larger monitoring coverage.

There has been a long line of work done on computing the traffic matrix within a network [28, 11, 23, 31, 32, 25, 24, 34]. While much of the previous work in this area was done using SNMP link loads [28, 31, 32, 24], there has been some recent interest in using data streaming techniques to measure the matrices [11, 25, 34]. Our algorithm is closer to these latter works in that it directly uses traffic data, rather than SNMP.

Entropy has recently been proposed, in several different contexts [10, 17, 29, 30], as a means for classifying and detecting anomalies in network traffic. Computing the entropy of OD-pairs was first proposed in [33], in which the authors propose the use of a sketch at each ingress and egress node in a network that can be used to compute the entropy of any arbitrary pair of nodes. The sketch in this paper is able to solve the same problem, but it is not restricted to solving just this single problem.

Recently, there is a line of work on *Compressed Counting* [18, 22], which applied *maximally-skewed stable random projections* to estimate the F_p frequency moment near $p = 1$ and then use the estimated F_p to approximate the Shannon entropy with a very high accuracy. For example, [22] conducted some comparisons with CRS to illustrate that, in order to achieve the same accuracy for estimating the Shannon entropy, Compressed Counting can reduce the required sample size of CRS by 2-fold to 113-fold (data-dependent).

6 Conclusions

In this paper we present and evaluate a sketch for computing any norm on the intersection of pairs of spatially separated streams. As data on the Internet gets more voluminous and more distributed, it will become increasingly important to be able to sketch and compare datasets at remote locations. The work in this paper is a first step towards addressing this challenging new problem.

The distinctive property of our sketch, as compared with prior work, is that it is not limited to a single type of query and can be used to execute arbitrary queries, even ones realized after the data has been collected. It is also designed to be lightweight, both in terms of memory requirements as well as update costs. We show that it is unbiased and that it performs well empirically by evaluating it on real Internet data collected at a tier-1 ISP.

References

1. Alon, N., Matias, Y., Szegedy, M.: The space complexity of approximating the frequency moments. Journal of Computer and System Sciences 58(1), 137–143 (1999)
2. Broder, A.: On the resemblance and containment of documents. In: Proceedings of the Compression and Complexity of Sequences (1997)
3. Carter, L., Wegman, M.N.: Universal classes of hash functions. J. Comput. Syst. Sci. 18(2), 143–154 (1979)
4. Cohen, E., Kaplan, H.: Bottom-k sketches: better and more efficient estimation of aggregates. In: SIGMETRICS (2007)
5. Cohen, E., Kaplan, H.: Summarizing data using bottom-k sketches. In: PODC (2007)
6. Duffield, N., Grossglauser, M.: Trajectory sampling for direct traffic observation. IEEE Transaction of Networking, 280–292 (June 2001)
7. Duffield, N., Lund, C., Thorup, M.: Estimating flow distribution from sampled flow statistics. In: Proc. ACM SIGCOMM (August 2003)
8. Duffield, N.G., Lund, C., Thorup, M.: Flow sampling under hard resource constraints. In: Sigmetrics (2004)
9. Estan, C., Varghese, G.: New directions in traffic measurement and accounting. In: Proc. ACM SIGCOMM (2002)
10. Feinstein, L., Schnackenberg, D., Balupari, R., Kindred, D.: Statistical approaches to DDoS attack detection and response. In: Proceedings ofthe DARPA Information Survivability Conference and Exposition (2003)
11. Feldmann, A., Greenberg, A., Lund, C., Reingold, N., Rexford, J., True, F.: Deriving traffic demands for operational IP networks: Methodology and experience. IEEE Transaction on Networking (June 2001)
12. Gunnar, A., Johansson, M., Telkamp, T.: Traffic matrix estimation on a large ip backbone-a comparison on real data. In: USENIX/ACM SIGCOMM IMC (2004)
13. Indyk, P.: Stable distributions, pseudorandom generators, embeddings, and data stream computation. J. ACM 53(3), 307–323 (2006)
14. Krishnamurthy, B., Sen, S., Zhang, Y., Chen, Y.: Sketch-based change detection: Methods, evaluation, and applications. In: IMC (2003)
15. Kumar, A., Sung, M., Xu, J., Zegura, E.: Data streaming algorithms for efficient and accurate estimation of flow size distribution. In: Proc. ACM SIGMETRICS (June 2005)

16. Kumar, A., Xu, J.: Sketch guided sampling-using on-line estimates of flow size for adaptive data collection. In: Proc. IEEE INFOCOM (March 2006)
17. Lakhina, A., Crovella, M., Diot, C.: Mining anomalies using traffic feature distributions. In: SIGCOMM (2005)
18. Li, P.: Improving compressed counting. In: UAI (2009)
19. Li, P., Church, K.W.: Using sketches to estimate associations. In: Human Language Technology and Empirical Methods in Natural Language Processing, HLT (2005)
20. Li, P., Church, K.W., Hastie, T.: Conditional random sampling: A sketch-based sampling technique for sparse data. In: NIPS (2006)
21. Li, P., Church, K.W., Hastie, T.: One sketch for all: Theory and application of conditional random sampling. In: NIPS (2008)
22. Li, P., Zhang, C.-H.: A new algorithm for compressed counting with applications in shannon entropy estimation in dynamic data. In: COLT (2011)
23. Medina, A., Taft, N., Salamatian, K., Bhattacharyya, S., Diot, C.: Traffic matrix estimation:existing techniques and new directions. In: SIGCOMM (2002)
24. Nucci, A., Cruz, R., Taft, N., Diot, C.: Design of igp link weight changes for estimation of traffic matrices. In: Proc. IEEE INFOCOM (March 2004)
25. Papagiannaki, K., Taft, N., Lakhina, A.: A distributed approach to measure traffic matrices. In: Proc. ACM/SIGCOMM IMC (October 2004)
26. Ramakrishna, M.V., Fu, E., Bahcekapili, E.: Efficient hardware hashing functions for high performance computers. IEEE Trans. Computers 46(12), 1378–1381 (1997)
27. Sekar, V., Reiter, M.K., Willinger, W., Zhang, H., Kompella, R.R., Andersen, D.G.: csamp: A system for network-wide flow monitoring. In: NSDI (2008)
28. Vardi, Y.: Internet tomography: estimating source-destination traffic intensities from link data. Journal of American Statistics Association, 365-377 (1996)
29. Wagner, A., Plattner, B.: Entropy Based Worm and Anomaly Detection in Fast IP Networks. In: Proceedings of IEEE International Workshop on Enabling Technologies, Infrastructures for Collaborative Enterprises (2005)
30. Xu, K., Zhang, Z.-L., Bhattacharya, S.: Profiling internet backbone traffic: Behavior models and applications. In: SIGCOMM (2005)
31. Zhang, Y., Roughan, M., Duffield, N., Greenberg, A.: Fast accurate computation of large-scale ip traffic matrices from link loads. In: Proc. ACM SIGMETRICS (June 2003)
32. Zhang, Y., Roughan, M., Lund, C., Donoho, D.: An information-theoretic approach to traffic matrix estimation. In: Proc. ACM SIGCOMM (August 2003)
33. Zhao, H., Lall, A., Ogihara, M., Spatscheck, O., Wang, J., Xu, J.: A data streaming algorithm for estimating entropies of OD flows. In: IMC (2007)
34. Zhao, Q., Kumar, A., Wang, J., Xu, J.: Data streaming algorithms for accurate and efficient measurement of traffic and flow matrices. In: SIGMETRICS (June 2005)

A Power Adjusting Algorithm on Mobility Control in Mobile Ad Hoc Networks

Jianrui Yuan* and Jintao Meng

[1] Department of Computer Science, Central China Normal University,
Changsha 410083, P.R. China
yuan.jianrui@gmail.com
[2] High Performance Computing Center, Shenzhen Institutes of advanced Technology,
Shenzhen 518055, P.R. China
meng.jintao@gmail.com

Abstract. Power saving is one of the key issues in mobile ad-hoc networks (MANET), while previous researches in MAC layer are mostly focused on improving the channel utilization by adopting variable-range transmission power control. In this paper we focus on the power savings in the network layer, and propose a power adjusting algorithm (we term it PAA). In the presence of mobile host's mobility, PAA is designed to conserve energy by adjusting the transmission power to maintain the route's connectivity and restarting the route discovery periodically to find the new better route dynamically. After analyzing the operations of PAA, we find that the length of route discovery restarted period is a critical argument which will affect power saving, so we propose an optimizing model which finds the optimal value of this argument by analyzing the energy consumption of this algorithm. PAA can handle the mobility of MANET by adjusting the transmission power and in the meantime save energy by restarting route discovery periodically to balance the energy consumption on route discovery and packets delivering. It is suggested that PAA can be implemented in the dynamic source routing protocol (DSR). Simulation results are provided, which demonstrate DSR embedded with PAA saves nearly 40 energy compared to DSR without PAA in the presence of high mobility.

Keywords: Mobile ad-hoc networks (MANETs), Power control, Dynamic Source Routing (DSR), Mobility control, Power efficiency.

1 Introduction

Mobile ad-hoc network (MANET) is a kind of wireless networks with mobile hosts (MHs), it was deployed without any fixed routers, and all nodes are capable of movement and can be connected dynamically in an arbitrary manner. Two mobile hosts can communicate with each other either directly or indirectly. Nodes of these networks function as routers which discover and maintain routes to other nodes in the network. Representative environments of the mobile ad-hoc network

---

* She is also with High Performance Computing Center, Shenzhen Institutes of advanced Technology, Shenzhen 518055, P.R. China.

E. Altman and W. Shi (Eds.): NPC 2011, LNCS 6985, pp. 214–231, 2011.

applications are fleets in oceans, natural disasters, and battle fields. Some or all of the nodes in a MANET may rely on batteries or other exhaustible energy resources. As such, one of the most important system design requirements in MANETs is power saving [1].

Power saving operations in MAC protocol is initially discussed in [2], [3]. By introducing the appropriate distributed active-sleep schedule for each node, the authors of [2] propose an efficient power saving MAC protocol for multi-hop mobile ad hoc networks called p-MANET, which avoids power consumption by activating mobile node during one beacon interval for every n interval, where n is the size of a super frame. The authors of [3] propose an on-demand power management framework for ad hoc networks. In this framework nodes that are not involved into delivering may go to sleep to adapt to the traffic load, which will save energy in the ad-hoc network. These two algorithms are both energy-saving schemes which are adaptive to traffic load. The present paper, however, studies the power saving issue in MANETs from a different perspective. Rather than adaptive to traffic load, our algorithm presented in this paper is adaptive to MHs' mobility, which can be implemented in the existing routing protocols in MANETs to achieve energy efficiency and maintain network connectivity simultaneously. Recent power control developments for MANETs also include the transmission power control mechanisms (e.g. [4], [5], [6]) for increasing channel utilization, and the distributed protocol [7] for interplaying between the MAC and network layers. Motivated by these works, in this paper we introduce a novel power control mechanism into the network layer to control the mobility, which can conserve energy and maintain network connectivity in MANETs. With the aid of this power control method, we are able to design an algorithm which is shown to be promising in conserving energy in both MAC layer and network layer when implemented in the routing protocols.

The recently routing protocols designed for wireless ad hoc network include the notable Dynamic Source Routing (DSR) Protocol [8] and Ad-hoc On Demand Distance Vector Routing (AODV) protocol [9]. DSR is a routing protocol for wireless ad hoc networks. This protocol uses source routing, in which all the routing information is maintained and dynamically updated at mobile nodes. It has two major phases, namely Route Discovery and Route Maintenance. These two functions work together to enable any host in the ad hoc network to dynamically discover and maintain a route to any other host in the network. The source broadcasts a Route Request (RREQ) message to find a route, Route Reply (RREP) is then generated if the message has reached the intended destination node. AODV builds routes using a route request & route reply query cycle. When a source node desires a route to a destination for which it does not already have a route, it broadcasts a RREQ packet across the network. A node receiving the RREQ may unicast a RREP back to its source or rebroadcasts the RREQ depending on if it is the destination or not. Nodes keep track of the RREQ's source IP address and broadcast ID. As the RREP propagates back to the source, nodes set up forward pointers to the destination. Once the source node receives the RREP, it may begin to forward data packets to the destination.

These routing protocols are usually sensitive to the mobility of MHs. The MH's mobility frequently cause the route to be broken, due to the fact that the receiver frequently moves out of the transmission range of the sender. In DSR, if some active link is broken, the downstream neighbor is currently unreachable. Then the node broadcasts a Route Error (RERR) packet back to the source, indicating that the route topology has changed, the source node must start route discovery by broadcasting the RREQ packet to find a new path in this case. In AODV, some periodic hello messages can be used to ensure symmetric links, as well as to detect link failures [14]. Once the next hop becomes unreachable, the node upstream of the break first repair the failed link locally, if it failed then the node propagates an unsolicited RREP to all active upstream nodes. Upon receiving notification of a broken link; source nodes can restart the discovery process if they still require a route to the destination. Even though there is certain mechanism of route maintenance implemented in these protocols to maintain network connectivity in the presence of mobility of MHs, it is still a challenge how to schedule the two schemes, namely route discovery and route maintenance so as to reach a state of global power saving. Therefore, this paper is aimed at designing an algorithm to control mobility and also save energy by balance the energy consumption on route discovery and packets delivering.

We apply power control into the routing protocol design in MANET for long lived flow, e.g. the TCP flow in MANET. We focus on the power saving in both MAC layer and network layer, and propose a power adjusting algorithm (PAA). The main techniques in PAA are

1. Conserving power in the routing protocol, this includes the power consumed on both route discovery and data transmission.

2. Adjusting transmission power in the presence of MHs' mobility to keep the route's connectivity when the packets are transmitting on this route.

3. Restarting the route discovery after an appropriate period to find a new better route for data transmission.

Therefore, PAA is essentially a period schedule which introduces the adjustable transmission power control, and periodically restarts the route discovery to balance the energy consumption on route discovery and packets delivering. This algorithm can be implemented within both DSR and AODV. In the simulation DSR is selected to be implemented with PAA for its simple schedule on route maintenance, and the simulation result shows that the DSR with PAA saved nearly 40% energy compared to the DSR without PAA.

The remainder of this paper is organized as follows. In Section 2, the propagation model, mobility model, and network assumptions used in this paper are introduced. Section 3 proposes and describes the power adjusting algorithm (PAA). Section 4 discusses the parameters of the PAA, where we propose an energy model to obtain the desired parameter for PAA in order to minimize the energy consumption. In Section 5, we implement the PAA and perform simulations to analyze and compare the DSR with PAA and DSR without PAA on the power saving performance. Finally, the conclusions are drawn in section 6.

2 Propagation Model, Mobility Model, and Network Assumptions

We first introduce the propagation model and mobility model used in this paper, and then some network assumptions and notations are listed which will help us simple the problems and models.

2.1 Propagation Model

Here we use free space propagation model to forecast the power level of sender and receiver within line of sight. Let P_t and P_r be the power level when the packet is transmitted at the sender and received at the receiver respectively, then the power level of the receiver, which is d away from the sender, can be given out by the Friis formula [10]:

$$P_r = \frac{P_t G_r G_t \lambda^2}{(4\pi)^2 d^2 L},\qquad(1)$$

where λ is the carrier wavelength, d is the distance between the sender and the receiver, L is the system wastage factor, G_t and G_r are the antenna gains at the sender and receiver respectively. Note that λ , L , G_t and G_r are constants in this formula.

As in the free space we let the path loss exponent is 2, and then the power consumed on the transmitter side by sending one unit of data is:

$$P_t = \varepsilon_{11} + \varepsilon_2 d^2,\qquad(2)$$

and the power consumed on the receiver side by receiving one unit of data is

$$P_r = \varepsilon_{12},\qquad(3)$$

here ε_{11} is the power to run the transmitter circuitry, ε_{12} is the power to run the receiver circuitry, and ε_2 is the power for the transmit amplifier to achieve an acceptable SNR (Signal to Noise Ratio).

Then the power consumed by the network to forward one unit of data can be calculate below:

$$P_f = P_t + P_r = \varepsilon_1 + \varepsilon_2 d^2,\qquad(4)$$

where we have denoted $\varepsilon_1 = \varepsilon_{11} + \varepsilon_{12}$.

As the power consumption on computation is less than the energy for radio transmission by order of magnitude, we ignore the power consumption on computation in this paper.

2.2 Mobility Model

Many mobility model (e.g. random walk model, pursue mobility model, ant mobility model) [11] are proposed in recent years, we use the random walk model to simplify our simulation here.

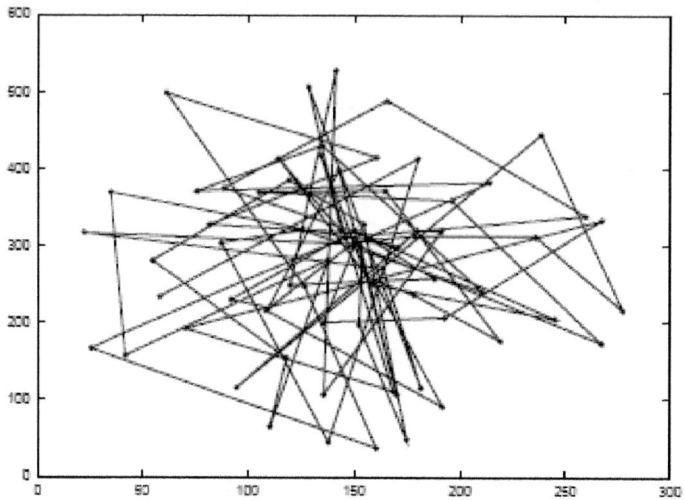

Fig. 1. Traveling pattern of a MH using the 2-D Random Walk Mobility Model

In the random walk model, a MH moves from its current location to a new location by randomly choosing a direction and speed in which to travel. The new speed and direction are both chosen from pre-defined ranges, $[0, maxspeed]$ and $[0, 2\pi]$ respectively. Each movement in the random walk model occurs in a constant time interval t, at the end of which a new direction and speed are calculated. If a MH which moves according to this model reaches a simulation boundary, it "bounces" off the simulation border with an angle determined by the incoming direction. The MH then continues along this new path. Figure 1 cited from [11] shows an example of the movement observed from this 2-D model. The MH begins its movement in the center of the $300m \times 600m$ simulation area or position $(150, 300)$. At each point, the MH randomly chooses a direction between 0 and 2 and a speed between 0 and 10 m/s. The MN is allowed to travel for 60 seconds before changing direction and speed.

2.3   Network Assumptions

1.There are N mobile hosts uniformly displayed in an area with radius R.

2. We adapt the random walk mobility model as our mobile host's mobility model.

3. The optimal transmission radius of the mobile host, which minimized the power consumption in the multi-hop ad hoc network, is characteristic distance [12], denoted as r_{char}, where$r_{char} = \sqrt{\varepsilon_1/\varepsilon_2}$.

4. We also make sure that r_{char} and n satisfy $\pi r_{char}^2 \geq \frac{\log n + c(n)}{n}$, this condition will keep network being connected [13].

5. The mobile host's max speed is set to be v_m m/s in the random walk model.

6. The data rate of the flow through the network is r_f packets/s.

7. The length of the message RREQ, RREP, DATA is L_{RREQ}, L_{RREP}, L_{DATA}, respectively.

8. The main cause to the break of route is the mobility of the mobile host, which means that when the receiver move out of the sender's transmission range, a link break will happen, and this will cause the route break. We ignore the result of host failure, unreliable channel, and network congestion in this paper.

3   The Power Adjusting Algorithm Design

In this section we will describe the power adjusting algorithm (PAA) which can be embedded in the existing routing protocols such as DSR for power conserving, and then some explications are list to illuminate this algorithm step by step.

3.1   Description of PAA

Now for a flow with data rate r_f originate from MH s and route to MH d, as PAA construct a periodic schedule on packet transmission, we simply let the time of sending every k packets to be one period T, where $T = \frac{k}{r_f}$, then after one period of sending k packets, the old route may not be energy efficient due to the mobility of hosts , then the new route need to be found, so route discovery is restarted to find a new route to the destination to instead the old one, Figure 2 has shown a route from MH 2 to MH 6 constructed by route discovery. Then after a period of T this route become less energy efficient as in Figure 3. At last In Figure 4, we need to find a new more energy efficient route $(2, 8, 1, 5, 6)$ by restarting route discovery.

According to the above discussion, we describe the algorithm of PAA as below:

Step 1. The source of this flow will start route discovery to find a route $(n_0 n_1 \ldots n_l)$ to the destination, where $n_0 = s$, $n_l = d$. In order to save power, we use the characteristic distance r_{char} as the transmission radius of the RREQ, and RREP messages.

Step 2. By analyzing the power level of RREQ and RREP messages received by the host, every host on the route path, will compute out the distance to its adjacent hosts, we denotes the initialed distance between adjacent MHs n_i and n_j on the route path to be d_{ij}^0 .

Step 3. Every $\frac{1}{r_f}$ seconds, one packet will be transmitted along this route, let us say this is the tth $(1 \leq t \leq k)$ packet on the fly, we forward it with the transmission radius of $(d_{ij}^{t-1} + 2\frac{v_m}{r_f})$ from n_i to n_j, where d_{ij}^{t-1} is the distance which was estimated when the $(t-1)$th packet passed through the adjacent hosts n_i and n_j on the route path.

Step 4. If there are no more packets, this flow should be canceled from the network.

Step 5. For every period of $T = \frac{k}{r_f}$ seconds, after sending every k packets, we restart the route discovery to find a new route $(n_0 n_1 \ldots n_l)$ to the destination host, and then go to Step 2 to continue.

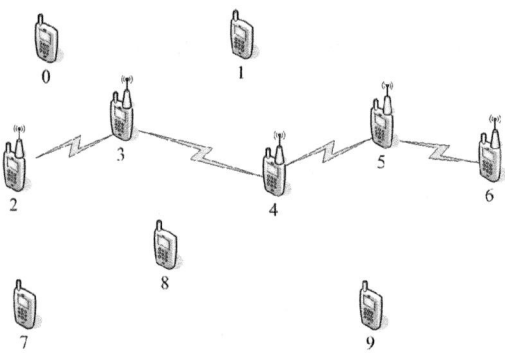

Fig. 2. A route $(2, 3, 4, 5, 6)$ constructed by route discovery

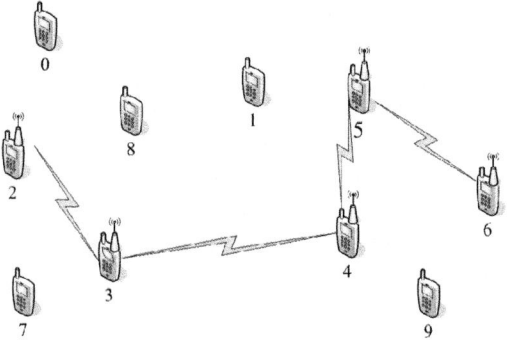

Fig. 3. The changing route $(2, 3, 4, 5, 6)$ caused by the mobility of the mobile hosts

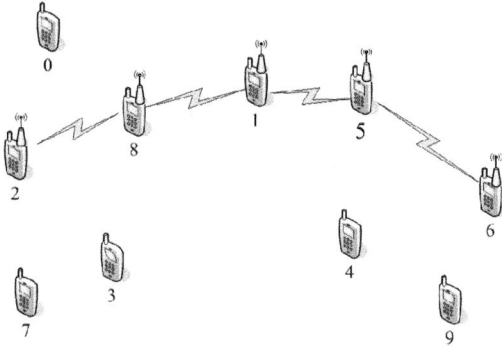

Fig. 4. A new better route $(2, 8, 1, 5, 6)$ found by restarting the route discovery

3.2   Analysis of PAA

In Step 1, the source broadcasts the RREQ messages to find the destination, after receiving the RREQ messages the desination will reply the source by sending a RREP message to construct a route $(n_0 n_1 \ldots n_l)$ from the source to the destination. By setting the transmission power to $P_t = \varepsilon_1 + \varepsilon_2 r_{char}^2$, the transmission radius of RREQ and RREP message will be r_{char}. Finally the route $(n_0 n_1 \ldots n_l)$ from the source to the destination is constructed by route discovery.

In Step 2, every host i on the route path will calculate the distance d_{ij}^0 to the downstream host j (except the source) by analyzing the power level of the RREQ or RREP message. In formula (1), the distance d_{ij}^0 can be calculated from the transmitted power level P_t and received power level P_r. As in Step 1, we set the transmission radius of RREQ and RREP message to be r_{char}, so the Sender's power level will be $P_t = \varepsilon_1 + \varepsilon_2 r_{char}^2$, and P_r can be get from the receiver side locally. Finally the initialed distance d_{ij}^0 between the sender i and the receiver j can be calculate as:

$$d_{ij}^0 = \frac{\lambda}{r\pi} \sqrt{\frac{P_t^i G_t G_r}{P_r^j L}}.$$

In Step 3, k data packets can be delivered to the destination within a period of $T = \frac{k}{r_f}$ seconds, and every $\frac{1}{r_f}$ seconds one packet will pass through the route. When the t-th packet passes through this route, we can estimate the distance d_{ij}^t between hosts n_i and n_j from the distance d_{ij}^{t-1} which is the distance when the packet $(t-1)$-th packet passes through $(t \geq 1)$, as the max speed the mobile host is v_m, so the distance d_{ij}^t satisfies

$$d_{ij}^{t-1} - 2\frac{v_m}{r_f} \leq d_{ij}^t \leq d_{ij}^{t-1} + 2\frac{v_m}{r_f}, \tag{5}$$

in order to make sure that the packet t can be successfully delivered to the host n_j from host n_i, we just let the host n_i's the RF power level cover a transmission distance of $d_{ij}^{t-1} + 2\frac{v_m}{r_f}$. Then after the transmission of packet t, we can estimate the distance d_{ij}^t from the transmitted power level P_t and the received power level P_r, and this new calculated distance d_{ij}^t can be calculated to estimate the transmission range of the packet $t + 1$. According to Equation (1), we can get d_{ij}^t as below:

$$d_{ij}^t = \frac{\lambda}{r\pi} \sqrt{\frac{P_t^t G_t G_r}{P_r^t L}},$$

here $P_t = \varepsilon_1 + \varepsilon_2 (d_{ij}^{t-1} + 2\frac{v_m}{r_f})^2$, and P_r is the receiver's power level when the $(t-1)$-th packet passes through the link (i, j).

In Step 4, when the flow has no packet to send, the network needs to cancel this flow.

In Step 5, when the final packet (packet k) was delivered along this route, the source will restart route discovery to find new route, which will find a new energy efficient route compared to the current one according to the current position of the mobile host in the network. Finally we will further discuss the parameter setting on k in a period in Section 4.

4   Parameters Setting of PAA

The length of a period is vital important in this algorithm, that means, if the period is too short, route discovery are restarted to frequently, which will waste more energy on route discovery, but if the length of period is too long, the link state along the route (eg. the route in Figure 3) will become more and more worse as the MH moves around in the network area, this will also waste much energy on delivering the packet along this energy inefficient route. Now we need to find an appropriate length of period for route discovery, that means when the energy wasted on the current route become unacceptable, the restarted route discovery will find a new better route to save as much energy as possible on delivering the packets.

Now before finding the optimal length of the period, we need first analyze the average distance of the MHs displayed in the network, then the energy consumption of the route discovery, and finally the distance variety between adjacent hosts on the route path in the present of MH's mobility.

4.1   The Average Distance of Any Two MHs

Lemma 1: Two vectors $v_1(r_1, \theta_1)$,$v_2(r_2, \theta_2)$ where $0 \le r_1, r_2 \le R$, $0 \le \theta_1, \theta_2 \le 2\pi$, are uniformly distributed in a circle with radius R, the sum of the two vector v_1, v_2 is v , that means $v = v_1 + v_2$, then the probability of v locating at (r, θ) (where $0 \le r \le R$, $0 \le \theta \le 2\pi$) is

$$P(r, \theta, R) = \frac{1}{\pi^2 R^2}(2 \arccos \frac{r}{2R} - \frac{r}{R}\sqrt{1 - (\frac{r}{2R})^2}). \tag{6}$$

Proof: In Figure 3, a vector $v(r, \theta)$ is located in a circle with radius $2R$, two small circles with radius R centered at the start point and the end point of the vector $v(r, \theta)$ are drawn in Figure 5. Then the sum of the two vectors $v_1(r_1, \theta_1)$, $v_2(r_2, \theta_2)$ with length R will be $v(r, \theta)$, and all the possibility position of vector v_1 should located in the overlapping regions of the two small circles. Then the area of the overlapping regions of the two small circles is

$$A = R^2(\theta - \sin(\theta)) = R^2(2\arccos \frac{r}{2R} - \frac{r}{R}\sqrt{1 - (\frac{r}{2R})^2}). \tag{7}$$

The variable area of the vector $v_1(r_1, \theta_1)$ or $v_2(r_2, \theta_2)$ is πR^2, so the probability of the sum of two vectors v located at (r, θ) is

$$P(r, \theta, R) = \frac{A}{\pi R^2 \pi R^2} = \frac{1}{\pi^2 R^2}(2 \arccos \frac{r}{2R} - \frac{r}{R}\sqrt{1 - (\frac{r}{2R})^2}). \tag{8}$$

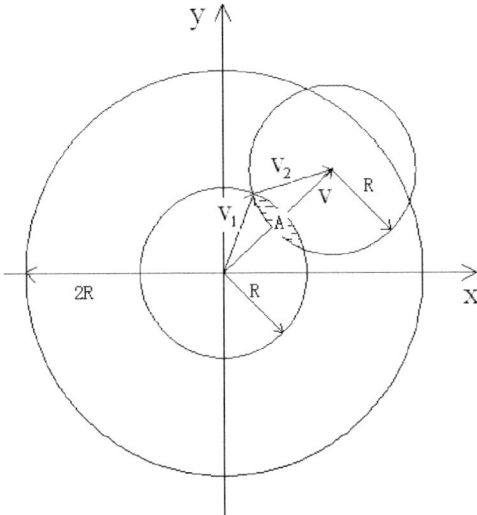

Fig. 5. Two vectors $v_1(r_1, \theta_1)$, $v_2(r_2, \theta_2)$ and their sum $v(r, \theta)$

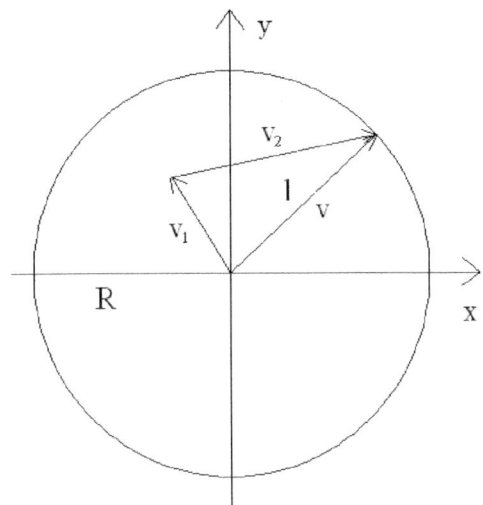

Fig. 6. Two vectors $v_1(r_1, \theta_1)$, $v_2(r_2, \theta_2)$ and their sum $v(r, \theta)$

Now for any two hosts uniformly displayed in the network with radius R, the location of the two host is $v_1(r_1, \theta_1)$, $v_2(r_2, \theta_2)$ respectively, where $0 \leq r_1, r_2 \leq R$, $0 \leq \theta_1, \theta_2 \leq 2\pi$. This can be seen from Figure 6, then the average distance l of this two MHs will be

$$E(l) = \int_0^{2R} \int_0^{2\pi} P(r, \theta, R) r^2 \, d\theta \, dr = \frac{128R}{45\pi}. \tag{9}$$

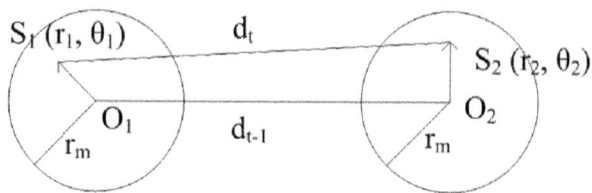

Fig. 7. The movement of two adjacent MHs n_i and n_j

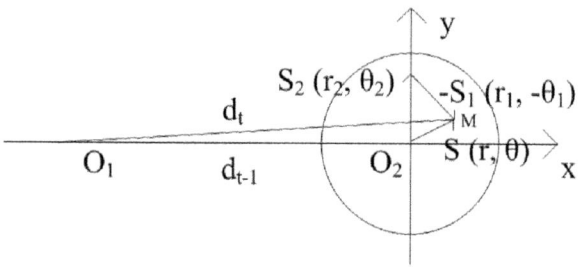

Fig. 8. The movement of MHs n_j from the view of host n_i

Therefore, for any two hosts which are uniformly located in a network area with radius R, their average distance is $\frac{128R}{45\pi}$.

4.2   Energy Comsumption on Route Dicovery

In a network with N MHs, the energy consumption of route discovery is mainly consumed by broadcasting the RREQ messages and unicasting the RREP messages, this means

$$E_{restart} = E_{RREQ} + E_{RREP}. \tag{10}$$

The source host broadcasting a RREQ message and this message will flood the whole network, so nearly every host will receive a RREQ message and they will rebroadcast the RREQ message to its neighbors. As the transmission range of the broadcasting is r_char which is suggested in PAA, then the energy consumption on broadcasting the RREQ message can be calculated approximately as follow

$$E_{RREQ} = NL_{RREQ}(\varepsilon_1 + \varepsilon_2 r_{char}^2). \tag{11}$$

The destination host will reply a RREP message after received a RREQ message, this RREP message will be unicasted back to the source, all the hosts who relay the RREP message will form a route $(n_0 n_1 \ldots n_l)$ from the source to the destination. As the routing protocol selects the route with minimum number of hops to be the final route, so the average number of hops of the active route $(n_0 n_1 \ldots n_l)$ will be

$$L = \lceil \frac{E(l)}{r_{char}} \rceil = \lceil \frac{128R}{45\pi r_{char}} \rceil. \tag{12}$$

Then the energy consumption of unicasting the RREP message can be calculated approximately as follows

$$E_{RREP} = LL_{RREP}(\varepsilon_1 + \varepsilon_2 r_{char}^2) = \lceil \frac{128R}{45\pi r_{char}} \rceil L_{RREP}(\varepsilon_1 + \varepsilon_2 r_{char}^2). \quad (13)$$

Finally the energy consumption of the route discovery is

$$E_{RREP} == (NL_{RREQ} + \lceil \frac{128R}{45\pi r_{char}} \rceil L_{RREP})(\varepsilon_1 + \varepsilon_2 r_{char}^2). \quad (14)$$

4.3   The Distance Variety between Adjacent MHs on the Routing Path

For any two objects randomly moving in the space, the distance between them will become larger and larger, this phenomenon is called diffusion in physics. Here we will estimate the distance variety of two adjacent MHs on the routing path, and this result will be used to build the energy consumption model of PAA in the next subsection, and then the optimal length of the period can be calculate out from this model.

The average distance of any two adjacent host n_i and n_j along the route path $(n_0 n_1 \ldots n_l)$ when packet $t-1$ and packet t comes are set to be d_{t-1}, $d_t$respectively. We define the distance variety to be $\Delta d = d_t^2 - d_{t-1}^2$. As the routing protocol selects the route with minimum number of hops to be the final route, the preliminary distance between any two adjacent hosts along the route path just after the route discovery restarted is nearly r_{char}, we just set $d_0 = r_{char}$ for simple.

As we have assumed the flow rate is r_f, so the time between any two continuous packets is $\frac{1}{r_f}$, and the MH's max speed in their random walk mobility model is set to be v_m, so the maximum distance that the MHs can move during the interim of two continuous packets is $r_m = \frac{v_m}{r_f}$.

The displacement of the two MHs n_i and n_j during the interim of two packets is denoted as $s_1(r_1, \theta_1), s_2(r_2, \theta_2)$ respectively, where $0 \le s_1, s_2 \le r_m$, $0 \le \theta_1, \theta_2 \le 2\pi$. The movement of the two hosts n_i and n_j can be seen in figure 7, and from the viewpoint of host n_i, the movement of host n_j can be seen in figure 8, and in figure 5 (b), the length O_1O_2 of is d_{t-1}, the length of O_1M is d_t . Then we can estimate distance variety Δd as follows

$$\Delta d = d_t^2 - d_{t-1}^2$$
$$= \int_0^{2r_m} \int_0^{2\pi} P(s, \theta, r_m)(d_{t-1}^2 + s^2 + 2d_{t-1}s\cos\theta - d_{t-1}^2)s\, ds\, d\theta, \quad (15)$$

where $P(s, \theta, r_m)$ is the probability of the final position of the MH n_j located at $s(r, \theta)$ from the viewpoint of MH n_i, here $s = -s_1 + s_2$, and

$$\sqrt{d_{t-1}^2 + s^2 + 2d_{t-1}s\cos\theta}$$

is the length of vector O_1M, which is the distance of the two host.

By some mathematical manipulations the equation (15) is reduced to the following equation:

$$\Delta d = d_t^2 - d_{t-1}^2 = r_m^2. \tag{16}$$

The above equation means that the distance variety of two adjacent MHs n_i and n_j is square of the maximum distance that the MH can move during the interval of two consecutive packets.

4.4   Finding the Optimal Length of the Period

In a period T, we let that k packets can be transmitted along the route, then the problem of finding optimal period T is transferred to find optimal number of packets can be transmitted in a period. Note the data rate r_f of the flow is assumed to be constant here.

After the route discovery, a route path $(n_0 n_1 \ldots n_l)$ from the source to the destination is constructed. As in Step 3 of PAA, the energy of delivering the t-th packet on this route path can be calculated in terms of

$$E(t) = \sum_{t=1}^{l} L_{DATA}(\varepsilon_1 + \varepsilon_2 d_t^2) = LL_{DATA}(\varepsilon_1 + \varepsilon_2 d_t^2). \tag{17}$$

Then the energy of delivering k packet in a period on an active route $(n_0 n_1 \ldots n_l)$ should be

$$E_p = \sum_{t=1}^{k} E(t) = LL_{DATA}(k\varepsilon_1 + \varepsilon_2 \sum_{t=1}^{k} d_t^2). \tag{18}$$

Now we need to minimize the average energy consumption on delivering one packet in a period, so this problem can be modeled as follow

$$Minimize \ \tfrac{1}{k}(E_p + E_restart) \tag{19}$$
$$Subjected \ to \quad d_0 = r_c har \tag{20}$$
$$d_1 = d_0 + 2v_m \tag{21}$$
$$d_t^2 = d_{t-1}^2 + v_m^2, \ \ 2 \le t \le k, \tag{22}$$

where $E_{restart}$ is the energy cost on route discovery, equation (19) means that we need to minimize the average energy consumption on delivering one packet. The conditions (21) is derived from step 3 of PAA, and (22) is derived from equation (16).

Now by substituting the conditions (22) into the object function (19) we will get the function below

$$E(k) = \frac{LL_{DATA}\varepsilon_2 r_m^2}{2} k + \frac{1}{k}\left(\frac{LL_{DATA}\varepsilon_2 r_m^2}{2} + E_{restart}\right) +$$
$$LL_{DATA}(\varepsilon_1 + \varepsilon_2(d_0 + 2v_m)^2 - \frac{3}{2}\varepsilon_2 r_m^2. \tag{23}$$

In order to get the optimal length of period, we need to minimize the energy consumption (23), to make the energy on delivering packet in the period minimized. So we can obtain the first order derivative of function (21) and then get the optimal number of packets delivering in a period

$$k_{opt} = \sqrt{1 + \frac{2E_{restart}}{LL_{DATA}\varepsilon_2 r_m^2}}, \tag{24}$$

when the parameters are determined, combining with equations (10),(11),(12), (14), we can get the optimal number of packet, then the length of the period in this network to restart the route discovery schedule will be $T = \frac{k_{opt}}{r_f}$.

5   Simulation Results

In this section, we have implemented the routing protocol DSR embedded with PAA and DSR without PAA. The parameter setting of these simulations is listed in Table I. In the simulation, 100 flows are randomly selected in a mobile ad-hoc network, and every flow needs to deliver 1000 packets through the network. First we verify the optimal number of packets can be sent in a period, then we compare the number of route discovery, the average energy consumption on delivering one packet, and the total energy consumption between the routing protocol DSR with PAA and DSR without PAA by changing the MH's maximum speed in the random walk mobility model. These results shows that the algorithm of PAA balances the energy consumed on route discovery and data delivering, this enable the routing protocol DSR with PAA conserve energy in the present of mobility.

Table 1. The parameters in the simulation

Parameter	Value
N	1000
R	$1000m$
ε_1	$180,000pJ/bit/m^2$
ε_2	$10pJ/bit/m^2$
L_{RREQ}	$16byte$
L_{RREP}	$16byte$
L_{DATA}	$512byte$
r_f	$1packet/s$

In Figure 9, as the number of packets k changes from 1 to 200, the average energy consumption on delivering one packet is plotted in this figure, here the max speed of the mobile host is set to be 10m/s. From this picture, we get that, when the number of packet k is in the range of $[20, 60]$, more energy will be conserved on packet delivering. The optimal value that computed from our model is 57, so the value computed from the model, will be acceptable in the algorithm of PAA.

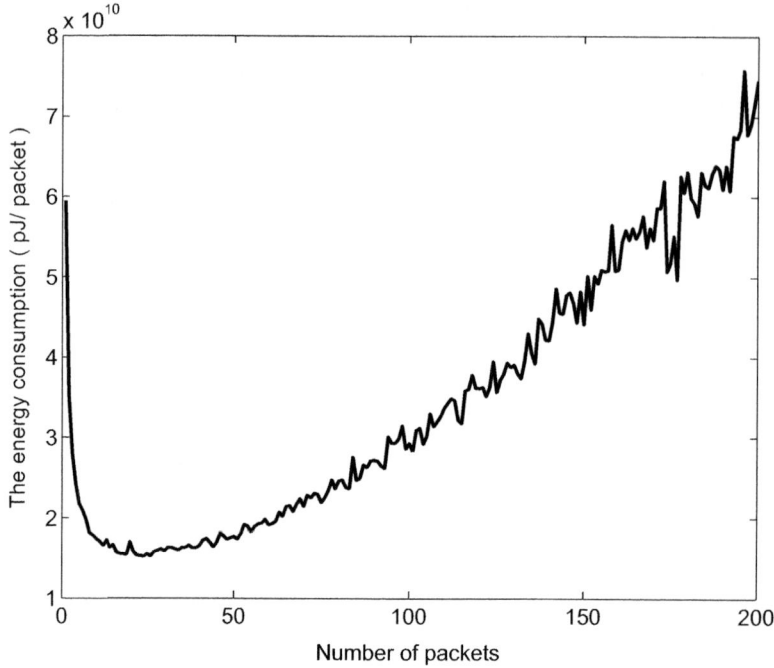

Fig. 9. Verification of the optimal length of period

By increasing the maximum speed of MHs from 1 m/s to 20 m/s in the mobility model, the number of restarted route discovery per flow, and the average energy consumption on delivering one packet are plotted in Figure 10, and Figure 12 respectively. In figure 6, the number of route discovery restarted is increased greatly in DSR without PAA compared to DSR with PAA. That's because the increasing max speed will enlarge the possibility of link break caused by MH's mobility along the route path in DSR without PAA, whereas this figure increases slowly in the DSR with PAA, that's because the number of route discovery restarted is largely decreased by adjusting the transmission power dynamically to adopt to the mobility of MHs.

Figure 7 demonstrates the route energy state on delivering packets. In this figure, the route energy state of DSR without PAA is always stable at $1.25 \times 10^{10}pJ$, while the route energy state of DSR with PAA increase as the MH's max speed increase. So the route energy state of DSR without PAA is maintained in good state, and the route energy state of DSR with PAA is becoming worse as the max speed increasing. As it has shown in figure 6, the good route state was maintained by DSR without PAA at the cost of much larger number of restarting route discovery, while PAA is aimed to reach a global balance not only in energy consumption on restarting route discovery but also on maintaining route energy consumption state on packet delivering. Clearly less number of route discovery leads to more energy consumption on packet delivering, here the number of

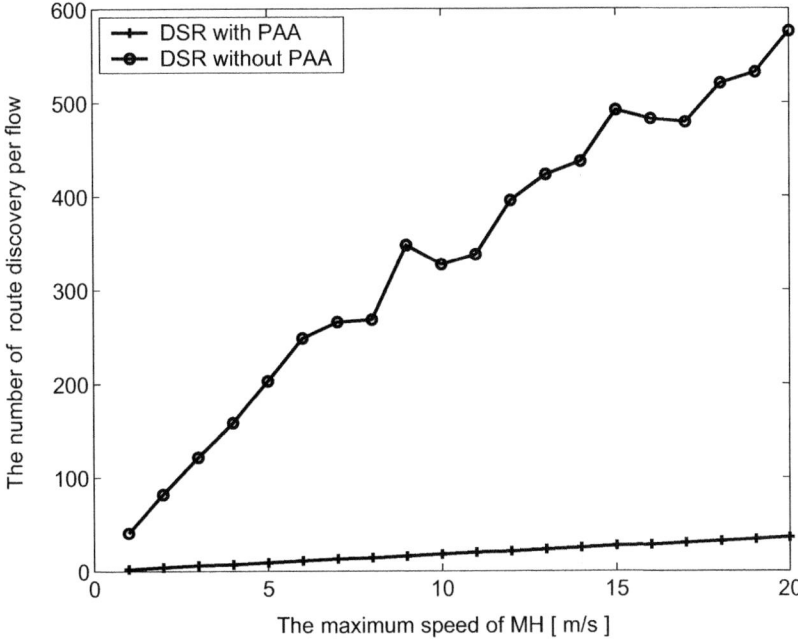

Fig. 10. The number of route discovery per ow on delivering 1000 packets

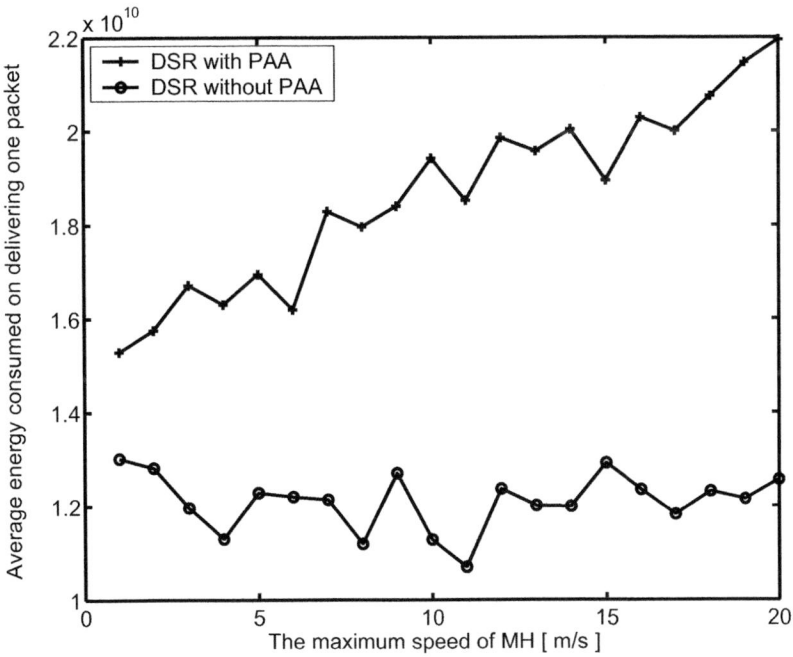

Fig. 11. The total energy consumption on delivering 1000 packets

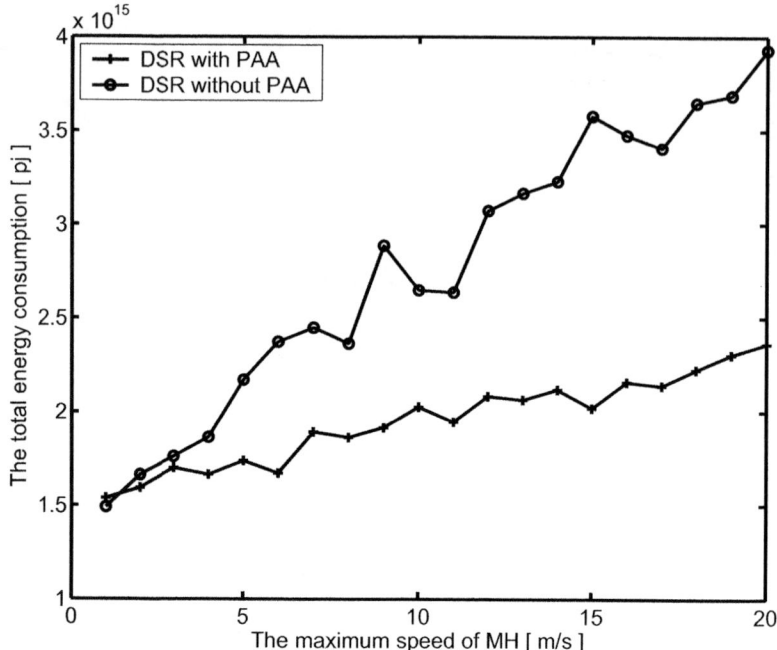

Fig. 12. Average consumption on delivering one packet

route discovery should be select carefully in PAA to minimize the total energy consumption.

The simulation result about the total energy consumption of the two protocols is plotted in figure 8. From the figure, you can see that 40protocol DSR with PAA when the max speed is becoming high. In the present of mobility of mobile host, the protocol DSR without PAA always restart the route discovery when a link break happens, it is suffering the mobility of MHs. While in the protocol DSR with PAA, the mobility of mobile host was under the control of PAA, and further more with the appropriate setting of the length of restarted period, the route discovery is restart to adjust the route path, which always balance the energy consumed on route discovery and packet delivering to reach a global power saving effect. Simulation results demonstrate that 40% energy was saved by using PAA to control the mobility of mobile host.

6   Conclusions

In this paper, we have proposed a power adjusting algorithm (PAA) which can be embedded in the routing protocol (e.g. DSR, AODV) to save power in the network layer. The algorithm of PAA introduced the adjustable transmission power control to control the mobility of MHs. By properly setting the length of period to restart the route discovery, PAA has the capability of balancing the energy consumption on route discovery and packets delivering to save power in network layer. By simulations, we first verified the optimal length of period calculated from our model, and then by analyzing the number of restarted route discovery and the route energy state, we also verified that PAA has indeed balanced the energy consumption on route discovery and packets delivering. Simulation results shows that the routing protocol DSR with PAA saves nearly 40% energy consumption under high speed mobility.

References

1. Corson, S., Macker, J.: Mobile Ad hoc Networking (MANET): Routing Protocol Performance Issues and Evaluation Considerations, IETF RFC2501 (January 1999)
2. Wang, C., Wu, C., Chen, G.: p-MANET: Efficient Power Saving Protocol for Multi-Hop Mobile Ad Hoc Networks. In: Proceedings of Third International Conference on Information Technology and Applications (ICITA 2005), Washington, USA, vol. 2, pp. 271–276 (2005)
3. Zheng, R., Kravets, R.: On-demand Power Management for Ad Hoc Networks. In: Proceedings of IEEE INFOCOM, vol. 1, pp. 481–491 (April 2003)
4. Wu, S., Tseng, Y., Sheu, J.: Intelligent Medium Access for Mobile ad hoc networks with busy tones and power control. IEEE Journal on Selected Areas in Communications 18(9), 1647–1657 (2000)
5. Gomez, J., Campbell, A.: A case for variable-range transmission power control in wireless ad hoc network. In: Proceeding of IEEE INFOCOM, vol. 2, pp. 1425–1436 (March 2004)
6. Monks, J., Bharghavan, V., Hwu, W.: A Power Controlled Multiple Access Protocol for Wireless Packet Networks. In: Proc. of IEEE INFOCOM, Anchorage, USA, vol. 1, pp. 219–228 (April 2001)
7. Zawodniok, M., Jagannathan, S.: A Distributed Transmission Power Control Protocol for Mobile Ad Hoc Networks. In: Proc. of the IEEE WCNC, pp. 1915–1920 (2004)
8. Johnson, D.B., Maltz, D.A.: Dynamic source routing in ad hoe wireless networks. In: Mobile Computing, pp. 153–181 (1996)
9. Perkins, C.: Ad-hoc On Demand Distance Vector (AODV) routing, intemet-Draft (November 1997)
10. Rappaport, T.: Wireless Communications: Principles and Practice. Prentice Hall, New Jersey (1996)
11. Camp, T., Boleng, J., Davies, V.: A survey of mobility models for ad hoc network research. In: Proceeding of Wireless Communications and Mobile Computing (WCMC 2002), vol. 2(5), pp. 483–502 (2002)
12. Bhardwaj, M., Garnett, T., Chandrakasan, A.: Upper bounds on the lifetime of sensor networks. In: Proceedings of IEEE International Conference on Communications, Helsinki, Finland, vol. 3, pp. 785–790 (June 2001)
13. Gupta, P., Kumar, P.: Critical Power for Asymptotic Connectivity in Wireless Networks. In: Stochastic Analysis, Control, Optimization and Applications, Boston, pp. 547–566 (1998)
14. Perkins, C.E., Royer, E.M.: Ad-hoc On-Demand Distance Vector Routing. In: Proceedings of the 2nd IEEE Workshop on Mobile Computing Systems and Applications, New Orleans, LA, pp. 90–100 (February 1999)

Power-Aware Run-Time Incremental Mapping for 3-D Networks-on-Chip[*]

Xiaohang Wang[1], Maurizio Palesi[2], Mei Yang[3],
Yingtao Jiang[3], Michael C. Huang[4], and Peng Liu[1,**]

[1] Zhejiang University, China
[2] Kore University, Italy
[3] University of Nevada Las Vegas, USA
[4] University of Rochester, USA
{baikeina,liupeng}@zju.edu.cn, maurizio.palesi@unikore.it,
{mei.yang,yingtao}@egr.unlv.edu,
michael.huang@rochester.edu

Abstract. 3-D Networks-on-Chip (NoCs) emerge as a powerful solution to address both the interconnection and design complexity problems facing future Systems-on-Chip (SoCs). Effective run-time application mapping on a 3-D NoC-based Multiprocessor Systems-on-Chip (MPSoC) can be quite challenging, largely due to the fact that the arrival order and task graphs of the target applications are not known a priori. This paper presents a power-aware run-time incremental mapping algorithm for 3-D NoCs that aims to minimize the communication power for each incoming application as well as reduce the impact of the mapped applications on future applications that are yet to be mapped. In this algorithm, if the vertical links are found to be shorter and provide higher communication bandwidth than horizontal links, more communications will be mapped to vertical links to reduce delay and power consumption. Extensive experiments have been conducted to evaluate the performance of the proposed algorithm and the results are compared with those obtained from the optimal mapping algorithm (branch-and-bound), a random mapping and a simple heuristic. When mapping a single application, the proposed algorithm is four orders of magnitude faster than the branch-and-bound algorithm at a small degradation of mapping quality. When mapping multiple applications incrementally, our algorithm can save 50% communication power compared to the random mapping and 20% communication power compared to the simple heuristic.

Keywords: Networks-on-chip, application mapping, 3-D IC.

1 Introduction

Advance in CMOS technology keeps driving the increase of the number of processing cores that can be integrated on a single chip. With the further increase of the number

---

[*] This work is supported in part by NSFC under the grants 60873112 and 61028004.
[**] Corresponding author.

E. Altman and W. Shi (Eds.): NPC 2011, LNCS 6985, pp. 232–247, 2011.

of processing cores, the integration limitations of SoCs become more significant. 3-D integration together with the NoC design paradigm provide a promising solution to overcome these limitations [1]. In the literature, several approaches exist for 3-D integration, e.g., wire bounded, microbump, through via and contactless [2]. 3-D integration can considerably reduce the global interconnection length, resulting in lower interconnection delay, power consumption and also the overall chip area [2]. Combining 3-D ICs and NoC can provide significant performance improvement and make the chip more power efficient.

The large number of processing cores integrated into 3-D NoC-based MPSoCs unquestionably offer high parallelism in computation. To better utilize these vast available computation resources, virtualization is applied to allow a single MPSoC to be shared by multiple applications which can be mapped to different networks of the chip at run time. However, the behaviors of the multiple applications vary so dramatically at run time, making it nearly impossible for these applications to be efficiently mapped offline. For these applications, run-time incremental mapping methods should be designed which could not only minimize the overall communication power but also consider future applications whose arrival orders are not known. In addition, in 3-D NoCs, the wire lengths of vertical links (in a few tens of μm) is much shorter than those of horizontal links (in a few thousand μm) [1][3]. As such, more communication could be mapped to vertical links to further reduce transmission delay and power consumption. In a simple word, a run-time mapping method for applications on 3-D NoC systems shall take multiple factors into consideration, namely the dynamic feature of applications with ever changing behaviors and the benefits of vertical links in 3-D NoCs.

Up to date, there is very little work on run-time 3-D NoC mapping reported in the open litterature. Existing approaches for offline 3-D NoC mapping [4] are not suitable for run-time mapping as they do not consider the shape of the mapped region and the impact on future applications. The 2-D NoC run-time incremental mapping algorithms [5, 6] cannot be directly applied to 3-D NoCs because the vertical links in 3-D NoCs are not an issue in those approaches.

In this paper, we propose a novel run-time incremental mapping algorithm which maps applications that can randomly enter and leave an embedded 3-D NoC system while considering the benefits of vertical links. The mapping algorithm tries to minimize overall communication power as well as minimize the impact on future applications (i.e., to reduce the fragmentation caused by small region of tiles). The proposed algorithm is composed of three steps: 1) *NoC region selection* which selects a cuboid region to reduce the impact on future applications; 2) *set matching* which allocates the application graph to the sub-regions in different layers such that the vertical links are used as much as possible; and 3) *CTG to NoC region mapping* which maps the IP cores to the tiles in different sub-regions with minimized total communication power. The higher bandwidth and lower delay properties of the vertical links in 3-D NoC are particularly exploited in set matching and region mapping steps. Experimental results have confirmed that the proposed algorithm saves up to 50% communication power over random mapping and about 20% over a simple heuristic.

The rest of this paper is organized as follows. Section 2 summarizes the related work. Section 3 provides the preliminaries and problem definition. Section 4 presents a motivating example and decomposition of the problem. Following the observations from the example, Section 5 presents the run-time mapping algorithm in detail. Section 6 presents the simulation results. Finally, Section 7 concludes the paper.

2   Related Work

Research in 3-D NoCs emerges in recent years. In [1], both the analytical model of zero-load latency and the power model for 3-D NoCs are provided. Different 3-D NoC designs are shown in [7, 8, 9]. In [7], a three-layer NoC is proposed where each layer has different network topology so that the planar topology on every layer could be customized to meet different cost-performance demands. In [8], both 3-D mesh-based architectures (symmetric 3-D mesh, stacked mesh, and ciliated mesh) and 3-D tree-based architectures are analyzed in terms of network performance and energy dissipation. The analysis shows that 3-D mesh-based architectures demonstrate significant performance gains with a small area overhead compared with 2-D meshes. In [3], the 3-D Dimensionally-Decomposed (DimDe) Router is proposed. The DimDe router features is a true 3D crossbar with two vertical interconnects spanning over all layers. As such, the crossbars of all the routers with the same vertical index are fused into one unit. With the fusion of crossbar, short vertical links could be utilized such that vertical transmissions among different layers only take one hop. In addition, the crossbar is decomposed to reduce complexity. Simulation results show that the 3-D mesh NoC constructed with DimDe routers achieves better throughput, latency and energy-delay product compared with a symmetric 3-D mesh built with 7-port routers extended from 5-port routers [3].

In the literature, a number of IP mapping algorithms have been proposed for 2-D NoCs with the objective of minimizing the overall communication power. However, most of these existing mapping algorithms designed for 2-D NoCs summarized in [10] cannot be used in run-time incremental mapping for 3-D NoCs as these algorithms do not consider the short vertical links featured in 3-D NoCs. The branch-and-bound algorithm [11][12] can be extended to run-time incremental mapping for 3-D NoCs. However, the extremely long running time is not suitable for run-time mapping. In [4], a genetic algorithm based thermal-aware 3-D offline mapping is proposed. Due to the complexity, it is also not suitable for run-time 3-D NoC mapping.

In terms of run-time incremental mapping for 2-D NoCs, several schemes have been proposed. In [13], a run-time task assignment algorithm is proposed for heterogeneous processors with the task graphs limited to a small number of tasks. A dynamic task mapping scheme is proposed for NoC-based MPSoCs in [14], aiming to improve the performance by minimizing the channel load. The incremental mapping algorithms proposed for 2-D NoCs [5, 6] may be helpful for 3-D NoCs. The general idea of these run-time mapping algorithms is to find a convex tile region first, followed by mapping the incoming application to the convex region. The convexity of the tile region helps to reduce communication within the region and the impact on future applications as the remaining tiles always form a continuous shape.

Run-time mapping algorithms in traditional parallel and distributed systems [15] do not suit for the on-chip application mapping as they do not consider on-chip power consumption.

3   Problem Formulation

In this paper, our study is focused on run-time mapping for 3-D mesh-based NoCs considering the regularity and advantage of the topology [8]. Fig. 1 shows the 3-D mesh-based NoC architecture, which is composed of N layers of IP cores and routers. Each IP core is indexed by (x, y, z) where $0 \le x \le M_x$, $0 \le y \le M_y$ and $0 \le z \le N\text{-}1$, (each layer is composed of a M_x x M_y mesh). At each layer, each IP core is on a single physical plane and connected to its router through a horizontal link. Due to its advantages, the 3-D DimDe router [3] is adopted here. As shown in Fig. 1, each router still has five horizontal ports, i.e., E, W, N, S and local. The guided flit queuing methods [3] are used to decompose the traffic into X, Y, and Z dimensions. The 5x5 crossbar in a 2-D mesh is split into two 4x2 crossbars to reduce the router complexity. Each vertical link has one input connection from its associated path set (PS) MUX and three output connections, one to the East-West crossbar, the North-South crossbar and the local port, respectively. Assume that the wire length of vertical links between adjacent layers is much shorter than the wire length of horizontal links between adjacent routers. The deterministic XYZ routing is assumed. A tile is defined to be an IP core with the corresponding part of the router on the same layer.

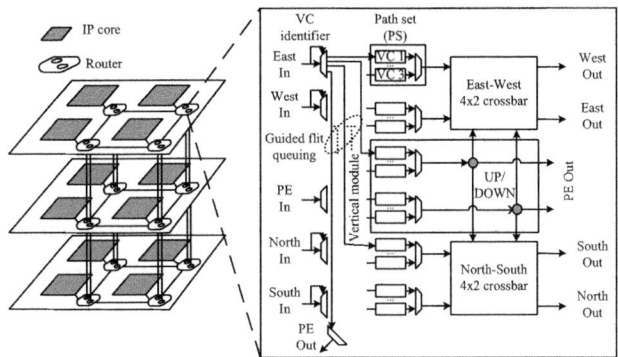

Fig. 1. The 3-D NoC architecture [3]

3.1   Communication Power Model

The communication energy needed for sending a flit from a source tile to a destination tile is composed of two parts, the energy consumed at the routers and the energy consumed on the interconnection links. The average energy consumption of sending one bit of data from tile t_i to tile t_j can be represented as

$$E^{t_i,t_j}{}_{bit} = E_R + E_L \tag{1}$$

where E_R and E_L are the energy consumed by the routers and links in the communication path from tile t_i to tile t_j. To be more specific,

$$E^{t_i,t_j}{}_{bit} = \eta E_{Rbit} + \eta_H E_{LHbit} + \eta_V E_{LVbit} \tag{2}$$

where E_{Rbit} is the energy consumed when transporting a flit at the router, η is the number of routers traversed from tile t_i to tile t_j, η_H and η_V are the number of horizontal and vertical links in the communication path, and E_{LHbit} and E_{LVbit} are the energy consumed on the horizontal and vertical links between tiles t_i and t_j. Following the wire model given in [7], $E_{Lbit} = dV^2 C_{wire}/2$, where d is the length of the link, V is the supply voltage and C_{wire} is the wire capacitance.

3.2 Application and Architecture Model

Each incoming application is represented by its communication trace graph defined below.

Definition 1. A *Communication Trace Graph* (CTG) $G=(P, E)$ is an undirected graph, where a vertex/node $p_k \in P$ represents a task, and an edge $e_i=(p_j, p_k) \in E$ represents the communication trace between vertices p_j and p_k.

- For edge e_i, $\omega(e_i)$ defines the communication bandwidth request between vertices p_j and p_k given in bits per second (bps).
- $\omega(e_i)$ sets the minimum bandwidth that should be allocated by the network in order to meet the performance constraints.

The 3-D NoC architecture is modeled by the architecture characteristic graph.

Definition 2. An *Architecture Characterization Graph* (ACG) $G'=(T, L)$ is an undirected graph, where each vertex $t_i \in T$ represents a tile and each edge $l_i \in L = (t_j, t_k)$ represents the link between adjacent tiles t_j and t_k. N is the number of NoC layers. For link l_i

- $bw(l_i)$ defines the bandwidth provided on link l_i between adjacent tiles t_j and t_k;
- $c(l_i)$ defines the link cost of l_i, i.e., power consumption for transmitting one bit data from t_j and t_k.

In this paper, we focus on NoC architectures which have $bw(l_i)=B$, $c(l_i)=C_V$ if l_i is a vertical link, $c(l_i)=C_H$ if l_i is a horizontal link for each $l_i \in L$, where B, C_V and C_H are constants. $h_{t_j,t_k j}$ is the set of links forming one of the shortest paths from tile t_j to tile t_k ($h_{t_j,t_k} \subseteq L$). We also assume that the IP core with index $(0, 0, 0)$ manages the whole mapping process.

3.3 Problem Description

The 3-D NoC run-time mapping problem is described as: Given the CTG of the incoming application and the ACG of the current 3-D NoC system, find a mapping function $M:P \to T$, with the objective of minimizing the communication power, i.e.,

$$Min(\sum_{\substack{i=0 \\ e_i=(p_j,p_k) \in E}}^{|E|-1} \omega(e_i) \cdot \sum_{\substack{m=0 \\ l_k \in h_{M(p_j),M(p_k)}}}^{|h_{M(p_j),M(p_k)}|} c(l_m)) \tag{3}$$

satisfying

$$\forall p_j \in P, M(p_j) \in T, \tag{4}$$

$$\forall p_j, p_k \in P \text{ and } p_j \neq p_k, M(p_j) \neq M(p_k), \tag{5}$$

$$\forall l_m, B \geq \sum_{e_i = (p_j, p_k)} \omega(e_i) \cdot f(l_m, h_{M(p_j), M(p_k)}), \tag{6}$$

where $f(l_m, h_{M(p_j), M(p_k)}) = \begin{cases} 1 \text{ if } l_m \in h_{M(p_j), M(p_k)} \\ 0 \text{ if } l_m \notin h_{M(p_j), M(p_k)} \end{cases}$.

Conditions given by (4) and (5) ensure that each task should be mapped exactly to one tile and no tile can host more than one task. The inequities given in (6) specify the bandwidth constraint for every link.

4 Motivating Example and Problem Decomposition

4.1 Motivating Example

A motivating example of mapping a newly incoming application to a 3-D mesh-based NoC (with 3x16 tiles) is given in Fig. 2 to illustrate the composition of the problem. Fig. 2(a) gives the CTG of an example application with 16 tasks. The black tiles in Fig. 2(b) are reserved for other applications already running in the system. Before mapping, as in run-time incremental mapping for 2-D NoCs [5, 6], a region of available tiles shall be selected. Intuitively, a cuboid region is preferred to minimize the impact to future applications. Fig. 2(b) shows such a region of 18 tiles (in grey color). Next, in the mapping process, the tasks which have high communication requests should be considered first [10]. Based on the definitions in Section 3, these tasks shall be allocated to the sub-regions in different layers such that the communications with high bandwidth requests can utilize vertical links. Fig. 2(c) shows an allocation result of the tasks which have high communication requests. Last, all tasks are mapped to the tiles in the sub-regions as shown in Fig. 2(d).

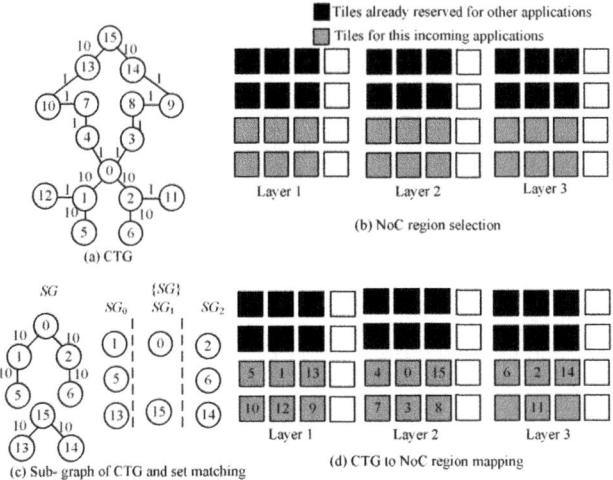

Fig. 2. Illustration of the whole problem

4.2   A Mapping Flow by Problem Decomposition

Based on the observations from this example, the run-time mapping problem for 3-D NoCs is divided into three sub-problems as shown in Fig. 3. The three sub-problems are described below.

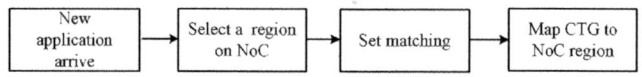

Fig. 3. The mapping process

(4.1.1) NoC Region Selection

First, a region is selected to map each incoming application. This region is composed of N sub-regions, one on each layer. To reduce the impact on future applications, these sub-regions should be rectangle in shape and the size of each of the sub-regions shall be made as close to each other as possible.

Given the CTG of the incoming application, the ACG of the 3-D NoC, and the current system behavior (i.e. the used and unused tiles), this sub-problem is to find a cuboid region $SR=\{SR_0, \ldots, SR_{N-1}\}$, where SR_w represents the sub-region of unallocated tiles on layer w, with the objective of:

$$Min\ (|\ SR_w|\cdot N - |G|),\ \text{for each } w=0, \ldots, N\text{-}1 \tag{7}$$

satisfying,

$$|SR_w|\cdot N \geq |G|, \tag{8}$$

$$|SR_w|=|SR_{w+1}|\ \text{for } w =0, \ldots, N\text{-}2, \tag{9}$$

Here $|G|$ gives the number of tasks in G and $|SR_w|$ gives the number of tiles in set SR_w.

(P2) Set Matching

The basic idea of set matching is to find the layers to be mapped for those tasks which have high bandwidth (BW) communication requests. When both vertical and horizontal links are available, according to the assumption that vertical links tend to be shorter than horizontal links, vertical links are thus preferred. That is, communication edges with high BW requests shall be allocated to vertical links if possible in order to reduce delay and power consumption.

Assume the edges in G are sorted in a non-increasing order in terms of their communication bandwidth request (i.e., $\omega(e_i)$). Let $SG\subset G$ be a sub-graph formed with the first $\alpha\%$ edges in the sorted edge list [10]. The objective is to allocate the vertices in SG into N subsets to be mapped to the corresponding N sub-regions found in (P1) such that the vertical links are used as much as possible. This sub-problem is formally defined as follows.

Given the sub-graph SG of the CTG and the sub-regions $SR_0, \ldots, SR_{N-1}$ obtained from region selection step described in (P1), allocate the vertices in SG into N sets $SG_0, \ldots, SG_{N-1}$, assuming vertical links are preferred, with the objective of:

$$Max \sum_{\substack{e_i=(p_j,p_k)\\p_j\in SG_u\\p_k\in SG_v\\u\neq v}} \omega(e_i), \tag{10}$$

satisfying,

$$SG_u \cap SG_v = \varnothing, \text{ for } u \neq v \tag{11}$$

$$|SG_u| \leq |SR_w|, \text{ for each } u=0,\ldots, N\text{-}1 \tag{12}$$

(P3) CTG to NoC Region Mapping

With the sub-regions and sets obtained in (P1) and (P2), the application is then mapped to minimize the communication power.

Given the CTG of the incoming application, N sets of the vertices $SG_0, \ldots, SG_{N-1}$ and a set of sub-regions $SR=\{SR_0, \ldots, SR_{N-1}\}$, find a mapping function $M: P \rightarrow SR$ with the objective:

$$Min \; (\sum_{\substack{i=0 \\ e_i=(p_j,p_k) \in E}}^{|E|} \omega(e_i) \cdot [MD_v(M(p_j), M(p_k)) \cdot C_V$$

$$+ MD_H(M(p_j), M(p_k)) \cdot C_H]), \tag{13}$$

satisfying

$$\forall p_j \in P, \; M(p_j) \in T, \tag{14}$$

$$\forall p_j, p_k \in P \text{ and } p_j \neq p_k, \; M(p_j) \neq M(p_k), \tag{15}$$

$$\forall \, l_m, B \geq \sum_{e_i=(p_j,p_k)} \omega(e_i) \cdot f(l_m, h_{M(p_j),M(p_k)}), \tag{16}$$

where $f(l_m, h_{M(p_j),M(p_k)}) = \begin{cases} 1 \text{ if } l_m \in h_{M(p_j),M(p_k)} \\ 0 \text{ if } l_m \notin h_{M(p_j),M(p_k)} \end{cases}$, $MD_H()$ and $MD_V()$ denote the

horizontal and vertical Manhattan distance between two tiles, respectively. Conditions given by (14) and (15) ensure that each task should be mapped exactly to one tile and no tile can host more than one task. The inequities given in (16) specify the bandwidth constraint for every link.

5   Algorithm Description

For each sub-problem listed in Section 4, an algorithm is introduced in each of following subsections. Before discussing these algorithms, the following assumption is made. All the edges of an incoming application's CTG are sorted in a decreasing order by the edge weight $\omega(e_i)$. The sorted edge list is represented as *SE*.

5.1   NoC Region Selection (P1)

As discussed in Section 4, a cuboid of NoC tiles shall be first found. This problem can be further divided into two small problems. First, given the incoming application's CTG G, a window with a size of size $l \cdot w$ should be found such that $N \cdot l \cdot w \geq |G|$ and $N \cdot l \cdot w - |G|$ is minimized. That is, the shape and size of sub-region should be chosen to minimize fragmentation. Second, after finding the $l \cdot w$ matrix, unallocated tiles which form the $N \cdot l \cdot w$ cuboid should be found (these tile regions are called NoC regions). A window sweeping process is used as in Fig. 4(a).

A window of size $l \cdot w$ starts from tile (0, 0, 1) and moves at the first layer. The window sweeps the whole layer until all of the tiles inside the window are found not allocated yet.

An example of applying this algorithm is shown in Fig. 2(b). The CTG shown in Fig. 2(a) has 16 tasks. Thus, a 3x2x3 cuboid is selected based on the window sweeping process (Fig. 2(b)).

The NoC region selection algorithm is shown in Fig. 4(b). The complexity of the algorithm is $xy+(|TV/N| \cdot x \cdot y) = O(|TV/N|)^2$.

```
NoC_region_selection(G, Q,G')
Input: (1) G: The CTG of the incoming application
        (2) Q: current unallocated tiles in NoC
        (3) G': The ACG of the NoC architecture
Output: (1) SR: a cuboid tile region allocated for the incoming application
Function: find the sub-regions of tiles for the incoming application
Procedure body:
{
    var: size_each_layer = ⌈|G|/N⌉;
    // 1. find the window size
    for (l=1; l< size_each_layer/2;l++)
        for (w=1; w< size_each_layer/2;w++)
            if (l·w > size_each_layer){
                break from the l-indexed loop;
            }
    // 2. find an N·l·w cuboid in Q for G,
    // use window sweeping at the bottom layer
    for (each tile ti in Q₀) {
        // suppose Q₀ is the free tile region in the bottom layer of 3-D NoC
        // suppose the coordinate of ti is (i, j, 0)
        // let R be the the rectangle tile region whose top left and bottom right ranges are (i, j, 0) and (i+l, j+w, 0)
        // let R ' be the rectangle tile region whose top left and bottom right ranges are (i, j, 0) and (i+w, j+l, 0)
        // m = 0,1,...N-1
        if (all the tiles in R are available) {
            SRₘ = R;
            break;
        }
        else if (all the tiles in R ' are available) {
            SRₘ = R ' ;
            break;
        }
    }
    Q = Q -SR
}
```

Window sweeping, size 3x3

■ Occupied tiles
□ Available tiles

(a)

(b)

Fig. 4. The NoC region selection algorithm

5.2   Set Matching (P2)

In the second step, the sub-graph of the CTG, i.e. *SG*, which includes the tasks with high communication BW requests should be allocated into the *N* sets, one for each layer. The sub-graph *SG* is formed by the first 50% edges (denoted as *SE'*) in *SE*, Vertical links are preferred for high BW communication edges. Hence, edges with larger weight will be first allocated to vertical links if possible. However, there is only one vertical link between the two tiles (x, y, z) and $(x, y, z+1)$, $z= 0, ..., N-2$. Thus, if a task is allocated to tile (x, y, z) and has two neighbors in layer $z+1$, it may result in higher power consumption than mapping one of the neighbors to the same layer z. Fig. 5 shows such an example. Given the CTG shown in Fig. 5(a), if tasks 1 and 2 are mapped to layer 1 (Fig. 5(b)), the energy cost is $10 \cdot (C_V+C_V+C_H)$ suppose the link energy cost are C_V and C_H for vertical and horizontal links, respectively. If task 2 is mapped to the same layer of task 0 (Fig. 5(c)), the energy cost is $10 \cdot (C_V+C_H)$ which is lower than that of Fig. 5(b). Thus, an observation is made that when vertical links are preferred, a task can be allocated to the same layer of its neighbor if the neighbor already has edges allocated to adjacent layers.

The algorithm works as follows. For each edge (p_j, p_k) in the sorted edge list SE',

- If neither of the two tasks is allocated, the tasks are checked to see whether one of them has degree in SG greater than 1. If so, the task with a larger degree in SG is allocated to SG_u with ($0<u<N-1$), i.e., to a layer whose tiles have two vertical links, up and down. Otherwise, the tasks are allocated to SG_u and SG_v with $u \neq v$ and $|u-v|$ minimized.
- If one of the tasks is allocated, e.g., p_j is allocated to SG_u, the unallocated task p_k is allocated to SG_v ($u \neq v$) such that $|u-v|$ is minimized, given that p_j has no neighbor in SG_v. Otherwise, p_k is allocated to SG_u.

Fig. 6 shows an example of the set matching processing based on the CTG given in Fig. 2(a). The sub-graph SG of this CTG is given in Fig. 6(a) and the size of region on each layer is 6. The sorted edge list of the sub-graph is $\{(0, 1), (0, 2), (1, 5), (2, 6), (13, 15), (14, 15)\}$. Fig. 6(b) shows that tasks 0 and 1 are first allocated to SG_1 and SG_0 as task 0 has a degree of 2 in Fig. 6(a). When allocating edge (0, 2), task 2 is allocated to SG_0 as task 0's neighbor task 1 is already allocated to SG_1 (Fig. 6(c)). When allocating edge (1, 5), task 5 is allocated to SG_0 as task 1's neighbor task 0 is already allocated to SG_1. Similarly, task 6 is allocated to SG_2 as in Fig. 6(d). Tasks 13, 14 and 15 are allocated similarly as in Fig. 6(e) and (f). The final result of the set matching problem for the vertices in SG is shown in Fig. 6(f).

The set matching algorithm is shown in Fig. 5(d). The complexity of the algorithm is $O(|E||N|^2)$.

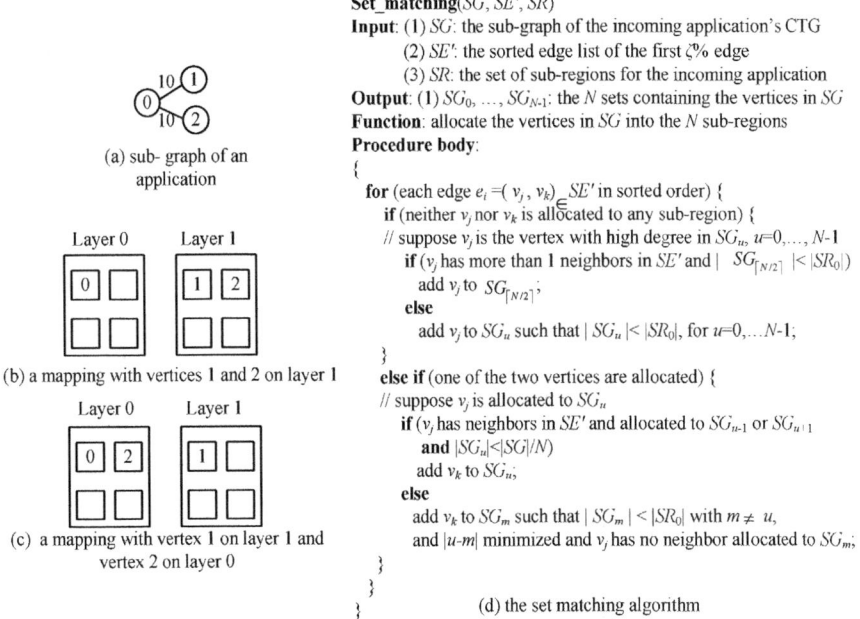

(a) sub- graph of an application

(b) a mapping with vertices 1 and 2 on layer 1

(c) a mapping with vertex 1 on layer 1 and vertex 2 on layer 0

Set_matching(SG, SE', SR)
Input: (1) SG: the sub-graph of the incoming application's CTG
   (2) SE': the sorted edge list of the first ζ% edge
   (3) SR: the set of sub-regions for the incoming application
Output: (1) SG_0, ..., SG_{N-1}: the N sets containing the vertices in SG
Function: allocate the vertices in SG into the N sub-regions
Procedure body:
{
 for (each edge $e_i = (v_j, v_k) \in SE'$ in sorted order) {
  if (neither v_j nor v_k is allocated to any sub-region) {
   // suppose v_j is the vertex with high degree in SG_u, $u=0,...,N-1$
   if (v_j has more than 1 neighbors in SE' and $|SG_{\lceil N/2 \rceil}| < |SR_0|$)
    add v_j to $SG_{\lceil N/2 \rceil}$;
   else
    add v_j to SG_u such that $|SG_u| < |SR_0|$, for $u=0,...N-1$;
  }
  else if (one of the two vertices are allocated) {
   // suppose v_j is allocated to SG_u
   if (v_j has neighbors in SE' and allocated to SG_{u-1} or SG_{u+1}
    and $|SG_u|<|SG|/N$)
    add v_k to SG_u;
   else
    add v_k to SG_m such that $|SG_m| < |SR_0|$ with $m \neq u$,
    and $|u-m|$ minimized and v_j has no neighbor allocated to SG_m;
  }
 }
}

(d) the set matching algorithm

Fig. 5. The set matching algorithm (P2)

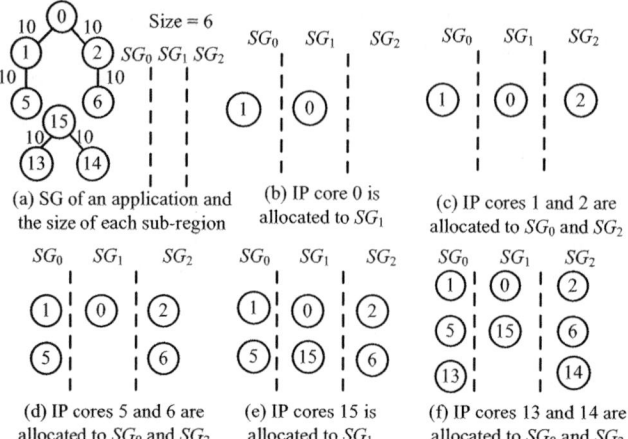

Fig. 6. An example of set matching when vertical links are preferred

5.3   CTG to NoC Region Mapping (P3)

After finding the set of tile regions *SR* and the allocation of the vertices in *SG* to the *N* set SR_0, ..., SR_{N-1}, all of the vertices in CTG should be mapped to *SR*. In this algorithm, a metric *Dist()* is used to find the weighted distance of two tiles. The *Dist()* metric is defined as: $Dist(t_a,t_b)=|x_a-x_b|C_H+|y_a-y_b|C_H+|z_a-z_b|C_V$, where (x_a,y_a,z_a) and (x_b,y_b,z_b) represent the coordinates of tiles t_a and t_b, respectively. As discussed in Section 3, *Dist()* reflects the power consumption of each communication edge after mapping the two tasks. The algorithm checks for each edge in *SE* of CTG and maps the tasks to minimize their distance. It works as follows. For each edge (p_j, p_k),

- If neither of the two tasks p_j, p_k are mapped. There are three cases to consider

  1)   Both tasks are already allocated to the *N* sets SR_0, ..., SR_{N-1}, e.g., p_j allocated to SG_u and p_k allocated to SG_v ($0 \leq u$, $v \leq N-1$). If p_j has high degree (>2) in *SG*, find a tile in SR_u with large number of free neighbor tiles. Otherwise, find an unused tile in SR_u for p_j. Then find a tile for p_k in SR_v to minimize the *Dist()* metric.

  2)   One of the two tasks already allocated to the *N* sets, e.g., p_j allocated to SG_u. If p_j has high degree (>2) in *SG*, find a tile in SG_u with large number of free neighbor tiles. Otherwise, find an arbitrary tile in SG_u for p_j. Then find a tile for p_k in *SR* to minimize the *Dist()* metric.

  3)   Neither of the two tasks allocated to the *N* sets yet. If p_j has high degree (>2) in *SG*, find a tile in *SR* with large number of free neighbor tiles. Otherwise, find an arbitrary tile in *SR* for p_j. Then find a tile for p_k in *SR* to minimize the *Dist()* metric.

- If one of the two tasks is mapped, e.g., p_j is mapped to tile *t*. If the unmapped task p_k is allocated to SG_u, find a tile in SR_u for p_k to minimize the *Dist()* metric. Otherwise, find a tile for p_k in *SR* to minimize the *Dist()* metric.

The CTG to NoC region mapping algorithm is shown in Fig. 7. The complexity of the CTG to NoC region mapping algorithm (P3) is $O(|E||T|^2)$. The total complexity of the run-time incremental mapping algorithm (combining the algorithms introduced in section 5.1 to 5.3) is $O(|E||T|^2)$.

Assume the vertical links are preferred for communications with high BW requests. Fig. 2(d) shows the mapping result given the CTG in Fig. 2(a) based on the results of NoC region selection (Fig. 2(b)) and set matching (Fig. 2 (c)).

```
CTG_to_NoC_mapping (G, SE, SR)
Input: (1) G: the CTG of the incoming application
       (2) SE: the sorted edge list of the CTG
       (3) SR: the set of sub-regions for the incoming application
       (4) SG₀, ..., SGN-1: the N sets containing the vertices in SG
Output: (1) MAP: mapping table for each IP core
Function: map each IP core to a tile in SR
Procedure body:
{
    for (each edge eᵢ =( pⱼ, pₖ)∈ SE) {
        if (neither pⱼ nor pₖ are mapped) {
            if (pⱼ ∈ SGᵤ and pₖ ∈ SGᵥ) { // u,v=0,...,N-1
                MAP[pⱼ] = tₐ s.t. tₐ∈ SRᵤ;
                // if pⱼ has more than two neighbors in SG,
                // find a tₐ have more than two free neighbor tiles
                MAP[pₖ] = t_b s.t. t_b∈ SRᵥ and Dist(tₐ, t_b) is minimized;
            }
            else if (suppose pⱼ ∈ SGᵤ) { // u =0,...,N-1
                MAP[pⱼ] = t_c s.t. t_c∈ SRᵤ;
                // if pⱼ has more than two neighbors in SG,
                // t_c should also have more than two free neighbor tiles
                MAP[pₖ] = t_d s.t. t_d∈ SR and Dist(t_c, t_d) is minimized;
            }
            else {
                MAP[pⱼ] = t_e s.t. t_e∈ SR;
                // if pⱼ has more than two neighbors in SG,
                // t_e should also has more than two free neighbor tiles
                MAP[pₖ] = t_f s.t. t_d∈ SR and Dist(t_e, t_f) is minimized;
            }
        }
        else if (only one IP core is mapped){
            // suppose pⱼ is mapped to tile t
            if (pₖ∈ SGᵥ) { // v=0,...,N-1
                MAP[pₖ] = t_g s.t. t_g∈ SRᵥ and Dist(t, t_g) is minimized;
            }
            else {
                MAP[pₖ] = t_h s.t. Dist(t, t_h) is minimized;
            }
        }
    }
}
```

Fig. 7. The CTG to NoC region mapping algorithm

6   Performance Evaluation

The proposed algorithms have been evaluated through extensive experiments. Two sets of experiments are performed. First, single random applications are mapped to a 3-D NoC architecture. In this set of experiments, our algorithm is compared against the branch and bound (BNB) algorithm in terms of the solution quality. BNB tries to exhaustively enumerate all possible mapping results where mapping results with higher power consumption are discarded by estimating upper and lower bounds. Second, multiple applications (including random applications generated by TGFF [16] and applications from E3S [17]) are incrementally mapped to a 3-D NoC architecture. In this set of experiments, our algorithm is compared against a random mapping algorithm and a simple heuristic algorithm, namely large communication first (LCF).

The power model is adopted from the DimDe router [3]. The network is assumed to be a 6x6x3 3-D mesh. The flit size is set to be 128-bit. To study the power consumption trend, vertical and horizontal links with different lengths are chosen. The wire parameters are adopted from [1], e.g., the unit wire capacitances (C_{wire}) for vertical and horizontal links are 600fF/mm and 332fF/mm, respectively. Table I lists the wire length combinations evaluated where vertical links are preferred over horizontal links. The Noxim simulator [18] is used as the NoC simulator.

Table 1. Different combinations of vertical and horizontal link length

Combinations	Length of vertical links between adjacent layers	Length of horizontal links between adjacent routers
I	60um	1mm
II	90um	1mm
III	120um	1mm
IV	60um	0.5mm
V	90um	0.5mm
VI	120um	0.5mm

6.1   Mapping Single Application to 3-D NoC

First, we show the single application mapping results of our algorithm compared to that of BNB. Two types of applications are evaluated: random applications and real applications. For random applications, TGFF is used to generate the CTGs. The numbers of tasks range from 12 to 20. The communication BW requests vary from 1 to 10. The tile regions selected for our algorithm and BNB are the same. The running time of BNB is more than one hour while the running time of our algorithm is within 1 sec. From Fig. 8, we can see that the increase in power consumption of our algorithm over BNB is within 11%.

Fig. 8 shows that, the results from our algorithm get closer to that of BNB when the energy cost ratio of horizontal links over vertical links (C_H:C_V) are smaller. The ratio of C_H:C_V is the largest for combination I and smallest for combination VI. The reason is due to the fact that, as the ratio of C_H:C_V becomes smaller, the difference in vertical and horizontal communications is reduced. The power consumption of horizontal links in the mapping result produced by our algorithm has less impact on the overall communication power consumption.

6.2   Mapping Multiple Applications Incrementally to 3-D NoC

In this section, our algorithm is compared against a random mapping (RM) and large communication first (LCF) with multiple applications. Due to the complexity of BNB, it is not used for runtime mapping. In RM and LCF, the NoC region selection step is the same as in our algorithm. RM maps the tasks to the tiles in the selected region randomly. LCF sorts the edges in the non-increasing order of BW request. Then the terminal vertices of the communication edge with higher bandwidth request are mapped to links with smaller $c(l)$ values. Both random and real applications are evaluated.

First, random applications are simulated with their CTGs generated from TGFF [16]. The numbers of tasks in these CTGs vary from 12 to 20. The communication BW requests vary from 1 to 10. For each combination in Table I, five experiments are performed for each number of tasks. In each experiment, 10 applications are mapped to a 6x6x3 network. The running time of each application is varied from 1 to 10 time units. Fig. 9 shows the normalized power saving of our algorithm over RM and LCF. Fig. 9(a) shows that our algorithm can save up to over 50% power compared to RM and up to 20% over LCF.

Real application CTGs, including auto-industry, consumer, networking, and office automation, are generated from E3S [17]. Again, for each combination in Table I, five experiments are conducted. Each experiment is composed of 10 applications which are mapped to a 6x6x3 network incrementally. Fig. 9(b) shows that our algorithm can save up to about 30~40% power compared to RM and up to 8~17% compared to LCF. The power saving in Fig. 9(b) is smaller than that in Fig. 9(a) since the CTG structures of the real applications from E3S are highly regular, e.g., mostly forming a chain-type structure. For such chain-type CTGs, RM and LCF will result in better results compared to non-regular structures.

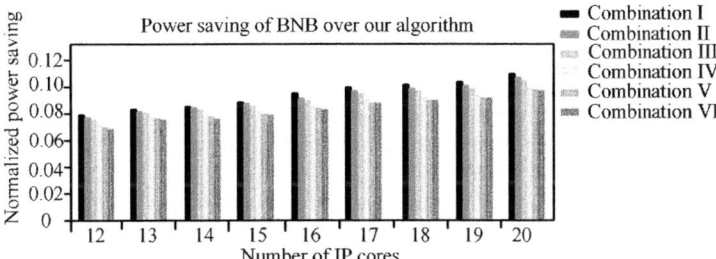

Fig. 8. Normalized power saving of BNB over our algorithm (normalized over the power consumtiopn of the results of BNB)

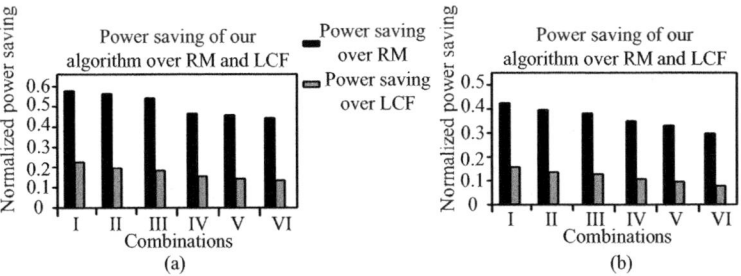

Fig. 9. Normalized power consumption of RM and LCF over our algorithm on TGFF (a) and E3S (b). Power consumption are normalized over the power consumtiopn of the results of our algorithm.

7 Conclusion

In this paper, we have proposed a power-aware run-time incremental mapping algorithm for 3-D NoCs with the objective of minimizing the communication power for each incoming application. In addition, the proposed algorithm attempts to reduce the fragmentation impact on future applications. The proposed algorithm is composed of three steps: 1) *NoC region selection* which selects a cuboid region to reduce the impact to future applications, 2) *set matching* which allocates the application graph to the sub-regions in different layers such that the vertical links are used as much as possible, 3) *CTG to NoC region mapping* which maps the tasks to the tiles in different sub-regions with minimized total communication power. Our experiment results have confirmed that the proposed algorithm is over four orders of magnitude run time efficient than BNB when mapping a single application. It has been shown that our algorithm can also achieve 50% power saving compared to random mapping and 20% compared to a simple heuristic when mapping multiple applications incrementally.

References

1. Pavlidis, V.F., Friedman, E.G.: 3-D topologies for networks-on-chip. IEEE Trans. Very Large Scale Integration Systems 15(10), 1081–1090 (2007)
2. Davis, W.R., Wilson, J., Mick, S., Xu, J., Hua, H., Mineo, C., Sule, A.M., Steer, M., Franzon, P.D.: Demystifying 3D ICs: the pros and cons of going vertical. IEEE Design and Test of Computers 22(6), 498–511 (2005)
3. Kim, J., Nicopoulos, C., Park, D., Das, R., Xie, Y., Narayanan, V., Yousif, M.S., Das, C.R.: A novel dimensionally-decomposed router for on-chip communication in 3D architectures. In: Int'l Symp. Computer Architecture, vol. 35, pp. 138–149 (2007)
4. Addo-Quaye, C.: Thermal-aware mapping and placement for 3-D NoC designs. In: IEEE Int'l SoC Conf., pp. 25–28 (2005)
5. Chou, C.L., Marculescu, R.: Run-time task allocation considering user behavior in embedded multiprocessor networks-on-chip. IEEE Trans. Computer-Aided Design of Integrated Circuits and Systems 29(1), 78–91 (2010)
6. Chou, C.L., Ogras, U.Y., Marculescu, R.: Energy-and performance-aware incremental mapping for networks on chip with multiple voltage levels. IEEE Trans. Computer-Aided Design of Integrated Circuits and Systems 27(10), 1866–1879 (2008)
7. Matsutani, H., Koibuchi, M., Amano, H.: Tightly-coupled multi-layer topologies for 3-D NoCs. In: Int'l Conf. Parallel Processing, pp. 75–85 (2007)
8. Feero, B.S., Pande, P.P.: Networks-on-Chip in a three-dimensional environment: a performance evaluation. IEEE Trans. Computers 58(1), 32–45 (2009)
9. Park, D., Eachempati, S., Das, R., Mishra, A.K., Xie, Y., Vijaykrishnan, N., Das, C.R.: MIRA: a multi-layered on-chip interconnect router architecture. In: Int'l Symp. Computer Architecture, pp. 251–261 (2008)
10. Wang, X., Yang, M., Jiang, Y., Liu, P.: A power-aware mapping approach to map IP cores onto NoCs under bandwidth and latency constraints. ACM Trans. Architecture and Code Optimization 7(1), 1–31 (2009)
11. Land, A.H., Doig, A.G.: An automatic method for solving discrete programming problems. Econometrica 28, 497–520 (1960)

12. Hu, J., Marculescu, R.: Energy-and performance-aware mapping for regular NoC architectures. IEEE Trans. Computer-Aided Design of Integrated Circuits and Systems 24(4), 551–562 (2005)
13. Smit, L.T., Smit, G.J.M., Hurink, J.L., Broersma, H., Paulusma, D., Wolkotte, P.T.: Run-time assignment of tasks to multiple heterogeneous processors. In: Progress Embedded System Symp., pp. 185–192 (2004)
14. Carvalho, E., Calazans, N., Moraes, F.: Heuristics for dynamic task mapping in NoC-based heterogeneous MPSoCs. In: IEEE/IFIP Workshop Rapid System Prototyping, pp. 34–40 (2007)
15. Lo, V., Windisch, K.J., Liu, W., Nitzberg, B.: Noncontiguous processor allocation algorithms for mesh-connected multicomputers. IEEE Trans. Parallel and Distributed Systems 8(7), 712–726 (1997)
16. TGFF: task graphs for free,
    http://ziyang.eecs.umich.edu/~dickrp/tgff/
17. Dick, R.: Embedded system synthesis benchmarks suite(E3S) (2002),
    http://ziyang.eecs.umich.edu/~dickrp/e3s/
18. Noxim, http://noxim.sourceforge.net/

WeLe-RAID: A SSD-Based RAID for System Endurance and Performance

Du Yimo, Liu Fang, Chen Zhiguang, and Ma Xin

Department of Computer Science, National University of Defense Technology,
Changsha, China
poshand@163.com, fangliu@nudt.edu.cn,
chenzhiguanghit@gmail.com, mxviking@yaho.com.cn

Abstract. Due to the limited erasure/program cycles of flash memory, flash-based SSDs need to prolong their life time using wear-leveling mechanism to meet their advertised capacity all the time. However, there is no wear-leveling mechanism among SSDs in RAID system, which makes some SSDs wear out faster than others. Once any one of SSDs fails, reconstruction must be triggered immediately. But, the cost of this process is so high that the reliability and availability is affected seriously. We propose WeLe-RAID which introduces Wear-Leveling mechanism among flash SSDs to enhance the endurance of entire SSD-based RAID system. As we know that under the workload of random access pattern, parity stripes suffer from much more updates because every update to the data stripe would cause the modification to the related parity stripe. Based on this principle, we introduce age-driven parity distribution scheme to guarantee the wear-leveling among flash SSDs. At the same time, because of age-driven parity distribution, it brings into the performance benefit with better load balance. Compared with conventional RAID mechanism, it significantly improves the life span and performance with ignorable overhead.

Keywords: SSD, RAID, wear-leveling, endurance, performance, reliability.

1 Introduction

SSD (Solid State Drive) exhibits higher speed and lower power consumption than disk. To some degree, it alleviates the I/O bottleneck in computer system by replacing disk. For the compatibility, it offers standard interfaces like disk, which can use previously calculated hardware and software based on disks. However, there are three critical technical constraints for flash memory [1]: (1) No in-place update, that means the whole block must be erased before overwriting data in any page; (2) No random write in a page, for the reliability, pages in a block need to be programmed in a sequential order rather than random writes. (3)Life limits, block will wear out after a certain number of program cycles. To cope with these obstacles, many strategies have been proposed respectively. In this paper, we mainly focus on the problem of the third constraint that flash memory has the limited erasure/program cycles. Actually, almost all the SSD products in the market supplied by kinds of vendors adopt the wear-leveling schemes to make all blocks in the SSD wear out evenly to guarantee their advertised capacity. Over

E. Altman and W. Shi (Eds.): NPC 2011, LNCS 6985, pp. 248–262, 2011.

provision of capacity also has the same goal, while not just meet the requirement of garbage collection. These two strategies work together to prolong the lifespan of SSD, although they cannot increase the total program cycles of all the blocks.

RAID mechanism has already been a very effective and popular method to construct high performance and reliable storage system since it is firstly published in 1988 [2]. It uses redundancy scheme to improve reliability and stripe scheme to promote throughput. In this case, using inexpensive disks with a little cost, it can construct a high performance storage system.

As SSD has wider applicable area, it would be a nature idea to construct storage system using the techniques mixed with RAID mechanism and state-of-the-art SSD. SSD has internal wear-leveling strategies to prolong its lifespan with advertised capacity. Once it cannot afford equivalent capacity as what vendors claimed in their product introductions, it no longer can supply the good service to meet users` requirements. So, wear-leveling is very necessary in SSD. As we know that, RAID controller does not have the wear-leveling mechanism to guarantee that all the SSDs in the RAID system wear out synchronously. Once a disk fails because of reaching its life limit, it costs too much time to replace it and reconstruct data on it using the algorithm based on parity. In this paper, we propose a novel method which adopts parity distribution based wear-leveling scheme among SSDs named WeLe-RAID to make the entire RAID system effectively work longer. The WeLe-RAID has three properties as follows:

(1) Age-driven parity distribution. As we know that, RAID4 assigns parity in unique device, and RAID5 assigns parity evenly which means every device has the same fraction of parity, while WeLe-RAID distributes parity according to its age dynamically. If some SSDs have higher erased number than others, and once this gap reaches the previously assigned critical value, we need reallocate the parity on these SSDs: more parity on younger SSDs and less parity on older SSDs.

(2) Less replacement in the lifecycle of entire RAID system. Since using the wear-leveling mechanism in the entire SSD-based RAID system, every device has afforded a part of workload so that all the devices can serve longer comparatively. It will be a long time until all the devices simultaneously approach their life critical value. Before that point, we have enough time to back up all the data on other new devices. Then totally replace the old ones. Consequently, in the lifecycle of the entire RAID system, less replacement needed than the previous system without weal-leveling mechanism among SSDs.

(3) Optimized addressing method with age-driven parity distribution. Conventional RAID mechanism adopts round-robin data layout [16], which the mapping relationship can be represented through simple function. However, age-driven parity distribution makes addressing more complex. In this paper, we give the original and optimized data layout and addressing method respectively. And the optimized one is much more effective.

The rest of the paper is organized as follows: Section 2 gives the motivation of this paper by analyzing previously main work which cannot meet the needed requirement. Section 3 describes the design and related algorithms in detail. Section 4 is the evaluation of WeLe-RAID. Section 5 introduces some related work. The last part is conclusion summing up the works in this paper.

2   Problem Description

2.1   Why Need Wear-Leveling

SSD has the internal wear-leveling mechanism to prolong its life span with the capacity advertised by the vendors. However, Diff-RAID [3] figures out that wear-leveling mechanism among SSDs will lead to high probability of correlated failures. On the contrary, it attempts to create and maintain the age difference among SSDs to guarantee at least some devices have lower bit error rate to avoid high correlated failure rate. We think it is very useful when the bit error rate of flash chip gradually rises in its whole life. Actually, for SLC, the bit error rate of flash chip does not have linear relationship with its age, even almost maintain zero until they reach their rated lifetime. For most MLC models, the bit error rate increases sharply shortly after their rated life times, and some start to increase sharply even earlier. Before they hit their rated lifetime, they can maintain comparatively stable bit error rate. And with the correctness of ECC, this climbing trend will be slowed down further [4]. In order to keep the age difference while the oldest SSD is retired, Diff-RAID has to replace the retired one with the new one, then reconstruct data and redistribute parity. We use a common equation 1 [10] to approximately evaluate the reliability of SSD-based RAID5 system. In this equation, MTTDL (Mean Time To Data Lose) is marked as the metric of system reliability. MTTF means Mean Time To Failure of single device. MTTR means Mean Time To Repair a failed device. From the equation 1, we can see that if the procedure of reconstructing data and redistributing parity is complex and high time-cost, it will be apt to loss data because any device failing at this moment could cause data corruption. If we use wear-leveling among SSDs, we can prolong the endurance of the entire system, which reduces the number of replacement to avoid more fragile moments.

$$MTTDL = \frac{MTTF^2}{N(N-1)MTTR} \tag{1}$$

Otherwise, wear-leveling among SSDs brings into the performance benefit with better load balance since parity stripes suffer from much more updates because every update to the data stripe would cause the modification to the related parity stripe.

2.2   Why Not RAID5

Through the above discussion, we know that, in most occasions, wear-leveling in the entire RAID system is useful and necessary. Since parity is the key factor of affecting wear-leveling because devices allocated more parity wear out faster, RAID5 adopting evenly parity distribution scheme may work well on wear-leveling in system level. However, through the experiment, we find that RAID5 cannot ensure the wear-leveling among devices either under some workloads. Figure 1 has proven that by showing the result of wear distribution under different workloads. This experiment is done on the simulator described in paper [6]. Set a counter in each SSD and increase itself when meet an erasure. After running the trace, total counter number on each device is its wear situation. This situation is resulted from that some workloads access some certain parity more often so that devices holding this parity suffer more updates and wear out faster than others.

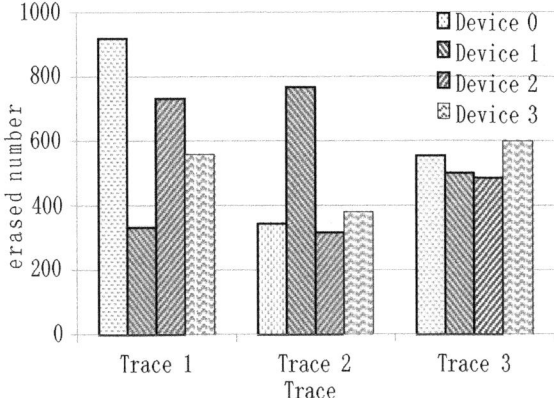

Fig. 1. Erased number of each SSD for RAID5. Here RAID5 consists of four SSDs.

2.3 Why Not other Schemes

Wear-leveling mechanism among SSDs in RAID system has been referred in previously paper. Kwanghee Par etc [7] give a brief design of wear leveling for SSD-based RAID5. It uses a big table to restore the erased number of stripe in each SSD respectively. When some parity hit the previously sat number, exchange the hot parity and cold parity with the greedy algorithm. This method costs much extra space and greedy algorithm is so complex that the performance is restricted seriously.

WeLe-RAID can balance the wear grade among devices based on parity distribution to prolong endurance and improve performance. Meanwhile it is simple to implement and has tolerable time cost and space cost.

3 WeLe-RAID

3.1 The Architecture of WeLe-RAID

Figure 2 illustrates the architecture of WeLe-RAID. WeLe-RAID has two controllers. One is RAID controller which manages a group of running SSDs called active devices in figure 2 to offer the service; the other is migration controller triggered when the entire system approaching the end of its lifetime to migrate the data from the active devices to the prepared ones, then replace the old devices with prepared ones. After replacement, prepared devices have become the active ones and new devices are brought in as prepared ones. Because wear-leveling scheme among SSDs is incorporated in our RAID mechanism, all SSDs of RAID system can be promised to maintain the same level of wear grade and can be totally replaced in one time. If any one of devices failed earlier before its life limit, the corresponding prepared one would replace it at once and reconstructing process would be triggered to resume the data on it.

Control flow and data flow both can be seen from figure 2. RAID controller administrates active devices below it and connects with migration controller to activate it when active devices nearly approach their life limits. Then migration controller put on the switch between active devices and prepared ones to create data path between them. In common cases, data flows merely through RAID controller to supply service for users. RAID controller has the implementation of basic RAID mechanism and our proposed parity distribution schemes. Migration controller doesn`t need much complex hardware because it only needs the function of migration which copies data from old devices to the same address of the new ones. Certainly, this process usually proceeds when the system is idle to avoid competition of responding I/O requests.

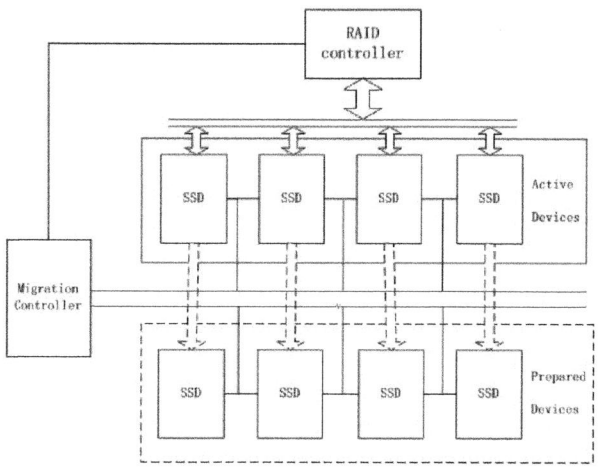

Fig. 2. The architecture of WeLe-RAID. Prepared devices in dash line frame are not in the system all the time. They are plugged in only when they are needed.

3.2   Data Layout

WeLe-RAID introduces dynamic age-driven parity distribution strategy like Diff-RAID [3]. We describe this relationship between parity distribution and age distribution quantitatively as follows. Given the age of RAID system consisting of n SSDs represented by a N-tuple $(a_1, a_2, \ldots a_n)$ which $a_1, a_2, \ldots a_n$ has no prime number, we can compute its variance (S) to evaluate its age difference. If it exceeds the critical value (CA), the process of parity redistribution must be called to make the entire RAID system retain the similar wear grade. The parity distribution represented with $(p_1, p_2, \ldots, p_n)$ can be made according to the age distribution through following two steps: 1. Sort $a_1, a_2, \ldots a_n$ in descend order; 2. p_k equals the k_{th} value in age`s descend order.

Figure 3 is the basic data layout of WeLe-RAID. It exhibits some characteristics. At the first beginning, we suppose the devices are new and their age distribution is (1, 1, 1, 1) shown in figure 3-(a). For wear-leveling, we make parity distribution be (1, 1, 1, 1). Actually, it is the RAID5 scheme assigning parity evenly across all devices. However, just like what we said in section 2.2, RAID5 cannot ensure wear-leveling completely among SSDs either. After a running period, the age gap among

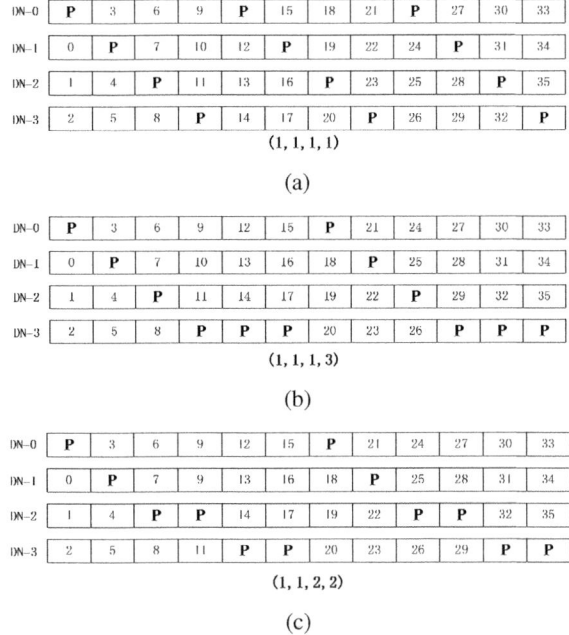

Fig. 3. Basic data layout of WeLe-RAID. (a) shows the data layout under parity distribution (1, 1, 1, 1); (b) shows the data layout under parity distribution (1, 1, 1, 3); (c) shows the data layout under parity distribution (1, 1, 2, 2).

SSDs appears which age distribution is (3, 3, 3, 1). The age difference can be described as variance (S) which the value is 3. If it exceeds CA, parity redistribution needs to be called to mitigate age difference: more parity on younger device and less parity on older device. Figure 3-(b) illustrates the data layout of new parity distribution (1, 1, 1, 3) made according to age distribution. Then, after another running period, the age distribution is (2, 2, 1, 1) whose variance is 1. Compared with last variance, its difference gap significantly becomes smaller. Suppose it still exceeds CA, then parity redistribution need to be called again. Figure 3-(c) shows the data layout of corresponding parity distribution.

In figure 3, data layout adopts round-robin striping scheme that has simple addressing policy but causes huge migration once parity distribution scheme changed. Figure 4 gives an improved data layout. Adopting this data layout, every parity redistribution operation brings small amount of shifts between data and parity. The procedure of parity shift from an original distribution to a new distribution can be depicted as follows:

1. Compute the region number. The region number is determined by computing the minimum common multiple of last region and sum of each fraction in new distribution. The first region is the sum of each fraction in the original parity distribution. From figure 4-(a) to figure 4-(b), we can compute the region number which is 12 equaling to minimum multiple common of 4 (sum of (1, 1, 1, 1)) and 6 (sum of (1, 1, 1, 3)).

2. Amplify the fraction in each part of parity distribution equation according the region number. So the parity distribution is changed from figure 3-(a) (1, 1, 1, 1) to figure 4-a (3, 3, 3, 3) and from figure 3-(b) (1, 1, 1, 3) to figure 4-(b) (2, 2, 2, 6).
3. Exchange the parity and data block in corresponding area according to the newly computed parity distribution.

Compared with basic data layout, improved data layout migrates less data. Although it cannot guarantee parity distribution according to age evenly in the finest grain, it is quite uniform from the point of the whole layout.

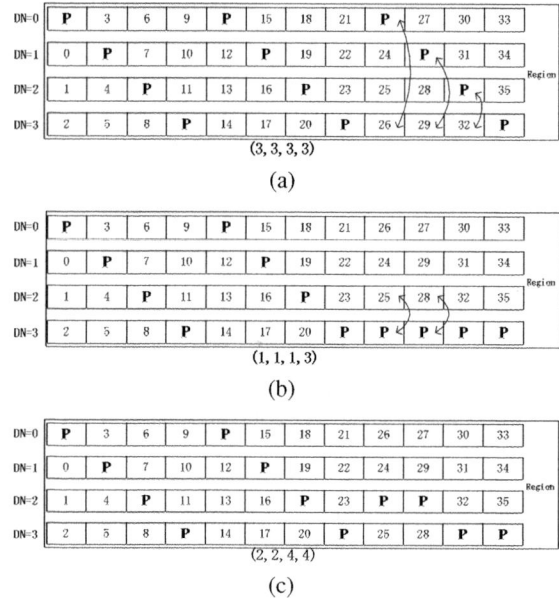

Fig. 4. Improved data layout of WeLe-RAID. (a) shows the data layout under parity distribution (1, 1, 1, 1); (b) shows the data layout under parity distribution (1, 1, 1, 3); (c) shows the data layout under parity distribution (1, 1, 2, 2).

3.3   Addressing Method

The key to implement WeLe-RAID is to design the mapping mechanism between logical address and physical address in the controller. When the controller receives an I/O request, it uses striping scheme to partition the data into several parts. And send the data and parity to the certain related devices according to the mapping relationship. Round-robin placement scheme is popularly used in RAID system. In this method, data layout is ascertained before. So any logic block address can be mapped to physical address easily through function without looking up operation. However, it lacks a little flexibility. The other method seldom used is mapping table. It is more flexible, but lead to high pressure on time cost and space cost. Usually, dynamic parity distribution like WeLe-RAID needs more flexible mapping data structure just like mapping table. But, in this paper, we use former method which still meets our requirement.

Traditional RAID scheme distribute parity either to a dedicated device like RAID4 or across all devices evenly like RAID5. From their different data layouts, we can compute the physical address using a linear function respectively. The addressing function of RAID4 can be summarized as follows:

$$SN = LBA / (N - 1)$$

$$PN = N - 1 \tag{2}$$

$$DN = LBA \bmod (N - 1)$$

In above equations, LBA means logical block address of the data unit after partition. N means the number of devices including data devices and parity devices. SN means stripe group number representing the stripe group allocated for the data. PN means the number of device that stores parity related with current data. DN means the number of device that stores current data. RAID5`s addressing function is displayed as follows:

$$SN = LBA / (N - 1)$$

$$PN = SN \bmod N$$

$$DN = \begin{cases} LBA \bmod (N - 1) + 1 & if \ LBA \bmod (N - 1) >= PN \\ LBA \bmod (N - 1) & if \ LBA \bmod (N - 1) < PN \end{cases} \tag{3}$$

For WeLe-RAID, in different time period, it has different parity distribution caused by age difference of devices. Every device`s age can be denoted by the average number of all blocks` age. If we use the data layout as figure 3 shows. The address function can be stated as follows:

$$SN = LBA / (N - 1)$$

$$PN = \begin{cases} 0 & if \quad SN \bmod (p_1 + p_2 + ... + p_n) <= p_1 - 1 \\ 1 & if \quad p_1 <= SN \bmod (p_1 + p_2 + ... + p_n) <= p_1 + p_2 - 1 \\ ... \\ N - 1 & if \quad p_{n-1} <= SN \bmod (p_1 + p_2 + ... + p_n) <= p_1 + p_2 + ... + p_n - 1 \end{cases} \tag{4}$$

$$DN = \begin{cases} LBA \bmod (N - 1) + 1 & if \ LBA \bmod (N - 1) >= PN \\ LBA \bmod (N - 1) & if \ LBA \bmod (N - 1) < PN \end{cases}$$

We have pointed out the drawback of data layout shown in figure 3. Then we present an improved data layout to reduce the data migration. With improved data layout, we can give the algorithm depicted in pseudo code 1 to solve addressing problem. This addressing algorithm is run when redistribution has been completed according to the layout depicted in last section.

In the algorithm, parity redistribution history and region history must be recorded as permanent variables. SN can be computed directly like any previous RAID mechanism. Because of exchange between parity and data when parity redistribution occurred, only using one function cannot meet the requirement of addressing parity device number (PN) and data device number (DN). Hence, we reserve all region history and parity distribution history in order to attain the current physical address of parity and common data through the algorithm described in pseudo code 1.

Pseudo Code 1

```
Algorithm: Address (LBA, t, p[t][N], region[t], SN, PN,
DN)
Input:
LBA: logical block address
t: redistribution times
p[t][N]: parity distribution history
region[t]: region history
Output:
SN: stripe group number
PN: parity device number
DN: data device number
1.  SN=LBA/(N-1)
2.  if (t=0)              //no parity redistribution happens
3.      PN=SN%N
4.      if LBA%N-1>=PN then
5.              DN=LBA%(N-1)+1
6.      else
7.              DN=LBA%(N-1)
8.  else
9.      mmn = minimum multiple number(region[t],
        region[t-1])
10.     x=mmn/region[t-1], y=mmn/region[t]
11.     for(j=0; j<N; j++) //amplify the fraction in
                        parity distribution expression
12.             d[j]=x*p[t-1][j]-y*p[t][j]
13.             for(j=0; j<N; j++)
14.                 if (d[j]>0)
15.                 for(k=N-1; k>=0; k--)   //exchange data
                                    and parity
16.                     if (d[k]<0)
17.                         if(PN==j)
18.                             PN=k
19.                         if(DN==k)
20.                             DN=j
21.     Address(LBA, t-1, p[t-1][N], region[t-1], SN, PN,
            DN)
```

Actually, there is another way to deal with addressing problem. We could use a table to reserve the number of device to which the data and correlated parity should be sent. Through looking up the table, we can get its physical address of any logical block. But the operation of looking up may cost too much time and the table must be huge to accommodate all the mapping relationship which causes extreme pressure to the space in the RAID controller. Compared with this mapping table method, what we proposed is more effective. We know that the time of redistribution is very few because it is only called when the age difference exceeds the critical value which is usually a little high. So the algorithm described in pseudo code 1 costs little time and absolutely saves space since it has no complex data structure.

4   Evaluation

We measure the performance, endurance and reliability of WeLe-RAID compared with other SSD-based RAID system. We have constructed a SSD simulator in paper [6]. In order to compare the performance and endurance between WeLe-RAID and other RAIDs, we implement these RAID schemes respectively in software RAID mode. Then we run some traces [9] collected from PC and servers under the real workloads. Through the simulation experiment, we can attain the average latency which can be used as a metric of performance. After running the traces, we check the average erased number of each block on each SSD which represents the endurance of the entire RAID system. For reliability, we adopts mathematic model to analyze the MTTDL (mean time to data lose) that is the common criteria to evaluate reliability.

4.1   Performance of WeLe-RAID

The performance experiment is done on the state that redistribution has been completed, and the data layout is stable. Figure 5 shows the average latency for different RAID mechanism under kinds of workloads. We can see from the figure that the performance of WeLe-RAID is better than another two: outperforms RAID5 about 10% and outperforms Diff-RAID 30% approximately sometimes even 40%. The reason for that is WeLe-RAID adopts age-driven parity distribution. Since the device that has the higher wear grade means it suffers from more writes, transforming some parity from older device to younger device, to some degree, balances the write workload. That is why it outperforms RAID5 although RAID5 distributes parity absolutely evenly. Diff-RAID distributes more parity on the older device to create age gap to improve reliability. However, it makes older device which has already been responsible for more requests to undertake more coming ones. It aggravates the unbalance of loads among SSDs and lead to the bottleneck of some certain device. Consequently, its performance is extremely influenced which is the worst among the three methods.

Parity redistribution is necessary in the WeLe-RAID and Diff-RAID. But this procedure must cost so much time that the performance is extremely decreased. Diff-RAID has not given the implementation of parity redistribution in detail. If it does not

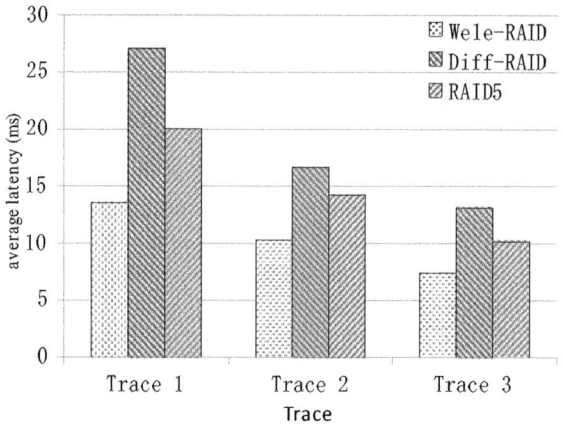

Fig. 5. Average latency of different RAID systems under various traces

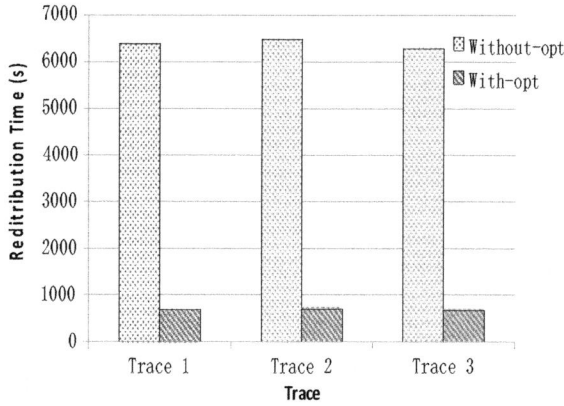

Fig. 6. Redistribution time of WeLe-RAID with unimproved data layout and improved data layout under various traces

make any improvement in parity migration, it will cost too much time. Figure 6 displays parity redistribution time of WeLe-RAID under different data layouts with optimization and without optimization. It shows that improved layout has much smaller overhead.

4.2   Endurance of WeLe-RAID

After running each trace, we collect the erased number of each block on each SSD. We use average erased number of total blocks in each SSD to represent the age of each SSD. Figure 7 displays the age difference of different RAID schemes under different workloads. We use standard deviation of all SSDs` erased number to evaluate the devices` age difference. Apparently, WeLe-RAID has the most uniform age distribution which means the endurance of entire WeLe-RAID system has been prolonged.

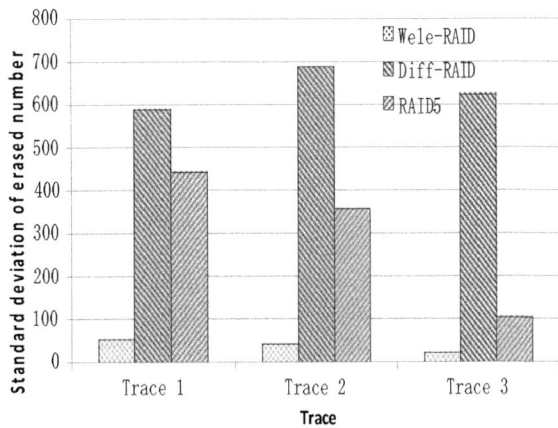

Fig. 7. Devices` age difference of different RAID under various traces

4.3   Reliability of WeLe-RAID

Currently, reliability is a tough problem for flash-based SSD. For one thing, reliability constrains the speed of market development of flash. For other thing, there is no dependable model on reliability for SSD. For traditional disks, some research has been done on their failure models. In term of these models, various methods have been proposed such as Markov model [10], simulation and shortcut method. [11] This paper analyzes the reliability of SSD-based RAID system with mathematic method.

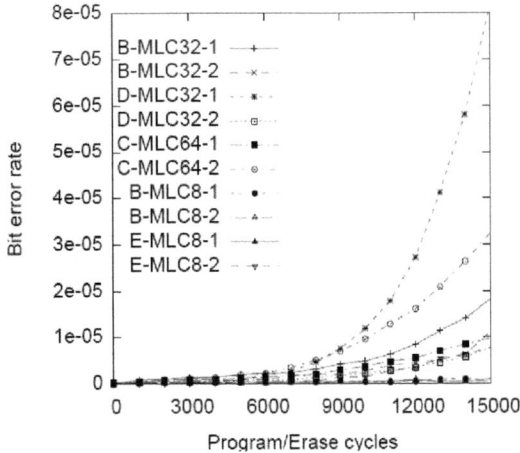

Fig. 8. Wear out and error rate for MLC flash device [4]

Before we measure the reliability of SSD-based RAID system, we must understand the reliability of single flash chip. Figure 8 shows the relationship between raw bit error rate (RBER) and age for MLC flash. RBER can be reduced prominently with ECC, which is called uncorrectable bit error rate (UBER). And UBER is some orders magnitude lower than RBER because ECC in every page can correct most errors.

WeLe-RAID and Diff-RAID are both one failure tolerant RAID like RAID5 belonging to 1-of-N system. For disk-based RAID5, we can use equation 1 referred in section 2 to estimate the reliability. When disks are replaced by SSD, the failure rate of each device cannot be treated as same constant any more. Due to the uniform age of each device in WeLe-RAID, we can assume the failure rates of all devices are the same. For SLC flash, RBER is stable before flash approaches its rated lifetime. Especially, it is almost changeless with ECC. For MLC, RBER rises along with the increase of the age. But the change is not obvious when it is far away from its rated lifetime, and ECC has narrowed down the changing speed. WeLe-RAID transforms data from old devices to prepared ones before they reach their life limits. So no device whose age approaches life limit is in service of storing data. Based on this point, we can use a constant to approximately express the failure rate. Therefore, we can still use equation 1 to evaluate the reliability of WeLe-RAID. The data loss possibility (DLP, reciprocal of MTTDL) of Diff-RAID converges to steady state after several replacements [3]. We can attain the DLP of Diff-RAID and RAID5 from paper of Diff-RAID. Given the UBER of flash used in Diff-RAID [3], we can compute the DLP of WeLe-RAID and compare it with Diff-RAID in table 1. We can see from table 1 that WeLe-RAID`s DLP is approaching the Diff-RAID`s.

Table 1. Reliability of Diff-RAID and WeLe-RAID

	Diff-RAID	WeLe-RAID
Data lose possibility	1e-06	5e-06

5   Related Work

RAID mechanism can improve the performance and reliability of storage system based on flash memory. We classify flash storage system as two categories according to the grain of device applied with RAID mechanism. One is coarse grain which uses RAID mechanism on SSDs. This mode is completely compatible to previous RAID technology including software and hardware. But while solid state disks hide the difference with hard disks by flash translation layer (FTL), the potential advantages of flash is hidden too. So the fine grain which uses RAID mechanism on flash chips can exploit the characteristic of flash totally.

Mao Bo, Jiang Hong etc [12] have designed a hybrid RAID4 named HPDA composed by disk and SSDs. It uses disk to respond to the write-intensive accesses as dedicated parity device which is the shortage of SSD. It improves the performance and reliability compared with RAID4 composed totally with SSDs. But it also has the drawback of traditional RAID4 that parity device is the bottleneck. Kadav Asim etc [3] have proposed a novel SSD-based RAID called Diff-RAID which has been discussed in detail in section 2.

Meanwhile, some research has been done on constructing RAID system with flash chips. Lee Yangsup etc [13] design a flash-aware redundancy array abbreviated FRA. It separates the parity updating from the write procedure, and deal with it when the system is idle. Thereby, this lazily parity updating method improves write performance prominently. Yu-Bing Chang etc [14] have proposed a self-balanced flash array. It encodes hot data into several replicas stored on different banks. Thus, requests on hot data can be directed to cold banks that are responsible for fewer requests. However, every update brings modification of parity extremely affecting the write performance and causing high space cost. Sooju Im etc [15] present a flash-aware RAID technique for dependable and high-performance flash memory SSD. It delays the parity update accompanied with every data write to decrease parity handling overhead.

6   Conclusion and Future Work

In this paper, we propose a novel SSD-based RAID called WeLe-RAID. It uses dynamic parity distribution scheme which is adaptive to age of SSD. Based on the principle that parity stripe suffers from more modification, we allocate more parity to younger SSD and less parity to older SSD which ensures wear-leveling among SSDs and to some degree alleviates unbalance of write loads on devices. We give the data layout and addressing algorithm of WeLe-RAID in detail. To implement this method, what we need is only some simple data structure to record a little redistribution history information. Through the experiment, we can see that with ignorable overhead, WeLe-RAID outperforms other RAIDs in average response time. And it has comparable reliability with Diff-RAID.

What this paper discussed is one device failure tolerant RAID such as RAID4 and RAID5. Two or more devices failure tolerant RAID like RAID6 has not been introduced currently. It is more complex because multiple parity in one stripe group. In future work, we will intend to design the good layout for RAID6 to decrease the migration when redistribution.

Acknowledgments. We appreciate Lipin Chang, Po Liang and Joshon for some of the traces, and anonymous reviewers for valuable suggestions to improve this paper. This work is partially supported by National Natural Science Foundation of China grants NSFC60736013 and NSFC60903040.

References

1. Chen, F., Luo, T., Zhang, X.D.: CAFTL: A Content-Aware Flash Translation Layer Enhancing the Lifespan of Flash Memory based Solid State Drives. In: Proceedings of FAST 2011, San Joes, USA (2011)
2. Patterson, D., Gibson, G., Katz, R.H.: A Case for Redundant Arrays of Inexpensive Disks (RAID). In: Proceedings of SIGMOD 1988, New York, USA (2011)
3. Balakrishnan, M., Kadav, A., Prabhakaran, V., Malkhi, D.: Differential RAID: Rethinking RAID for SSD reliability. In: Proceedings of Eurosys 2011, Salzburg, Austria (2011)

4. Grupp, L.M., Caulfield, A.M., Coburn, J., Swason, S., Yaakobi, E., Seigel, P.H., Wolf, J.K.: Characterizing flash memory: anomalies, observations, and applications. In: Proceedings of MICRO 2009, New York, USA (2009)

5. Thomasian, A., Blaum, M.: High Reliablity Redundant Disk Arrays: Organizations, Operation, and Coding. ACM Transaction on Storage 5(3), Articale 7 (2009)

6. Du, Y.M., Xiao, N., Liu, F., Chen, Z.G.: A Customizable and Modular Flash Translation Layer(FTL) Design and Implementation. Journal of Xi'an Jiaotong University 44(8), 42–47 (2010)

7. Park, K., Lee, D.H., Woo, Y., Lee., G.Y.: Reliability and Performance Enhancement Technique for SSD array storage system using RAID mechanism. In: Proceedings of ISCIT 2009, Incheon, Korea (2009)

8. Zheng, W.M., Zhang, G.Y.: FastScale: Accelerate RAID Scaling by Minimizing Data Migration. In: Proceedings of FAST 2011, San Jose, USA (2011)

9. Chang, L.P., Kuo, T.W.: An Adaptive Stripping Architecture for Flash Memory Storage Systems of Embedded Systems. In: Proceedings of IEEE Eighth Real-Time and Embedded Technology and Applications Symposium (RTAS), San Jose, USA (2002)

10. Geist, R., Trivedi., K.: An analytic Treatment of the Reliability and Performance of Mirrored disk subsystems. In: Proceedings of Twenty-Third Inter. Symp. on Fault-Tolerant Computing, FTCS-23 (1993)

11. Thomasian, A.: Shortcut method for reliability comparisons in RAID. The Journal of Systems and Software 79, 1599–1605 (2006)

12. Mao, B., Jiang, H., Feng, D., Wu, S.Z., Chen, J.X., Zeng, L.F., Tian, L.: HPDA: A Hybrid Parity-based Disk Array for Ehnaced Performance and Reliability. In: Proceedings of IPDPS 2010, San Atlanta, USA (2010)

13. Lee, Y., Jung, S.: Song. Y.H.: FRA: A Flash-aware Redundancy Array of Flash Storage. In: Proceedings of CODES+ISSS 2009 (2009)

14. Chang, Y.B.: Chang. L.P.: A Self-Balancing Striping Scheme for NAND-Flash Storage Systems. In: Proceedings of the 2008 ACM Symposium on Applied Computing (2008)

15. Soojun, I.M., Shin, D.K.: Flash-Aware RAID Techniques for Dependable and High-Performance Flash Memory SSD. IEEE Transaction on Computers 60(1), 80–92 (2011)

16. Zhen, W.M., Zhang, G.Y.: FastScale: Accelerate RAID Scaling by Minimizing Data Migration. In: Proceedings of FAST 2011, San Joes, USA (2011)

Reorder the Write Sequence by Virtual Write Buffer to Extend SSD's Lifespan

Zhiguang Chen, Fang Liu, and Yimo Du

School of Computer, National University of Defense Technology
Changsha, China
chenzhiguanghit@gmail.com, liufang@nudt.edu.cn, poshand@163.com

Abstract. The limited lifespan is the Achilles's heel of Solid State Drive (SSD) based on NAND flash memory. NAND flash has two drawbacks that degrade SSD's lifespan. One is the out-of-place update. Another is the sequential write constraint within a block. To extend the lifespan, SSD usually employs a write buffer to reduce write traffic to flash memory. However, existing write buffer schemes only pay attention to the first drawback, but fail to overcome the second one. We propose a virtual write buffer architecture, which covers the two aspects simultaneously. The virtual buffer consists of two components, DRAM and the reorder area. DRAM is the normal write buffer which aims at the first drawback. It endeavors to reduce write traffic to flash memory as much as possible by pursuing higher hit ratio. The reorder area is actually a part of SSD's flash address space. It focuses on reordering write sequence directed to flash chip. Reordering write sequence helps to overcome the second drawback. The two components work together just like the virtual memory adopted by operating system. So, we name the architecture as virtual write buffer. Our virtual write buffer outperforms traditional write buffers because of two reasons. First, the DRAM can adopt any existing superior cache replacement policy, it achieves higher hit ratio than traditional write buffers do. Second, the virtual write buffer reorders the write sequence, which hasn't been exploited by traditional write buffers. We compare the virtual write buffer with others by trace-driven simulations. Experimental results show that, SSDs employing the virtual buffer survive longer lifespan on most workloads.

Keywords: flash memory, SSD, lifespan, virtual write buffer, storage.

1 Introduction

Flash memory is of hot topic in recent years. Solid State Drives (SSDs) based on NAND flash have been widely deployed in storage systems. Different from hard disks, flash memory is absolute semiconductor chip without any mechanical components. Flash chip is hierarchically organized. Typically, a chip is comprised of thousands of blocks. A block is further divided into tens of pages. Flash memory supports three basic operations, write, read and erase. Write must be preceded by the erase. An alternation between write and erase is named as an E/W (Erase/Write) cycle. Read and write are performed at the granularity of page, while, erase is performed at block level.

E. Altman and W. Shi (Eds.): NPC 2011, LNCS 6985, pp. 263–276, 2011.
© IFIP International Federation for Information Processing 2011

Even though flash memory exhibits some superior features, there still exist some critical drawbacks, which hinder much wider deployment of SSDs. We focus on three of these drawbacks. One is the limited lifespan of flash memory. Generally, each block could only survive limited E/W cycles. When a block has been written and erased too many times, it becomes unreliable and even leads to bit flips. Another concerned drawback is the out-of-place update. It's unable to directly overwrite a page for flash memory. If a page that has already contained data will be rewritten again, it must be erased beforehand. Exactly, the whole block containing the page must be erased because erase is performed at block level. The last concerned drawback is the sequential write constraint within a block. Pages in a physical block cannot be written randomly. They must be written one by one in the same order as they are arranged in the block.

To overcome the first drawback discussed above, SSD employs a write buffer to reduce write traffic, thus extends its lifespan. Correspondingly, various write buffer management schemes have been proposed [e.g. 1, 2, 3, 4, 5, 6 and 7]. These schemes mostly aim at decreasing the write traffic directed to flash memory. However, the number of write requests is not the only one factor affecting lifespan. Actually, SSD's lifespan is impaired by both out-of-place update and sequential write constraint, which are the last two drawbacks as discussed above, respectively. Unfortunately, existing write buffer schemes mostly pay attention to the out-of-place update. They endeavor to reduce the quantity of updates to flash memory, but neglect to optimize the write sequence.

In this paper, we propose a novel virtual write buffer architecture to extend SSD's lifespan. The virtual write buffer consists of two components. One is the DRAM, which is also employed by traditional write buffers. The other is a part of SSD's address space. Actually, our virtual buffer is the same with virtual memory employed by Operating Systems (OS). These two components focus on the two factors affecting SSD's lifespan, respectively. DRAM is used to overcome the out-of-place update drawback. It buffers the frequently updated pages to reduce write traffic directed to flash chips. The flash based component is responsible for reordering the write sequence, which helps to overcome the sequential write constraint.

The DRAM can adopt any existing high performance cache replacement policy, such as 2Q [8], ARC [9], and LIRS [10]. So, it achieves higher hit ratio, therefore reduces write traffic significantly compared with other SSD-oriented write buffers. The flash based component reorders the write sequence directed to flash memory. This optimization is neglected by traditional write buffers completely. As the virtual buffer covers both two factors affecting the lifespan, it's not surprising that, our virtual buffer outperforms other write buffers constantly. We carry out trace driven simulations to evaluate our virtual buffer. Experimental results show that, the virtual write buffer erases less blocks on most workloads compared with CLC [1], PUD-LRU [2], and BPLRU [4]. Operating Systems name the part of hard disk used for virtual memory as swap area. Similarly, the flash based component in the virtual write buffer is named as *reorder area*, just as its function implies.

The rest of paper is organized as follows. Section 2 introduces the backgrounds and related works. Section 3 presents the principle of our virtual buffer elaborately. Section 4 evaluates different write buffers. The last section concludes our work.

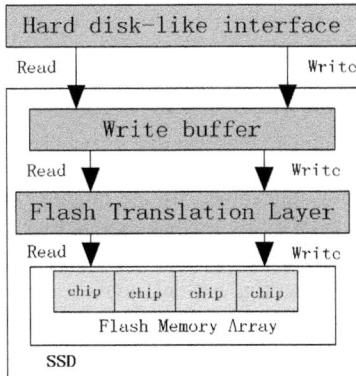

Fig. 1. Overall architecture of SSDs

2   Backgrounds and Related Works

The first subsection reviews the typical architecture of SSDs briefly. The second subsection analyzes the negative impacts imposed on SSD's lifespan by the two drawbacks of flash memory. They are the motivations of our work. The last subsection introduces some related works.

2.1   SSD Overview

Compared with hard disks, flash memory has some peculiarities. It cannot be applied to traditional storage system directly. To be compatible with existing software stack, several flash chips are packaged into an SSD. A typical architecture of SSD is shown in Figure 1. SSD exhibits the same interface with hard disks by employing the Flash Translation Layer (FTL). FTL hides these peculiarities of flash memory. Due to the out-of-place update characteristic, flash memory can't overwrite a page. An alternative method to accommodate updates is to direct updated data to other free physical pages. The original pages are marked as invalid. In other words, a logical page can be written to any free physical page. Correspondingly, a logical address would point to a new physical page once its data are updated. The dynamic mapping relationship between logical and physical addresses is maintained by FTL. Ideally, a logical address can map with any physical page. However, the fully-associative mapping between physical and logical pages requires a large table to maintain the mapping entries. Instead, practical SSDs usually map a logical block with a physical block. Logical pages (in the logical block) and physical pages (in the physical block mapping with the logical block) that have the same offset in respective blocks maps with each other by default. This mapping scheme is usually named as block-level mapping. This coarse-grained mapping scheme leads to a more compact mapping table. Besides the address mapping, FTL is also responsible for reclaiming invalid pages. As updated data is directed to other free pages, the original data is invalid. FTL must convert these invalid pages to be free to guarantee that, SSD supplies constant storage capacity to users. The erase operation is used for converting invalid pages to be free. The process reclaiming invalid pages is called garbage collection.

As shown in Figure 1, there is a write buffer between SSD's interface and FTL. Write buffer is mostly used for decreasing write traffic to flash array. Since the write requests are reduced, fewer pages become invalid. Garbage collection erases fewer blocks to reclaim these invalid pages. Thus, SSD's lifespan is extended. However, we argue that, the lifespan is not determined by the quantity of write traffic completely. Usually, SSD's lifespan is depleted by inner-generated write traffic, rather than user's write requests. Reducing the inner-generated write traffic is a more attractive way to extend SSD's lifespan. Supposing that a block contains some invalid pages, to reclaim these invalid pages, the whole block must be erased (erase operation is performed at block level). Unfortunately, the block still contains some valid pages, which must be moved to other locations. Moving these valid pages leads to additional write requests generated by SSD itself, rather than by user. This phenomenon is called write amplification [11]. So, write buffer should not only reduce write traffic, but also overcome write amplification.

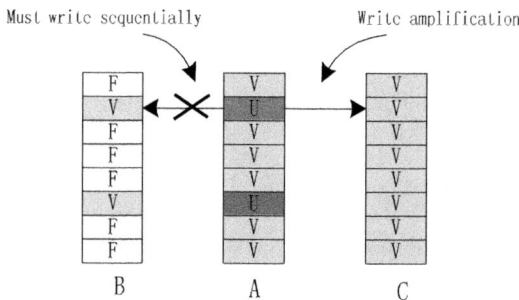

Fig. 2. Write amplification induced by out-of-place update and sequential write constraint

2.2   Write Amplification Analysis

Practical SSDs usually map physical address with logical address at the granularity of block. Pages in the two blocks are mapped sequentially. Block is the atomic unit of address management. So, updates to any page in a logical block lead to rewriting the entire block to another physical block. Figure 2 shows this drawback elaborately.

Figure 2 presents the negative impacts imposed on SSD's lifespan by out-of-place update and sequential write constraint. As shown in the figure, we assume that a block contains 8 pages. Pages marked by V contain valid data. Pages marked by U had been updated. Pages marked by F are free and have not been written.

In Figure 2, all pages of block A are originally valid. Two pages (marked by U) are to be updated. Since flash cannot overwrite these pages, it must direct updated data to other pages. Consequently, another block B is allocated to accept the updates. As block-level mapping scheme demands that two pages (coming from logical and physical blocks, respectively) with the same offset map with each other, ideally, we expect that updates are directed to the new block with their page offset unmodified. As shown in block B, two pages contain valid data. Unfortunately, this is not permitted by flash memory due to the sequential write constraint. Pages in a block must be written sequentially beginning from the first one. Instead, we update the two pages in another manner illustrated by block C. In this manner, not only are the updated pages written to block C, but also these unchanged pages are moved to block C as well. This update policy conforms to the principle of block-level mapping scheme. Pages in physical and logical blocks are mapped with their offsets unmodified. However, this policy requires moving valid pages. Even though there are only two pages updated, SSD moves six additional pages. The process of moving these still valid pages to the new block is named as padding [4]. Padding leads to write amplification directly.

Based on the discussion, we can conclude that, two factors lead to write amplification. One is out-of-place update. The other is the sequential write constraint. The first factor requires that, updated data must be written to a new block. The second factor does not allow writing the new block randomly. Ultimately, it needs to rewrite the whole block, which results in write amplification. Write amplification impairs the lifespan remarkably. Write buffer is an effective way to reduce write amplification. But, existing write buffer management policies mostly focus on reducing write traffic, which helps to reduce the chance of out-of-place updates. They scarcely pay attention to overcome the sequential write constraint. The next subsection will introduce some typical write buffer policies in detail. By contrary, our virtual write buffer not only reduces the updates, but also makes write sequence to be sequential. So, it achieves superior performance.

2.3   Related Works

Write buffers for SSDs are different from buffers of hard disks. Buffers of hard disks try to encapsulate several trivial requests into a long sequence, reducing the chance of seek and rotation of disk heads. Buffers of SSDs aim at reducing write traffic and alleviating write amplification. The first goal requires frequently updated pages to be kept in write buffer for as long time as possible. The last goal demands to reduce padding. They conflict with each other sometimes. Write buffers for SSDs mostly compromise between the two.

CFLRU. Clean first LRU (CFLRU) [13] is a policy used for managing the cache of both write and read requests. For flash memory, write is more expensive than read, so, write requests should be kept in cache for a longer time. CFLRU always attempts to select a clean page as the replaced victim. Dirty pages are protected. CFLRU is found to be able to reduce the average replacement cost by 26% compared with LRU. But, it deals with the cache containing both read and write. The scope of this paper is constrained to write buffer only.

FAB. Flash aware buffer (FAB) [5] is also a policy for write buffer of SSDs. In the write buffer, all pages coming from the same block are packed into a group. All the groups are organized into an LRU list. Once a group is accessed, or a new page joins the group, the group is moved to the MRU-end (most recently used). If replacement is needed, FAB selects the group having most pages as the victim. If more than one groups meet this demand, the least recently used group is evicted. FAB evicts the group with most pages to reduce padding pages, despite that the evicted group may be accessed frequently. The arbitrary policy may lead to thrash.

BPLRU. Just like FAB does, Block Padding LRU (BPLRU) [4] also packs pages belonging to a block into a group. It selects the least recently used group as the victim. Maybe, some pages of the block are not in write buffer. BPLRU reads them from flash memory and pads the block, then writes the whole block to flash memory. PBLRU pads blocks explicitly before they are written to flash.

CLC. FAB evicts the largest group. BPLRU evicts the least recently used group. CLC [1] incorporates these two policies together. It divides the write buffer into two parts. One part employs BPLRU policy, the other employs FAB. Compared with FAB, it protects some of the recently used large groups. Compared with BPLRU, it gives higher priority to large groups to be replaced, because replacements of large groups reclaim more free capacity for write buffer.

PUD-LRU. Hu et. al. proposed a new erase-efficient write buffer management algorithm called PUD-LRU, PUD-LRU [2] divides blocks in the write buffer into two groups based on a combined measure of frequency and recency, Predicted average Update Distance (PUD). One group is used for keeping frequently or recently updated blocks. The other is used for selecting replaced blocks. It evicts the block with the largest PUD value, because the block is considered to be the least frequently and recently updated. By doing so, PUD-LRU maximizes the efficiency of destaging operation.

Wu. [3] et. al. proposed a hybrid page/block write buffer architecture along with an advanced replacement policy, called BPAC [3]. BPAC also divides the buffer into two parts. One exploits temporal locality, the other exploits spatial locality. BPAC analyzes the workloads constantly and adapts to workloads dynamically. Sun. et. al. had made use of Phase Change Random Accessed Memory (PCRAM) as SSD's write buffer [6]. Griffin [7] extends SSD's lifespan by disk-based write buffer.

In conclusion, write buffers described above mostly focus on reducing write traffic by caching frequently updated pages. Some of them reduce padding pages by evicting the block containing the most updated pages. All of them fail to optimize write order.

3   The Virtual Write Buffer Architecture

Our virtual write buffer consists of two components. The DRAM is used to cache frequently updated pages, thus reduce write traffic. The reorder area is responsible for reordering write sequence, thus decreasing padding pages. They are introduced in the next two subsections, respectively.

3.1   The DRAM Component

DRAM used in the virtual write buffer is absolutely a traditional cache. It attempts to achieve as higher hit ratio as possible. By contrary, write buffer management schemes described above do not center around hit ratio completely. Take CLC as an example, it not only pursues higher hit ratio, but also tries to evict the largest group to decrease padding pages. These two goals may conflict with each other. Therefore, write buffers adopting CLC usually obtain poor hit ratio.

To achieve higher hit ratio, we manage the DRAM at page level (Contrarily, several write buffers described above pack some pages belonging to a block into a group, they are managed at block level). Only frequently accessed pages are prevented from being evicted. As the DRAM purely exploits temporal locality, which is also pursued by traditional caches, so, some classical cache replacement policies, such as 2Q [8], ARC [9], and LIRS [10], can be reused. This is an important superiority of our virtual buffer over the others. Exactly, we adopt ARC [9] as the replacement policy for DRAM. ARC is so superior a cache replacement policy that, it has been adopted by ZFS [14] and IBM DS8000 storage server. The rationale of ARC is explained as follows.

ARC is well-known due to its simplicity and high performance. It maintains two caches, a physical cache and a virtual cache (the virtual cache is also named as ghost cache). The physical cache is organized into two lists. One list focuses on frequency, the other focuses on recency. The ghost cache contains pages that had been evicted out of the physical cache recently. Actually, the ghost cache only keeps the index entries of these pages. Data in these pages are discarded. In other words, the ghost cache just stores replaced history. Replacements in the physical cache are guided by the feedback of the ghost cache. If a page hits in ghost cache, and it had been evicted from the recency list in physical cache, it means that pages in the recency list are more valuable. ARC gives priority to replacing the pages in frequency list. On the other hand, if an access hits in the ghost cache, and the target page had been evicted from the frequency list in physical cache, ARC is prone to replace pages in the recency list. ARC adapts itself to the workloads continually and dynamically by changing the size of each list. So, it achieves high hit ratio on most workloads.

Compared with conventional write buffers of SSDs, the DRAM achieves high hit ratio for two reasons. The first is to manage the buffer at page level, which helps to exploit temporal locality aggressively. The second is to inherit the classical high performance cache replacement policy. Higher hit ratio means that, the write traffic is reduced significantly.

3.2   Reorder Area

The reorder area is a part of SSD's flash address space. It is used for accommodating out-of-order updates. To explain the reordering process clearly, we first introduce a concept, *prior page*. For a given page, its prior pages are those belonging to the same block, but their page offsets are smaller than that of the given page. For example, in logical block 0, Page 2 has smaller offset than Page 3 does, Page 2 is one of the prior pages of Page 3. Similarly, Page 1 is also a prior page of Page 3. The rationale of reordering write sequence can be summarized as follows. When a page is evicted from DRAM, the virtual write buffer detects whether there are some prior pages of the evicted page existing in DRAM. If there is such a page in DRAM, the evicted page cannot be written to its physical block sequentially, because a page prior to it hasn't been written to the block. Instead, the page is written to the reorder area to wait for the right sequence. The process will be explained in detail by resorting to Figure 3. In the figure, there are seven scenarios denoted by S_i, where i belongs to $\{0, 1, 2, 3, 4, 5, 6\}$. On each scenario, DRAM evicts a page out.

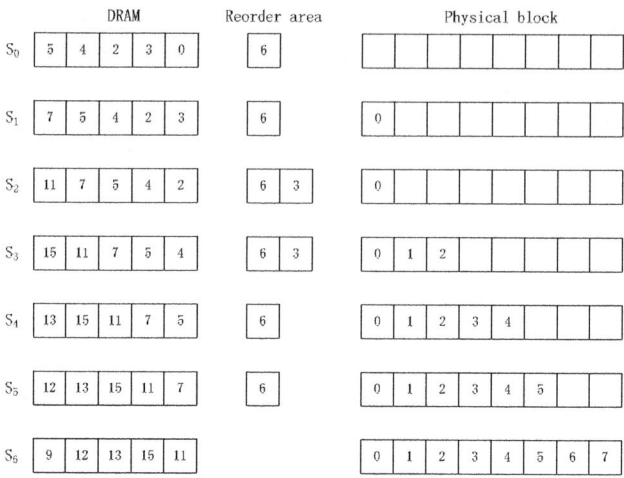

Fig. 3. The process of reordering

On Scenario 0, the size of DRAM is five pages. The page numbered by 6 is in the reorder area. In another word, Page 6 had been written to flash due to its out-of-order update. A free physical block is prepared for accepting replaced pages. As DRAM is full, the page numbered by 0 is going to be replaced.

On Scenario 1, Page 0 is replaced. As it is the first page of a logical block, it should be written to the first page of a physical block as well, because a page in the logical block has to locate in the same offset in corresponding physical block for block level mapping scheme. Since there is no prior page of Page 0 in DRAM, Page 0 can be written to its physical block directly. There is no need to write it to the reorder area.

On Scenario 2, Page 3 is replaced. However, Page 2 is still in DRAM, and it is a prior page of Page 3. Therefore, Page 3 cannot be written to the physical block sequentially. Instead, it's directed to the reorder area.

On scenario 3, Page 2 is replaced from DRAM. As none of the pages prior to it (such as Page 0 and 1) is in DRAM, Page 2 could be written to its physical sequentially. However, it requires reading Page 1 from flash memory to pad the block. As shown in the figure, Page 1 and 2 are written to the physical block sequentially. Reading Page 1 and writing it back to flash are I/O requests generated by SSDs, rather than by users.

On Scenario 4, Page 4 is replaced. In order to write Page 4 in the physical block sequentially, it needs to pad Page 3 beforehand. As a result, Page 3 and 4 are written to the physical block. So, when Page 5 is replaced, it can be written to the block directly, as presented on Scenario 6. When Page 7 is replaced from the DRAM, we pad Page 6 as well, as shown on the last scenario.

In conclusion, the DRAM doesn't concern about the write sequence. It evicts pages depending on temporal locality and the adopted cache replacement policy. If a page is replaced, the write buffer considers whether it is able to be written sequentially. If so, the page is written to flash directly, otherwise, the page is directed to reorder area, which is also a part of flash address space. Whether a page can be written to flash directly is determined by whether there are some prior pages in the DRAM. If there are no prior pages in DRAM, the replaced page can be written to flash directly. But maybe, it needs to pad some pages.

The virtual buffer can be compared with other write buffers as follows. For a write buffer mentioned in the related works, when a page is evicted out of buffer, the entire block containing the page is replaced. All the absent pages are padded to the block. Then, the block is written to flash. For our virtual write buffer, replacement of a page does not influence other pages in the same block. This is the first improvement to traditional write buffers. We don't write the entire block to flash arbitrarily, but write its pages one by one. For a given page, its prior pages won't be padded to the block until the given page is replaced from DRAM. As these prior pages haven't been written to the target physical block, updates to them will not lead to write amplification. Delaying page padding as late as possible is the second improvement to traditional write buffers. To keep the sequential write order, we employ the reorder area to register these out-of-order replaced pages.

Actually, the reorder area is a part of flash address space. Directing out-of-order replaced pages to reorder area still shortens SSD's lifespan. But, as the DRAM is able to filter more updates than other write buffers do, and the padding pages is less as well, our virtual buffer erases less blocks all the same compared with others, as shown in the next section.

4 Performance Evaluation

This section evaluates the performance achieved by our virtual write buffer. The first subsection introduces the experimental setup. Subsection 2 compares our virtual write buffer with other buffers. Actually, the virtual buffer is similar with an FTL called FAST (Fully Associative Sector Translation) [15]. The last subsection compares the virtual write buffer with FAST.

4.1 Experimental Setup

We evaluate different write buffers by trace driven simulations. Write buffers mostly aim at extending SSD's lifespan, so, performance is measured by the number of erased blocks. We expect that the erased blocks are as few as possible.

Characteristics of adopted traces are listed in Table 1. They are all enterprise class traces delegating typical applications. Among these traces, *SRC*, *USR*, *Proj* and *Proxy* were gathered from servers at Microsoft Research Cambridge. *LiveMaps* was gathered from *LiveMaps* backend server for duration of 24 hours. *Develop* was collected from Developers Tools Release server for a duration of a day. *MSNFile* was collected from MSN Storage file server for duration of 6 hours. *Exchange* was collected from Exchange Server for duration of 24 hours. All the traces can be downloaded from internet [16]. They were used by Dushyanth N. [17].

The flash chip configuration adopted in experiments is summarized as follows. The size of a page is 4KB. A block contains 64 pages. These parameters come from the specification of a flash chip with small blocks from Sumsung [18].

Table 1. Characteristics of trace

Traces	Read	Write	R/W
USR	41362884	3837166	10.78/1
SRC1	43544675	2155325	20.2/1
SRC2	21110497	16289503	1.3/1
Proj	47281632	9818368	4.82/1
Proxy	110389290	58210710	1.9/1
LiveMaps	38616344	11033656	3.5/1
Develop	12324273	5865727	2.1/1
MSNFile	19725455	9614545	2.05/1
Exchange	25246721	31823279	1/1.26

4.2   Comparison with Other Buffers

We compare the virtual write buffer with BPLRU [4] and PUD-LRU [2]. BPLRU is a classical write buffer policy for SSDs. It has been extensively evaluated. PUD-LRU is a recently proposed policy achieving high performance. It inherits the design principle of classical cache replacement policies.

The experimental results are presented in Figure 4. As shown in the figure, SSDs employing the virtual write buffer erase the least physical blocks on most workloads. To further explain why the virtual buffer achieves higher performance, we compare the hit ratios and the numbers of padding pages related to different write buffers, which are presented in Figure 5 and 6, respectively. Higher hit ratio means that the write traffic is reduced more remarkably. So, we expect the hit ratio to be as high as possible. Inversely, padding pages are additional write traffic generated by background operation. A superior write buffer should help to reduce padding pages, thus alleviate write amplification. So, we expect that padding pages are as few as possible. As padding a block indicates migrating pages from one physical block to another, hereafter, we refer padding pages as *padding pages* or *migrated pages*, interchangeably.

BPLRU and PUD-LRU pack updated pages in a logical block into a group. Groups are the atomic units for replacement in write buffer. BPLRU organizes these groups into an LRU list. It always replaces the least recently updated group. Hu et al. argued that, the LRU list only focuses on recency, but neglects access frequency [2]. They proposed PUD-LRU to exploit both of the two aspects. PUD-LRU improves BPLRU by employing a new measurement called Predicted average Update Distance, rather than the simple recency. So, PUD-LRU usually erases less blocks compared with BPLRU, as shown in Figure 4. Actually, the importance of frequency is extensively evaluated in the research domain of cache replacement policy.

Policies discussed above mostly aim at improving hit ratio and reducing write traffic to flash memory. But, as shown in Figure 5, hit ratios achieved by different write buffers are low. Even when the cache size is 64MB, the write buffer still cannot reduce write traffic significantly. Only on workloads *Prxy*, the erased blocks are reduced with the expanding of buffer size. So, simply using write buffer to reduce write traffic is not an effective way to extend SSD's lifespan.

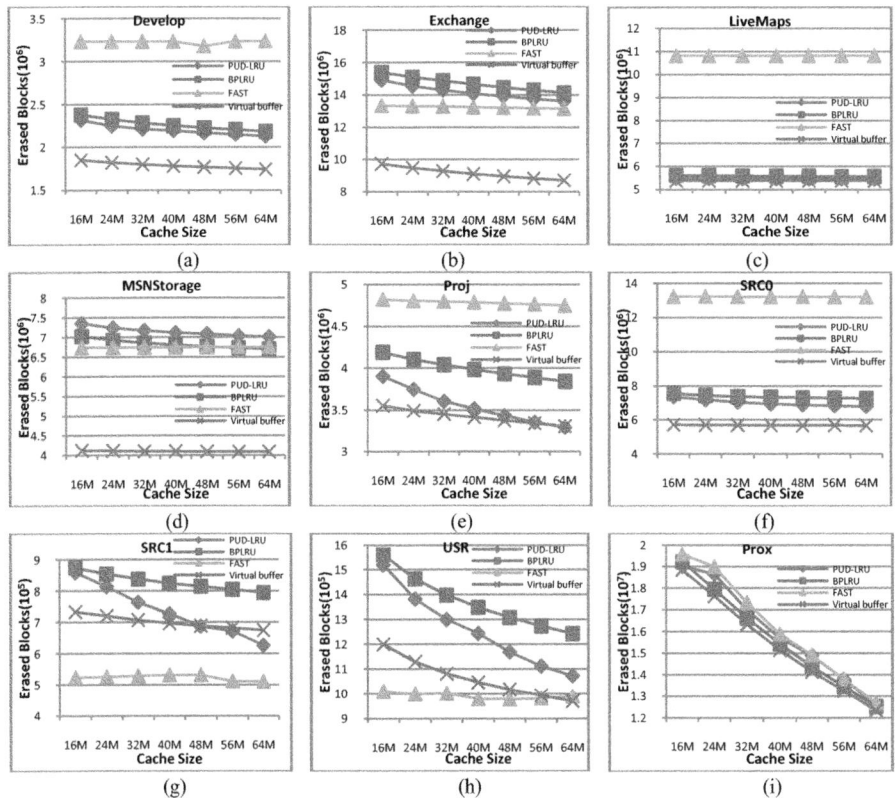

Fig. 4. SSDs employing our virtual write buffer erase the least blocks on most workloads. That's because our virtual write buffer optimizes both cache replacement and write sequence.

We propose to reorder the write sequence in virtual write buffer. Reordering write sequence avoids writing physical blocks randomly. Usually, random write results in write amplification, which will shorten SSD's lifespan. As shown in Figure 6, SSDs employing the virtual write buffer move the least pages for padding. It means that the write amplification is prohibited. That's why SSDs equipped with the virtual buffer erase fewer physical blocks. Actually, out-of-order written pages are directed to the reorder area, which is a part of flash address space. These pages also deplete SSD's lifespan. But, these pages can be written to any physical pages in flash chips. There is no need to migrate any page for them. They will not bring about write amplification. So, the erased blocks induced by out-of-order written pages are negligible.

Except for the reordering optimization, our virtual buffer does not neglect hit ratio. The DRAM devotes to improving hit ratio. DRAM is managed at the page level. It is able to exploit temporal locality completely. Furthermore, it can reuse existing high performance cache replacement policies. So, the DRAM achieves higher hit ratios on most workloads, as shown in Figure 5. Higher hit ratio means to reduce write traffic. This is pursued by traditional write buffers. Based on the two aspects (higher hit ratio and reordering optimization), the virtual write buffer reduces erased blocks.

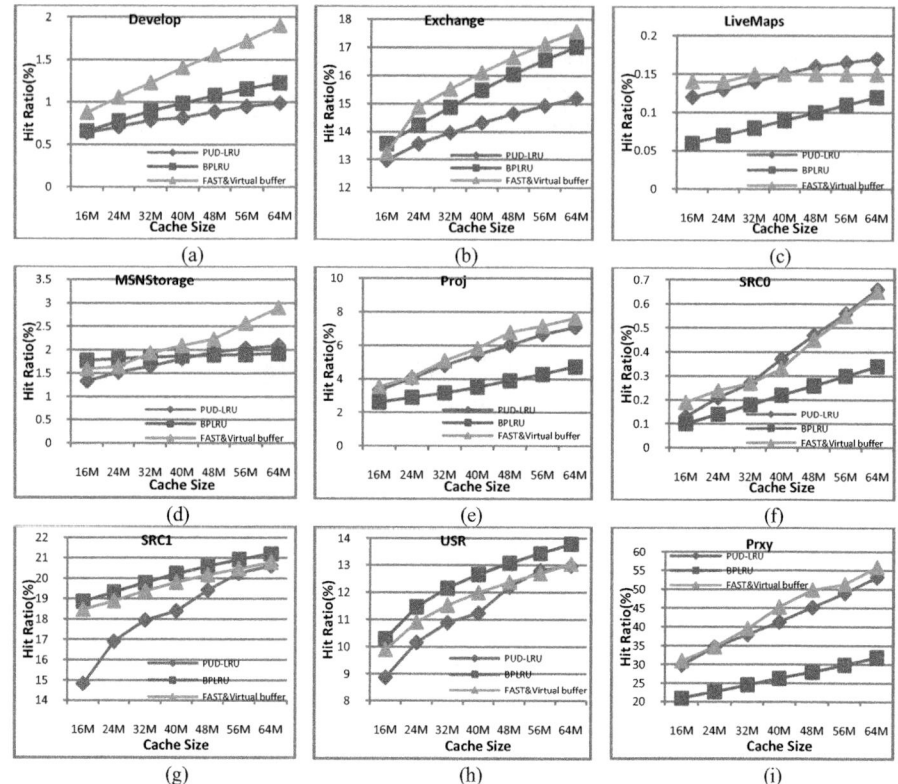

Fig. 5. The virtual write buffer achieves higher hit ratio than others do

4.3   Comparison with FAST

Reorder area is similar with the log area adopted by FAST [15]. So, we compare the virtual write buffer with FAST further. The rationale behind FAST can be described as follows. FAST allocates a set of blocks called log blocks. Left blocks used by users are called data blocks. Data blocks contain most of the user's data. Log blocks are prepared to accept updated pages. The log set is shared by all data blocks. Updates to any data blocks are directed log blocks sequentially. If the log set is used up, FAST merges valid data in the log set to data blocks. And another log area is allocated. These log blocks are similar with the reorder area adopted by our virtual write buffer. To compare the two schemes fairly, we assume that FAST is equipped with the same DRAM as our virtual write buffer owns. And it adopts ARC [9] as the cache replacement policy as well. The difference between two schemes relies on the direction of updated pages evicted from DRAM. For FAST, pages evicted from DRAM are written to log blocks arbitrarily. When the log set is used up, log blocks are merged with data blocks. For our virtual buffer, SSD tries its best to write pages to data blocks directly. Only when a page is evicted from DRAM in out-of-order manner, the page is written to the reorder area.

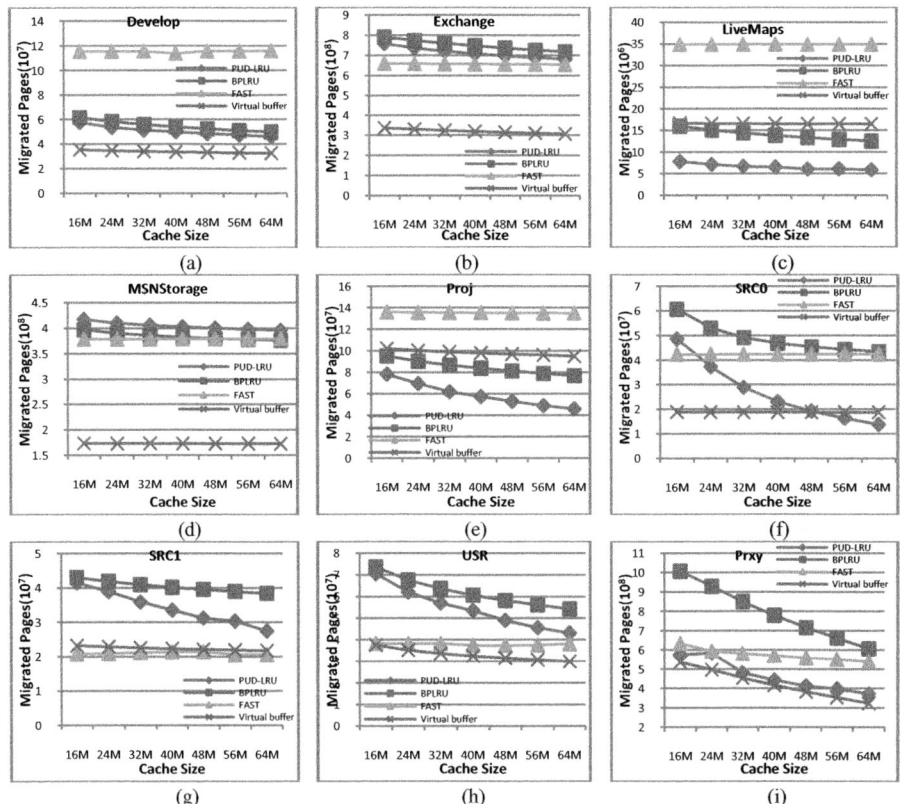

Fig. 6. SSDs employing the virtual write buffer migrate the least number of pages

As two schemes adopt the same cache replacement policy to manage DRAM, they achieve the same hit ratios. But, the virtual buffer usually erases fewer blocks. FAST writes all updates to log area arbitrarily. When the log area is used up, it merges log blocks with data blocks. The merge operation requires to moving many pages. As shown in Figure 6, FAST usually moves more pages than the virtual write buffer does. On the contrary, the virtual buffer gets rid of merge operation. It reorders the write sequence, and then writes pages of a logical block to a physical block with page offset unchanged. There are no page migrations except for padding. So, the virtual buffer erases less blocks.

5   Conclusion

SSDs usually employ write buffer to extend the lifespan. However, existing write buffers haven't optimized the write sequence. We propose a virtual write buffer. The buffer consists of two components, the DRAM and reorder area. DRAM devotes to improving hit ratio, as pursued by traditional write buffers. Since DRAM is managed at page level and adopts existing superior cache replacement policy, it gets higher hit ratio.

The reorder area reconfigures the write sequence, thus prohibits write amplification. Based on the two optimizations, the virtual write buffer enables SSDs to erase less physical blocks, and thus to extend the lifespan.

Acknowledgments. We are grateful to the anonymous reviewers for their valuable suggestions to improve this paper. This work is supported by the National Natural Science Foundation of China (NSFC60736013, NSFC60903040, NSFC61025009), Program for New Century Excellent Talents in University (NCET-08-0145).

References

1. Kang, S., Park, S., Jung, H., Shim, H., Cha, J.: Performance trade-offs in using nvram write buffer for flash memory-based storage devices. IEEE Transactions on Computers 58(6), 744–758 (2009)
2. Hu, J., Jiang, H., Tian, L., Xu, L.: PUD-LRU: An Erase-Efficient Write Buffer Management Algorithm for Flash Memory SSD. In: MASCOTS 2010 (August 2010)
3. Wu, G., Eckart, B., He, X.: BPAC: An Adaptive Write Buffer Management Scheme for Flash-based Solid State Drives. In: MSST 2010 (May 2010)
4. Kim, H., Ahn, S.: Bplru: A buffer management scheme for improving random writes in flash storage. In: FAST 2008 (2008)
5. Jo, H., Kang, J.U., Park, S.Y., Kim, J.S., Lee, J.: Fab: flashaware buffer management policy for portable media players. IEEE Transactions on Consumer Electronics 52(2), 485–493 (2006)
6. Sun, G., Joo, Y., Chen, Y., Niu, D., Xie, Y., Chen, Y., Li, H.: A hybrid solid-state storage architecture for the performance, energy consumption, and lifetime improvement. In: HPCA 2010, pp. 141–153. IEEE, Los Alamitos (2010)
7. Soundararajan, G., Prabhakaran, V., Balakrishnan, M., Wobber, T.: Extending ssd lifetimes with disk-based write caches. In: FAST 2010. USENIX (February 2010)
8. Johnson, T., Shasha, D.: 2Q: a low overhead high performance buffer management replacement algorithm. In: VLDB 1994, Santiago de Chile, pp. 297–306 (1994)
9. Megiddo, N., Modha, D.S.: ARC : a self-tuning, low overhead replacement cache. In: FAST 2003, San Francisco, pp. 115–130 (2003)
10. Jiang, S., Zhang, X.D.: LIRS: an efficient low inter-reference recency set replacement policy to improve buffer cache performance. In: SIGMETRICS 2002, pp. 31–42 (2002)
11. Hu, X.Y., Eleftheriou, E., Haas, R., Iliadis, I., Pletka, R.: Write amplification analysis in flash-based solid state drives. In: SYSTOR 2009 (2009)
12. Park, C., Kang, J.-U., Park, S.-Y., Kim, J.-S.: Energy-aware demand paging on NAND flashbased embedded storages. In: ISLPED 2004, New York, NY, USA, pp. 338–343 (2004)
13. Park, S.-Y., Jung, D., Kang, J.-U., Kim, J.-S., Lee, J.: CFLRU: a replacement algorithm for flash memory. In: CASES 2006, New York, NY, USA, pp. 234–241 (2006)
14. ZFS Introduction, http://en.wikipedia.org/wiki/ZFS
15. Lee, S., Park, D., Chung, T., Lee, D., Park, S., Song, H.: A Log Buffer based Flash Translation Layer Using Fully Associative Sector Translation. IEEE Transactions on Embedded Computing Systems 6(3), 18 (2007) ISSN 1539–9087
16. http://iotta.snia.org/traces
17. Narayanan, D., Donnelly, A., Rowstron, A.: Write Off-Loading: Practical Power Management for Enterprise Storage. In: FAST 2008 (2008)
18. K9WBG08U5M-KCJ0 Datasheet, http://www.samsung.com

Memory-Side Acceleration for XML Parsing

Jie Tang[1], Shaoshan Liu[2], Zhimin Gu[1], Chen Liu[3], and Jean-Luc Gaudiot[4]

[1] Beijing Institute of Technology, Beijing, China
[2] Microsoft, Redmond, WA
[3] Florida International University, Miami, Florida
[4] University of California, Irvine, California
tangjie.bit@gmail.com, shaoliu@microsoft.com, zmgu@x263.net,
chen.liu@fiu.edu, gaudiot@uci.edu

Abstract. As Extensible Markup Language (XML) becomes prevalent in cloud computing environments, it also introduces significant performance overheads. In this paper, we analyze the performance of XML parsing, identify that a significant fraction of the performance overhead is indeed incurred by memory data loading. To address this problem, we propose implementing memory-side acceleration on top of computation-side acceleration of XML parsing. To this end, we study the impact of memory-side acceleration on performance, and evaluate its implementation feasibility including bus bandwidth utilization, hardware cost, and energy consumption. Our results show that this technique is able to improve performance by up to 20% as well as produce up to 12.77% of energy saving when implemented in 32 nm technology.

1 Introduction

One of the main challenges in cloud computing environments is data exchange between different platforms. XML is emphasized for its language neutrality and application independency, and thus it has been adopted as the data exchange standard in cloud computing environments. When data is in XML, thousands of existing software packages can handle that data. Data in XML is universally approachable, accessible, and usable. Although XML exhibits many benefits, due to its verbosity and descriptive nature, XML parsing has incurred heavy performance penalties [1, 2]. Studies have shown that servers spend a significant portion of their execution time on processing XML documents. A real world example would be Morgan Stanley's Financial Services system, which spends 40% of its execution time on processing XML documents [3]. This is only going to get worse as XML data get larger and more complicated. Generally, in cloud computing environments, XML parsing is memory and computation intensive, it consumes about 30% of processing time in web service applications [4], and has become a main performance bottleneck in real-world database servers [5].

To improve performance of XML processing, many have proposed computation-side acceleration techniques. In this paper, we find out that memory accesses actually incur significant performance overheads in XML parsing. Therefore, different from previous studies which focus on computation acceleration, we propose to accelerate

E. Altman and W. Shi (Eds.): NPC 2011, LNCS 6985, pp. 277–292, 2011.

XML parsing from memory side. Unlike computation acceleration, which has a strong dependency on the parsing model, memory-side acceleration is generic and can be effective across all parsing models. We believe the combination of computation-side and memory-side acceleration will largely relieve the performance pressure incurred by XML parsing. In our vision, cloud computing services can be hosted by one many-core chip, such as Intel's SCC chip [6]. Within this many-core chip, we should have at least one core act as the Data Exchange Frontend (DEF), which is dedicated to and optimized for XML parsing; and this DEF core should incorporate special instructions for computation-side acceleration as well as dedicated prefetchers for memory-side acceleration.

Within this context, we aim to answer three questions in this paper: first, what is the performance bottleneck of XML parsing? Second, can memory-side prefetching techniques improve the performance of XML parsing? Third, is it feasible to implement these techniques in hardware? The rest of this paper is organized as follows: in section 2, we review XML parsing techniques and related research work; in section 3, we discuss the methodology of our study; in section 4, we study the performance of XML parsing under native and managed environments; in section 5, we aim to answer the first question by evaluating the performance of XML parsing and identify the performance bottleneck of XML parsing; in section 6, we aim to answer the second question by delving into memory-side acceleration of XML parsing; In section 7, we aim to answer the third question by studying the implementation feasibility of the memory-side acceleration. At the end, we conclude and discuss our future work.

2   Background

In this section, we review XML parsing techniques as well as related studies on software and hardware acceleration of XML parsing.

2.1   XML Parsing Techniques

Based on how data is processed, there are two categories of XML parsing models: event-driven parser and tree-based parser. Event-driven parsers first parse the document, and then through callbacks, they notify client applications about any tag they find along the way. It transmits and parses XML infosets sequentially at runtime. As a result, Event-driven parsers don't cache any information and have an enviably small memory footprint. However, it does not expose the structure of the XML documents, making them hard to manipulate. Furthermore, according to how events are delivered, event-driven model can be divided into two classes: pull parser and push parser. In pull parsing, clients pull XML data when it is needed. In push parsing, an XML parser pushes XML data to the client as new elements are encountered. Simple API for XML (SAX) [7] is the industry standard for push based event-driven model. As shown in upper part of Figure 1, SAX processes the XML document and then pushes the XML information into Application in terms of SAX Events.

On the other hand, tree-based parsers read the entire content of an XML document into memory and create an in-memory tree object to represents it. Once in memory,

DOM trees can be navigated freely and parsed arbitrarily for the duration of the document processing, providing maximum flexibility for users. However this flexibility pays great costs of a potentially large memory footprint and significant processor requirements. Document Object Model (DOM) [8] is the official W3C standard for tree-based parser. As shown in bottom part of Figure 1, DOM parser processes XML data, creates an object-oriented hierarchical representation of the document and offer the full access to the XML data.

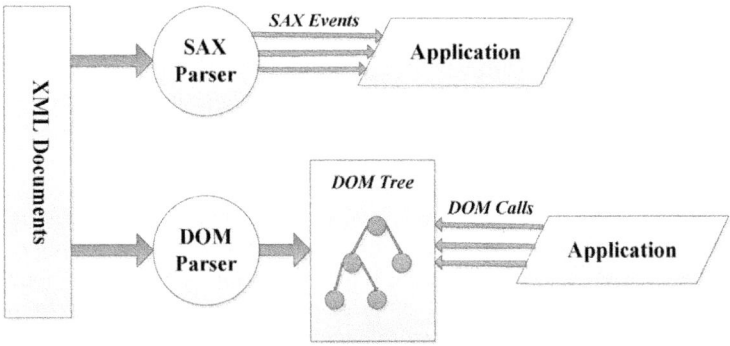

Fig. 1. SAX and DOM Parsing Flow

2.2   Related Research Work

There have been several proposals on mitigating the performance overheads of XML processing. In software community, several researcher groups employed the concept of binary XML to avoid performance bottleneck of XML parsing [1, 9, 10]. Specifically, VTD-XML parser [10] parses XML documents and creates 64-bit binary format VTD records. However, the major shortcoming of this approach is that the parsed binary data can't be used by other XML applications directly. On the other hand, some researchers focus on parallelizing the parsing process. Pre-scanning based parallel parsing model [11] builds a skeleton of the XML document to guide partitioning of the document for data parallel processing. Also, in [12] researchers exploited the parallelism by dividing XML parsing process into several phases, so that they can schedule working threads to execute each parsing phase in a pipeline model. In addition, Parabix employs the SIMD capabilities of commodity processors to process multiple characters at the same time [13].

In the hardware community, based on the profiling analysis, researchers incorporate new instructions with special hardware support to speedup certain frequently-used operations of XML parsing [14]. In [15], researchers presented a technique to automatically map regular expressions directly onto FPGA hardware and implemented a simple XML parser for demonstration. Their technique could be not sufficient to solve all problems since XML syntax rule is not a regular language. XOE [16] use an Offload Engine to accelerate XML document parsing. Some fundamental parsing functionality like tokening is offloaded to XOE. XPA [17] is another XML Parsing Accelerator implemented on FPGA capable to do XML well-formed checking, schema validation, and tree construction. It can reach up to1

Cycle-Per-Byte throughput for XML parsing. Nevertheless, their design works only for tree-based parsers. As we show in the following sections, memory access is one of the major bottlenecks of XML parsing, thus we may be able to generate extra performance gain from memory-side acceleration. In addition, unlike computation-side acceleration that targets specific parsing model, memory-side acceleration is generic and can be effective regardless of the parsing model.

3   Methodology

In this section, we discuss our methodology to study the performance of XML parsing, the effectiveness of memory-side acceleration, and implementation feasibility.

3.1   XML Parsers and Benchmarks

In order to make fair comparison, we choose XML parser implementations of both event-driven and tree-based model from Apache Xerces [18]. Apache Xerces provides SAX and DOM XML parsers, and it has implementations of these two models in both native (C++) and managed (Java) environments. This allows us to perform a thorough study to understand the performance of SAX and DOM models in different execution environments. As for inputs to the XML parsers, we have selected seven real world XML documents with varying sizes (from 1.4 KB to 113 MB) and complexities as input data and they are listed in Table 1. Specifically, *personal-schema* is a very simple document with flat structure, thus the parsing process is straightforward; on the other hand, *standard* is a long document with deep structures, which complicates the parsing process.

Table 1. Benchmarks

Name	Size (KB)	Description
long	*65.7*	*sample XML SOAP file*
mystic-library	*1384*	*Information of library books*
personal-shema	*1.4*	*personal information data*
physics-engine	*1171*	*configuration data for physics simulation*
resume_w_xsl	*51.8*	*personal resume*
test-opc	*1.8*	*xml test file for web services gateway*
Standard	*113749*	*bank transaction records*

3.2   Prefetchers

In this study, we evaluate how different prefetching techniques impact the performance of XML parsing. In order to make a comprehensive investigation, we have selected eight hardware prefetchers, which utilize different techniques and algorithms. We summarize these prefetchers in Table 2: *cache hierarchy* indicates the coverage of the prefetching, which means if the prefetching is applied at L1 cache, L2, cache, or both; *prefetching degree* suggests whether the aggressiveness of the prefetcher is statically or dynamically adjusted. Usually, the dynamic prefetching degree can adapt itself to the phase change of the application so as to produce more efficient prefetching; *trigger L1* and *trigger L2* respectively show the trigger set for covered cache hierarchy respectively, in this case *demand access* stands for access requests from upper memory hierarchy regardless whether it is a miss or hit and *N/A* means no prefetching is applied. Since *demand access* trigger set contains more opportunity to invoke the prefetching, it always yields more aggressiveness. Besides, all selected prefetchers can filter out redundant access requests.

Table 2. Summary of Prefetchers

	Cache Hierarchy	Prefetch Degree	Trigger L1	Trigger L2
n1	*L1 & L2*	*dynamic*	*Miss*	*Access*
n2	*L1*	*Static*	*Miss*	*N/A*
n3	*L1 & L2*	*dynamic*	*Miss*	*Miss*
n4	*L1*	*Static*	*N/A*	*N/A*
n5	*L2*	*Static*	*N/A*	*Miss*
n6	*L1 & L2*	*dynamic*	*Miss*	*Miss*
n7	*L2*	*Static*	*Miss*	*Access*
n8	*L2*	*Static*	*N/A*	*Access*

The aggressiveness of the prefetching is the co-production of all these four metrics and prefetching algorithms. The first prefetcher *n1* can tolerate out of order memory accesses by making prefetching based on the recent memory access pattern. The second prefetcher *n2* exploits various localities in both local and global cache-miss streams, including global strides, local strides and scalar patterns. A multi-level prefetching framework is applied in *n3*: it uses a sequential tagged prefetcher at L1 cache and either an adaptive prefetcher or a sequential tagged prefetcher at L2 cache. With the observation that memory accesses often exhibit repetitive layouts spanning large memory region, *n4* is the optimized implementation of Spatial Memory Streaming (SMS) including a novel mechanism of pattern bit-vector rotation to reduce SMS storage requirement. Combining the storage efficiency of Reference Prediction Tables and high performance of Program Counter/Delta Correlation (PC/DC) prefetching, *n5* can substantially reduce the complexity of PC/DC prefetching by avoiding expensive pointer chasing and re-computation of the delta buffer. The sixth prefetcher *n6* applies a hybrid stride/sequential prefetching schema at both L1 and L2 cache levels. Metrics such as prefetcher accuracy, lateness and memory bandwidth contention are fed back to adapt the aggressiveness of prefetching. By understanding and exploiting a variety of memory access patterns, *n7* combines global history buffer and multiple local history buffers to improve the coverage of prefetching. Finally, *n8* is a stream-based prefetcher with several enhancement techniques including constant stride optimization, noise removal, early launch of repeat stream and dead stream removal.

3.3   Performance and Memory Modeling

To study the performance of the memory-side acceleration, we utilize CMP\$IM [19], a binary-instrumentation based cache simulator developed by Intel. CMP\$IM is able to characterize cache performance of single-threaded, multi-threaded, and multi-programmed workloads. The simulation framework models an out-of-order processor with the basic parameters as outlined in Table 3.

Table 3. Simulation Parameters

Frequency	1 GHz
Issue Width	4
Instruction Window	128 entries
L1 Data Cache	32KB, 8-way, 1cycle
L1 Inst. Cache	32 KB, 8-way, 1cycle
L2 Unified Cache	512 KB, 16-way, 20 cycles
Main Memory	256 MB, 200 cycles

To understand the implementation feasibility of these memory-side accelerators, we also study the energy consumption of these designs. To model the energy consumption of these prefetchers, we utilize CACTI [20], an energy model which integrates cache and memory access time, area, leakage, and dynamic power. Using CACTI, we are able to generate energy parameters of different storage and interconnect structures implemented in different technologies. Note that the overall system energy consumption consists of two sources: static power and dynamic power. Static power is generated by the leakage current of the transistors, and it persists regardless of whether the transistors are actively switching or not. On the other hand, dynamic power is incurred only when the transistors are actively switching. In this paper, we use CACTI to model both static and dynamic energy to evaluate the implementation feasibility of memory-side accelerators.

4   Native vs. Managed Execution

In this section, we study the performance of XML parsing in both managed and native environments. We executed XML parsers on a dual-core machine running at 2.2 GHz and used the Intel Vtune analysis tool [21] to capture the overall execution time. The results are shown in Figure 2, in which we take the performance of native execution as the baseline. The x-axis shows the seven benchmarks and the y-axis shows the percentage of the excess execution time incurred by the managed layer (in this case JVM). It is obvious that when parsing with SAX model, managed execution produces high performance overhead. For instance, when parsing *test-opc* and *mystic-library*, the managed middle layer contributes 41.67% and 38% performance overhead respectively. Even in the best case, *long*, the middle layer still incurs 20.73% performance overheads. The situation is even worse when using DOM parsing model. Even the best case has incurred 25.93% performance overheads. In the worst case, *test-op*, it incurs up to 52.08% performance degradation.

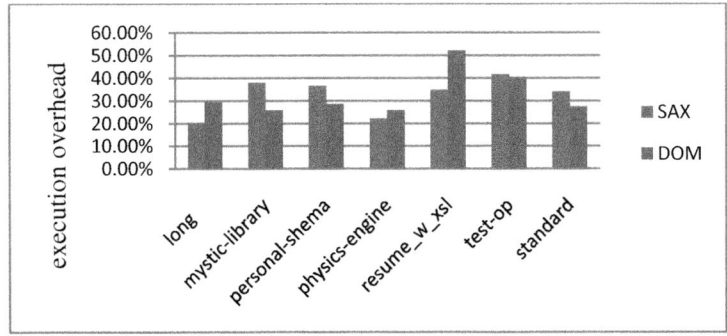

Fig. 2. Managed Execution vs. Native Execution

Although managed environment is able to reduce development time, in cloud computing environments, XML parsers reside at the data exchange frontend and many other components in the system may have dependency on the outputs of the XML parsers. Therefore, the performance overheads incurred by the managed layer would largely hinder the performance of the whole system. This result indicates that managed execution of XML parsing is not suitable in cloud computing environments and we focus on native execution of XML parsing in the rest of this paper.

5   Performance Analysis of XML Parsing

In this section we aim to determine the performance bottleneck of XML parsing by studying the throughput of XML parsing at different parts of the system, including network data exchange, disk I/O, and memory accesses. Figure 3 shows the data flow of XML parsing: first, data is loaded from either network or local hard disk. Then, data flows into the memory subsystem: main memory, L2 and L1 caches. At the end, the processor fetches data from cache and performs the actual XML parsing computation.

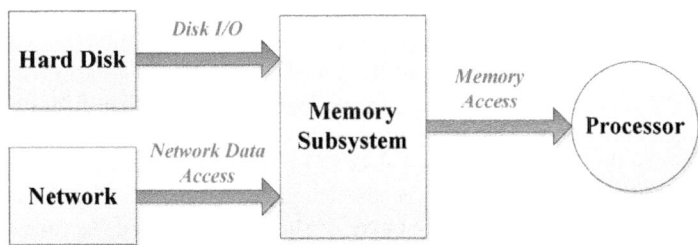

Fig. 3. Data flow of XML data parsing

5.1   Network Data Exchange

Some previous work has demonstrated that network data exchange would incur significant performance overheads [23, 27]. In this subsection, we measure the data exchange throughput of different cloud data services. In Table 4, we summarize our measurements of two popular categories of cloud data services: *Content Distribution Network* (CDN) and *Cloud Storage*; and for each category, we measured the data exchange throughput of four service providers. Note that CDN services contain several copies of data in network to maximize bandwidth, whereas Cloud Storage services provide online storage where people can require their storage capacity for their data hosting needs. On average, the data exchange throughput to CDN services can reach 29.26 Mb/s. When employing the CDN service provided by Amazon CloudFront, the rate can reach 48.85 Mb/s. On the other hand, the average data exchange throughput to Cloud Storage services is 12.56 Mb/s and its best case, provided by Amazon S3 – US East, can reach 21.8 Mb/s. In our experiment, our machine contains a 100 MB/s Network Interface Card and network it connected to has a bandwidth limit of 100Mb/s, which is far greater than the throughput provided by cloud data services. That indicates the network I/O interface is not fully utilized, and thus the network interface is not likely to be the bottleneck of XML parsing operations.

Table 4. Cloud Service Data Rate

CDN Service		Cloud Storage Service	
Provider	*Rate (Mb/s)*	*Provider*	*Rate (Mb/s)*
Akamai CDN	27.50	Amazon S3 - US East	21.80
Amazon CloudFront	48.85	Amazon S3 - US West	10.31
Cotendo CDN	27.72	Azure-South Central US	6.97
Highwinds CDN	12.97	Nirvanix SDN	11.17
AVG	29.26	AVG	12.56

5.2   Disk Data Loading

In order to study the disk I/O throughput, we used the XPerf Performance Analyzer tool [26] to capture disk I/O throughput when running the XML parsers using the *standard* benchmark, and the collected results are shown in Figure 4: the x-axis shows the execution timeline in seconds and the y-axis shows the amount of triggered disk I/O during the execution. The gray curve overlaid on top of the bar diagram shows the CPU usage information. The peak of the curve means the CPU is fully utilized. Figure 4 shows that most of the time disk I/O is in the underutilized state; that is to say that the I/O subsystem rarely needs to reach its full capacity. Besides, when looking into the overlaid CPU usage curve, it shows that most of the time the CPU is fully utilized, running at 100%. Once in a while, the CPU utilization drops down, probably due to high-latency memory accesses. It indicates that in this case most of the time CPU is fed with enough data from the I/O subsystem. Based on these observations, it can be concluded that disk I/O is also not likely to be the bottleneck of XML data processing. We also ran the XML parsers with other benchmarks shown in Table, and the results were similar.

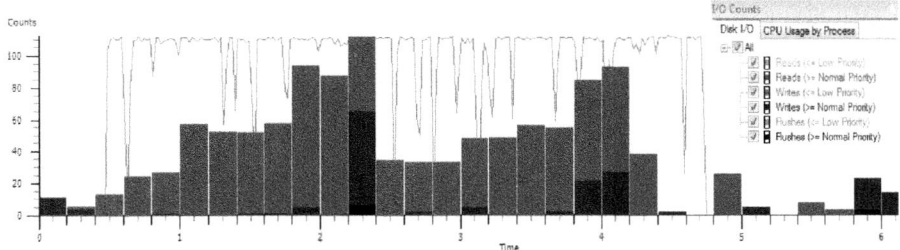

Fig. 4. Disk I/O counts and CPU Usage

5.3   Data Loading from Memory Side

Finally, we studied the overhead produced by memory data loading stage. Here, memory data loading refers to the data flow starting from main memory, going through each cache layer and finally fetched into CPU. Making a comparison, we measured the CPI (cycle per instruction) of *Speed-test*, which is a computation intensive CPU stress test application with negligible memory access; and we measured the CPI of native XML parser using the *standard* benchmark, which is the large XML document with a lot of memory accesses. The CPI of *Speed-test* is 0.80. Using the SAX parser, the CPI of *standard* is 1.27, which introduces nearly 50% overheads compared to *Speed-test*; using the DOM parser, the CPI of *Standard* becomes 1.42, which nearly doubles that of *Speed-test*. In addition, when using other benchmarks shown in Table 1, we obtained similar performance data as that of *standard*.

As a further validation, we measured the miss count per kilo instructions (MPKI) of both L1 and L2 cache layers, which are nearly 10 and 2 respectively. That is to say that for every 1000 instructions there comes about ten L1 and two L2 cache misses. The large number of cache misses mainly contributes to the CPI increase of XML parsing. Compared with the CPI of *Speed-test*, the extra cycles consumed by XML parsing may indicate that memory data loading stage incurs a significant amount of overhead to the execution.

5.4   Summary

In summary, the results from the previous three subsections show the following: first, network I/O throughput can easily reach over 15 MB/s, and this is far below the 100 MB/s network bandwidth limit, showing that network I/O is far from being stressed and network data exchanging is not likely to be the bottleneck of XML parsing. Second, our experiment results show that the disk I/O subsystem is under-utilized most of the time, which means disk data loading of XML data parsing is within the coverage of disk I/O subsystem and cannot be the bottleneck of execution as well. At last, comparing CPI data of XML parsing workloads and a CPU stress test, we have found that in some case the CPI of XML parsing almost double that of the CPU stress test. Upon further analysis, we have found that the high cache miss rate on both L1 and L2 caches is the main contributor to this CPI increase. These results indicate that the performance bottleneck of XML parsing is memory data loading stage; in other word, the overheads introduced from memory subsystem really hit the pain point of

XML data parsing. Therefore, in order to speed up the XML parsing execution, it is imperative to turn around the focus of acceleration and reduce the overheads incurred by the memory subsystem.

6   Memory-Side Acceleration

We have identified that memory accesses impose significant overheads in XML parsing workloads. Similarly, a study released by Intel verifies that memory accesses contribute to more than 60% execution cycles of the whole parsing process [22]. Furthermore, another empirical study done by Longshaw *et al.* has shown that loading an XML document into memory and reading it prior to parsing may take longer than the actual parsing time [24]. Consequently, instead of optimizing specific computation of parsing model, we explore acceleration from memory side; that is to say, accelerate the XML data loading stage.

Table 5 summarizes the reduction of cache misses as a result of applying the prefetchers (please refer to section 3.2 for the details of the prefetchers). Note that different prefetchers may target different cache levels; in this table, we show the cache miss reduction of the lowest level cache that the prefetcher is applied to. For example, n1 is applied to both L1 and L2 caches, we show the cache miss reduction of L2 cache; n2 is applied to only L1, so we show the cache miss reduction of L1 cache. The results indicate that prefetching techniques are very effective on XML parsing workloads, as most prefetchers are able to reduce cache miss by more than 50%. In the best case, n3 is able to reduce L2 cache miss by 82% in SAX and 85% in DOM.

In Figure 5, we show how the cache miss reduction translates into performance improvement on SAX parsing: it shows the performance of the eight prefetchers (n1-n8) as well as the average performance. The X-axis lists the seven benchmarks we used and the Y-axis shows the percentage of performance improvement (in terms of execution time reduction). The results indicate that prefetching techniques are able to improve SAX parsing performance by up to 10%. For instance, on average, the parsing time of *personal-schema* has been reduced by 7.24%. Even in the worst case, *standard*, prefetchers are still able to reduce execution time by 3%. Looking into each prefetching technique, we observe that n3 shows greatest power in improving the performance by 2.58% to 9.72% across different benchmarks. This is because n3 is the most aggressive prefetcher and covers both L1 and L2 cache level, thus resulting in the best average performance.

Similarly, Figure 6 summarizes the performance impact of prefetching on DOM parsing. The results indicate that prefetching techniques are able to improve DOM parsing performance by up to 20%. For instance, when averaging the results, memory-side acceleration produces 13.74% execution cycle reduction for *mystic-library*. It is obvious that the most effective prefetcher is still n3 : even in the worst case, n3 can still reduce execution time by 6%. Note that different from SAX parsing, DOM must construct inner data structure in memory for all elements. The bigger the document is the more space it would consume, and the more cache miss it would induce. As a result, large sized benchmarks such as *mystic-library*, *physics-engine* and *standard* can get a higher performance gain from memory side acceleration from 7.65% up to 13.75%. These results confirm that memory-side acceleration can be effective regardless of the parsing models.

Table 5. Cache Miss Reduction

	n1	n2	n3	n4	n5	n6	n7	n8
SAX	0.69	0.43	0.82	0.82	0.51	0.4	0.73	0.77
DOM	0.77	0.52	0.85	0.85	0.61	0.52	0.77	0.84
Cache Level	L2	L1	L2	L1	L2	L2	L2	L2

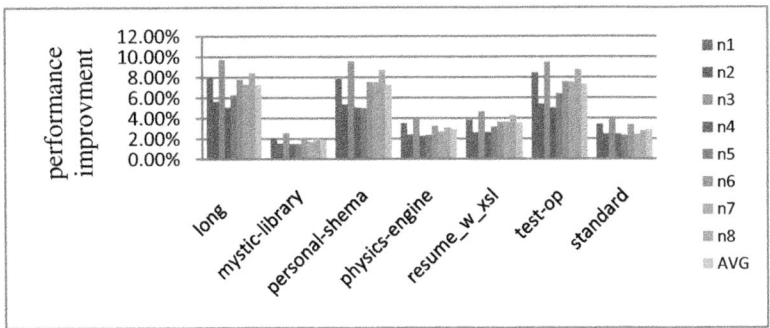

Fig. 5. Performance improvement for SAX parsing

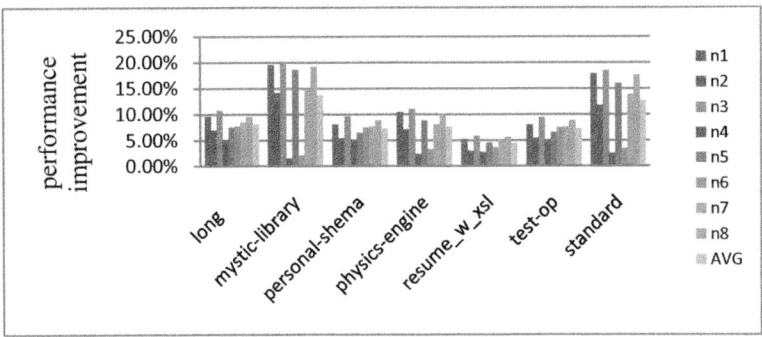

Fig. 6. Performance improvement for DOM parsing

7   Implementation Feasibility

By now we have shown that memory-side acceleration can significantly improve XML parsing performance. However, the conventional wisdom is that prefetching requires extra hardware resource, competes for limited bus bandwidth, and consumes more energy. Thus, many would argue that it is not worthwhile to implement memory-side accelerators for XML parsing. In this section, we address these doubts by validating the feasibility of memory side acceleration in terms of bandwidth utilization, hardware cost and energy consumption.

7.1   Bandwidth Utilization

Contention for limited bus bandwidth often leads to serious performance degradation. Prefetching techniques result in extra bus traffic and thus require extra bus bandwidth. If the application itself has used up all the bus bandwidth, then the contention brought in by memory-side acceleration might hinder rather than improve performance. Hence, we study the bandwidth utilization of XML parsing workloads and the results are summarized in Table 6. The results show that bus bandwidth utilization without prefetching is far away from exhaustion.   On average, bus utilization for SAX and DOM parsing are only 3.72% and 5.51% respectively.   This indicates the performance of XML parsing is hurt by the latency but not the throughput of memory subsystem, and thus confirming that prefetching would be effective.

Table 6. Bandwidth consumption without prefetching

	SAX	DOM
long	*4.09%*	*5.55%*
mystic-library	*4.38%*	*7.46%*
personal-shema	*4.94%*	*6.31%*
physics-engine	*4.07%*	*6.08%*
resume_w_xsl	*0.97%*	*1.03%*
test-opc	*1.01%*	*5.25%*
Standard	*6.58%*	*6.89%*

7.2   Hardware Cost and Energy Consumption

We summarize the hardware cost of the eight prefetchers in Table 7. On average, these prefetchers require about 28000 bits of memory space. For instance, n6 consists of a 14080 bits L1 prefetcher, a 4096 bits L2 prefetcher and eight 20 bits counters producing 32416 bits hardware cost. All of their hardware cost is below 4KB, which is not a significant amount of hardware resource in modern high-performance processor design.

Table 7. Hardware cost of prefetcher

n1	*32036 bits*	*n2*	*20329 bits*	*n3*	*20787 bits*	*n4*	*30592 bits*
n5	*25480 bits*	*n6*	*32416 bits*	*n7*	*30720 bits*	*n8*	*32768 bits*

Next we study how these memory-side accelerators impact system energy consumption. Using our simulation framework consisting of CMP$IM and CACTI, we can generate energy parameters of different storage and interconnect structure implemented in different technologies. Here, we focus on the implementation with 32 nm technologies and the results are summarized in Figures 7 and 8. In these Figures, we select energy consumption with no prefetching as our baseline, thus a positive number indicates that the prefetcher consumes extra energy, and a negative number indicates otherwise. Note that in 32 nm technology, static energy is comparable to dynamic energy [25].   The prefetchers generate extra memory requests and bus transactions, thus adding dynamic energy consumption.   On the other hand, prefetchers accelerate XML parsing execution, resulting in reduction of static energy consumption.   If the static energy reduction surpasses the dynamic energy addition, then the prefetcher results in overall system energy reduction.

As shown in Figure 7, in SAX parsing, most prefetchers lead to more energy consumption: It is due to the increase of dynamic energy dissipation coming from excess memory accesses incurred by prefetching. Nevertheless, looking into details, n5 always leads to energy efficiency, resulting in 1% to 4.5% energy saving across the benchmarks. Similarly, n1 results in energy saving in about half of the cases. This is because n1 and n5 are relatively conservative prefetching techniques: they either prefetch at only one cache level or prefetch a small amount data each time.

In Figure 8, we summarize how acceleration impacts energy consumption in DOM parsing. Identical with Figure 7, n5 is still the most energy efficient prefetcher which archives 12.77% energy saving in *mystic-library*. Even when running its worst case, *resume_w_xsl*, n5 can still reduce overall energy by almost 3%. Different from the results in SAX parsing, most prefetchers become energy-efficient in many cases due to their ability to further reduce execution time in DOM parsing. Note that static energy is the product of static power and time, since static power is constant, by reducing execution time, we can reduce static energy as well.

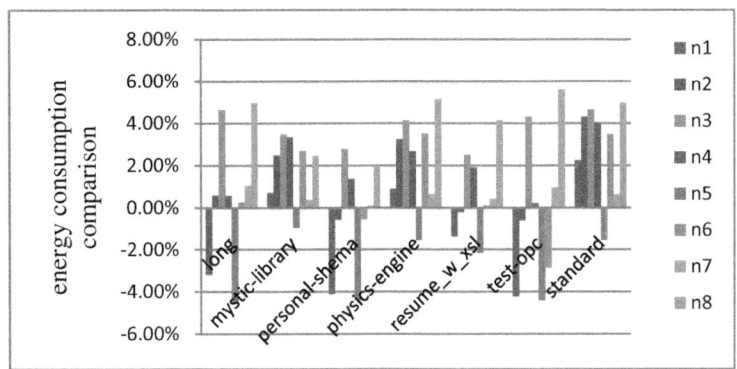

Fig. 7. Energy consumption of SAX parsing

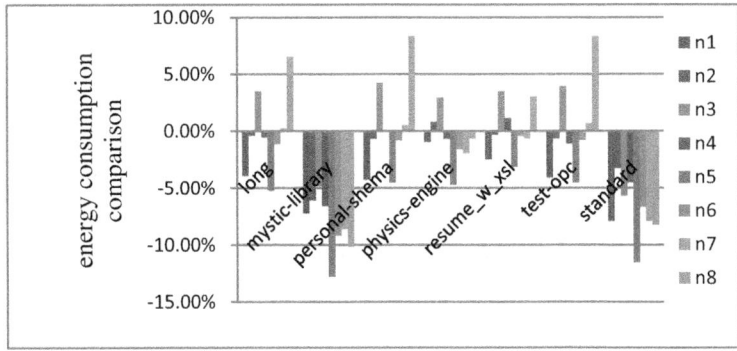

Fig. 8. Energy consumption of DOM parsing

8   Conclusions

XML has been adopted in cloud computing environments to address the data exchange problem. While XML has brought many benefits, XML parsing also imposes heavy performance penalties. As XML processing often resides at the data exchange frontend, different parts of the system would have dependency on the outputs of XML parsing, making it critical to system performance. While previous research work has focused on computation acceleration of XML parsing, we have identified memory access as one of the performance bottlenecks. Motivated by this finding, in this paper, we have done a study on the effectiveness and feasibility of memory-side acceleration of XML parsing. The results are encouraging, we have demonstrated that memory-side acceleration is effective regardless of the parsing model and is able to reduce cache miss by up to 80%, which translates into up to 20% of performance improvement.

On implementation feasibility, we have identified that XML parsing performance is hurt by the latency but not by the throughput of the memory subsystem, thus verifying that memory-side acceleration is not likely result in resource contention. In addition, we have shown that the memory-accelerators require an insignificant amount of extra hardware resources, and more importantly, in many cases they are indeed able to reduce the overall system energy consumption. These results confirm that memory-side acceleration of XML parsing is not only effective but also feasible.

In our vision, cloud computing services can be hosted by one many-core chip, and within this many-core chip, one or more cores act as the Data Exchange Frontend (DEF). Our next step is to incorporate memory-side and computation-side accelerations into the DEF cores and evaluate its performance in many-core environments.

Acknowledgements. This work is supported by the National Science Foundation under Grant No. CCF-1065448, the National Natural Science Foundation of China under Grant No. 61070029, as well as the China Scholarship Council. Any opinions, findings, and conclusions as well as recommendations expressed in this material are those of the authors and do not necessarily reflect the views of the National Science Foundation.

References

1. Chiu, K., Govindaraju, M., Bramley, R.: Investigating the limits of soap performance for scientific computing. In: Proceedings of the 11th IEEE International Symposium on High Performance Distributed Computing HPDC-11 (2002)
2. Head, M.R., Govindaraju, M., van Engelen, R., Zhang, W.: Grid scheduling and protocols—benchmarking xml processors for applications in grid web services. In: SC 2006: Proceedings of the 2006 ACM/IEEE Conference on Supercomputing, p. 121. ACM Press, New York (2006)

3. Apparao, P., Iyer, R., Morin, R., Naren, N., Mahesh, B., Halliwell, D., Striberg, W.: Architectural characterization of an XML-centric commercial server workload. In: 33rd International Conference on Parallel Processing (2004)

4. Apparao, P., Bhat, M.: A detailed look at the characteristics of xml parsing. In: BEACON 2004: 1st Workshop on Building Block Engine Architectures for Computers and Networks (2004)

5. Nicola, M., John, J.: XML parsing: A threat to database performance. In: Proceeding of the 12th International Conference on Information and Knowledge Management (2003)

6. Intel Single-Chip Cloud Computer,
   `http://techresearch.intel.com/ProjectDetails.aspx?Id=1`

7. SAX Parsing Model, `http://sax.sourceforge.net`

8. W3C, Document object model (DOM) level 2 core specification,
   `http://www.w3.org/TR/DOM-Level-2-Core`

9. Chiu, K., Devadithya, T., Lu, W., Slominski, A.: A binary xml for scientific applications. In: Proceedings of e-Science 2005. IEEE, Los Alamitos (2005)

10. XimpleWare, VTD-XML: The Future of XML Processing,
    `http://vtdxml.sourceforge.net` (accessed March 10, 2007)

11. Lu, W., Chiu, K., Pan, Y.: A Parallel Approach to XML Parsing. In: Proceedings of The 7th IEEE/ACM International Conference on Grid Computing, Barcelona, Spain (September 2006)

12. Head, M.R., Govindaraju, M.: Approaching a Parallelized XML Parser Optimized for Multi-Core Processor. In: SOCP 2007, June 26, ACM, Monterey (2007)

13. Cameron, R.D., Herdy, K.S., Lin, D.: High Performance XML Parsing Using Parallel Bit Stream Technology. In: Proceedings of the Conference of the Center for Advanced Studies on Collaborative Research, Ontario, Canada (October 2008)

14. Zhao, L., Bhuyan, L.: Performance Evaluation and Acceleration for XML Data Parsing. In: Proceedings of the 9th Workshop on Computer Architecture Evaluation using Commercial Workloads, Texas, USA (2006)

15. Moscola, J., Lockwood, J.W.: Reconfigurable Content-based Router using Hardware-Accelerated Language Parser. The ACM Transactions on Design Automation of Electronic Systems 13 (2008)

16. Nag, B.: Acceleration techniques for XML processors. In: XML Conference & Exhibition (November 2004)

17. Dai, Z., Ni, N., Zhu, J.: A 1 Cycle-Per-Byte XML Parsing Accelerator. In: FPGA 2010 (2010)

18. Apache Xerces, `http://xerces.apache.org/index.html`

19. Jaleel, A., Cohn, R.S., Luk, C.K., Jacob, B.: CMP$im: A Pin-Based On-The-Fly Multi-Core Cache Simulator. In: MoBS (2008)

20. Shivakumar, P., Jouppi, N.P.: CACTI3.0: an integrated cache timing, power, and area model, WRL Research Report (2001)

21. Intel Vtune, `http://software.intel.com/en-us/intel-vtune/`

22. XML Parsing Accelerator with Intel® Streaming SIMD Extensions 4 (Intel® SSE4) (December 15, 2008), `http://software.intel.com/en-us/articles/xml-parsing-accelerator-with-intel-streaming-simd-extensions-4-intel-sse4/`

23. Lee, S., Ro, W.W.: Accelerated Network Coding with Dynamic Stream Decomposition on Graphics Processing Unit. The Computer Journal

24. Longshaw, A.: Scaling XML parsing on Intel architecture. Intel Software Network Resource Center (November 2008),
http://www.developers.net/intelisnshowcase/view/537
25. Power vs. Performance: The 90 nm Inflection Point,
http://www.xilinx.com/publications/archives/solution_guides/power_management.pdf
26. Windows Performance Analysis Tool,
http://msdn.microsoft.com/en-us/performance/cc825801
27. Park, K., Park, J.S., Ro, W.W.: On Improving Parallelized Network Coding with Dynamic Partitioning. IEEE Transactions on Parallel and Distributed Systems 21(11), 1547–1560 (2010)

Hardware Performance Monitoring for the Rest of Us
A Position and Survey

Tipp Moseley[1,2,*], Neil Vachharajani[2,3,*], and William Jalby[1]

[1] Université de Versailles Saint-Quentin-en-Yvelines
[2] Google Inc.
[3] Pure Storage Inc.

1 Introduction

Microprocessors continue to make great strides in performance and scalability, yet hardware performance monitoring remains an area of dissatisfaction amongst those interested in better understanding the interactions of hardware and software. HPM technology has, at best, maintained the status quo for over a decade, though hope for better answers still remains. As it is, HPM is well-suited for some purposes, and everyone else tries to make the most of what is available. HPM will never be everything to everyone, and as new features are added, new users will adopt them in unforeseen ways.

HPM means different things to different people, so before proceeding we will give it a definition. Hardware performance monitoring refers to any hardware mechanism that enables (not necessarily by design) insight into how software performs on a microprocessor. This definition includes features as simple as timer-based interrupts, but also a broad range of things like event counters, last branch buffers, instruction-based samples, and many more.

Defining perspective is equally important. Performance tuning for any party involves identifying hot and representative code and determining whether the code is satisfactory relative to some notion of peak performance. When code does not achieve peak performance, the perspective of a hardware architect and software developer are quite different. From a hardware architect's perspective, some hardware unit performs poorly due to an instruction which cannot be changed. From a software developer's perspective, some instruction performs poorly due to some hardware unit which cannot be changed. Understanding this distinction is important for deciding how information is to be collected and presented. We describe HPM from a software perspective in hopes of influencing hardware architects to consider this viewpoint in future designs.

When tuning an application, either manually or automatically, there comes a point when further performance gains can only be achieved by truly understanding the minute details of the microarchitecture. Due to the effort required, however, this is one of the last stages of application tuning. Figure 1 illustrates this phenomenon.[1] Of course, some strategies can fit into multiple regions. Conveniently, the graph has no scale. The curve is segmented into three stages:

1) Application Insight. The biggest performance gains come from identifying and understanding the behavior of the hot portions of the code to apply better algorithms, refactor code, or choose the best data structures [1].

---

[*] Current affiliation.

[1] This figure comes completely from the authors' imaginations.

E. Altman and W. Shi (Eds.): NPC 2011, LNCS 6985, pp. 293–312, 2011.

Simply knowing where an application spends its time is the most valuable piece of information available. Yet this seemingly simple task is still an area of active research, even for natively compiled programs [2, 3]. In the managed world, the state of things is comical (though here, HPM is not at fault) – one of our colleagues tested several different Java profiling tools and found the relative execution time attributed to specific functions can differ by an order of magnitude!

Software engineering can expedite development, but opacity can lead to terrible performance for even small programs. The authors of a binary decision diagram (BDD) based potential parallelism detection tool discovered a 12X speedup simply by tuning parameters of their BDD library's garbage collector [4]. For linear solvers, choosing the correct software package can be of similar importance. A performance engineer at a large company helped application developers achieve a 1000X speedup by integrating a library call that used fork/exec repeatedly. None of these programmers are stupid; they are simply ignorant to the entire behavior of their program.

Though we somewhat disagree with his conclusion, Zilles's "Benchmark Health Considered Harmful" [5] is a must-read for compiler and architecture researchers. The health benchmark is often used to tout significant gains from compiler and architectural optimizations targeting linked lists. Instead, Zilles modifies the program's algorithms and data structures to produce the same result with 200X better performance. Zilles concludes health probably does not represent any real benchmark, while we fear it may be more common than anyone would like to admit.

The purpose of this group of anecdotes is not to argue that HPM does not matter. To the contrary, HPM can provide useful information to help uncover these types of *hardware independent* performance sinks and assist the developer in fixing them.

2) Application + Architectural Insight. Here, we make a distinction between architecture and microarchitecture. We use the term architecture to describe any aspect of performance that requires some knowledge of how modern processors are designed (i.e., with branch predictors, TLBs, and caches), and microarchitectural for things that pertain to a specific processor implementation (e.g., Core i7's unaligned vector operations will perform better when given aligned data, but Core 2's vector operations perform the same in either case).

Since all high performance CPUs have caches, it is important to structure data access patterns with their behavior in mind. For example, on a Core 2, loop interchange for matrix multiplication provides a 10X performance improvement.

Though the complexity varies greatly, branch predictors are also a ubiquitous piece of hardware and can be a critical performance bottleneck. Moseley et al. show an example from 445.gobmk where a clever software transformation to reduce branch mispredicts leads to an 8X performance improvement on a Pentium 4 [6].

The measurable impact of each of the previous anecdotes could vary in magnitude, but they represent common pitfalls that are significant on any piece of modern hardware. As such, HPM should provide simple and accessible features to access architectural performance information.

3) Microarchitectural Insight. HPM can be of assistance at every point on the curve, but without a simulator, it becomes *necessary* for microarchitectural insight. At this

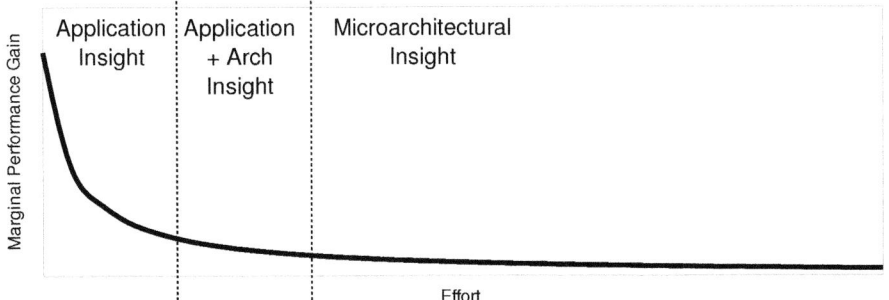

Fig. 1. Additional tuning effort versus marginal performance improvement

level, very subtle and often undocumented features such as queue sizes, specific latencies, alignment issues, μops, and coherency protocol idiosyncrasies come into play. Mytkowicz shows that simply altering a program's initial stack alignment by modifying the size of an environment variable can often affect performance by around 30%, and in one case, 300% [7].

Because their scope is typically limited, microarchitectural optimizations are often automated by compilers, libraries, and runtime systems. Building these systems is left to the top experts, and they must have intimate knowledge of processor-specific features, techniques for measuring such features, and limitations of measurement.

Understanding microarchitectural interactions comes at a high cost of both education and tedious analysis, yet the potential gains are diminished. An increasingly popular solution is to simply guess a lot and choose the best solution [8–11], though the guessing process (also known as search or learning) can take a long time, and defining the parameters to use may still require an understanding of the underlying microarchitecture.

Interestingly, the three-stage model can be observed in compilers and operating systems as well. The first steps of the compiler are transformations like inlining, constant propagation, and common subexpression removal. Next are vectorization and loop unrolling, and finally instruction alignment, scheduling, and peephole optimizations are performed.

We believe that HPM capabilities should mirror the three-stage model. Today, low-level information, while necessarily concrete, does not cover everything compiler, OS, and VM designers care about. Stages 1 and 2 are even worse off because an expert-level of understanding is often required to collect and apply HPM data; hardware and software must improve to provide more abstract information for the earlier stages of performance tuning.

Motivation. The common desktop computing experience is enough to see that most programs do not get past stage 1. From that perspective, it is hard to motivate designing HPM with application tuning in mind. As it is, HPM is clearly designed to give hardware designers the feedback they need to understand their own decisions. However, Figure 2 highlights an important trend in hardware sales[2]; end customers who

---

[2] This figure is also imaginary.

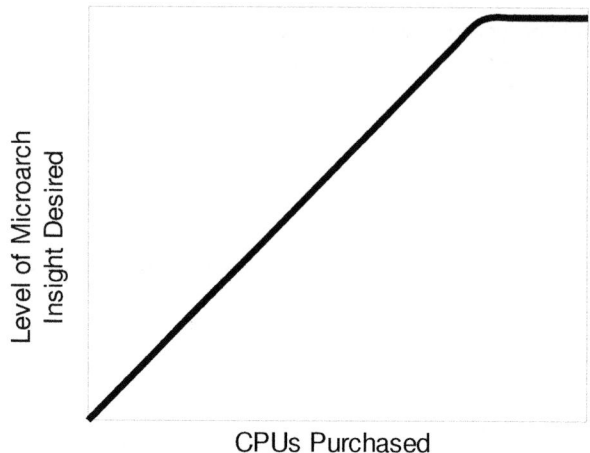

Fig. 2. CPUs purchased versus level of microarchitectural insight desired

purchases more hardware have higher expectations of how well they will be able to understand and monitor the hardware. Note that the curve levels off at no more knowledge about the processor can be gained (though customers will still continue to buy more hardware after that point). Furthermore, a [real] study by HP [12] concluded that the performance increase from using counters is more effective than simply waiting for a faster processor.

For instance, when AMD's Lightweight Profiling [13] is released, we believe it alone will drive some percentage of our colleagues cluster purchasing decisions, if only for research potential. For supercomputing and datacenter customers, even the smallest gains can translate to millions of dollars of savings on energy costs. HPM that enables developers to realize these savings adds real value.

The rest of this paper is organized as follows. Section 2 gives an overview of modern HPM hardware. Section 3 discusses issues facing current and future designers and users. Section 4 proposes some alternatives and opportunities for improvement. Section 5 proposes a paradigm shift from the current course. Finally, Section 6 concludes.

2   Background

This section gives a brief overview of the types of hardware that exist today (or have existed in the past). It is far from complete, but it covers most of what is currently available.

2.1   Event-Based Sampling (EBS)

Event-based sampling involves configuring a counter to interrupt every Nth time an event occurs. When the interrupt occurs, the program counter (PC) can be recorded. Ideally, EBS can be used to identify instructions that most frequently cause a specific event.

However, due to the out-of-order (OoO) nature of modern processors, the reported PC may be quite far (tens of instructions) from the instruction that actually triggered the interrupt.

Time-based Sampling (TBS). Logically, time-based sampling is event-based sampling where the event is time. It may use a high-frequency interrupt (or an event like CPU_CLK_UNHALTED) to collect information at specific time intervals. TBS can be used to get an estimate of where time is spent in the system [14, 15], though more weight will be given to long-latency instructions. In conjunction with other counters, it can be used to get an overall sense of bottlenecks in a program [16].

TBS is the most basic form of HPM and needs no special hardware support (for low fidelity).

Precise Event Based Sampling (PEBS). Several generations of Intel x86 machines have included a feature called Precise Event-Based Sampling [17]. For a small subset of possible events (and until Core i7, only a subset of counters), PEBS will report the entire architectural state (i.e., register contents), and the PC is claimed to be within one instruction of the actual culprit.

POWER processors have a mode called random sampling which is similar to PEBS, but it gives the actual PC associated with an event.

2.2   Instruction Based Sampling (IBS)

Due to the imprecise nature of EBS, Digital introduced ProfileMe [18] in the Alpha 21264, which has since inspired Instruction-based Sampling included on AMD's x86 offerings since 2007 [19]. IBS works by tagging random instructions and recording useful properties of their journey through the pipeline. Unlike ProfileMe, which did not have to deal with μops, IBS has two modes: fetch and op sampling. Fetch sampling reports the instruction's address, whether a fetch was completed or aborted and how long it took to complete, and flags for which levels of cache or TLB were missed. Op sampling reports the instruction's address, tag-to-retire cycles, completion-to-retire cycles, and flags for branch misprediction and many memory-system related flags.

2.3   Event Address Registers (EAR)

Debuting in Intel Itanium Processors, event address registers [20] can be configured to sample detailed information including precise PC and linear address for fetches or loads (but not stores) that miss in specified caches or TLBs.

Load Latency Filtering (LLF). Load latency filtering [17] is a mechanism introduced with Intel Core i7 processors and works in conjunction with PEBS. LLF is similar to EARs, though it is more flexible and in some aspects more informative. It works by randomly tagging load (but not store) ops, and when a load exceeds a specified threshold, it reports the linear address along with fields denoting where the data came from (e.g., local L2/L3, remote cache, local/remote DRAM). LLF is more powerful than EARs because it provides more details on the source of the data. Since it is a PEBS facility, the PC may be off by up to one instruction.

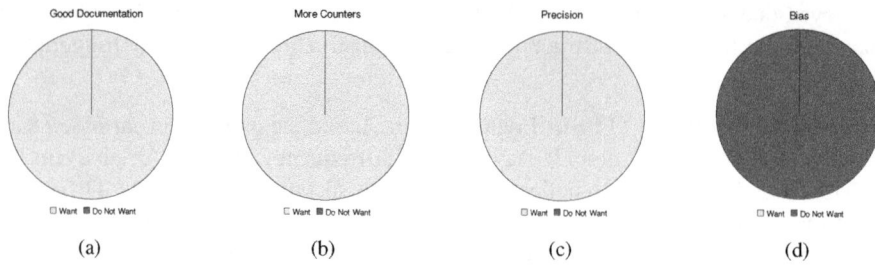

Fig. 3. Survey of HPM users (sample size = 3)

2.4   Last Branch Record (LBR)

A last-branch record is a buffer containing the most recently seen branch instructions and targets (ranging from 4 to 16 branches) [17]. It can also be configured to filter based on branch type (e.g., call, return, conditional). In conjunction with PEBS, it can be used to give the path leading up to a cache miss.

2.5   Lightweight Profiling (LWP)

Though not yet available at the time of writing, AMD has released an official specification for Lightweight Profiling [13], which represents a refreshing and radical departure from currently available hardware. LWP is configurable entirely from userspace and can be configured to generate interrupts or simply be polled. Instead of interrupting every time an an event threshold is reached, LWP uses a ring buffer so events can be processed in batch. An event record is precise; the record contains the PC responsible for generating an event. Each type of event has a unique record format (e.g., branch events have information about predictions and directions).

LWP can currently be configured to count instructions retired, branches retired, dcache misses, CPU clocks unhalted, and CPU references clocks unhalted – all simultaneously, if desired. The main limitation at this point for LWP appears to be coverage. Even events as important as TLB misses, icache misses, and FPU operations are not yet monitored.

3   Issues Facing HPM

HPM has long been an issue of contention between users and hardware designers, and all of the issues are well known (if not well quantified). In addition to discussions with our colleagues, we found the "Hardware Performance Monitor Design and Functionality" workshop [21] associated with HPCA in 2005 as well as a recent Linux kernel thread [22] to be excellent sources of information. One of the most unsettling trends we notice is that the HPM solutions have remained relatively unchanged for over a decade, yet machines have grown significantly in complexity. Since none of the insights here are new, we will instead try to motivate them with examples.

Inherent Complexity. Modern processors are inherently complex, and many interacting factors can significantly impact performance. We previously described how stack alignment can affect performance by up to 300% [7], but instruction alignment can be a significant factor as well:

- Across weekly revisions of a compiler, the variance in performance for 176.gcc on Core 2 is much higher than for Pentium 4, largely due to an increased importance in instruction alignment.
- Aligning a loop such that it will be used by the loop-stream detector (LSD) can result in 2X performance improvement.
- Branch prediction fetches are larger than instruction fetches, so in some cases a bigger alignment boundary for loops with multiple branches can reduce branch prediction bubbles for a 50% speedup on Core 2.
- The data prefetcher can be confused by IP aliasing, resulting in 8% performance drop on 189.lucas.
- Branch aliasing can result in 5-10% performance differences across an application, and 40% for a small kernel.

With subtle issues like these, analysis can take days for each one, and some can only be uncovered using a simulator. Considering that these examples only cover alignment issues in the front-end, the number of ways a program can encounter performance corner cases is frightening.

Examples like this are uncommon except when the working set is small because a few long latency memory operations usually overshadow these issues. Thanks to this, average and even advanced users rarely deal with them. In fact, most users probably do not know they exist. Even we were surprised to learn the magnitude of some of the anomalies. Because of the knowledge required for a relatively small speedup, even if HPM did make understanding these types of issues easier, it is unlikely users would spend more time focusing on them. It is still the more common issues that matter, and HPM should cater to optimizations in stages 1 and 2 first and foremost.

Precision. From an manual performance tuning standpoint, there are two critical pieces of information: the location of problem, and what it is. **Knowing the location of a problem is more important than knowing what the problem is.** IBS is nice. PEBS is not. Knowing the location of a long-latency instruction is usually enough to reason about the cause. However, simply knowing the cause of performance problems gives the programmer no indication of where to look. Think of it this way: if you manage a datacenter with thousands of nodes and dozens of applications, would you rather know the instruction that spends the most time stalled, or that cache misses are a problem for an application?

Just the name Precise Event-based Sampling (PEBS) is surreptitiously misleading. Under most conditions, a PEBS sample gives you precisely the next instruction. On variable-length ISAs, it is non-trivial just to figure out where the previous instruction actually starts. What if the previous instruction was a branch? Prior to load-latency filtering, PEBS was less trustworthy for non-scientific applications for address profiling because for instructions like `mov eax, [eax]`, the source operand is clobbered and its memory contents are given in the PEBS buffer. With the advent of the load latency record, the correct linear address is always provided. Furthermore, PEBS sampling itself can be asymmetric during bursts of retirement events – the distribution of events is not uniform, so for frequently occurring events, some instructions can receive orders of magnitude more samples than others. Furthermore, under rare conditions, PEBS is not always precise. We have learned, through a paper review of all places, that there is an undocumented mechanism to know when PEBS will be precise. The potential for nonuniform distribution and imprecision makes PEBS quite difficult to trust. Figure 3c shows users are extremely dissatisfied with imprecision.

ProfileMe was developed for Alpha to address this problem, and in our opinion it remains the most elegant solution. It may not always be helpful in solving extremely complex microarchitectural performance problems, but it addresses the simple ones in a natural way.

In many cases, the processor is a black box, and performance tuning is like playing a game of Clue; there is a room with a dead body and 10 people who could be guilty. Imprecise profiling tells us the murder weapon but never who committed the crime. Precise profiling will always give us the perpetrator and many times (but not all) the murder weapon as well. Programmers need to know the culprit, but hardware designers are much more concerned with knowing the weapon so they can devise ways to make it less potent. For programmers, simply knowing where stalls are occurring should be easy (but is not on all hardware). Knowing that, programmers can intelligently (or blindly [9]) tweak parameters until it works.

Bias. One of the trickiest issues with event-based sampling is bias, which can come in many forms. Bias is most deceptive because to even measure it we need multiple ways to measure the same data (or be able to predict it), and that is often not an option. Suppose we want to use HPM to estimate the relative frequency of execution for each basic block. One approach might be to use EBS to count INST_RETIRED, but this approach does poorly for many reasons. Sampling *skid* means the interrupt will report a PC that occurs some variable number of instructions after the instruction that triggered it. *Synchronization* effects with constant sampling periods (even when prime relative to a loop body!) can result in sample counts 3X different from those expected, and random sampling still yields sample counts with up to 50% from what they should be. Instructions that trigger long-latency stalls are subject to over counting via *aggregation effect* because they sit at the head of the instruction queue for more cycles. Consequently, the instructions in the *shadow* of a stall are under sampled. Note that these effects are common to all OoO machines.

PEBS hardware on Intel chips is an enticing alternative, but in some cases it actually has worse bias. PEBS does not support randomization of sampling intervals, so it is more susceptible to synchronization effects, and, as we previously mentioned, PEBS is not always precise and PEBS samples are not evenly distributed.

Another appealing approach is IBS, but it, too, is insufficient. Using op-sampling mode would require the user to know how many μops each instruction decodes to, and fetch-mode is biased to wrong-path instructions.

Of course, the best approach would be to use the last-branch record, but the omission of an event for taken branches retired on Core i7 prohibits this. The LBR does generally work well on Core 2, where the event exists, but there are still anomalies where some branches get significantly oversampled.

Figure 3d shows surveyed users find bias not to be a desirable feature of HPM.

Number of Events and Counters. When we developed a driver for the Pentium 4 performance counters, we cursed its arcane restrictions. We beg for forgiveness. Having 18 counter registers was great for accelerating the measurement process and allowed much better correlation of time-based samples since there was no need for interpolation. Exacerbating the problem, the number of events is growing faster than the number of counters. Two counters on Core 2 and four counters on Core i7 simply is not enough, and Figure 3b shows that 100% of users agree. However, 100% of designers say adding more counters is very challenging, so we may be at a stalemate. Perhaps a distributed approach like the Pentium 4 and proposed by others [23] is worth revisiting.

The increasing number of events can be viewed as a good thing, but it steepens the learning curve and often means multiple complex events must be counted to obtain one aggregate, more meaningful value. With so many hundreds of events, the user needs a good idea of what the problem is a priori. An oft-heard quote from internal performance tuners on more complex problems is, "we used a simulator to find the problem, but we now know could have used counter X". Machine learning is becoming increasingly popular to deal with the abundance of information available [16, 24].

Common advice is that multiplexing the counters across time will yield statistically valid results. In the absence of more counters, hardware support for multiplexing would be extremely helpful. Yet, as we have found, even a well-chosen constant sampling period results in strong bias for a single event. **There is a disturbing lack of research describing best practices for sampling and multiplexing.**

Design Philosophy. Users have long suspected that HPM features are at best a second-class citizen of processor design. Events are what is convenient to connect to a wire, rather than what is useful to understand the program. It is hard to argue, given that the designer of the Pentium Pro and Pentium 4 counters endorses this claim as well [25], although others disagree [12]. IBM's POWER4 PMU was allegedly "verified" by an intern, though its importance has increased dramatically in subsequent revisions. Either way, the fact remains that HPM will never satisfy all desires.

Perhaps it is the fault of those who are dissatisfied that are to blame; the dearth and difficulty still associated with software drivers indicates there is not a huge demand for advanced features. When users do not fully utilize current hardware, the case for return on investment may not yet be strong enough to dedicate the resources required for more robust HPM.

Verification. Also relating to design philosophy, verification of performance counters seems to be an afterthought. Even on Intel's newest x86 processor, the Core i7, most of the events relating to the L1 data cache are incorrect. There is an event on Core i7 which over counts by a factor of 3, and another on POWER5 which over counts by a factor of 4! A previous version of VMWare's replay system attempted to rely on a counter for branches retired to schedule when to intervene in native execution, but the counter was so inconsistent across processor revisions the approach was abandoned. If the standard

ISA features had defects like those found in HPM, processors would be unusable. Perhaps this is the reason more features are not architected. As it is, revealing unverified features or broken features without proper errata is worse than not revealing the features at all. Verification can be costly, so it should be focused on the most worthwhile events.

Features and Use Cases. Despite much research in the area, the two most widely used applications of HPM continue to be architectural characterization [26, 27] and application performance tuning. This is likely because the hardware best supports these applications. In fact, with respect to these two applications, we have no *fundamental* complaints about the assortment of hardware currently available, though no single processor has everything we would like and the list of secondary complaints is long.

Even with current hardware, research applications for hardware introspection are plentiful; researchers have used HPM for profile-guided optimization [24], dynamic optimization [28], adaptive power management [29], thread scheduling for shared resources [30], path profiling [31], user-aware design [32], and others.

Researchers propose going much further. Adaptive thread coscheduling would benefit from duplicated performance counters for SMT contexts (but so would everyone else). Coscheduling could also benefit from per-thread utilization metrics for each shared resource. Others call for cache-line monitors to measure locality and contention in caches, buses, and NUMA systems [33–35], using bits for memory state checking [36], using branch predictor history for path profiles [37]. Eyerman et al. propose a fundamentally different HPM architecture to collect more meaningful CPI stacks for OoO machines. Shotgun profiling [38] proposes an approach to measure the interaction cost of parallel instructions, though with the abundance of cores now available, better core-to-core communication mechanisms would probably be sufficient.

From a cynical standpoint, an academic motivation for HPM is to enable writing more papers, even if there is little rationale for the proposal to actually be implemented in hardware. Some have even proposed a specialized coprocessor to analyze ProfileMe-like data [39]. We wonder how the coprocessor's performance will be modeled. With so many divergent proposals that all look compelling in research papers, we pose this question: how are architects to decide which direction to pursue?

Parallel Programs. With respect to HPM, we do not believe parallel programs have any fundamental disadvantage relative to sequential programs. The biggest factor in parallel performance is sequential performance, but some events begin to be bigger factors. For example, cache misses limit the performance of sequential programs, but their effects are amplified for parallel programs when shared caches, buses, and interconnects become contended. The same is true for any shared resource and becomes increasingly important in SMT processors.

Issues specific to parallel programs include bus contention, false sharing, true sharing, and lock contention. With features like IBS, precise attribution of cache misses is helpful, but the real problem can be difficult to identify without value profiling. Here, we would expect load latency filtering to be quite powerful; for a cache miss, it reports the linear address accessed along with where the data came, which can be used to distinguish between true and false sharing and identify other instructions that are competing for the same cache line. Interestingly, an Intel performance expert informed us that regular PEBS sampling configured with the proper coherency-related events is more useful for identifying the false sharing that most hurts performance.

Portability and Abstraction. Aside from a small, yet increasing, set of architected counters, subsequent generations of Intel processors are deceptively diverse. For example, we can count cache misses and references on Core 2, but hits and misses on Core i7. In conjunction with the last-branch record, it is necessary to use a counter for taken branches retired (because the LBR only stores taken branches) to get unbiased samples. This exists on Core 2, but the event does not exist (they forgot?) on Core i7! On the Pentium 4, `fldcw` counts as two instructions, but on all other x86 implementations, it counts as one [40].

When counting system-wide (user and kernel) events, there may be many instructions executed between a counter interrupt and actually reading the counter value. Some systems support an atomic freeze that stops counting on an interrupt until it is reset, yet some do not. For those that do not, tools must estimate the perturbation error due to over counting.

Users are very rarely interested in monitoring exactly one platform. Typically, they are trying to collect the same type of data across a heterogeneous fleet of machines. This is true in supercomputing, this is true in data centers, and this is true for client applications. Even on a single machine, there is a steep learning curve and validation phase to gather event counts. The diversity of counters and subtle semantic differences across generations make data collection many times more challenging. IBM has recognized this problem and architected 32 counters in POWER6 that will be available on subsequent revisions.

Software Support. VTune and PTU are decent if you want to profile few applications/inputs on a single machine, but they do not scale well. Most performance tuning for Intel architectures probably occurs on Linux machines, but the vanilla kernel only supports OProfile [15]. OProfile is good for system-wide event sampling, but it does not support any features beyond basic EBS. Perfmon is a very nice interface, but it has been struggling to become part of the vanilla kernel for years. Patching and recompiling the kernel is an involved process, and it is a showstopper if the machine administrators are unwilling to do the work.

Even with good interfaces like Perfmon installed, you have to be an expert to do most things. PAPI [41] does provide some nice abstractions and an API to poll performance counters from within an application. There are group of Linux kernel developers who are trying to make the world simple and uniform with the `perf_event` project, but that approach does not capture the subtleties in the counters or expose advanced PMU features.

From another perspective, Linux users have all the luxury. FreeBSD has no support for Core i7. Windows tools for Intel x86 start and end with VTune and PTU.

We need tools that scale from the novice to the expert, and we need more than one for each layer. Lower level interfaces like Perfmon should be flexible and enable programming of every HPM feature, and they need to be open source. Low-level controls are by far the most important aspect, and it is a shame they are not better supported by the processor manufacturers. Higher level tools should abstract features so we can ask, for example, how many L2 cache misses were there? It should be able to respond with a breakdown of misses caused by instructions, by page table walks, DMA traffic, coherence traffic, etc. Some of these things may be measurable, but some may have to be guessed based on the available counters. If such a tool exists, it might provide guidance for future PMU designers to see what is most important to get right.

Virtualization. Virtualization is becoming increasingly commonplace, especially in markets like datacenters where performance analysis is paramount. However, currently, other than the LWP specification, no system we are aware of has support for virtualization.

Overhead. To read performance counters, at least one context switch to the kernel is required and may cost 1000 cycles itself. Beyond that, the cost of reading a single counter register varies greatly between microarchitectures: Opteron 1.4: 14 cycles, Athlon64: 20 cycles, Pentium IV (model 3/2): 226/146 cycles, PentiumPro: 33 cycles, PPC750: 2 cycles [42]. If they are to be read frequently, there is a high potential for perturbation and bias simply from reading the counters.

Some HPM features like LWT and LBR support buffering, but most do not. It is rarely the case that the user wants to react when a specific event happens. More often, the interrupt handler just buffers information somewhere else. Sampling overhead in general could be reduced with more HPM features supporting buffering.

User-level Access and Management. Needing root access to measure performance (or at least, install suid performance-measuring software) is a significant barrier to entry, as is needing to compile modules or recompile the Linux kernel for support for many features. AMD's LWT avoids these issues entirely by allowing full userspace control over its features. Some hardware currently allows user processes to read performance counters if they are mmapped into user memory, but user processes cannot perform any configuration or modification. Some may argue that hardware events are a security threat and can be used to exploit timing attacks in other processes. We envision few systems where such a threat really is a concern, and suspect those which are do not give users shell access to begin with. If they in fact do, features like LWT could be disabled by the kernel or BIOS. Other metrics, like instruction mix counters or last branch records, offer no threat if virtualized within a process.

Documentation. HPM documentation is critical, and the documents need to specify exactly what is getting counted. However, the documentation (and possibly, the HPM itself), seems to be outsourced to the legal department. Many times, documentation is intentionally vague to avoid liability and expectations from users. Any time we want to count something, we first develop a microbenchmark to see if the counter meets our expectations. Usually, our first attempt is wrong. It seems that many people do this, so the work is unnecessarily duplicated, and better documentation or open microbenchmarks might save everyone some effort. For Intel architectures, there are the official docs in Volume 3B of the x86 manuals, then there is the most up to date information which is hidden in a VTune. The disconnect is due to the lag time to update the official manuals. Sprunt proposes encoding HPM descriptions and specifications in XML to avoid this disconnect [43].

We have recently done some experiments trying to understand the effects of the `prefetchnta` instruction so that we can do some memory optimizations. Using some microbenchmarks, and we could not even make the cache miss numbers add up. Depending on how one counted L1 misses (there are multiple ways), different numbers are produced. One of those sets of numbers agreed with the number of L2 references, the other did not. However, the one that did not match our intuition about how many times the program should miss in the L1 cache. It seems one counter counts only misses caused by load instructions, while the other also includes misses caused by hardware page table walks. These kind of omissions are commonplace.

In another example documented by Sprunt [25], the architects event definition may not be fully understood by the designer, resulting in events that are too broken to be useful. On the P6, the architect specified to count memory references that miss the DTLB, but the designer interpreted it as count the times the DTLB is referenced, with no match. This is problematic because canceled, conditional μops for string instructions all miss the DTLB, so DTLB miss counts can be unpredictably too high.

If there is still any doubt, consider this: Figure 3a shows that 100% of people want better documentation. A plausible theory is that vague documentation is an attempt to conceal details about a chip's microarchitecture, but discussions with internal engineers reveal that their resources are no better. It is wonderful that there are events to count nearly every aspect of the processor (and off-core systems as well), but the length of event descriptions is not commensurate with their complexity. Similar events need differentiation. Obscure events need better descriptions. Broken events need errata, and the event descriptions should refer to the errata if it is in a separate location. Subtle feature limitations, like PEBS not always being precise, must be disclosed.

Improved documentation of the HPM features is not enough; for users to leverage HPM, they must know more detail about how the hardware actually works. Researchers have invested their time to reverse engineer cache attributes and policies for Core i7 that should simply be in the manual [44]. Hardware optimizations like the loop stream detector need to be well-documented if vendors would like anyone other than their own employees to take advantage of them.

Interpretation. CPI stacks are nice for identifying the biggest performance bottlenecks, but they are difficult to construct for OoO machines. The information that is available is usually in the form of ratios like last-level cache misses per cycle or branch mispredicts per instruction. For non-experts, these ratios have very little qualitative meaning; how does one know when something is "bad"? Of course, latencies can be masked, so there is not a true measure of an event's cost, but an event's documentation should provide some guidance about what ranges can be considered mildly, moderately, or highly problematic. For HPC codes, peak floating point performance is the goal, but for most other codes there is no notion of peak.

For any metric, defining a qualitative value is a challenge in itself. One approach is Intel's Platform Modeling Tool (PMT) [16] with machine learning. PMT uses many application runs to sample a large set of performance counters and uses the data to identify which events are most correlated with instruction throughput. Another approach would be to create a synthetic benchmark to stress each event and define that as a high water mark for the event. Alternately, high water marks from standard benchmarks could be used as well.

4   Opportunities and Alternatives

4.1   A Pragmatic Proposition

To quote Douglas Adams, via Robert Fowler, "their fundamental design flaws are completely hidden by their superficial design flaws" [45]. Let us return to the fundamentals.

The previous section details our grievances with many different aspects of hardware performance monitoring. Here, we propose a few tenable changes that would alleviate much of the burden in performance tuning.

One issue, trust, lies at the heart of the HPM debate, and it relates directly to each of the issues above. Features frequently have vague documentation, unforeseen bias, or are outright broken, so users are often measuring something different from what they expect. For adoption of HPM to increase broadly beyond vendors' own tools, only the reliable features should be exposed and documented along with any caveats that may exist.

Remember the Average User. A significant amount of recent research is devoted solely to collecting unbiased edge, path, and call stack profiles [31, 37, 46, 47], and one such paper even won the best paper award at PLDI 2009 [2]. This ostensibly simple feature should have long ago become a commodity, programmable and accessible from user space.

Cache, TLB, and branch misses are historically, and will continue to be, the largest performance sinks. Each of these can of course be broken down into many subcomponents, and that is the problem – it is sometimes hard for the user to decide which of the hundreds of events should be used to measure a simple thing. But it should be easy. This problem spans hardware, software, users, and documentation, so each of these groups should be involved in a solution.

In addition to precision, IBS provides average latency and flags for events like cache/TLB/branch misses. For tuning stages 1 and 2, this is incredibly powerful. Some may argue that long latency instructions are not necessarily performance bottlenecks because OoO hides latencies, but we have never met a cache miss we liked – especially a frequently occurring one.

Forget the Expert. In being able to count a plethora of events, expert users are already well-served, but experts, too, are hindered by the same challenges as average users.

Free the Software. Processor vendors have their own internal tools and drivers for controlling HPM, and they underlie tools like VTune and CodeAnalyst [48]. They should be decoupled (or the underlying tools should be documented), and they should be free and open source. **We contend that open sourcing tools and drivers will add more value to the underlying hardware than selling closed-source tools.**

Many HPM tools are easy to run, but they require the user to specify which events will be counted. Instead, there should be a default mode that requires no parameters and collects an overview of where time is spent *and* what critical architectural events occur.

Drivers like Perfmon should be finally pushed into OS kernels because installing it is a day-long chore or more. Once installed, root access should not be required to use the tools.

4.2 Feature Requests

We would be thrilled to see LWP and ProfileMe-like features offered on Intel x86 hardware. With increasingly complex hardware, instruction-based sampling could use a renovation as well. Extensions approach that allow programmable fields and filtering for instruction samples would be a killer features.

The PAPI model is very popular amongst programmers, not just for its abstraction, but because it allows caliper-style measurement of regions of code. PAPI has drawbacks, though. For small code regions, there is a relatively high overhead for system calls to read counters. Also, simply adding PAPI function calls to the code can alter register allocation, stack alignment, heap alignment, and instruction alignment, so there is potential for serious measurement perturbation. Instead of hardware, it would require compiler support to be easy to use, but we would like to see a feature that uses patching or breakpoints to perform PAPI accounting.

5 An Adventurous Approach

Consumers want hardware to collect and manage complex information, and they all want something different. Hardware designers want to count what is easily countable and have software synthesize conclusions. Clearly, the complexity must be handled somewhere. In over a decade, we have not seen any real advancement in the capabilities of HPM. At the same time, we have seen great advances in software instrumentation tools [49–53].

We propose to abandon HPM entirely in favor of a purely software profiling model. There is already some movement in this direction [54, 55]. Few people probably remember this, but DCPI/ProfileMe also used an interpretation mode to do value profiling to better understand dependences and complex interactions. Prior to DCPI [14] and Morph [56], it was done entirely this way, and we believe the shift to multicore processing makes it more feasible now than before. Techniques like bursty tracing [57, 58] and shadow profiling [59] enable long execution traces to be collected with overheads around 1%, which is comparable to current continuous profiling infrastructures.

Collecting execution traces is cheap and easy, and the real challenge lies in analyzing the traces. To the extreme, this involves a full pipeline simulation of the underlying microprocessor. For most common performance issues, simpler models of hardware will suffice.

One could even imagine a scenario where users upload execution traces to hardware vendors and the vendors' internal simulation tools are used to generate a detailed report breaking down stalls and interactions for a variety of ISA-compatible microarchitectures. In this arrangement, both parties win. The users can better tune their code, even for architectures they do not have access to. The vendor does not have to reveal the inner-workings of its design and effectively crowdsources collection of a previously unimaginable wealth of workloads to design future architectures. The workload distribution would even be biased toward those who care most about performance. If the system were to become popular, users could be given a certain number of free runs and charged for more intensive use. We anticipate customers from Wall St., datacenters, and HPC domains would pay for this type of service.

This type of thing actually happens regularly in practice. A developer with a particularly troublesome performance anomaly will send a trace (or the whole application) to an vendor's engineer for analysis. No data would be necessary with the traces, though some clients may desire very protective agreements for the instructions as well.

More realistically, we do not expect companies to publish these details, but fortunately, most performance issues are microarchitecture-independent. Hoste et al. show that a selection of architectural metrics like instruction mix, data stride patterns, and register conflicts can be used to predict relative processor performance with a 0.89 correlation coefficient [60]. In fact, much microarchitecture-specific tuning is done automatically or blindly anyway [9, 24], and the biggest issue is often data organization to benefit the memory hierarchy [11]. The variety of hardware underlying large-scale computing increases the appeal of generalized profiling.

Pure software profiling may be limited in modeling unpublished microarchitectural details, so it will have its own sources of bias. But to the user, complexity is greatly reduced. Any metrics of interest can be measured and correlated simultaneously, and precision is guaranteed. Program introspection enables heap [61] and locality analysis as well. Much more powerful analyses, like idealized execution [62–64] can also be performed. With a little cooperation from the hardware designers, even things like prefetching and subtle anomalies like those described in Section 3 can easily be modeled.

A less radical approach might employ synergy between hardware and software. HPM can be used to report issues that are too complex to model in software, precisely attribute where time is spent, and identify troublesome spots where tracing should be done. Hardware could even offer logging features to expedite tracing, especially for multithreaded programs.

6   Conclusion

HPM can provide invaluable insight into application performance, but it is unreachable, overly complex, or easily misinterpreted by many users. Volume hardware purchasers tend to also be performance experts, but even they have tremendous difficulty measuring seemingly simple information. This paper highlights the key problems with HPM from an application performance tuning perspective and proposes potential improvements. The fundamental problem with HPM today is measuring simple things is just as difficult as measuring complex things. The complexity of data collection should be commensurate with the complexity of data collected.

Acknowledgment. Many of the examples and positions in this paper were documented with the help of Zia Ansari (Intel), Lee Baugh (Intel), Mickaël Ivascot (U. de Versailles), Todd Mytkowicz (U. of Colorado), Naveen Neelakantam (U. of Illinois, Intel), Sonny Rao (IBM), Alex Shye (Northwestern, AMD), Manish Vachharajani (U. of Colorado, LineRate Systems), Stéphane Zuckerman (U. de Versailles). David Levinthal (Intel) was instrumental in keeping us honest.

References

1. Liu, L., Rus, S.: Perflint: A context sensitive performance advisor for c++ programs. In: IEEE/ACM International Symposium on Code Generation and Optimization. IEEE Computer Society, Los Alamitos (2009)
2. Tallent, N.R., Mellor-Crummey, J.M., Fagan, M.W.: Binary analysis for measurement and attributionof program performance. In: PLDI (2009)
3. Moseley, T., Connors, D.A., Grunwald, D., Peri, R.: Identifying potential parallelism via loopcentricprofiling. In: Proceedings of the 2007 International Conference on Computing Frontiers (May 2007)
4. Price, G.D., Giacomoni, J., Vachharajani, M.: Visualizing potential parallelism in sequential programs. In: PACT (2008)
5. Zilles, C.B.: Benchmark health considered harmful. SIGARCH Computer Architecture News (2001)
6. Moseley, T., Grunwald, D., Peri, R.V.: Optiscope: Performance accountability for optimizing compilers. In: CGO 2009: Proceedings of the International Symposium on Code Generation and Optimization. IEEE Computer Society, Seattle (2009)
7. Mytkowicz, T., Diwan, A., Hauswirth, M., Sweeney, P.F.: Producing wrong data without doing anything obviously wrong! In: ASPLOS (2009)
8. Moseley, T., Shye, A., Reddi, V.J., Iyer, M., Fay, D., Hodgdon, D., Kihm, J.L., Settle, A., Grunwald, D., Connors, D.A.: Dynamic run-time architecture techniques for enabling continuous optimization. In: Proceedings of the 2005 International Conference on Computing Frontiers (May 2005)
9. Knights, D., Mytkowicz, T., Sweeney, P.F., Mozer, M.C., Diwan, A.: Blind optimization for exploiting hardware features. In: Conference on Compiler Construction (2009)
10. Pan, Z., Eigenmann, R.: Fast, automatic, procedure-level performance tuning. In: PACT 2006: Proceedings of the 15th International Conference on Parallel Architectures and Compilation Techniques, pp. 173–181. ACM Press, New York (2006)
11. Whaley, C.R., Dongarra, J.J.: Automatically tuned linear algebra software. In: Supercomputing 1998: Proceedings of the 1998 ACM/IEEE Conference on Supercomputing, CDROM (1998)
12. Callister, J.: Confessions of a performance monitor hardware designer. In: Workshop on Hardware Performance Monitor Design and Functionality Colocated with HPCA (2005)
13. Amd lightweight profiling specification, http://developer.amd.com/cpu/LWP/Pages/default.aspx
14. Anderson, J.M., Berc, L.M., Dean, J., Ghemawat, S., Henzinger, M.R., Leung, S.-T.A., Sites, R.L., Vandevoorde, M.T., Waldspurger, C.A., Weihl, W.E.: Continuous profiling: where have all the cycles gone? In: SOSP 1997: Proceedings of the Sixteenth ACM Symposium on Operating Systems Principles, pp. 1–14. ACM Press, New York (1997)
15. OProfile, http://oprofile.sourceforge.net
16. Intel platform modeling tool with machine learning, http://software.intel.com/en-us/articles/intel-platform-modeling-with-machine-learning/
17. Intel64 and IA-32 Architectures Software Developer's Manual - Volume 3B, Intel Corporation
18. Dean, J., Hicks, J.E., Waldspurger, C.A., Weihl, W.E., Chrysos, G.Z.: Profileme: Hardware support for instruction-level profiling on out-of-order processors. In: International Symposium on Microarchitecture, pp. 292–302 (1997), citeseer.ist.psu.edu/dean97profileme.html

19. Drongowski, P.: Instruction-based sampling: A new performance analysis technique for amd family 10h processors (2007)
20. Intel Corporation, Intel Itanium 2 processor reference manual: For software development and optimization (May 2004)
21. Workshop on hardware performance monitor design and functionality colocated with hpca (2005), http://lacsi.rice.edu/workshops/hpca11
22. v2 of comments on performance counters for linux, pcl (2009), http://lkml.org/lkml/2009/6/16/432
23. Hunter, H.C., Nair, R.: Refining performance monitor design. In: Proceedings of the 2004 Workshop on Complexity Effective Design, WCED (2004)
24. Cavazos, J., Dubach, C., Agakov, F., Bonilla, E., O'Boyle, M.F., Fursin, G., Temam, O.: Automatic performance model construction for the fast software exploration of new hardware designs. In: International Conference on Compilers, Architecture, And Synthesis For Embedded Systems (CASES 2006) (October 2006)
25. Sprunt, B.: Performance monitoring hardware will always be a low priority, second class feature in processor designs until. In: Workshop on Hardware Performance Monitor Design and Functionality Colocated with HPCA (2005)
26. Moseley, T., Kihm, J.L., Connors, D.A., Grunwald, D.: Methods for modeling resource contention on simultaneous multithreading processors. In: Proceedings of the 2005 International Conference on Computer Design (ICCD) (October 2005)
27. Ould-Ahmed-Vall, E., Woodlee, J., Yount, C., Doshi, K.A., Abraham, S.: Using model trees for computer architecture performance analysis of software applications. In: ISPASS (2007)
28. Dai, X., Zhai, A., Hsu, W.-C., Yew, P.-C.: A general compiler framework for speculative optimizations using data speculative code motion. In: CGO 2005: Proceedings of the International Symposium on Code Generation and Optimization (2005)
29. Canturk Isci, M.M., Contreras, G.: Hardware performance counters for detailed runtime power and thermal estimations: Experiences and proposals. In: Workshop on Hardware Performance Monitor Design and Functionality Colocated with HPCA (2005)
30. Moseley, T.: Adaptive thread scheduling for simultaneous multithreading processors, Boulder, CO. (March 2006)
31. Shye, A., Iyer, M., Moseley, T., Hodgdon, D., Fay, D., Reddi, V.J., Connors, D.A.: Analyis of path profiling information generated with performance monitoring hardware. In: INTERACT 2005: Proceedings of the 9th Annual Workshop on Interaction between Compilers and Computer Architectures, pp. 34–43. IEEE Computer Society, Washington, DC (2005)
32. Shye, A., Özisikyilmaz, B., Mallik, A., Memik, G., Dinda, P.A., Dick, R.P., Choudhary, A.N.: Learning and leveraging the relationship between architecture-level measurements and individual user satisfaction. In: ISCA (2008)
33. Tikir, M.M., Buck, B.R., Hollingsworth, J.K.: What we need to be able to count to tune programs. In: Workshop on Hardware Performance Monitor Design and Functionality Colocated with HPCA (2005)
34. Tuduce, I., Gross, T.: Efficient collection of information on the locality of accesses. In: Workshop on Hardware Performance Monitor Design and Functionality Colocated with HPCA (2005)
35. Brantley, B.: The NUMA challenge. In: Workshop on Hardware Performance Monitor Design and Functionality Colocated with HPCA (2005)
36. Rishi, A., Masamitsu, J.A.: Us patent no. 5953530. method and apparatus for run-time memory access checking and memory leak detection
37. Conte, T.M., Patel, B.A., Menezes, K.N., Cox, J.S.: Hardware-based profiling: an effective Technique for profile-driven optimization. Int. J. Parallel Programming (1996)
38. Fields, B.A., Bodik, R., Hill, M.D., Newburn, C.J.: Interaction cost and shotgun profiling. ACM Trans. Architecture Code Optimization (2004)

39. Zilles, C.B., Sohi, G.S.: A programmable co-processor for profiling. In: HPCA (2001)
40. Weaver, V.M., McKee, S.A.: Can hardware performance counters be trusted? In: IISWC (2008)
41. Mucci, P., Smeds, N., Ekman, P.: Performance monitoring with papi using the performance Application programming interface. Dr. Dobb's (2005), http://www.ddj.com/developmenttools/184406109
42. Mucci, P.: Towards a flexible and realistic hardware performance monitor infrastructure. In: Workshop on Hardware Performance Monitor Design and Functionality Colocated with HPCA (2005)
43. Sprunt, B.: Managing the complexity of performance monitoring hardware: The brink andabyss Approach. Int. J. High Perform. Comput. Appl. (2006)
44. Daniel Molka, R.S., Hackenberg, D., Mller, M.S.: Memory performance and cache coherency effects on an intel nehalem multiprocessor system
45. Fowler, R.: Performance hardware if i ran the world. In: Workshop on Hardware Performance Monitor Design and Functionality Colocated with HPCA (2005)
46. Levin, R., Newman, I., Haber, G.: Complementing missing and inaccurate profiling using a minimum cost circulation algorithm. In: Stenström, P., Dubois, M., Katevenis, M., Gupta, R., Ungerer, T. (eds.) HiPEAC 2007. LNCS, vol. 4917, pp. 291–304. Springer, Heidelberg (2008)
47. Todd Mytkowicz, D.C., Diwan, A.: Inferred call path profiling. In: OOPSLA (2009)
48. AMD Code Analyst, http://developer.amd.com/cpu/CodeAnalyst/Pages/default.aspx
49. Luk, C.-K., Cohn, R., Muth, R., Patil, H., Klauser, A., Lowney, G., Wallace, S., Reddi, V.J., Hazelwood, K.: Pin: building customized program analysis tools with dynamic instrumentation. In: PLDI 2005: Proceedings of the 2005 ACM SIGPLAN Conference on Programming Language Design and Implementation, pp. 190–200. ACM Press, New York (2005)
50. Nethercote, N., Seward, J.: Valgrind: A framework for heavyweight dynamic binary instrumentation. In: Proceedings of ACM SIGPLAN 2007 Conference on Programming Language Design and Implementation (PLDI 2007), San Diego, California, USA (2007)
51. Dyninst: An application program interface (api) for runtime code generation, http://www.dyninst.org
52. Bruening, D.L.: Efficient, transparent, and comprehensive runtime code manipulation. Ph.D. dissertation, Cambridge, MA, USA (2004)
53. Magnusson, P.S., Christensson, M., Eskilson, J., Forsgren, D., Hllberg, G., Hgberg, J., Larsson, F., Moestedt, A., Werner, B.: Simics: A full system simulation platform. Computer (2002)
54. Valgrind's tools suite, http://valgrind.org/info/tools.html
55. Hoste, K., Eeckhout, L.: Microarchitecture-independent workload characterization. IEEE Micro 27(3), 63–72 (2007)
56. Zhang, X., Wang, Z., Gloy, N.C., Chen, J.B., Smith, M.D.: System support for automated profiling and optimization. In: SOSP (1997)
57. Hirzel, M., Chilimbi, T.: Bursty tracing: A framework for low-overhead temporal profiling. In: 4th ACM Workshop on Feedback-Directed and Dynamic Optimization, FDDO-4 (2001), citeseer.ist.psu.edu/hirzel01bursty.html
58. Arnold, M., Ryder, B.G.: A framework for reducing the cost of instrumented code. In: SIGPLAN Conference on Programming Language Design and Implementation, pp. 168–179 (2001), citeseer.ist.psu.edu/arnold01framework.html
59. Moseley, T., Shye, A., Reddi, V.J., Grunwald, D., Peri, R.V.: Shadow profiling: Hiding instrumentation costs with parallelism. In: CGO 2007: Proceedings of the International Symposium on Code Generation and Optimization. IEEE Computer Society, San Jose (2007)

60. Hoste, K., Phansalkar, A., Eeckhout, L., Georges, A., John, L.K., Bosschere, K.D.: Performance prediction based on inherent program similarity. In: PACT (2006)
61. Shaham, R., Kolodner, E.K., Sagiv, M.: Heap profiling for space-efficient java. In: PLDI 2001: Proceedings of the ACM SIGPLAN 2001 Conference on Programming Language Design and Implementation (2001)
62. Djoudi, L., Barthou, D., Carribault, P., Lemuet, C., Acquaviva, J.-T., Jalby, W.: Exploring application performance: a new tool for a static/dynamic approach. In: Los Alamos Computer Science Institute Symp., Santa Fe, NM (October 2005)
63. Iyer, M., Ashok, C., Stone, J., Vachharajani, N., Connors, D.A., Vachharajani, M.: Finding parallelism for future epic machines. In: Proceedings of the Fourth Workshop on Explicitly Parallel Instruction Computer Architectures and Compiler Technology, EPIC (2005)
64. Fursin, G., O'Boyle, M., Temam, O., Watts, G.: Fast and accurate method for determining a lower bound on execution time. Concurrency: Practice and Experience 16(2-3), 271–292 (2004)

An Efficient Architectural Design of Hardware Interface for Heterogeneous Multi-core System

Xiongli Gu[1], Jie Yang[1], Xiamin Wu[2], Chunming Huang[1], and Peng Liu[1,*]

Department of Information Science and Electronic Engineering,
[1] Zhejiang University, Hangzhou, 310027, China
[2] UTStarcom Co.Ltd., Hangzhou, 310053, China
{guxiongli2010,mckeyyang,alonewoo}@gmail.com,
hcm198611@yahoo.com.cn, liupeng@zju.edu.cn

Abstract. How to manage the message passing among inter processor cores with lower overhead is a great challenge when the multi-core system is the contemporary solution to satisfy high performance and low energy demands in general and embedded computing domains. Generally speaking, the networks-on-chip connects the distributed multi-core system. It takes charge of message passing which including data and synchronization message among cores. The size of most data transmission is typically large enough that it remains strongly bandwidth-bound. The synchronization message is very small which is primarily latency bound. Thus the separated networks-on-chip are needed to transmit the above two types of message. In this paper we focus on the network for the transmission of synchronization messages. A hardware module – message passing unit (MPU) is proposed to manage the synchronization message passing for the heterogeneous multi-core system. Compared with the original single network approach, this solution reduces the run-time object scheduling and synchronization overhead effectively, thereby, improving the whole system performance.

Keywords: data flow graph (DFG); multi-core system; parallel programming.

1 Introduction

Nowadays multi-core system becomes a popular solution for obtaining higher performance, short developing period, and low cost in the application system design. The multi-core system has its advantages but it also brings new problems: the run-time concurrency and synchronization among tasks are crucial if the high system performance is pursued [1].

We use the data flow graph (DFG) programming model to guide the parallel programming [2] in our work. The compiled inter-processor tasks are statically mapped

---

* Corresponding author.

E. Altman and W. Shi (Eds.): NPC 2011, LNCS 6985, pp. 313–323, 2011.
© IFIP International Federation for Information Processing 2011

to the distributed processors and the synchronization message passing among inter processors are needed for the parallel running of tasks on different processors. Usually the size of synchronization message is small which shall be transmitted among processors with lower latency. But the traditional networks-on-chip is usually designed for the data transmission and is not efficient to manage the synchronization message passing among inter cores.

In this paper we suggest a hardware module called message passing unit (MPU) which transmits the scheduling and synchronization message for the lightweight distributed multi-core system without shared memory. The aim of this work is to reduce the inter processor communication overhead. We consider that NoC shall not only play the role of data transmission but also help to manage part of the application scheduling and synchronization work for the multi-core system. The constructs in the application program for handling coordination and synchronization between the threads are transferred to the control signals that shall be sent and/or received by the processors during runtime. The control signals are short and they shall be transmitted fast with less overhead. If they are transmitted in the same network as data the average overhead is expensive which is usually unacceptable. So in the NoC design space we specify two sub layers in the link/network layer: the data transmission sub layer manages the data communication. The control sub layer - MPU manages the control signal flow and messages passing for handling the coordination and synchronization among threads which is efficient for the heterogeneous multi-core system.

The rest of the paper is organized as follows: Section 2 gives an overview of related work. Section 3 explains our MPU proposal. Section 4 describes the implementation details of object scheduling and synchronization flow. Section 5 discusses the evaluation methodology and gives the evaluated results. Finally conclusions are made.

2 Related Work

In the literature, there are some prior work have been done to accelerate the synchronization message passing among inter cores. In [3], the MultiFlex uses the object request broker (ORB) to connect client task to the server task. The aim is to accelerate the scheduling and synchronization message passing among tasks. In [4], the MLCA adopts universal register file (URF) to exchange the scheduling and synchronization message passing among inter-core tasks. But the ORB and URF have the same problem: they transmit the scheduling and synchronization message in the general NoC. The general NoC is designed for data transmission among inter cores, which usually has large bit-width and the complicated protocol to assure the correct data transmission. As a result, the complicated protocol will bring overheads. Thus the traditional NoC is not efficient to manage the small size synchronization message passing among inter-core tasks. In [5], DMA based message passing mechanism is applied in Cheng's work to transmit the synchronization messages among inter-core tasks which is also inefficient for the transmission of synchronization message.

3 Construct of MPU

3.1 Application Model

Before describing the proposed MPU, the application model is firstly introduced. The tasks of a data-driven workload can be modeled as a data flow graph.

Definition 1: A *data flow graph* (*DFG*) [6] is a directed graph DFG(*V, E, D*), where each node $n_i \in V$ represents a task and a directed edge $e_k=(n_i, n_j) \in E$ represents the communication between nodes n_i and n_j.

The tasks are mapped onto processors statically at compile time. All tasks are executed in a self-timed manner [7] as follows: a task can be invoked if (1) it receives the data from all its predecessors and (2) its output data buffers are valid. The above two operations are based on message passing mechanism. So the MPU shall manage the message passing for these two operations of message passing architecture. The tasks are executed atomically and in this paper we define the atomic task as object.

3.2 MPU Structure

A hardware/software implementation for the object scheduling, synchronization and data transmission between objects is proposed. Essentially the function of real-time operating system (RTOS) task/thread management is partly realized in hardware, which is named message passing unit (MPU) and situated in the link/network layer of NoC. As described in Section 1, MPU is also the control sub net of NoC, which takes advantage of the multi-core system's characteristics and transmits the control signals and messages for object scheduling and synchronization efficiently.

The task/thread management is the controller of the scheduler. The producer processor informs MPU that its object execution has been completed and then MPU wakes up the consumer objects to start processing the incoming data. This message passing mechanism realized in the control sub net guides the scheduling and synchronization of the different objects. The DMA tasks are also set by MPU to transfer the data between the producer and consumer objects.

3.2.1 MPU Hardware Architecture

The hardware module of MPU supports four functions, (1)receive and response to the producer object information, (2)wake up the available consumer objects for execution, (3)synchronize the different objects execution, and (4)initialize the DMA tasks for data transmission between the different objects. The hardware block diagram of MPU is

An object scoreboard entry

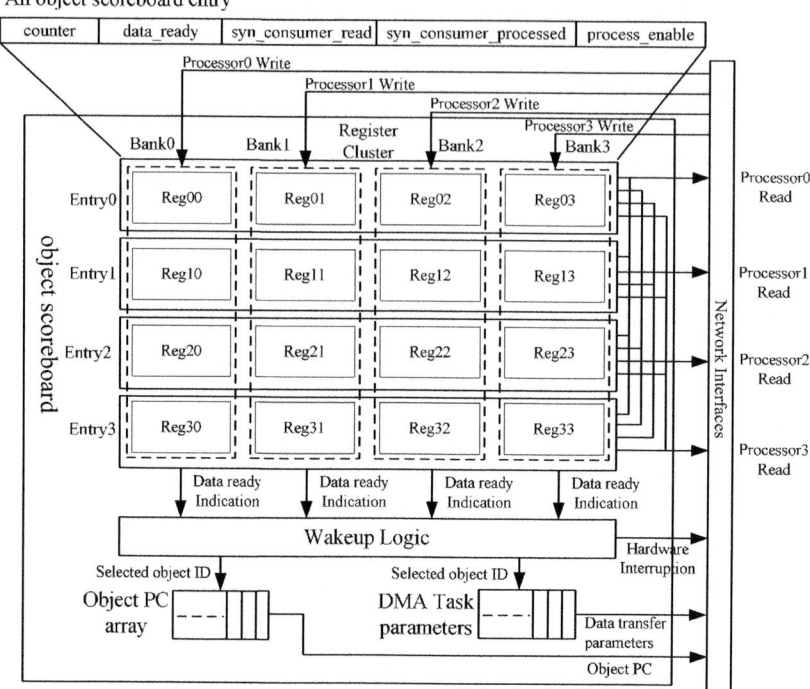

Fig. 1. Block diagram of MPU hardware

illustrated in Fig. 1, which consists of four parts: an object score board, a wakeup logic, an object program counter (PC) array, and a DMA task parameters buffer.

(1) The object scoreboard records the status of objects which are running or pending in the multi-core system. It is the kernel part for message interchange. Each processor in the multi-core system has one corresponding entry (in Fig. 1 it is supposed that the system has four processors) in the object scoreboard, which records the status of the objects assigned to this processor. The length of entry is decided by the maximum number of objects that can be mapped to the processor. Each processor or object can write data in one bank of register cluster, and each processor (or object) can read every entry of the register cluster. So the message passing among tasks are realized in this way. Each entry includes five fields: counter, data_ready, syn_consumer_read, syn_consumer_processed, and process_enable.

i) Counter field

The counter field records the input data port number of the objects allocated on this processor.

ii) Data_ready field
This field is set by the related producer objects allocated in the other processors, which is used to inform the consumer objects that the input data has been ready.

iii) Syn_consumer_read field
The syn_consumer_read field is designed to realize the synchronization for data reading.

iv) Syn_consumer_processed field
This field is served as the synchronization point to assure the synergistic working of the producer and consumer objects pair in the multi-core system.

v) Process_enable field
In our execution model the object shall be executed atomically. When one object is in its execution, the other objects cannot interrupt it. This is realized by tag set in the process_enable field.

(2) The wakeup logic selects the available objects for execution.

(3) The object program counter array records the starting addresses of objects.

(4) The DMA task parameter buffer is used to store the DMA operation parameters which the global memory address, the local memory address, the data length and the data format are set in its entries. Directors call for the DMA operation when the input data is ready.

3.2.2   Operating System Interface for MPU

We design four functions in RTOS for MPU to manage the task/thread running of multi-core system. These functions include *Write_MPU()*, *Syn_consumer_read()*, *Syn_consumer_processed()*, and *Check_MPU()*.

(1) The *Write_MPU* function is used by the director of producer object to set and clear its consumer object's data ready fields in the entry of object scoreboard.

(2) The *Syn_consumer_read* function is called by the director of consumer object to set its syn_consumer_read field of the object scoreboard.

(3) The *Syn_consumer_processed* function is used by the director of consumer object to clear its syn_consumer_processed field.

(4) The *Check_MPU* function is applied to check the object status in an entry of object scoreboard.

These four functions constitute main part of the task/thread management of RTOS, which handles the objects operation in the multi-core system.

4   Object Scheduling and Synchronization Flow

The scheduling and synergistic synchronization management for the running of the parallel program are partly performed by the hardware MPU and partly by software - the director in RTOS. The hardware MPU manages the object waken-up and part of the operation of synergistic synchronization for the objects execution in the multi-core

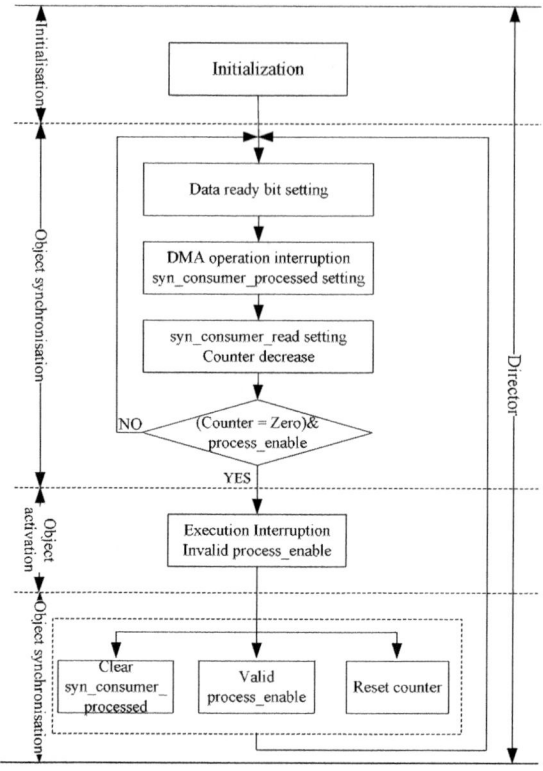

Fig. 2. MPU scheduling and synchronization flow

system. After the object scoreboard entries have been set by the producer object which completed its execution, the DMA operation will be called first to transfer the produced output data to the local memories of the consumer objects. Then the consumer objects which have all the input data ready can be selected for execution by the wakeup logic. The whole flow includes the following steps.

(1) The syn_consumer_processed bit becomes unavailable after the data ready bit has been set. The MPU sends the DMA operation interruption signal to the corresponding consumer object director to initiate the data transfer between the producer and consumer objects. When the DMA operation is over, the director of consumer object will set syn_consumer_read bit and decrease the number by one in the corresponding counter. Later the data ready bit will be cleared by the producer object.

(2) The wakeup logic scans the counters to find out the ready objects for execution. If the processor of the ready object is free (process_enable bit is available) the highest priority ready object will be activated, MPU sends execution interruption signal to the

corresponding processor. Then this processor fetches the program from the address indicated by the PC array.

(3) After the scheduled object finishes its execution the result data will be written to the global memory and its consumer objects' entries in the object score board will be set if they have completely processed the former produced data (all the syn_consumer_processed bits of its consumer objects are cleared). Then this producer object's syn_consumer_processed bit is cleared, process_enable is reset to valid and the counter is reset to its input data number by hardware.

Thus it means that the parallel program has finished its execution for one batch of its input data, the process mentioned above will be repeated cyclically for the successive batches of the input data. The MPU scheduling flow is depicted in Fig. 2.

5   Experimental Results

5.1   Evaluation Methodology

In order to evaluate the proposed MPU performance two applications – FFT program [8] and eigenvalue of matrix – Jacobi algorithm [9] program are adopted in the experiment. The experimental platform integrates one 32-bit integer RISC core - RISC32E [10] and eight 32-bit integer DSPs - MediaDSP3200 [11-12]. A 3x3 mesh topology NoC connects them and the DMA engine is also included. Each core has a local memory and the SDRAM is used as the global data buffer for the application. Each DSP has one allocated director and RTOS is running on the RISC processor. The MPU and software directors (proxy of RTOS) manage the object scheduling and synchronization for this multi-core system.

5.2   The Fast Fourier Transform (FFT)

The fast Fourier transform (FFT) is the fast algorithm for DFT and one of the most popular algorithm is the Cooley-Turkey algorithm which is written as below:

$$X[k_1,k_2]=\sum_{n_2=0}^{N_2-1}W_{N_2}^{n_2k_2}\left(\underbrace{W_N^{n_2k_1}\sum_{n_1=0}^{N_1-1}x[n_1,n_2]W_{N_1}^{n_1k_1}}_{\underbrace{N_1\text{ - point DFT transfer}}_{x[n_2,k_1]}}\right)=\underbrace{\sum_{n_2=0}^{N_2-1}W_{N_2}^{n_2k_2}\overline{x}[n_2,k_1]}_{N_2\text{ - point DFT transfer}}$$

$$n=N_2n_1+n_2\begin{cases}0\le n_1\le N_1-1\\0\le n_2\le N_2-1\end{cases},k=k_1+N_1k_2\begin{cases}0\le k_1\le N_1-1\\0\le k_2\le N_2-1\end{cases},N=N_1N_2.$$

In the experiment 64-point FFT is applied as the test algorithm. The 64-point FFT on platform is arranged as $N_1=N_2=8$ and Fig.3 shows its parallel programming process and synchronizations among objects.

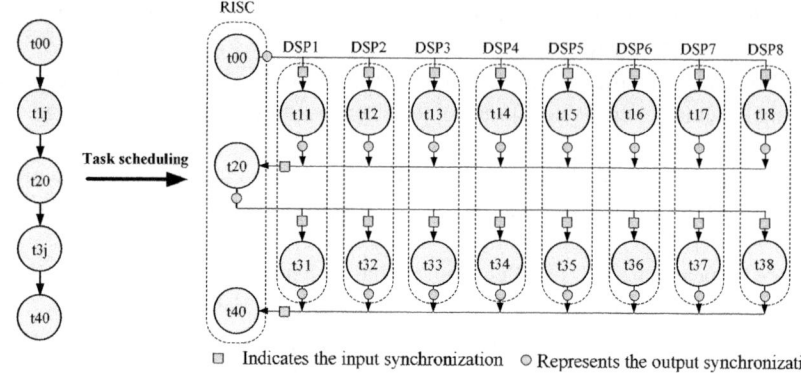

□ Indicates the input synchronization ○ Represents the output synchronization

(a) task graph   (b) mapped graph

Fig. 3. Parallel programming process and synchronizations in FFT

1) The object t_{00} is the predecessor for the inter-processor objects t_{1j} (j=1...8), which calculates the indexes for original data. It is allocated to the control RISC.

2) The objects t_{1j} (j=1...8) calculate the inner summation algorithm of the

$$\text{FFT} \sum_{n1=0}^{N_1-1} x[n_1,n_2] W_{N_1}^{n_1k_1}$$ by using the FFT algorithm. The objects are allocated to DSPs.

3) The object t_{20} calculates the $W_N^{n_2k_1}$ which multiplies by input data and finishes the data permutation operation from the order of $x[k_1,n_2]$ to $x[n_2,k_2]$. It is allocated to the control RISC.

4) The objects t_{3j} (j=1...8) calculate the summation algorithm of the

$$\text{FFT} \sum_{n2=0}^{N_2-1} W_{N_2}^{n_2k_2} \overline{x}[n_2,k_2]$$ by using the FFT algorithm. The objects are allocated to

DSPs.

5) The object t_{40} manages the output data permutation to the frequency domain parameter and is allocated in control RISC.

Table 3. FFT experimental result

Overhead Scheduler	RTOS kernel on RISC(Kbytes)	Director on processor(Kbytes)	Kernel delay/ total execution time (cycles)
Software Director	10	1.884	6716/21299
MPU	9	0.584	1435/16018

The experimental results are shown in Table 3. From Table 3 we can see that the MPU solution has less memory space requirement for RTOS kernel and directors. It takes an average time consumption of 16018 cycles for one time 64-point FFT. The kernel delay for the scheduling and synchronization of MPU approach takes up 8.96% and for software director the percentage is 31.53%. Thus the MPU efficiently reduces the kernel delay for the multi-core system which improves the system efficiency by 24.79%.

5.3   Eigenvalue of Matrix

The eigenvalue λ of matrix $\mathbf{A}$ is defined as $\mathbf{Au} = \lambda\mathbf{u}$, where $\mathbf{A}$ is an n x n matrix, λ is a real number and $\mathbf{u}$ is the n dimensional characteristic vector of matrix $\mathbf{A}$. The Jacobi matrix algorithm is applied to solve this problem. In experiment a 64*64 matrix is applied as the test algorithm. The Fig. 4 shows its parallel programming process and the synchronizations among objects.

1) The object t_{00} assigns the matrix coefficients of $\mathbf{A}$ to the DSPs, which is the predecessor of objects t_{1j} (j=1...8). It is allocated to control RISC.

2) The objects t_{1j} (j=1...8) divide the assigned coefficients into upper diagonal and lower diagonal classes. They are the predecessors of object t_{20} which are allocated to DSPs.

3) The thread t_{20} finds the maximum value from the collected biggest values, which is the predecessor of objects t_{60} and t_{3j}. It is allocated to control RISC.

4) The objects t_{3j} (j=1...8) calculate the tangent of rotating angle θ of hyper plane (g, h), cos θ and sin θ, which are the predecessors of objects t_{5j} (j=1...8) and are allocated to DSPs.

5) The object t_{40} broadcasts the matrix coefficients of row g and column h to the DSPs, which is the predecessor of objects t_{5j} (j=1...8). It is allocated to control RISC.

6) The objects t_{5j} (j=1...8) performs multiplication of the former result ($\mathbf{P}_{gh}^{(1)}$ $\mathbf{P}_{gh}^{(2)}...\mathbf{P}_{gh}^{(k-2)}$) by $\mathbf{P}_{gh}^{(k-1)}$, which are the predecessors of t_{1j} and are allocated to DSPs.

7) The object t_{60} get the final results, which is allocated to control RISC.

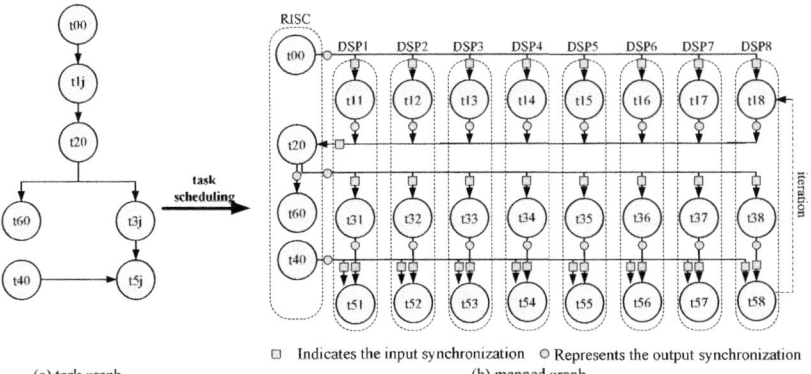

(a) task graph   (b) mapped graph

Fig. 4. Parallel programming process and synchronizations in Jacobi matrix algorithm

Table 4. Jacobi matrix algorithm experimental result

Overhead Scheduler	RTOS kernel on RISC(Kbytes)	Director on processor(Kbytes)	Kernel delay/ total execution time (cycles)
Software Director	10.298	2.182	15870/59182
MPU	9.494	0.974	5633/48945

The eigenvalue of matrix's result is shown in Table 4. Similarly, the memory space requirement of MPU is less than the software director's. The one-time 64*64 Jacobi matrix algorithm calculation needs 48945 cycles so that the kernel delay of MPU approach takes up about 11.51% of the whole time consumption and for software director the percentage is 26.82%. Thus the MPU scheme reduces the kernel delay which improves the system efficiency by 17.30%.

5.4   Physical Parameters of MPU

The hardware cost of MPU depends on the scale of multi-core system and the maximum number of threads/objects which are allocated on the processors. Here the scale of MPU is for nine processors multi-core system so that there are nine entries in the object scoreboard. For a limited number of threads exploited in the program it is supposed that each processor has no more than four threads/objects. In the multi-core system each object may have maximum eight producers and eight consumers so every object needs 27-bit for the entry. At the same time a 32-bit program counter and a 128-bit DMA task parameter buffer are needed for one object. So a 187-bit width hardware register is needed for one object in total. The 3x3 mesh topology NoC is used which the channel width is 64-bit and the depth of the FIFO is 8. We synthesize the MPU module and NoC module using Synopsys v-2003.6 and the TMSC90 CMOS process technology. The physical parameters of MPU and NoC are listed in Table 5. From Table 5 we can see that the MPU module can work at the NoC frequency and the area cost of MPU takes up 14.5% of the whole NoC area.

Table 5. Physical parameters of MPU and NoC (TSMC90: worst case, voltage 1.08v, temperature 125°C)

Parameter Component	Delay (ns)	Frequency (MHz)	Gate count	Dynamic power (mW)
MPU	0.85	1176	97096	6.42
NoC	1.30	769	669634	80.82

6 Conclusion

The hardware/software approach – message passing unit interface offers an efficient way to manage the object scheduling and synchronization for the multi-core system to reduce the communication overhead. Compared with the software director, it not only cut down the average delay for object scheduling and synchronization but also reduces the code size for RTOS and director, which is usually important for the limited memory space of the embedded system. The physical parameters imply that the hardware MPU module has the characteristic of relatively higher frequency and small area. Compared with the software approach the MPU approach improves the system efficiency by 24.79% in FFT application and 17.30% in Jacobi matrix algorithm with the hardware area increase of 14.5%.

Acknowledgment. This work is supported by NSFC under grant 60873112.

References

1. Mignolet, J.-Y., Baert, R., Ashby, T.J., Avasare, P., Jang, H.-O., Son, J.C.: MPA: parallelizing an application onto a multicore platform made easy. IEEE MICRO 29(3), 31–39 (2009)
2. Robert, G., Babb II: Parallel processing with large grain data flow techniques. Computer 17(7), 55–61 (1984)
3. Paulin, P.G., Pilkington, C., Langevin, M., Bensoudane, E., Lyonnard, D., Benny, O., Lavigueur, B., Lo, D., Beltrame, G., Gagne, V., Nicolescu, G.: Parallel programming models for a multiprocessor SoC platform applied to networking and multimedia. IEEE Transactions on Very Large Scale Integration (VLSI) Systems 14(7), 667–680 (2006)
4. Abdelrahman, T., Abdelkhalek, A., Aydonat, U.: The MLCA: a solution paradigm for parallel programmable SoCs. In: IEEE North-East Workshop on Circuits and Systems, pp. 253–253 (2006)
5. Cheng, X.M., Yao, Y.B., Zhang, Y.X., Liu, P., Yao, Q.D.: An object oriented model scheduling for Media-SoC. Journal of Electronics (CHINA) 26(2), 244–251 (2009)
6. Sinnen, O.: Task scheduling for parallel systems, pp. 60–61. John Wiley & Sons press, New Jersey (2007)
7. Bekooij, M., Hoes, R., Moreira, O., Poplavko, P., Pastrnak, M., Mesman, B., Mol, J., Stuijk, S., Gheorghita, V., Meerbergen, J.V.: Dataflow analysis for real-time embedded multiprocessor system design. In: Dynamic and Robust Streaming in and Between Connected Consumer-Electronic Device, pp. 81–108. Springer, Dordrecht (2006)
8. Cooley, J.W., John, W.T.: An algorithm for the machine calculation of complex Fourier series. Mathematics of Computation 19(90), 297–301 (1965)
9. Golub, G.H., van der Vorst, H.A.: Eigenvalue computation in the 20th century. Journal of Computational and Applied Mathematics 123(1/2), 35–65 (2000)
10. Xiao, Z.B., Liu, P., Yao, Y.B., Yao, Q.D.: Optimizing pipeline for a RISC processor with multimedia extension. ISA. Journal of Zhejiang University-Science A 7(2), 269–274 (2006)
11. Liu, P., Yao, Q.D., Li, D.X.: 32-bit media digital signal processor. China Patent ZL200410016753.8 (2004)
12. Shi, C., Wang, W.D., Zhou, L., Gao, L., Liu, P., Yao, Q.D.: 32b RISC/DSP media processor: MediaDSP3201. In: Embedded Processors for Multimedia and Communications II. SPIE, vol. 5683, pp. 43–52 (January 2005)

Evaluations on Effectiveness of Bump-Slot over DAP-NAD-Based Tactical Wideband Wireless Networks[*]

Sewon Han and Byung-Seo Kim

Dept. of Computer and Information Communications Engineering, Hongik University,
300 Shinan-ri, Jochiwon-ub, Yeongi-gun,
Chungcheongnam-do, Korea
hansewon@gmail.com, jsnbs@hongik.ac.kr

Abstract. MIL-SD-188-220 standard has specified the operations and functions of narrowband-based tactical networks. While the conventional tactical networks have mainly dealt with voice and short message data services, the future tactical networks are evolving towards broadband and multimedia-enabled wireless Ad-Hoc networks. Therefore, this paper evaluates a network access method of the standard from the wideband network perspective, not narrowband perspective. In this paper, Deterministic Adaptable Priority Net Access Delay (DAP-NAD), one of the channel access methods specified in MIL-STD-188-220D with Change 1 standard, is simulated and evaluated over Wideband Networking Waveform–like environments in terms of Urgent precedence traffic. The simulation results conclude that unlike the narrowband environments, Bump-Slot, which is a unique time slot specified by the standard, does not play a critical role to enhance the performance in transmitting Urgent traffic over the wideband networks.

Keywords: MIL-STD-188-220, Tactical networks, DAP-NAD, Bump-Slot.

1 Introduction

MIL-STD-188-220 standard specifies physical, data link, and intranet protocol layers for tactical communication devices using narrowband channels [1]. The standard has been versioned up from MIL-STD-188-220A to MIL-STD-188-220D with Change 1 (Hereinafter, MIL-STD-188-220 standard means MIL-STD-188-220D with Change 1 throughout the paper). In general, main traffic over tactical networks are voices and short messages. However, because the future tactical environment is moving towards network-centric warfare, the tactical communications and networks are also evolved to obtain and to utilize various types of tactical information through multimedia traffic including voice, video, and a large-sized data traffic over wideband

---

[*] This research was supported in part by the National Research Foundation of Korea (NRF) grant funded by the Korea government (MEST) (2011-0005360) and in part by the MKE (The Ministry of Knowledge Economy), Korea, under the ITRC (Information Technology Research Center) support program supervised by the NIPA (National IT Industry Promotion Agency" (NIPA-2011- (C1090-1121-0011)).

E. Altman and W. Shi (Eds.): NPC 2011, LNCS 6985, pp. 324–333, 2011.

communication channels. Therefore, the networks provide the better awareness on the current battlefield situations and as a consequence, the better command and control are achieved. Furthermore, the network topologies are evolving to be flexible and scalable without any infrastructure and centralized nodes like mobile ad-hoc networks. In the summary, unlike narrowband infrastructure-based conventional tactical networks in the past, the future tactical networks have been evolved as wideband wireless ad-hoc networks with multimedia services.

This trend of the future tactical networks is proved by Joint Tactical Radio Systems (JTRS) which has been planned to be the next-generation voice-and-data radio used by the U.S. military in the field operations [2]. JTRS is a wideband mobile ad-hoc network with a software-defined radio technology to work with various military and civilian radio. Fig. 1 shows tan overview of JTRS network architectures [3]. JTRS specifies several types of waveforms. One of the forms is Wideband Networking Waveform (WNW). WNW has been proposed and developed to provide the wider channel bandwidth and the higher data rate to the tactical wireless networks [4]. Based on the specification provided by Spectrum company in [4], WNW support the high data rates from 100 Kbps to 23Mbps using OFDM-based physical layer over 1.2 ~ 10MHz bandwidths as shown in [4]. Besides, Software Defined Radio (SDR) and Cognitive Radio (CR) are also extensively researched for the opportunistic communications over scarce frequencies. While the efforts to enhance the physical layer for the tactical networks has mainly focused in the past decade such as WNW, SDR, and CR, the data link protocol to efficiently deliver the data to multi users is not extensively studied.

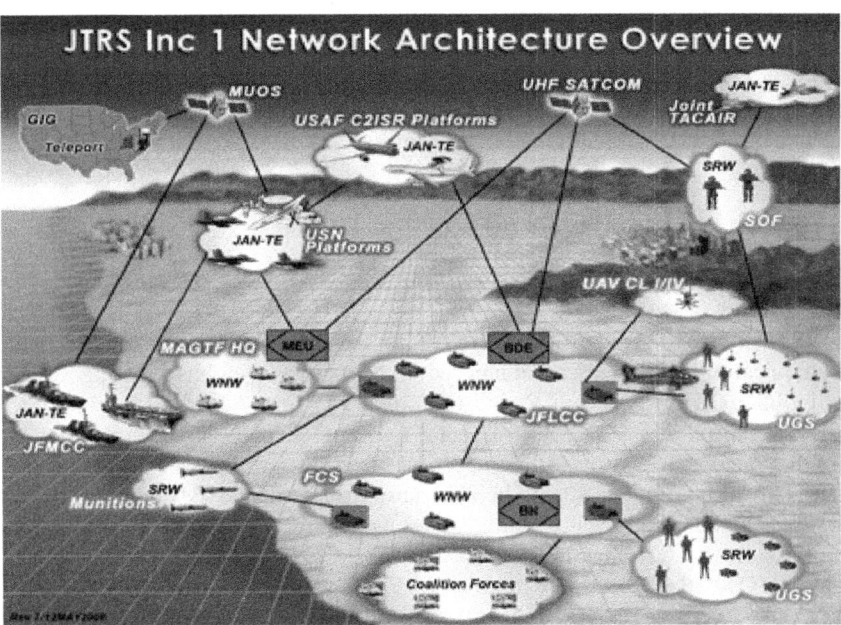

Fig. 1. An overview of JTRS networks architecture [3]

The researches in the past regarding the data link protocols based on different versions of MIL-STD-188-220 standards have used the network parameters for old-type tactical communication environments, not for the future environment such as wide bandwidth, high data rate, and multimedia traffic types [5]-[12]. Recently, [13] has compared two of 6 channel access methods specified in MIL-STD-188-220 standard to Carrier Sense Multiple Access and Collision Avoidance (CSMA/CA) protocol over IEEE802.11a-based physical layer which is 20MHz wideband channel. The two methods of MIL-STD-188-220 standard are Random net access delay (R-NAD) and Deterministic adaptable priority net access delay (DAP-NAD). The research shows that while R-NAD has worse performance than CSMA/CA protocol has, DAP-NAD has better performance than CSMA/CA protocol has. However, the paper does not analyze the behavior of the DAP-NAD method itself over the sideband systems.

Even though the channel access methods in MIL-STD-188-220 standard are designed for the old-fashioned narrowband systems, it is needed to evaluate the methods for the future tactical wideband systems. The reason is because using the methods over the WNW may have advantages in terms of reducing the cost to develop new protocols, providing interoperability new communication devices with the old devices, and simplifying communication specifications over all tactical communication devices.

Therefore, this paper evaluates the DAP-NAD channel access method over the wideband network scenarios and clams a issue using a Bump-Slot which is a time slot for a specific purposes mentioned in Section 2.2.

In this paper, Section 2 introduces the specifications on the data link protocols specified in MIL-STD-188-220 standard and reviews the previous researches regarding on the protocol. Particularly, one of medium access control (MAC) methods in the standard is illustrated in details. Furthermore, a potential issue is claimed. In Section 3, DAP-NAD method is simulated and the claimed issue is evaluated through the simulation results. Finally, the conclusions are made in Section 4.

2   MIL-STD-188-220D with Change 1

2.1   Network Access Control (NAC)

MIL-STD-188-220 standard defines NAC to arbitrate the transmissions of multiple communication nodes. NAC is composed of 4 functions; Net busy sensing, Response Hold Delay (RHD), Timeout Period (TP), and Network Access Delay (NAD). Net Busy Sensing is a way to detect a signal over the channel, RHD defines the times from the data transmission to the reception of an acknowledgement packet, and TP defines a waiting time of a node before transmitting a data. NAD defines how many slot-times a node has to wait before making its transmission and how to act before its transmission after TP is expired.

MIL-STD-188-220 standard defines 6 different NADs including Random-NAD (R-NAD), Prioritized-NAD (P-NAD), Hybrid-NAD (H-NAD), Radio Embedded-NAD (RE-NAD), Deterministic Adaptable Priority NAD (DAP-NAD), and Data And Voice NAD (DAV-NAD). Moreover, MIL-STD-188-220 standard defines three precedences for the traffic: Urgent, Priority, and Routine precedence. Urgent precedence is the highest precedence and Routine precedence has the lowest precedence. P-NAD, DAP-NAD, and DAV-NAD are designed to provide the better transmission opportunities to the higher precedence traffic.

The paper in [5] compares R-NAD with P-NAD in terms of the average network access delay and the collision rate with varying the packet size and load balancing. The paper concludes R-NAD has better performance than P-NAD does. Researches in [6] and [7] shows DAP-NAD has better performance than RE-NAD has in terms of the end-to-end delay and the network utilization. In addition, in [8], DAP-NAD is compared with DAV-NAD in terms of the latency and the network utilization and concludes DAP-NAD provides the better performance. As a consequence of aforementioned previous researches, this paper focuses on DAP-NAD method among 6 NADs.

2.2 DAP-NAD

In DAP-NAD method, nodes access a medium and transmit their data in a pre-scheduled its time slot like TDMA system, but the length of time slot is varied whose size is the same as the packet length. The transmission order is re-scheduled after the completion of one sequence. However, unlike TDMA system, there are unique characteristics in DAP-NAD as follows.

First of all, the transmission order is not decided by a central scheduler, but by nodes themselves. Participating nodes are assigned with a unique Identification (ID) number when nodes join the networks and the ID itself defines the transmission order using the round-robin manner. For example, if there are 3 nodes and their IDs are 1, 2, and 3, then the transmission order of nodes is 1, 2, and 3. All nodes have their slots in a round. If one node with ID 1 transmits its own time slot, then the next round starts with node with ID 2 and the sequence is 2, 3, and 1.

Secondly, as aforementioned above, each packet has one of the three precedences. Each transmission sequence also has a *network-precedence*, which means that only a node having a packet with same precedence as the current *network-precedence* can transmit during its own time slot. Node can transmit its packet at its turn only if the precedence of its pending packet is the same as or higher than the *network-precedence*. During a round of the transmission sequence, if there is no transmission with the current *network-precedence*, then the *network-precedence* of the next round sequence is downgraded. For example, let's assume that the *network-precedence* of the first round is Urgent. If there is no Urgent packet transmissions during the transmission round, then *network-precedence* is Priority that means node having Urgent or Priority precedence can send their packet in their time slot in that round. However, if there is transmission with the precedence the same as the *network-precedence,* then the current *network-precedence* is maintained for the next round.

Thirdly, there is unique time slot, called Bump-Slot. The slot follows right after any slot in which any actual transmission completes. Any node having only an Urgent packet can transmit its packet during the Bump-Slot regardless of its transmission turn only if the current *network-precedence* is not Urgent. If there is any transmission in the Bump-Slot, the *network-precedence* for the next round is updated to Urgent. Therefore, the Bump-Slot is used to give more transmission opportunity to a node with Urgent packet, so that it improves the performance of Urgent packet. Like TDMA-based medium access, in general, the transmission is performed in the contention-free manner. However, the transmission during the Bump-Slot is based on slotted aloha medium access. That is, collisions occur only during Bump-Slot in DAP-NAD.

An example of DAP-NAD channel access method is illustrated in Fig. 2.

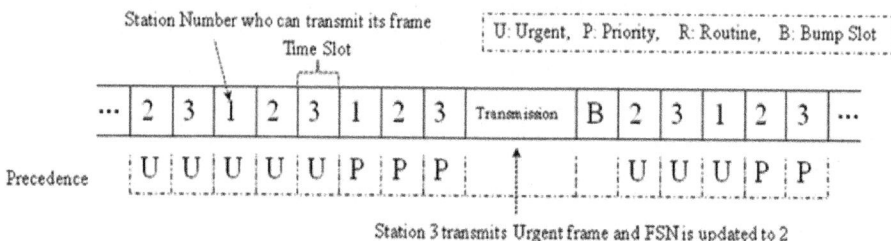

Fig. 2. An example of DAP-NAD access method

2.3 Motivations

As mentioned before, the channel access method in Bump-Slot is a slotted aloha method, so that it causes collisions among nodes having Urgent packets. The collision in the slot generally increases as the number of nodes with the Urgent packets increases. The conventional tactical communication devices using DAP-NAD method has been operating with the low data rates over the narrow bandwidth channels. The low data rate requires relatively longer transmission time than the high data rate over the wide bandwidth channel does. In addition, this makes a slot time longer because the duration of each time slot in DAP-NAD is the same as the duration of packet transmission time unlike constant time slots in TDMA-based cellular networks. Therefore, over the communication environments of the conventional tactical networks, increasing the number of nodes prolongs the waiting time of nodes that are waiting their reserved time slots. Such a long waiting time might be critical for the Urgent packet transmissions which has a delay constraint. To prevent from this, the Bump-Slot resets the *network-precedence* to Urgent. Therefore, the nodes with Urgent packets have more transmission opportunities so that it reduces the transmission delay of the Urgent packet. That is, the Bump-Slot is essential to enhance the performance of Urgent packet transmissions over the narrow bandwidth channels.

On the other hand, the future tactical networks are operating over the wide bandwidth channels. Thus, it might be considerable if the Bump-Slot is also effective over the wide-bandwidth channel. Over the wideband networks, the transmission time is reduced due to the high data rates and as a consequence the transmission delay is shortened. In addition, the time to take that a node waits its scheduled time slot becomes much shorter in the wideband networks than that in the narrow-bandwidth channels. Therefore, the Bump-Slot might not be necessary because the transmission delays of Urgent packets over the wide-bandwidth channels may not be so bad. Besides, because the Bump-Slot causes collisions and there is more urgent traffic over the wideband system, it may make the performance of the Urgent packet worse. Therefore, in the next section, the performance of DAP-NAD with the Bump-Slot is compared to that of the DAP-NAD without the Bump-Slot over wideband channel environments throughout the extensive simulations.

3   Simulations and Evaluations

3.1   Simulation Environments

In this section, the effectiveness of the Bump-Slot over the wideband networks is evaluated through the extensive simulations. Note that the objective of this paper is to evaluate the only channel access mechanism over wideband networks with multimedia traffic. In addition, it is also hard to obtain exact network parameters for the wideband tactical networks due to confidentiality. Therefore, the simulation uses some parameters that can be obtained from the public resources and assumed to be similar to the future wideband tactical networks.

For this evaluations, it is assumed that DAP-NAD method operates over Orthogonal Frequency Division Multiplexing (OFDM)-based WNW illustrated in [3] as a physical layer. Because the exact specification of WNW is confidential and is not revealed in the public, the information on the possible data rates and bandwidths for WNW is obtained from the open source such as [3]. For the simulations, the data rate is set to 3Mbps with 10MHz bandwidth. Furthermore, the well-known OFDM-based wireless data network is IEEE802.11-based wireless local area networks (WLANs). Thus, the network parameters for the simulations are adopted from in IEEE 802.11a standard [14]. Because the paper focuses on the performance of channel access method itself, the parameters including frame format, processing time, propagation delay (which is set to 0), the sizes of preamble and header and so on uses those of IEEE802.11a unlike system parameters used by [5]-[12] and MIL-STD-188-220 standard. On the other hand, because the lowest data rate of IEEE802.11a standard is 6Mbps with 20MHz bandwidth and the simulation uses 3Mbps rate with 10MHz bandwidth, most of parameters in IEEE 802.11a are expanded two times longer than the original values. For instance, the duration of Short InterFrame Space (SIFS) is doubled comparing to the value specified in IEEE 802.11a.

Table 1. Simulation parameters

Parameter	Value
Data Rate	3Mbps
Preamble	32us
Physical layer header	16us
MAC header	272 bits
Default Slot Time	18 us
ACK packet	88us
SIFS	32us

Default Slot Time in the Table 1. indicates the minimum time duration taken to decide if the channel is busy and it is set to the same time as backoff slot time in IEEE 802.11a. That is, if no transmission is detected during the time, the next time is automatically started. There is SIFS between the end of transmitted packet and the beginning of the next time slot.

The detailed parameters used in the simulation are shown in Table 1.

The error-free channel is used for the simulations. The number of nodes is set to 100 and it is assumed that all nodes are in one-hop radio range, so that all nodes can hear one another. The total number of nodes in the simulation is 100. The number of nodes generating Urgent, Priority and Routine precedence traffic are set to 30, 35, and 35 nodes, respectively. All nodes generate their packets with the exponential distribution with 500 byte-average length and with Poisson-distributed inter-arrival time with $1/\lambda$ average time. The lifetime of the packet at the MAC layer is set to 150ms which is recommended in International Telecommunication Union (ITU) as shown in [15][16]. As a performance metrics, the average End-to-End delay, the average Packet Delivery Ratio (PDR), and the average throughput are measured at the MAC layer.

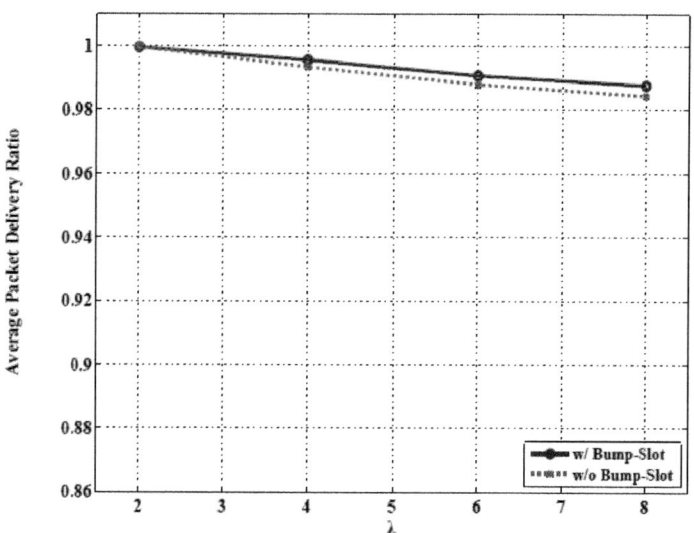

Fig. 3. Average packet delivery ratio of Urgent precedence traffic as a function of λ

3.2 Performance Evaluations

The average packet delivery ratios and end-to-end delays of DAP-NAD with Bump-Slot, named "w/ Bump", and without Bump-Slot, named "w/o Bump", as λ increases are shown in Fig. 3 and Fig. 4, respectively. The average end-to-end delay takes into account only the delays of successfully transmitted packets, not the dropped packets. The performances are only for Urgent traffic. The performance of the two methods are similar each other cross over all values of λ.

Regarding packet delivery ratio, both of methods provides almost same performance as shown in Fig. 3. The differences of the performance of both methods are less than 1%. On the other hand, the average packet delay of the method with Bump-Slot shows the 40% higher than that of one without Bump-Slot. However, the average end-to-end delays of both methods are much less than 150*ms* requirements specified in [15] and [16]. Therefore, in terms of the delay requirement, even the relative high delay of the method without Bump-Slot is acceptable.

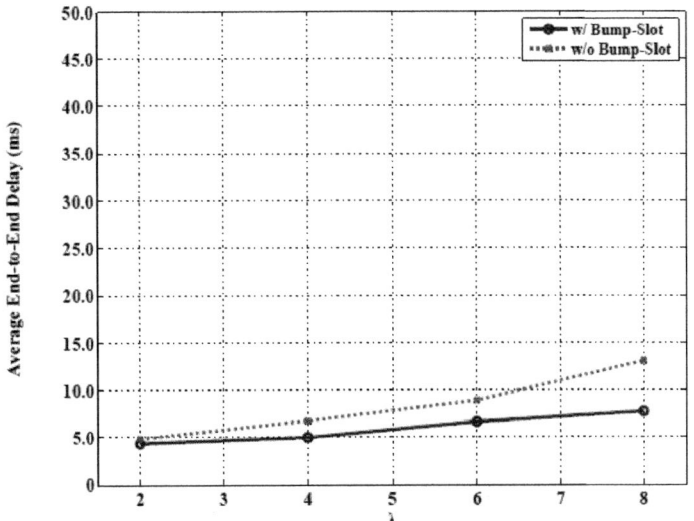

Fig. 4. Average end-to-end delay of Urgent precedence traffic as a function of λ

Fig. 5 shows the average packet delivery ratios of Priority and Urgent traffic using DAP-NAD with Bump-Slot and without Bump-Slot as λ increases. The performance of the both methods is almost similar, but the performance of DAP-NAD without Bump-Slot has better performance than that of one with Bump-Slot. The results are clear because the role of Bump-Slot increases only the performance of the Urgent traffic by scarifying the other traffic. However, as shown in Fig. 3 and 4, the improvement of the Urgent traffic is hardly seen.

In Fig. 6, the average Bump-Slot Utilization and the collision rate in Bump-Slots are shown. As shown in the figure, the utilization of Bump Slots decreases after λ is 6. The reason of this decrease is that even though Bump-Slots are generated after all transmissions, no node sends its packet because the *network-precedence* of the most transmission round is Urgent. As the standard [1] specifies, Bump-Slot is uses only when the *network-precedence* is lower than Urgent. In addition, the Collision ratio increases as the traffic increase and it deteriorates the performance of Urgent transmissions.

As results, the overall performance of DAP-NAD with Bump-Slot is hardly improved comparing to one without Bump-Slot because of the increase of collisions in the slots and the low utilization of Bump-Slots.

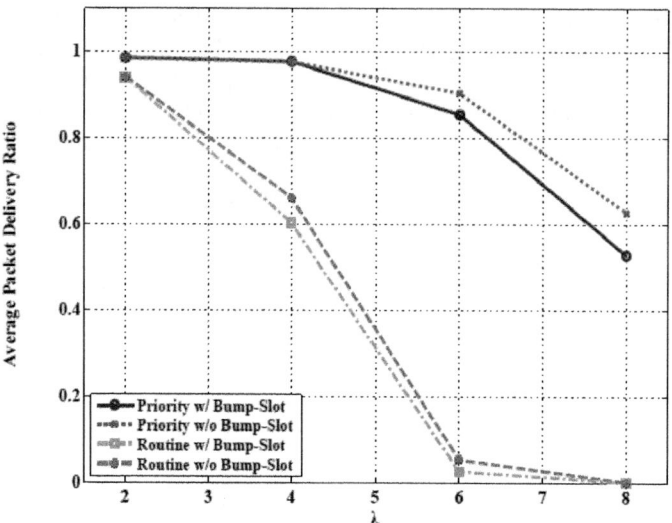

Fig. 5. Average packet delivery ratio of Priority and Routine precedence traffic as a function of λ

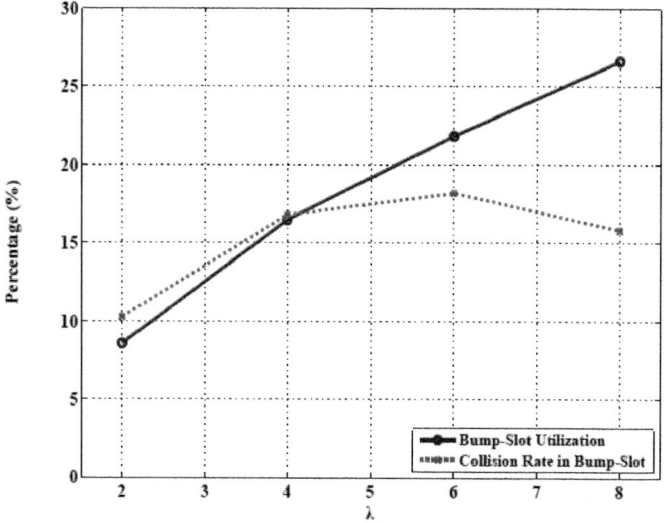

Fig. 6. Average Bump-Slot utilization and collision rate in Bump-Slots as a function of λ

4   Conclusions

The future wireless tactical networks are evolving to serve wideband multimedia traffic. MIL-STD-188-220 standard specifies the channel access method over the voice-based narrowband networks. Using the methods in the future tactical networks provides some advantages in terms of providing the interoperability with the legacy systems and the simplicity on the development of the future systems. In this paper, one of channel access method specified in MIL-STD-188-220, named DAP-NAD, is evaluated over wideband environment and points out the problem of using Bump-Slot. The Bump-Slots resets the *network-precedence* to Urgent to give more transmission opportunity to the Urgent traffic. However, over the wideband environments, using the Bump-Slots hardly improves the performance of DAP-NAD networks because of many collisions and the low utilizations on the Bump-Slots. Therefore, this paper claims the effectiveness of Bump-Slots in DAP-NAD method is lost over the wideband networks and there are new methods to improve the performance of Urgent traffic because of the importance of the traffic in the battlefield.

References

1. MIL-STD-188-220D with Change1 Digital Message Transfer Device Subsystem (June 23, 2008)
2. JPEO JTRS Standard, http://sca.jpeojtrs.mil
3. Abacus Programming Corporation, http://www.abacuscorp.com/se.htm
4. Spectrum Signal Processing by Vecima, http://www.spectrumsignal.com/products/pdf/wnw_starter_kit.pdf
5. Burch, R.G., Chamberlain, S.C.: Performance evaluation of MIL-STD-188-220 interoperability standard for digital message transfer device subsystems. In: 14th Military Communications Conference, pp. 427–432 (1995)
6. Thuente, D.J., Borchelt, T.E.: Simulation studies of MAC algorithms for combat net radio. In: 16th Military Communications Conference, pp. 193–199 (1997)
7. Thuente, D.J., Borchelt, T.E.: Simulation model and studies of MIL-STD-188-220A. In: 17th Military Communications Conference, pp. 198–204 (1998)
8. Thuente, D.J., Borchelt, T.E.: Efficient data and voice media access control algorithm for MIL-STD-188-220B. In: 19th Military Communications Conference, pp. 115–121 (2000)
9. Thuente, D.J., Whiteman, J.K.: Modified CSMA/Implicit token passing algorithm for MIL-STD-188-220B. In: 20th Military Communication Conference, pp. 838–844 (2001)
10. Thuente, D.J.: Improving quality of service for MIL-STD-188-220C. In: 21st Military Communication Conference, pp. 1194–1200 (2002)
11. Yang, J., Liu, Y.: An improved implicit token passing algorithm for DAP-NAD in MIL-STD-188-220C. In: 2nd International Conference on Wireless Communications, pp. 1–4 (2006)
12. Liu, Y., An, J., Liu, H.: The modified DAP-NAD-CJ algorithm for multicast applications. In: 4th International Conference on Wireless Communications, Networking and Mobile Computing, pp. 1–4 (2008)
13. Kim, B.-S.: Comparative Study of MIL-STD-188-220D Standard over IEEE802.11 Standard. SK Telecommunications Review 20(1) (2010)
14. Part 11: Wireless LAN Medium Access Control (MAC) and Physical Layer (PHY) specifications, IEEE Std. 802.11 (June 12, 2007)
15. Calyam, P., Sridharan, M., Mandrawa, W., Schopis, P.: Performance Measurement and Analysis of H.323 Traffic. In: Barakat, C., Pratt, I. (eds.) PAM 2004. LNCS, vol. 3015, pp. 137–146. Springer, Heidelberg (2004)
16. International Telecommunication Union, http://www.itu.int/itudoc/itu-t/workshop/qos

Access Path Based Source Address Validation in Mobile IPv6

Min Zhu, Ke Xu, and Qi Li

Tsinghua National Laboratory for Information Science and Technology,
Department of Computer Science and Technology, Tsinghua University,
Beijing, China
{zhumin,xuke,liqi}@csnet1.cs.tsinghua.edu.cn

Abstract. Mobile IPv6 runs high risk of being attacked by IP spoofing due to the introduction of mobility and route optimization. In this paper, an authentic IP address validation scheme is proposed to protect mobile nodes in Mobile IPv6 against IP spoofing attack. The mobile nodes' historical traffic information is leveraged to validate the authenticity of its claimed home address in the scheme. Compared with other authentication schemes, this scheme is much simpler to implement and easier to deploy based on the usage of real data, and does not require additional computational overhead. It also solves the address ownership problem and the unauthenticated binding update issue in Mobile IPv6. Real traces are used to demonstrate the applicability of the scheme in this paper. The experimental results show that only three consecutive historical packet records are required to construct a unique authentication key, which can identify forged home address efficiently.

1 Introduction

As an enhancement to IPv6, Mobile IPv6 provides more flexible and open communication with support of the binding update protocol and the route optimization protocol, which allows mobile nodes to roam freely in the network with two addresses[7]. When the mobile node is in the home subnet, it is identified by its home address. When it moves to a foreign subnet, it obtains a new address as care of address. The key point of mobile node is to notify the home agent and the correspondent node its current care of address in a reliable and timely way through binding update request.

However, exploiting the security vulnerability of unauthenticated binding update, an attacker can masquerade as a mobile node (MN) and send a binding update request to the home agent (HA) and the correspondent node (CN) easily[10]. As IP address plays an important role in Internet, it is a disaster if such request is trusted and accepted: the normal traffic direction in the network will be changed, and the network resources will be consumed. Moreover, the victim's confidential information may be stolen[5]. Obviously, mechanisms to authenticate the identity of the mobile nodes are crucial to network communication and management.

E. Altman and W. Shi (Eds.): NPC 2011, LNCS 6985, pp. 334–349, 2011.

The IETF has proposed IPsec[2] and return routability (RR)[7] mechanism to verify the identity of the mobile nodes. Some cryptography-based mechanisms with the mobility support such as AIP[1] and CGA[3] have also been proposed to generate accountability address in order to verify the identity of the source address. But these mechanisms have not been widely applied yet, because of their computation complexity, heavy storage overhead and long communication latency. As a result, further studies on source address validation in Mobile IPv6 are strongly needed.

The main reason behind the success of masquerade attack in Mobile IPv6 is that the home agent and the correspondent node cannot determine the ownership of the address claimed by the mobile node with unauthenticated binding update. If the mobile node can prove its identity after its move, the masquerade attack can be distinguished. SAVA[16,17] is the first method that proposed authentic source IP address. SAVA guarantees address authenticity in a hierarchical way. First, it completes the source address validation in local subnet by exploiting the dynamic binding relationship between the switch port and the valid source IP address. Second, it completes authentication at Intra-AS level through the ingress/egress filtering. Finally, it completes Inter-AS source address validation by alliance. SAVA has currently been deployed in CNGI-CERNET2[1], which is a large-scale pure IPv6 backbone. However, SAVA does not consider the authentic source IP address issue in Mobile IPv6. Our work is an extension of SAVA, and we will solve the authentic source address validation problem in Mobile IPv6 in this paper.

Identity authentication is not unique to network security, but exists in our daily life. For example, in credit cards customer service, some authentication questions will be asked to verify our identity, such as credit card number, home address, phone number, and the amount of recent consumption. These information together forms a key for a certain card holder. Following the same logic, our study attempts to address the following questions:

- Is there any information only known to the mobile node and the home agent or correspondent node that can be used to verify the node's identity?
- How does a mobile node use such information to signal its ownership of an IP address?
- How to determine the effectiveness of the authentication information?

In this paper, we try to extract authentication information from historical traffic generated by users (or end hosts/nodes). This is possible because users' traffic is private and very diverse in certain dimensions. For example, our analysis of the data collected from DragonLab[2] (Dataset 1 described in Section 5) suggests that different users access the Internet at different time and sequence (Section 2). The result shows that although 67.11% of the access behaviors are concentrated on only 2 of the 21 monitored destinations, the online activities of different users actually happen at very different times and in very different sequences.

---

[1] http://www.edu.cn/cernet2_7948/
[2] http://dragonlab.org/

As a result, users in Dataset 1 need no more than two consecutive packets to differentiate themselves from each other. If the mobile node can tell when and what it has done correctly, its identity can be verified.

Such evidence allows us to propose an authentic source address validation scheme in Mobile IPv6 based on the historical traffic of the mobile nodes. To implement this scheme, we first collect the mobile nodes' traffic at both the home agent and the mobile node, and then construct the consecutive packets of each mobile node in time as access path. We also employ some storage techniques to strengthen the security of the access path to defend against the eavesdropped traffic used by the attackers. Such access path can serve as authentication key to validate the ownership of the home address claimed by the mobile node after its move (Section 3). Theoretical analysis on performance shows that our scheme has light overhead and is able to complete the source address validation in a secure way(Section 4). Our experimental results with real traces demonstrate that the access path with only three consecutive packets can differentiate a mobile node in a subnet completely under reasonable settings (Section 5). Our scheme has the following advantages:

- Accountability: The mobile node can prove the ownership of its claimed home address efficiently using access path generated from its historical traffic.
- Light overhead: Without using cryptography, our scheme has no computational overhead. It has light storage overhead also because it needs a few packets for validation.
- Easy to implement: Leveraging the real traffic generated in the network, the implement and the deployment of the scheme is easy. Minimum data collection is required in this scheme.

The rest of the paper begins with the motivation for our research in Section 2. Section 3 describes the trustable communication architecture in Mobile Ipv6, the construction of the access path, and the source address authentication details. The performance and security analysis of our scheme are presented in Section 4. The applicability of the scheme is demonstrated in Section 5 with real traces. Section 6 introduces related work. Section 7 concludes the paper.

2   Problem Statement

Since it is a complicated and daunting task to generate a key to complete authentication with cryptography and PKI's support, we look for alternative ways in this paper.

As is commonly known, numerous historical traffic will be generated in the network when the nodes access the Internet. However, only information that satisfies the three criteria of privacy, uniqueness and anti-replay attack ability can be used for the authentication purpose. Our mission in this paper is to extract information from the historical traffic to generate the authentication key satisfying above three criteria.

Since it is impossible for attackers to monitor the network all the time, we can assume that the traffic is only known to the nodes that send it and the devices that collect it. Even though some traffic may be eavesdropped by attackers, we can use some techniques to make them useless to attackers. In essence, we assume that the traffic information is not known to attackers in authentication.

It is a great challenge to ensure the uniqueness of the authentication key generated from the historical traffic because the traffic of different nodes can be same at the same time. However, our analysis based on real traces reveals that online activity differences always occur among individual users even though they may behave exactly the same at some time (Figure3 and Figure 8). For example, only 1.81% of 2856 users in Dataset 1 have exactly the same access behavior at some particular point of time, and all the nodes can be differentiated with access behaviors of two visits. Therefore, it is feasible to construct a unique authentication key according to time (access sequence) and space (packet composition information) properties of the traffic.

The ability of anti-reply attack is important to validation because attackers may eavesdrop the traffic in the network. In general, there are two classes of methods to protect the authentication key. One is using encryption, and the other is generating a new key whenever it is needed. The volume of the traffic information in the network allows us to take the second approach because the nodes usually generate a large number of packets every day.

In summary, it is possible to construct authentication key from mobile nodes' historical traffic that satisfying the three criteria of privacy, uniqueness, and anti-reply attack ability.

3   Access Path Based Trust Communication Architecture in Mobile IPv6

The purpose of this paper is to validate the home address claimed by the mobile node using its historical traffic after its move. There are three important issues to address. The first is what traffic we should collect, where to collect it and how to store it for easy access. The second is how to construct the authentication key. And the third is how to validate the home address of the mobile node according to the authentication key. We discuss these issues in this section.

3.1   Overview

Figure 1 presents our trustable communication architecture based on mobile nodes' historical traffic information. It consists of two modules. The first one is collecting module, which resides in the home agent and the mobile node. This module decides what information to collect and how to store it. The second one is communication module. This module accomplishes the mobile nodes' authentication after its move. It involves binding update authentication both to the home agent and to the correspondent node. We elaborate on the function of each module below.

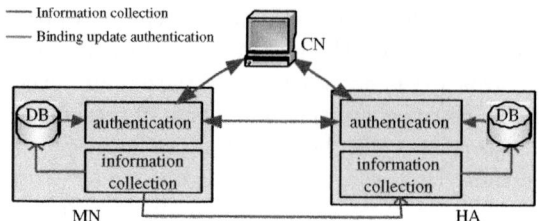

Fig. 1. Historical traffic based trustable communication architecture in Mobile IPv6

3.2   Information Collecting and Recording

As the basis of our scheme, traffic collection is a crucial part in our study. We think that the best location to collect and record the traffic is the home agent and the mobile node because of their positions. Packet is chosen as the collection unit because it is easy to collect by both the home agent and the mobile node. Because of the privacy and overhead issues, we will not collect packet payload in this paper.

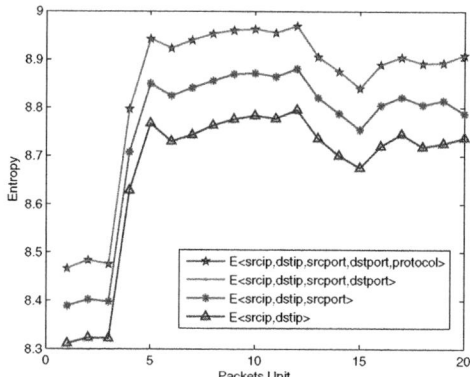

Fig. 2. The entropy of traffic which is composed of different tuples

Generally, we need use a 5-tuple <srcIP,dstIP,srcport,dstport,protocol> to denote a flow in the traffic. But in this paper, we only need use the 4-tuple <srcIP,dstIP,srcPort,dstPort> to construct the authentication key because we find that the information *protocol* has marginal effect in determining the distribution of the traffic. This can be seen from the entropy statistics of Dataset 2 shown in Figure 2. Entropy is a concept to measure the probability of particular information in information theory. It has been shown to contribute to network monitoring[6] recently. The smaller the entropy is, the more regular the information distribution is. Therefore, it is more difficult to distinguish between mobile nodes when the entropy is low. From Figure 2, we can see that the traffic's entropy of 5-tuples is almost identical to that of 4-tuples and the entropy of 4-tuples is bigger than the others. This suggests that the choice of 4-tuple is the most suitable one to construct the authentication key because the packets of 4-tuples is much easier to differentiate. We will verify this conjecture with real data in Section 5.

To guarantee the consistency between the traffic collected in the home agent and that collected in the mobile node, we collect the traffic through the asynchronous transmission. We also focus on the packet order instead of the precise time in the procedure of authentication to further reduce the impact of time difference between the traffic in the home agent and that in the mobile node.

After determining the information to be collected, the home agent and the mobile node find a way to store the collected traffic in easy-to-access types. The traffic collected is usually stored in a database in the home agent. However, it is inconvenient to access such information if all users' traffic is stored in one table. So, each home agent in our work builds a table for each mobile node to record their traffic in time order. To reduce the access time, the home agent also creates a hash table to maintain the relationship between the mobile nodes and their traffic table. Compared with traffic storage in the home agent, the traffic storage in the mobile node is much simpler. Each mobile node only needs maintaining its own traffic table in time order.

As there is so much traffic in the network, it is impossible to collect all the packets generated by the mobile nodes. In our work, we use stationary space to store the traffic for each mobile node. Meanwhile, we apply several strategies to reduce the frequency and quantity of data collection.

First, we reduce the collection frequency by just collecting special data. Some measurements based on mobile circumstance find that the traffic generated by the mobile nodes largely focuses on individual ports and services[8,14], such as port 80 or web service. This allows us to collect the packets of special application, such as the packet whose destination port is 80. This collection strategy not only reduces the storage overhead but also reduces the risk of attackers' eavesdropping, as attackers need more time and energy to get the special application information they want.

Second, we update the storage depending on the availability of the space and the frequency of collection. Once the storage space is full, the collection will be stopped temporarily. So, even if the nodes do not access the Internet for a long time, or they have a prolonged absence from the local subnet, the traffic records will be sustained unless the space is full and new collection begins. This collection method increases the difficulty of attackers' eavesdropping because they do not know what information to collect and what sequence to store it.

3.3 Access Path Construction

As shown in Figure 3, there may be many nodes in a subnet and they may exhibit the same online activities at a particular point of time. Therefore, it is insufficient to use just one packet to differentiate different users. However, we can combine the time and space properties of the traffic to construct the authentication key. In order to do so, we define the list of consecutive packets from one mobile node N as its access path indicated by

$Apath_{N,timestart} = \{(number_i, P_i)\}$, where,
$P_i = \{srcIP_i, dstIP_i, srcPort_i, dstPort_i\}$.

The parameter *timestart* represents the collection time of the first packet in the access path. The parameter $number_i$ indicates the sequence number of the packet in the storage. It is an auxiliary parameter to strength the security of the authentication key in the construction of the access path. The parameter P_i is used to denote the packet in the list and it is represented by a 4-tuple. P_1 is named starting point of the access path. We call the length of the access path access hop in our paper, which is equal to the number of packets in the list. The most important question for our architecture is how many hops we should use to construct a unique access path. We answer this question in Section 5.

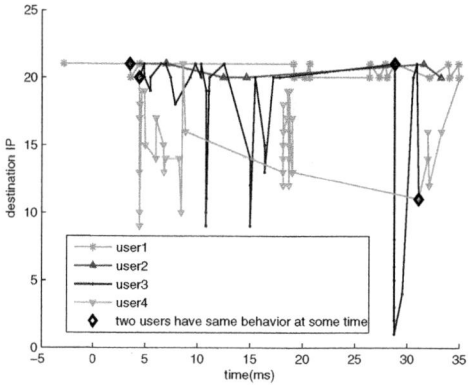

Fig. 3. The map sites access path of five users in some time interval in Dataset 1

3.4   Access Path Based Authentic Source Address Validation

The access path based source address validation includes two parts, as shown in Figure 4.

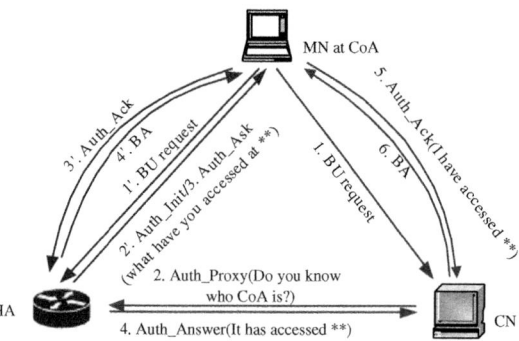

Fig. 4. The procedure of home address validation. In this way, the home agent and the correspondent node can authenticate the binding update and distinguish the ownership of the home address claimed by the mobile node.

In the first part, the home agent validates the home address of the mobile node once it receives a binding update request from the mobile node. It searches through traffic records table according to the home address claimed by the mobile node, constructs a challenge question and sends it to the mobile node with message Auth Init as shown in Figure 4. After the mobile node gets the question, it looks for the answer in its own storage table, builds the corresponding authentication key, and returns the key back to the home agent through message Auth Ack to prove its identity. The home agent can compare the answer from the mobile node with the records in its own table to validate the identify of the mobile node.

In the second part, the correspondent node needs to validate the identity of the mobile node as well after it receives a binding update request from the mobile node. The authentication to the correspondent node is more complicated because it has no records of mobile nodes' historical traffic. Usually, the correspondent node is a server that has large access volumes. The cost of monitoring and collection on the correspondent node is very expensive. However, the correspondent node can depend on the home agent to complete validation. The procedure is shown in Figure 4. After the correspondent node receives a binding update request, it sends an authentication request to the home agent through message Auth Proxy. The home agent then sends a new challenge question to the mobile node through message Auth Ask. At the same time, the home agent also sends the correspondent node the hash value of the right answer to the challenge question. After the correspondent node receives the answer from the mobile node through message Auth Ack, it computes the hash value of the answer and compares the result with that from the home agent. Such comparison allows the correspondent node to distinguish the identity of the mobile node.

How to construct the challenge question is an important task in authentication. Since our validation is based on the access path, it is easy to construct a challenge question. For example, we can ask "what information do you have between number 5 and 8?" or "what did you do after you accessed the 120.23.*.* at port 80 at 11:00?". Since neither storage order nor the accurate content can be known by the attacker, a right answer must come from the right mobile node. Of course, we can ask more than two questions to strengthen the security.

4   Performance and Security Analysis

4.1   Storage overhead

We illustrate the storage overhead of our scheme using the example of our campus network (see Section 5). Suppose all 48,000 users in the campus network are mobile nodes, and each packet record in our case is 40B. The relationship between the storage overhead and the number of packet records for each mobile node is shown in Figure 5.

From Figure 5, we can see that only 0.076MB of overhead is needed to store 2000 packet records for each mobile node, and only 3.58G of overhead is needed to store all the packet records for all mobile nodes in the home agent. Obviously, this

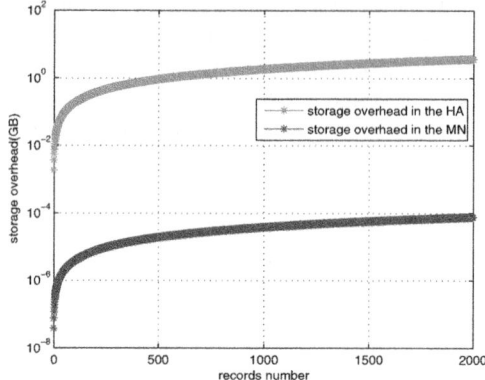

Fig. 5. Storage overhead in the home agent and the mobile node

light storage overhead will not lead to overhead burdens on the home agent or the mobile nodes. Since our experimental results show that only three consecutive packets are sufficient to complete validation (see Section 5.2), the actual overhead in real practice should be much smaller than that in Figure 5.

4.2   Security Analysis

Attackers are most likely to eavesdrop at three locations in the network: on the path between the home agent and the correspondent node (HA-CN path), on the path between the home agent and the mobile node (HA-MN path), and on the path between the mobile node and the correspondent node (MN-CN path). We analyze the security of our scheme under scenarios of attacks to these three paths.

– On HA-CN path: The only useful message to the attacker on the HA-CN path is the hash value of the authentication key generated by the home agent. Even if the attacker is able to get the hash value, it is almost impossible for the attacker to decode the original authentication key from it.
– On HA-MN path: In our scheme, the messages transmitted on the HA-MN path include the mobile nodes' traffic, the binding update request, the challenge question and the authentication key. The authentication key is useless for attackers, because it changes all the time. The mobile nodes'traffic is also useless for attackers, because the attackers cannot know the sequence number of the packets required to construct the access path unless they collect the traffic continuously from the very beginning. But this is impossible.
– On MN-CN path: The eavesdropping on the MN-CN path is not a concern to our scheme because that the authentication key will change in every communication under our scheme.

4.3   Feasibility Analysis

The authentication key used in our scheme comes from real traffic data. No additional device or software is needed except for a collection module. As a result, it is simple to deploy our scheme in practice. Moreover, most core routers have collected the historical traffic passing by for the purpose of measurement and management. Our scheme can use the data collected by routers directly, or add some additional features to the collecting function of routers without introducing too much overhead.

5   Experimental Study

In this section, we demonstrate the optimal choice of access hops in the construction of authentication key. We use two datasets collected from Campus Network of Tsinghua University (TUNET), which serves for about 40,000 hosts and 48,000 connected end users. TUNET connects to the CERNET (China Education and Research Network) that connects to the Internet through a 2 Gbps full-duplex link.

One dataset was collected from the platform of DragonLab (Dataset 1). It monitored the Web/HTTP traffic of TUNET that interacts with online map sites including Google Map, Microsoft Live Maps, Yahoo Maps, Baidu Maps, Koubei Maps, Sogou Maps, Edushi and Dushiquan. This dataset consists of about 2GBs of map traffic data for the 18 days between April 7th and 24th of 2009.

The other dataset was collected by a core router in TUNET (Dataset 2). It includes all the packets without payload for ten minutes between 16:40 and 16:50 on December 7th of 2006. The size of the data is around 2GBs.

Notice that these datasets are used for methodology analysis, other datasets with packet records can also be used.

5.1   Effectiveness Evaluation Algorithm

Before determining how many access hops are needed to construct a unique authentication key, we first propose a standard used to evaluate the effectiveness of an access path. In order to do so, we design an access path based forest through three steps (To strengthen the security, we do not consider the packet sequence number of the access path in the construction of the forest):

- Create an access path graph for the nodes that have the same behaviors at the same point of time.
  We first create a graph to cluster all the nodes that have the same behaviors at the same point of time. In the graph, each point (node) represents a packet in the access path, which is denoted by Pi; and each directed link reflects the sequence of packets. We illustrate the graph construction with an example. Suppose we need to validate a mobile node N1. First, an access path $Apath_{N1,t0} = \{P1, P2, P3, P4\}$ is chosen from the home agent's records table randomly and a graph is constructed as shown in Figure 6. Next, all the nodes that have the same packet $P1$ around the same point of time are extracted from the database. Suppose four nodes are found and their access paths are $Apath_{N2,t0} = \{P1, P2, P3, P5\}$, $Apath_{N3,t0} = \{P1, P2, P6, P7\}$,

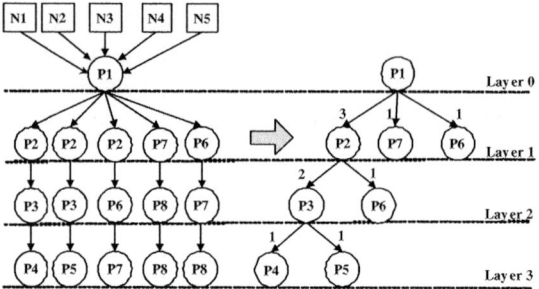

Fig. 6. The construction of the access path graph and forest. Each node represents a packet and the directed link denotes access order.

$Apath_{N4,t0} = \{P1, P7, P8, P8\}$ and $Apath_{N5,t0} = \{P1, P6, P7, P8\}$ respectively. These access paths are then inserted into the directed graph one by one as shown in Figure 6. In order to improve the security, we do not require other nodes to access $P1$ exactly at $t0$ as node N1 does, but allow other nodes to access $P1$ between $t0 - l$ and $t0 + l$, where t is a threshold (We use 0.5 second as the threshold in this paper).

– Construct the access path forest. The forest can be constructed according to the following steps:
First, we make layers for the access path graph shown in Figure 6. The layer of the starting point $P1$ is defined as layer 0. The layer number is one less than the corresponding access hops.
Second, we set the starting point of the access path as the origin node of the forest and define the number of mobile nodes in the access path graph as the in-degree of the origin node. As shown in Figure 6, the in-degree of the point $P1$ is 5.
Third, we consolidate the points in the graph layer by layer to construct the forest. The same points at the same layer in the graph are consolidated into one point in the forest at the same layer. The in-degree of the point in the forest is the number of the mobile nodes that have accessed this point at the same layer of the graph. In effect, the in-degree of the point means the number of users that have the same starting point and the same access path up until this point. We call points whose in-degree is one as "leaf nodes", and we do not add points under them in the next layer of the forest. Point $P6$ in Figure 6 is an example of leaf point.

– Compute the effectiveness of the access path.
The ultimate goal of constructing the access path forest is to determine how many hops are needed to construct an effective authentication key. Based on the in-degree of the points in the forest, the effectiveness of the access path with hops i can be defined as follows:

$$Disc_i = \begin{cases} 0 & \text{(if i=1 \& N>1);} \\ 1 & \text{(if i=1 \& N =1) ;} \\ \frac{\sum_{k=1}^{(} i-1)(leaf_k)}{N} & \text{(if i>1);} \end{cases} \tag{1}$$

In formula (1), the parameter N represents the in-degree of the origin node, the parameter $leaf_k$ denotes the number of leaf points at layer k, and $Disc_i$ defines the effectiveness of the access path with i hops. The result of $Disc_i$ allows us to find the most suitable access hops needed for authentication purpose. For example, the effectiveness of the access path in Figure 5 is illustrated in formula (2). The result suggests that the access hops must be at least 4 in order to construct an authentication key to identify node N1 or differentiate all the mobile nodes. However, the number of access path hops can be less under certain circumstances.

$$Disc_i = \begin{cases} 0 & (\text{i}=1); \\ 40\% & (\text{i}=2); \\ 60\% & (\text{i}=3); \\ 100\% & (\text{i}=4); \end{cases} \tag{2}$$

5.2 Choice of Access Hops

The authentication key constructed with different information may have different effects on validation efficiency. In this section, we detect the optimal number of access hops under different tuples to construct the authentication key. To evaluate the impact of alternative choices of tuples on authentication key, we change the definition of packet from 2-tuple to 4-tuple to calculate the distribution of mobile nodes' traffic for both Dataset 1 (as shown in Figure 7(a)) and Dataset 2 (as shown in Figure 7(b)). In both Figures, each column in the m-tuple group represents the frequency of a m-tuple packet re-appear (does not consider $srcIP$ information since it is the producer of the packet). In fact, it reflects the number of mobile nodes that have the same behaviors at the same point of time. For example, the first column of the first group in Figure 7(a) stands for the number of unique 2-tuple <srcIP,dstIP> packets in Dataset 1; and the second column stands for the number of 2-tuple <srcIP,dstIP> packets that is common to 2

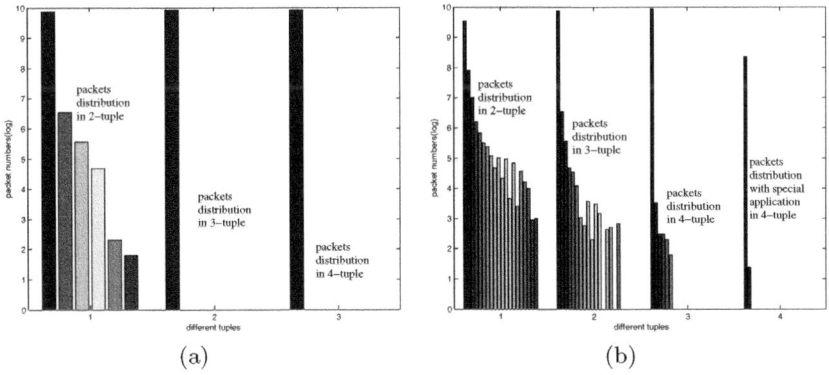

(a)   (b)

Fig. 7. Packets distribution under different tuples in Dataset 1(a) and Dataset 2(b)

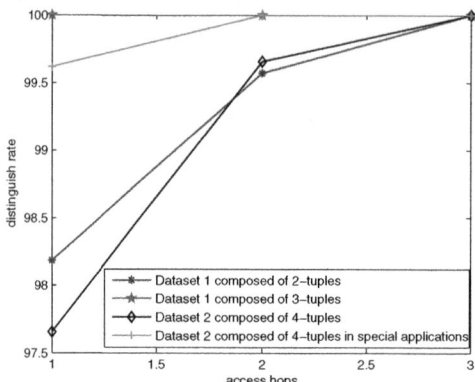

Fig. 8. Nodes' discrimination rate in different hops

different mobile nodes in their access history at some point of time. Apparently, the 4-tuples packets have a lower probability to re-appear than others.

Using the effectiveness evaluation algorithm discussed earlier, we compute the smallest number of access hops needed to construct the authentication key as the choice of the tuples changes for both Dataset 1 and Dataset 2. The result is shown in Figure 8.

We can see that most nodes (98.19%) in Dataset 1 can be distinguished by one 3-tuple <srcIP,dstIP,dstPort> packet, and all nodes can be distinguished by one 4-tuple <srcIP,dstIP,srcPort,dstPort> packet. For Dataset 2, at most three access hops are needed to construct a unique authentication key. We can also notice from Figure 8 that the access hops needed for Dataset 2 is much longer than that for Dataset 1. This is because the traffic in Dataset 1 is more special. In general, the access hops based on special application traffic is always much shorter. However, it may need more time to collect.

6   Related Work

The IETF uses the IPsec[2] to assure the authenticity of the binding update to the home agents. It is secure in theory. However, it has not been widely deployed because of its complexity and computational overhead.

The IEFT has also proposed return routability (RR)[7] mechanism to overcome the security vulnerability introduced by the route optimization. The RR mechanism uses reachable check to assure the right mobile node is sending the binding update message. When the mobile node moves to a new location, it sends two Init messages to the correspondent node through two paths. One is sent directly to the correspondent node. The other is sent via the home agent. The correspondent node generates two tokens for these two Init messages according to a secret only known by himself and sends them back to the mobile node through the same two paths. After that, the mobile node sends back a binding management key (named kbm in IETF) that is constructed from these two tokens to the correspondent node to prove its identity. Although it is difficult for attackers to intercept on two paths at the same time, some have managed to do so[13]. [9,12,15] propose some improvements to RR mechanism, but they have not been able to make it applicable to a larger extent.

Our scheme shares some similarities with RR mechanism in design. Both RR mechanism and our scheme rely on the home agent to help the correspondent node to complete the binding update authentication. However, there are two essential differences in our scheme. First, the source of the authentication key is different in these two mechanisms. It is generated by the mobile node in our scheme but generated by the correspondent node in RR mechanism. This makes our scheme more secure than RR mechanism. For example, if the attackers manage to eavesdrop on the HA-CN path, they are able to obtain one token of the RR mechanism. If they obtain the other token directly from the correspondent node, they can generate kbm to win the correspondent node's trust. While our scheme has no such kind of risk. Second, the implementation of RR mechanism requires the support of the security tunnel between the home agent and the mobile node. However, the security tunnel such as IPsec has not been deployed widely because of its complexity. As a result, RR mechanism is not widely employed although the concept of security tunnel is theoretically sound. In the contrast, our scheme does not require the support of a pre-created security tunnel.

The idea of accountability is widely applied in IPv6 to validate the identity of the nodes, such as in AIP[1], CGA[3] and HIP[11]. These mechanisms often bind the source address onto public key to generate a self-certification address, and most of them support mobility as well. However, the computational complexity caused by encryption limits their deployment. For example, the CGA(Cryptographically Generated Addresses) is composed of subnet prefix (64 bits) and interface identifier (64 bits) that is generated by two hash changes according to the address owner's public key and some CGA parameters. The corresponding private key and the interface identifier that is unchanged no matter how host roaming assert the senders identity in mobility. Unfortunately, the time required for generating a valid high secure CGA address is overwhelming from a practical perspective[4]. In this paper, the scheme we proposed also builds on the notion of accountability. However, our scheme only requires existing data in the network, which solves the overhead and deployment issues of traditional cryptography-based mechanisms.

7 Conclusion

In this paper, we propose an authentic source IP address validation scheme in Mobile IPv6. Using historical traffic generated by the mobile nodes, our methodology generates a unique authentication key to validate the home address claimed by the mobile node after its move. This key is a sequence of access paths composed by 4-tuple <srcIP, dstIP, srcPort, dstPort> packets. It is difficult for attackers to forge because the access path and the sequence number of the packets in the storage is only known by mobile nodes and the home agent. In addition, any effort from attackers to extract authentication key is meaningless because authentication key is changing all the time.

Our experiment with real traces demonstrates that a unique authentication key can be constructed using only three 4-tuple <srcIP, dstIP, srcPort, dstPort> packets. Compared with other cryptography-based methods, our scheme consumes no computational overhead and less storage overhead. Most important of all, it is easy to deploy using available data existing in the network.

Acknowledgment. We are greatly indebted to Wenlong Chen for fruitful discussion. We also owe our deepest gratitude to Bingqing Xu and Kaijun Zhang for data collection support.

References

1. Andersen, D., Balakrishnan, H., Feamster, N., Koponen, T., Moon, D., Shenker, S.: Accountable internet protocol(aip). In: Proceedings of ACM SIGCOMM (2008)
2. Arkko, J., Devarapalli, V., Dupont, F.: Using ipsec to protect mobile ipv6 signaling between mobile nodes and home agents. RFC 3776 (June 2004)
3. Aura, T.: Cryptographically generated addresses(cga). RFC 3972 (March 2005)
4. Bos, J.W., Ozen, O., Hubaux, J.: Analysis and optimization of cryptographically generated addresses(cga). In: Proceedings of ISC (2009)
5. Elgoarany, K., Eltoweissy, M.: Security in mobile ipv6: a survey. Information Security Technical Report 12(1), 32–43 (2007)
6. Hu, Y., Chiu, D.-M., Lui, J.C.S.: Entropy based adaptive ow aggregation. IEEE/ACM Transactions on Networking(TON) 17(3), 115–139 (2009)
7. Johnson, D.B., Perkins, C., Arkko, J.: Mobility support in ipv6. RFC 3775 (June 2004)
8. Kivi, A.: Mobile data adoption in finland 2005-2006. In: Proceedings of the 6th Conference on Telecommunication Techno-Economics(CTTE), Helsinki, Finland (June 2007)
9. Li, J., Zhang, P., Sampalli, S.: Improved security mechanism for mobile ipv6. International Journal of Network Security 6(3), 291–300 (2008)
10. Mankin, A., Patil, B., Harkins, D., Nordmark, E., Nikander, P., Roberts, P., Narten, T.: Threat models introduced by mobile ipv6 and requirements for security in mobile ipv6. IETF draft-ietf-mipv6-scrty-reqts-02.txt (2001)
11. Moskowitz, R., Nikander, P.: Host identity protocol (hip) architecture. RFC 4423 (May 2006)
12. Nikander, P., Aura, T., Arkko, J., Montenegro, G.: Mobile ip version 6 (mipv6) route optimization security design. In: Proceedings of the IEEE Vehicular Technology Conference Fall 2003 (2003)
13. Ren, K., Lou, W., Zeng, K., Bao, F., Zhou, J., Deng, R.H.: Routing optimization security in mobile ipv6. Computer Networks: The International Journal of Computer and Telecommunications Networking 50(13), 2401–2419 (2006)
14. Riikonen, A.: Mobile internet usage - network traffic measurements. Master's Thesis. Department of Communications and Networking, Helsinki University of Technology, Espoo (September 2009)

15. Song, S., Choi, H.-K., Kim, J.-Y.: A secure and light weight approach for routing optimization in mobile ipv6. EURASIP Journal on Wireless Communications and Networking (2009)
16. Wu, J., Bi, J., Li, X., Ren, G., Xu, K., Williams, M.: A source address validation architecture (sava) testbed and deployment experience. RFC 5210 (June 2008)
17. Wu, J., Ren, G., Li, X.: Source address validation: Architecture and protocol design. In: Proceedings of ICNP (2007)

Improve Google Android User Experience with Regional Garbage Collection

Yunan He, Chen Yang, and Xiao-Feng Li

China Runtime Technologies Lab, Intel Corporation
{yunan.he,chen.yang,xiao-feng.li}@Intel.com

Abstract. Google Android is a popular software stack for smart phone, where the user experience is critical to its success. The pause time of its garbage collection in DalvikVM should not be too long to stutter the game animation or webpage scrolling. Generational collection or concurrent collection can be the effective approaches to reducing GC pause time. As of version 2.2, Android implements a non-generational stop-the-world (STW) mark-sweep algorithm. In this paper we present an enhancement called Regional GC for Android that can effectively improve its user experience. During the system bootup period, Android preloads the common runtime classes and data structures in order to save the user applications' startup time. When Android launches a user application the first time, it starts a new process with a new DalvikVM instance to run the application code. Every application process has its separate managed heap; while the system preloaded data space is shared across all the application processes. The Regional GC we propose is similar to a generational GC but actually partitions the heap according to regions instead of generations. One region (called the class region) is for the preloaded data, and the other region (called the user region) is for runtime dynamic data. A major collection of regional GC is the same as DalvikVM's normal STW collection, while a minor collection only marks and sweeps the user region. In this way, the regional GC effectively improves Android in both application performance and user experience. In the evaluation of an Android workload suite (AWS), 2D graphic workload Album Slideshow is improved by 28%, and its average pause time is reduced by 73%. The average pause time reduction across all the AWS applications is 55%. The regional GC can be combined with a concurrent GC to further reduce the pause time. This paper also describes two alternative write barrier designs in the Regional GC. One uses page fault to catch the reference writes on the fly; the other one scans the page table entries to discover the dirty pages. We evaluate the two approaches with the AWS applications, and discuss their respective pros and cons.

Keywords: Small Device, Runtime System, Memory Management, Garbage Collection.

1 Introduction

Recent advances in computing technology are enabling the widespread use of smarter mobile computing devices. Here smarter means more powerful software stack that

E. Altman and W. Shi (Eds.): NPC 2011, LNCS 6985, pp. 350–365, 2011.
© IFIP International Federation for Information Processing 2011

supports a variety of applications. Garbage Collection (GC) is a key component of the systems to provide automatic memory management. GC helps to improve both the application developers' productivity and the system's security. However GC is not without drawbacks. In performance wise, automatic memory management could be less efficient than well-programmed explicit memory management. In user experience wise, the GC pause time cannot be too long to stutter the game animation or webpage scrolling. The user experience is more critical for smart devices since most of the applications are user-inactive.

Google Android is an excellent software stack for mobile computing system. Android user applications are programmed in Java language, built on top of a Java-based application framework and core libraries, deployed in bytecode form and running on a virtual machine called DalvikVM. Android memory management has a two-level design. Underlying is the dlmalloc module managing the process virtual memory. DalvikVM has a garbage collector built on the dlmalloc to manage the runtime objects life cycles. As of version 2.2, Android implements a non-generational stop-the-world (STW) mark-sweep GC. The occasional pauses of garbage collections sometimes are long enough to be noticeable to the users, which is not pleasant user experience.

There are usually two ways to reduce the collection pause time, i.e., generational GC or concurrent GC. Generational GC is designed based on the "generational hypothesis" that most objects die young. A generational GC partitions the heap into regions (generations) for different ages of objects. When a generation space becomes full, the objects referenced from older generations and root set are promoted to next older generation. In this way, only one generation space needs to be collected in one collection cycle, thus the collection time is reduced compared to the entire heap collection. A common generational GC design requires write barrier to catch the cross-generation references, and usually copies the surviving objects for promotion. Since Android GC is built on dlmalloc, which does not allow moving objects, it is hard to enhance it to be generational.

A concurrent GC usually has a dedicated thread running in parallel with the application execution. It tries not to pause the application when possible. Concurrent GC can achieve much shorter average pause time than STW GC, but it requires write barrier to catch the reference updates in order to maintain the correctness of the concurrent execution. Thus concurrent GC has lower overall performance than STW GC. A concurrent GC actually is a superset design of a STW GC. Under certain conditions it falls back to STW collection. For example, when the system available free memory is not enough to sustain the application's execution before the concurrent GC finishes scanning the object graph, it has to suspend the application for GC to recycle the memory. The maximal pause time of a concurrent GC can be longer than its STW counterpart.

In this paper, we propose a regional GC for Android. The regional GC is similar to a generational GC but partitions the heap into regions according to the different regions' properties. It does not require copying objects from one region to another hence it is easy to implement in Android on top of dlmalloc. The regional GC can achieve the benefits of a generational GC in that it mostly collects only one region so the pause time is reduced largely. Compared to concurrent GC, the regional GC development is much simpler. More importantly the regional GC not only achieves shorter pause time, but also achieves higher performance than the original STW GC, which is impossible with a concurrent GC. The major contributions of this paper include:

- It discusses the design of Android GC, and then proposes a regional GC that exploits the Android heap properties.
- The paper evaluates the regional GC with a set of Android Workload Suite (AWS) to understand its characteristics.
- The paper also describes and evaluates two alternative write barrier designs in the Regional GC. One is to use page protection at user level; the other is to scan the page table entries in the OS kernel.

2   Related Work

McCarthy invented the first tracing garbage collection technique: the mark-sweep algorithm in 1960 [1] and Marvin Minsky developed the first copying collector for Lisp 1.5 in 1963 [2]. Many tracing garbage collectors have been developed to manage the entire heap with mark-sweep or copying algorithm in a stop-the-world manner. GC spends considerable time in scanning the long-live objects again and again.

Generational GC [3] segregates objects by ages into two or more generations. Since "most objects die young" [3][4][5], it is cost-effective to collect the young generation more frequently than the old generation, hence to achieve higher throughout. The variants of the generational collection include older-first collection [13] and the Beltway framework [14]. By collecting only a part of the heap, the pause time can be reduced as well. Another similar approach is Garbage-First GC [15]. Garbage-First GC partitions the heap into a set of equal-sized heap regions and the remembered sets record the cross-region pointers from all regions. So it allows an arbitrary set of heap regions to be chosen for a collection. The regional GC in this paper is similar to the generational GC in the concept of heap partitioning, but the regional GC partitions the heap according to the region properties instead of the object ages.

In order to further reduce the pause time of the STW collections, concurrent garbage collections have been developed [6][7][8][15]. Concurrent GC uses dedicated GC thread(s) to run concurrently with the mutator thread(s). Compared to a STW GC, since the total workload for a collection is the same and write barrier has runtime overhead, concurrent GC usually achieves shorter pause time but degrades the application overall performance.

There have been some efforts to share the data and/or code across different runtime instances. The Multi-tasking VM from Oracle has explored a few solutions [9]. They find the J2SE is not a good environment to justify the data sharing; instead, it is useful for J2ME environment, because the memory is scarce on small devices, and a large fraction of the footprint is taken by the runtime representation of classes. In these circumstances, a JVM that shares most of the runtime data across programs can be extremely valuable.

The most common write barrier implementations proposed include the techniques of remembered sets [4], card marking [10][11], and etc. One variant of card marking leverages the page protection mechanism provided by the operating system [7].Meanwhile the GC community have investigated the possibility of using page dirty bits to replace the page fault handling for write barrier implementation [12]. Although a user-level page table dirty bit could be favorable, we have not seen actually implementation. In regional GC, we implemented two different write barriers. One uses the page fault handling mechanism and the other uses a system call to read the page dirty bits.

3 An Overview of the Regional GC

The regional GC is designed specifically for the heap layout of DalvikVM in Google Android 2.2. In Android system, a demon process called Zygote is created during the system initialization. Zygote preloads system classes and some common data. A new application is started by Zygote forking a new process that runs the new application code in a new DalvikVM instance. The new process shares Zygote's space at the forking point. In this way, all the application processes in Android share a same space with Zygote in copy-on-write manner. This space holds the preloaded data and is seldom modified. We call this space the Class Region. After the new application is started, it then creates a new space for the application's private dynamic data. The application only allocates objects in this space and a collection is triggered when it is full. We call this space the User Region.

The default GC in DalvikVM is a mark-sweep collector. In marking phase, it scans the object graph from root set references to identify the live objects in both class and user regions. In sweeping phase, the collector sweeps only the user region. The class region and user region have following properties:

1. The class region is usually much larger than the user region for common Android applications. That means the marking time in the class region is much bigger than in the user region. We give more data in the evaluation section.
2. The class region is seldom written. The most data in this region are class objects. The class static data are stored outside of the region. The user region has all the runtime objects generated by the applications.
3. The class region is much more expensive to write than the user region. A first write to a page in this region triggers the copy-on-write handling in the OS kernel to allocate a new page for the writing process.
4. It is too expensive to sweep (i.e., write) the class region, so the class region is only scanned in marking phase for correct reachability analysis, but not swept in sweeping phase. The user region is both scanned and swept.

Our regional GC exploits the regional heap layout in Android. It has two kinds of collections as a generational GC: minor collection and major collection. The minor collection in the regional GC only collects (mark-and-sweep) the user region. The major collection behaves the same as the default Android GC.

Similar to a generational GC, write barrier is used to ensure the correctness. During the application execution, the write barrier tracks the cross-region references from other regions to the user region, and records them in a remembered set. When the heap is full, a collection is triggered. The remembered set is scanned together with the root set. The object graph traversal does not enter other regions except the user region.

The major collection is similar to the original mark-sweep GC. The remembered set is cleaned at the beginning of the major collection because it scans the all the regions from the root set. The only difference is that regional GC needs to remember all the cross-region references discovered in the marking phase. The remembered set is used for next minor collection together with those cross-region references caught by the write barrier.

By default the regional GC always triggers the minor collection except two cases. One is when the remembered set has no free slot available; the other case is when a minor collection does not return enough free space.

The idea of regional GC is to reduce the marking time. It is orthogonal to the STW or concurrent collection, and can be used to reduce their marking time.

4   Regional GC Design Details

In this section we describe the details of our regional GC implementation in Android. We implement the regional GC in Android 2.2.

4.1   The Heap Layout

Figure 1 illustrates the heap layout of DalvikVM, where two applications' process heap is shown. Each process heap has a class region and a user region. The class region is shared across the processes.

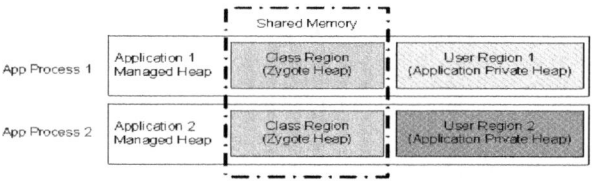

Fig. 1. Regional heap layout designed in DalvikVM

Class region is created and populated by the initializing Zygote process. The Zygote process is the parent process of all the application processes. All of them share the Zygote heap, i.e., the class region. The objects in the class region are mostly the class objects preloaded by the zygote process, and some other common system objects necessary for the initialization. An application never allocates objects in its class region.

The user region is created when an application is started and it is private to each application. An application allocates objects in the user region. The virtual memory management of the region is delegated to the underlying dlmalloc library.

A heap region is a contiguous space. Mark-bit tables are allocated outside the heap to indicate the objects status in the heap.

4.2   The Minor Collection

The minor collection is the default collection of the regional GC. It only scans and sweeps the objects in the user region. To ensure the collection correctness, all the references from outside of the user region are recorded in the remembered set by the write barrier during the application execution.

The Root Set And Remembered Set
In the regional GC, a minor collection starts tracing from the root set and remembered set.

- Root set

As any other GC, the regional GC enumerates the root set from the runtime stack and global variables. Different from other GC, the regional GC does not enumerate the class static variables, because the regional GC wants to avoid the scanning of the class region. A class' static data is allocated with dlmalloc outside of the class region when the class object is loaded. There is no specific region for the class static data in Android, so the class static data can only be accessed via the class objects in the class region. Because the regional GC wants to avoid scanning the class region, it has to catch the references in the class static data with write barrier.

- Remembered set

The remembered set has the references to the user region from outside. It includes the references from the class region and from the class static data. Both of them are caught by the write barrier.

Since the remembered set is used by the minor collection, it must be prepared before a minor collection. There are following scenarios for the remembered set to record the references:

1. At the beginning of the application execution, the remembered set is empty. It starts to record the references to the user region from outside with the write barrier;
2. When the user region is full, and a minor collection is triggered, the remembered set is used together with the root set, but the content of the remembered set is kept during the collection. After a minor collection, the remembered set continues to record the references;
3. When a major collection is triggered, the remembered set is cleared, and only the root set is used for tracing the live objects. During the collection, the references to the user region from the external are recorded in the remembered set. This is prepared for the next minor collection.

The Write Barriers
During the application execution, when the mutator modifies the object reference field (the field address is called the slot), write barrier is triggered and checks the positions of the source object and the target object. If source object is outside of the user region and the target object is in the user region, the reference slot is recorded in the remembered set. There are two kinds of write barriers in the regional GC. One is to track the static data updates, and the other is to track the class region update.

- Write barrier for the static fields

As we have explained above, in DalvikVM design, the static data of the classes are allocated outside the class region, and we have to use write barrier to catch the writes in reference slots. We instrument the VM execution engine (such as the interpreter and/or JIT compiler) with write barrier for static field operations, including opcode sput-object. The write barrier records the static reference slots in the field remembered set.

- Write barrier for the class region

For the class region, the regional GC uses page protection to catch the reference slots updates. The page protection write barrier is a variant of card marking. It depends on the underlying OS support to trap the writes to the protected virtual memory pages.

At the beginning of the application execution, a user-level signal handler for SIG_SEGV is registered. At a point before the first object allocated in the user region and also at a point after a major collection, the class region pages are protected to be read-only. Whenever there is a write into the class region, a page fault is triggered. The OS kernel then delivers a SIG_SEGV signal to the user application. When the execution exits from the page fault handling in the kernel, it enters the user registered signal handler. The signal handler changes the page protection mode to be read-write and records the virtual memory address of the page in the page remembered set.

Figure 2 illustrates how the page protection write barrier works.

- Step 1. The steps 1.a, 1.b and 1.c show the process of page protection. There are three objects A, B and C in three pages of the class region. D is allocated in the user region.
- Step 2. When the application executes C.m=D, the page fault is triggered.
- Step 3. The SIG_SEGV signal handler reads the fault address of the reference field C.m. And then changes Page 3 to be writable and remember it in the page remembered set.
- Step 4. When a minor collection happens; only the objects in Page 3 are scanned. Other pages of the class region are untouched in the collection.

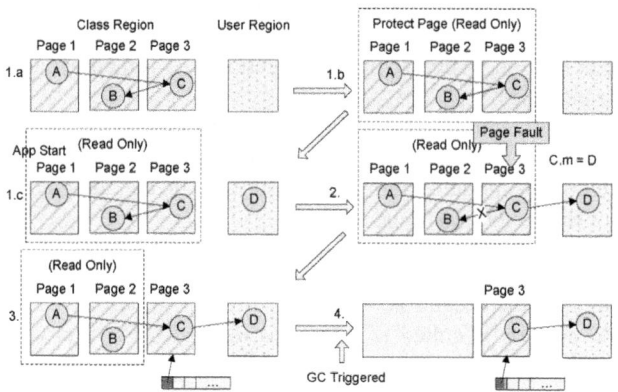

Fig. 2. Page-protection write barrier

In order to reduce the runtime overhead of page fault, we also implement an alternative write barrier for the class region. We call it PTE-scan write barrier.

- PTE-scan write barrier

The PTE-scan write barrier is different from the page protection write barrier; it does not depend on page fault signal handling. Instead, it implements a new system call in the Linux kernel to iterate the page table entries to track the dirty pages.

| iterate_pte(pmd_t *pmd, unsigned long from, unsigned long to, func* operation)
{
　pte_t *pte = get_pte(pmd, from);
　for(addr=from; addr != end; addr += pagesize)
*operation(pte ++, addr);
}

iterate_PMD(pud_t *pud, unsigned long from, unsigned long to, func* operation)
{
　//iteate PMD, it's similar to iterate_PGD
} | iterate_PUD(pgd_t *pgd, unsigned long from, unsigned long to, func* operation)
{
　//iterate PUD, it's similar to iterate_PGD
}

iterate_PGD(unsigned long from, unsigned long to, func* operation)
{
　pgd_t *pgd = get_pgd(from);
　for(addr = from; addr != end; pgd++, addr=next){
　　next = start_address_in_next_pgd(addr, end);
iterate_PUD(pgd, addr, next, operation);
　}
} |

Fig. 3. Pseudo code of iterating memory area

In the regional GC implementation, the new system call "dirty_pages" scans all page table entries (PTE) belongs to the class region and checks the dirty bit in the PTE. If the dirty bit is set, the virtual memory address of the page is recorded. The system call records the dirty page addresses in an array and then copies the array back to the user space as the page remembered set.

The system call has two functionalities, one is to iterate the heap to record the dirty bit and the other one is to reset the dirty bit for the memory area. Both of them needs to recursively walk the page table for the memory area. It starts from PGD and scans the PUD, PMD and PTE in depth first order. Figure 3 is a pseudo code of walking the PTE.

During walking the memory area, the call back function is called for very page table entry. In clean dirty mode, if the pte dirty bit is set, then system erase the dirty bit. In get dirty mode, it record the address in array. Below is the pseudo code:

```
clear_dirty_callback (pte_t *pte, unsigned long addr){
    if(pte_dirty(*pte)) set_pte(pte, pte_mkclean(ptent));
}
dirty_page_callback(pte_t *pte, unsigned long addr){
    if(pte_dirty(*pte)) dirty_array[count++] = addr;
}
```

In the regional GC, the dirty_pages system call is invoked when a minor collection starts. Another system call "clear_dirty" is invoked at the beginning of the application exection and right after a major collection.

Marking Phase

When the user region is full, a minor collection is triggered and the application threads are paused. The first phase of the collection is the marking phase that identifies the reachable objects. The object graph tracing algorithm is a depth-first algorithm and similar to traditional mark-sweep GC, and reuses the Android GC infrastructure.

A mark-bit table is used to track the objects status. Since the objects in the heap are 8-bytes aligned, one bit in the mark-bit table maps to 8 bytes in managed heap. The marking phase firstly prepares the root set and remembered set to start from, and then traces the object graph to mark the live objects.

• Root set and remembered set preparation

The regional GC marks all the objects referenced by the root set in the mark-bit table. It then marks all the objects referenced by the field remembered set in the mark-bit table. Then the GC iterates the page remembered set. For each page in the set, the GC marks all the objects in the mark-bit table according to the allocation-bit table. (The allocation-bit table is similar to the mark-bit table. Whenever the mutator allocates an object, it marks a correspondent bit in the allocation-bit table.) This initial set of the marked objects are the root objects for object graph traversal.

• Object graph traversal

In this step, the regional GC iterates the mark-bit table from the beginning to the end, tracing the live objects in depth-first order. The first step is processing root objects. For each marked object in the mark-bit table, the GC scans its reference fields to find out the referenced objects. If the referenced object is in the user region, the GC pushes the referenced objects in the mark stack. The next step is processing the mark stack. The GC gets a object from mark stack. If the object is in the class region, the GC does not proceed to scan it. If it's in user region, the GC put all the referenced objects in the mark stack. This process continues until the mark stack is empty. Figure 4 shows the execution flow of the process.

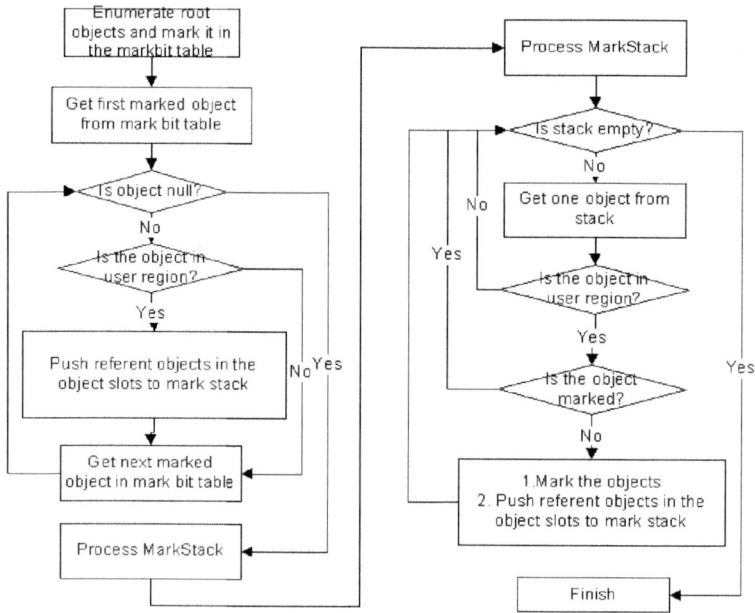

Fig. 4. Execution flow of the marking phase

The Sweeping Phase

The sweeping phase in the regional GC is similar to the traditional mark-sweep GC. The regional GC only recycles the free space in the user region. To find out all the dead objects in the user region, the GC performs "xor" operation on the bits of the mark-bit table and allocation-bit table. The results of the operation keep in the mark-bit table. All the dead objects are marked with 1. The GC iterates the mark-bit table in the area of the user region. All the dead objects are freed by passing them to dlmalloc free routine. The size of the free space is accumulated during the sweeping phase. If the free space is smaller than 20% of the total heap size, the next collection is scheduled to be a major collection.

4.3   The Major Collection

The regional GC needs the major collection to trace the entire heap from time to time to recycle the possible floating garbage retained by the cross-region references in the remembered set. The major collection in the regional GC has longer pause time than the minor collection since it traces both the class region and the user region. It also clears the remembered set before the collection, and rebuilds the set during the collection.

The major collection is expected to happen infrequently. It is triggered in two situations.

1. When the reserved space for the remembered set is full during the application execution, the next collection has to be a major collection to ensure the correctness;
2. When the size of the free space after a collection is smaller than 20% of the total heap size, the next collection is scheduled to be a major collection.

The Marking Phase

Similar to the marking phase of the minor collection, the application is paused during the major collection. The content of remembered set is discarded at the beginning of the major collection in order to trace both the class region and the user region. The live objects are identified by traversing from the root set references and marked in the mark-bit table.

During the marking process, all the references to the user region from external are recorded in the remembered set. The remembered set is prepared for the next collection, since a minor collection is the default to be scheduled for the next collection.

- Root set preparation

At the beginning of the major collection, the regional GC cleans the remembered set, including the field remembered set and the page remembered set. It then enumerates the entire root set references from the runtime stack and global variables. Those objects referenced in the root set are marked in the mark-bit table. The regional GC finishes this step with all the root objects marked in both the class region and the user region.

- Object graph traversal

Similar to the minor collection, the regional GC iterates the root objects in the mark-bit table from the beginning to the end, and traces the object graph in depth-first order. For each marked object in the mark-bit table, the GC scans its fields to find out the referenced objects and then scans those referenced objects recursively. If a live object in the class region has a field that contains a reference to the user region, the reference slot is recorded in the remembered set. The remembered set is prepared for the next collection.

The Sweeping Phase
The sweeping phase is the same as in the minor collection. The regional GC only sweeps the dead objects in the user region. It does not sweep the class region, because to recycle one dead object may trigger a copy-on-write for one page. The benefit is negative.

When the sweeping phase is done, the regional GC should reset the dirty pages in the class region to prepare for the next minor collection. For the page-protection write barrier, the GC protects the virtual memory in the class region to be read-only. For the PTE-scan write barrier, the system call "clear_dirty" is invoked to clear all the dirty bits in the page table entries.

5   Experimental Results

We evaluate the regional GC with Android Workload Suite (AWS) 1.0. AWS 1.0 is a client side workload suite including 15 workloads with 23 scenarios for 2D/3D graphics, media, browser, productivity and VM engine. The AWS 1.0 is not designed for GC evaluation but a comprehensive workload suite for Android platform evaluation. We choose AWS 1.0 intentionally so that the data are representative for the real usages. We use the page-protection write barrier by default in the evaluation of the regional GC.

5.1   Overall Performance Impact

In figure 5, the overall performance impact of the regional GC is presented. Compared with the Froyo default GC, the regional GC has 3% performance gain in average across the 23 workloads/scenarios. As expected, performance of the object-intensive workloads has been improved significantly. For example, the graphic 2D workload Album Slideshow and the productivity workload PDF Viewing get 28% and 8% performance gains respectively. Meanwhile, the regional GC does not visibly impact the non-object-intensive workloads. For most of the browser and media workloads, the performance difference between the default GC and the regional GC is within ±1%.

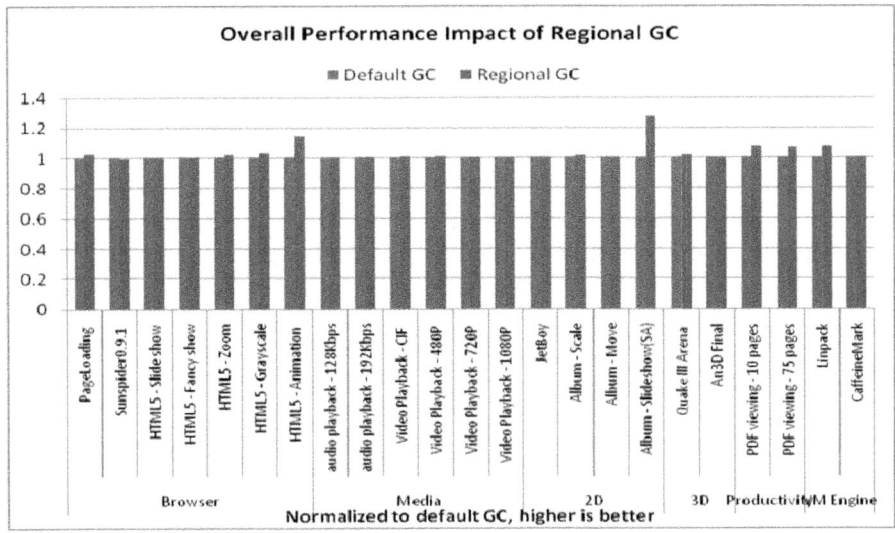

Fig. 5. Overall performance impact

5.2 Collection Pause Time Reduction

For the smart phone consumers, the user experience is sometimes more important than the pure performance. The GC related user experience metrics include the average pause time of the collections, the maximal pause time and the number of pauses.

The average GC pause time is shown in Figure 6(A). The average GC pause ti of the regional GC is reduced by 55% compared to that of the default GC. None of

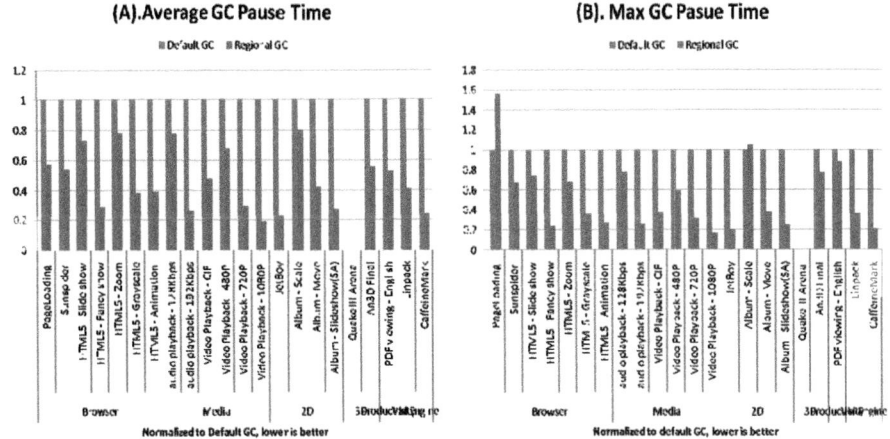

Fig. 6. GC pause time reduction

workloads has bigger average pause time with the regional GC. This is reasonable since the regional GC omits the marking time for the class region in the minor collections. QuakeIII Arena does not have any collection happening.

We show the maximal collection pause time for each applicaiton in Figure 6(B). The JetBoy and audio workloads has largely reduced maximal GC pause time significantly, because all the collections during these workloads execution are minor collection. The Pageloading and Album Scale workload has longer maximal GC pause time with the regional GC. We find that the longest pause time happens in major collections, and the marking time in them happens to be long due to application's execution dynamics.

5.3   Write Barrier Overhead

We implement the two alternative page write barriers in the regional GC: the PTE-scan write barrier and the page-protection write barrier. First, we measure the overhead of one page fault handling, including the signal processing, for the page-protection write barrier. We also measure the overhead of one round PTE scanning with different heap sizes. The data is given in Fig. 7(A).

The dash line is for the page fault processing overhead, and the dotted line is for the PTE scanning overhead, along with different heap sizes. From the chart, we can see that the overhead of one page fault handling is a constant with different heap sizes, while the overhead of the PTE scanning is proportional to the page table size, or the heap size. The two curves have an intersection point at heap size 3.5MB.

When a workload executes, the total PTE-scan write barrier overhead is roughly equal to the total collection counts multiplying the time of one round PTE scanning. The total overhead of the page-protection write barrier is roughly equal to the dirty page number multiplying the time of one page fault processing. We collect the d page number, collection count and average heap size in table 1.

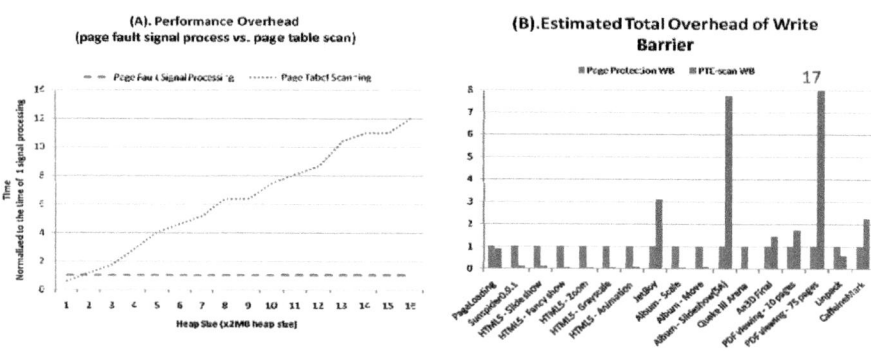

Fig. 7. Overhead of Write Barrier

Table 1. Workload statistics: dirty page number, collection counts and used heap size

Workload	Dirty Page Num	GC counts	Average Heap Size (MB)	Workload	Dirty Page Num	GC counts	Average Heap Size (MB)
PageLoading	484	180	6.4	Album – Scale	66	2	3.2
Sunspider0.9.1	102	9	3	Album - Move	63	3	3
HTML5 - Slideshow	133	10	3	Album - Slideshow(SA)	65	500	2.7
HTML5 - Fancyshow	106	3	3	Quake III Arena	0	0	0
HTML5 - Zoom	85	2	3	An3D Final	83	45	7.2
HTML5 - Grayscale	109	2	3	PDF viewing - 10 pages	93	87	4.9
HTML5 - Animation	86	4	3	PDF viewing - 75 pages	93	724	5.8
JetBoy	63	2	2.7	Linpack	81	12	5.7
				CaffeineMark	44	89	3

Based on the data in Table 1, we compute the estimated write barrier overhead in Figure 7(B). The data are normalized to the page-protection write barrier overhead. We can see that the workloads have different preferences over the write barrier solution. The workloads such as the HTML5-related have very small PTE-scan write barrier overhead because they usually consume small heap size and seldom trigger the collections. For the workloads that have large heap size and frequent collections, the page-protection write barrier outperforms the PTE-scan write barrier.

We also measure the true runtime overhead of the write barriers. Figure 8(A) is the overall performance comparison between the two kinds of write barriers. We cannot see obvious difference between them. It is because the total runtime overhead of the write barrier is quite small with AWS 1.0, as shown in figure 8(B). Te page-protection write barrier overhead is within ±1% of the total execution time. Thus the performance impact of the different write barrier implementations is negligible.

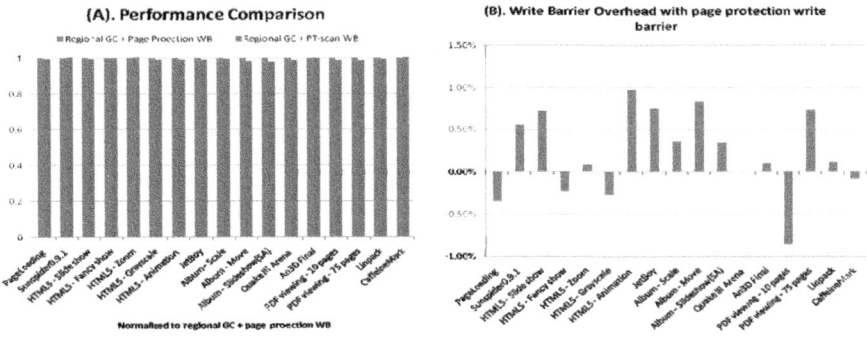

Fig. 8. Performance Comparison and Overhead

6   Conclusion

For smart phone software stack, the GC algorithm should consider both the pure performance and the pause time, in order to achieve best user experience. In this paper we present a Regional GC for Android that can effectively improve both application performance and user experience. The Regional GC we propose is similar to a generational GC but actually partitions the heap according to heap layout regions instead of the object ages.

A major collection of the regional GC is the same as DalvikVM's normal STW collection, while a minor collection only marks and sweeps one of the heap regions. In the evaluation with Android workload suite (AWS), the performance of 2D graphic workload Album Slideshow is improved by 28%, and its average pause time is reduced by 73%. The average pause time reduction across all the AWS applications is 55%. The regional GC can be combined with a concurrent GC to further reduce the pause time.

This paper also describes two alternative write barrier designs in the Regional GC. One is page-protection based, and the other is PTE-scan based. We evaluate the two approaches with the AWS applications, and find their overhead is not visibly impactful to the application performance.

As the next step, we are evaluating the applicability of the regional GC to a concurrent GC in Android, and further investigate the balance between the pure performance and user experience. The other work we are doing is to design an adaptive memory scheduling algorithm that can automatically balance the memory allocations among all the running applications.

Acknowledgments. We would like to thank Ying Gao whose work in PTE-scanning enlightened us to apply the similar idea to the regional GC design.

References

1. McCarthy, J.: Recursive functions of symbolic expressions and their computation by machine. Communications of the ACM 3(4), 184–195 (1960)
2. Minsky, M.: A LISP garbage collector algorithm using serial secondary storage. A.I.Memo 58. MIT Project MAC, Cambridge (1963)
3. Lieberman, H., Hewitt, C.: A real-time garbage collector based on the lifetimes of objects. Communications of the ACM 26(6), 419–429 (1983)
4. Ungar, D.M.: Generation scavenging: A non-disruptive high-performance storage reclamation algorithm. In: ACM SIGSOFT/SIGPLAN Software Engineering Symposium on PSDE, pp. 157–167. ACM Press, New York (1984)
5. Shaw, R.A.: Empirical Analysis of a Lisp System. Ph.D thesis, Standford University, Palo Alto, California, Technical Report CSL-TR-88-351, Standford University Computer Systems Laboratory (February 1988)
6. Doligez, D., Leroy, X.: A concurrent generational garbage collector for a multi-threaded implementation of ML. In: Conference Record of the 20th ACM Symposium on Principles of Programming Languages (January 1993)
7. Boehm, H.-J., Demers, A.J., Shenker, S.: Mostly parallel garbage collection. SIGPLAN PLDI 26(6), 157–164 (1991)

8. Azatchi, H., Levanoni, Y., Paz, H., Petrank, E.: An on-the-fly mark and sweep garbage collector based on sliding views. In: 18th Annual ACM SIGPLAN Conference on OPSLA 2003, Aneheim, CA (2003)

9. Heiss, J.J.: The Multi-Tasking Virtual Machine: Building a Highly Scalable JVM (March 22, 2005) http://java.sun.com/developer/technicalArticles/ Programming/mvm/

10. Wilson P.R., Moher, T.G.: Design of the opportunistic garbage collector. In: Proceedings of the Conference on OOPLSA, New Orleans, Louisiana, pp. 23–35 (October 1989)

11. Sobalvarro, P.: A Lifetime-based Garbage Collector for LISP system on General-Purpose Computers. Massachusetts Institute of Technology, Cambridge, MA (1998)

12. Hosking, A.L., Hudson, R.L.: Remembered sets can also play cards. In: OOPSLA 1993 Workshop on Garbage Collection and Memory Management (1993)

13. Stefanovic, D., McKinley, K.S., Eliot J., Moss, B.: Age-based garbage collection. In: Proceedings of the Conference on OOPSLA, N.Y, pp. 370–381 (November 1999)

14. Blackburn, S.M., Jones, R., Mckinley, K.S., Eliot, J., Moss, B.: Beltway: Getting Around Garbage Collection Gridlock. In: Proceedings of the ACM SIGPLAN 2002 Conference on PLDI, Brelin, Germany (June 2002)

15. Detlefs, D., Flood, C., Heller, S., Printezis, T.: Garbage-First Garbage Collection. In: Proceedings of the 4th ISMM, Vancouver, BC, Canada (October 2004)

Author Index